# THE
# JOHN MACARTHUR
# HANDBOOK

*of*

# EFFECTIVE BIBLICAL
# LEADERSHIP

# THE
# JOHN MACARTHUR
# HANDBOOK

*of*

# EFFECTIVE BIBLICAL
# LEADERSHIP

## JOHN
## MACARTHUR

GENERAL EDITOR

HARVEST HOUSE PUBLISHERS
EUGENE, OREGON

Cover by Bryce Williamson, Eugene, OR

Cover photos © Lubushka, Lava4images / Getty Images

**The John MacArthur Handbook of Effective Biblical Leadership**
Copyright © 2019 Grace Community Church
Published by Harvest House Publishers
Eugene, Oregon 97408
www.harvesthousepublishers.com

ISBN 978-0-7369-7630-5 (hardcover)
ISBN 978-0-7369-7631-2 (eBook)

Compilation of:

*The Shepherd as Preacher*
Copyright © 2015 Grace Community Church
ISBN 978-0-7369-6207-0

*The Shepherd as Leader*
Copyright © 2016 Grace Community Church
ISBN 978-0-7369-6209-4

*The Shepherd as Theologian*
Copyright © 2017 Grace Community Church
ISBN 978-0-7369-6211-7

**Printed in the United States of America**

19 20 21 22 23 24 25 26 27 / Bang-RD / 10 9 8 7 6 5 4 3 2 1

# CONTENTS

# Introduction

The first Shepherds' Conference was held on March 19, 1980, at Grace Community Church, where 159 men gathered to focus on the theme of pastoral ministry. From the beginning, the goal was to live out Paul's mandate to Timothy: "The things which you have heard from me in the presence of many witnesses, entrust these to faithful men who will be able to teach others also."

What started as a small event has, by God's grace, blossomed into an international movement with thousands in attendance each spring. Over the years, pastors from every state and nearly 100 countries have come to the conference to be challenged and encouraged in areas of preaching, theology, leadership, discipleship, and counseling. My own heart has been deeply blessed by the faithful men I've met and fellowshipped with at the conference.

Since its inception, the Shepherds' Conference has featured hundreds of sermons specifically directed at pastors and church leaders. Because the truth of God's Word is timeless, those messages are still as rich and powerful today as when they were first preached.

This volume brings together a collection of the most memorable Shepherds' Conference messages on the topics of preaching, leadership, and theology. Nothing is more urgently needed in today's church than ministers and leaders who are committed to fulfilling their roles according to principles found in God's Word, and the contents of this book have been brought together to equip men like you in that very endeavor. The chapters that follow have been edited as minimally as possible so that they reflect the original content of the Shepherds' Conference messages.

My ongoing desire has been for the Shepherds' Conference to contribute to the multiplication of "faithful men who will be able to teach others also." May this book help you, whether you've been to the Shepherds' Conference or not, to think more deeply and purposefully about the calling God has given you. As you read it, my prayer is that your passion for truth will burn brighter and your resolve for Christ's glory will grow stronger as you seek to serve and lead His church.

For the Great Shepherd,
John MacArthur

# PART 1:

# THE SHEPHERD
# AS PREACHER

# 1

# PREACH THE WORD

*John MacArthur*
*Shepherds' Conference 1998*

*2 Timothy 3:1–4:4*

There is a text of Scripture that is beloved by me, and one upon which I have preached numerous times through the years. It is a text that my father wrote inside the flyleaf of a Bible that he gave to me when I told him I felt called to preach. The text is 2 Timothy 4:2: "Preach the word; be ready in season and out of season, reprove, rebuke, exhort with great patience and instruction."

That brief verse defines biblical ministry in one central command: "Preach the Word." Along with this command you could add 1 Timothy 3:2, which says pastors, overseers, and elders are to be skilled in teaching and preaching. We are to preach the Word skillfully. That is our calling, and this verse is definitive because it speaks so concisely, calling us to "preach the Word."

Now you will notice that the apostle Paul addresses the time and the tone of our preaching. The time is "in season and out of season." We could debate what that means, but if I can lead you to a simple conclusion, the only possibilities are to be in season or out of season; therefore, it means all the time. We are to preach the Word all the time. There is no time when we change that commission, no time when that method of ministry is set aside for something else. Preaching the Word is to be done all the time.

As for the tone, it is twofold: There is the negative aspect of reproving and rebuking, and there is the positive aspect of taking God's truth and exhorting people with great patience and instruction. Negatively we are to confront error and sin. Positively we are to teach sound doctrine and godly living. We are to exhort people to be obedient to the Word, and we are to have great patience and allow them the time to mature in their obedience.

---

**If every word of God is true and pure, and every word is food for the believer, then every word is to be proclaimed.**

---

This is a simple command: Preach the Word all the time. Jesus said, "Man shall not live on bread alone, but on every word that proceeds out of the mouth of God" (Matthew 4:4). That truth calls us to an expository ministry in which we deal with every word that proceeds out of the mouth of God. If every word of God is true and pure, and every word is food for the believer, then every word is to be proclaimed.

People are starving for God's Word but they don't know it. They are hungry, they are reaching out, they are grasping. They realize the hollow places in their life, the shallowness, the lack of insight, the lack of understanding. They cannot solve the problems of life. They are starving for God's Word and are being offered substitutes that do not help. God has ordained that His Word be brought to them because it alone can feed them, and the delivery method is preaching. Paul wrote, "How will they hear without a preacher?" (Romans 10:14). Martin Luther said, "The highest worship of God is the preaching of the Word."[1] God

is revealed through His Word; therefore, preaching His Word is preaching His character, His will, and all that defines Him in true terms and exalts Him as He is to be exalted.

Our mandate then comes not from the culture, it comes from heaven. It is the God of heaven who has mandated us through the pages of Scripture to preach the Word, to preach every word, and to bring to starving souls the only food that feeds—the truth of God. The Bible is the inerrant and infallible Word of the living God. It is sharper than any two-edged sword, and every word in it is pure and true. We are to preach God's Word in its entirety and to unfold all its truth. That is the command.

This concise, clear, and unequivocal command to preach the Word is supported by five potent realities that motivate us in this endeavor. Even though these five realities are potent enough individually to motivate a man to preach the Word of God, together they provide a formidable set of motivations like no other text of Scripture.

### Preach the Word Because of the Danger of the Seasons (3:1-9)

First, we are to preach the Word because of the danger of the seasons. In 2 Timothy 3:1 Paul prefaced his instruction by telling Timothy, "Realize this, that in the last days…" The last days began when the Messiah came the first time. The apostle John said, "Children, it is the last hour" (1 John 2:18). Paul wrote, "…in the last days difficult times will come" (2 Timothy 3:1). The phrase "difficult times" can be translated "seasons" rather than "times." It is not a reference to clock time or calendar time. The word used here in the original Greek text is *kairos,* which means seasons, epochs, or movements. The word translated "difficult" could have been translated "dangerous," or even "savage." Dangerous, perilous times will come. These times will threaten the truth, the gospel, and the church. According to 2 Timothy 3:13, they will increase in severity because "evil men and impostors will proceed from bad to worse, deceiving and being deceived." From the beginning of the last days until Jesus comes, there will be an escalating severity and frequency of these dangerous epochs.

We are talking about movements and epochs that began when Jesus came and started the church, and they have continued cumulatively. They do not come and go; rather, they come and stay, and increase in frequency, so that there is greater danger now than there has ever been. These epochs define for us the danger that threatens the life of the church and the truth. Let's look at some of them, suggested by J.W. Montgomery in his book *Damned Through the Church.*[2]

### The Dangerous Epochs
#### Sacramentalism

The first and most prominent epoch of danger thrust upon the church began in the fourth century—sacramentalism. This began with the development of the

Holy Roman Empire and Constantine, which blossomed into the Roman Catholic system of salvation by ritual. The church became a surrogate Christ—that is, people were connected to the church and to the system rather than to Christ through a personal relationship with Him. Sacramentalism became the enemy of the true gospel, the enemy of grace and faith, and led to the persecution and execution of true believers. It was not until the Reformation in the sixteenth century that sacramentalism began to weaken.

#### Rationalism

Not long after the Reformation came the second epoch of danger—rationalism. As people came out of the Reformation and entered the Renaissance and Industrial Revolution, they broke away from the monolithic institution of Roman Catholicism and got their own identity back and began to think for themselves. They began to discover, invent, and develop things and feel their freedom. They began to worship their own minds, and human reason became god. Thomas Paine wrote *The Age of Reason,* in which he debunked the Bible and affirmed that the human mind is god, and the Bible became a slave to rationalism. Rationalists assaulted Scripture and denied its miracles, its inspiration, the deity of Christ, and the gospel of grace—all in the name of scholarship and human reason.

These epochs have not disappeared. We still have sacramental religions all around the world, and we still have rationalism. Rationalism has destroyed every seminary in Europe. I will never forget visiting St. Salvator's Chapel at the University of St. Andrews in Scotland and standing in the pulpit where John Knox launched the Scottish Reformation. At a time when Rome was in power, John Knox came and preached the gospel of grace and faith in the midst of a works-based system. He took his stand against this massive and powerful system that held people in religious bondage.

Outside that little chapel, on one of the cobblestone streets nearby, there are three sets of initials. These initials represent the names of three young students who, in their late teens, heard the preaching of John Knox, believed the gospel, and turned to Jesus Christ by faith. Consequently, they were burned at the stake by the Catholic authorities. As a tribute to these students, their initials were inscribed on the street at the spot where they were burned. Right across the street is the theological college at the University of St. Andrews. Every day, the faculty of that school walks to the pub across the street, stepping on the initials of the martyrs who died for the truth that these rationalist theologians reject. They worship the god of human intellect and deny the veracity of Scripture.

## Orthodoxism

Rationalism was followed by orthodoxism—a cold, dead, and indifferent orthodoxy. Although in the nineteenth century huge strides in printing technology allowed for mass production of Bibles, many people were indifferent to it because their orthodoxy was dead and cold. Their spirituality was either shallow or nonexistent.

## Politicism

Then came politicism. The church became preoccupied with gaining political power. It developed the social gospel, reconstruction, and liberation theology all in an attempt to bring change through human means rather than through salvation in Christ.

## Ecumenism

Ecumenism was the fifth dangerous epoch, and it erupted during the 1950s. Everyone was talking about unity and setting aside dogma to prevent divisions over doctrinal issues. This produced sentimentalism, and along came a new hermeneutic for interpreting Scripture called "the Jesus Ethic." Jesus was defined as a nice guy who would have never said anything harsh, so the proponents of ecumenism took judgment and retribution out of the Bible. Evil was tolerated and doctrine was disdained, which led to a lack of discernment.

## Experientialism

The sixth epoch was experientialism, which characterized the 1960s. Truth was defined as a feeling that originated in intuition, visions, prophecies, or special revelations. One no longer looked to the objective Word of God to determine truth, but rather, to some subjective intuition. This perspective posed an immense danger to the church and drew people away from the Word of God.

### Subjectivism

The seventh epoch was subjectivism. In the 1980s, psychology captured the church and many believers got into narcissistic navel gazing. They were concerned about whether they could bump themselves up the comfort ladder a little bit and become more successful and make more money. They developed man-centered and needs-based theology. As a result, personal comfort became the ultimate goal.

### Mysticism

Mysticism was the eighth epoch, developing in the 1990s and permitting people to believe in whatever they wanted. Concurrently, pragmatism allowed people to define ministry. The church was said to exist to serve people. A minister determined his plan of ministry by distributing a survey to find out what people wanted. Truth became the servant of what works. Expository preaching was viewed as a pony-express method of delivery in a computer age to a lot of folks who did not want it in the first place. The key to effective ministry was said to be image or style rather than content.

### Syncretism

The ninth epoch was syncretism—the belief that all monotheistic religions worship the same God, and all monotheists are going to heaven. Our culture likes to suppose that heaven will be occupied by followers of Confucius, Buddha, Mohammed, orthodox Jews, and even atheists because they all sought the truth. That's syncretism.

As you can see, the church has faced one dangerous epoch after another and they never go away. Rather, they stay and accumulate so that the church is dealing with all of them. As a shepherd, you are facing a formidable set of fortresses (2 Corinthians 10:4-5). They are strong and well-designed ideological fortifications that must be countered skillfully with God's truth. This requires that you be effective in your handling of the Word. It is not easy to be discerning, to understand the issues that face us, and to bring the appropriate portion of Scripture to bear upon the imminent dangers all around us. Most of Christianity does not care, but we who bear the responsibility as shepherds of God's flock do. These dangers are accumulating and worsening, resulting in a lack of discernment and a growing disdain for doctrine.

### The Guilty and the Gullible

Starting in 2 Timothy 3:2, Paul further defines these dangerous seasons by describing the people who are behind them. They are "lovers of self, lovers of money, boastful, arrogant, revilers, disobedient to parents, ungrateful, unholy, unloving, irreconcilable, malicious gossips, without self-control, brutal, haters of good, treacherous, reckless, conceited, lovers of pleasure rather than lovers of God" (3:2-4). Now if you applied that list to anyone today, would it not be politically incorrect? Can you imagine someone confronting another individual in error and going through that list? It reminds me of Jesus' approach. He went up to the religious leaders of His day who were in error and said, "You snakes, you vipers, you dogs, you filthy, stinking, wretched tombs painted white." How well would that work today?

In 2 Timothy 3:5, Paul reveals that false teachers have a form of godliness. The face that they want to portray is of godliness, but power is absent. They do not have the power of God because they do not know God. Second Timothy 3:6 goes on to say they "enter into households and captivate weak women weighed down with sins, led on by various impulses." Today they enter homes through the media as well as in person, and they target women, whom God designed to be protected by faithful men. They captivate weak women who are weighed down with sins and teach them error. Just like Jannes and Jambres, the two magicians in Egypt who opposed Moses, these men oppose the truth. These false teachers have depraved minds, and they should be rejected.

We need godly men who can go into the fray, men who understand the Word of God clearly. Satan's deceptions are not without subtlety. It is not always obvious on the surface what is actually going on.

That's why we need formidable men who understand God's Word. We need men who understand the issues of their time, who have a holy courage, and who are willing to step into the battle so they can assault the enemy graciously and relentlessly with the truth.

In 2 Corinthians 10:4, Paul says our job as shepherds is to smash ideological fortresses and bring everyone who is captive into obedience to Christ. We want to set free those who are held captive in the fortresses that these dangerous epochs have erected. We are called to guard the truth and preach the truth. We cannot do either if we do not understand the truth. It takes well-trained men to stand against the subtleties and nuances of Satan's devices.

## Preach the Word Because of the Devotion of the Saints (3:10-14)

The second reason we must preach the Word is because of the devotion of the saints. In 2 Timothy 3:10-11, Paul charged Timothy, "Now you followed my teaching, conduct, purpose, faith, patience, love, perseverance, persecutions, and sufferings." In other words, "Timothy, you followed me, you were my disciple and I went through the patterns of ministry for you. You saw my purpose and my ministry duty—teaching and living—so proclaim and live the truth in Jesus' name. You saw how I taught it and I lived it; that is my integrity." Paul was relentlessly focused on the responsibility he had to proclaim the truth. And

Timothy saw Paul's faithfulness to this purpose. He persevered in his love for people and God even in the face of persecution and suffering.

In summary, Paul said, "You saw how I ministered. You saw the way I did it. I did it with love. I did it with focus. I did it relentlessly. I did it patiently. I did it lovingly. I took the flack. I took the pain. I took the suffering. I took the imprisonments. I took the beatings, the whippings, and the stonings. You were with me at Antioch, Iconium, and Lystra; you saw all that."

Paul then challenged Timothy to "continue in the things you have learned and become convinced of, knowing from whom you have learned them" (2 Timothy 3:14). He said, "Timothy, you just do exactly what I told you to do." Many people today want to reinvent ministry, have you noticed? But Paul said, "Do it exactly the way I told you to do it."

In 2 Timothy 3:17 Paul went on to call Timothy the "man of God." That is a technical term used only twice in the New Testament, both times in Timothy. It is used over 70 times in the Old Testament, and every time it refers to a preacher. Paul was saying, "Timothy, you are just another man of God. There is a long line of these men of God—men called by God and gifted by Him to proclaim His truth. You cannot get out of step. You cannot go your way or invent your own approach. You are one man in a long line of men who are called to preach the Word. That is what you are to do."

That is how I look at my own life, and it brings to mind a childhood memory about my grandfather. He was a faithful preacher of the Word of God all through his ministry right up until his death. While he was on his deathbed at home, my father and I were there, and my father asked him, "Dad, is there anything you want?" My grandfather responded, "Yes, I want to preach one more time." While dying from cancer, he wanted just one thing: to preach one more time. He had prepared a sermon he had not preached. That is hard for a preacher to handle; that is fire in his bones. He needs to get it out.

My grandfather had prepared a sermon on heaven and died without ever being able to preach it. So my dad took his notes, printed them, and passed them out to everybody at the funeral. In that way, my grandfather preached on heaven from heaven. That incident had a tremendous effect on me as a young boy. What a faithful man—right down to the last breath, all my grandfather wanted to do was preach the Word one more time.

The same was true about my father. All throughout his ministry he was diligent to preach the Word. As I mentioned earlier, he gave me a Bible in which he wrote on the flyleaf, "Preach the Word." Eventually I went to Talbot Seminary because I wanted to study under Dr. Charles Feinberg. Dr. Feinberg was the most brilliant Bible scholar I knew. For example, he taught himself Dutch in two weeks so he could read a Dutch theology. He studied 14 years to be a rabbi and ended up being converted to Christ. He then attended Dallas Theological Seminary, where he earned his PhD. Dr. Lewis Sperry Chafer, who was the president of Dallas Theological Seminary at that time, said of Dr. Feinberg that he was the only student who came to the seminary knowing more when he arrived than when he left.

Subsequently, Dr. Feinberg attended Johns Hopkins University to earn a PhD in archaeology. He had an immense and brilliant mind and he loved the Word of God. He read through the Bible four times a year and he was absolutely committed to the fact that every word of Scripture is inerrant, inspired, and true. He was the man I wanted to influence my life.

During my first year in seminary, my first class under Dr. Feinberg was Old Testament introduction. It was a demanding course that included a lot of tedious material which was hard to absorb for a college athlete who was suddenly exposed to academia. The first day a student asked a question, Dr. Feinberg dropped his head, never looked up, and said, "If you do not have a more intelligent question than that, do not ask any more questions. You are taking up valuable time." There were no more questions that semester! He had all the time to himself. He was dead serious about the things of God and Scripture.

That same year, I was assigned by Dr. Feinberg to preach a text before the student body and the faculty. I worked countless hours on this sermon. The faculty would sit behind you and write notes while you were preaching and then afterward they gave you their criticisms. I preached the message and thought I had done fine. When I was done, Dr. Feinberg handed me a sheet of paper with red writing across the front: "You missed the whole point of the passage."

How could I do that? How could I miss the whole point? That was the greatest lesson I ever had in seminary. Dr. Feinberg was upset and called me into his office because he wanted to make an investment in me and he did not appreciate what I had done. After all, handling God's Word correctly is the whole point of ministry. That day, I received a lecture I have never forgotten. Ever since, Dr. Feinberg has sat on my shoulder and whispered, "Do not miss the point of the passage, MacArthur!"

On graduation day, Dr. Feinberg called me into his office and said, "I have a gift for you." He picked up a big box, and in it were all 35 volumes of Keil and Delitzsch, a Hebrew Old Testament commentary set. He said, "This is the set I have used for years and years. I have all my notes in the margins; I want to give it to you as a gift." This was an expression of his love for me, but it was also another way of saying, "Now you have no excuse for missing the point of an Old Testament passage."

One of the highlights of my life was when Dr. Feinberg's family asked me to speak at his funeral. Somewhere along the line he must have told them that he thought I had finally gotten to the place where I could figure out the point of a passage. He is with the Lord now, but I do not want to do anything differently. I just want to continue doing what faithful prophets, apostles, preachers, evangelists, pastors, and missionaries have done through the ages. I am astonished at the boldness of people in ministry today who are quick to discard the God-ordained, scripturally mandated pattern of preaching and invent their own. What audacity! Who do they think they are?

So, preach the Word because of the devotion of the saints who came before you. Get in line, take the baton, and run your lap.

## Preach the Word Because of the Dynamic of Scripture *(3:15-17)*

The third reason we preach the Word is because of the dynamic of Scripture. Paul wrote to Timothy, "From childhood you have known the sacred writings" (2 Timothy 3:15). From the time Timothy was a baby in his mother's arms, he was introduced to "the sacred writings." That is a Greek-Jewish term referring to the Old Testament, *hiera grammata*. Paul said, "You have known the [Old Testament, which is] able to give you the wisdom that leads to salvation through faith which is in Christ Jesus."

Although Timothy's parents were Jewish and Gentile, he still had the influence of the Old Testament law in his family. Paul was saying that since Timothy was a child, the law had been preparing him for the gospel. The Jews used to claim that their children "drank in" the law of God with their mother's milk and it was so imprinted on their hearts and minds that they would sooner forget their names than forget God's law.

The law was the tutor that led to Christ, and Timothy had been raised on the sacred writings of the Old Testament. He had been given the wisdom he needed so that when the gospel was preached, he apprehended it because his understanding of the Old Testament law prepared him for it. Ultimately, Paul was saying, "You know that the Word of God has the power to lead you to salvation. What else would you preach?" For it is sharper than any two-edged sword (Hebrews 4:12). Peter declared, "You have been born again…through the living and enduring Word of God" (1 Peter 1:23). It is the power of the Word that converts the soul and produces salvation.

You commit to preaching the Word when you understand that it is the power that converts the soul. If you do not preach the Word, then it's because you do not believe it is the only source of salvation and sanctification, no matter what you might claim otherwise. In 2 Timothy 3:16-17 we read, "All Scripture is inspired by God and profitable for teaching, for reproof, for correction, for training in righteousness; so that the man of God [and everyone who follows His pattern] may be adequate [or complete], equipped for every good work."

It is the power of the Word that saves and sanctifies. It provides doctrine, it reproves error and sin, it sets upright, and it trains in the path of righteousness. That's the sequence.

Through preaching the Word you lay a foundation of doctrine and it reproves error and sin. In the original Greek text, this speaks of setting upright someone who has fallen down. You pick him back up, correct his error and his iniquity, and then put him on the path of righteousness. You train him to live an obedient life. It's the Word that makes the man of God and everybody who follows His pattern complete. It prepares them spiritually. This is what we call the sufficiency of Scripture—God's Word completely saves and completely sanctifies. What else would you use? I cannot fathom why anyone would use anything other than the Word that saves and sanctifies.

### Preach the Word Because of the Demand of the Sovereign (4:1-2)

Next, we preach the Word because of the demand of the Sovereign. Second Timothy 4:1 is a frightening verse that strikes me with holy fear. It should terrify every preacher. This verse helps us to understand why John Knox, before he ascended the pulpit to preach, fell on his face and burst forth in tears of fear. He was reverently afraid of misrepresenting the truth and knew he was under divine scrutiny. Paul wrote, "I solemnly charge you in the presence of God and of Christ Jesus, who is to judge the living and the dead, and by His appearing and His kingdom: preach the Word." The command "I solemnly charge you" is dead serious. Paul was commanding Timothy—and all preachers—with all solemnity and all seriousness.

"My friend," Paul said, "you are under the scrutiny of God, the one who will judge all who are alive and all who have died." The Greek construction here can be rendered "in the presence of God, even Jesus Christ," since He is introduced as the judge in the verse. We are preaching under the scrutiny of the omniscient and holy judge. I agree with what Paul wrote in 1 Corinthians 4:3-4: "It is a very small thing that I may be examined by you, or by any human court…the one who examines me is the Lord." A preacher cannot build his sense of faithfulness on whether his listeners like his sermon. He can appreciate his listeners' commendations and hear their criticisms, but in the end, he should preach to honor the One who is the judge. It is Christ who will reveal the secret things of the heart. He will give a reward to those who are worthy of it, and only His judgment matters.

A reporter once asked me, "For whom do you prepare your sermons?" I said, "To be truthful with you, I prepare them for God. He is the judge whom I have to stand before. He is the one who really matters. I want to get the message right before Him. I do not want to take the Word of the living God and somehow corrupt it, or replace it with foolish musings of my own."

Hebrews 13:17 says, "Obey your leaders and submit to them, for they keep watch over your souls as those who will give an account." Every minister will have to give an account someday before the Lord. I want to give my best to the Lord and build on the foundation with gold, silver, and precious stones (1 Corinthians 3:12). I want to receive that reward that evidences my love for Him, a reward I can cast at His feet in honor and praise. Someday we will all stand before that judgment seat for that time of reward for our labors.

It is a very serious thing for me, this matter of preaching. Sometimes people say to me, "You spend so much time in preparation. Why?" Because God's Word deserves it! We could probably get by with doing less because our listeners don't have high expectations. Frankly, with most listeners a few good stories will do it. But with God, the task of preaching is a different matter. When we preach, we must have Him in mind and the honor of His truth.

## Preach the Word Because of the Deceptiveness of the Sensual (4:3-4)

Yet another reason we are to preach the Word is because of the deceptiveness of the sensual. The great enemy of the Word of God is anything outside the Word of God—the word of Satan, the word of demons, and the word of man. We are living in dangerous seasons concocted by seducing spirits and hypocritical liars. In 2 Timothy 4:3, Paul identifies for us that which makes it possible for false teachers to be successful: "The time will come when they will not endure sound doctrine." People will not want to hear healthy, wholesome teaching. They will not want the sound, solid teachings of the Word. They will just want their ears tickled. They will be driven by the sensual and not the cognitive. They won't be interested in truth or theology. Instead, they will want ear-tickling sensations rather than the great truths that save and sanctify. According to 2 Timothy 2:16, people will want to hear worldly and empty chatter that produces ungodliness and spreads like gangrene.

We are in such a season now. People say that teaching doctrine and being clear about the Word of God is divisive, unloving, and prideful. The prevailing mood in postmodern Western culture is that everyone determines truth for himself and everyone's opinion is as valid as everyone else's. There is no room for absolute, authoritative doctrine. That is one other "ism" you can add to the list of dangerous seasons—relativism.

---

**There will be no church left to fight anything if we do not preserve the truth.**

---

Even the evangelical Christian church has fallen victim to this agenda.

Many Christians are willing to speak up against abortion, homosexuality, and euthanasia. They are willing to fight for religious freedoms in America and, among other things, to preserve prayer in the schools. But the worst form of wickedness is the perversion of God's truth—that is, wrong doctrine and false teaching. The church today treats spiritual error with indifference as if it was harmless, as if a right interpretation of Scripture was unnecessary. While many Christians are fighting peripheral issues, they are giving away the essential truths that define our faith. That is suicide. There will be no church left to fight anything if we do not preserve the truth.

The ability to distinguish between truth and error is absolutely critical. You cannot speak truth or guard it if you do not understand it. That's why at our church we started The Master's Seminary—to train up men who can do that. These men do not worry about figuring out what is culturally relevant. They go all over the world with the Word of God, sort through the issues, and bring God's truth to bear upon the society in which they live. No matter what language you speak or where you live, everyone around you is in the same needy condition, spiritually destitute before God. And the truth of God transcends all cultures.

We live in a time when false teachers do not want to tell people the truth. They do not want to call error "error"; they do not want to confront sin because "they love you." But false teachers do not love

their listeners. If they did, they would seek everyone's best and highest good and proclaim the truth of God's Word.

If I say, "I do not think it is loving to confront," then I do not love people. Rather, I am loving myself—I am more concerned about people liking me than about speaking the truth. It's more loving to confront people's error and show them the truth that can lead them to the blessings and well-being that produces God's greatest good in their lives. Instead we have a loss of truth, loss of conviction, loss of discernment, loss of holiness, loss of divine power, and loss of blessing—all because people want to get their ears tickled. "Tell me a little about success. Tell me a little about prosperity. Give me some excitement. Elevate my feelings of well-being, self-esteem, and give me emotional thrills." Second Timothy 4:3 says these people "will accumulate for themselves teachers in accordance to their own desires." The market creates the demand.

As Marvin Vincent said in *Word Studies in the New Testament*, "In periods of unsettled faith, skepticism and curious speculation in matters of religion, teachers of all kinds swarm like flies in Egypt. The demand creates the supply. The hearers invite and shape their own preachers. If the people desire a calf to worship, a ministerial calf maker can always be found."[3]

I was in Florida back when people were being rocked by the craziness that was going on in the name of revival and people were flipping and flopping around and diving on the floor and gyrating and speaking in bizarre and unintelligible ways. They kept saying, "This is all a work of God." Can I be straightforward with you? Such behavior is an offense to our rational, truth-revealing God. It is an offense to the true work of His Son. It is an offense to the true work of the Holy Spirit to use the names of God or of Christ or of the Holy Spirit in any mindless, emotional orgy marked by irrational, sensual, and fleshly behavior produced by altered states of consciousness, peer pressure, heightened expectation, or suggestibility. That is socio-psycho manipulation and mesmerism, and it is a prostitution of the glorious revelation of God taught clearly and powerfully to an eager, attentive, and controlled mind.

That which feeds sensual desires pragmatically or ecstatically cannot honor God. You have to preach the truth to the mind. That is where the real battle is fought. So we who are preachers are to bring God to people through His Word. That is the only way we can do it. People are starving for the knowledge of God—they just do not know it. But when we start delivering the truth, they find out. It was said of Bible expositor Martyn Lloyd-Jones, by J.I. Packer, "He brought more of the sense of God than any other man."[4] What a commendation!

# PRAYER

Father, we thank You that we do not need to wander in some fog about the direction of life in ministry. We thank You that You have clarified it to us. We thank You that You are raising up men who will proclaim the truth. We thank You, Father, for their devotion and commitment to the fulfillment of this command.

O Lord, grant them power and faithfulness and integrity of life and effectiveness as they endeavor to serve You and carry out this commission. We thank You for men who will face the dangerous seasons, who maintain the devotion to the saints who went before them and were faithful, who will express the dynamic of the Word, who will discharge their responsibility before You as their Sovereign, and who will confront the desires of the sensual world with the powerful and rational truth of Scripture. Father, continue to raise them up, and we give You all the glory in Christ's name. Amen.

# 2

# THE CALL OF GOD

*Mark Dever*

*Shepherds' Conference 2002*

*Ezekiel 1:28–3:15*

I pastor a church in Washington, DC, of about 350 members, and we have approximately 400 to 500 attendees each Sunday morning. Because the church is located in the inner city, we have members from about 30 different countries. Our visitors range from congressmen to ambassadors. For a while we had one high-ranking official from the Chinese embassy who, for two years, celebrated Thanksgiving with my family. He had never attended a Christian church before visiting Capitol Hill. Ministering in this context has provided great opportunities for spreading the gospel.

I've also learned that diplomats are some of the most fascinating people in Washington. Historian Will Durant said, "To say nothing, especially when speaking, is half the art of diplomacy."[1] Now

diplomats may think Durant's observation is harsh, but over the years I've read a few statements that support the point Durant was making. For example, President McKinley once asked an assistant secretary of state how to say no to six European ambassadors who were coming to see him about a certain matter. The career diplomat instantly grabbed an envelope and wrote this on the back of it:

The government of the United States appreciates the humanitarian and disinterested character of the communication now made on behalf of the powers named, and for its part is confident that equal appreciation will be shown for its own earnest and unselfish endeavors to fulfill a duty to humanity by ending a situation, the indefinite prolongation of which has become insufferable.[2]

The president read the message to each one of the ambassadors, and they were satisfied.

Another American president, Franklin Roosevelt, felt quite certain that politicians and diplomats rarely listen to each other. To prove his point, during a diplomatic reception, Roosevelt resolved to greet his guests who were standing in line by saying, "I murdered my grandmother this morning."[3] The story goes on to say that with only one exception, the president received very polite responses.

We're making sport of this a bit, but diplomacy is a serious matter—not just for Washington, but for everyone. We who are Americans tend to lean toward what's called "Wilsonianism," named after Woodrow Wilson, which advocates the idea that there's an underlying good in people and all we need to do is help reassert it. Henry Kissinger wrote a serious and important book on this topic entitled *Diplomacy*,[4] in which he argued against this ideology. Kissinger spent his career contending for Americans to have a more realistic outlook on humanity, assuming that even in the best of worlds there will still be clashes of interests.

Because conflict exists, we need diplomats—professional representatives who work sometimes for short-term advantage and sometimes for long-term interest. And as we turn our attention to the

book of Ezekiel, we see the backdrop is a political conflict between the Babylonian Empire and Judah. Babylon had absorbed the little nation of Judah and begun to exile some of its citizens. However, the book of Ezekiel is not just about the conflict between Israel and Babylon, but more fundamentally about the conflict between Israel and God. As God's rebellious people continued in their insurgence, how would God react?

Some assume that God engages in a kind of religious diplomacy—that He calls on religious professionals who read the latest polling information and use focus groups to determine how to market religion. These professionals usually conduct diplomacy on behalf of God by exacting a concession here and making a compromise there, equivocally bargaining for God and hoping something good may come out of it. This type of mindset deems that an individual strives to appear more reasonable and more diplomatic for God. If that's your idea of how God interacts with His people, then our study of Ezekiel should be of interest to you, particularly as a pastor.

Let's begin by reading Ezekiel 1:28–3:15:

> Such was the appearance of the likeness of the glory of the LORD. And when I saw it, I fell on my face and heard a voice speaking.
>
> Then He said to me, "Son of man, stand on your feet that I may

speak with you!" As He spoke to me the Spirit entered me and set me on my feet; and I heard Him speaking to me. Then He said to me, "Son of man, I am sending you to the sons of Israel, to a rebellious people who have rebelled against Me; they and their fathers have transgressed against Me to this very day. I am sending you to them who are stubborn and obstinate children, and you shall say to them, 'Thus says the Lord GOD.' As for them, whether they listen or not—for they are a rebellious house—they will know that a prophet has been among them. And you, son of man, neither fear them nor fear their words, though thistles and thorns are with you and you sit on scorpions; neither fear their words nor be dismayed at their presence, for they are a rebellious house.

"But you shall speak My words to them whether they listen or not, for they are rebellious. Now you, son of man, listen to what I am speaking to you; do not be rebellious like that rebellious house. Open your mouth and eat what I am giving you." Then I looked, and behold, a hand was extended to me; and lo, a scroll was in it. When He spread it out before me, it was written on the front and

back, and written on it were lamentations, mourning and woe.

Then He said to me, "Son of man, eat what you find; eat this scroll, and go, speak to the house of Israel." So I opened my mouth, and He fed me this scroll. He said to me, "Son of man, feed your stomach and fill your body with this scroll which I am giving you." Then I ate it, and it was sweet as honey in my mouth.

Then He said to me, "Son of man, go to the house of Israel and speak with My words to them. For you are not being sent to a people of unintelligible speech or difficult language, but to the house of Israel, nor to many peoples of unintelligible speech or difficult language, whose words you cannot understand. But I have sent you to them who should listen to you; yet the house of Israel will not be willing to listen to you, since they are not willing to listen to Me. Surely the whole house of Israel is stubborn and obstinate. Behold, I have made your face as hard as their faces and your forehead as hard as their foreheads. Like emery harder than flint I have made your forehead. Do not be afraid of them or be dismayed before them, though they are a rebellious house." Moreover, He said to me, "Son of man, take into your heart all My words which I will speak to you and listen closely. Go to the exiles, to the sons of your people, and speak to them and tell them, whether they listen or not, 'Thus says the Lord GOD.'"

Then the Spirit lifted me up, and I heard a great rumbling sound behind me, "Blessed be the glory of the LORD in His place." And I heard the sound of the wings of the living beings touching one another and the sound of the wheels beside them, even a great rumbling sound. So the Spirit lifted me up and took me away; and I went embittered in the rage of my spirit, and the hand of the LORD was strong on me. Then I came to the exiles who lived beside the river Chebar at Tel-abib, and I sat there seven days where they were living, causing consternation among them.

At the outset of our study, we need to recognize that our call to be a pastor was not exactly like Ezekiel's call. Too often when we go to the Old Testament we attempt to draw direct correlations between biblical characters and ourselves—correlations that aren't necessarily accurate. A look at the Old Testament for exemplary purposes is fine, for Paul sanctioned this in his letter to the Corinthians when he said, "These things happened as examples for us" (1 Corinthians

10:6). Yet at the same time, we will not find exact parallels between Ezekiel's commission and ours. Even so, there are some details in this text that are instructive for us. If we are called to be messengers, ministers, and teachers of God's Word, then we must consider four statements from this passage that will benefit us, our ministries, and those to whom we minister.

### The Message Must Be the Word of God

A very important aspect of our calling as pastors is that the message we proclaim must be the Word of God. One who serves as a messenger is not called to be inventive. Rather, he is commissioned to give God's words alone. One reason I like the Puritans so much is that they valued plainness. If you were to tell a Puritan pastor that you thought he was painful, pathetic, and plain, you'd be giving him a high compliment. *Painful* entails taking pains in ministry. *Pathetic* entails feeling for the flock. *Being plain* means not drawing attention to yourself, but dealing straight with another's soul.

It is this kind of plainness that God was calling Ezekiel to demonstrate. Ezekiel was to be, if you will, the donkey on which Christ sat to ride into Jerusalem. The prophet was simply to bear the Word of God, and the scroll mentioned in Ezekiel 2:9 symbolized this. The scroll is a picture of God's Word, which came to Ezekiel before it went out to the people. The question, however, was this: Would Ezekiel receive the Word of God?

Unlike the rebellious house of Israel, Ezekiel was obedient to God's instructions. He passed the test. Let's look at the details of his reaction in Ezekiel 1:28–2:2:

> When I saw it, I fell on my face and heard a voice speaking. Then He said to me, "Son of man, stand on your feet that I may speak with you!" As He spoke to me the Spirit entered me and set me on my feet.

God set Ezekiel on his feet because He wanted the prophet to be clear-headed and able to concentrate in order to understand the message he was about to receive. Unlike what happens in pagan religious experiences, Ezekiel would be required to have a clear mind. He was not to be in a trance or a frenzy, but instead, in a heightened state of alertness. As a result, the prophet would need to get up on his feet and listen.

The Word given to Ezekiel included lament and woe:

> "Now you, son of man, listen to what I am speaking to you; do not be rebellious like that rebellious house. Open your mouth and eat what I am giving you." Then I looked, and behold, a hand was extended to me; and lo, a scroll was in it. When He spread it out before me, it was written on the front and back, and written on it were lamentations, mourning and woe (Ezekiel 2:8-10).

Sometimes the message God has for His people is a difficult one, but friend, if it is God's Word, we do His people no service by altering it or refusing to give it.

The pastor and evangelist A.B. Earle said that the text he found most blessed of God for the conversion of souls in his ministry was Mark 3:29: "Whoever blasphemes against the Holy Spirit never has forgiveness, but is guilty of an eternal sin."[5] Jonathan Edwards said he found Romans 3:19 to be most used by God for the conversion of souls in his ministry: "Now we know that whatever the Law says, it speaks to those who are under the Law, so that every mouth may be closed and all the world may become accountable to God."[6] God's people need to know the whole truth. He will use the message that we preach, even when the content is burdensome. We must know and teach the things our people don't want to hear. We need to make sure that our message is the Word of God, and nothing more. We have to be willing to say, "God, whatever You're speaking, I will give out. If it's in Your Word, I will preach it, and I will not go beyond it by presenting something that is *not* the Word of God as *the* Word of God."

God was not commissioning Ezekiel to go around and give religious lectures on whatever topics he desired. Ezekiel was a messenger of God only as long as he gave God's message. If he had begun to declare anything else, then he would have ceased to be God's herald. You see this in the following passages:

Ezekiel 2:4—"I am sending you to them who are stubborn and obstinate children, and you shall say to them, '*Thus says the Lord* GOD.'"

Ezekiel 3:4—"Go to the house of Israel and speak with *My words* to them."

Ezekiel 3:11—"Go to the exiles, to the sons of your people, and speak to them and tell them, whether they listen or not, '*Thus says the Lord GOD*'" (emphasis mine).

God told Ezekiel to listen, to eat, to take heart, and then to go and speak. It was not that Ezekiel was extremely insightful and so God decided that he should go on the lecture circuit. No, Ezekiel was a priest trained in God's law and had been taken into captivity and exile in Babylon, but God called him to be a prophet. He received this calling not because of his own insight, but because of God's will.

> **Anyone who claims to be called to ministry has to realize that he is God's messenger only as long as he gives His message.**

If you are a minister of God's Word, beware of the danger in misusing your position. Anyone who claims to be called

to ministry has to realize that he is God's messenger only as long as he gives His message. We're not called to be preachers in a sense that we can preach whatever we want, any more than we would appreciate it if our mailman started scribbling notes to us and then sending them through our door or mailbox. The mailman is valuable to us only as long as he faithfully delivers to us the mail that others have sent.

I hope you haven't been scribbling down your own thoughts and presenting them to God's people as if they were God's words. If there's one person in the universe whose mouth I would not want to put my words into, it would be God. When you are standing in front of God's people, make sure it is God's Word you are giving to them. Be careful of the things that you identify as an essential part of Christianity which are not, and be careful of the things that you claim His Word is saying.

### The Messenger Must Be Sympathetic

A French diplomat was on the verge of taking up a new ambassadorship when he visited President Charles de Gaulle and said to him, "I'm filled with joy at my appointment," to which De Gaulle responded with a frown, "You are a career diplomat, joy is an inappropriate emotion in your profession."[7] In our passage, we see that Ezekiel was no diplomat. He was not called to be a casual professional in his negotiations between God and His rebellious people; instead, as the messenger, he was to be sympathetic. That's the second statement we must consider as ministers.

In this passage, Ezekiel is sympathetic to the recipients of the message. It's interesting that though Ezekiel says that God's Words tasted "sweet as honey in my mouth" (3:3), his reaction afterward was that he "went embittered in the rage of my spirit" (verse 14). Why is that?

I think Ezekiel went away in bitterness because he was sad for his people. The message Ezekiel was called to bear, at least initially, was a tough one, and he doesn't have any *Schadenfreude*—that is, enjoyment over someone else's pain. Instead, Ezekiel has sympathy. It's only natural that he didn't want to be a bearer of bad news. Likewise, sin or the denunciation of it is never something to delight in. Consider your own ministry—when you see a brother or sister caught in sin, do you savor the thought of needing to confront him or her? Of course you delight in the fact that God loves His people and that they can be freed from their sin. But do you relish the actual work of being that messenger?

In a similar fashion, Ezekiel didn't relish being the messenger to a stubborn and obstinate people. God told Ezekiel that He had an important message for the people of Israel, yet the people wouldn't listen to it. Ezekiel could not have appreciated this aspect of his task. Yet the reality is that God doesn't only want His Word to go to white fields of harvest. His purpose is for His Word

to go everywhere—even to some of the most difficult, dangerous, and unresponsive people in the world.

We should expect to experience dread when we find it necessary to counsel parents with intractable children or minister to people who are caught in sin. It's difficult when we know the people we are about to address are likely to be resistant or unresponsive. So we can relate to why Ezekiel would have a bitter spirit toward the task he was being called to, or why he felt overwhelmed by it.

I remember attending a conference a number of years ago at which the speaker gave a very clear talk on hell. I recall walking out afterward and hearing people say in a lighthearted manner, "Wasn't it great to hear such a clear word on hell?" I knew what they meant because we hear so little with regard to the topic of hell today, and the message was beneficial. But there was nothing qualifying that in their voices. I thought, *Surely these people couldn't have contemplated the reality of exactly what they had just heard.* To clarify, I didn't disagree with the speaker at all, and I too was thankful to have heard his message. But I couldn't imagine being happy about it in the way other people were. The thought of hell and what it means for unrepentant sinners must provoke sympathy.

Please understand that I agree with Jonathan Edwards when he says that God will be glorified in the damnation of sinners.[8] But I am not in heaven yet. My heart is not yet perfectly holy and my sympathies are not yet entirely where they should be. Our Lord Jesus, while hanging on the cross and displaying God's glorious justice and mercy, did not laugh as He was bearing our sorrows. Rather, He was sympathetic, and we who are God's messengers should likewise have sympathy toward those to whom we're proclaiming God's Word. Even though our message may be an unfavorable one, we must not be harsh with the recipients.

Ezekiel's sympathy toward his audience was motivated by another factor—God's sympathy. As an individual meditates on Scripture, his mind and heart become conformed to God's mind and heart. Similarly, as Ezekiel took in the message of God's judgment, he began to be conformed to God's feelings toward His people. Ezekiel internalized this word of judgment and was compelled to feel as God felt about the people's disobedience. At the same time, he did not let his feelings bend God's hard truths. He was true to God's message, and we should be as well. We must be faithful for the sake of our people, and we must also be faithful for God's sake.

As a pastor, will you direct all your sympathies toward people and none to God? Are you tempted to condemn God as being too harsh when you read certain passages of Scripture? Let me suggest that instead of trying to exculpate God and make Him not guilty of something that you perceive Him to be guilty of, why not pause and try to have sympathy toward God? Assume for a moment that He is right, that He is infinitely holy, and that He can justly require everything of us, and then see what that does to your assessment of the situation. As God's messengers, we should have sympathy with God. I'm not saying God needs to be the object of our pity. Rather, we must share our Father's perspective. We must have a concern for His name, glory, and honor.

When it is necessary to confront someone, don't become preoccupied with how that person might be offended by your message. Instead, think about how God is hurt, how He is offended. After all, sin is a personal revolt against God and His lordship. If we are to be His messengers, we must be sympathetic not only to people but also to God, our Creator and Redeemer.

## The Messenger Must Know that God Will Supply

If the heart and soul of our ministry is preaching the Bible, then we don't have to worry about running out of things to say. God's Word is inexhaustible, and He is fully sufficient to supply everything needed. As we've seen, God supplied His Word to Ezekiel, and we read in Ezekiel 3:14 that He also supplied a way: "The Spirit lifted me up and took me away." God took the prophet to a specific location and promised to empower him to fulfill his mission. He equipped Ezekiel with the courage to address a hard and stubborn people:

THE CALL OF GOD

As for them, whether they listen or not—for they are a rebellious house—they will know that a prophet has been among them. And you, son of man, neither fear them nor fear their words, though thistles and thorns are with you and you sit on scorpions; neither fear their words nor be dismayed at their presence, for they are a rebellious house (2:5-6).

God went on to tell Ezekiel, "The house of Israel will not be willing to listen to you, since they are not willing to listen to Me. Surely the whole house of Israel is stubborn and obstinate. Behold, I have made your face as hard as their faces and your forehead as hard as their foreheads. Like emery harder than flint I have made your forehead" (3:7-9).

Because Israel was rebellious, God promised to harden Ezekiel so he would be prepared to carry out his task. What God begins He will complete—He will provide the strength His messenger needs to stay the course. When God told Ezekiel to speak, He gave Ezekiel the words. When God told Ezekiel to go, He took him to the location. When God told Ezekiel that the people would be hard, He promised to make Ezekiel harder still. As a result, Ezekiel's determination to speak was tougher than the people's refusal to listen.

Pastors cannot rely on their own ability, but on God's. Augustine prayed, "Give me the grace to do as You command,

and command me to do as You will."[9] That should be our prayer as well.

I'm reminded of an interaction I had with someone early in my pastoral ministry. During a church potluck, I sat down next to one of the older members of the church—someone who didn't seem to like me. This member turned to me and said, "I don't like young pastors." I calmly responded, "Really?" and continued to eat. Then he said, "Well, I might make an exception in your case." I turned and said, "I guess you've seen a good number of pastors come and go, haven't you?"

"Yes," he replied.

At which time I said, "Well, I think you may have met your match." Then I turned back to eating my meal.

Sometimes a holy resolve, not a discourteous hardness, is exactly what the Lord calls us to. If He has made you a messenger to a hard and obstinate people, He must in some ways make you harder and more obstinate. I'm not encouraging you to indulge in sinful selfishness, arrogance, impatience, or immaturity as you carry out your task. But understand that when the way is hard, God will supply the stamina you need. You have never been and you will never be in a situation beyond what God can enable you to bear. Pray that He will enable you to endure, and know that He will supply.

## The Messenger Must Expect Rejection

The final statement we must consider is that the messenger of God must expect rejection. One of the more interesting details about the book of Ezekiel is the frequent use of the title "son of man." It's used 93 times, and scholars have spilt endless amounts of ink speculating on what all might be involved in its meaning. The title "son of man" seems to mean mortal or subject to death, and it often tends to be associated with rejection. Ezekiel refers to himself as "son of man" because he understood himself to be the rejected ambassador of a rejected King.

Ezekiel was not the only one in the Old Testament who faced rejection. Isaiah presented the Suffering Servant as a rejected individual: "He has no stately form or majesty that we should look upon Him, nor appearance that we should be attracted to Him. He was despised and forsaken of men, a man of sorrows and acquainted with grief; and like one from whom men hide their face He was despised, and we did not esteem Him" (53:2-3). In this way Isaiah prophesied that the Messiah would be despised and rejected. So it's no surprise that it was common for Jesus to refer to Himself by the title "Son of Man." For example, we read in Mark 8:31, "He began to teach them that the Son of Man must suffer many things and be rejected by the elders and the chief priests and the scribes, and be killed, and after three days rise again."

A little later in Mark 9:31 we read, "He was teaching His disciples and telling them, 'The Son of Man is to be delivered into the hands of men, and they will kill Him; and when He has been killed,

He will rise three days later.'" Jesus then used this title again in Mark 10:33-34:

> Behold, we are going up to Jerusalem, and the Son of Man will be delivered to the chief priests and the scribes; and they will condemn Him to death and will hand Him over to the Gentiles. They will mock Him and spit on Him, and scourge Him and kill Him, and three days later He will rise again.

By adopting the title "Son of Man," Jesus was affirming a long tradition of rejection, a rejection that He explained by quoting Psalm 22:1, "My God, my God, why have You forsaken me?" and Psalm 118:22, "The stone which the builders rejected has become the cornerstone." If you want to survive in the ministry, you must witness the rejection that Jesus experienced. You must reflect on His ministry. You must not allow the carnality in your own heart to entice you to find a way to be more successful in ministry than Jesus was.

Suffering is common to believers. The entire letter of 1 Peter was written to disperse any confusion Christians had with regard to their trials. Confusion exists because suffering seems to be counterintuitive. The logic some have is that when we turn to God, we should experience blessings and not trials. But Scripture tells us the people in the first-century church experienced suffering.

Peter encouraged some of these people by saying to them in 1 Peter 2:20-21, "When you do what is right and suffer for it [and] you patiently endure it, this finds favor with God. For you have been called for this purpose, since Christ also suffered for you, leaving you an example for you to follow in His steps."

In other words, "Don't be discouraged because of your suffering. If you're suffering for doing good, that's a sign you're on the right path. Look at who you're following. What happened to Him? Did He receive universal acceptance and acclaim? No, He knew rejection and suffering."

Appealing to Christ's example, Peter then charged his fellow believers with the following words:

> Beloved, do not be surprised at the fiery ordeal among you, which comes upon you for your testing, as though some strange thing were happening to you; but to the degree that you share the sufferings of Christ, keep on rejoicing, so that also at the revelation of His glory you may rejoice with exultation (1 Peter 4:12-13).

Now it's true that some of the suffering we face is due to our own stupidity. Even a great minister like Jonathan Edwards made foolish mistakes as a pastor. When he was fired from his church in North Hampton, it wasn't only because he was faithful to preach God's Word.

He had also publicly summoned some of the children of the prominent families to talk to him in connection with a scandalous matter, unintentionally implying that the kids were guilty of some heinous crime. Edwards made relatively small pastoral mistakes that resulted in major consequences.

---

**If you are presenting the gospel in a way that makes it attractive to a carnal person, then you're setting your church up to misunderstand what it means to follow Christ.**

---

Although some of the suffering we experience is brought upon ourselves, there's still more that's encountered in the midst of faithful ministry. It is normal for the messenger of God's Word to face rejection in a fallen world. If you are presenting the gospel in a way that makes it attractive to a carnal person, then you're setting your church up to misunderstand what it means to follow Christ. The faithful preaching of God's Word will result in some rejection.

Now, even though rejection is normal, it is not final. Praise God for such a hope! Read with me another reference to the title "Son of Man"—one that appears in Daniel 7:13-14:

> I kept looking in the night visions,

and behold, with the clouds of heaven One like a Son of Man was coming, and He came up to the Ancient of Days and was presented before Him. And to Him was given dominion, glory and a kingdom, that all the peoples, nations and men of every language might serve Him. His dominion is an everlasting dominion which will not pass away; and His kingdom is one which will not be destroyed.

In the New Testament we see who this "Son of Man" is. When Jesus was asked whether He was the Messiah, He said to the high priest, "I am; and you shall see the Son of Man sitting at the right hand of power, and coming with the clouds of heaven" (Mark 14:62). The Suffering Servant is also the glorious King. The pattern you see in the teaching of Jesus, in the book of Acts, in 1 Peter, and in other places in the Bible is suffering, *then* glory. Beware when someone comes preaching just glory. But you also don't want someone who preaches just suffering. For suffering is followed by glory.

There is nothing we will suffer in the ministry that we will not be repaid for infinitely. From the shores of heaven we will look back and say, "Oh, it was worth it a thousand times over." That's why we look at Jesus' entrance into Jerusalem during the passion week and we call it the triumphal entry. We know He's going to be betrayed and killed, but we also know that it is not the whole story. Jesus would rise from the dead, ascend into heaven, and will reign there until He comes back and gathers the universe to worship Him.

So if you have been called to serve as one of His messengers, remember these words: "Let us…[fix] our eyes on Jesus, the author and perfecter of faith, who for the joy set before Him endured the cross, despising the shame, and has sat down at the right hand of the throne of God. For consider Him who has endured such hostility by sinners against Himself, so that you will not grow weary and lose heart" (Hebrews 12:2-3).

# PRAYER

God, You know the weariness that Your messengers can feel—a weariness that goes far beyond the physical. We pray, Lord, that any opposition that we have experienced from sinful men will be put in perspective as we consider Him who endured such opposition. O God, give us hearts that are fixed on the presentation of the Lord Jesus Christ in Your Word. Give us the time, patience, and discipline to meditate on Christ. Help us to understand further how to follow Christ and to be Your messengers. Work in our hearts by Your Spirit in a way that You would never work through the eloquence of a speaker or through the accuracy of descriptions in a book, but only as Your Holy Spirit can work through our hearts, through each one of our situations, so that you may receive all the glory. In Jesus' name we pray, Amen.

# 3

## Epitaph of a Faithful Preacher

*John MacArthur*
*Shepherds' Conference 2003*

*2 Timothy 4:6-8*

The words of dying men tend to be stripped of all hypocrisy—they tend to reveal what resides within a man's heart. For example, Napoleon, on his deathbed, said, "I die before my time and my body will be given back to earth to become the food of worms, such is the fate which so soon awaits the great Napoleon."[1] It was Mahatma Gandhi who said, at the edge of his death, "My days are numbered. For the first time in fifty years I find myself in a slew of despond, all about me is darkness, I am praying for light." What's interesting is that the phrase "slew of despond" comes from *The Pilgrim's Progress*, which Gandhi had read but not believed. It was Charles Maurice de Talleyrand, a prominent French diplomat of the nineteenth century, who wrote on a piece of paper that was found after his death, "What cares, what agitation, what anxieties, what ill will, what sad complications, and all this without other results except great fatigue of mind, and body, and a profound sentiment of discouragement with regard to the future, and disgust with regard to the past."[2] Such miserable ways to die! Yet there are better ways to die.

I remember, in my childhood, visiting Christ Church in Philadelphia. As I wandered around the church grounds I found the gravestone of Benjamin Franklin. I cannot vouch for the purity of his religion, but I liked the epitaph he wrote for himself—so much so that I memorized it:

The Body of
B. Franklin, Printer.
Like the Cover of an old Book,
Its Contents torn out,

And Strip of its Lettering
& Gilding,
Lies here, Food for Worms.
But the Work shall not be lost:
For it will, as he believ'd,
appear once more
In a new and more elegant
Edition,
Corrected and Improved
By the Author.[3]

Like Ben Franklin, the apostle Paul wrote his own epitaph. Here's what he said:

I am already being poured out as a drink offering, and the time of my departure has come. I have fought the good fight, I have finished the course, I have kept the faith; in the future there is laid up for me the crown of righteousness, which the Lord, the righteous judge, will award to me on that day; and not only to me, but also to all who have loved His appearing (2 Timothy 4:6-8).

**Faithful to the End**

I want to take you not to the next few years of your ministry, but to the end of your life. I want you to think about what your epitaph will say. Second Timothy 4:6-8 contains the epitaph of God's greatest servant among men; here we find Paul's own assessment of his life. When he wrote it, he was on the brink of death—his trial had taken place, his sentence was death, and his execution was imminent. Paul knew his present imprisonment would be his last, and that he was on his way to martyrdom.

I suppose by human standards it wasn't a good time for Paul to leave the world. I am sure that among many believers in the early church, there was a deep and profound love and affection for this apostle. After all, many Gentile believers were able to trace their spiritual lineage back to his ministry—they were indebted to him because he had introduced them to Christ as their Savior. Who could ever replace him? He was the last of the apostles, and there was no apostolic succession after him. Paul had firsthand experiences with the risen Jesus on several occasions, the first being on the road to Damascus. There was nobody like him, and yet it was now time for him to go.

Paul's departure took place at a seemingly inappropriate time for the church. For example, the church at Ephesus, where Timothy was pastoring, had fallen upon difficult times. Paul had started this church, and it had gotten to the point where people were deviating from the truth and abandoning the pursuit of holy things, and corrupt leaders were leading people astray. As a result, the church was erring in doctrine and conduct. That's why Paul had left Timothy in charge—he hoped that Timothy would set things right. But the resistance from within the church and persecution from outside evidently had caused Timothy to waver.

In the beginning of the letter that bears his epitaph, Paul wrote to Timothy, "I am mindful of the sincere faith within you" (2 Timothy 1:5). That's an interesting statement—it's like writing a letter to someone and saying, "Dear friend, I know you're a Christian, but…" Why else would Paul remind Timothy that the young disciple was in the faith, unless there were certain things happening that might call that into question?

Paul then went on to explain why he mentioned Timothy's "sincere faith": "For this reason I remind you to kindle afresh the gift of God, which is in you" (1:6). He was saying, "Timothy, you have a gift for preaching and ministry, which was affirmed by the elders of the church. Stir it up." Paul was rightly concerned because Timothy had evidently faltered in the use of his gifts. Because of pressure from the inside and persecution from the outside, he was beginning to collapse. That's why, in the next verse, Paul gave this exhortation: "God has not given us a spirit of timidity" (1:7). When Paul spoke of Timothy's "timidity," he was referring to cowardice. This was very serious—not only because Paul, the last of the apostles, was on the verge of leaving, but because Paul's replacement, Timothy, was waning. It had gotten to the point Paul found it necessary to say, "Don't be a coward. Keep doing what you've been gifted to do." In verse 8 Paul added, "Don't be ashamed of the testimony of our Lord."

A few verses later Paul urged, "Retain the standard of sound words. Guard, through the Holy Spirit who dwells in us, the treasure which has been entrusted to you" (1:13-14). When you're under persecution from outsiders and resistance from within the church, you'll find yourself tempted to change your doctrine and compromise so that you can ease up some of the pressure on you. But Paul told Timothy to combat that temptation and guard what had been entrusted to him.

We get a sense for how dire the situation might have been when Paul added, "You are aware of the fact that all who are in Asia [have] turned away from me" (1:15). The implication is, "Timothy, are you also going to turn away?"

This is strong language from Paul. It reveals the condition of Timothy's heart and the health of the Ephesian church. Paul had given Timothy the responsibility of leading in Ephesus and being an example to the other churches. Yet Timothy was drifting toward weakness. That's why in 2 Timothy 2:1 Paul wrote, "You therefore, my son, be strong in the grace that is in Christ Jesus." In the verses that follow he urged, "Be a soldier," "Be an athlete," "Be a hardworking farmer," "Be a diligent workman," "Be a vessel for honor and flee youthful lusts," and "Be a slave of the Lord." Paul commanded Timothy to not give in, fail, or compromise.

In the next chapter, Paul wrote, "Continue in the things you have learned" (3:14). Contextually, it is important to remember that in 2 Timothy 3:16 Paul reminded Timothy that all Scripture was inspired by God and was profitable for every good work. Then in 4:2 Paul exhorted this young man to "preach the word." This entire epistle of 2 Timothy was an attempt by the apostle Paul, under the inspiration of the Holy Spirit, to infuse strength into a weakened Timothy.

You can see, then, that from a human perspective, this was not the optimal time for the apostle Paul to depart. Yet Paul went on to express a quiet confidence as he prepared to step aside and let Timothy succeed him. After boldly confronting Timothy, Paul then exhibited an attitude of triumphant victory as he summed up his life with these words: "I have fought the good fight, I have finished the course, I have kept the faith" (4:7). In essence, Paul was saying, "I am ready to go."

You can't control the next generation, and you can't determine what will happen after you're gone. As it turned out, Paul's concern about the church at Ephesus proved to be legitimate. By the time the book of Revelation was written, we learn that this church had left its first love. This prompted Jesus to say, "I am coming to you and will remove your lampstand out of its place—unless you repent" (Revelation 2:5).

Even when Paul had plenty of reason for concern, he faced death triumphantly. He was able to look back over his life and say, "I did what the Lord asked me to do, and that's all I can do. I can't guarantee the future; I can't guarantee the successor. I can only do what I was given to do."

## Paul's Epitaph

In his epitaph, Paul viewed his life from three perspectives: the present, the past, and the future. He looked to the close of his life, the course of his life, and the future of his life. He did this not merely to provide information for Timothy, but to motivate him. There was nothing subtle about what Paul wrote to this young man who was likely wavering: "I am going to run and fight to the end. I am going to keep the faith." Such words would have served as a strong encouragement to Timothy.

---

**For a soldier to have motivation to fight in the moment, he needs to have victory in view at the end.**

---

The New Testament tells us that Paul was put in prison for his faithfulness. In this way he was an effective role model for Timothy, and that should be true for us as well. Paul is our example when it comes to finishing strong. I can't think about the next week or next month of my life without thinking about the end. It's what I want to be at the end that keeps me on course right now.

The metaphors Paul used in 2 Timothy 2 reaffirm this idea. For a soldier to have motivation to fight in the moment, he needs to have victory in view at the end. For an athlete to exert himself in the middle of a race, he needs to keep in mind the reward that comes with winning the race. Any steward given a responsibility finds it helpful to remember he will have to give an account for how he guarded what was entrusted to him. It's our view of the end that sustains us in the present.

When ministers default doctrinally or morally—when they wander away from their calling—it's usually because they've lost sight of the end. They've stopped looking ahead to the final victory, the final reward, the final affirmation.

If you have a clear view of the way you want to finish, then you will know how to move forward. If you care about winning, then you will know how you need to run. With that in mind, let's look at Paul's three perspectives for finishing well.

### The Close of Paul's Life: Poured Out as an Offering

In his epitaph, Paul looked first at the present aspect of his life: "I am already being poured out as a drink offering, and the time of my departure has come" (2 Timothy 4:6). The confidence he expressed here is remarkable. He said, "It's over. I am being poured out, and the time has come." In the original Greek text the word translated "time" is *kiros*, which is not a reference to time as measured on a clock, but to an epoch or an

era. Paul was saying, "The season of my departure has come."

Note that Paul said he was "being poured out as a drink offering." Here, he used Jewish language from the Old Testament. When the children of Israel went into the land of Canaan, God gave them instructions on how to conduct worship. This included guidelines for the burnt offering (Numbers 15). This was an offering for sin—it was recognition on the part of the people that the wages of sin was death, and that there was a need for a sacrifice to pay for their sins. This sacrifice pointed toward the Lord Jesus Christ, the one and only true sacrifice. But before Christ's death on the cross, the burnt offering involved putting a slain animal on the altar as an offering to God.

But the slain animal wasn't placed alone on the altar. Poured over the offering was flour mixed with oil, which produced a sweet aroma. And wine was added to all this as well. Paul had this imagery in mind when he said, "I gave myself as a burnt offering. I put my whole life up there—all of it from the Damascus Road onward. For the last three decades I've been up there on that altar, offering up my life and taking no thought for myself. For me, to live is Christ and to die is gain. If I live, I live to the Lord and if I die, I die to the Lord. Whatever happens, I am the Lord's."

This imagery is beautiful. The burnt offering symbolizes Paul's life, and the drink offering symbolizes his death. Paul understood sacrifice, and that's why he could live the way he did. That's why he could fight the good fight, run the race, and maintain his stewardship all the way to the end—he had never viewed his life as his own. For Paul, life wasn't about success or accolades or prestige. It was about sacrifice.

In Romans 12:1, Paul wrote, "Present your bodies a living and holy sacrifice, acceptable to God, which is your spiritual service of worship." He practiced what he preached and gave his body as a living sacrifice wholly acceptable to God. When you approach life that way, there's no disappointment when things don't go according to plan. Rather than pursue comfort, you're more concerned about giving your life away—and as a result, you're not worried about becoming burned out.

Earlier, in Philippians 2:17, when Paul wrote "Even if I am being poured out as a drink offering," he was speaking hypothetically. But here in 2 Timothy 4:6, the language is not hypothetical; it is real. Don't think for a moment there was anything easy about what Paul faced. He was in prison, winter was coming, and it would soon be very cold. That's why in 2 Timothy 4:13 he said, "Bring the cloak which I left at Troas." If Paul survived through the winter before his execution, it was going to be cold and he wouldn't have anything to read, so he asked for both his cloak and "the books, especially the parchments."

As if that weren't enough, Paul also faced serious opposition: "Alexander the coppersmith did me much harm" (4:14). Timothy was to watch out for Alexander because he vigorously opposed biblical teaching. Paul then added, "At my first defense no one supported me, but all deserted me...But the Lord stood with me" (2 Timothy 4:16-17). Paul had been abandoned and was lonely. This had to be difficult for him. Is this how the great apostle ended his ministry? Nobody was naming cathedrals after him then. He was alone, forsaken by Demas and others. Because he was lonely, Paul asked for Mark and for something to read. Even at the end of his life, Paul was an offering on the altar.

Paul then said, "The time of my departure has come" (2 Timothy 4:6). "Has come" is in the perfect verb tense in the original Greek text, which means it had already come, or it had already arrived. The clouds of death were already hovering over Paul. I love his use of the word "departure" (Greek, *analyseōs*)— that's a great way to view death. When we use the word *departure*, we don't usually think about it in the context of death. Rather, we use the word in the sense of leaving one location and going to another. That's exactly what Paul meant, but he had his death in mind. It's interesting to note that in the New Testament, *analyseōs* was used in a number of ways that fit with the point Paul was making.

First, *analyseōs* was used to speak of unyoking an animal from the shaft of a plow. Paul viewed death as being unhooked from all the toil he had exerted here on earth. He would soon be able to lay down his heavy load of ministry.

Second, *analyseōs* was used in reference to the loosening of chains, fetters, or bonds that held a prisoner. In essence, Paul was saying, "Not only am I going to be loosed from the burden of my labor, I'm also going to be loosed from the chains of my fallenness, my persecution, and all else that binds me. I will be released from the confines of my flesh and this Roman prison and enter into the glorious liberty of the courts of heaven."

Third, *analyseōs* was used to speak of bringing down a tent. The nomadic people in Bible lands would put up a tent, live in that location for a brief time, then take their tent down. Paul was saying, "I'm about to take this tent down, and I won't be putting it up again. I'm going to live in a place where there aren't any tents. I'm going to the dwelling place prepared for me in the Father's house, where I will live in the glories of heaven forever."

Fourth, *analyseōs* was used in connection with the loosening of a ship's mooring ropes. Many times during his missionary journeys crisscrossing the Mediterranean, Paul had stood on a deck and watched the ropes fall away as the ship began to move out to sea. This, however, would be the last time Paul set sail, launching him into the greatest deep of all—crossing the waters of death and arriving at the port of heaven.

For the Christian, death means laying down every burden and labor in exchange for a rest that lasts forever. It also means the laying aside of all the sins and difficulties that bind and pull. Death is striking camp, as it were, to take up residence in a permanent place, an eternal home. It is casting off the ropes that bind us to this world and sailing into God's world, where we will live in His presence forever. And here in 2 Timothy 4, Paul declares, "I'm ready for that!"

Wouldn't it be great to come to the end of your life and be able to say, "I'm done, Lord. What is the delay?" This reminds me of Robert Browning's poem about a young soldier who came flying from the battlefield to report to Napoleon the victory at Ratisbon. Though he was wounded, the soldier was eager to bring the good news to his chief. Napoleon noticed the man's wounds and the poem ends with these now-famous lines:

> "You're wounded!" "Nay,"
>     the soldier's pride
> Touch'd to the quick, he said:
> "I'm kill'd, Sire!" And his
>     chief beside,
> Smiling the boy fell dead. [4]

The soldier's message was, "No sir, I'm not wounded, I'm proud to be dead for your cause." The apostle Paul was saying something similar: "I've done my duty; now I lay down my life."

### The Course of Paul's Life: Committed to a Fight

In 2 Timothy 4:7 Paul looked to his past and said, "I have fought the good fight, I have finished the course, I have kept the faith." In the original Greek text, all those verbs are in the perfect tense, describing actions completed in the past and bearing present results. Actually, the order of the words in the Greek text is "The good fight I have fought, the course I have finished, the faith I have kept." In each case, the object is placed before the verb so that the emphasis is on the object. That was how Paul viewed ministry: as a course, a faith, a body of truth, a race to run, and a battle to fight.

Wouldn't it be great to look back over your life and have no regrets? No sadness, no lack of fulfillment, no feeling of having left things unfinished? Paul faced death with complete satisfaction and triumph. I can't think of a more glorious way to leave this world. I don't know how you think about death, but I assume most people think about it in terms of its physical reality. People exercise, eat healthy, and do whatever it takes to protect their heart and body and ensure they don't die young. They do whatever they can to protect themselves physically.

When it comes to death, I don't know how I'm going to go—that's all in God's hands. But when I consider death, I don't think so much about the physical aspect of it. Rather, I'm more concerned with the spiritual aspect. Where will I be in terms of my faithfulness when my time comes? That's the issue for me. I have absolutely no control over how I die, but I do have responsibility for how I go spiritually. God has given me the means of

grace, the power of the Holy Spirit, and the truth of the Word to keep me on course. I want to look at my life the way Paul looked at his life—I want to finish well spiritually. Paul said, "It doesn't matter to me if I live or die. What matters is that faithfulness marks my life to the end." Having that perspective is one way to ensure you stay on course.

*Fighting the Good Fight*

Note particularly how Paul described his life of ministry: "I have fought the good fight." Recognizing that you are in a fight will help motivate you to finish well. In the original Greek text, "have fought" (*ēgōnismai*) and "fight" (*agōna*) speak of an intense struggle—it could be translated, "I have agonized the agony." Paul understood that this life is an ongoing, agonizing war that requires an immense amount of energy.

Many Christians assume that life should be easier as a believer, but it's not. It requires giving yourself as a sacrifice and placing yourself on the altar. It's a lifelong battle. So we shouldn't be surprised when things get difficult. In fact, we should worry when they aren't. A moment of peace is nice but it's also frightening, for that could mean there's a sneak attack coming up. It's always better to know where the battle is taking place.

Over my years of church ministry I've had people come up to me and say, "I hate to tell you this, but we have a problem over here." My response has always been, "You know what's worse than you telling me we've got a problem? Not knowing that the problem exists." That's because when we know about a problem, we can do something about it.

As long as Satan is active, we will be engaged in spiritual warfare. That's why we can expect the work of ministry to be hard, and it's going to take every effort we have to hang in there and endure. You cannot expect to go through life comfortably with everything going exactly the way you want it to. If you take that expectation into the ministry, you'll be a casualty because you can't wander in blissful ignorance in the middle of a battlefield without getting shot.

From the time Paul became a believer, he was at war. He fought against Satan, principalities, spiritual wickedness, Jewish and pagan attacks, fanaticism among the Thessalonians, incipient Gnosticism among the Ephesians and the Colossians, his own heart, his own disappointments, and on top of all of that he battled against his own flesh, which caused him to do what he didn't want to do. The Christian life is a never-ending battle. You can't ever take a rest; you can't ever let down your guard. Life is an ongoing spiritual struggle that demands supreme commitment and effort. And after all he had been through, Paul was able to declare, "I fought it all the way to the end."

Note that Paul called this fight "the good fight." Many of us consider ourselves to be patriotic and we enjoy hearing the national anthem. We are inspired by what the flag stands for and we feel the nobility behind it and our nation's history. That's also how we as Christians should feel every time we see a Bible. While we may be glad to take a stand for noble causes, our labor for God is the cause of all causes.

The word translated "good" in 2 Timothy 4:7 is the Greek word *kalon*—it means that the fight is noble, beautiful, profitable, excellent, delightful, and distinguished. I especially like the word *noble*. Paul was saying, "I fought a noble fight." It's the most noble of all fights—the fight for the honor of Jesus Christ, for the glory of the gospel, for the integrity of God's Word.

The men who come to the end of their life victoriously and are able to face the Lord with confidence are those who are faithful in the ministry God has called them to. They realize they are in a noble war, and they are fully committed to facing the battle head-on.

*Finishing the Course*

Paul then moved from the battlefield metaphor to a race metaphor—in 2 Timothy 4:7 he wrote, "I have finished the course." The word translated "course" is the Greek term *dramas*, which refers to an athletic race. Paul said, "I started the race, I ran it, I stayed on course, and I finished." He didn't run aimlessly. He stayed on the course and aimed for the finish line. He was focused and didn't waver.

This course Paul spoke of begins at conversion and ends in glory. He had begun the race on the road to Damascus and was soon going to cross the finish line. Along the way, he never lost sight of what God wanted him to do. The key to doing this is found in Hebrews 12:1-2: "Let us run with endurance the race that is set before us, fixing our eyes on Jesus, the author and perfecter of faith." Jesus was the model runner, and Paul followed after Him.

Have you ever run a race? I used to run sprints in my college days. I ran the 100 meter, the 200 meter, and occasionally the 400 meter races. I was rarely the winner, but I gave my best and my objective was to stay as close as possible to whoever was in the lead. Likewise, the winner of this spiritual race is Jesus Christ and right behind Him is Paul, and I'm endeavoring to stay with those two. They're my objective. This was the focus Paul had—one that reminds me of Rudyard Kipling's line:

> If you can talk with crowds and keep your virtue, or walk with kings and not lose the common touch, if neither foes nor loving friends can hurt you, if all men count with you but none too much; if you can fill the unforgiving minute with 60 seconds worth of distance run, yours is the earth and everything that's in it, and which is more you'll be a man, my son.[5]

The focused life is undisturbed by everything going on around you. Run the race well all the way to the end.

The apostle Paul also recognized the need to use his time well. If you're going to run the race so as to win it, then don't waste the time God has given you. In Ephesians 5:16, Paul wrote about "making the most of your time, because the days are evil." He was committed to running hard and fast so he could finish strong. What can you do to make Paul's epitaph your own? Follow his example!

### Keeping the Faith

Paul saw life not only as a war and a race, but also as a stewardship: "I have kept the faith" (2 Timothy 4:7). The Lord put Paul into battle, and gave him a lane to run in and a trust to keep. Paul kept it faithfully. What was this trust? He had kept "the faith"—not a subjective faith, but the Christian faith, "the faith which was once for all handed down to the saints" (Jude 3). Paul was unwaveringly faithful to the Word of God.

---

**You have been given a sacred trust—that of taking God's truth and making sure it gets safely into the hands of the next generation.**

---

That should be the passion of your life as well. Not only are you a preacher of God's Word, you are also called to be its guardian. You have been given a sacred trust—that of taking God's truth and making sure it gets safely into the hands of the next generation. It's a guardianship for which you will answer to God. According to Hebrews 13:17, there will come a day when you have to give an account to God for what He entrusted to you. That's why you should become deeply grieved when you see people play fast and loose with Scripture, and it's why you should jump into the battle to defend God's Word whenever the need to do so arises.

In my preaching ministry, I am concerned that people take the Word of God seriously. I don't ever want to misinterpret Scripture, and I don't ever want to put words into God's mouth. People ask me, "Why do you study so much when you prepare your sermons?" It's because I want to get the passage right. I don't want to say, "God said" when He didn't say something. And I want to know how to protect God's Word from erroneous attacks. That is my stewardship.

What is my life? It's nothing but a sacrifice on an altar. The sacrifice is me giving up my life to fight God's battle, run His race, and keep His truth. That's what I'm called to do. I'm not reluctant about this calling, and I'm extremely grateful for it because it is the most noble of all callings.

### The Crown of Paul's Life: Reward for Faithfulness

After Paul wrote about the past and present aspects of his life, he turned his attention to what was to come: "In the future there is laid up for me the crown of righteousness, which the Lord, the righteous Judge, will award to me on that day; and not only to me, but also to all who have loved His appearing" (2 Timothy 4:8). Isn't that amazing? When we go to heaven, the Lord will reward us.

What will we do with the crowns given to us? Cast them at Jesus' feet! Everything we do is possible only because of the glorious goodness of our Lord. Our righteousness comes from His righteousness, which He was able to give to us because Jesus Christ paid the penalty for all our sins. We're not able to fight the good fight, finish the course, and keep the faith on our own. It's all God's doing.

Note that Paul said this "crown of righteousness" was coming "not only to me, but also to all who have loved His appearing." What does that mean? Some might assume it refers to having an interest in prophecy, but that's not what Paul was talking about. Just because you read all sorts of books about Bible prophecy and you know every detail of what is to come doesn't mean that you love His appearing. There's nothing wrong with studying about the end times, but to love His appearing means having in your heart a longing for Jesus' second coming. If you can't wait for His return and you're saying, "Come, Lord Jesus," then that's testimony that you desire to be found faithful when He comes.

So look at your life like Paul did. Fast-forward to the end and ask yourself, "What will my epitaph be?" And this isn't just for pastors or ministry leaders; it's for every Christian. Wouldn't you like your epitaph to read like the apostle Paul's?

Maybe you're feeling discouraged because somewhere along the way, as you fought the good fight and you ran the race, you blew it. You let down your guard, you strayed from the course, you weren't a good steward of what God entrusted to you. If that's the case, don't think that means it's all over. God is a God of grace—Psalm 103:12 says, "As far as the east is from the west, so far has He removed our transgressions from us." So think of it this way: Today is the beginning of the rest of your life. From here onward, you will fight, you will run, and you will maintain the steward-ship of God's truth. And when you're all done, the Lord will say, "Well done, good and faithful slave" (Matthew 25:23). And you will enter into the full reward that God has prepared for those who love Him.

# PRAYER

Father, it brings joy to our hearts to know that You have prepared for us an eternal reward even though there are times when we fail You. Even Paul had times when he stumbled. But You have forgiven our sins, and we understand what You mean by faithfulness to the very end. You aren't talking about perfection, but faithfulness. May You find us always a faithful soldier, always a striving runner, always a careful steward of the treasure of Your truth to the very end. May it be true of us so that we can enter the fullness of the reward that You've prepared for all who love You. We pray in Your Son's name, Amen.

# 4

# Bring the Book

*Steven J. Lawson*
*Shepherds' Conference 2006*

*Nehemiah 8:1-18*

All the people gathered as one man at the square which was in front of the Water Gate, and they asked Ezra the scribe to bring the book of the law of Moses which the Lord had given to Israel. Then Ezra the priest brought the law before the assembly of men, women and all who could listen with understanding, on the first day of the seventh month. He read from it before the square which was in front of the Water Gate from early morning until midday, in the presence of men and women, those who could understand; and all the people were attentive to the book of the law. Ezra the scribe stood at a wooden podium which they had made for the purpose. And beside him stood Mattithiah, Shema, Anaiah, Uriah, Hilkiah, and Maaseiah on his right hand; and Pedaiah, Mishael, Malchijah,

Hashum, Hashbaddanah, Zechariah and Meshullam on his left hand. Ezra opened the book in the sight of all the people for he was standing above all the people; and when he opened it, all the people stood up. Then Ezra blessed the Lord the great God. And all the people answered, "Amen, Amen!" while lifting up their hands; then they bowed low and worshiped the Lord with their faces to the ground. Also Jeshua, Bani, Sherebiah, Jamin, Akkub, Shabbethai, Hodiah, Maaseiah, Kelita, Azariah, Jozabad, Hanan, Pelaiah, the Levites, explained the law to the people while the people remained in their place. They read from the book, from the law of God, translating to give the sense so that they understood the reading.

Then Nehemiah, who was the

55

governor, and Ezra the priest and scribe, and the Levites who taught the people said to all the people, "This day is holy to the LORD your God; do not mourn or weep." For all the people were weeping when they heard the words of the law. Then he said to them, "Go, eat of the fat, drink of the sweet, and send portions to him who has nothing prepared; for this day is holy to our Lord. Do not be grieved, for the joy of the LORD is your strength." So the Levites calmed all the people, saying, "Be still, for the day is holy; do not be grieved." All the people went away to eat, to drink, to send portions and to celebrate a great festival, because they understood the words which had been made known to them.

Every great season of reformation in the church, and every great hour of spiritual awakening, has ushered in a recovery of biblical preaching. J.H. Merle d'Aubigne, the noted historian of the Reformation in Geneva and Europe, wrote, "The only true reformation is that which emanates from the Word of God."[1]

Such was certainly the case in sixteenth-century Europe, which witnessed the recovery of biblical preaching by men like Martin Luther, John Calvin, and John Knox. These Reformers

turned the European continent upside down with their pulpit expositions. Such was the case in the golden Puritan era in the seventeenth century, which also witnessed the recovery of biblical preaching in Scotland and England under the likes of John Owen, Jeremiah Burroughs, Samuel Rutherford, Thomas Watson, and an entire army of biblical expositors. These Puritan divines shook the English monarchy with their bold, biblical preaching. Such was the case in the Great Awakening through the biblical preaching of Jonathan Edwards, George Whitefield, and Gilbert Tennent. These preachers took New England by storm and electrified the Atlantic seacoast with the preaching of the Word. Every great reformation, every great awakening, and every great revival has been ushered in by the recovery of biblical preaching. The noted church historian Phillip Schaff wrote:

Every true progress in church history is conditioned by a new and deep study of the Scripture. While the humanists went back to the ancient classics and revived the spirit of Greek and Roman Paganism, the reformers went back to the Sacred Scriptures. In the original language, *ad fontes*, back to the fountain and revived the spirit of Apostolic Christianity. They were fired by an enthusiasm for the gospel, such as had not been seen since the days of Paul.[2]

Sola Scriptura and the preaching of the Scripture ushered in the Reformation. Describing that time, James Montgomery Boice wrote,

> Calvin had no weapon but the Bible. From the very first, his emphasis had been on Bible teaching. Calvin preached from the Bible every day and under the power of that preaching, the city began to be transformed. As the people of Geneva acquired knowledge of God's Word and were changed, the city became as John Knox said, "the most perfect school of Christ since the days of the Apostles."[3]

This is what is so desperately needed—a recovery not just of preaching, but of biblical preaching, expository preaching, and true preaching. That is why I love Nehemiah chapter 8—it puts its arms around what God has called you and me to do, which is to be expositors of the Word of God.

Here is the setting: the date is 445 BC and the place is Jerusalem. It has been less than one week since God's people rebuilt the wall around the city of Jerusalem under Nehemiah's leadership. It is a time in which the whole nation has come together to celebrate the Feast of Tabernacles. The temple has been restored and the city wall has been built. The people are back in the land after 70 years of captivity, but they need more than a mere building program and more than a crowd. They now need the preaching of God's Word to ignite their souls so that they may grow in the holiness with which God has called them to live.

In this passage, we examine a case for biblical preaching. In the first verse, Nehemiah presents the *cry* for biblical preaching. Then in verses 2 through 8, the *characteristics* of biblical preaching are delineated. Finally in verses 9 through 18, the *consequences* of biblical preaching are laid out.

**The Cry for Biblical Preaching**

The narrative begins where every revival and reformation must begin—with a cry and hunger for the preaching of the Word of God. In verse 1 the narrator wrote, "All the people gathered as one man at the square which was in front of the Water Gate." There were upwards of 42,000 people assembled by the water gate on the east side of Jerusalem near the Gihon Spring (Ezra 2:64).

Nehemiah 8:1 indicates that the people gathered as "one man," meaning they were intent on one purpose. They had come together for the right reason. They were there to make their plea, to cry out to their leaders to bring them the Word of God. Verse 1 continues, "And they asked Ezra the scribe to bring the book of the law of Moses which the LORD had given to Israel." This was remarkable. This plea came from the crowd—in a sense, from the pew. They were crying out, "Bring the Book! Bring the Book!"

Moses commanded in Deuteronomy 31:10-13 that the people of Israel were to come together every seven years for a corporate, public reading of God's Word. The Israelites had been in captivity for 70 years, and they were long overdue for this type of public gathering in the Holy City. They were eager to hear the Pentateuch read to them and the explanation to be given to them. They were under the heightened awareness of this reality and they cried out, "Bring the Book!" Ezra was the right man to step forward with the Book. It was 14 years earlier that Ezra himself had returned from captivity to Jerusalem to begin this ministry of teaching the Word. God had been preparing Ezra 14 years for this revival. He had been preparing the man for the moment, and the moment for the man.

### A Singular Focus

No doubt you are familiar with Ezra 7:10: "Ezra had set his heart to study the law of the Lord and to practice it, and to teach His statutes and ordinances in Israel." This was Ezra's philosophy of ministry. He had "set his heart," which means that he was resolved and fixed. He was a man of one thing—he was a man of the Book. Notice the passage says that Ezra was "set...to study the law," which means he was ready to seek something through careful inquiry. This term carries the connotation of digging out, as

a miner who digs out riches that are beneath the earth's surface.

---

**Studying the truth is where any meaningful ministry begins.**

---

This was the ministry to which God had called Ezra. He was a student of the Word. He had been doing this for at least 14 years leading up to this revival. Studying the truth is where any meaningful ministry begins. In 2 Timothy 2:15 Paul wrote, "Be diligent to present yourself approved to God as a workman who does need not to be ashamed, accurately handling the word of truth." The revival began with Ezra in front of an open scroll as he studied the Word of God. The man whom God calls into the ministry to be a preacher of the Word is supernaturally given an insatiable desire to study the Word of God.

I grew up in the home of an academician. My father was a professor in medical school. He was a brilliant man. Every morning, he rose early before I got up and was already off to the university. He had his laboratory. He did his research. He wrote his periodical articles. And he taught his classes. My brother is a professor at Vanderbilt Medical School, a cardiologist, and he too is a brilliant man. My mother was the valedictorian in her graduating class. My sister is an accomplished teacher. In contrast, while growing up, all I wanted to do was play football. When football season was over, I played on the basketball team. When basketball season was over, I played on the baseball team. While playing baseball, I also ran on the track team and lifted weights with the football team. During the summer I played golf, and in the fall my cycle repeated. That was my life. I did not want to study and I did not want to read.

During my senior year of high school, I signed a full scholarship to play football for Texas Tech University. When I signed that scholarship, I thought I would never have to study again. However, for my father, academia was the core value of being a Lawson. Right before I graduated from high school, my father sat me down and lectured me on the importance of academics, but I did not want to have anything to do with it. I went to Texas Tech and majored in finance, but ultimately I was there to play football. My whole life was immersed in athletics. I read CliffsNotes to pass classes and don't think that I even owned a book.

A couple years ago, my father visited my study at the church. The office walls were covered with books, and as my father stood in the middle of the room and looked around, he said, "Now I know there is a God in heaven. My son, the student." Then he walked over and hugged me. My father is a believer, and he rightly concluded that for me to become a student was a transformation only God could do in me. I had been primarily an athlete,

but when God calls you into the ministry, He gives you an insatiable desire to dig into the text. It is a supernatural work of God, and if you do not have it, you have not been called. If God wants you to fly, He will give you wings. If God wants you to preach, He will give you a great hunger and desire for His Word. When He summons you, you will become a student of the Word. You will dig, dig, and dig into it, knowing that you must plunge into the depths of His inerrant, inspired, and infallible Word.

Ezra can be described with the same words that Charles Spurgeon used to describe John Bunyan: "Why, this man is a living Bible! Prick him anywhere—his blood is bibline, the very essence of the Bible flows from him."[4] Bunyan was a walking Bible, Ezra was a walking Bible, and you and I must be walking Bibles. We have nothing to say apart from the Word of the living God.

### A Strenuous Pursuit

Not only did Ezra set his heart to study the Word, he was also determined "to practice it" (Ezra 7:10). He became a living epistle of what he was reading and learning. Ezra lived out the Word of God and put it into practice. This word "practice" is used elsewhere in the Old Testament and carries the idea of expending great energy in the pursuit of something. It's the word that was used to speak of Noah's strenuous effort in building the Ark. With diligent effort, Ezra was building the Word of God into his life. He was not passive in his sanctification. He was bringing his life under the authority of Scripture. He was striving to be an incarnation of the Book that he was reading.

### A Strong Passion

In addition to studying and practicing God's Word, Ezra was committed to "teach[ing] His statutes and ordinances in Israel" (Ezra 7:10). This word "teach[ing]" indicates the image of instructing by goading and prodding, as a master would his ox. Not only was Ezra laying out information for those who were in front of him, but there was also a purpose to declaring the truth. He was pushing the people toward the will of God as he was teaching the truth.

This is what God has called us to be—students. We are to dig into the Word. Likewise, we are to be believers who live out the message. Moreover, we are to be preachers who teach it. The revival at the Water Gate began 14 years earlier when Ezra was alone with God, with the scrolls of Scripture unraveled before him, studying the Word, digging into the text, grasping its meaning, capturing its thunder, incorporating it into his soul, applying it in his life, and teaching it faithfully. This revival began with the people crying out for biblical preaching, and Ezra was prepared.

In like manner, the people in your congregation who truly know God and love Him are crying out to you in their hearts, "Preacher, bring the Book!" Sadly,

there are pastors all over this country who instead of hearing the cry of their people are going to conferences where they are told, "Go out and survey unbelievers and give them what they want." If you go survey lost people, they are not going to say, "We want more Bible exposition." That is because "the natural man does not accept the things of the Spirit of God, for they are foolishness to him; and he cannot understand them, because they are spiritually appraised" (1 Corinthians 2:14). The unbelievers want entertainment and drama, and when we cave in to their carnal demands, we sin before the almighty God.

Yet among the faithful few, there is a cry for biblical preaching. Open your ears and you will hear it in your own congregation. This is the yearning that always precedes a great movement of God in reformation, awakening, and revival. Imitate Ezra's commitment to being a man who studies and digs in order to feed your people the Word of God.

## The Characteristics of Biblical Preaching

As we build a case for biblical preaching, it is helpful to look at the characteristics of biblical preaching. Martyn Lloyd-Jones wrote, "What is it that always heralds the dawn of a reformation or of a revival? It is a renewed preaching. Not only a new interest in preaching but a new kind of preaching."[5]

Ezra's preaching was a specific kind

of preaching. As we examine it, I want to point out five indispensable characteristics of biblical preaching. These should form the paradigm for our sermon preparation and delivery.

*A Biblical Reading*

The first characteristic of biblical preaching is to maintain a reading of the Word of God. Nehemiah 8:3 tells us Ezra's starting point when he proclaimed the Book to God's people: "He read from it before the square, which was in front of the Water Gate." Ezra began his exposition with a simple reading of the Book because he knew that the Bible is living and active and sharper than a two-edged sword (see Hebrews 4:12). As Ezra spoke, he had passion in his voice. This was not a monotone mumbling of the Word. In the original Hebrew text, the word "read" is *kara*, which means "to cry out, to call aloud, to roar, to proclaim." In fact it is the word used in Jonah 3:2 when God said, "Arise, go to Nineveh the great city and *kara*." Proclaim! And that's what happened: "Jonah began to go through the city one day's walk; and he cried out [*kara*]" (verse 4).

When Paul instructed young Timothy, he said, "Until I come, give attention to the public reading of Scripture, to exhortation and teaching" (1 Timothy 4:13). This is how you begin the exposition of the Word of God—with a reading of the passage. Public reading of Scripture is in keeping with Jesus' own practice. In the Gospel of Luke, Jesus entered a synagogue in Nazareth and took the scroll of Isaiah and read from it, then said, "Today this Scripture has been fulfilled in your hearing" (Luke 4:21).

Similarly, Paul challenged the Colossians to read Scripture aloud: "When this letter is read among you, have it also read in the church of the Laodiceans; and you, for your part read my letter that is coming from Laodicea" (Colossians 4:16). The pastor is to stand in front of the congregation and read the Word of God. In 1 Thessalonians 5:27 Paul said, "I adjure you by the Lord to have this letter read to all the brethren." John wrote in Revelation 1:3, "Blessed is he who reads and those who hear the words of the prophecy, and heed the things which are written in it."

This practice of a public reading of Scripture has long slipped away from the worship service. Yet it is the only part of the worship service that is perfect. When you do this, you are making these statements to everyone who is listening, that your sermon content originated from a specific text of Scripture. What God has to say is far more important than what any man has to say.

When you step into the pulpit, you are an ambassador of the King and you have arrived with His Book. You need to conduct yourself like a man of God. You need to be like Ezra and open the Bible and read from the text. When you read the Bible in preaching, you are making a statement to everyone who sits under you that you are a man who has nothing but the Word of God to bring to the hearts of people.

### A Lengthy Treatment

The second characteristic of true biblical preaching is to present a lengthy treatment of the passage. Nehemiah 8:3 continues, "He read from it...from early morning until midday, in the presence of men and women, those who could understand; and all the people who were attentive to the book of the law." From sunrise to high noon, from 6:00 a.m. to 12:00 p.m., Ezra provided a full treatment of God's Word.

In order for there to be authentic Bible exposition, there has to be sufficient time for an introduction, transitions, homiletical points, and an explanation of the text. A genuine sermon involves word studies, cross-references, historical background, thematic context, authorial intent, application, illustration, exhortation, persuasion, and conclusion. Early in my pastoral ministry, one of the matriarchs in our church said, "Pastor, your sermons are becoming too long." I said, "Well ma'am, it all depends upon the size of the cup you bring to church. If you bring a little thimble to church, it will not take me long to fill it up. May God enlarge your heart for the things of His kingdom."

Sometimes I am asked to speak in a seminary chapel and the dean will say to me, "I want you to model Bible exposition. You have 22 minutes to preach." I cannot model Bible exposition in a compressed period of time—not true exposition of the Scripture. Ezra offered a lengthy treatment. Yes, there are variables you must consider when it comes to sermon length, such as your own giftedness and where your congregation is spiritually. Still, your responsibility is to provide a full disclosure of the truth.

### An Authoritative Posture

The third characteristic of biblical preaching is an authoritative posture. In Nehemiah 8:4 we read, "Ezra the scribe stood at a wooden podium which they had made for the purpose." He is not sitting on a stool and casually sharing. He is not walking around gabbing. He is standing at a wooden pulpit, and the reason he is standing there is because the Word is opened before him. I become nervous when a pastor walks around the stage without a Bible in his hand. The preacher needs to be where the Bible is. If you are walking away from the pulpit, you better take the Bible with you because I am not going to listen to you without an open Bible in your hand.

Verse 4 also tells us Ezra's wooden podium was large enough to hold 14 people. Ezra mounted the platform in order to be seen and heard. He had six men on one side and seven men on the other. There was solidarity in this leadership team.

Nehemiah 8:5 goes on to say that "Ezra opened the book in the sight of all the people for he was standing above all the people." For Ezra to stand above the people was intentional. There was a transcendence about this moment. It was a way to indicate that God's message was not on their level. The message is coming down from above. Notice as well how the people reacted when Ezra opened the Book: "All the people stood up." When the preacher is serious about the Word of God, it becomes contagious. When you believe the Book and are ready to die for the Book, the people take notice. In Ezra's case, when he opened the Scriptures in front of all the people, they stood up. This is in response to the authoritative posture of the preacher.

> **When the preacher is serious about the Word of God, it becomes contagious.**

It is worth noting the people's response to Jesus' preaching when He taught the Sermon on the Mount. Matthew said "the crowds were amazed at His teaching; for he was teaching them as one having authority" (7:28-29). Peter took a similar posture in his first sermon on the day of Pentecost when he stood up and said, "Men of Judea and all you who live in Jerusalem, let this be known to you and give heed to my words" (Acts 2:14).

There must always be an authoritative nature about the preaching of the Word of God. Martin Luther once said, "The pulpit is the throne for the Word of God."[6] It is from the throne of the pulpit that the Word of God is to reign. Phillip Brooks, in his famous 1877 preaching lecture series at Yale, said, "If you are afraid of men and a slave to their opinion, go and do something else. Go and make shoes to fit them. Go even and paint pictures, which you know are bad, but which suit their bad taste. But do not keep on all your life preaching sermons which say not what God sent you to declare."[7] The man who will preach the Word of God must understand that there is an authoritative nature to true biblical preaching.

### A God-Exalting Thrust

The fourth characteristic of biblical preaching is a God-exalting thrust. In Nehemiah 8:6 we read that Ezra "blessed the Lord the great God." There seems to be an eclipse of the glory of God in the church today, but when Ezra brought the Book, he blessed the Lord and there was an unveiling of the glory of God. What happened in response? "All the people answered, 'Amen, Amen!' while lifting up their hands" (verse 6). The raising of the hands was emblematic of receiving the Word coming down from heaven. The response to such a God-glorifying moment was that "they bowed low and worshiped the LORD with their faces to the ground" (Nehemiah 8:6).

The Lord was magnified, and the

response was worship. This should be the effect of true expository preaching. When you are elevating God, you are lowering man. At the same time, you are magnifying the grace of God which spans that wide chasm. The more you lower God and the more you raise man, the more you trivialize the grace of God. But when you put God in His proper place, you put His grace on display.

### A Faithful Explanation

A fifth characteristic of biblical preaching is faithful explanation. Ezra involved the Levites in his preaching. They were spread among the 42,000 people to help explain the Scriptures. It was like a relay—Ezra read the Word of God and they explained it. There is a proper emphasis on the mind in true biblical preaching, and we see this all through Nehemiah chapter 8. In verse 2 we read, "understanding"; in verse 3, "understanding"; in verse 7, "explained"; in verse 8, "understood"; in verse 12, "understood"; and in verse 13, "insight." The emphasis of all true Bible exposition is on a precise explanation of the text.

John MacArthur has said, "I like to say that the meaning of the Scripture is the Scripture. If you do not have the interpretation of the passage right, then you do not have the Word of God, because only the true meaning is the Word of God."[8] He continues,

Authentic Christianity…is concerned first and foremost with truth. The Christian faith is not primarily about feelings, although deep feelings will surely result from the impact of truth on our hearts. It is not about human relationships, even though relationships are the main focus in many of today's evangelical pulpits. It is not about success and earthly blessings, no matter how much one might get that impression from watching the programs that dominate religious television these days. Biblical Christianity is all about truth. God's objective revelation (the Bible) interpreted rationally yields divine truth in perfectly sufficient measure…God wrote only one book—the Bible. It contains all the truth by which He intended us to order our spiritual lives.[9]

This is Bible exposition. The preacher gives the authorial intent of the text and explains the text. He persuades with the text, exhorts with the text, and then moves to the next text.

As Ezra preached the text, the Levites explained it. Nehemiah 8:8 says, "They read from the book, from the law of God, translating to give the sense." This was necessary because (1) the Israelites had been exiled for many years in Babylon, so for some of them it was difficult to understand the Hebrew text, and (2) the foreign culture of Babylon had influenced the Jewish way of life, making it necessary to explain the meaning of God's Word. The Levites were going beyond mere translation and were explaining the text's meaning. This is at the heart of expository preaching. If you do not explain the text in order to let God speak through that text, you do not have expository preaching.

**The Consequences of Biblical Preaching**

When the Word of God is preached in the power of the Spirit of God, there is a powerful effect. Although the consequences are not always instant, God's Word does not return void (see Isaiah 55:11-12). Sometimes God calls us to labor faithfully for many years before we see results. I remind you that "the eyes of the LORD run to and fro throughout the earth that He may strongly support those whose heart is completely His" (2 Chronicles 16:9). God is looking for congregations and pulpits where His Word is given a fair hearing and His people are called to a complete commitment to it.

*The Weeping of Repentance*

In Nehemiah 8 we notice that the preaching of God's Word has an impact on the people: "Then Nehemiah, who was the governor, and Ezra the priest and scribe, and the Levites who taught the people said to all the people, 'This day is holy to the LORD, your God; do not mourn or weep.'" Why did he say that? Because "all the people were weeping

when they heard the words of the law" (verse 9). The Word of God is a mirror that allows us to see ourselves for who we are. It enables us to see ourselves as God sees us. It removes our self-deception and allows us to see our sin and our need for grace. In this instance, as the Israelites came under this revelation, they began to weep and mourn.

George Whitefield was a prominent preacher whom God used mightily during the Great Awakening. On one occasion he preached to coal miners in Scotland. As Whitefield declared, "You must be born again," he noticed that their faces, which were covered with black soot, had white channels created by their trails of tears. These rough and vulgar men, after hearing the Word, came under conviction over their sins. The work of the Spirit, through the preaching of God's Word, pierces the hearts of men. It produces repentance and tears people down before it builds them up.

*The Rejoicing of Restoration*

Then after this repentance comes rejoicing. In Nehemiah 8:10, Ezra said to the people, "Go, eat of the fat, drink of the sweet, and send portions to him who has nothing prepared; for this day is holy to our Lord. Do not be grieved." Ezra no longer desired for the people to mourn; instead, he wanted them to realize that the joy of Lord was their strength. Ezra encouraged them by pointing them to the greatness of God, and a supernatural joy flooded their souls because their hearts had been cleansed through the ministry of God's Word. Verse 11 tells us, "The Levites calmed all the people, saying, 'Be still for the day is holy.'" The Word of God, when it is preached with power, brings a unique effect upon the souls of men.

That brings us to Nehemiah 8:12, where we see the apex of expository preaching: "All the people went away to eat, to drink, to send portions and to celebrate a great festival, because they understood the words which had been made known to them." Ezra's life of devotion to the Word of God preceded this moment for at least 14 years in Jerusalem, and the consequences were amazing. He had been digging and studying such that some say that he is the author of Psalm 119. Others say he memorized the entire Old Testament. What we do know with certainty is that Ezra was a man of the Word and a walking Bible. He stood up before the people of Israel and gave a proper instruction of the Word. As a result, the people were revived and transformed.

### The Call

This is what God has called you to do. Do you hear the people who are crying

in your church? The people who want to be fed and who desire for their souls to be nourished? Nehemiah 8 reveals for us the characteristics of biblical preaching and the consequences of biblical preaching. So bring the Book to your people.

In 1517, Martin Luther lit a match that ignited the fires of the Reformation that spread through the continent of Europe. Its flames soon leaped across the English Channel. Scotland and England were caught up in this Protestant movement, in which people were coming back to the fountain of the Scriptures. They asked Luther this question: "How did you bring about the Reformation? How did you turn Europe upside down?" He answered, "I simply taught, preached and wrote God's Word. Otherwise, I did nothing. When I slept, the Words so greatly weakened the papacy that never a prince or emperor inflicted so much damage upon it. I did nothing. The Word did it all."[10]

Each of us has the same instrument in his hand. You are called by God to exposit it, to preach it, and to proclaim it. The more you study it, the more you live it, and the more you declare it, the more you will see this world change.

# PRAYER

God, I pray that in this hour, in this place, You would raise up from this conference men who would be so committed to biblical preaching that they would literally storm the gates of hell. I pray that they would hold fast to sound doctrine, that they would give themselves to the deep study of the text, that they would be men of holiness and purity who would live the very message that they proclaim. As they step into the pulpit, may You be in the pulpit with them, to undergird them and strengthen them as they declare Your Word. Bring about another revival as You did in the days of Ezra. May it shake this country and shake every continent in the world. We pray this to the glory of Him who suffered, bled, and died for us upon the cross. In Jesus' name we pray, Amen.

# 5

## PREACHING AND
## THE SOVEREIGNTY OF GOD

*R.C. Sproul*
*Shepherds' Conference 2004*

*Romans 9:10-16*

Not only this, but there was Rebekah also, when she had conceived twins by one man, our father Isaac; for though the twins were not yet born and had not done anything good or bad, so that God's purpose according to His choice would stand, not because of works but because of Him who calls, it was said to her "The older shall serve the younger." Just as it is written, "Jacob I loved, but Esau I hated."

What shall we say then? There is no injustice with God, is there? May it never be! For He says to Moses, "I will have mercy on whom I have mercy, and I will have compassion on whom I have compassion." So then it does not depend on the man who wills or the man who runs, but on God who has mercy.

In the 1960s a friend of mine, John Guest, came to the United States from Liverpool, England. He came with a guitar slung over his back and had decided to give his life to a ministry of evangelism in the States. During his early weeks in America he spent time trying to familiarize himself with the country's culture and history. He visited Independence Hall, went and saw the Liberty Bell, and he visited the antique stores in the Germantown section of Philadelphia.

Many of these stores carry Revolutionary War memorabilia. As John went through them, he noticed placards that dated back to the eighteenth century which proclaimed, "Don't tread on me," and "No taxation without representation." He told me that in one of those stores he looked at a wall and a specific placard caught his eye—it said, "We serve no sovereign here." He said to me, "I was terrified when I read that—so much so, that I almost wanted to take the next ship back to England. I thought, *How can I possibly come to a people proclaiming the kingdom of God when they have a built-in allergy to sovereignty in their culture?*" I'll never forget the insight this stranger to our shores offered, for it was and is a fair assessment of our culture, even with regard to the evangelical church.

I do want to clarify that I've never met a professing Christian who would answer "No" to the question, "Do you believe in the sovereignty of God?" Every Christian I've ever asked has responded with a resounding, "Yes, of course I believe." What could be more axiomatic for a Christian to affirm than the sovereignty of God? We all understand that if God is not sovereign, He is not God. An affirmation of sovereignty is simply an affirmation of theism.

Now, even though people are quick to say, "Yes, I believe God is sovereign," I've discovered that if you scratch that affirmation just a bit—if you begin to probe it by asking two or three penetrating questions—you soon find out that the matter of God's sovereignty is a loosely held concept.

As a preacher of God's Word, I don't want you to be uncertain, but instead to be confident in and sure of God's sovereignty. To do that, there are three specific

areas of sovereignty at which I would like to look. Although they do not exhaust the application of the sovereignty of God, they are a good place to begin.

## God's Sovereignty over His Creation

The first area of sovereignty we need to discuss is with respect to our affirmation of God's control over His creation. God rules over nature, and He rules over history. This may seem elementary, but it is an aspect of God's sovereignty that is often overlooked.

> Part of the reason we make so many mistakes in our thinking about God is because we have been reared in a pagan culture.

As pastors, we're fragile and sometimes erroneous in our thinking. I'm sure that in my beliefs I have theological errors, and the response I receive to that statement is generally, "Why don't you get rid of them?" If I knew which ones they were, I would. Nevertheless, I affirm the things that I believe because I'm convinced that they are accurate. However, somewhere in that theology there will surely be some mixture of error.

I believe part of the reason we make so many mistakes in our thinking about God is because we have been reared in a pagan culture. Every single day we are bombarded by ideas that are pagan. From kindergarten to adulthood, in the movies we watch, in the novels we read, and in the television shows we observe our minds are being assailed with ideas, many of which get into our heads because we accept them without critical thinking.

Often we don't realize that some of the ideas we have been taught are antithetical to the Christian faith. When we are born again, we aren't instantly sanctified, nor do we suddenly have the mind of Christ. Instead, we have excess baggage that we carry through our Christian pilgrimage, and one of the most common notions that invades our thinking is a pagan view of nature.

Let me try to illustrate this: Imagine that I am holding a pair of glasses and I am going to throw them into the air and hope that I don't break them. What will make these glasses go up into the air, and why is it that they won't hover and stay in the air? Why is it that after they reach their apogee they will follow the law that says, "What goes up, must come down"? In a pagan view of nature, we say that what happened in this little experiment is that the glasses obeyed the fixed laws of a mechanistic universe—a universe whose physics operate according to inherent powers and forces. What will make these glasses go up is the exertion of energy and power from my wrist and arm, and what will make them come back down is the law of gravity, which is a force that is inherent in nature. If that's what you believe to be the case, you're thinking like a pagan.

## God Is the Power Supply of the Universe

One of the most profound principles in the Word of God is a pronouncement the apostle Paul made in Athens on Mars Hill. Paul affirmed to the Athenians that "in Him we live and move and have our being" (Acts 17:28). After the Reformation, the theologians of the seventeenth century who were concerned about the way in which God relates to His universe and creation made a very important distinction in theology. The distinction was between primary and secondary causality. Primary causality represents the ultimate causal power for anything that takes place in the universe. Scripture universally affirms this power supply for all living and moving beings to be the sovereign power of the almighty God. Without that primary causal power, which rests in God, there can be no living, there can be no moving, and there can be no being.

At the same time, the Reformers understood that there are causal forces that are real and take place in nature. When I exercise my force to pick up the pair of glasses, I exert real force that produces a real causal action. I'm the one who moves, but the point is that I can't move my hand, I can't grab these glasses, I can't throw them into the air, let alone hope that they come back to the earth, apart from the sovereign power of the almighty God. But because of our pagan context, we adopt a view of a nature that operates independently from the sovereignty of God.

We must grasp the doctrine of providence. This doctrine was vividly displayed in the book of Genesis when Joseph confronted his brothers. Upon learning of his identity, they were terrified that Joseph, in his position of power, would exact revenge against them. But on the contrary he told them, "Do not be afraid, for am I in God's place? As for you, you meant evil against me, but God meant it for good in order to bring about this present result, to preserve many people alive" (Genesis 50:19-20). Joseph was saying that in this drama of history, there was more than one player on the stage. There were the actions, the causal power, and the intentionality of his brothers, but above and beyond their intentions was the ultimate forethought of God. Does not the Bible say the same thing with respect to the passion of Christ? Jesus was delivered into the hands of a mob by the determinant counsel of God (Acts 2:23).

This is not to say that human actions are inconsequential, but rather that they are secondary. Although secondary causes are real, we still need to make the distinction that there can be no secondary causality without the primary cause. You and I couldn't do a thing apart from the power of God. After the tragic events of September 11, 2001, the question I was often asked was, "Where was God on 9/11?" My response: "He's in the same place He was on 9/10 and on 9/12. He's the Lord God omnipotent who reigns and holds all of nature in His hand. He is the one who raises up nations and brings them down, and He rules over people and impersonal nature."

### How Free Is My Free Will?

Another myth that is pervasive in our culture is the pagan view of human free will. How many times have you heard the dispute regarding divine sovereignty and human freedom or free will? I have heard people, including professing Christians, say, "God's sovereignty is limited by human freedom." Have you ever heard that? That's like me saying to my son when he was in sixth grade, "My authority ends where your will comes into play." Instead, I said to him, "Son, you have a free will and I have a free will; but mine is more free than yours." A person's freedom, which is real and true, is always and everywhere limited by the freedom of God. That's what we mean when we talk about sovereignty—God is the one who is sovereign, not us.

Proponents of Reformed theology do not deny human free will. I don't know of anyone in the history of Reformed theology who denies that even after the fall the faculty of the will remains intact and we are able to still make choices. However, fallen humans always choose according to their strongest inclination; they have the power to choose whatever they want. However, as Calvin is said to have stated, "If that's all we mean by free will, then free will is far too grandiose a term to apply to mortals."

The notion of free will that the world

teaches us is that human beings are creatures who have equal power to do good and evil. However, this pagan view of free will is on a collision course with the Bible's teaching that the fallen human will is enslaved to sin. We can still do what we want to do, but the problem is with the "want to." The Bible tells us over and over again that we don't want God in our thinking. We want to be sovereign, we want to be autonomous, we want to rule, we want to reign, and we want to do evil.

The Bible teaches that without Christ, we can do nothing. Martin Luther is said to have remarked on Jesus' words, "Apart from Me you can do nothing" (John 15:5) by saying that "nothing" is not "a little something." Jesus taught Nicodemus that unless he was born of the Holy Spirit, he could not even see the kingdom of God, let alone enter it (John 3:1-8). But there is this pervasive view, not only in the world but in the church, that unregenerate people can see the kingdom, can choose the kingdom, and can enter the kingdom all apart from God's sovereign work of grace in their souls. We must reject this notion and acknowledge that God is the primary cause of all things. As preachers, we must believe this and teach it.

## God's Absolute Authority to Bind the Conscience

The second area of sovereignty we need to consider is God's absolute authority to bind the consciences of His creatures. God has the right to impose obligations upon us, and He can say to

His creatures, "Thou shall, or thou shall not." We claim to believe this, but every time you and I sin, we challenge the truth of this proposition. When we disobey, we contradict the idea that God has the right to bind our consciences absolutely, for even in the slightest sin that we commit we are involved in an act of cosmic treason. Sin is the raising up of the human will and desire against the Lord God omnipotent and the rejection of His preceptive will.

It is surprising how quickly Christians strip God of His sovereignty when it comes to the matter of salvation. If Christians affirm the truth that God is sovereign over the universe and there's not a single maverick molecule running loose in His creation apart from His sovereign control, and if they affirm that God is sovereign in ruling over all people and their actions, then the next affirmation should be the sovereignty of God's grace in salvation. However, even when people agree that God is sovereign over creation, nature, history, and law, they still deny Him the exercise of His sovereignty when it comes to His purposes in salvation. It is this third area of God's sovereignty that I would like to examine in the rest of this chapter.

## God's Sovereignty over Salvation

In Romans 9:10-16, Paul wrote about the purposes of God. After explaining the gospel, he wrote in verse 10, "Not only this, but there was Rebekah also, when she had conceived twins by one man, our father Isaac; for though the twins were not yet born and had not done anything good or bad..." Paul wanted his original recipients, as well as us, to understand that according to the purposes of God, there were two children who had the same parents, were in the same environment, lived in the same culture, and were even womb-mates. Paul belabored the point that prior to their birth, prior to their behavior, prior to their human decisions, and prior to their human actions, the purposes of God according to election already stood firm. God decreed that the elder would serve the younger (Romans 9:12).

Although Paul's affirmation was explicit, the popular view of election held in the culture and the church today attempts to soften the doctrine. But whether you like it or not, if you believe the Bible, you have to believe in some kind of doctrine of predestination because the term wasn't invented by Calvin, or Luther, or Augustine, it was the apostle Paul who used the language of election, choosing, and predestination. For example, in Ephesians 1:3-6 we read,

> Blessed be the God and Father of our Lord Jesus Christ, who has blessed us with every spiritual blessing in the heavenly places in Christ, just as He chose us in Him before the foundation of the world, that we would be holy and blameless before Him. In love He predestined us to adoption as sons through Jesus Christ to Himself, according to the kind intention of His will, to the praise of the glory of His grace, which He freely bestowed on us in the Beloved.

Therefore, if you're going to be biblical, you must affirm some view of the doctrine of predestination.

### The Foreknowledge View of Predestination

The most popular view of this doctrine is a prescient or foreknowledge view that advocates that God looked down the corridor of time and saw who was going to make the right choice and on the basis of that choice He selected who would come to salvation. But this view doesn't explain the biblical doctrine of predestination, it denies it. I don't see how anyone can look seriously at what Paul taught in Romans chapter 9 and hold that position. Romans 9 is the most neglected text in all of Scripture by semi-Pelagians of all eras—they just don't want to deal with it. It was Romans 9 that brought me kicking and screaming into the Reformed understanding of predestination because Jonathan Edwards kept rubbing my nose in that text. I tried to get away from it with this logic: "Since the prescient view takes place before Jacob and Esau are born, I'm not denying that the decree of predestination took place before their birth; therefore, I can be an Arminian and still believe that part of the text." However, as we will see below, this logic was flawed.

In Romans 9:11-14 we read, "The twins were not yet born and had not done anything good or bad, so that God's purpose according to His choice would stand, not because of works, but because of Him who calls, it was said to her, 'The older will serve the younger.' Just as it is written, 'Jacob I loved, but Esau I hated.' What shall we say then? There is no injustice with God, is there?" In this passage, Paul was employing an ancient debating technique called *reductio ad absurdum*. Zeno of Elea, a fifth-century BC Greek philosopher, implemented this approach by standing in his opponent's shoes for a few moments, adopting the position of his opponent, and then taking that position to its logical conclusion, which revealed the absurdity of that position. In using this technique, the goal is to anticipate your opponent's objections and then state those objections in a more convincing and eloquent fashion than your opponent. After you've done that, then you dismantle that objection and reduce it to absurdity.

There was no greater master of this technique than the apostle Paul. For example, in 1 Corinthians chapter 15, in response to people who were denying the resurrection, Paul said, and I paraphrase, "Well let's look at the implications. If Christ was not raised, then what would that mean?" He then took that position to the point of absurdity in verses 13-19.

I used to teach pastors and lay people the same approach as we went through *Evangelism Explosion*.[1] We would go through the gospel presentation, and I would teach that when you get to a person's need for salvation, don't start by saying, "God is holy and God is a God of justice." Don't start there because the entire time you're telling a person that God is a God of justice, they are ready with their rebuttal, "God is a God of love." Therefore, start with that statement "God is a God of love," and talk about how incredible the love of God is and how marvelously the Bible communicates the idea that God is a God of love. Tell it better than the person has ever heard it, so then you can turn the corner and tell him or her that the same source that teaches about the love of God also teaches about His justice and that He will never clear the guilty. Then you're ready to discuss the cross. That is the technique the apostle Paul used in Romans 9:14.

After Paul introduced God's purpose according to election, he raised the question, "How do we respond to this, and what shall we say to this; is there unrighteousness with God?" I embraced the Reformed faith more than 40 years ago. Do you know how many times I have presented the case for the Reformed doctrine of election? And how many people have raised the objection, "That's not fair"? The objection is "If this doctrine is true, then it's not fair, and God is not righteous."

I don't think any Arminian in history has ever had to answer the objection. If you embrace Arminianism, you're teaching something that casts a shadow on the righteousness of God. Have you heard of any Arminian response to this objection? If you follow Arminianism, what could be fairer than for God to make the decision as to who gets saved when that decision is ultimately based on what people do? In Arminianism, if a person rejects the gospel, there is no notion of blaming God, for if the person's eternal destiny wasn't up to Him, it was the person's choice and therefore his or her fault.

Paul anticipated that some people would say, "That's not fair" in response to what he was teaching in Romans 9. At this point we're tracking with the apostle, for our view of election also provokes that response. Paul was anticipating the very objection that every semi-Pelagian in history has raised against an Augustinian understanding of grace: the false notion that there is unrighteousness in God if He elects only some people.

So how did Paul answer his own question? In Romans 9:14 he wrote, "What shall we say then? There is no injustice with God, is there?" Did Paul say, "Well, maybe," or "Sure looks like it here"? No, he gave the strongest negative response one can possibly give to a rhetorical question in the Greek language. Some translators render the original Greek text, "Certainly not!" Others put it this way: "God forbid!" To ask the question "Is there unrighteousness in God?" is to blaspheme, for there is no unrighteousness in God.

Paul elaborated on his argument by demonstrating that this teaching went back to Moses' writings. In Romans 9:14-15 he wrote, "May it never be! For He says to Moses, 'I will have mercy on whom I have mercy, and I will have compassion on whom I have compassion.'" Paul pointed to Moses to remind his readers that God's grace has always been sovereign. The Lord God Almighty is not bound by any law outside of Himself to dispense His grace to anyone; and if He gives it to one individual, He is not required to give it to another, He has absolute authority with regard to the granting of His executive clemency. God's sovereignty in salvation is not a New Covenant invention. Rather, it is an Old Covenant concept.

## "That's Not Fair"

I would like to reinforce this truth with an illustration. Back in the 1960s I taught at a Christian college in New England. I was a Bible teacher, teaching the Old Testament, and my first class had 250 freshmen in it. The only classroom big enough to fit all the students was the chapel, so that's where we met.

On the first day of class I went over the syllabus for the course, and said, "You have three small papers due at various points throughout the semester. The first one is due September 30, and it must be on my desk by noon. The only exceptions to late papers are a death in the immediate family or if you're confined to the hospital."

I made the rules clear, and when September 30 came, 225 students turned in their term papers. The other 25 were trembling in their boots: "Professor Sproul, we didn't finish our papers; please don't give us an F for this assignment! Won't you give us a few more days to finish it? We haven't made the adjustment from high school to college, but we promise we'll never let it happen again."

I said, "You can have two days, but no more. Don't let it happen again."

October 30 came, and this time 200 students turned in their term papers and 50 did not. I said to the 50, "Where are your papers?"

The students said, "We had midterm exams, and it was homecoming week. We didn't prepare properly, and we didn't budget our time. Please don't fail us, Professor Sproul. Give us one more chance!"

I said, "All right. But this is the last time."

The students responded with overwhelming joy. In fact, they spontaneously broke out in song: "We love you Prof Sproul, oh yes we do!"

I was the most popular professor on the campus until November 30. On that date, 150 students turned in their term papers and 100 did not. I looked at the 100 and said, "Where are your term papers?"

They replied, "Hey, Prof, don't worry about it. We'll have them to you in a couple of days."

I said, "Johnson, where's your paper?"

He said, "I'm not done with it yet, but I'll get it to you."

I then took out every student's nightmare, the little black grade book. I said, "Johnson, you don't have your paper?"

He said, "No."

"Fine," I said, "that's an F. Harrison, where's your paper?"

He said, "I don't have it."

I made a mark in my grade book and said, "F."

With one voice a chorus of protests echoed through the chapel. Guess what the students said? "That's not fair!"

I said, "What did you say?"

They answered, "That's not fair."

I then looked at Johnson and said, "Did you say 'That's not fair'?"

"Yes sir."

"Okay, so it's justice that you want?"

"Yes," he said.

I continued, "Well, I remember that you were late with the last paper, weren't you?"

"Yes."

I said, "Okay, I'm going to erase last month's grade and give you an F for that one too."

Suddenly the room became quiet. No one mumbled another word.

"God forbid that I not be just." I declared. "Now, who else wants justice?"

After more silence, I said, "Maybe we should all sing the song, 'I've grown accustomed to His grace.'"

**Amazing Grace**

You see, when we experience God's grace once, we're grateful. When we experience it a second time, we become a bit jaded. By the third time, not only do we expect God's grace, but we demand it. We harbor in our souls the idea that if God doesn't choose us, there's something wrong with Him rather than with us.

---

**The minute you get the idea that God is obliged to show His grace to you, you're no longer thinking about grace.**

---

In Romans 9, Paul reminds us that God reserves to Himself the absolute sovereign right to pardon whom He will and to give justice to whom He will. Not one person in this universe deserves the grace of God. The minute you get the idea that God is obliged to show His grace to you, you're no longer thinking about grace. Grace, by definition, is something God is not required to give. That's the mystery of election.

One question many students ask me is this: "Why doesn't God give all people equal grace? Why isn't He an equal opportunity redeemer?" But that's the wrong question. The question every Christian should ask is, "Why me? Why did God bring me out of darkness and into light?" Think of your own conversion, and how God, in His grace, rescued you by His mercy and compassion,

by a grace that is sovereign. "Hallelujah" should be your response.

The sad reality is that we sing "Amazing Grace," but we're not amazed by it. We must not only be amazed by grace, but we must be continually astonished by it. I still can't get over the fact that God chose me. One thing I know is that He didn't choose me because of anything He saw in me. God's choosing me was a gift to His Son so that the Son could see the travail of His soul and be satisfied (Isaiah 53:11).

This is the message we need to preach with regard to the passion of Christ; it was impossible that Christ could go through His sufferings to no avail. The idea that Christ came into the world to die on the cross to make salvation "possible" is blasphemous. He came into this world to make salvation absolutely certain for those whom the Father had given Him from the foundation of the world.

God's sovereign grace is love that is unfathomable. That's why when the apostle Paul talked about this doctrine of grace he broke out into doxology. In Romans 11:33 he wrote, "Oh, the depth of the riches both of the wisdom and knowledge of God! How unsearchable are His judgments and unfathomable His ways!"

As preachers, we must believe, teach, and find comfort in God's sovereignty over creation, history, our lives, our deaths, the salvation of our souls, and the salvation of the souls of those to whom we preach. May you preach and trust that God is sovereign to save.

## PRAYER

Our Father and God, please forgive us when we presume upon Your grace. Let us always remember that we are saved by grace, through faith, and even that faith is not of ourselves, but is of You. So that salvation is not of him who decides, nor of him who runs, nor of him who wills, but of Thee who shows us mercy. Amen.

# 6

# HAS ANY PEOPLE HEARD THE VOICE OF GOD SPEAKING...AND SURVIVED?

*Albert Mohler Jr.*
*Shepherds' Conference 2008*

*Deuteronomy 4:32-40*

What an honor it is to be here among you men. As I stand in Pastor MacArthur's pulpit, I think about how many people have been affected by messages declared from this very location. I suppose there is no time when his voice is not being heard somewhere around the world, and it is John MacArthur's faithful example we are drawn to.

I've spoken to several pastors at this conference and have heard that some of you make it through the year in order to get here once again. I know that as I look out at you, I'm looking at preachers who find tremendous encouragement by being here in the company of other preachers. There is something precious and sweet about this conference and there is nothing else quite like it. This is one of the few places where you don't have to explain what you do for a living. It's one of the few places where you don't have to defend preaching. It's one of the few places where when individuals find out that you're a preacher, their faces light up. And it's one of the few places where you can come and make so many friends of fellow preachers.

## The Task At Hand

There's no doubt that we are living in strange times. One of the hallmarks of our generation is the fact that there is a crisis in preaching. It would be an exercise of mass delusion if we were to act like there isn't a problem in our midst. Let me ask you a question in order to diagnose this current epoch: How likely is one to hear an expository sermon if he were to take a seat in an evangelical church? A candid answer to this question indicates that you really do not have the assured expectation that most evangelical churches practice the exposition of God's Word.

Do you believe that as time moves forward, it's becoming more likely or less likely for people to hear an expository message? To help you answer this question, look at the preaching literature published in the Christian world. Look at the resources available at popular conferences and seminars, and you'll see how little exposition there is. But by God's grace this is not true everywhere, and it's not true here among us—yet it is increasingly true in the church at large.

Once we diagnose this crisis and recognize that it exists, we have to ask why it's happened. It's almost as if by some form of strategy there has been a unilateral disarmament of the evangelical church when it comes to expository preaching. The exposition of the Scriptures should be the easiest thing in the world to understand. As a matter of fact, you have to be clever to mess it up. In Nehemiah 8:1-8 we see a display of what preaching is all about:

All the people gathered as one man at the square which was in front of the Water Gate, and they asked Ezra the scribe to bring the book of the law of Moses which the Lord had given to Israel.

Then Ezra the priest brought the law before the assembly of men, women and all who could listen with understanding, on the first day of the seventh month. He read from it before the square which was in front of the Water Gate from early morning until midday, in the presence of men and women, those who could understand; and all the people were attentive to the book of the law.

Ezra the scribe stood at a wooden podium which they had made for the purpose. And beside him stood Mattithiah, Shema, Anaiah, Uriah, Hilkiah, and Maaseiah on his right hand; and Pedaiah, Mishael, Malchijah, Hashum, Hashbaddanah, Zechariah and Meshullam on his left hand. Ezra opened the book in the sight of all the people for he was standing above all the people; and when he opened it, all the people stood up. Then Ezra blessed the Lord the great God. And all the people answered, "Amen, Amen!" while lifting up their hands; then they bowed low and worshiped the Lord with their faces to the ground.

Also Jeshua, Bani, Sherebiah, Jamin, Akkub, Shabbethai, Hodiah, Maaseiah, Kelita, Azariah, Jozabad, Hanan, Pelaiah, the

Levites, explained the law to the people while the people remained in their place. They read from the book, from the law of God, translating to give the sense so that they understood the reading.

Now, I didn't say that the exposition of Scripture was an easy task to do, but rather that it was straightforward and simple to understand. We see that "they read from the book, from the law of God, translating," or explaining, "to give the sense so that they understood the reading" (8:8). How is it possible to misunderstand that? What is it in the Book that we are capable of misunderstanding? The task at hand is simple: You read the Book and you explain it.

**Simple Instructions**

I want you to note carefully the expository pattern. This is not a scene from "the Ezra code." There's nothing hidden here. As an expositor, you are called to read and explain—that's fairly simple, isn't it? I heard someone the other day say that there's still a fellow locked in the shower somewhere because the instructions on the shampoo say, "Lather, rinse, repeat." Likewise, exposition is all about reading the text, explaining the text, going home, coming back, and again reading and explaining the text.

I recognize that instructions are often inadequate. I'm the kind of person who goes to a department store, buys a bicycle, and pays the store to put it together. I

simply don't have the patience to struggle through the mistranslations of the English language into which the instructions have been written. A friend of mine, and his wife, when they were expecting their first child, went out to buy a crib. The father, in a moment of absolute commitment, said, "Tonight, I will put this crib together." And he did. There was only one problem—after a few hours of putting it together, he realized the instructions lacked a key bit of information: "Assemble the crib in the room where it will be used." He had to completely dismantle the crib, move it into the baby's room, and put it all together again.

Instructions can be confusing or inadequate, but when it comes to expository preaching the directions are clear: You are to read the Book and explain it.

Of course there is a bit more to preaching in terms of background. Scripture tells us that the messenger must be called. We read this in Ezra 7:6: "This Ezra went up from Babylon, and he was a scribe skilled in the law of Moses, which the Lord God of Israel had given; and the king granted him all he requested because the hand of the Lord his God was upon him." It isn't just anyone who is assigned to take up the instructions and fulfill the command. The hand of the Lord falls upon certain men who are called to preach. We need to recognize that calling is important and indispensable.

How do we know when a man is called to this task? We observe in Ezra

7:10 that Ezra was the man for the job because "Ezra had set his heart to study the law of the LORD and to practice it, and to teach His statutes and ordinances in Israel." Along with calling, studying was very much a part of what made Ezra a preacher. Ezra is described as being "learned in the words of the commandments of the LORD and His statutes to Israel" (verse 11). A preacher is one whom God has called and one whom the congregation recognizes that the hand of the Lord is upon him; and his response to this call is demonstrated by his preparation and his dedication to study, all of which is done in order to become skilled in the Word of God.

We have instruction in the New Testament as well. In 2 Timothy 4:1-2 the apostle Paul, delivering his final message to Timothy, sets forth that greatest priority of the pastoral calling, which is the preaching of the Word of God: "I solemnly charge you in the presence of God and of Christ Jesus, who is to judge the living and the dead, and by His appearing, and His kingdom: preach the word; be ready in season and out of season; reprove, rebuke, exhort, with great patience and instruction." I ask you again: How clever do you have to be to understand this? Paul used straightforward words and there aren't many polysyllabic constructions in this verse. The command is to preach the Word in season and out of season, reprove, rebuke, exhort, and patiently teach. This is the pattern.

> **If you're not reading the text and explaining, reproving, rebuking, exhorting, and patiently teaching, then you're not preaching.**

Why is it not happening? Why is it that the exposition of the Scriptures is evacuated from so many of our churches, missing from so many of our pulpits, and alien to so many preachers? I understand preaching takes place all across the world, but is it expository preaching? According to the Bible, exposition is preaching. According to the Bible, if it isn't exposition, it isn't preaching.

You may call it a sermon, you may be called a preacher, and what you do may be called preaching, but if you're not reading the text and explaining, reproving, rebuking, exhorting, and patiently teaching, then you're not preaching. We have to stop saying, "I prefer expository preaching," and just say, "I'm a preacher. I read the text, explain it, go home and study it, and I come back and do it again." It's so simple, yet it's so tragically absent.

### The Theology Behind the Instructions

The essence of the problem is not faulty technique but faulty theology. Since this problem is deeply theological, I want us to focus our thoughts on Deuteronomy chapter 4. I want us to think together about a theology of expository preaching, I want us to see what is at stake, I want us to see a means of recovery, and I want us to feel the urgency of this text as it applies to the exposition of the Word of God. Read with me Deuteronomy 4:32-40:

> Indeed, ask now concerning the former days which were before you, since the day that God created man on the earth, and inquire from one end of the heavens to the other. Has anything been done like this great thing, or has anything been heard like it? Has any people heard the voice of God speaking from the midst of the fire, as you have heard it, and survived? Or has a god tried to go to take for himself a nation from within another nation by trials, by signs and wonders and by war and by a mighty hand and by an outstretched arm and by great terrors, as the LORD your God did for you in Egypt before your eyes? To you it was shown that you might know that the LORD, He is God; there is no other besides Him. Out of the heavens He let you hear His voice to discipline you; and on earth He let you see His great fire, and you heard His words from the midst of the fire. Because He loved your fathers, therefore He chose their descendants after them. And He personally brought you from Egypt by His great power, driving out from before you nations greater and mightier than you, to bring you in and to give you their land for an inheritance, as it is today.
>
> Know therefore today, and take it to your heart, that the LORD, He is God in heaven above and on the earth below; there is no other. So you shall keep His statutes and His commandments which I am giving you today, that it may go well with you and with your children after you, and that you may live long on the land which the LORD your God is giving you for all time.

When you read the first-person singular in this passage, it is God speaking through Moses, and then Moses providing a commentary and reflection on what God has done and said. Deuteronomy is so intentionally theological that scholars of the Old Testament identify what they call the Deuteronomic Theology. It is the book of the Pentateuch that Jesus quotes from most often. And it is the third-most-quoted Old Testament book in the New Testament, next to Psalms and Isaiah.

The historical context of Deuteronomy is that the children of Israel are in the wilderness. Moses is preparing them to enter the Land of Promise. Behind them is the history of the Exodus, Sinai, and the rebellion at Kadesh Barnea. Before them is the River Jordan and on the other side of the river is the Land of Promise. This is the generation that will enter the land. But because the people will enter this land without Moses, the Lord is speaking to His people through Moses in order to prepare them for the challenges ahead.

The book of Deuteronomy is the second giving of the law. God has given His people the opportunity to be faithful rather than unfaithful and obedient rather than disobedient. How will they be readied and prepared? You'll notice that the book of Deuteronomy doesn't prepare the people with a military briefing, a demographic analysis, or a geography overview. Instead, the book concentrates on the Word of God. It's about the glorious truth that God has spoken. It's about the necessity and regularity with which God's people need to hear His voice. It's about the mandate to obey what God has said.

The theme of Deuteronomy chapter 4 is "hearken back to Horeb." After three chapters of introduction, the intensity of the text is raised in chapter 4 with the first words being "Now, oh Israel" (verse 1). In the Old Testament, especially in the book of Deuteronomy, this phrase is similar to the New Testament word "therefore," which aims to link future information with previous instruction. In other words, on the basis of what has been said in the first three chapters, the people must now be prepared to hear what follows. In Deuteronomy 4:1 Moses charges Israel to

"listen"—listen to God because hearing His word is not a matter of success, but a matter of survival, life, and death. The entire theology of Deuteronomy comes down to the fact that God has spoken. Hearing and obeying is life, while disobeying is death. Moses wants the children of Israel to know that life and death hang in the balance of the Word. The pattern of the book is this: hear, listen, obey, and you will live. Refuse to listen and disobey, and you will perish.

I would submit to you that perhaps the central problem in our crisis of preaching is that somehow we believe this pattern has changed. Somehow we believe that God's Word was a matter of life and death in the wilderness, but it's a matter of something less in our churches. The only diagnosis I can offer of why expositional preaching is in decline, if not absent from so many pulpits, is the absence of the belief that the Word of God comes as a matter of life and death. But the truth is that it is *always* a matter of life and death, and woe to the preacher who forgets this truth.

With that in mind, in the rest of the chapter we will make four observations regarding the Deuteronomic pattern of preaching.

### The Pattern of Preaching
#### The God Who Speaks

The first observation on preaching from Deuteronomy is that the true and living God is the God who speaks.

We know who God is not because we were smart enough to figure Him out or because we were clever enough to entice Him into revealing Himself, but because out of His own love, grace, and mercy, He has spoken to us. The true and living God is the God who speaks.

Back in the 1970s, Francis Schaeffer wrote a powerful book titled *He Is There and He Is Not Silent*.[1] That book made a significant impression on my life because those two assertions actually frame the beginning of all Christian theology, of any Christian worldview, and of any understanding of who God is and what He would expect of us. We preach because He is not silent. What is the confidence in our preaching? Our confidence is that out of His Word, which is living and active and sharper than any two-edged sword, He still speaks. This is the miracle of revelation that I fear we give inadequate attention to in our churches, in our teaching, and in our preaching. God manifests His love for us in actually speaking to us, and in Deuteronomy 4:10-19 Moses makes this very clear:

> Remember the day you stood before the LORD your God at Horeb, when the LORD said to me, "Assemble the people to Me, that I may let them hear My words so they may learn to fear Me all the days they live on the earth, and that they may teach their children." You came near and stood at the foot of the mountain, and the mountain burned with fire to the very heart of the heavens: darkness, cloud and thick gloom. Then the LORD spoke to you from the midst of the fire; you heard the sound of words, but you saw no form—only a voice. So He declared to you His covenant which He commanded you to perform, that is, the Ten Commandments; and He wrote them on two tablets of stone. The LORD commanded me at that time to teach you statutes and judgments, that you might perform them in the land where you are going over to possess it.
>
> So watch yourselves carefully, since you did not see any form on the day the LORD spoke to you at Horeb from the midst of the fire, so that you do not act corruptly and make a graven image for yourselves in the form of any figure, the likeness of male or female, the likeness of any animal that is on the earth, the likeness of any winged bird that flies in the sky, the likeness of anything that creeps on the ground, the likeness of any fish that is in the water below the earth.
>
> And beware not to lift up your eyes to heaven and see the sun and the moon and the stars, all the host of heaven, and be drawn away and worship them and serve

them, those which the LORD your God has allotted to all the peoples under the whole heaven.

Moses declared, "Remember when you were there at Horeb? Remember when you heard the voice of God speaking from the midst of the fire?" What's interesting is that many of those who were listening to Moses speak were not present at Horeb, and yet he tells them that they heard the voice of God. They were not there physically because many of them were not yet born, but they are under the Word just as their fathers and their forefathers were.

Moses stresses that they heard the voice of God. To prevent any confusion, he continues, "You heard the sound of words, but you saw no form—only a voice" (Deuteronomy 4:12). The context here makes it clear that the great danger is always idolatry. We have not progressed beyond Old Testament idolatry; we've just become more sophisticated in it. The issue is always idolatry because in our fallen state we would rather have an image than a word. We would rather have an image we can control, because we can put an idol over here, dress it, and speak to it. This is the major distinction between the one true God and the false gods in the Old Testament—while the pagans speak to the idols, the one true and living God, who has no form, speaks to His people.

Elijah referenced this distinction when he confronted the pagan priests at Mount Carmel. In 1 Kings 18:29, we read, "When midday was past, they raved until the time of the offering of the evening sacrifice; but there was no voice, no one answered, and no one paid attention." Just think about those haunting words for a moment, and consider where we would be if God had not spoken. We would be in the same predicament as those pagan priests. We could do whatever we want, we could light whatever fire we want to light, we could come up with whatever creative message we desired, we could draw a crowd, we could even call it a church; but if God has not spoken, we are just as damned, dead, and lost as those priests.

Jeremiah spoke of idols in the same manner as Elijah when he said, "Like a scarecrow in a cucumber field are they [idols], and they cannot speak" (Jeremiah 10:5). It comes down to this: You either have the Word of God or a scarecrow in a cucumber field. It's either the God who speaks or it's an idol. Paul, in 1 Corinthians 12:2, wrote, "You know that when you were pagans, you were led astray to the mute idols." Now, Paul's challenge to remember is very different from Moses' challenge to the Israelites to remember. Paul asked the Gentile Christians in Corinth to remember that they were led astray and worshipped idols that don't speak, while Moses asked the children of Israel to recall when God spoke. In both instances, the emphasis is on the one God who speaks and reveals himself.

Revelation can be defined in this

way: "Revelation is God's gracious self-disclosure, whereby He forfeited His own personal privacy, that His creatures would know Him."[2] The God who needs nothing, who is sovereign in His majesty and infinite in His perfections, forfeited His own personal privacy that we might know Him. Wouldn't you assume that the recipients of that revelation would live by it, be nourished by it, and cling to it? Wouldn't the natural response of those who are called to preach that Word be to read it and explain it?

Paul's reminder in Romans is similar—God reveals Himself to all the peoples everywhere through general revelation. There isn't an atom or a molecule in all of creation that doesn't cry out the majesty of the Creator. There isn't a single human being, made in the image of God, who does not have a conscience that cries out the knowledge of a Creator, and beyond that, the moral sensibility that one has violated His divine law. Paul also makes clear in Romans that mankind's problem is perpetual idolatry. The consequence of the fall is that there is not a single human being who by general revelation is going to come to a saving knowledge of the Lord Jesus Christ. This is where we are absolutely dependent not upon general revelation, but special revelation, which came in the form of a voice as God spoke.

However, if you think that God's speaking was all in the past, then resign from preaching. I say that with dead seriousness. If you do not believe that God now speaks from His Word, what do you think you're doing? Furthermore, if you do not have the confidence that God is speaking through you, insomuch as you rightly read and rightly explain the Word of God, then quit. We are completely dependent upon supernatural revelation, and as God spoke in times past, what we have now is the Scripture. This book we call the Bible is written, inspired, and God-breathed revelation. Through the Scriptures we have God speaking to His people now, even as He spoke to His people in times past.

The Bible is the inerrant and infallible Word of God, and if you believe that it's anything less than perfect, then you believe that even if God speaks, He speaks haltingly and falteringly. You believe that His voice is in there somewhere, rather than hearing it in every single word of Scripture. We must realize that God's voice is in every word, and just as "He spoke long ago to the fathers in the prophets in many portions and in many ways, in these last days has spoken to us in His Son" (Hebrews 1:1). His Word makes all the difference between true and false religion and between life and death.

What if God had not spoken? What if God had not called unto Moses from the burning bush, which was not consumed? What if God had not spoken to His children gathered there at Horeb? What if God had not spoken through the law? What if God had not spoken through the prophets? What if God had not spoken in these latter days through His Son? Then we would be lost in an aimless, meaningless, and nihilistic cosmos. If God has not spoken and if God does not speak now, then eat, drink, and be merry, for tomorrow you die. But God has spoken, and as a result, that message is a matter of life and death. That message is death to those who will not hear and life to those who do.

### God's People Hear God Speak and Obey

The second observation on preaching from Deuteronomy is that God's true people are identified as those who hear God's words. The doctrine of revelation is essentially tied, not only in terms of epistemology and authority, to the doctrine of election. How do you recognize God's people? It's because He speaks to them. God did not speak to all the nations of the earth, but to Israel. He chose them from among the nations, and their election was confirmed by receiving revelation. Moses would remind Israel time and time again, "Remember that Yahweh didn't speak to everyone, but He spoke to you." The intent was not to produce an arrogant, self-confident people, but a nation who understood that it's only by grace and mercy that God chose to reveal Himself.

### Chosen for God's Own Possession

In Deuteronomy 4:32-34, Moses asked a series of four questions to further support the truth that Israel was God's chosen people. The first question

he asked was concerning the Exodus, the giving of the law, and the entirety of Israel's history. Had anything like these events occurred before? The answer, of course, is no.

Moses moved to the second question and asked, "Has anything been heard like it?" No other people could claim that they had a God who spoke to them, who did miracles for them, and who was creating in them a people for His own glory. Israel was alone among the nations to whom this had occurred—it hadn't even been rumored to have happened elsewhere.

The third question, in Deuteronomy 4:34, asked Israel if "a god tried to go to take for himself a nation from within another nation by trials, by signs and wonders and by war and by a mighty hand and by an outstretched arm and by great terrors, as the LORD your God did for you in Egypt before your eyes?" The world knew that Israel was God's chosen people and that they had been freed by God's hand from captivity and now existed for His good pleasure because of her redemption. This is similar to what is written in Joshua 4:6: "What do these stones mean to you?" The answer is in verse 7: "So these stones shall become a memorial to the sons of Israel forever." In the Old Testament, the people of God were constantly reminded that they were once captives to Pharaoh and Egypt but God Almighty had freed them by His mighty hand.

The fourth and final question Moses

asked is in Deuteronomy 4:33, which becomes the primary focus of our discussion. It's one of the sweetest, most powerful, most incredible questions asked anywhere in Scripture. God, speaking through Moses, asked the children of Israel, "Has any people heard the voice of God speaking from the midst of the fire, as you have heard it, and survived?" How do the people of Israel know that they are God's people? How do they know that God has chosen them and that they are His? Because no other people had heard the voice of the transcendent, almighty, sovereign, omniscient, and omnipotent God speak from the fire and survived. If He just uttered His voice to us we would be annihilated, but instead He lowers His voice and He speaks to us as a Father to His children. Israel was there at Mount Horeb and the Lord God almighty spoke as a Father to His children so that they would live. These questions demonstrate that Israel came to know its privileged position, calling, election, and place in God's plan of salvation.

This level of privilege with regard to receiving the revelation of God is not just an Old Testament reality; it is also found in the New Testament. In Matthew 13:11, Jesus said to the disciples, "To you it has been granted to know the mysteries of the kingdom of heaven, but to them it has not been granted." This privilege was bestowed on the disciples not because of their intelligence, giftedness, or personality, but because God's sovereignty determined to glorify Himself through them.

Jesus said to His disciples that the way you know you are Mine is because "to you it has been granted to know the mysteries of the kingdom of heaven, but to them it has not been granted." Jesus continued, "Blessed are your eyes, because they see; and your ears, because they hear. For truly, I say to you that many prophets and righteous men desired to see what you see, and did not see it, and to hear what you hear, and did not hear it" (Matthew 13:16-17).

## Chosen to Testify

For the modern-day reader, how do you know that you're a believer in the Lord Jesus Christ? To answer that question, let me ask you two qualifying questions. How do you explain why you're a believer? We are saved by grace through the hearing of His marvelous message of salvation: "Blessed are your ears for they hear, and your eyes for they see. It has been granted to you to know the mysteries of the kingdom of heaven, but to them it has not been granted." This is no different than God saying to Israel, "I'm speaking to you as My chosen people. Out of all the nations, I am picking you." It's not about Israel's power, glory, wisdom, talents, or potential. God chose this tiny people group who couldn't even draw a straight line through the wilderness in order to show His glory as the redeeming, saving God who is faithful to His promises.

The reason is the same for why God chose us and allowed us to hear His revelation. Paul told the Corinthians, "God has chosen the foolish things of the world to shame the wise, and God has chosen the weak things of the world to shame the things which are strong" (1 Corinthians 1:27). It's because of the grace and mercy of God. This must produce humility and not arrogance and it should lead to witness—"So keep and do them, for that is your wisdom and your understanding in the sight of the peoples who will hear all these statutes and say, 'Surely this great nation is a wise and understanding people'" (Deuteronomy 4:6-8). God's special revelation was not just about Israel even as it's never just about us.

This kind of testimony will lead the nations to ask the following question: "What great nation is there that has a god so near to it as is the LORD our God whenever we call on Him?" (Deuteronomy 4:7). And furthermore, "What great nation is there that has statutes and judgments as righteous as this whole law which I am setting before you today?" (Deuteronomy 4:8). With these two response questions God was saying, "Israel, it's not about you. It's about what I'm going to do through you. When My covenant with you is made clear and you obey Me and follow My statutes, the other nations of the earth are going to say, 'What in the world is going on there? What nation has a God so gracious as to give this people such just laws? What nation is this that has heard from the one true and living God, and yet survives?'"

In all of this revelation, God's sovereign purpose is to create a people by saving them with the blood of His Son for His own glory. We are identified by the same mercy that Israel received—we've heard Him speak.

### God's People Survive by Hearing God's Word

The third observation about preaching we can make from Deuteronomy is that God's people survive by hearing His Word, for it is a matter of life and death. This observation is found in the concluding portion of the book of Deuteronomy. We read,

> This commandment which I command you today is not too difficult for you, nor is it out of reach. It is not in heaven, that you should say, "Who will go up to heaven for us to get it for us and make us hear it, that we may observe it?" Nor is it beyond the sea, that you should say, "Who will cross the sea for us to get it for us and make us hear it, that we may observe it?" But the word is very near you, in your mouth and in your heart, that you may observe it (30:11-14).

Moses communicated God's message that Israel did not find God's word by searching for it; it came to Israel and now it's very near to her. Similarly, the preacher finds answers that lead directly back to the Word of God. We have this Word, and this Word has consequences:

> See, I have set before you today life and prosperity, and death and adversity; in that I command you today to love the LORD your God, to walk in His ways and to keep His commandments and His statutes and His judgments, that you may live and multiply, and that the LORD your God may bless you in the land where you are entering to possess it. But if your heart turns away and you will not obey, but are drawn away and worship other gods and serve them, I declare to you today that you shall surely perish. You will not prolong your days in the land where you are crossing the Jordan to enter it and possess it. I call heaven and earth to witness against you today, that I have set before you life and death, the blessing and the curse. So choose life in order that you may live, you and your descendants, by loving the LORD your God, by obeying His voice, and by holding fast to Him; for this is your life and the length of your days, that you may live in the land which the LORD swore to your fathers, to Abraham, Isaac, and Jacob, to give them (Deuteronomy 30:15-20).

For Israel, the Word was like manna.

They had to have it fresh every day in order to survive. They lived as God's people by His Word and it became their help, blessing, and identity.

In 2 Timothy 3:16-17, Paul provided us with a similar and eloquent testimony of Scripture. He wrote, "All Scripture is inspired by God and profitable for teaching, for reproof, for correction, for training in righteousness; so that the man of God may be adequate, equipped for every good work." Nothing else is adequate except for the written revelation of God. Paul's testimony spoke not only to the authority, perfection, inerrancy, and infallibility of the Word of God, but also to its sufficiency, for it alone will accomplish these things.

We have to live by the Word, just as much as Israel had to live by the Word, for that's how we know who we are and who God is. It's in this Word that we find the testimony of Christ—He spoke of the perfect and enduring quality of Scripture in Matthew 5:17-18: "Do not think that I came to abolish the Law or the Prophets; I did not come to abolish but to fulfill. For truly I say to you, until heaven and earth pass away, not the smallest letter or stroke shall pass from the Law until all is accomplished."

How are we going to know who we are? How are we going to know that we are His? How are we going to know how to live? How are we going to know the life-and-death issues of obedience and disobedience? How are we going to grow in grace? It is only through the ministry of the Word.

### God-Honoring Preaching Is a Matter of Life and Death

The fourth and final observation about preaching we perceive from Deuteronomy is that it is always a matter of life and death. Since God's people survive by hearing God's Word, preaching must be the exposition of the Scriptures, because nothing else will do. Preaching is not merely about growing our churches, inspiring our people, or making people live more faithfully than before. God-honoring preaching is a matter of life and death. We either believe that or we don't. As Deuteronomy 30:19 says, "I have set before you life and death, the blessing and the curse. So choose life in order that you may live."

**When it is the Word of God that speaks through the preacher, then it is God who speaks.**

### So Who Will Speak—the Preacher or God?

We have the Bible. If we know the Bible to be the perfect and God-breathed written Word, then we must view it in its proper perspective. It comes down to the question of who is going to speak: the preacher, or God? There are a whole lot of preachers doing a whole lot of speaking, but when it is the Word of God that speaks through the preacher, then it is God who speaks. That's the difference between life and death. Do we arrogantly think that God's redeemed people can live on our words? Or do we realize that life is found only in the Word of God?

We live only because He is there and He is not silent. Those who are called to preach are commissioned to study, stand before God's people, read the text, explain the text, reprove, rebuke, exhort, and patiently teach. We are called to keep doing this until Jesus comes or we die. Our hope and prayer in this endeavor is for our people, as they leave the church building, to turn and say to one another, "Did we really hear the voice of God speaking from the midst of the fire and survive?"

# PRAYER

Our Father, I pray that You will raise up an army of expositors who will preach in season and out of season, through whom You will speak through Your Word. Father, may we have nothing to do with anything less or with anything other. May we see Your glory. May we see Your church recovered by preaching. May we see You bring glory to Your name as You honor Your Word. We pray this in the name of our Savior, the Lord Jesus Christ, Amen.

# 7

# THE PASSION AND POWER OF APOSTOLIC PREACHING

*Steven J. Lawson*
*Shepherds' Conference 2007*

*Acts 2:14-24*

I want to persuade you to be an expository preacher. I am not referring to just any kind of expositor, but a preacher who has the thunder of the apostles as they heralded and proclaimed the Word of the living God. The church does not need any more mild and meek preachers in pulpits. We need men of God to stand up, to speak up, and to herald the full counsel of God. We need the passion and the power of apostolic preaching to be upon our lives.

## Two Dangers

As the church advances into the twenty-first century, I see two deadly dangers that concern me greatly—dangers that are threatening the very lifeblood of modern preaching.

The first threat is the devaluation of preaching in many churches. In this radical paradigm shift, biblical preaching is being displaced in favor of other alternatives. Exposition, once the main staple of the pulpit, is now being replaced with entertainment. Theology is giving way to theatrics. Sound doctrine is being exchanged for sound checks. The unfolding drama of redemption is becoming substituted for just plain drama. God-exalting and soul-awakening preaching is out and casual dialogues are in. The straightforward exposition of Scripture is being demoted to secondary status.

This threat worries me, but it is not my greatest concern. The other danger lies entirely on the opposite end of the preaching spectrum. It is a threat far more subtle and one that endangers those who value biblical preaching. It is a stifling danger that is encroaching upon those whose exegesis is sound, whose study is deep, whose cross-references are dotted, and whose manuscripts are prepared. The problem is that their expository preaching is all exposition with no preaching. It is little more than a data dump. It is a lifeless lecture on the Bible. Their preaching has become clinical, cold, sterile, and stagnant. It is all light and no heat; it is precision without power. It is this second problem that most concerns me. Richard Baxter, the great Puritan minister, once said, "Nothing is more indecent than a dead preacher speaking to dead sinners, the living truth of the living God."[1]

R.C. Sproul has rightly said, "Dispassionate preaching is a lie, it denies the very content it conveys."[2] Walter Kaiser has weighed in on this and said, "Away with all the mediocre, lifeless, boring, lackluster orations offered as pitiful substitutes for the powerful Word of the living God. If that Word does not thrill the preacher and fill him with an intense desire to glorify God, how shall he ever expect it to have any effect upon his hearers?"[3] Martyn Lloyd-Jones has defined preaching as theology coming through a man who is on fire for God.[4] I believe that this is what must be recaptured among us who are called into ministry. We are not in danger of giving up the pulpit and inviting entertainment into our worship service. It is us, who believe in the authority of the Word of the living God, who all too often are lifeless in our exposition of the Scriptures.

We must look to the apostolic preaching that burst onto the scene in the first century. Every reader of Acts should be impressed with how dominant, powerful, and passionate apostolic preaching was. There are 19 major sermons or defenses of the faith in the book of Acts. It has been suggested that Acts could just as easily be entitled, "The Sermons of the Apostles." There are eight sermons by Peter, one sermon by Stephen, one by James, and nine sermons by Paul—five that are messages, and four that are defenses. Twenty-five percent of the book of Acts is devoted to recording the words of apostolic preaching in the early church. One out of every four verses in the book of Acts is a sermon or a defense of the faith. That underscores to us how important apostolic preaching was. It also suggests to us the kind of preaching that we are to emulate. One of the reasons these sermons are recorded in Acts is so that we might follow their timeless pattern in our preaching.

**What Is Needed**

It is not just expository preaching that we need, but expository preaching of a certain tone and with a certain thrust. What we need is apostolic expository preaching. We need to bring the thunder back into the pulpit. As we look in Acts chapter 2, I want to bring to your attention four marks of apostolic preaching that ought to direct every expositor who preaches the Word of God.

---

**This is the preacher's greatest glory—to set forth the majesty and supremacy of the Lord Jesus Christ.**

---

First, preaching must be authoritative. Second, preaching must be text-driven. It must start with Scripture, continue with Scripture, stay with Scripture, and conclude with Scripture. The preacher never deviates nor departs from the central thrust of the Word of God. Third, preaching must be Christ-centered. It is a magnification and exaltation of the presentation of the person and work of Jesus Christ; this is the preacher's greatest glory—to set forth the majesty and supremacy of the Lord Jesus Christ. And fourth, preaching must be heart-piercing.

These four marks are found in the sermon Peter delivered on the day of Pentecost, and I suggest that as preachers we are to stand on the shoulders of the apostles and not only preach what they preached, but also preach as they preached. This will involve the following:

### Preaching Must Be Authoritative

The first mark of apostolic preaching is that it is preaching with authority. As Peter stepped forward to preach, he did not offer suggestions to his listeners. He was not laying out mere options for them. On the contrary, Peter was assertive, emphatic, confident, commanding, directional, outspoken, and compelling. In fact, he was arrested for his preaching. Luke records this in Acts 2:14-24:

> Peter, taking his stand with the eleven, raised his voice and declared to them: "Men of Judea and all you who live in Jerusalem, let this be known to you and give heed to my words. For these men are not drunk, as you suppose, for it is only the third hour of the day; but this is what was spoken of through the prophet Joel: 'And it shall be in the last days,' God says, 'That I will pour forth of My Spirit on all mankind; and your sons and your daughters shall prophesy, and your young men shall see visions, and your old men shall dream dreams; even on My bondslaves, both men and women, I will in those days pour forth of My Spirit and they shall prophesy. And I will grant wonders in the sky above and signs on the earth below, blood, and fire, and vapor of smoke. The sun will be turned into darkness and the moon into blood, before the great and glorious day of the Lord shall come. And it shall be that everyone who calls on the name of the Lord will be saved.'"

As Peter stood before this crowd, his listeners had to decide which way they would go as a result of hearing his proclamation. Notice how the narrative begins in verse 14: "Peter, taking his stand with the eleven…" Peter took his stand as he stepped forward to preach. Luke's use of this verb translated "taking a stand" means far more than merely arising from a sitting position to stand on one's feet. What is being described here is Peter arising to take a firm stand and establish himself. John Calvin commented on Luke's description of Peter in this scene, saying, "He had something very serious to say and wanted to be heard."[5] Peter assumed an authoritative posture by standing with the other apostles, who flanked him on both sides. Their presence added to the sense of Peter's authority as he declared the Word of God.

Luke also wrote in verse 14 that Peter "raised his voice." He was passionate, assertive, and sure. He had been trained by the Lord Jesus Christ himself. In John 7:37, it was Jesus who similarly expressed passion in His preaching when He taught at the Feast of the Tabernacles. John recorded that moment and wrote, "Jesus stood and cried out, saying, 'If anyone is thirsty, let Him come to me and drink.'" As Peter stepped forward and raised his voice, he did so as he had seen his Lord do so many times. This is not to say you need to be loud in order to be passionate, for there must be an ebb and flow in your volume as you speak the Word of God. Yet there must be a deep intensity conveyed.

I remember an incident in a class on preaching at Dallas Theological Seminary that highlights the importance of passion in preaching. In a preaching lab, a student was mumbling out his sermon as he preached to his fellow students. Professor Howard Hendricks interrupted his message in front of the class and said, "You do not believe that." The student responded, "Well I do." Hendricks said again, "Apparently, you do not." As this went on, the student became worked up and frustrated. He began to speak with deep conviction. Hendricks then said, "All right, get up there and preach it just like that. Let us know that you believe what you are saying. Once you convince us that you believe this, then maybe we will buy what you are selling." So it must be with every preacher.

Luke continued his description of Peter's sermon by noting his delivery: "Peter…declared to them" (Acts 2:14). Here Luke employed the term "declare" to describe the clarity of Peter's message. He was plainly heard and clearly understood. If there was to be a problem with those who were listening, it would not be because they had misunderstood Peter, but because they had heard exactly what he had to say. The word "declare" carries the idea of speaking seriously with gravitas. There was a gravity and a sobriety about Peter as he stepped forward to preach. He preached as if lives depended on it, as if souls were hanging in the balance.

Peter was confident and bold. There was no equivocation nor hesitation in his delivery. He said, "Men of Judea and all you who live in Jerusalem, let this be known to you" (verse 14). Peter spoke as a man who had been given a mandate by God and sent as the Lord's ambassador to be His mouthpiece upon the earth. Peter was not like those preachers who stroke their chin and say, "Well, it seems to me…" You do not want to listen to anyone who says that. You want to listen to a preacher who says, "Let this be known to you."

Peter then said, "Give heed to my words" (verse 14). He demanded that he be heard. He was saying, "Listen up, pay attention, and do not ignore me." That is the manner in which we are to stand up and preach God's Word. Peter then became corrective and showed his listeners the error of their ways when he said to them, "These men are not drunk, as you suppose, for it is only the third hour of the day" (verse 15). He reproved the crowd for wrongly assuming that the apostles were drunk.

Peter's authoritative approach continued through the rest of his sermon. In verse 22 he said, "Listen to these words." In verse 29 he asserted himself again when he said, "Brethren, I may confidently say." And finally in verse 36, he maintained certainty about his message: "Let all the house of Israel know for certain." The tone of Peter's entire sermon was characterized by authority and conviction.

Every gospel preacher and every true expositor must preach with the same authoritative boldness. We must speak the truth in love, but we must speak the truth. That is how Jesus taught and preached. At the very end of the Sermon on the Mount, "When Jesus had finished these words, the crowds were amazed at His teaching; for He was teaching them as one having authority, and not as their scribes" (Mathew 7:28-29). Where are the men who are marked by authority when they speak from the Word of the living God?

Paul taught Titus to preach in the same way: "These things speak and exhort and reprove *with all authority. Let no one disregard you*" (Titus 2:15, emphasis mine). This necessitates that our preaching be commanding and authoritative. Yes, we are to be kind, loving, patient, and long-suffering. But as we stand with the Word of God in our hand, we are to be exactly as Peter was—we are to be bold, we are to raise our voice, we are to declare to our listeners, and we are to call for a verdict. In 1 Corinthians 16:13, Paul wrote, "Stand firm in the faith, act like men, be strong." Too many men are tripping over their skirts in the pulpits because there is a feminization of the pulpit today.

The problem with preachers today is that nobody wants to kill them. Peter was crucified. James was beheaded. Stephen was stoned to death. Paul was imprisoned and beheaded. All of the apostolic preachers died a martyr's death but one—John, who was held in confinement on the island of Patmos. The apostles were persecuted for what they believed and boldly declared. If there are people in your church who are in your ear urging you to tone it down, by the grace of the Holy Spirit do not listen to them. Instead, preach the full counsel of God in all that it says and affirms. That is what God has called us to do—our preaching must be bold and authoritative.

### Preaching Must Be Text-Driven

The second mark of apostolic preaching is that it must be text-driven. The text itself is the real authority of the sermon and the preacher. Apostolic preaching is rooted in the Word of the living God. The sermon must be thoroughly biblical and entirely expository. In Peter's sermon there were five major citations of Old Testament Scripture that he weaved together. Note that Acts 2:17-21 is simply a reading of Joel 2:28-32. In Acts 2:25-28 we see Psalm 16:8-11. In Acts 2:30 he quoted Psalm 132:11. In Acts 2:31 Peter went back to Psalm 16:10. Finally, in Acts 2:34-35 Peter referenced Psalm 110:1. His entire message was rooted in the Scripture that he knew and had available to him. It is from this that I want us to observe five features of a text-driven sermon.

### Read the Text

The first feature of a text-driven sermon is to read the text. Notice that Acts 2:16 begins, "This is what was spoken of through the prophet Joel." Expository preaching is not to begin by calling attention to what happened to you on the way to church. Rather, it is about calling attention to the Word of God. The preacher has nothing to say apart from the Word of God, for the preacher is a parrot of the Word. We are a cave that God has spoken into and our task is to echo His revelation.

Beginning a message with the reading of the Word is exactly what Ezra did in Nehemiah chapter 8: "Ezra the priest brought the law before the assembly of men…He read from it" (verses 2-3). It is what our Lord did in the synagogue in Nazareth: "The book of the prophet Isaiah was handed to Him. And He opened the book and found the place where it was written…" (Luke 4:17). It is what Paul told Timothy to do in 1 Timothy 4:13: "Give attention to the public reading of Scripture, to exhortation and teaching." Peter did what Ezra had done, what Christ had done, and what Paul had told every preacher to do.

Every preacher must begin with a reading of the Word of God because everything that will be said must originate from the text of Scripture. In Acts 2:16 Peter said, "This is what was spoken of through the prophet Joel." As Peter pointed out the occurrence of the pouring out of the Holy Spirit on the day of Pentecost, he used the Word of God to explain what had just happened and bring into focus the events with biblical support. Peter stood up, announced his text, and began, "'And it shall be in the last days,' God says…"

(Acts 2:17). As a side note, notice the dual authorship of Scripture here. Verse 16 says Joel was the speaker, and verse 17 says God was the speaker. In the inspiration of Scripture, there is a primary Author and a secondary author. Joel was the secondary author; he was the instrument God used to record His message. Peter affirmed this in verse 17 when he clarified that it was God who was speaking what Joel had said. In other words, the real preacher on the day of Pentecost was not Joel or Peter, but God Himself.

God is speaking in this text, and the proof is in the personal pronouns that were used. For example, in verse 17 God said, "I will pour forth of My Spirit," and in verse 19 He said, "I will grant wonders in the sky above." The personal pronoun "I" refers to God; Joel and Peter are secondary to God, who is primary. In verse 18 we read, "Even on My bond-slaves, both men and women, I will in those days pour forth of My Spirit." There, the personal pronoun "My" refers to God. So God is the real preacher here. He is the one preaching on the day of Pentecost. Peter is simply a mouthpiece for what Joel has written, and Joel was inspired by God.

*Explain the Text*

After you read the text, you must explain the text. As we continue, we observe Peter explaining the Scriptures. He said, "It shall be that everyone who calls on the name of the Lord will be saved" (Acts 2:21). Then in verse 22 Peter explained the previous verse. We see an inseparable connection between the two verses. After challenging his audience to call on the name of the Lord, Peter provided the name they must call on for their eternal salvation. In verse 22 he stated the name of the Savior, Jesus the Nazarene. He then explained the ministry of this Savior: "A man attested to you by God with miracles and wonders and signs which God performed through Him in your midst, just as you yourselves know" (verse 22).

Peter finished his explanation of the Savior with the following words: "This Man, delivered over by the predetermined plan and foreknowledge of God, you nailed to a cross by the hands of godless men and put Him to death. But God raised him up again, putting an end to the agony of death, since it was impossible for Him to be held in its power" (verses 23-24). In Luke's account, these verses are merely an explanation of Joel 2:32. This is what expository preaching is—you read the text, then you explain the text. You explain it as it was meant to be interpreted, conveying the meaning of what the original author said, the historical setting in which it was said, and the grammatical sense of what was said.

*Support the Text*

After reading and explaining the text, the preacher is to support the text from other passages. Peter supported the central theme of his argument by tracing it throughout the Old Testament. He provided four strategic cross-references that bolstered his explanation of who the Savior is. The apostle was able to do this because the full counsel of God speaks with unity and clarity. Beginning in verse 25, Peter said, "David says of Him...," and with this statement he introduced a quote from Psalm 16:8-11:

> I have set the LORD continually before me; because He is at my right hand, I will not be shaken. Therefore my heart is glad and my glory rejoices; my flesh also will dwell securely. For You will not abandon my soul to Sheol; nor will You allow Your Holy One to undergo decay. You will make known to me the path of life; in Your presence is fullness of joy; in Your right hand there are pleasures forever.

Peter used Scripture to support Scripture and reinforce what he was saying. He defended the resurrection of the Lord Jesus Christ, which was mentioned in verse 24: "God raised Him up again." Then Peter said, "For David says of Him, 'I saw the Lord always in my presence'" (verse 25). Peter's intention is to alert his audience, as well as us, to the reality that David was not speaking of himself, but of a future and greater descendant of David who would come in the Messianic line, Jesus Christ Himself. In Psalm

16, David was looking beyond himself and beyond his own time to the coming of the Messiah.

Looking at Acts 2:25 in full, Peter said, "For David says of him, 'I saw the Lord always in my presence; for He is at my right hand, so that I will not be shaken.'" The passage speaks of Jesus' trust in God the Father as He approached the cross and hung upon it. Jesus knew the Father was with Him and would remain with Him until that time at high noon when God blocked out the sun and Jesus said "My God, My God, why have You forsaken Me?" (Matthew 27:46). For the first three hours upon the cross, Jesus knew that the Father was with Him. So in Acts 2:26 we read the Messiah proclaiming, "Therefore my heart was glad and my tongue exulted; moreover my flesh also will live in hope." The hope referred to here is the joy that was set before Jesus as He endured the cross (Hebrews 12:1-3). That is to say, Jesus knew that He would not die in vain, but that His death would secure the eternal salvation of all those for whom He was dying.

Peter's support of his assertion continues in verse 27, where he exposes an inter-Trinitarian conversation. Luke records what the Son is saying to the Father, "You will not abandon my soul to Hades, nor allow your Holy One to undergo decay. You have made known to me the ways of life; you will make me full of gladness with Your presence."

Jesus knew that on the other side of death, His Father would raise Him from the grave. There would be a resurrection, and in that resurrection there would be fullness of joy and gladness in the presence of the Father.

The reason we know that Peter was speaking of Jesus and not David is because in verse 29 we read, "I may confidently say to you regarding the patriarch David that he both died and he was buried, and his tomb is with us to this day." Peter, with deep conviction, preached that David was not speaking of himself, for David is still in the grave. However, the grave of greater Son of David, the Lord Jesus Christ, is empty.

The second cross-reference Peter included in his sermon is Psalm 132:11: "God had sworn to him with an oath to seat one of his descendants on his throne" (Acts 2:30). Peter was undergirding what he had said in verse 24 regarding the resurrection of Jesus Christ. In verses 33-34 he continued, "Therefore having been exalted to the right hand of God, and having received from the Father the promise of the Holy Spirit, He has poured forth this which you both see and hear. For it was not David who ascended into heaven but he himself says…" Peter then quoted yet another text of Scripture, Psalm 110:1: "The Lord said to my Lord…" The first mention of "Lord" refers to God the Father, while "my Lord" refers to God the Son. The intent of this citation is to support what was said in Acts 2:21: "Everyone who calls on the name of the Lord will be saved." Peter is aiming to link the sermon very tightly with the salvation found in Christ—in the resurrection of Christ and the exaltation of Christ.

*Synthesize the Text*

The fourth feature of a text-driven sermon is the synthesis of the text. In Acts 2:36, Peter directs us to the conclusion of his message when he says, "Therefore let all the house of Israel know for certain that God has made Him both Lord and Christ—this Jesus whom you crucified." This expository sermon—this apostolic sermon—is not a compilation of disconnected theological thoughts with unrelated verses. In this message is a precise progression of logical and orderly thought. The Lord whom the people must call upon in verse 21 is the very Lord whom they have crucified in verse 23, the very Lord whom God has raised from the dead in verse 24, and the very Lord of whom God the Father has made both Lord and Christ in verse 36.

*Apply the Text*

The final feature of a text-driven sermon is application. Before Peter even had the opportunity to finish speaking, the people listening to him came to the startling realization, through the illuminating ministry of the Holy Spirit, that with their own hands they had put to death the Prince of Life: "Now when they heard this, they were pierced to the heart, and said to Peter and the rest of the apostles, 'Brethren, what shall we do?'" (verse 37). Peter had not even finished preaching, but the sermon was so arresting that the sinners were giving the invitation: "Brethren, what shall we do?" The people interrupted Peter's preaching because they were under the deep conviction of the Word of God. So in verse 38, Peter uses the second-person plural pronoun "you" and tells them, "Repent, and each of *you* be baptized in the name of Jesus Christ for the forgiveness of *your* sins; and *you* will receive the gift of the Holy Spirit" (emphases mine).

Like Peter's proclamation, our preaching must be personal and directional. We must give the application that spells out what the sinner and the saint must do. Expository preaching involves persuasion, appeal, invitation, begging, pleading, warning, and exhortation. Peter, in this sermon, exhorted the audience's will. He called for the verdict, and he pleaded for their decision.

It was said of Jonathan Edwards that his great preaching was used by God to spark the Great Awakening. This preaching included both doctrine and application, for the common Puritan sermon consisted of two main sections—doctrine, then application. It was said that in the doctrinal portion of his sermons Jonathan Edwards was merely bringing his cannons into place and packing in the gunpowder, and it was in the application portion that he fired them. I wonder how many times we fall short of firing our cannons

as we set forth the doctrinal truths found in Scripture. Our sermons must include the imperative mood—they must incorporate the "you" that calls for a response. Text-driven preaching includes the application that God requires of His listeners.

### Preaching Must Be Christ-Centered

The third mark of apostolic preaching, in addition to being authoritative and text-driven, is that it is Christ-centered. Peter's sermon was riveted on the person and work of Jesus Christ. In verse 22 we see the affirmation of Jesus as the Christ: "Men of Israel, listen to these words: Jesus the Nazarene, a man attested to you by God with miracles and wonders and signs which God performed through Him in your midst, just as you yourselves know…" Every miracle that Jesus performed was the finger of God from heaven pointing and saying, "This is My beloved son; hear Him."

Not only did Peter emphasize Jesus' qualification to be the Messiah, but he also taught about His foreordained death. Peter proclaimed that Jesus was "delivered over by the predetermined plan and foreknowledge of God" (Acts 2:23). Jesus Christ, the Lamb of God, was slain from before the foundation of the world. He was foreknown by the Father, and it was the Father's eternal decree that Jesus Christ would bear the sins of His people as He was nailed to the cross by the hands of godless men. Peter binds his audience's conscience and holds them directly accountable to God for the most heinous sin of all human history—the first-degree murder of the sinless Son of God. Peter then moves to the resurrection in verse 24: "But God raised him up again." In other words, Peter was saying to his listeners, "You thought you could put Him to death. You thought you would not have to deal with Him anymore. You thought you could wash your hands of the matter. You thought you could bury Him, and it would all be over. But God has raised Him from the dead."

Peter next moves to Jesus' exaltation. In verse 33 we read that Jesus was "exalted to the right hand of God." He was elevated to the place of highest honor, the place of absolute unrivaled sovereignty over heaven and hell. Thus, Jesus has the authority to send the Holy Spirit; He has the authority to convert His enemies; He has the authority to overcome circumstances; He has the authority to open eyes, ears, and hearts; He has the authority to grant repentance; He has the authority to bestow saving faith; and He has the authority to build His church. Peter declared the person and work of Jesus Christ on the day of Pentecost. This is what Paul was speaking of when he said we preach "Jesus Christ, and Him crucified" (1 Corinthians 2:2). Peter did just that: "Therefore let all the house of Israel know for certain that God has made Him both Lord and Christ" (Acts 2:36).

Peter is not alone in church history with regard to preaching the centrality of Jesus Christ. Iain Murray, in his extraordinary book *The Forgotten Spurgeon*,[6] reveals that C.H. Spurgeon's ministry was focused entirely on preaching of the Lord Jesus Christ. Murray writes of an incident in which Spurgeon went into the Crystal Palace in London during the week in preparation of preaching there. One of the workers asked him, "Say something so we can test the acoustics." What came from Spurgeon's mouth was what was supreme in his heart—he said, "Behold the Lamb of the God who takes away the sin of the world." There was a worker up on the roof who heard the words and did not know Spurgeon was in the building. He thought he had heard the voice of God speaking to him. Startled, he went into the building, saw Spurgeon, and said to him, "I must be saved; I've heard the voice of God." Spurgeon responded, "What did He say?" The man answered, "Behold the Lamb of God who takes away the sin of the world."

There is another illustration of Spurgeon's fixation on the centrality of Jesus in preaching. In 1855 he preached a sermon entitled "Eternal Name." In the course of that sermon, Spurgeon depicted what would become of the world if the name of Jesus were to be removed from it. Unable to restrain his feelings, Spurgeon declared, "I would have no wish to be here without my Lord. And if the gospel be not true, I should bless God to annihilate me this instant, for I would not care to live if ye would destroy the name of Jesus Christ."[7]

> Apostolic preaching is an arrow
> that is fired like a laser to the target
> of the heart to magnify the
> glory of Jesus Christ.

Many years later, Mrs. Spurgeon reflected upon that night when her young husband preached that sermon. She reminisced about how her husband knew no greater joy than to preach the name of the Lord Jesus Christ. She remembered that at the end of the sermon, after an entire hour of magnifying, elevating, and exalting the supreme Lordship of Jesus Christ, Spurgeon made a mighty effort to recover his voice, which had become hoarse. But all she could hear was him whispering, "Let my name perish but let Christ's name last forever. Jesus, crown Him Lord of all. You will not hear me say anything else."[8] Then Spurgeon fell backward into the chair that was behind the pulpit in exhaustion. It was Spurgeon's greatest glory to preach the name, the person, the work, and the terms of the Lord Jesus Christ. Apostolic preaching is an arrow that is fired like a laser to the target of the heart to magnify the glory of Jesus Christ.

### Preaching Must Be Heart-Piercing

The fourth and final mark of apostolic preaching is that it must be heart-piercing. In Acts 2:37 Luke records the response of the audience to Peter's preaching and says, "When they heard this, they were pierced to the heart." In other words, Luke is saying the audience felt as if they had been stabbed with a knife. This is the only kind of preaching that brings about such a soul-rending result.

Dramatic plays and video clips are not going to produce this type of response. Nor a man-centered sermon series on how to have a happy vacation. Only bold and authoritative preaching that is text-driven and Christ-centered can bring about this effect in the hearts of sinners. When Peter's listeners "were pierced to the heart," they cried out, "Brethren, what shall we do?" (Acts 2:37). And Peter answered by preaching repentance to them. He told the people to acknowledge and turn from their sin, renounce self and self-righteousness, and throw themselves upon the mercy of the Lord Jesus Christ. Earlier in the sermon he had promised, "Everyone who calls on the name of the Lord will be saved" (verse 21), and he repeated this at the end: "The promise is for you and your children and for all who are far off, as many as the Lord our God will call to Himself" (Acts 2:39).

Peter relied upon the sovereign election of God to call out those sinners who were elect before the foundation of the world. He believed in the sufficiency of God's Word and the sufficiency of the Holy Spirit to uphold the text and uphold Christ so that God would be pleased to call sinners to Himself.

## The Preaching God Honors

We must ask the question, Did God honor this preaching? The answer is in Acts 2:41: "So then, those who had received his word were baptized; and that day there were added about three thousand souls." God is pleased to honor the preaching of His Word that lifts up the name of the Son of God. Richard Baxter said, "I preached as never sure to preach again; and as a dying man to dying men."⁹ Every time you step up to the pulpit, may you preach as though it is the final sermon you will ever proclaim.

This is the passion and the power of apostolic preaching. Such preaching is bold, text-driven, Christ-centered, and heart-piercing. May God raise up expositors who will herald the Word far and wide.

# PRAYER

Father, thank You for the glories and the majesty of Christ. Thank You for our Savior and Your predetermined plan that commissioned Him into this world. Thank You that at the fullness of time He was born under the law to perfectly keep every demand and every requirement of the law. Thank You for His determination to set His face like a flint toward Jerusalem and to be lifted up from the earth upon that cross for us.

Thank You, Father for taking our sins and transferring them to Christ that He might make them His very own. We thank You that He bore our sin, absorbed Your wrath, and was raised in glory. As You send us into the world to proclaim the great message of salvation, may we preach as Peter preached on the day of Pentecost. May there be passion and urgency as we lift high that name that shall endure forever, the name of our Lord Jesus Christ. In His name we pray, Amen.

# PREACHING IN THE SPIRIT'S POWER

*Tom Pennington*
*Shepherds' Conference 2010*

*1 Corinthians 2:1-5*

We are painfully aware of our inadequacy as preachers. Many Sundays in the moments before I enter the pulpit, I find myself repeating the words Martin Luther often prayed before he preached: "Dear Lord God, I want to preach so that you are glorified...Although I probably cannot make it turn out well, won't you make it turn out well?"[1] More often my prayer comes from the words of Paul in 1 Corinthians 2:5—"Father, help me to preach in demonstration of the Spirit and of power." That must be the goal and the prayer of every true preacher of the Word of God. Those remarkable words are the heart of the clearest statement of Paul's philosophy of preaching found anywhere in his letters.

The apostle Paul visited the Greek city of Corinth on his second missionary journey in AD 51. According to Acts 18, he stayed there for 18 months. Three years after Paul had departed from Corinth, while he was in Ephesus, he heard some troubling news. A prominent member of the church, Chloe, wrote to Paul or perhaps even travelled across the Aegean Sea to bring the report that serious divisions had erupted in the church at Corinth.

## Enamored with the Method

Paul began his letter to the Corinthians by addressing that serious problem. He wrote, "Now I mean this, that each one of you is saying, 'I am of Paul,' and 'I am of Apollos,' and 'I am of Cephas,' and 'I of Christ'" (1 Corinthians 1:12). Why this division? In verse 17, Paul elaborated on the issue that was dividing the church, which had to do with "cleverness of speech." The problem in Corinth was not primarily about doctrine, but style. It was not about what was preached, but how it was preached. Ultimately, what divided the church in Corinth was something that the people had embraced from the culture around them—they were enamored by eloquent rhetoric.

Scholars who have researched the situation in first-century Corinth say that Corinth was home to a very popular school of Greek rhetoric promoted by a group called the Sophists.[2] The Sophists were itinerant intellectuals who taught rhetoric for a fee. They traveled from city to city trying to amaze people with their speaking in order to attract paying students.

Philosophically, the Sophists were relativists. That is, they were not convinced about the certainty of truth. For the Sophists, then, communication was more about style than substance, which set this school of rhetoric against even the great philosophers Aristotle and Plato.

The Sophists were also pragmatists. They contextualized their message to get the results they wanted. They were primarily after personal advancement, applause, status, and the wealth that came with these things. They intentionally chose content and the form of that content which would most please the crowd. Their intent was to build their own personal prestige and their greatest concern was results, not truth.

Duane Litfin, in his book *St. Paul's Theology of Proclamation*, describes their priority this way: "The orator began by

determining what results he wanted to achieve and then he shaped his message accordingly. The message was the manipulated variable…and it was up to the orator by the sheer power of his rhetorical gifts, his training, his experience, to create a message that would produce those results."[3] This group in Corinth was selling what one writer called "an applause-generating, consumer-oriented rhetoric."[4]

Nothing was more important in Greek culture than the ability to speak in a way that persuaded others. If you could speak with some measure of eloquence, then you were considered to be intelligent, cultured, and high-class. In fact, the English word *sophisticated* comes from the Greek word *sophos,* which means "skilled" or "wise." Tragically, the believers in Corinth played right into the hands of these teachers and were attracted to those who spoke eloquently. First Corinthians 1 says there were some believers who rallied around Apollos—their slogan was, "We're of Apollos." There were others who were impressed by Paul's ability to speak. Their slogan was, "We are of Paul." Still others claimed Peter or Christ as their favored orator.

Paul, however, explained to the Corinthians that they were wrong in being enamored with any one person's speaking style. In 1 Corinthians 1, he said God intentionally wanted to save sinners in a way that would demolish any reason for human pride and wisdom. To accomplish this task, God chose a foolish message—the gospel. He chose a foolish method—preaching. And He chose foolish people to redeem—a bunch of nobodies.

All through 1 Corinthians chapter 1, Paul made it clear that in matters related to the gospel and salvation, God's ultimate goal was to remove any reason for human pride and to bring all glory to Himself. That's the message through the end of chapter 1. Paul then said that when he came to preach to the Corinthians, he had done so in a way that complemented God's goal. Christ had not sent Paul to preach the gospel in cleverness of speech, for Paul's success in Corinth had nothing to do with him, his ingenuity, or his technique. Paul's preaching and the response it generated was entirely a work of the Spirit.

In 1 Corinthians 2:1-5, Paul contrasted his approach to preaching with the techniques the Sophists used in their rhetoric:

> When I came to you, brethren, I did not come with superiority of speech or of wisdom, proclaiming to you the testimony of God. For I determined to know nothing among you except Jesus Christ, and Him crucified. I was with you in weakness and in fear and in much trembling, and my message and my preaching were not in persuasive words of wisdom, but in demonstration of the Spirit and of power, so that your faith would not rest on the wisdom of men, but on the power of God.

Paul's message in these verses is clear and direct: Preaching that exalts God must always be "in demonstration of the Spirit and of power." The question is, how do we preach like that? In this text we discover the personal commitments Paul made in his own preaching—commitments that enabled him to rely completely on the Spirit's power and not his own. He was not dependent on his personality, the power of his own gifts, or some human technique.

---

**If we are going to preach in demonstration of the Spirit and of power, we must focus on the message and not our own glory.**

---

### Keys to Preaching in the Spirit's Power

So what are the crucial commitments we need to make to preach in a way that demonstrates the Spirit's presence and power?

#### Focus on God's Message and Not Personal Glory

The first commitment we must make is to focus on God's message and not personal glory. Paul wrote in 1 Corinthians 2:1, "When I came to you, brethren, I did not come with superiority of speech or of wisdom, proclaiming to you the testimony of God." The Greek word translated "superiority" literally means "a projection or something that rises above what is around it." The verb form of the word means "to stand out, to rise above, to outdo, to excel." Paul did not come to Corinth attempting to make his speech or wisdom stand out from that of other orators. His aspiration wasn't to outdo anyone, nor did he preach in an attempt to distinguish himself. Paul's philosophy of preaching was this: "We do not preach ourselves but Christ Jesus as Lord, and ourselves as your bond-servants for Jesus' sake" (2 Corinthians 4:5).

If we are going to preach in demonstration of the Spirit and of power, we must focus on the message and not our own glory. The Scottish pastor James Denney understood this philosophy of preaching. To help him remember, he had these words framed and hung in his church: "No man can bear witness to Christ and to himself at the same time. No man can give the impression that he himself is clever, and that Christ is mighty to save."[5] Similarly, Paul refused to promote his own cleverness. In his *speech*—that is, his style of speaking. Or in his *wisdom*—that is, his content.

As Paul made his point, he used the very terms the orators in Corinth loved. He said, "I didn't come to exalt myself, to excel in some way, to distinguish myself. Instead, my focus was on God and His message. I came proclaiming to you the testimony of God." The Greek word translated "proclaiming" was used often in the first century to speak of an official or authoritative announcement. We are not called to "share" the Word and we certainly aren't called to be "part of a conversation" about the Word. We are called to *proclaim* the Word, and to do so with authority.

## Announcing Christ

What are we to announce? First Corinthians 2:1 says, "The testimony of God." Like Paul, we are to declare with authority God's own testimony—especially the testimony about His Son. Paul elaborated on this in verse 2: "I determined to know nothing among you except Jesus Christ, and Him crucified." Some people think that in this passage, Paul was announcing a change in his preaching style. They say that when the apostle went to Athens, his message was more philosophical. But then after his "failure" on Mars Hill, he realized he should change his approach.

But there's no evidence in Acts 17 that Paul was disappointed with his ministry in Athens. Preaching Christ and Him crucified was Paul's message from day one, when he met the risen Savior on the Damascus Road. Notice what Paul wrote in his very first New Testament letter, the book of Galatians. He described the Galatians as those "before whose eyes Jesus Christ was publicly portrayed as crucified" (3:1). Paul, from the beginning of his ministry, preached Jesus Christ and Him crucified. This was always his approach, and he never deviated from it.

What does it mean to preach Christ and Him crucified? It doesn't mean that all Paul taught about was Jesus and the cross. For example, in Acts 18:11, we learn that Paul settled in Corinth for a year and half and taught all of the Old Testament scriptures to the Christians there. Surely his ministry in Corinth was similar to what he had done in Ephesus. Remember what he said to the Ephesian elders in Acts 20:27? "I did not shrink from declaring to you the whole counsel of God."

To preach Christ and Him crucified does not mean to declare the simple gospel message and nothing else. If we do that, we are missing out on the purpose of corporate worship, and we will also starve the sheep. Instead, Paul was saying that everything we preach must ultimately be rooted in and founded upon the truth that Jesus is the Messiah. Paul's preaching found its center in Jesus Christ and Him crucified.

## Staying Focused

Twenty years ago, I was diagnosed with the eye disease glaucoma. Once or twice a year I take a visual field test that checks my peripheral vision to make sure I have no additional optic nerve damage. During the test, the technician props my head onto a device that holds my chin still, and tells me to keep my eyes focused on a red pinpoint of light directly in front

of me. As I stare at that red light, one at a time little pinpoints of white light begin to show up in my peripheral field of vision. When I see a white light, I'm supposed to push a button. I dislike this test because it's very intense, and after several seconds of staring at that red light and not seeing any pinpoints of light in my peripheral vision, I wonder if maybe I missed one, so I'm tempted to push the button just in case.

What's interesting about this test is that if your eyes wander from the red light for even a second, a buzzer sounds to tell you that you've lost your focus. You have to stay focused on the center so that any other lights you see are visible only in your peripheral vision. That illustrates what Paul meant when he said, "We must keep our preaching centered on Christ." Whatever our subject may be or whatever passage we are preaching from, we must keep our eyes centered on Christ and His cross. I don't mean we ought to distort a text by spiritualizing it to include Christ. However, the great theme of the Bible is that God is redeeming a people by His Son, for His Son, to His own glory. Whatever your passage, it's somehow developing that theme. Our responsibility, then, as ministers of the New Covenant, is to show our listeners how that theme is interwoven in the text we preach.

Charles Spurgeon loved to tell his students the story of a young preacher who gave a sermon while an older and more experienced preacher sat in the audience.

Afterward, the young preacher asked the older man, "What did you think of my message?"

The older pastor replied, "It was a very poor sermon, indeed."

The young man said, "I don't understand. I studied a long time. I pored over the text. Was my explanation wrong? Were my arguments weak? Were my illustrations inappropriate?"

The older pastor said, "No, all those things were fine. But it was still a poor sermon."

Exasperated, the young preacher said, "Tell me why."

The older preacher answered, "Because there was no Christ in it."

The young man responded, "Christ wasn't in the text. You have to preach the text."

"Don't you know," said the older man, "that from every town and every village in England there is a road to London? So also from every text in Scripture there is a road to Christ. Your business, when you get to a text, is to say, 'What is the road to Christ?' and then make sure your sermon follows that road."[6]

Every sermon we preach must ultimately point to Christ and Him crucified. That means our sermons need to include not only the historical facts of the crucifixion and resurrection, but also the meaning of Jesus' death and resurrection, and the nature of the atonement. Throughout his letters, Paul explained Jesus' death and used profoundly rich theological terms to do so—terms that

today are foreign to many professing Christians. For example, there's *substitution*—Jesus, the innocent one, died in the place of the guilty. There's *imputation*—God credits to the sinner the righteousness of Christ, and He credits to Christ the sin of the one who believes.

There's also *propitiation*—during those six hours on the cross, Christ satisfied the infinite wrath of God against the sin of everyone who will ever believe. Then there's *justification*—we are declared right before God, the Judge, on the basis of the righteousness of Jesus Christ that we receive by faith.

Paul taught both the historicity of the cross and the theological implications of it. He wasn't concerned that someone might think his teaching was the moral equivalent of divine child abuse, as some people claim. The heart of Paul's ministry of the Word was Jesus Christ *and* the facts, nature, and ramifications of His death.

Paul didn't try to contextualize the gospel message to make it more palatable to people. In fact, in Corinth, Paul dwelt on the very element of the Christian message that was most in conflict with the surrounding culture. The Corinthians thought the message was foolish, and yet that's the message Paul preached.

The sad truth is that a portion of today's evangelical church has allowed its focus to drift. Some pastors and churches have taken their eyes off the pinpoint of light at the center and let their focus wander to things that should only be in the periphery. Paul wanted us to understand that ultimately, our preaching must focus on the person of Jesus Christ and the doctrine of the atonement. What that means, in practical terms, is that we must not choose our next sermon series based on what we think will draw the largest crowd. For example, Paul didn't focus on how to have better relationships or how to communicate better. We are called to preach the Scriptures, and when we do, we are to do so without letting our eyes wander from the focal point, which is Jesus Christ and His death and atonement.

Having Christ and Him crucified at the center of our preaching will also determine the boundaries of our fellowship. The truth of the gospel ought to be more important to us than becoming cobelligerents, even on important issues like abortion, the sanctity of marriage, or social justice. We should be more concerned about protecting the gospel than the planet. We should be more passionate about defending the atonement than the environment. We cannot allow any cause to become more important to us than Christ—not our personal glory, not some pet doctrine or program, not church growth, not a social agenda, and not some façade of Christian unity.

D.A. Carson was right when he said, "Whenever the periphery is in danger of displacing the center, we are not far removed from idolatry."[7] If we want our preaching to put the power of God's Spirit on display, then we first have to make the same commitment that Paul made: to focus on God's message and not on personal glory.

### Depend on God's Grace and Not Personal Ability

There's a second commitment Paul made that we also need to make: We must depend on God's grace and not personal ability. In 1 Corinthians 2:3 Paul transitioned from the content of his preaching to the content of his heart. He said, "I was with you in weakness and in fear and in much trembling."

There are two primary ways to understand this verse. Paul may have been referring to his physical circumstances. It's possible that he was physically weak when he arrived in Corinth, perhaps because he was ill. Or it's possible that Paul was afraid for his own safety when he came to Corinth (see Acts 18). But based on the context, it's best to see Paul again contrasting himself and his attitude with the Sophists. Paul was not referring to his physical weakness, but to his own attitude about preaching: "I was with you in weakness and in fear and in much trembling." In Ephesians 6:5, Paul used two of these words, "fear and trembling," when he told slaves to obey their earthly masters. Paul was describing a kind of conscientious anxiety. That's the attitude necessary for properly declaring the Word of God.

Personal danger did not make Paul tremble. It was the weight of responsibility that he shouldered in his preaching ministry. As Bible commentator Gordon Fee said, "Paul seems overwhelmed by the task before him."[8] When Paul preached, he was painfully aware of his own weakness. He had a deep sense of his inadequacy for doing what the Lord had called him to do. It was with fear and trembling that Paul came into the pulpit.

It's important to remember that when Paul came to Corinth, he had already been preaching the gospel for some 20 years. Yet he still had an attitude of humility. What's notable is that Paul's attitude was exactly the opposite of the attitude exuded by the speakers whom the Corinthians so greatly admired. One of the distinguishing traits of the Sophists was their supreme self-confidence when they got up to speak. In that culture, self-assurance was considered an essential for an effective orator. One ancient writer described the attitude of one Sophist this way: "He appeared before his audience as one who was entering to win glory for himself, and was confident that he could not fail."[9]

Paul, however, felt inadequate for the task of proclaiming the testimony of God. He stated this frequently. In 1 Corinthians 15:10 he said, "By the grace of God I am what I am, and His grace toward me did not prove vain; but I labored even more than all of them"—that is, more than all the apostles—"yet not I, but the grace of God with me." The reason Paul was able to labor so effectively had nothing to do with him. Rather, it was the grace of God in him.

Paul reaffirmed this in 2 Corinthians 2:14, where he revealed that he had been given the responsibility to manifest "the sweet aroma of the knowledge of [Christ] in every place." In verse 16 we see that in some cases that sweet aroma brings death, and in other cases it brings life. Paul added, "Who is adequate for these things? For we are not like many, peddling the Word of God, but as from sincerity, but as from God, we speak in Christ in the sight of God" (verses 16-17). We see this again in 2 Corinthians 3:4-6: "Such confidence we have through Christ toward God. Not that we are adequate in ourselves to consider anything as coming from ourselves, but our adequacy is from God, who also made us adequate." Like Paul, we are utterly inadequate to do what God has called us to do. Our only hope is in His grace.

Martin Luther understood the inadequacy of the preacher. In May 1532, Luther was trying to encourage his friend Anthony Lauterbach, who had been called as pastor of the Castle Church in Wittenberg. Luther looked back at his own experience at the beginning of his ministry and explained "how I feared the pulpit." He continued, "I advanced more than 15 arguments to Dr. Staupitz, and with them I declined my call, but they did me no good. When I finally said, 'Dr. Staupitz, you are taking my life. I shall not live a quarter year if you make me preach.' He replied, 'God needs wise people in heaven, too.'"[10] Luther understood his inadequacy and his inability.

Paul came to the pulpit with that same

sense of fear and humility. Is this our attitude when we preach? If we're honest with ourselves, I think we are all tempted to believe that we can preach God's Word in our own ability—that we have the capacity and the tools to understand the Bible in all its depth and richness. We can even convince ourselves that somehow, by our own skill, we can take that Word and make people understand it, respond to it, and be changed by it. Whenever such thoughts cross our mind, we need to repent in sackcloth and ashes.

John Calvin wrote, "Those who intrude themselves confidently, or who discharge the ministry of the Word with an easy mind, as though they were fully equal to the task, are ignorant both of themselves and of the task."[11] Self-confidence is deadly in a preacher of the gospel. We see this in the story of the preacher who entered the pulpit with great confidence. When he was done, it was clear to everyone that the sermon was a terrible disappointment. He came out of the pulpit greatly humbled, and later, an elder of the church gave him this wise advice: "If you had entered the pulpit the way you left it, you would have left the pulpit the way you entered it."

Our confidence cannot be in ourselves—in our personality, our ability to communicate, in our skills with the original languages, our intellect, our experiences, or our education. We must depend on God's grace to preach in a way that demonstrates the Spirit's power. Like Paul, we need to cultivate an

awareness of our own weakness and inadequacy. We must surrender every shred of self-confidence and approach the Word of God with fear and trembling. When we are weak, God manifests His power; and only then does He get all the glory. As 2 Corinthians 4:7 says, "We have this treasure in earthen vessels, so that the surpassing greatness of the power will be of God and not from ourselves." To preach in the demonstration of the Spirit and of power, we must focus on God's message and not personal glory. We must depend on God's grace and not personal ability.

### Trust in the Spirit's Power and Not Any Human Method or Technique

The third commitment a preacher must make is to trust in the Spirit's power and not in any human method or technique. Note what Paul said: "My message and my preaching were not in persuasive words of wisdom, but in demonstration of the Spirit and of power" (1 Corinthians 2:4). Paul made sure that the power of his persuasion didn't rest in him, his form, or his delivery. When he said "my message," he was referring to the content of his preaching. And "my preaching" refers to the style with which he presented his message. Paul intended these two words as a kind of hendiadys—that is, two words that combine into one idea, like "sick and tired."

Paul was saying that nothing about his preaching—content, form, or delivery style—was done with persuasive words of human wisdom. If you had been sitting in first-century Corinth, hearing these words from Paul would have shocked you. As we saw earlier, the Sophists' primary goal was to use their wisdom and delivery to persuade people—and the people of Corinth were enamored by this. By contrast, Paul wrote, "My message and my preaching were not in persuasive words of wisdom, but in demonstration of the Spirit and of power." The Greek word translated "demonstration" is a word that the Sophists loved. It occurs only here in the New Testament, but in Greek rhetoric it was a technical term used to speak of compelling evidence or proof.

Here's what Paul wants us to understand: The compelling factor in preaching is not our personal powers of persuasion. It is not the brilliance of our arguments. It does not lie in the structure of our message. It doesn't rest in the manner of our delivery. The compelling demonstration in our preaching must always be the Spirit and His power working through the message.

Very few of us today are tempted to use the techniques of first-century Greek rhetoric in an attempt to persuade an audience. But we're still faced with the temptation to rely on human methods and techniques of persuasion rather than depend on the power of the Spirit.

We need to search our hearts and honestly ask ourselves, "What human methods or techniques are we tempted to rely on? What do we believe really persuades people when we preach?"

Maybe our confidence is in the style of our delivery. Perhaps we figure that if we expend a lot of energy, pump up the volume, sweat through a couple of handkerchiefs, use catchy sayings, and close the service with an emotional story, we'll persuade people. Then there are those who believe the best approach is to speak with a quiet and intense sincerity. The goal is to make the sermon sound like a conversation. While our style of communication ought to be a natural expression of who we are, we cannot think for a moment that's where the power lies when it comes to preaching.

Still others are tempted to put their confidence in the visual arts, drama, the right lighting, or some other visual or experiential approach. There's a big emphasis on setting the right atmosphere.

> If our confidence for persuading people is in anything but the power of the Spirit, we will never know His power in our preaching.

Even those who are committed to biblical exposition can end up relying on some human technique or method. Expositors can be tempted to put their confidence in long hours of study, careful exegesis, syntactical analysis, homiletical skills, parallel outline points, and passionate delivery. As Martyn Lloyd-Jones has said, "We can easily become pulpiteers rather than preachers."[12]

Henry Ward Beecher had a name for sermons designed to put our preaching skills on display—he called them "Nebuchadnezzar sermons; is this not Babylon the great, that I have built myself, by the might of my power and for the glory of my majesty?" Beecher went on to say, "Would to God that these preachers would go, like Nebuchadnezzar, to grass for a time. If like him, they would return sane and humble."[13]

While it's true that careful exegesis and diligent sermon preparation are essential, still, if our confidence for persuading people is in anything but the power of the Spirit, we will never know His power in our preaching, for He will not share His glory with us.

## Preaching in the Spirit's Power—Proclaiming God's Word

What exactly is preaching in the demonstration of the Spirit and of power? Some respected men in the history of the church have thought of preaching in the Spirit's power as some kind of a special experience—they speak of a special anointing to preach. It's true that the New Testament uses two different Greek word groups to speak of two kinds of Spirit-filling. One of them speaks of a condition of the soul. According to Ephesians 5:18, we are to allow the Spirit to fill us with the Word of God (cf. Colossians 3:16). The other describes a filling with the Spirit that is a special empowering, a

divine enablement to fulfill a specific task at a designated time. And some ministers interpret 1 Corinthians 2:4 as saying, "I ought to seek a special empowerment to preach."

However, the context of 1 Corinthians 2:4 makes it clear that's not what Paul had in mind. Here Paul directly linked preaching in the demonstration of the Spirit's power to the Word of God. In the rest of 1 Corinthians 2, he emphasizes that the Spirit revealed the Word of God, inspired the Word of God, and illumines our understanding of the Word of God. Paul's point was that the Spirit's power is demonstrated *through* the Word. He said this to the church in Thessalonica as well: "Our gospel did not come to you in word only, but also in power and in the Holy Spirit" (1 Thessalonians 1:5). In other words, the Holy Spirit was manifesting His power through the words of the gospel that Paul preached.

How can you and I preach in demonstration of the Spirit and His power? Not by seeking some mystical experience, but *by preaching the truth the Spirit inspired, and doing so in complete dependence upon Him.* As a result, the Spirit will take that Word preached and He will do what you and I could never do. He will illumine, He will give life, and He will change minds and hearts. When Paul speaks of preaching in demonstration of the Spirit and of power, he is not referring to power that resides in the preacher, a powerful experience that happens to him, or some powerful technique he employs. Rather,

Paul means the power that is in God's Word when it is accurately preached and energized by the Spirit.

In the first two chapters of 1 Corinthians, we learn that God has a great eternal plan for redeeming sinners. He decided on this plan so that no human being would be able to boast before Him. God chose a message that undermines all human wisdom. And He chose for preaching to be the method by which this message would spread—a method that cuts across human wisdom in every age. Why? So that He alone would get the glory.

When you and I change the emphasis of the message away from Christ and Him crucified or the means of delivering that message, terrible things happen. The cross of Christ is made void (1 Corinthians 1:17)—that is, we empty the message of the cross of its power. When we change the method or the message, we also rob God of His glory (1 Corinthians 1:30-31). In 1 Corinthians 2:5 Paul adds yet another terrible outcome of tampering with the message and the method. He declared that the reason he did not preach persuasive words of human wisdom was "so that your faith would not rest on the wisdom of men, but on the power of God." When we elevate ourselves rather than God's message, when we depend on our own abilities rather than God's grace, and when we trust in human methods or techniques rather than the Spirit's power, then we cause people's faith to rest on human wisdom and not God's power.

Gordon Fee, commenting on this passage, challenges us all: "Paul's point needs a fresh hearing. What he is rejecting is not preaching, not even persuasive preaching; rather, it is the real danger in all preaching, self-reliance."[14] The danger lies in forgetting that lives are changed when the gospel is proclaimed through human weakness and accompanied by the powerful work of the Spirit.

We live in a culture that is almost identical to that which existed in Corinth. We are faced with the very same dilemma that confronted Paul when he first arrived in that city. May God help us to follow the preaching philosophy of the apostle Paul, who preached in the power of the Spirit by (1) focusing on God's message and His Son instead of personal glory, (2) depending on God's grace and not our personal ability, and (3) trusting in the Spirit's power and not any human method or technique. When we approach preaching with these commitments, then it will be in demonstration of the Spirit and of power.

# PRAYER

Father, forgive us for the times when we handle Your Word with a sense of self-confidence and we trust in something other than Your Word and Your Spirit. We repent and we ask that You would give us, through this passage, a fresh reminder of how we are to approach the task of preaching.

Lord, none of us are comparable to the apostle Paul, and yet he realized the inadequacies in his own life. May we embrace our weaknesses and frailty, and may we realize that when we acknowledge our insufficiency we are opening ourselves for the work of the Spirit. Father, use us to build Your church—to see people come to faith in Christ and see believers grow and be edified. We pray that You would do this in demonstration of the Spirit and His power. Amen.

# THE ART OF CRAFTING A LIFE-CHANGING SERMON

*Rick Holland*

*Shepherds' Conference 2010*

*Selected Scriptures*

In order to refine my preaching, I've tried to place myself into situations where I'm stretched as a preacher. For example, earlier in my ministry, I served in a couple of youth pastoral positions that allowed me the opportunity to preach on a weekly basis to students. This experience was invaluable—if you really want to learn how to preach, then you should preach to junior high, high school, and college students. They don't have the courtesy to pretend that you're interesting when you're not. Likewise, preaching to young people helped me to figure out the dynamic of bringing the exegetical and delivery aspects of a sermon together in an environment where gaining people's interest is very difficult and clarity demands simplicity.

I've also had the privilege of studying at The Master's Seminary and Southern Baptist Theological Seminary. At both schools, I learned under the example of excellent preachers who have served as role models for my own pulpit practices.

Even with these helpful experiences, I still find myself learning how to preach more effectively. There's always room for us as preachers to develop better outlines, propositions, introductions, transitions, illustrations, applications, implications, and conclusions. There is no end to the work of mastering the art of delivering a good sermon.

There are some Sundays when, after giving a sermon, I feel like writing a letter of resignation. If you haven't felt that level of discouragement before, then you haven't preached long enough. I can usually tell how I did on a Sunday based on how my wife reacts during the drive home. If she says something to me about the sermon in the parking lot, I did okay. If we pass a certain landmark before she says anything, then it was "iffy." If we get to the highway before she speaks, there were problems in the sermon that she wants to talk about. And if we make it all the way home without her saying anything, then that usually indicates something bad.

Yet I still come back to the pulpit week in and week out because there's nothing else I would rather do than preach the Word of God. I aspire to excel still more in preaching, and my goal is to help you do the same.

## Preaching and the Current Culture

As if our own idiosyncrasies weren't enough of a barrier to preaching well, we also live in a culture that does not hold expository preaching in high regard. This is nothing new. For example, in 1928, Harry Emerson Fosdick published an essay in *Harper's Magazine* that was entitled, "What's Wrong with Preaching?" He was one of the most prominent liberal ministers of his day, and he called for a type of preaching that was more relevant and involved more congregational experiences. Here's what he wrote:

Many preachers indulge habitually in what they call expository sermons. They take a passage from the Scripture, and proceeding on the assumption that the people attending church that morning are deeply concerned about what the passage means, they spend their half hour or more on historical exposition of the verse or chapter, ending with some upended practical application to the auditors. Could any procedure be more surely predestined to dullness and futility? Who seriously supposes that, as a matter of fact, one in a hundred of the congregation cares to start with about what Moses, Isaiah, Paul, or John meant in those special verses, or came to church deeply concerned about it. Nobody else who talks to the public so assumes that the vital interests of the people are located in the meaning of words spoken 2,000 years ago.[1]

Almost a century later, this sentiment is still prevalent in many churches today. There are pastors who, like Fosdick, disdain expository preaching. At the same time, Fosdick gives voice to what many people today are asking: "How is it that the things that happened in the Bible have any relevance, bearing, or meaning to my life today?"

This surfaces a divide that exists between the scholar and the listener. Scholars are mostly concerned with what the text of Scripture meant. They focus on what happened back in Corinth, in

Rome, or in Hosea's time. Those who sit in the congregation, on the other hand, are mainly interested in what the text means to them in their own world. Broadly, scholars care about what the text *meant*; those who listen in the pew care about what it *means*. And it's the pastor who stands in between those two worlds and brings them together in a sermon. He does so by explaining what the text meant and showing its relevance for today. And he should be controlled by this mammoth principle—the text can never *mean* something today that it did not *meant* originally.

The preacher's job is to move from the past to the present, from the historical to the contemporary, from the particular to the universal. He has the difficult task of moving from the specifics in the Word to the principles that can be preached. Our homiletics must come from our hermeneutics. In fact, preaching is public hermeneutics. Every time a preacher opens the Bible and tells his people what it says and means, he is teaching them, by example, how they are to approach Scripture in their devotional time and personal Bible study. He is providing a pattern for how people are to understand and apply God's Word.

---

**When you preach, your people...need to understand the original context of the text before they can apply what it means for them today.**

---

If I have one criticism of preaching today, it is that it starts with the contemporary and tries to go backward, instead of beginning with the past and moving forward. Historian George Marsden wrote this about the critics of the Great Awakening, who did not see the value in preaching the historical context of a biblical passage:

> In the midst of the Great Awakening, Edwards made a revealing comment about the effects of preaching. During intense periods of awakenings, evangelists often preach to the same audience daily or even more frequently, multiple times a day. Opponents of the awakening argued that people could not possibly remember what they heard in all these sermons. [2]

Jonathan Edwards responded to these critics with the statement: "The main benefit that is obtained by preaching is by the impression made upon the mind in the time of it, and not by the effect that arises afterwards by a remembrance of what was delivered." [3] Edwards was right—preaching is designed to shock people with the living reality of God, and to take them from their contemporary world back into the Bible. When you preach, your people need to go back, put on sandals, and "experience the humidity" of that day. They need to understand the original context of the text before they can apply what it means for them today.

As preachers, it's so easy for us to come to a text, find a little lesson, get up, talk about it, illustrate it, apply it, cry, laugh, tell a joke, leave, get a pat on the back, and think we've done a great job. In contrast, I want to talk about life-changing preaching that builds a bridge from exegesis to an artfully crafted sermon that truly affects people. We're going to look at ten principles of life-changing preaching, each beginning with the letter *I*.

## Principles of Life-Changing Preaching

### Indisputable Preaching

*Preaching God's Word God's Way, for God's People*

The first *I* of life-changing preaching is *indisputable preaching*. Indisputability comes from preaching God's Word, God's way, to God's people, for God's glory. It's being accurate, clear, and making sure to present the meaning of the biblical text rather than human opinions. Indisputable preaching can only come from discerning and explaining the authorial intent of the biblical author. The crown jewel of all exposition—the result of all exegesis—is being able to answer the question, "What did this text originally mean to those to whom it was originally written?"

The only way our preaching will be indisputable is if we get to this crown jewel. If our content is what the Bible says, all

that the Bible says, and no more than what the Bible says, we are speaking an audible articulation of God's voice. As preachers, our mandate is to preach the truth—the Word. Therefore, if someone has an argument with what we say, it ought to be an argument with what the Book says.

I've had firsthand experience with an extremely conservative church that lacked indisputability. As a recently converted high school student, I was excited about the Lord and had an older man disciple me. One day when he took me out to lunch he reprimanded me for about an hour because some of my hair was touching the top of my ear. The conversation grieved my conscience and I was so overwhelmed that I got a haircut the next day. As I continued attending the church, I was given plenty of other "corrections" that had no umbilical cord attached the Bible. I could dispute much of what was said because the church attempted to say more than what the text said.

Our job as pastors is to rely only on the text that's in front of us and mine the original meaning from it. We must understand what Moses meant, what Haggai meant, and what Paul meant in the original context to the original readers. By contrast, there are some who say, "Well, you can't possibly know that; the Bible is so old." This attitude leads to a reader-response methodology in which the meaning of a passage is ultimately based on what the reader wants it to mean. The objective truth then becomes completely subjective. Sadly, that kind of thinking has made its way into the pulpit, where many pastors are now attempting to create an experience that lets people interpret God's Word any way they want to. These preachers say the Bible is all about "what it means to you."

But that wasn't God's intention when He wrote the Bible. He wants the reader to understand the authorial intent. There's a test I apply to myself whenever I prepare a sermon. For example, while I was preaching through Proverbs, whenever I made my final pass through my notes I asked the question, "What would Solomon say if he heard this sermon? Would he agree with me, or would he stand up and say, 'I'm sorry, but that's not what I meant when I said that.'"

When you preach, do you explain to your people what the author meant? If your response is that there's no way you can possibly know that, then you have just said the Bible has no authority.

God was very clear when He wrote His Book. It's not that difficult to understand it. Even though it's good for a pastor to have a mastery of Hebrew, Greek, and all the exegetical nuances, we have to acknowledge that someone with a basic secondary school education can comprehend the English Bible pretty well. Now, don't mistake this to mean you can neglect your study of Greek and Hebrew, because part of understanding the original meaning of a text has to do with knowing how to correctly interpret the original languages.

So use your Greek and Hebrew

knowledge to show the authorial intent and the meaning of a passage, but don't use it so much that the sermon becomes a mere academic exercise. Instead, teach your people how to get the authorial intent so they can benefit as fully as possible from their reading of the Bible.

Here's an illustration you might find helpful: Let's say I call a florist and order a dozen roses to be delivered to my wife as a symbol of her meaning the world to me. The deliveryman then takes those roses, shows up at my house, and knocks on the door. When my wife opens the door, the deliveryman says, "Hello, these roses are from Rick." Imagine she replies, "Oh, thank you, but what do they mean?" The man then says, "The message he's trying to send is that you're a thorny pain, you fade in the midday sun, and you smell good in the morning, but you give off a stench at night."

Who is it that determines what the roses mean—the giver, or the deliveryman? The giver, of course. Likewise, your job as a preacher is not to provide your listeners with a "What does this mean to me?" interpretation of God's Word. Rather, you are to communicate the authorial intent. And when you do, then your preaching will be indisputable.

### Informational Preaching
*Data Necessary for Understanding*

The second *I* of life-changing preaching is *informational preaching*. This is the teaching part of the pastor's role, and by this I mean information is the salient data necessary to understand the ancient text in a contemporary context. If you look at the words used in the New Testament to speak of preaching, you'll learn that these terms are predominantly used of evangelism.

When you read through the book of Acts, you see that preaching is a proclamation that leads to a presentation of the gospel. The apostle Paul said, "Woe is me if I do not preach the gospel" (1 Corinthians 9:16). We should always include the gospel in our preaching. I understand that the gospel is not in every text, but the gospel should be in every sermon. Don't shoehorn the gospel in places that it's not, but strive to teach in a manner that eventually leads to an opportunity to present the gospel.

We should give our people information that reveals the beauty of the good news, and this informational preaching can only come from being well-studied. Most of what we do as expositors is akin to what the New Testament calls "teaching." It is the provision of information that comes from Scripture. It informs, instructs, enlightens. Life-changing preaching includes teaching the listener something unknown before. Or, something unclear that becomes lucid.

### Important Preaching

#### Application and Implications

The third *I* of life-changing preaching is *important preaching*. If you want to deliver a life-changing sermon, then it

needs to be an important sermon. Importance is conveyed when the sermon is relevant, and relevance is achieved when application and implication are made.

At this point you may be asking, "What is the difference between application and implication?"

Let me explain the distinction through an example. I was over at a friend's house when an incident occurred at the dinner table and my friend had to deal with his kids. I respected this man and wanted to learn from how he handled his children. When I walked away from that encounter, I found myself applying certain implications. I wasn't going to do exactly what he did, because my family context varied from his. But seeing how he applied certain biblical principles to his children helped me to discover implications that were different yet based on the same principles.

If you're too specific in your sermon application, then you will rob your people of the opportunity to be convicted by the Holy Spirit's implications. For example, if you're preaching on self-control and you say, "Hey, do you love cinnamon rolls? The next time you have one, I want you to get all the way down to the last bite and then don't eat it—just stare at it." People might respond, "I get it—I can develop better self-control by not eating everything I want to eat." But if your listener is lactose intolerant, he'll say, "Cinnamon rolls have dairy product in them, so I guess the message doesn't quite apply to me." You see, application is a great tool for the preacher, but it needs to be used sparingly and wisely.

If you explain with clarity the original contextual meaning of a biblical text, it will implicate your people in such a way that they say, "I see where the Lord would have me apply that principle." As a result, they're not stuck with the specific applications you gave at the end of the sermon, but there is freedom for the Holy Spirit to work in their hearts however He wishes.

Does this mean you should never provide applications? Absolutely not. However, you are on safer and more helpful ground when you explain the text in such a manner that your hearers are implicated by what it says, for the Holy Spirit who wrote the Scriptures works in the lives and the hearts of those who are hearing it. If you properly preach the text, your people will learn how to figure out the authorial intent and the implications for their own lives. Therefore, you want to apply sparingly yet implicate constantly.

## Insightful Preaching

### Explanation that Generates Clarity

The fourth *I* of life-changing preaching is *insightful preaching*. Insight is achieved by an explanation that increases understanding and generates clarity. It produces an "aha moment" in which listeners say, "I've read that before, but I've never seen that." However, you don't want to read too much into a passage and have people say, "I've read that before and

I see what you're saying, but I don't think I'll ever see that again." Give insight, but don't resort to overstating the obvious and employing the preaching technique, "Weak point, yell here!"

An example of insightful preaching is taking a phrase like "As Jesus was about to go up to Jerusalem…" (Matthew 20:17) and instead of stating the obvious that can be gleaned from a first reading of the text, you provide a noteworthy detail. You say, "Jericho is so many feet below Jerusalem. It's a fourteen-mile climb from Jericho to Jerusalem, and that's what is meant when the text says Jesus was about to 'go up.'" It's information like this that enhances your listeners' understanding of what's happening.

## Interesting Preaching

### Arouses Curiosity, Gets Attention, and Provokes Thought

The fifth *I* of life-changing preaching is *interesting preaching*. All preachers can be self-indicted on this point, but for sermons to have impact, they have to be riveting. And interest is created and maintained by preaching that arouses curiosity, gets attention, and provokes thought. If you're going to be boring, pursue another calling, because preaching should never be boring.

When I was 18, I drove from Tennessee to California with a friend. During our cross-country trip we stopped at the Grand Canyon. It was my first visit, and I was completely overwhelmed by what I saw. I wanted to get the full experience of this majestic wonder, so I boarded a tour-guided tram. The guide, in a detached, monotone voice, said, "There's the rock that looks like an alligator. We call that formation 'The Alligator.' The canyon is three thousand feet deep here, and at the bottom you'll see the Colorado River, which is carrying silt." The entire time he was talking I was thinking, *Why does he sound so bored? Everything we're looking at is so remarkable!* Evidently the guide was so used to the beauty that it no longer amazed him. And that affected his presentation. John Piper, in his book *The Supremacy of God in Preaching*, made this observation: "A bored and unenthusiastic tour guide in the Alps contradicts and dishonors the majesty of the mountains."[4]

As preachers we must heed that critique. We need to be interesting, and our listeners will find us more fascinating when we are personally captivated by the text. One of the practical ways to keep your audience's interest is by not using canned illustrations. When you start giving an illustration, you don't want the people in your church to think, *Yeah, I've heard that one before.* Instead, put some thought into your preparation and come up with original illustrations. The best ways to find quality sermon illustrations is by doing a lot of reading and being observant of the world around you. Be enamored with your text and be creative with your illustrations, and you will retain your people's attention.

## Intense Preaching

### Creating Urgency by Preaching with Passion

The sixth *I* of life-changing preaching is *intense preaching*. Intensity is creating urgency by preaching with passion. I love how Alex Montoya explains this: "I am passionate because God's Word makes me so, because man's condition demands it, and ultimately because the nature of preaching deserves it."[5]

Now, when it comes to passion, I'm not talking about turning up the volume, because if everything is emphasized, then nothing is emphasized. Consider the range of passion that you show in your own personal communication. Your son scores his first basket, and you yell at the top of your lungs. But there's also the whisper on your wedding anniversary, when you're holding your wife's hand during a candlelit dinner and you say, "Sweetheart, I love you."

---

**Don't resort to an artificial passion. The passion will come when you are excited about the text and you genuinely care about your listeners.**

---

In both situations, you express passion. And if you faithfully follow the nuances of the biblical text, it will demand both the emphatic and quieter expressions of passion. If you find yourself inclined to be too vocal, learn to develop a subtle demonstration of passion. And if you tend to be too calm and reserved, then work on ramping up your energy levels.

Whatever you do, don't resort to an artificial passion. The passion will come when you are excited about the text and you genuinely care about your listeners. And in the midst of all this, you must be natural and let whatever personality God has given you be manifest in your preaching.

### Imperatival Preaching

#### Commands and Responses

The seventh *I* of life-changing preaching is *imperatival preaching*. Your preaching must find the imperative voice that demands a response. Paul told Timothy, "Prescribe and teach these things" (1 Timothy 4:11). Preachers are not to suggest or instruct on their own initiative. Rather, they are to declare what the Lord has commanded. For you to be faithful to the apostolic mandate, your sermon must find its way to the imperative voice.

Sadly, some preachers read, "Thou shall not commit adultery," and then say, "Yeah, it's probably a good idea for you not to commit adultery. You will end up hurting your spouse. I hope you don't do it." But that's not what God meant when He said, "Thou shall not commit adultery." God was not offering a suggestion. He was prescribing a command, and as His ambassadors we are to do the same.

Yet we must also preach imperatively with kindness and grace. "The Lord's bond-servant must not be quarrelsome, but be kind to all, able to teach, patient when wronged, with gentleness correcting those who are in opposition" (2 Timothy 2:24-25). Sometimes we can become mean, old, angry preachers who just bark out commands instead of being shepherds who lead our sheep to fairer lands of obedience. Remember that the shepherd's crook has two functions— the curved hook at one end that helps to coddle the sheep back into the fold, and the rod portion that helps to discipline those who go astray.

### Impossible Preaching

#### Communicates the Need of God's Sanctifying Work

The eighth *I* of life-changing preaching is *impossible preaching*. This kind of preaching communicates a righteousness that is not attainable without the regenerating and sanctifying work of God. If people can do what we say by their own efforts, we have not preached faithfully because obedience, justification, and sanctification are impossible without the enabling power of the Spirit of God. There is a drastic difference between genuine heart change and behavior modification.

To illustrate, there are religions that do nothing more than shape a person's external behaviors with no change taking place in the heart. The same is true of psychology—it teaches how to condition people to act in specific ways without bringing about true, internal transformation. Only a magnificent vision of a glorified God who sent His Son to die for wretched sinners can change a heart of stone into a heart of flesh. Impossible preaching challenges the audience to be and to do what they are not and cannot be. It casts a vision, gives hope, and connects to the divine by saying, "Your hope is only in Christ. Now turn to Him, trust Him, and obey Him."

This change, biblically speaking, involves both God's sovereign intervention and man's responsibility. In Philippians 2:12, Paul wrote, "Work out your salvation with fear and trembling." That is a command that calls for effort on the part of the Christian. Then Paul mentions God's part: "For it is God who is at work in you, both to will and to work for His good pleasure" (verse 13).

Paul states the same principle in Colossians 1:29: "For this purpose also I labor." If the verse ended there, I'd be very discouraged because I know I'm not capable of good. But thankfully, the verse doesn't end there: "For this purpose also I labor, striving according to His power, which mightily works within me." In your preaching, you call people to labor and trust that God will work mightily within them. We don't know exactly how this works out, but we are to call people to depend on, pray to, and lean on the Holy Spirit, who causes them to change, causes them to have different affections, causes them to have different motivations, and causes them to take different

actions. If you want your preaching to be life-changing, it needs to be impossible preaching.

### Invitational Preaching

#### Inviting Listeners to Make a Decision

The ninth *I* of life-changing preaching is *invitational preaching*. This entails provoking people to make a decision about their justification or sanctification in Christ. The apostle Paul reinforces this in 1 Corinthians 9:16: "Woe is me if I do not preach the gospel." Do you know what Paul was saying? By using the word "woe," he meant, "Let me be cursed and damned if I don't preach and proclaim the gospel."

When you preach, you must always assume there are unbelievers in your audience. If there aren't, then the believers in your congregation will be edified by hearing the gospel again. On a personal note, I challenge you to examine yourself against the teaching of Matthew 7:13-29. This passage reveals there will be people who make it all the way to the judgment seat of Christ thinking they're right with God. They will exclaim, "Lord, didn't we do all these things in Your name?" The Lord will say in return, "I never knew you; depart from Me" (verse 23).

Are you too proud to beg for people to come to Christ?

That leads me to bring up a point about giving invitations after a service. When I first came to Grace Community Church, I was encouraged to hear how Pastor MacArthur concluded a service.

He tells everyone in the congregation, "The prayer room is up front to my right. If you want to talk to someone about a relationship with Christ, we have men and women who are waiting for you." Now, I admit that the first few times I heard that, I thought, *No one's going to get saved that way. What are you thinking? Do you know how much God needs your help to get them into the prayer room?*

But that's carnal thinking—God doesn't need our help. We are to invite people with truth that affects the emotions, not emotional appeals through which we hope to give them the truth. Be cautious about how you handle your public invitations, yet be sure that your preaching is invitational.

### Integral Preaching
*Avoiding Hypocrisy and Inaccuracy*

The tenth and final *I* of life-changing preaching is *integral preaching*. The message must be integrated into the messenger's life, and he ought to be a model of what he's proclaiming. The preacher must experience the conviction of working through a text all week, having it pierce his heart, and getting up Sunday morning thinking, *I am undone. I'm going to tell people to be what I'm not.* If your message isn't affecting you, then you have reason to be concerned. Our sermons must change us because preaching without integrity makes us hypocrites; and the two greatest threats to effective preaching are hypocrisy and inaccuracy. Have integrity and be faithful not only

in how you preach a text, but in how you apply that text to your own life.

### An Example of Inaccuracy

Now that we've looked at the ten *I*'s of life-changing preaching, I want to reinforce once again the importance of finding the authorial intent in a text. Let me put it this way: Suppose you're teaching through the Gospel of Matthew. You preach your way through the genealogy, the Christmas story, and the ministry of John the Baptist. Then you get to Matthew chapter 4, which recounts Jesus' temptation, and you preach a series on how to fight temptation. And you're delighted because the congregation is responding positively.

However, the problem is that Matthew didn't write chapter 4 with the intent that it serve as a guide to fighting temptation. As he was writing, he didn't think, *Since I've provided three chapters of Messianic Christology, I need to add a practical chapter on how to conquer sin.* The authorial intent of Matthew 4 is to fortify the truth that Jesus is the Savior who was tempted in every way like us and yet did not sin.

The application and implication of the wilderness temptations are, "Hallelujah, what a Savior," not a behavior modification plan. Does that mean that you can't include some applications for enduring in the midst of temptation? No, you can preach that because we are called to imitate Christ. However, that's a collateral subordinate application. If you want to preach in a way that is faithful to the Word and changes lives, you must preach the intent of the text and provide an opportunity for your people to be implicated by it.

**A Final Impression**

Earlier, I quoted this statement about preaching that came from Jonathan Edwards: "The main benefit that is obtained by preaching is by impression made upon the mind in the time of it, and not by the effect that arises afterwards by a remembrance of what was delivered."[6] Is Edwards saying that a sermon should never be remembered? Of course that's not his intention, for he printed his sermons for people to have, to read, and to remember. What he's saying is that something unique occurs when the people of God come under the preacher's leadership, passion, personality, giftedness, study, exegesis, and experience in order to hear the message that God has perfectly ordained for that moment. Those who hear biblical preaching will walk away saying, "What a God and what a gospel."

Your people must see you as a man of the Book, a man who loves the Scriptures and is dedicated to communicating the authorial intent of the text every single week. Their impression must be that you believe that the Bible is the absolute source of authority and your mission is to explain it faithfully. With that in mind, commit yourself to doing what it takes to preach well-crafted sermons that will change people's lives.

# PRAYER

Father, give us grace to study and to proclaim Your Word in a way that's accurate and that portrays Your intention. We ask for grace to experience the preaching moment that Edwards wrote of, where for that allotted time, people sit suspended between heaven and earth with a gaze toward You, the living Savior. Encourage us through our interaction with Your truth and implicate us for our own application. In Jesus' name, Amen.

# 10

# Preaching as a Dying Man to Dying Men[1]

*Alex Montoya*
*Shepherds' Conference 2012*

*Selected Scriptures*

In 2 Timothy 4:1-4, Paul exhorted Timothy,

I solemnly charge you in the presence of God and of Christ Jesus, who is to judge the living and the dead, and by His appearing and His kingdom: preach the word; be ready in season and out of season; reprove, rebuke, exhort, with great patience and instruction. For the time will come when they will not endure sound doctrine; but wanting to have their ears tickled, they will accumulate for themselves teachers in accordance to their own desires, and will turn away their ears from the truth and will turn aside to myths.

These are solemn words that impress upon preachers and teachers the urgency of declaring God's Word. As preachers, it must be our ambition to take God's Word and proclaim it verse by verse and chapter by chapter. Yet we may erroneously think of exposition as an end in itself, but preaching is really a means to an end. The purpose of proclaiming the Bible is so that individuals might repent of their sins, come to saving faith, and be transformed into the image of Christ. Paul taught this truth in Colossians 1:28: "We proclaim Him, admonishing every man and teaching every man with all wisdom, so that we may present every man complete in Christ." The purpose of ministry, then, is creating disciples of Christ, and preaching is a means to that end. How do we preach with this vision in mind? How do we preach, as Richard Baxter said, "as a dying man to dying men"?[2] In this chapter we will examine certain features that must characterize our preaching so that it may achieve this purpose.

## Errors to Avoid

Before we look at these features, we must first recognize the types of major errors that can arise in our preaching. There are six I would like to highlight.

### The Long Sermon

The first error we need to avoid is the long sermon. Some preachers have the notion that longer is better—that somehow the length of the sermon also determines its quality. I was having dinner a few years ago with a pastor and his wife, and I asked him, "What are you preaching on tomorrow?" He responded, "I'm preaching on John chapter six." I said, "Oh, what portion of the chapter are you preaching?" He said, "I'm preaching the whole chapter," and his wife exclaimed, "Oh no!" Your people may be saying the same thing if you're preaching long sermons. Longer is not necessarily better because you need to be an awfully great communicator to hold the attention of your listeners for an extended period of time.

### The Dump Truck Sermon

A second error we must steer clear of is the dump truck sermon. This is when the preacher spends 20 to 30 hours a week in exegetical studies, and then backs up the truck on Sunday morning and dumps large quantities of data onto the people of God. More is not always better. An example of this is eating a steak dinner. An eight-ounce fillet mignon is a great piece of meat. Maybe if you're a little bit of a glutton, you enjoy a twelve-ounce slab. However, a fourteen-pound fillet mignon is just too much. Similarly, we don't want to overload our people and assume they can handle large quantities of information.

### The Sausage Sermon

Third, we should not preach sausage sermons. These are sermons in which you just continue the exposition from the exact point where you left off the previous week. You'll go for 40, 50, or 60 minutes and when your time is up, you cut it off just like you cut sausage. You never introduce or conclude; you just continue on. This approach doesn't usually go as well as one would like it to go.

### The Deep Sermon

The fourth error to avoid is the deep sermon, and by this I mean too complex. Some preachers spend large quantities of their teaching time discussing the original Hebrew and Greek texts and other academic details.

I once had a discussion with a pastor who received a poem from one of his church members. The two-page poem was beautifully written and criticized the pastor's preaching. The man was livid and upset. I read through the poem and said, "This person is doing you a favor. Normally when folks don't like your preaching they don't write you a poem. But this individual is letting you know that you're going so deep in your preaching that she can't make heads or tails out of it."

Sometimes we're so deep that no one knows what we're talking about. We've forgotten that clarity is important when we preach.

### The Nowhere Sermon

A fifth error to avoid is the nowhere sermon. In the San Gabriel Mountains near Los Angeles there is a bridge called the Bridge to Nowhere. It spans more than 100 feet above a large crevice and goes absolutely nowhere; ironically, it was built to go nowhere. Sometimes our sermons are like that bridge—they go nowhere. The preacher ends up just occupying a space of time because there's no real purpose in the sermon. Some may attempt to defend themselves by saying, "I don't need a purpose because I'm just going through a book of the Bible." But the reality is that each book has a purpose, and so must your sermons.

---

The Bible is the most exciting book that has ever and will ever exist, and you are to preach it effectively and passionately.

---

### The Boring Sermon

The sixth and ultimate error made in preaching is the boring sermon. Some men are under the impression that boring somehow equates to holiness. The more boring a sermon is in its delivery, the more holy it is. On the contrary, as a preacher, for you to preach a boring sermon is a great sin. Preachers are entrusted with the oracles of God. The Bible is the most exciting book that has ever and will ever exist, and you are to preach it effectively and passionately. You must preach with great fire and energy.

That leads us to the first characteristic that must mark our preaching if we wish to preach as a dying man to dying men.

### What It Takes to Preach with Passion

Jerry Vines describes passion in preaching in this way: "We need a return to heart preaching. Perhaps some would use other terminology. Perhaps you would prefer the term 'sincere.' Or maybe you like the word 'earnest.' Whatever you choose to call it, we desperately need it."[3] Martyn Lloyd-Jones, in his wonderful book *Preaching & Preachers*, stressed passion in this way:

> This element of pathos and of emotion is, to me, a very vital one. It has been so seriously lacking in the present century, and perhaps especially among Reformed people. We tend to lose our balance and to become over-intellectual, indeed almost to despise the element

of feeling and emotion. We are such learned men, we have such a great grasp of the truth, that we tend to despise feeling. The common herd, we feel, are emotional and sentimental, but they have no understanding![4]

Passion in preaching is the power, the drive, the energy, and the life in the delivery of the sermon. Without passion the sermon becomes just a lecture, an address, a moral speech; and God is not calling us to that. God calls us to preach fervent sermons that declare the unsearchable riches of Christ.

John Broadus, an earnest proponent of expository preaching, wrote, "The chief requisite to an energetic style is an energetic nature. There must be vigorous thinking, earnest if not passionate feeling, and the determined purpose to accomplish some object, or the man's style will have no true, exalted energy."[5] Charles Spurgeon illustrated passion in preaching in *Lectures to My Students* in this way: "We must regard the people as the wood and the sacrifice, well wetted a second and a third time by the care of the week, upon which, like the prophet, we must pray down the fire from heaven. A dull minister creates a dull audience."[6]

Lloyd-Jones reinforced this idea when he said,

I would say that a "dull preacher" is a contradiction in terms; if he is dull he is not a preacher. He may stand in a pulpit and talk, but he is certainly not a preacher. With the grand theme and message of the Bible dullness is impossible. This is the most interesting, the most thrilling, the most absorbing subject in the universe; and the idea that this can be presented in a dull manner makes me seriously doubt whether the men who are guilty of this dullness have ever really understood the doctrine they claim to believe, and which they advocate. We often betray ourselves by our manner.[7]

Finally, W.A. Criswell, the great Baptist pastor and preacher, said the following about passion in preaching:

You cannot read the New Testament without sensing that the preachers were electrified by the power of the gospel and swept off their feet by the wonder of the great revelation which had been committed to their trust. There is something wrong if a man charged with the greatest news in the world can be listless and frigid and dull. Who is going to believe that the glad tidings brought by the preacher means literally more than anything else on earth if they are presented with no verve or fire or attack, or if the man himself is apathetic, uninspired, afflicted with spiritual coma in unsaying by his attitude what he says in words. [8]

These remarks are convicting because we can be dull and boring in the pulpit. God is calling us to preach with great passion and great energy. Now sometimes people who hear me teach on passion in preaching respond by saying, "Montoya, you're Hispanic. You're just passionate by nature. I, however, am not like that."

But passion is not a matter of ethnicity! I want to encourage you today to go through a metamorphosis. I'm not talking about going through a ritual or some mystical act, but simply committing yourself to developing an energetic nature. As a teacher and preacher of God's Word you must learn to develop passion in your heart, your soul, and your life.

With that in mind, I'd like to identify five ways you can bring more passion into your preaching.

### Preach with Spiritual Power

The first way to preach with passion is to preach with spiritual power. The English word *enthusiastic* comes from a combination of two Greek words that mean "to be in God" or "God to be in you." To be enthusiastic means to be filled with all that God is. For us to preach with great passion we must be dependent on spiritual power. We must be energized and empowered by God Himself so that the message we preach is coming from Him.

This cannot be artificially produced—it has to be something that becomes part of our nature. To learn to preach with spiritual power, we need to develop contrition of the soul and be men who are deeply underneath the shadow and view of God. We must know that we're simply sinners saved by grace. The great Reformer Martin Luther prayed, "O Lord God, dear Father in heaven, I am indeed unworthy of the office and ministry in which I am to make Thy glory and to nurture and to serve this congregation."[9]

Are you overwhelmed with the weight of the calling that God has entrusted to you? Whether it is 5 teenagers or 500 members you meet with on Sunday morning, they're both a gift, and you ought to be overwhelmed by the fact that you are able to stand before them and preach God's Word.

*Clean vessels for master's use.* Moreover, if we are to preach with spiritual power, we must approach God as clean preachers. How often have we attempted to continue serving in ministry with sins that have not been confessed, sins that have not been taken care of? We should understand that there can be no fire, no passion, no divine energy if we are before God with unclean hands and an impure heart. You may not be the most learned preacher or the most gilded vessel in the cupboard. In fact, you may be a cracked vase. But above all, you must be a clean vase. Bring to God a clean vessel, and He will honor your resolve. I would encourage you to determine to never go into the pulpit with unclean hands and an impure heart. Take time to confess sins to ensure that you're always a sincere preacher in the pulpit.

*Maintain a deep communion with God.* As you examine your dependence on God, remember that preaching with spiritual power comes from deep communion with God. You must spend time in His Word. The Puritan minister Richard Baxter said, "Content not yourselves with being in a state of grace, but be also careful that your graces are kept in vigorous and lively exercise, and that you preach to yourselves the sermons which you study, before you preach them to others."[10] Heed that counsel and let your sermons work in your own heart first before they are delivered to others.

Robert M'Cheyne wrote, "In great measure, according to the purity and perfections of the instruments, will be the success. It is not great talent which God blesses so much as great likeness to Jesus. A holy minister is an awesome weapon in the hand of God."[11] As you know, there are too many examples in the media of ministers who have fallen and disqualified themselves. Resolve today that you will stand and preach as a holy vessel of God.

*Learn to worship.* Another aspect of generating preaching that is spiritually powerful is learning to worship. The worship services at your church should be designed to not only benefit your

people, but also to feed and encourage you. Don't ever think that the sermon is the only important portion of your worship service, because it's not. Every part of the service is significant.

I've attended churches where the preacher thinks that everything before the sermon is preliminary—the opening prayer, the hymns, the special number, and the taking of the offering are all just fillers. That is an erroneous mind-set, for when there's an anthem sung to God, it is worship of God. Therefore, worship God along with your people. When an individual sings before the congregation, it is not simply to buy time for the preacher to get ready. Rather, the intent is to bring glory to God. Let the songs that are sung, the words that are said, and the prayers that are prayed feed your soul so when you get up to preach it's from a soul that has been nourished.

*Feed yourself.* On a similar note, it is not enough to study in preparation of your preaching; you must also study to feed yourself. Some pastors make the mistake of reading their Bibles only for sermon preparation. But it's important for you to read the Word simply for your own benefit so that out of the fullness of the soul there will be an abundance of power to preach.

*Remember your calling and commission.* A final element of preaching with spiritual power is knowing that you've been called and commissioned by God. This awareness must cause you to rely on

God completely and marvel in the wonderful task that He has set before you. I constantly thank the Lord for calling me into ministry. I can't think of anything else that I would rather do. The explanation behind such commitment is the knowledge that God has mandated me to preach. Therefore, I can't resign, I can't retire, and I can't change my calling until the Commander-in-Chief gives me orders to do so.

Ministry is not a profession. It is a call given by God. Be one who preaches with passion by learning to preach with spiritual power.

### Preach with Conviction

The second way to preach with passion is to preach with conviction. Men hold opinions, but convictions hold the man. Convictions are spiritual instincts that drive you to action regardless of the circumstances. You can't preach with great passion unless you develop deep convictions.

*Trust the Word of God.* The Book that we preach from is the inspired Word of God. Thus, it is without error from cover to cover. This truth was reaffirmed in my life when I took a class in seminary called New Testament Introduction. The course was taught by a beloved professor, Dr. Robert Thomas, who had a reputation for being ruthless as an instructor. He was the sweetest little man who ever slit a throat and scuttled a ship. He was a nice professor, yet his class was extremely difficult because of the large quantities of assigned reading and memorization. In his class we learned about the liberalism that attempts to deny the authority of God's Word through critical methodology. There was so much information for us to remember that many of us came out of the class paralyzed with fear. I remember leaving that class not being able to remember many of the details, but knowing confidently one thing: that the Bible is the inherent, infallible, God-breathed Word.

Convictions fuel passion, and they are cultivated when you trust the perfect and unbreakable Word of God. Therefore, if you're going to preach with the great conviction, you need to preach what the text says. When the preacher studies the text by utilizing and applying sound exegetical tools, the result is the identification of the main point of the text. Consequently, that main point becomes the focal point of your sermon. When you go through a text and the heart of that text becomes clear, you can get excited about preaching it because you are preaching what God intended you to preach.

However, you have to be careful about letting your exegetical studies spill over into your preaching. Every now and then my wife will ask me, "What are you preaching on this Sunday?" We have a standing joke where I reply, "I'm thinking about preaching on the sixteen implications of the iota subscript."

She replies, "Wow, it's going to be deep." Unfortunately, that's the way some ministers really do preach. If you are guilty of preaching technical material that doesn't really matter in your people's lives, then how can you expect your people to get excited about what you're saying?

*Address the people's needs.* When it comes to ministering to the people in your church, God hasn't asked you to write exegetical commentaries for them. He's commanded you to preach sermons that help them understand God's Word and how it meets their needs. I understand that every word in the Bible is inspired, but I can assure you that when the believers in Rome had the opening line of Paul's letter read to them—"Paul, a bond servant of Christ Jesus called as an apostle"—they did not sit through 15 sermons expounding on the name *Paul.* The preacher must give his people content they can meditate upon and use in their lives.

*Be diligent.* If you're going to preach with great conviction, then you must be zealous in preparing for the task. Follow Paul's mandate to Timothy in 2 Timothy 2:15: "Be diligent to present yourself approved to God as a workman who does not need to be ashamed, accurately handling the word of truth." Commit yourself to understanding and rightly dividing God's truth. If you need more training, there are seminaries that can help you. Don't reject crucial preparation for ministry by circumventing the

seminaries or your personal study of God's Word, because there are no shortcuts to being a great preacher.

---

**If your sermon doesn't excite you, how is it going to excite anyone else?**

---

*Experience the text.* Finally, if you're going to preach with conviction, you need to gain an experiential understanding of the text. I try to make sure every sermon I preach keeps me awake on Saturday nights because I can hardly wait to preach it. If your sermon doesn't keep you awake at night, maybe it's not worth preaching. If it doesn't excite you, how is it going to excite anyone else?

The modern world persuades us to be apathetic, to lack convictions and standards, to be spineless preachers. But we are called to take a stand and preach with powerful conviction. When we do, we'll find ourselves preaching with great passion.

### Preach with Compassion

The third way to preach with passion is to preach with compassion. It's been said, "To love to preach is one thing. To love those to whom we preach is another."[12] Some ministers love to preach, yet they don't love the people whom they preach to. If that's the case for you, then you're not a preacher. Ministers are entrusted by God to tend and love the flock. That's why Jesus said to Peter, "Peter, tend My lambs" (John 21:15). Peter's commission was to love and care for God's people.

Love is an attitude that often takes effort to develop because some church members are difficult to love; and yet they're the ones most in need of love. I've been asked, "How do you respond to people when they tell you that you preached a great sermon?" My response is, "Did I help you?" If I've helped someone, then I've succeeded in preaching with compassion. Even with what I've written in this chapter my intent is to help you. If I can contribute to you becoming a better teacher and preacher, then I have accomplished my task. I love you and want you to succeed in your ministry.

*Preach to convert.* A big part of preaching with compassion is preaching with a heart for converting people to Christ. As you preach, always be in love with bringing lost souls to Christ. You can also preach to correct the ignorant. There are people out there who do not know up from down. It's interesting to note that the apostle Paul addressed the Galatians as "you foolish Galatians" (Galatians 3:1). The apostle corrected this church out of deep care and love for them. Still another way to show compassion is by reproving the wayward. There are some people who are going the wrong way, and you need to exhort them to turn around. I'm

reminded of the deacon who came up to the pastor, who had been preaching to reprove, and said, "Pastor, I think you're stroking the cat the wrong way." The pastor replied, "Well, turn the cat around."

*Preach to heal.* Not only are we to correct the ignorant and reprove the wayward, we are also to preach to heal the broken. While it's true that we are called to preach in a way that convicts, we must also remember that there are people who are already broken. We need to preach so that we can bring healing to the wounded.

*Preach to teach.* A compassionate preacher is one who keeps the teaching simple so people will learn. J. Vernon McGee was such a preacher. Though he is now with the Lord, his sermons are still broadcasted all around the world. McGee was known for saying, "Place the cookies on the lower shelf." We need to preach simple sermons, because clarity is the chief requisite in oratory. If people don't understand what you are saying, then you are wasting their time.

*Preach to inspire.* Another way to show compassion is by preaching to inspire the weary. Many of our people live one day at a time. They come every Sunday with one cry: "Pastor, give me hope for one more day." There's an elderly woman who comes to our church and sits in the back and sneaks in and out every Sunday. Although I do not know her well, I do know that she's very sick and I know she comes with this prayer: "Give me hope for one more week." When you preach, be aware that there are people who are knocking on the gates of heaven and they need hope for one more day.

*Preach to yourself first.* You might be asking, "How do you stir up compassion?" I don't have an easy answer for you, but here is what I recommend: First, study your own heart and preach to yourself. Every sermon I preach, I preach first to myself. I know who I am, I know what I need, and I know that I'm like the rest of humanity. You are cut from the same cloth as your congregation, so you too need to be corrected, inspired, and encouraged. So start by preaching to yourself.

*Know your congregation.* Some pastors are afraid to live among their people. They want to be as far away from their people as possible and don't want to be involved in their lives. But if we're going to preach with compassion, we need to live among our people. How can you gain compassion for the people in your church if you don't know who they are? Get out there and live among them. Interact with them, and make them yours.

How are you going to win people to the Lord or help them if you avoid them? You have to be with your people. As you live among them, you will grow in your love and compassion for them. Do not fall into the trap of thinking that you can hide from the people and still be an effective preacher, because you can't. Instead, learn to listen to their groaning and cries.

Preach with a moist eye, and keep your heart sensitive before God. Then you will learn what it means to preach with compassion.

## Preach with Authority

The fourth way to preach with passion is to preach with authority. Timothy was given the charge, "Preach the word" (2 Timothy 4:2). Likewise, God commands all preachers to faithfully preach the Word with great influence. Don't misinterpret this as permission to be an authoritarian or egocentric pulpiteer. Rather, this is a commission to come before the people of God—whether through a sermon or a simple interaction with one soul—and say to them, "Thus says the Lord." We are not called to give suggestions, opinions, or make frivolous remarks. Instead, our mandate is to speak on behalf of God.

*Believe what you preach and fulfill your commission.* From a practical standpoint, how do you come to preach with authority? First, you need to believe what you preach. The apostle Paul wrote, "We also believe, therefore we also speak" (2 Corinthians 4:13). You must follow the example of the apostle and speak what you believe. You preach with authority when you preach as one who believes.

Second, to preach with authority means you speak as an ambassador. Martyn Lloyd-Jones wrote,

The preacher should never be

apologetic, he should never give the impression that he is speaking by their leave as it were; he should not be tentatively putting forward certain suggestions and ideas. This is not to be his attitude at all. He is a man, who is there to "declare" certain things; he is a man under commission and under authority. He is an ambassador, and he should be aware of his authority. He should always know that he comes to the congregation as a sent messenger.[13]

You are a sent messenger; therefore, when you execute your ministry, you execute it as an ambassador. Many churches today are in total disarray with people who are in auto-rebellion against God, His authority, and His Word because there are preachers who have lost their valor.

As preachers, we cannot be cowards. For example, I seek out members of my congregation who haven't attended church for a lengthy period of time. I show up at their house, knock on the door, and when the door opens, I say, "Hi, I've come to see if everything is okay." Typically these visits are difficult because they involve me calling someone to repentance, but I make them because I am a commissioned ambassador of God.

Every once in a while I'll ask my secretary to set appointments with a list of people who are having difficulties. As soon as she starts calling, the responses are, "What does he want? Well, tell him I can't." But you don't stop pursuing those who have wandered because as an overseer, that is part of your job description. You are expected to shepherd the flock of God with loving authority.

Showing this kind of authority doesn't always come naturally. I found this out during the third year of my pastorate at the same church I've been serving now for 40-plus years. There was an uprising in the church because some of the leaders wanted to fire me. There were some who didn't like the idea that I wanted the people to live by God's Word. As soon as I heard about their plan, I got up in the pulpit the next Sunday morning and said, "I've heard that some of you are thinking of firing me, but I want to let you know that you're not going to do that." I continued, "I'm here for the long haul, and I'm going to bury you." Back in those days, I was in my late twenties and most of the other leaders were older, so I knew I was going to outlast them and officiate their funerals. Now if you know me and my personality, you know that is very unlike me—that kind of authority does not come naturally. However, I do what I need to do because God has called me to shepherd His flock. When I'm in the pulpit, I am no longer Alex Montoya; I am an ambassador who proclaims God's Word with authority.

As a pastor, you are to preach the

truth in such a way that people realize it must be obeyed.

*Preach as a scholar.* If you want to preach with authority, you need to preach as a scholar—as one who knows the Bible well. There is much that I don't know, but there is one thing I absolutely must know: the Bible. I don't know much about basketball, football, or baseball. I don't know anything about celebrities, and my knowledge of pop culture is limited. But ultimately, there's one area in which I need to be an expert, and that is the Scriptures.

Perhaps you know the scores of every game and the stats of every player, but you have not mastered your Bible. As a messenger of God, your time must be consumed with the Bible. When a parishioner asks you a question, you must be ready to give him chapter and verse. Do your homework, and preach with a mastery of the Bible.

*Preach as a saint.* To preach authoritatively, you should strive to preach as a saint. This simply means to practice what you preach. You can know the Bible thoroughly and you can preach it as an ambassador, but if you're a hypocrite, people will not listen to you. As a pastor, you're living in a fishbowl and everyone is watching you. Make sure you're a clean fish in a bowl with no dirt in it, for a pure life carries with it authority.

*Master the art of preaching.* If you are to preach with authority, you must speak as a skilled artist. Preaching should

be your hobby, and you should master the art of preaching. Churches are dying because preachers can't preach, and they can't preach because they don't bother to put in the effort to preach well.

It's easy for us to think we are good at preaching when the reality is that we're not. Have you read a book on preaching since you finished seminary? Do you listen to your own sermons to see whether they might be homiletically deficient? Do you ask others for advice, or work to perfect your sermons? If a musician wants to be taken seriously, he has to practice playing his instrument hours upon hours. Likewise, if you want to be taken seriously, you need to be a practiced, skilled communicator.

If people are leaving your church and going down the street to a place where heresy is taught, it could be because that preacher has mastered the art of communicating. You shouldn't fault that man; rather, he ought to fault you because you have the truth and yet you don't bother to think about how to properly deliver it. You need to keep working on your preaching ability and perfecting your skills.

When it comes to boring sermons, some pastors might use the excuse, "Well, the people in my church aren't willing to endure deep truth." Or they say, "My congregation is getting soft." But don't assume that reluctance toward deep truth is necessarily the problem. If people are zoning out or falling asleep on you, it may be because of your preaching. You've got to preach in a way that makes people want to listen. Learn to speak as a skilled communicator.

### Preach with Urgency

The fifth way to preach with passion is to preach with urgency. David Eby wrote,

> Preaching today is so often passive, apathetic, impotent, soft, spineless and lame. It lacks fervor, heat, and heart. It is passionless. Preachers must become gospel maniacs. Preachers must become captivated and re-captivated by the Lord Jesus Christ and the Gospel. No intoxication for the gospel, no mania for the good news means no fire. No fire means no power preaching.[14]

You could say that passion is a sanctified madness that is driven by a deep sense of urgency. When you preach, you need to develop a certain sense of desperation by always thinking of God's future judgment for unbelievers. Sin is an enemy of the soul and of God, and the consequence of sin is eternal torment and judgment. This should provoke you to preach with urgency. Each time you step into the pulpit, remember that people are on the verge of dying and going to hell. C.H. Spurgeon wrote, "The awful and important thoughts of souls being saved by our preaching or left to perish,

to be condemned to hell through our negligence always dwell upon our spirits."[15] May that be true of you—may you preach with desperation and preach toward a verdict.

A sermon should never be a bridge to nowhere, but instead a persuasive plea for the salvation of souls. Some will criticize this kind of thinking by saying, "It's not my job to persuade people. That's God's job." My reply is, "Have you read the Bible? Paul, knowing the terror of the Lord's judgment, said, 'We persuade men'" (2 Corinthians 5:11).

If people aren't changing under your preaching ministry, maybe it's because you're not expecting them to change. If your preaching is apathetic, lifeless, and lacking passion, then of course nothing will happen. But if you preach toward a verdict, you'll preach with a sense of urgency that recognizes your listeners might not have a second chance. The Lord will bless that kind of preaching.

### Making a Statement

I want to conclude on a note of exhortation. In the Orient, when a man wants to make a statement to the world, he takes gasoline, pours it on himself, and then lights a match. His consumed life becomes a vivid and bold declaration.

As a preacher, you can do the same. You can take your Bible, drench yourself in it, light a match, and burn with passion every single Sunday by preaching with great fervency for the glory of

God. That's the kind of preaching that is passionate—and that changes lives. We should make it our consuming desire to develop a passionate heart that results in a passionate life for God that results in a passionate preacher who then preaches passionate sermons. There is no reason, there can be no excuse, for the lack of passionate preaching. If we have no definite desire to benefit God's people through the passionate preaching of His Word, then we have no right to ascend into the sacred pulpit to declare the eternal truths found in Scripture. Only a man set aflame by the Word of God should ever enter the pulpit to burn himself out in preaching to change lives and bring eternal glory to God. May you be that man.

# PRAYER

Lord, take us and mold us into great preachers for Your honor and Your glory. May we preach the unsearchable riches of Christ with passion, power, and a sense of urgency. Holy and merciful Father, may we look upon this world of ours and may we feel as our Lord Jesus felt toward scattered sheep, afflicted and without a shepherd. Help us to feel deeply about them, to care for them, to yearn for their eternal salvation and spiritual good. God, place Your passion for the world into our hearts so that we can preach Your eternal Word with passion. We ask this in Jesus' name, Amen.

# 11

# APOLLOS: AN AUTHENTIC MINISTER OF THE GOSPEL

*Albert Mohler Jr.*

*Shepherds' Conference 2011*

*Acts 18:24-28*

Faithfulness, steadfastness, and resolute dedication to ministry in the kingdom of God demands models, mentors, and examples. There's a sense in which today's generation is rather reluctant to make this admission. This generation would like to sometimes believe that they can do very well on their own, but this kind of thinking is a recipe for disaster. The Scriptures provide us with many models, and it's important for us to understand their function in our lives. For example, the apostle Paul said, "Be imitators of me, just as I also am of Christ" (1 Corinthians 11:1). The believers in Corinth needed a model, and they had one in the apostle Paul. Along with Paul, there are many positive models whom we want to emulate, but there are also tragic examples that God knows we need to learn from. The Scriptures mention King David, who was described as a man after God's own heart (1 Samuel 13:14), but it also reminds us of Saul, a paranoid and faithless man lurking and brooding in the background, similar to Shakespeare's King Lear or US President Richard Nixon in his last days.

If we want to be faithful until the end, then we're going to need models to follow. I would like to take a look at one of the most neglected figures in the New Testament—I invite you to look with me at Acts 18:24-28 so we can learn from Apollos and his ministry. Let's read together the Word of God:

Now a Jew named Apollos, an Alexandrian by birth, an eloquent man, came to Ephesus; and he was mighty in the Scriptures. This man had been instructed in the way of the Lord; and being fervent in spirit, he was speaking and teaching accurately the things concerning Jesus, being acquainted only with the baptism of John; and he began to speak out boldly in the synagogue. But when Priscilla and Aquila heard him, they took him aside and explained to him the way of God more accurately. And when he wanted to go across to Achaia, the brethren encouraged him and wrote to the disciples to welcome him; and when he had arrived, he greatly helped those who had believed through grace, for he powerfully refuted the Jews in public, demonstrating by the Scriptures that Jesus was the Christ.

It's a mystery in many ways as to why Apollos is so neglected. He is somewhat of an enigma. In the entire Bible, there are only ten verses that make reference to Apollos, and most of them simply mention his name. Yet in this passage we will witness the things that are said of him that are said of no other character in the New Testament. In this very crucial passage, we learn a great deal about this man and why he should be among our models for ministry.

**The Historical Context**

The author of our chosen text is the great historian, Luke. In the book of Acts, Luke shares with us details about the embryonic church in its earliest development, as well as the leaders who were important contributors to that growth. Luke teaches us about a time when the gospel is being hammered out in terms of its proclamation, when the church is coming together and learning what it means to be the people of God, and when the Holy Spirit is infusing Christ's church with power and sending it out into the world as a mighty missionary force. In Acts, Luke depicts Christ calling men to serve His church in a way that is absolutely spectacular and unbelievably powerful.

Before continuing with our study of Apollos, we must recognize that Luke's authorial technique in Acts is similar to his approach in the Gospel of Luke. Although the Bible is the inerrant and infallible Word of God, God's glory is demonstrated by His use of men as the authors of sacred Scripture. The Holy Spirit worked within human authors to produce the text of the Word of God. Yet the Spirit didn't use these authors robotically; instead, in His sovereignty, He created each author, He determined the context of each author's experiences, and He formed each author's heart in such a way that it was the Holy Spirit who led the human author to write Scripture.

Viewing Scripture through this prism,

we are reminded that Matthew should be understood, at least in part, for the theme of subversion. When we read the Gospel of Matthew, we come to understand that Matthew loves seeing things flipped on their head. Matthew enjoys showing the principalities and the powers—or for that matter, the Pharisees and the Sadducees—get thrown into a rodeo where everything is upside down. Mark, of course, has the feature of urgency as he often used the word "immediately." John, in terms of his Gospel, demonstrates majestic prose that is filled with much irony. And Luke's writings to Theophilus provide an orderly and factual account of the story of Jesus and the church.

As we read the historical narrative of Acts we are susceptible to rushing too quickly over little pieces of embedded language. For instance, chapter 18 begins with Paul leaving Athens and going to Corinth, where he is introduced to Aquila and his wife Priscilla, strategically placed by God in that city for the purpose of ministry. In verse 4 Luke presents Paul as reasoning in the synagogue every Sabbath as his customary missiology, "trying to persuade Jews and Greeks." In verse 5 Luke writes, "When Silas and Timothy came down from Macedonia, Paul began devoting himself completely to the word." If you're going to be a preacher, make sure you're occupied with the Word.

Paul's priority was clear. He was preoccupied with the Word and nothing else. Brother, may it be that when your people find you, they find you preoccupied with the Word. Paul, as our model and mentor, is found devoted to the Word. This holistic commitment harkens back to the earlier chapters in Acts and the need for deacons. This goes right back to the priority of the teaching office in the church. It goes back to the preeminence of the ministry of the Word. Paul was not to be troubled with lesser matters, for he was occupied with the Word.

This ministry of the Word got Paul into trouble and led to hostility from enemies of the truth. We read in Acts 18:6, "When they resisted and blasphemed, [Paul] shook out his garments and said to them," going back to Ezekiel, "Your blood be on your own heads! I am clean. From now on I will go to the Gentiles."[1] Now this is a great turning point in the book of Acts, for from this time forward, Paul's ministry is to the Gentiles.

We come to understand, as the story further progresses, that there's an escalating conflict God was preparing Paul for: "The Lord said to Paul in the night by a vision, 'Do not be afraid any longer, but go on speaking and do not be silent'" (Acts 18:9). Even in the midst of rejection, the apostle is commanded to continue declaring the truth. This, in turn, cultivates more conflict, as we see in Acts 18:12-15:

> While Gallio was proconsul of Achaia, the Jews with one accord rose up against Paul and brought him before the judgment seat,

saying, "This man persuades men to worship God contrary to the law." But when Paul was about to open his mouth, Gallio said to the Jews, "If it were a matter of wrong or of vicious crime, O Jews, it would be reasonable for me to put up with you; but if there are questions about words and names and your own law, look after it yourselves; I am unwilling to be a judge of these matters."

Paul demonstrated his faithfulness to do exactly what God called him to do by opening his mouth, but Gallio, when he heard the greatest theological debate imaginable, responded with, "Just words. No intervention for me needed here. No decision or determination from the proconsul is required. Just go off and fiddle with your words."

In this chapter we have a great contrast between Paul, who is preoccupied with the Word, and Gallio, who sees Paul's message as just empty words. This same contrast is very much evident in our world today. There are those who know that the Word of God is that which must occupy us above all, and there are others who think the Bible is just filled with words. This is the background for the story of Apollos.

### Introducing Apollos

In Acts 18:24 we are introduced to Apollos with these words: "Now a Jew named Apollos, an Alexandrian by birth, an eloquent man, came to Ephesus." In writing this narrative, Luke makes it a point to highlight Apollos' ethnicity—he was a Jewish man with a Greek name. There's something immediately jarring to the Jewish reader in hearing that a Jewish man had a pagan Greek name. As we continue to read Luke's description we come to realize why this is the case—Apollos was from Alexandria, the first location where the Jewish diaspora resided in the first century. It was also the most important intellectual center of the Mediterranean world, especially after the fall of Athens. Alexandria's culture was defined by its museum and library, which was the greatest library in the ancient world. Because Alexandria was a center of learning and the Jewish people were a people of learning, it was natural for many of the Jewish diaspora to come to Alexandria, for they were drawn to the kind of learning that this city provided. This Hellenistic learning center was Apollos's hometown.

In addition to being the center of ancient pagan knowledge, intellectual activity, and achievement, Alexandria was the city where the Septuagint, the Greek edition of the Old Testament, was translated in the second century BC. As a Jewish boy, Apollos would've been raised in the Alexandrian context of Hellenistic Judaism and trained in the Greek translation of the Holy Scriptures. This was a facility and ability that gave him a tremendous missionary advantage in the Greek culture. This was God's providence at work, overseeing his life to prepare him for future ministry in the Gentile world.

## Marks of an Authentic Minister

In addition to these two introductory details concerning Apollos, Luke makes six commendations of Apollos that are rarely said of anyone else in Scripture, and no one else in Scripture has all six of these commendations attributed to him. As we review them, let us consider Apollos as a model to follow.

### Eloquent

The first commendation that Luke makes about Apollos is that he was "an eloquent man." That's an important detail to know when you're talking about a figure in the first-century Greco-Roman culture. To be an eloquent man in that historical context is to say Apollos was educated, sophisticated, gifted, and consequential for public meeting.

Eloquence was the ticket into public significance. It was necessary for a public figure to have the ability to make an argument and hold an audience's attention. In Greco-Roman culture, the sign of having an orderly mind was the ability to speak orderly words that were articulated in accordance to the ancient canons of rhetoric.

This, of course, raises a question. You may recall that the apostle Paul said to the Corinthians, "When I came to you, I did not come with lofty words of human wisdom. I did not come to you arguing on the basis of the canons of classical

rhetoric in order that my rhetoric would impress you, but rather that the simplicity of the gospel would impress you" (my paraphrase, 1 Corinthians 2:1). As Paul was making his argument against the canons of classical rhetoric, he was still using them. Was Paul being double-minded? No! He was making the point that although ministry is not all about eloquence, it's difficult to be heard if you can't communicate.

In his famed and precious *Lectures to My Students*, Charles Spurgeon spoke about this in terms of the call to ministry. Spurgeon made it clear that if an individual is unable to speak in public, then he is not called to preach.[2] If the last thing you want to do is to get up and speak, preaching is not God's call for your life. If you're worth your salt, you read a text like 1 Corinthians 2:1 and you want to say, "Get out of the way; let's at least make this event a preaching tag team." However, if your temptation is to run into the foyer and bite your nails, you're not called to preach. Yet at the same time we realize that eloquence is not enough. If that were all that had been said about Apollos, it couldn't possibly explain why he had fulfilled such a crucial role in this turning point of church history.

One of the failures of the church today is that eloquence is not encouraged. There are far too many preachers who glory in a lack of eloquence—not because they fear their rhetoric might get in the way of the gospel, but because they just don't want to put in the effort to learn how to speak effectively. A second failure is that there are many leaders who aren't training young men in eloquence. God bless the pastor who looks at a 15-year-old and says, "I want you to make an announcement." I understand that public speaking may be the last thing a kid wants to do, but that's why you're there to guide him.

I recall being in a school gymnasium with a giant swimming pool. Nearby was a father who was teaching his nine-year-old son how to swim. The father leaned over to his son and said, "I want you to know and remember two things: I love you, and you're not going to die." Then I heard a large splash as the boy hit the water, and the father said, "We've got us a swimmer!" A person learns from hands-on experience. Eloquence is developed through experience, and we learn from Luke that Apollos was an eloquent man.

---

**In the relationship between a pastor and the congregation, there must be a level of trust in the preacher's ability to rightly divide the Word of truth.**

---

### Mighty in the Scriptures

Luke's second commendation of Apollos is that he was "mighty in the Scriptures" (Acts 18:24). Our eyes are drawn to this phrase because this is exactly what we want to be. Luke indicates that Apollos was powerful, dynamic, and at home in the Scriptures. He not only knew the Scriptures but had facility, expertise, and a level of dynamic power in the Scriptures—so much so that when he and the Scriptures came together, the power of God was shown. It's not enough to be mighty in the Scriptures in terms of your own study; God calls you to be dynamic and show how His Word can take a hold of a congregation.

The pattern we find in the book of Acts is that competence in the Scriptures is necessary if a congregation is going to trust a preacher. In the relationship between a pastor and the congregation, there must be a level of trust in the preacher's ability to rightly divide the Word of Truth. The congregation must know that the preacher is a trustworthy exegete who is a competent interpreter of Scripture. It is expected of the man of God that when he stands behind the pulpit, proper biblical exposition will be the result.

There are far too many pulpits that are simply a piece of furniture because they are not the launching pad for a dynamic preaching ministry. Since exegesis is both an art and a science, ministers must be prepared. That is why Paul told Timothy to study rather than sit in the room and hum a sacred syllable. Timothy needed to study in order to prove himself to be someone who was not ashamed as he rightly divided the Word of Truth (2 Timothy 2:15).

APOLLOS: AN AUTHENTIC MINISTER OF THE GOSPEL

## Instructed in the Way of the Lord

Luke's third commendation of Apollos is that he was "instructed in the way of the Lord" (Acts 8:25). The implication is that Apollos was instructed in the Old Testament. His parents must have raised him in the admonition of God. Yet he surpassed that knowledge and came to know the things concerning Jesus as well. It may not be possible to retrace his education down to his mentors, but we should be reminded that the Christian church has been an instructional people from the beginning. The church has always been instructed by the Scriptures. Where you find Christians, you will find instruction. Teaching is absolutely necessary to the Christian faith.

The Christian faith is not passed on by osmosis or by proximity. Rather, it is passed on by the cognitive transmission of biblical truth, which requires an instructor in order for there to be instruction. Many churches today will implement everything into their program except for instruction, and if you happen to find instruction, most likely it isn't instruction from the Scriptures. This is a sad reality because in order to have an Apollos, you need someone who will train him to be competent in the Scriptures, someone who will instruct him in the way of the Lord.

## Fervent in Spirit

The fourth commendation said of Apollos is that he was "fervent in spirit"

(Acts 8:25). There are many things we might infer from the phrase "fervent in spirit," which is why biblical exegesis is not about inference. In a situation like this it may be beneficial to let Scripture interpret Scripture. In Romans chapter 12 Paul wrote about the ideal Christian, and in verse 11 he mentioned this specific mark of such a Christian: "Not lagging behind in diligence, fervent in spirit, serving the Lord." Fervency is not about an attitude of excitement but about a zeal for the things of God that is translated into action. To be fervent in spirit is in contrast to being slothful. Where you find a man of God, you will find a man who is working, who is diligent, and who is fervent. He understands what is at stake and is motivated by the power of the gospel to fulfill gospel ministry. Someone who's fervent is always found busy, just like Paul was found occupied with the Word and Apollos was found busy serving the Lord.

In my academic career, I've seen students whom I felt like I wanted to jolt just to make sure they were alive. The minister of the gospel is supposed to look alive. He doesn't look alive just because his eyes are open and his chest is moving as he breathes, but because he's diligent in action. Fervency in spirit is clearly demonstrated in the fact that Apollos didn't just wash up in Ephesus. Instead, he was there because of his aspiration to serve the Lord. Every once in a while students tell me, "I can't find a place to serve." My response to them is, "Don't find a place to serve. Find a need and fill it!"

I discovered my call to teach when I was 16 years old. It was a Saturday night and my father, who was a Sunday school director, came into my room and said, "I'm short a teacher for Sunday morning." He then looked at me and said, "You're going to teach first-grade Sunday school in the morning." He gave me the material and told me to be prepared. I sat down and began to study the Word in a different way than I had ever studied it before. That night I discovered there is a difference between studying the Word and studying the Word to teach it.

I was pretty pumped on Sunday morning and I even dressed up for the occasion. I walked into the Sunday school room and it was filled with six-year-olds swarming around like ants looking for a crumb. After I assessed the situation, I asked them to sit down and began to teach. Since that day, there has hardly been a Lord's day when I did not teach. I didn't volunteer; it was foisted upon me, and it turned out to play an instrumental role in me recognizing my calling.

Find a need and fill it. Be fervent in spirit.

### Speaking and Teaching Faithfully

Fifth, Luke describes Apollos as someone who "was speaking and teaching accurately the things concerning Jesus" (Acts 18:25). We certainly hope there is some eloquence in us; we certainly want to be found powerful in the Scriptures; we want to be fervent in spirit; but how we must long to be men who speak and teach accurately the things concerning Jesus.

Avoiding heresy isn't merely a decision you can make and thus protect yourself from such a tragedy. There are men who would have never willfully decided, "I'm going to teach heresy" who are currently teaching it. Sometimes the difference between orthodoxy and heresy is so microscopically small that it can be reduced to a diphthong or a vowel. A vowel divided the Roman Empire as it was the difference between saying that Jesus is of a similar substance with the Father, or that He is of the same substance as the Father. That took place in Nicaea in AD 325, where the church came together to hear Athanasius confront the heresy of Arius. It wasn't about getting a sentence wrong. It wasn't about getting a phrase wrong. It wasn't about getting a diphthong or a vowel wrong. It was about an error which meant that the Jesus of Arius was a Jesus who could not save.

Apollos is commended because he "was speaking and teaching accurately the things concerning Jesus." We need to recognize with brokenheartedness that we do not have to look hard to find heresy. Heresy draws an enormous audience and virtually every time it sounds sweet to the ear of the one who does not know the truth. Heresy is a dangerous lure. It's a false gospel that elevates an idol rather than Jesus Christ. Therefore we must understand that it takes work, dedication, theological expertise, doctrinal grounding, and convictional commitment to speak and to teach accurately the things concerning Jesus.

### Speaking Boldly

The sixth and final word of commendation is that Apollos is bold (Acts 18:26). We are told that "he...[spoke] boldly in the synagogue." Apollos was audacious and courageous and willing to face the fear of opposition and to conquer it.

I love reading history, especially military history. One of my favorite stories is about General George Patton pressing into Nazi-occupied territory and liberating village after village. He was moving so quickly that he was ahead of his communication lines, and a modern military cannot operate without communication lines. At one point, Patton was riding in a jeep up to the front lines where there were Messerschmitt fighter planes diving down right over the American troops. As the fighter planes were shooting, there was a 17-year-old private on top of a tree putting up a telephone line. Patton, upon seeing him said, "Son, if I only had an army of you. You're not afraid of anything." With a cracking voice the private said, "Yes I am, sir." Patton said, "What are you afraid of?" The boy responded, "You, sir."[3]

Everybody is afraid of something, and that's not a problem. However, an unwillingness to conquer the fear is a problem, for it shows a focus on the self that is unhealthy. As preachers, we must be bold—not because we have

confidence in ourselves but because we have confidence in the One who has called us, confidence in the One who has sent us, and confidence in the One who is worthy. Because of our confidence in the Lord, we can be bold, audacious, and with courage face our fear and conquer it. The preacher must be found doing what he is called to do, especially in the face of opposition.

### Teachable and Humble

In addition to Luke's six commendations of Apollos, in Acts 18:25 we are told indirectly that Apollos was a humble and teachable man. Luke writes, "He was speaking and teaching accurately the things concerning Jesus, being acquainted only with the baptism of John." The second half of that verse reveals a serious problem, but one that is understandable considering Apollos's biography. Earlier we saw that he grew up in Alexandria in the context of Hellenistic Judaism, and yet somehow he heard the gospel. However, the gospel he heard was partial—similar to the gospel that was understood by the disciples of John.

It was at this point that Priscilla and Aquila entered the narrative to help Apollos. The Lord sovereignly placed Priscilla and Aquila in Ephesus at the exact moment that Apollos and the church needed them. Luke presents this couple as Paul's friends from Corinth: "After these things he [Paul] left Athens and went to Corinth. And he found a Jew named Aquila, a native of Pontus, having recently come from Italy with his wife Priscilla, because Claudius had commanded all the Jews to leave Rome" (Acts 18:1-2).

This is the couple who "took him [Apollos] aside and explained to him the way of God more accurately" (18:26). This verse is precious to us because here we have an unprecedented model of theological correction in the New Testament. Here we have a man who's described as fervent in spirit, eloquent, competent, and mighty in the Scriptures, and yet he doesn't know everything he needs to know about the gospel. It's possible to be mighty in the Scriptures and to be wrong on a point of doctrine and need correction. In all this, we learn that Apollos was teachable and humble.

*The Need for Correction*

Priscilla and Aquila heard Apollos and they recognized a problem. They realized that though he taught accurately the things concerning Jesus, when he spoke about baptism, he was left with a baptism of repentance not a baptism that points to regeneration. Apollos didn't have the complete picture, so the couple took him aside—that is to say, they did not confront him publicly. They didn't shame him or embarrass him before the congregation. Instead, in the love of Christ, they taught him the things of God more accurately. We need a church that is filled not only with the likes of Apollos but with the likes of Priscilla and Aquila as well. We desperately need Christians who have the ability

to hear what is not accurate and are willing to correct it.

> **Good intentions are not enough when it comes to gospel ministry. Gospel ministry demands accuracy.**

Apollos boldly proclaimed Christ in the synagogue, and in boldness Priscilla and Aquila corrected him. We live in an era in which it is considered a matter of bad etiquette to tell someone he is wrong. In this intellectually demilitarized age, we have declared doctrinal self-surrender. We're not supposed to tell people they're wrong. However, good intentions are not enough when it comes to gospel ministry. Gospel ministry demands accuracy. As a result, we need people like Priscilla and Aquila.

*Correcting with Grace*

I recall an incident that occurred when I was 26 years old. I was trained in a liberal theological seminary at which I now serve as president. By the grace of God, over the years I had the opportunity to lead this seminary through a process of reformation so that now it stands for the true faith. I was trained by my parents, church, and faithful men who invested in me so that I was saved from the poison of theological liberalism. I had to learn how to listen to discern, but I didn't catch everything. I was taught in seminary that

God was an equal-opportunity employer, and thus the office of pastor was said to be open to women as well as men. I had not read a single argument against that, and I picked up that teaching like a virus. One of the men who challenged my thinking on this was the evangelical theologian Carl F.H. Henry. He became a personal mentor, teacher, and friend. I had the opportunity to edit his writings and get to know him as a colleague.

The first time I met Dr. Henry, I was asked to be his host. He wasn't my colleague then, but rather a titanic theological figure. While we were walking across the campus he questioned me on everything from Process Theology to Liberation Theology. He inquired of my views on the inerrancy of Scripture and he was seemingly satisfied with everything he heard. But then he turned to me and asked, "What do you think about women in ministry?" With youthful audacity, I told him what I thought. He simply looked at me and said, "One day, this is going to be a very embarrassing conversation."

After finishing my responsibility to host him, I went to the library. I attempted to find every book I could on the subject, but the resources on biblical manhood and womanhood were scarce. The excellent book *Recovering Biblical Manhood and Womanhood*[4] hadn't been written yet, and the Council of Biblical Manhood and Womanhood had not yet been established. So I started reading the only thing I could find, which was a book by a confused Catholic Charismatic who argued against women serving as priests. The book prompted me to spend the rest of the night ransacking the Scriptures, and it didn't take all that long for me to be persuaded. When I met Dr. Henry the following morning, I told him of my quest and where I ended up. His response was, "Didn't take long, did it?" I said, "No, sir!" This was no small doctrinal issue, but Dr. Henry was gracious to me.

Dr. Henry later asked me to coauthor a work with him. It requires grace and courage to face someone and say, "That's wrong," and then say, "Come with me." That is what Priscilla and Aquila did with Apollos—they confronted him, and then taught him.

## What Will Be Said of You?

Whenever Paul referred to Apollos in his writings, he always did so with positive comments. For example, he wrote, "I planted. Apollos watered" (1 Corinthians 3:6). Toward the end of 1 Corinthians we read that Paul encouraged Apollos to visit the Christians in Corinth (16:12). When Paul wrote to Titus some years after the Corinthian correspondence, he said, "Make sure Apollos lacks for nothing" (see Titus 3:13). Apollos's reputation among the leaders of the first-century church was exemplary. He was spoken highly of, and as Luke says, "he greatly helped those who had believed through grace…for he powerfully refuted the

Jews in public, demonstrating by the Scriptures that Jesus was the Christ" (Acts 18:27-28).

May the things that were said of Apollos by Luke be said of you as well. Something will be thought of you, said of you, inscribed of you on your tombstone. May others say that you were an eloquent man, competent in the Scriptures, instructed in the way the Lord, and fervent in spirit. May you be known for speaking and teaching accurately the things concerning Jesus, and for speaking these things boldly.

# PRAYER

Father, we thank You for this text. Make us humble in spirit such that we accept the correction of those who are friends to the gospel. And may our congregations bear the marks of a church that would produce an Apollos and be filled with Priscillas and Aquilas, and may all the glory be Yours. We pray in the name of Jesus Christ our Lord, Amen.

# 12

# A TALE OF TWO PREACHERS

*John MacArthur*
*Shepherds' Conference 2013*
*Matthew 26–27*

Through all the years of my ministry, I have been concerned by a disturbing reality—the fact that the church is occupied by people who aren't really saved. I have written many books on this subject, including *The Gospel According to Jesus*, *The Gospel According to the Apostles*, *Ashamed of the Gospel*, *The Truth War*, and *Hard to Believe*. These books highlight that the church is full of people who are on their way to hell. If we are to throw our bodies in front of perishing sinners, then we have to start in the church. We can't make assumptions.

In the mid-twentieth century, there were two young and gifted evangelists. They came onto the scene in the United States at the same time. They were called the "Gold Dust Twins."[1] One of those two young evangelists you know very well, Billy Graham. His story is common knowledge and as of this writing is still being lived out. The other young evangelist was Charles Templeton, whom you probably don't know about.

It was Charles Templeton, Billy Graham, and Torrey Johnson who founded Youth for Christ. By all accounts, Charles Templeton was the more gifted preacher of the Gold Dust Twins. Intelligent, handsome, winsome, eloquent, oratorical, brilliant, persuasive, and effective—all those words were used to describe him. In fact, in 1946, the National Association of Evangelicals gave him an award—the "Best Used of God" award.

For a time, Charles Templeton overshadowed Billy Graham. He was considered a better and more effective speaker. The two of them went on an evangelistic tour of Europe. They preached in England, Scotland, Ireland, Sweden, and a few other places. They alternated as they went preaching to large audiences. Charles Templeton was given an opportunity to have weekly television programs on NBC and CBS in the 1950s. In the United States, he preached to as many as 20,000 people a night. He often preached in youth rallies with thousands of young people. He attended Princeton Seminary. He became a church planter, a pastor, and an evangelist with the Presbyterian Church. He even had opportunity to do a week of gospel preaching at Yale University. Charles Templeton was a formidable man.

But in 1957, Charles Templeton declared himself an agnostic. He rejected both the Bible and Jesus Christ. He attached the firmness of that rejection to reading Thomas Paine and other authors. He said that in ten days' time he read Voltaire, Bertrand Russell, Robert Ingersoll, David Hume, and Aldous Huxley. By the end of those ten days, he determined to leave the ministry. With $600 in his pocket, he returned to Canada and became a journalist. After being a journalist for a while, he became a politician, and almost became the prime minister of Canada. In 1957, he stepped into the eternal blackness of apostasy, blasphemed Christ, and signed off with a book, *Farewell to God*. So formidable!

Do you think there are other preachers like him? My dad was an evangelist. He ministered in Europe with another

evangelist, preaching day after day, night after night in a very intense, prolonged series of evangelistic meetings. The other preacher was doing the same in another part of this great European city. When my dad came home, he said it was one the most horrible experiences of his life because this fellow evangelist was involved with drunkenness and prostitutes. How common a problem is this?

The guy who ran next to me in the backfield on our college football team, a co-captain, went to seminary and subsequently denied the faith. When I went to Talbot Seminary, I was friends with a young man whose father was the dean of the seminary. We graduated together. I launched into Christian ministry, and he ended up putting a Buddhist altar in his home. Over the years, I have witnessed ministers who remained faithful and ministers who rejected the faith.

## The Two Preachers

I want to tell you another story, a tale of two preachers. These two you know very well. Both were called by Jesus personally. Both answered the call, forsook everything, and followed Him. Both declared repeatedly their personal devotion to Christ. Both were personally taught and trained by Jesus for preaching ministry. Both were intimately acquainted with Him every hour of the day, every day of the week, for years. They were taught by Him with perfect clarity, power, and conviction that had no parallel or ever will. They were taught by example and everything He ever taught them He lived to perfection. They were taught to know the will of God. They were taught the Word of God—to know it, believe it, live it, love it, and preach it.

Both saw the miracles of Jesus day after day as He banished illness from the land of Israel. No one has ever had a teacher who is equal, not even close. Both clearly saw the revelation of His divine nature. They saw His power over demons, disease, nature, and death. Both of them heard Jesus respond to every theological question perfectly. His answers always ended the discussion; there was never a need to say, "Could You clarify a little?" He answered profoundly, perfectly, and truthfully.

Both were confronted daily with the reality of their sin by living with the sinless one. Both were told day after day that every sinner needs salvation. Both were told about the reality of eternal heaven and eternal hell. Both received and used the very power the Lord Jesus delegated to them to preach effectively, to do healings, and to cast out demons. Both exercised that power and both preached Jesus as Messiah, Savior, Son of Man, and Son of God.

They shared all of this together. They were exposed to Jesus in identical ways. And there's more: Both were sinners, and they knew it. Both were so aware of their sin that they were overwhelmed with guilt to a crushing level. Both gave themselves over to Satan and took up Satan's cause. In the end, both of them betrayed

Jesus boldly, emphatically, openly, publicly, and resolutely. They both did this at the end of all their training and experience. Just before Jesus was crucified, both of them were completely devastated by what they had done.

One of them, in spite of his wicked betrayal of the Savior, is considered so honorable, so noble, and such a grand figure that millions of people have been named after him—Peter. There's even a feminine form of his name across the world, *Petra*. The other man…not so much. He is considered so dishonorable and so despicable that although his name means "praised," very few people have it. His name is hated and reviled by many.

One of those preachers ended his life a suicide, hanging himself, and being eternally banished. The other ended his life a saint, crucified upside down, but eternally blessed. One of them we will meet in heaven. The other one will be met in hell by those who reject Christ. You'd have to go to hell to meet Judas and other apostate and defecting preachers.

The bottom line for every person is this: What do you think of Christ?

Two men, side by side with each other and with Jesus for three years, and then separated from each other for all eternity. One of them is the first name in each of the four New Testament lists of the apostles. The other one is the last name in every list. One of them is enthroned in highest heaven, and the other one is consigned to lowest hell. One of them will be honored forever, and the other will be tortured forever. Amazingly, both betrayed the Lord Jesus, and both regretted what they had done; both were sorry. All this brings us to an important point: Salvation can't be by works because they both did the same works; they both did miracles. Salvation can't be by knowledge; they both had the same information. So what was the difference between the two?

### What Do You Think of Christ?

Let me tell you what the difference was. It's important for you to know because every minister should make it a high priority to be sure that the people in his church are genuinely saved. What accounted for the difference? Their attitudes toward the Lord Jesus. The bottom line for every person is this: What do you think of Christ? That's what explains the difference between Peter and Judas, and we need to be aware of that when it comes to the people in our churches today. Every church is full of Peters and Judases. They are full of people hearing the same messages, experiencing the same worship, and seeing the same power on display in people's lives, but they're going to end up in two extremely different destinations.

Isn't that what Jesus said would happen? At the end of the Sermon on the Mount, He said, "Many will say to Me

on that day, 'Lord, Lord.'" And to a large number of them He will respond, "I never knew you" (Matthew 7:21-23). It all comes back to one's attitude toward Jesus Christ.

Through the years, people have asked me, "Why are you so stuck on preaching Christ?" It's because I know that what saves people from hell is a right attitude toward Jesus Christ. I can't preach enough of Him. That's the point of all of Scripture—to point to Him. I make no apology for following my mentor, the apostle Paul, who preached Christ and was determined "to know nothing among you except Jesus Christ, and Him crucified" (1 Corinthians 2:2).

### Setting the Stage

To see these two preachers in action, let's look together at Matthew 26. Matthew opened the chapter with "When Jesus finished all these words…" That is, Jesus had just given the great Olivet Discourse, the sermon on His second coming. Then He said, "You know that after two days the Passover is coming, and the Son of Man is to be handed over for crucifixion" (verse 2). He had told this to the Twelve before—back in Matthew 16:21, we read, "From that time Jesus began to show His disciples that He must go to Jerusalem and suffer many things from the elders and chief priests and scribes, and be killed, and be raised up on the third day."

This was too much for Peter to swallow. "Peter took Him aside and began to rebuke Him, saying, 'God forbid it, Lord! This shall never happen to You.' But He turned and said to Peter, 'Get behind me, Satan!'" (verses 22-23). Jesus repeatedly told the disciples that He was going to die, and He even gave them details about what would happen—how He would be treated, who was going to do it, and that the plan was in motion.

Going back to Matthew 26, in verse 3 we read, "Then the chief priests and the elders of the people were gathered together in the court of the high priest, named Caiaphas; and they plotted together to seize Jesus by stealth and kill Him." That was the plan—capture and kill Jesus. In the meantime, Jesus was in Bethany, at the home of Simon the leper. While He was there, "a woman came to Him with an alabaster vial of very costly perfume, and she poured it on His head as He reclined at the table. But the disciples were indignant when they saw this, and said, 'Why this waste? For this perfume might have been sold for a high price and the money given to the poor" (Matthew 26:7-9). Though we are told the disciples said this, John 12:4 more specifically reports it was Judas who said it. He was the protestor.

**Judas, a Master Hypocrite**

Here is the first time in the Gospel record that Judas reveals his inner character. Up to this point, we know quite a bit about Peter, James, and John, but we don't have much information about Judas. There was no reason to suspect anything was amiss. Judas didn't seem to respond any differently than the rest of the Twelve to what Jesus said or did. There was no suspicion regarding Judas's character, but here in Matthew 26 Judas questions a woman's use of expensive perfume, making it evident he wanted the money that could have been obtained by selling the perfume.

In His rebuke to the disciples, Jesus said, "When she poured this perfume on my body, she did it to prepare me for burial" (Matthew 26:12). But Judas wasn't thinking about that. He had his own agenda—he wanted money, power, and prestige. He wanted to be in the power seat when Jesus set up His kingdom, and his ambitions were being smashed by all this talk of crucifixion, death, and burial. This was massively disappointing to Judas.

Look at what happened next: "Then one of the twelve, named Judas Iscariot, went to the chief priests and said, 'What are you willing to give me to betray Him to you?' And they weighed out thirty pieces of silver to him. From then on he began looking for a good opportunity to betray Jesus" (verses 14-16). Judas went to the chief priests, and they weighed out 30 pieces of silver. This, according to Exodus 21:32, was the price of a slave. This is just shocking—Judas, who had been trusted with a great stewardship along with the other disciples, was going to betray the Son of God for the price of a slave.

We continue in verses 17-19: "Now on the first day of Unleavened Bread the disciples came to Jesus and asked, 'Where do You want us to prepare for You to eat the Passover?' And He said, 'Go into the city to a certain man, and say to him, "The Teacher says, my time is near; I am to keep the Passover at your house with My disciples."' The disciples did as Jesus had directed them; and they prepared the Passover." The Passover was established back in Exodus 12, and they were going to observe this annual event together.

You know the rest of the story: "Now when evening came, Jesus was reclining at the table with the twelve disciples. As they were eating, He said, 'Truly I say to you that one of you will betray me.'" This came as a total shock to the group. "Being deeply grieved, they each one began to say to Him, 'Surely not I, Lord.'" Notice the disciples suspected themselves before they suspected anyone else, including Judas. Nothing had happened yet that would cause them to look at him.

Then Jesus said, "He who dipped his hand with Me in the bowl is the one who will betray Me" (verse 23). During the Passover supper, they ate their meal using a communal bowl into which they could dip their bread. Jesus continued, "'The Son of Man is to go, just as it is written of Him; but woe to the man by whom the Son of Man is betrayed! It would have been good for that man if he had not been born.' And Judas, who was betraying Him, said, 'Surely it is not I, Rabbi?' Jesus said to him, 'You have said it yourself'" (verses 24-25).

Judas had already made the deal, and now he was waiting for the opportune moment to betray Jesus. This may be one of the most horrendous moments in human history. Nobody suspected Judas, and he thought he could get away with another statement of hypocrisy. He was a master of hypocrisy.

**The Betrayal**

After the Passover meal, Jesus departed with the disciples for the Garden of Gethsemane. We are told that "after singing a hymn, they went out to the Mount of Olives" (verse 30). When they arrived at the garden, Jesus said to His disciples, "Sit here while I go over there and pray" (verse 36). Then He went a bit further with Peter and the two sons of Zebedee, asking them to keep watch and pray. But the three disciples could not stay awake and ended up falling asleep. When Jesus returned, "He came to the disciples and said to them, 'Are you still sleeping and resting? Behold, the hour is at hand and the Son of Man is being betrayed into the hands of sinners. Get up, let us be going; behold, the one who betrays Me is at hand!'" (verses 45-46).

Judas goes into action, and as he does, we are reminded in verse 47 that he was "one of the twelve." Every time Judas and the betrayal are mentioned together in the Gospels, the passage always identifies him as one of the Twelve. This underscores just how shocking and inconceivable his betrayal was.

John informs us that it was at this

point that Satan entered Judas (John 13:27). Jesus was never fooled. He knew all along that Judas was the son of perdition. In fact, in John 6:70, Jesus said, "Did I Myself not choose you, the twelve, and yet one of you is a devil?"

So Jesus was in the garden, and Judas showed up with a massive entourage that included the chief priests, the elders, the temple police with their clubs and swords, and no doubt some of the Romans. They were all coming to arrest Him.

Verse 48 continues, "Now he who was betraying Him gave them a sign, saying, 'Whomever I kiss, He is the one; seize Him.' Immediately Judas went to Jesus and said, 'Hail, Rabbi!' and kissed Him." Jesus responded by addressing Judas as "friend" (verse 50). In the original Greek text, this is not the usual word for friend. Instead, Jesus used a word that speaks of an associate—it is more technical than personal, as if He were saying, "Associate, do what you have come for." Then the people "came and laid hands on Jesus and seized Him" (verse 50).

Matthew 26:57-60 tells what happened next:

Those who had seized Jesus led Him away to Caiaphas, the high priest, where the scribes and elders were gathered together. But Peter was following Him at a distance as far as the courtyard of the high priest, and entered in, and sat down with the officers to see the outcome. Now the chief priests

and the whole Council kept trying to obtain false testimony against Jesus, so that they might put Him to death. They did not find any, even though many false witnesses came forward.

What was the outcome of the trial? Verse 65 says that "the high priest tore his robes and said, 'He has blasphemed! What further need do we have of witnesses?'" They were outraged by Jesus' comments and declared that He deserved death. So they began to mistreat Jesus: "They spat on His face and beat Him with their fists; and others slapped Him, and said, 'Prophesy to us, You Christ; who is the one who hit You?'" (verses 67-68).

Matthew 27 opens with the following scene:

Now when morning came, all the chief priests and the elders of the people conferred together against Jesus to put Him to death; and they bound Him, and led Him away and delivered Him to Pilate the governor.

Then when Judas, who had betrayed Him, saw that He had been condemned, he felt remorse and returned the thirty pieces of silver to the chief priest and elders, saying, "I have sinned by betraying innocent blood." But they said, "What is that to us? See to that yourself." And he threw the pieces of silver into the temple sanctuary and departed; and he went away and hanged himself. The chief priests took the pieces of silver and said, "It is not lawful to put them into temple treasury, since it is the price of blood." And they conferred together and with the money bought the Potter's Field as a burial place for strangers.

For this reason that field has been called the Field of Blood to this day. Then that which was spoken through Jeremiah the prophet was fulfilled: "And they took the thirty pieces of silver, the price of the one whose price had been set by the sons of Israel; and they gave them for the Potter's Field, as the Lord directed me" (verses 1-10).

It wasn't lawful for the chief priests and the elders to do what they had done to Jesus, but that didn't bother them. Now, you may wonder why this passage identifies Jeremiah as the source of the Old Testament quote. It's actually Zechariah, but the reason Jeremiah is identified is because the Old Testament is divided into three sections. You have the Law, the Writings, and the Prophets. Jeremiah was the first book of the Prophets in the Hebrew text, and so Jeremiah became the title for that section.

The historical account continues as we see the horrible tragedy of Judas unfold. He hung himself. Acts 1:18 says he died by "falling headlong...and all his intestines gushed out." Evidently

when he hung himself, either the rope or branch broke and his body was dashed against the ground. What a horrible and unparalleled tragedy. In fact, this is the greatest tragedy in human history because Judas had unequalled opportunity to see Jesus up close.

Yet Judas remained greedy, materialistic, earthly, and motivated by personal ambition. His desire for riches was so great that he ignored the truth that was in his face. Judas went to hell on purpose. He knew there was a hell, and he made the choice to send himself there. It's as if he said, "The agony is too great. I want relief. I'm going to send myself to hell." His downfall came because he loved himself too much, he rejected salvation too easily, and he resented Jesus too strongly. The same sun that melts the wax hardens the clay.

**Betrayed Again**

Next we direct our focus to Peter. Going back to Matthew 26:17-19, we read,

Now on the first day of the Unleavened Bread the disciples came to Jesus and asked, "Where do You want us to prepare for You to eat the Passover?" and He said, "Go into the city to a certain man, and say to him, 'The Teacher says, "My time is near, I am to keep the Passover at your house with My disciples."'" The disciples did as Jesus had directed them; and they prepared the Passover.

Jesus planned the Passover in such a way that Judas didn't know where it was going to take place. This meant he couldn't lead people there to arrest Jesus.

Verse 26 continues, "While they were eating, Jesus took some bread, and after a blessing, He broke it and gave it to the disciples, and said, 'Take, eat; this is my body.'" And with these words Jesus transitions the Passover into the Lord's Supper. Then after they sang a hymn they went to the Mount of Olives. As they did so, Jesus said, "You will all fall away because of Me this night, for it is written, 'I will strike down the shepherd, and the sheep of the flock shall be scattered.' But after I have been raised, I will go ahead of you to Galilee." But Peter said to Him, 'Even though all may fall away because of You, I will never fall away'" (26:31-33).

Jesus told the Twelve they would all defect, but Peter thought more highly of himself than he should have. Jesus responded, "Truly I say to you that this very night, before a rooster crows, you will deny me three times" (verse 34). Peter protested, "'Even if I have to die with You, I will not deny You.' All the disciples said the same thing too" (verse 35).

But as we well know, Peter went on to deny Christ. His crime was as evil, resolute, and public as Judas's. He wouldn't know it, however, until the rooster crowed.

Let's look at what happened: "Now Peter was sitting outside in the courtyard, and a servant-girl came to him and said, 'You too were with Jesus the Galilean.'

But he denied it before them all, saying, 'I do not know what you're talking about'" (verse 69). Peter then shuffled off to the entrance near the courtyard, where another servant girl saw him and said,

"This man was with Jesus of Nazareth." And again he denied it with an oath, "I do not know the man." A little later the bystanders came up and said to Peter, "Surely you too are one of them; for even the way you talk gives you away." Then he began to curse and swear, "I do not know the man!" (Matthew 26:71-74).

In the third encounter, when Peter "began to curse and swear," he pronounced a death curse on himself. He was saying, "If I'm lying, kill me." That's as bold as you can get, isn't it? Peter's denial was blatant.

Right after Peter's outburst, "immediately a rooster crowed" (verse 74). In that instant, Peter remembered Jesus' words: "Before a rooster crows, you will deny Me three times" (verse 34). He had pronounced a death sentence on himself—"Take my life if I'm lying"—even though he had already lied.

What did Peter do? Did he hang himself? No, he went out and wept bitterly. Luke provides an amazing detail here for us. He says that when the rooster crowed, "The Lord turned and looked at Peter" (22:61). When Judas looked into Jesus' eyes in the garden, he kissed Jesus with the hatred of a hypocrite. When Peter looked into Jesus' eyes, he broke out in tears.

Crushing sadness without repentance led Judas to suicide. Crushing sadness with repentance led Peter to restoration.

How did Peter get to the place where he would end up denying Jesus? How could he do this after living beside Jesus for three years?

First, Peter boasted too much. Earlier, he told Jesus, "Even though all may fall away because of You, I will never fall away" (verse 33). In fact, he went so far as to say, "Even if I have to die with You, I will not deny You" (verse 35).

Second, Peter prayed too little. Remember what happened in the Garden of Gethsemane? Jesus came back to the disciples and found them asleep: "So, you men could not keep watch with me for one hour?" (verse 40).

Third, Peter acted too quickly. When the crowd arrived to arrest Jesus, "one of those who were with Jesus reached and drew out his sword, and struck the slave of the high priest and cut off his ear" (verse 51). This was Peter's doing. "Then Jesus said to him, 'Put your sword back into its place'" (verse 52).

Fourth, Peter followed too far. When Jesus was led away to the high priest, Peter tagged along from a distance. This led to the three encounters with people who accused him of being one of the Twelve—encounters in which Peter ended up denying Jesus (verses 69-74).

## The Restoration

After the crucifixion and resurrection, Peter had gone back to fishing, which he wasn't supposed to do. He should have gone to Galilee and waited for Jesus to appear after they had met in the Upper Room after the resurrection. Jesus told the disciples to go to Galilee and wait. Instead, Peter had gone back to his boat and nets. He had returned to his old ways. Jesus showed up and confronted Peter, asking him three times, "Do you love me?"

What was Peter's attitude toward Jesus? It's very clear: "Yes, I love You. Yes, Lord. You know I love You." Notice that Peter even called on Jesus' omniscience. Why would he do that? Because it wasn't obvious that Peter loved Jesus: "You know I love You. You know everything. You know I love You."

The difference between Judas and Peter, then, was that Peter truly loved Christ. As the apostle Paul said, "If anyone does not love the Lord, he is to be accursed" (1 Corinthians 16:22). Later on, John wrote, "We love, because He first loved us" (1 John 4:19). Both Peter and Judas were present in the Upper Room when Jesus said, "He who has My commandments and keeps them is the one who loves Me; and he who loves Me will be loved by My Father, and I will love him and disclose Myself to him" (John 14:21). That night, Jesus talked to the Twelve about loving Him. But as it turned out, Judas hated Him—for dashing his ambitions.

In John 14:23-24, Jesus said, "If any-one loves Me, he will keep My word; and My Father will love him, and We will come to him and make Our abode with him. He who does not love Me does not keep My words; and the word which you hear is not Mine, but the Father's who sent me." It's all about loving Christ. As Jesus said in John 14:28, "You heard that I said to you, 'I go away, and I will come to you.' If you loved Me, you would have rejoiced because I go the Father, for the Father is greater than I."

When Jesus spoke about His disci-ples' love for Him, He wasn't referring to some sort of emotional sentiment, some sort of buzz that He wanted them to experience. Note carefully how Jesus defined this love: "Whoever loves Me keeps My commandments." True love for Jesus responds to Him in disciplined acts of obedience.

The more you know about Christ, the more irresistible He becomes and the more you will love Him. Sadly, not every-one responds to Jesus the same way. In John 6, after a crowd of disciples heard some difficult teachings from Jesus, they walked away. Jesus then turned to the Twelve and said, "'You do not want to go away also, do you?' Simon Peter answered Him, 'Lord, to whom shall we go? You have the words of eternal life. We have believed and come to know that You are the Holy One of God'" (verses 66-68).

Peter had the potential for disastrous betrayal, but he was different than Judas because he loved Christ. For this reason,

God went on to use Peter in powerful ways.

**Captivated by Love**

In light of the comparison between Judas and Peter, here's an important prin-ciple to remember: Sin and guilt do not produce true repentance. You can have powerful guilt, overwhelming remorse, agonizing regret, and still end up killing yourself. You can have an awareness of your sin and understand it fully, but that is not enough. Acknowledging your sin, feeling remorse over what you have done, and bearing the full temporal punishment for that crime doesn't necessarily produce repentance. The horror of Judas's sin did not make him repent. And the horror of Peter's sin did not make him repent.

The ugliness of sin is not enough to make the sinner repent. It can be enough to break you, to make you cry, to make you kill yourself, but it's not enough to make you repent. What is required to make you repent is a vision of Christ that elicits a captivating love. Peter loved Jesus. When their eyes met that night after the rooster crowed, Peter was crushed and driven to tears. His response was prompted by love. This reflects the mind of a true believer.

Peter later gave this testimony in his first epistle:

Blessed be the God and Father of our Lord Jesus Christ, who according to His great mercy has caused us to be born again to a living hope through the resurrection of Jesus Christ from the dead, to obtain an inheritance which is imperishable and undefiled and will not fade away, reserved in heaven for you, who are protected by the power of God through faith for a salvation ready to be revealed in the last time. In this you greatly rejoice, even though now for a little while, if necessary, you have been distressed by various trials, so that the proof of your faith, being more precious than gold which is perishable, even though tested by fire, may be found to result in praise and glory and honor at the revelation of Jesus Christ; and though you have not seen Him, you love Him (1 Peter 1:3-8).

When it comes to the people who attend your church, you are looking for genuine salvation. It shows up in a love for Christ that produces delight and obedience. Your responsibility, then, is to hold up Christ all the time—Christ, who is the most lovely, the most winsome, the most beautiful, the most glorious, the most magnificent, and the most perfect One of all. You can't offer people anything better.

---

*There is tremendous joy in having a congregation that loves Christ, because that love compels the people to honor and serve Him.*

---

## Giving People a Hunger for Christ

After I finished preaching through the entire New Testament I asked the people in my church, "Well, what do you want now?" They said, "Show us Christ in the Old Testament." I went to the Old Testament and for months, we learned about the pre-incarnate Christ. Then I said, "What now?" The church said, "Preach through the Gospel of John *again*." So we went back to the Gospel of John. Why? Believers want to see Christ. It's His beauty that overwhelms them. He's the one they love. Like Peter, they love Christ.

There is tremendous joy in having a congregation that loves Christ, because that love compels the people to honor and serve Him. So don't give your congregation some emotional, sentimental buzz. As a preacher, it is your duty and privilege to show them Christ.

That concludes our tale of two preachers. Until the end, Judas and Peter were indistinguishable to their close friends. But as it turned out, Judas belonged to Satan, and Peter belonged to the Savior.

## Last Words

Charles Templeton died in 2001 at the age of 86. We have only one quote from him as he was dying. He said of Jesus, "I miss Him."[2] I think that's what Judas will say forever as well: "I miss Jesus."

You don't need to miss Jesus. You can be in His presence forever. Don't be a defecting preacher. Hold up Jesus for your people so they can love Him like you love Him.

# PRAYER

Father, we thank You for the beauty, power, and clarity of Scripture. We are so blessed. This Book is overwhelming in its power. Thank You for the tale of two preachers that You've reminded us of once again. One day, we want to gather with all those preachers who are around Peter. May no one in this place meet Judas; and may You help us to lift up Christ to our people so they can see the one to whom they can give all their love forever. We thank You. We love You. Though we don't love You as we should, help us to love You more. Amen.

# Notes

## Chapter 1—Preach the Word (John MacArthur)

1. Martin Luther, as quoted in John Blanchard, comp., *Gathered Gold* (Welwyn, England: Evangelical Press, 1984), 238.

2. John Warwick Montgomery, *Damned Through the Church* (Minneapolis: Bethany Fellowship, 1970).

3. Marvin Richardson Vincent, *Word Studies in the New Testament*, vol. 4 (New York: Charles Scribner's Sons, 1887), 321.

4. Christopher Catherwood, *Five Evangelical Leaders* (Wheaton, IL: Harold Shaw, 1985), 170.

## Chapter 2—The Call of God (Mark Dever)

1. Evan Esar, *20,000 Quips & Quotes* (Basking Ridge, NJ: Barnes & Noble, 1994), 224.

2. James Rankin Young, *History of Our War with Spain* (Chicago: Monroe Book Company, 1898), 73.

3. Clifton Fadiman and Andre Bernard, *Bartlett's Book of Anecdotes* (New York: Little, Brown, 2000), 465.

4. Henry Kissinger, *Diplomacy* (New York: Simon & Schuster, 1994).

5. James Gilchrist Lawson, *Deeper Experiences of Famous Christians* (Anderson, IN: The Warner Press, 1911), 303.

6. Jonathan Edwards, *Sinners in the Hands of an Angry God*, 1741.

7. Fadiman and Bernard, *Bartlett's Book of Anecdotes*, 160.

8. Jonathan Edwards, *The Justice of God in the Damnation of Sinners*, 1734.

9. Augustine, *Confessions*, X, 31.

## Chapter 3—Epitaph of a Faithful Preacher (John MacArthur)

1. Napoleon Bonaparte, cited in Samuel Austin Allibone, *Great Authors of All Ages* (Philadelphia: J.B. Lippincott Company, 1889), 293.

2. Cited in Samuel Clement Fessenden, *Selections from the Speeches, Sermons, Addresses, Etc.* (New York: Wm. P. Tomlinson, 1869), 172.

3. Benjamin Franklin wrote this epitaph while he was still alive. It appears not on his original gravestone, but on a memorial plaque.

4. Robert Browning, "Incident of the French Camp," cited in Edmund Clarence Stedman, ed., *A Victorian Anthology, 1837-1895*, vol. 2 (Cambridge: Riverside Press, 1895), 346.

5. Rudyard Kipling, *The Works of Rudyard Kipling* (Hertfordshire, Great Britain: Wordsworth Editions Limited), 605-06.

## Chapter 4—Bring the Book (Steven J. Lawson)

1. J.H. Merle D'Aubigne, *The Reformation in England*, ed. S.M. Houghton, vol. 1, reprint (Edinburgh: The Banner of Truth, 1972), 143.

2. Philip Schaff, "Modern Christianity: The German Reformation," in *History of the Christian Church*, vol. 6, 2nd edition (New York: Charles Scribner's Sons, 1901), 17.

3. James Montgomery Boice, *Whatever Happened to the Gospel of Grace?* (Wheaton, IL: Crossway, 2009), 83-84.

4. "Mr. Spurgeon as a Literary Man," in *The Autobiography of Charles H. Spurgeon, Compiled from His Letters, Diaries, and Records by His Wife and Private Secretary*, vol. 4, 1878–1892 (Cincinnati, OH: Curtis & Jennings, 1900), 268.

5. Martyn Lloyd-Jones, *Preaching and Preachers* (Grand Rapids: Zondervan, 1971), 24-25.

6. Martin Luther, as cited in *More Gathered Gold: A Treasury of Quotations for Christians*, comp. John Blanchard (Hertsfordshire, England: Evangelical Press, 1986), 243.

7. Phillips Brooks, *Lectures on Preaching* (New York: Dutton, 1877), 59.

8. John MacArthur, *Why One Way?* (Nashville: W Publishing Group, 2002), 34.

9. MacArthur, *Why One Way?*, 41-42.

10. Martin Luther, "On God's Sovereignty," in *Luther's Works*, 51:77.

## Chapter 5—Preaching and the Sovereignty of God (R.C. Sproul)

1. D. James Kennedy, *Evangelism Explosion* (Wheaton, IL: Tyndale, 1977).

## Chapter 6—Has Any People Heard the Voice of God Speaking…and Survived? (Albert Mohler Jr.)

1. Francis A. Schaeffer, *He Is There and He Is Not Silent* (Carol Stream, IL: Tyndale, 1972).

2. Carl F.H. Henry, *God, Revelation, and Authority*, 6 vols. (Wheaton, IL: Crossway, 1999).

## Chapter 7—The Passion and Power of Apostolic Preaching (Steven J. Lawson)

1. Richard Baxter, as cited in Charles Bridges, *The Christian Ministry* (London: Banner of Truth, 1967), 318.

2. R.C. Sproul, *The Preacher and Preaching*, ed. Samuel T. Logan Jr. (Phillipsburg, NJ: Presbyterian & Reformed, 1986), 113.

3. Walter C. Kaiser, *Toward an Exegetical Theology* (Grand Rapids: Baker, 1981), 239.

4. Martyn Lloyd-Jones, *Preaching and Preachers* (Grand Rapids: Zondervan, 1972), 97.

5. John Calvin, *Acts*, The Crossway Classic Commentaries, eds. Alister McGrath and J.I. Packer (Wheaton, IL: Crossway, 1995), 33.

6. Iain H. Murray, *The Forgotten Spurgeon* (Edinburgh: Banner of Truth, 2009).

7. See at http://www.spurgeon.org/sermons/0027.html/. Accessed July 1, 2014.

8. Charles Spurgeon, "The Eternal Name," preached May 27, 1855 at Exeter Hall.

9. Richard Baxter, as cited in Lloyd-Jones, *Preaching & Preachers*, 100.

## Chapter 8—Preaching in the Spirit's Power (Tom Pennington)

1. Meuser, Fred W., *Luther the Preacher* (Minneapolis: Augsburg Publishing House, 1983), 51.

2. Stephen Pogoloff, *Logos and Sophia: The Rhetorical Situation in 1 Corinthians* (Atlanta, GA: Scholars Press, 1992), Duane Litfin, *St. Paul's Theology of Proclamation* (Cambridge: Cambridge University Press, 1994), Michael Bullmore, *St. Paul's Theology of Rhetorical Style* (San Francisco: International Scholars Publications, 1995).

3. A. Duane Litfin, *St. Paul's Theology of Proclamation: 1 Corinthians 1–4 and Greco-Roman Rhetoric* (Cambridge: Cambridge University Press, 1994), 207-8.

4. Anthony C. Thiselton, *The First Epistle to the Corinthians* in The New International Greek Testament Commentary, eds. I. Howard Marshall and Donald A. Hagner (Grand Rapids: Eerdmans, 2000), 218.

5. John Stott, *Between Two Worlds: The Challenge of Preaching Today* (Grand Rapids: Eerdmans, 1994), 325.

6. Charles H. Spurgeon, *Christ Precious to Believers* (March 13, 1859), a sermon given at Music Hall, Royal Surrey Gardens.

7. D.A. Carson, *The Cross and Christian Ministry: An Exposition of Passages from 1 Corinthians* (Grand Rapids: Baker, 2004), 26.

8. Gordan D. Fee, *The First Epistle to the Corinthians* in The New International Commentary on the New Testament (Grand Rapids: Eerdmans, 1987), 94.

9. Litfin, *St. Paul's Theology of Proclamation*, 209.

10. Ewald M. Plass, *What Luther Says* (St. Louis, MO: Concordia Publishing House, 2006), 1131.

11. John Calvin, *Commentary on the Epistles of Paul the Apostle to the Corinthians* in Calvin's Commentaries, vol. 20, trans. Rev. John Pringle (Grand Rapids: Baker, 2003), 99.

12. Stott, *Between Two Worlds*, 320.

13. Stott, *Between Two Worlds*, 321.

14. Fee, *The First Epistle to the Corinthians*, 96.

## Chapter 9—The Art of Crafting a Life-Changing Sermon (Rick Holland)

1. Harry Emerson Fosdick, "What Is the Matter with Preaching?" in Mike Graves, ed. *What's the Matter with Preaching Today?* (Louisville: Westminster John Knox Press, 2004), 9.

2. George Marsden, *The Salvation of Souls* (Wheaton, IL: Crossway, 2002), 11-12.

3. Jonathan Edwards, as cited in Marsden, *The Salvation of Souls*, 11-12.

4. John Piper, *The Supremacy of God in Preaching* (Grand Rapids: Baker, 2004), 57.

5. Alex Montoya, *Preaching with Passion* (Grand Rapids: Kregel, 2000), 151.

6. Jonathan Edwards, as cited in Marsden, *The Salvation of Souls*, 12.

## Chapter 10—Preaching as a Dying Man to Dying Men (Alex Montoya)

1. For a more complete treatment on the subject of preaching, see Alex Montoya's book *Preaching with Passion* (Grand Rapids: Kregel Academic, 2007).

2. D. Martyn Lloyd-Jones, *Preaching & Preachers* (Grand Rapids: Zondervan, 2011), 100.

3. Jerry Vines and Jim Shaddix, *Power in the Pulpit: How to Prepare and Deliver Expository Sermons* (Chicago: Moody Press, 1999), 347.

4. Lloyd-Jones, *Preaching & Preachers*, 93.

5. John Broadus, *On the Preparation and Delivery of Sermons* (New York: Harper & Row, 1944), 252-53.

6. Charles H. Spurgeon, *Lectures to My Students* (Grand Rapids: Zondervan, 1954), 307.

7. Lloyd-Jones, *Preaching & Preachers*, 87.

8. W.A. Criswell, *Criswell's Guidebook for Pastors* (Nashville: Broadman & Holman, 1980), 54.

9. David L. Larsen, *The Company of Preachers* (Grand Rapids: Kregel, 1998), 159.

10. Richard Baxter, *The Reformed Pastor* (Edinburg: Banner of Truth Trust, 1974), 61-63.

11. Robert Murray M'Cheyne, *The Works of Rev. Robert Murray McCheyne: Complete in One Volume* (New York: Robert Carter & Brothers, 1874), 211.

12. Lloyd-Jones, *Preaching & Preachers*, 92.

13. Lloyd-Jones, *Preaching & Preachers*, 83.

14. David Eby, *Power Preaching for Church Growth* (Fearn, UK: Mentor, 1996), 49.

15. Spurgeon, *Lectures to My Students*, 309.

## Chapter 11—Apollos: An Authentic Minister of the Gospel (Albert Mohler Jr.)

1. See Ezekiel 18:13; 33:4.

2. Charles H. Spurgeon, *Lectures to My Students* (Peabody, MA: Hendrickson, 2011), 29-32.

3. As told in a 1943 UP news story, cited in Charles M. Province, *The Unknown Patton* (New York: Random House Value Publishing, 1988), 8-9.

4. John Piper and Wayne Grudem, *Recovering Biblical Manhood and Womanhood* (Wheaton, IL: Crossway, 1991).

## Chapter 12—A Tale of Two Preachers ( John MacArthur)

1. Marshall Frady, *Billy Graham: A Parable of American Righteousness* (New York: Simon & Schuster, 2006), 161.

2. Lee Strobel, *The Case for Faith: A Journalist Investigates the Toughest Objections to Christianity* (Grand Rapids: Zondervan, 2000), 18.

# PART 2:

# THE SHEPHERD AS LEADER

# 1

# HUMILITY: AN ESSENTIAL FOR MINISTRY

*John MacArthur*
*Shepherds' Conference 2005*

*Luke 9:46–56*

It is easy to be proud when we are right. Our theology is right. Our understanding of the Word of God is right. Our view of Scripture as the inerrant revelation of the holy God is right. Our understanding of the gospel is right. We have the right message to preach to the world. It is difficult to be humble when we are right, for we can then become intolerant and heavy-handed. The reminder to be humble is a helpful one. The reminder to speak the truth in love and to be patient is necessary. Ironically, we live in a world that exalts self-love, self-satisfaction, self-promotion. For the world, it is considered virtuous to exalt self. But as pastors, we are forced to live in a counterculture way by being models of selfless humility in a world that sees that as a weakness.

## The Perils of Pride

Children of God are commanded to be humble because Scripture sees pride as an ugly sin that the devil committed along with the other angels who joined his rebellion. Pride is the sin that led to Adam and Eve being thrown out of the Garden. It is that damning sin that produced rebellion against God and His law, for it was pride that sought to dethrone God, strike at His absolute perfect sovereignty, and replace Him with self. This kind of pride naturally grips every human heart.

Pride is the reason it is difficult to come to Christ. After all, who wants to hate and deny self? Yet Jesus taught just that message—a message that one cannot come into His kingdom if he does not hate himself. It is tough to refuse to associate any longer with the person you are—to set aside your own desires, ambitions, dreams, goals, and come empty-handed, broken, and contrite to Christ.

It wasn't too many years ago when a wide-eyed first-year seminary student asked me, "Dr. MacArthur, how did you finally overcome pride?" A genuine but silly question because no one will ever overcome pride until this fallen flesh is forsaken. Battling pride will continue until the day of glorification. However, this does not give people an excuse to hold onto their pride. Pride has to be broken for individuals to be saved, and it has to be continually broken for individuals to be sanctified.

### The Pastor's Pride

My fear is that pastors who attend conferences like the Shepherds' Conference, who read the right books, and who accumulate the right knowledge may be motivated and energized to go out and fight the battle for the truth in the wrong way. I fear that well-equipped pastors are often too ready to pound on people who are slow to learn and accept certain truths. Pastor, the more you know and the more mature you are, then the more impact your ministry has, the more blessing you experience upon your life, and the more likely you are to feed your pride.

This is what the apostle Paul wrote about in 2 Corinthians when the Lord sent him a messenger of Satan; I believe

that is a reference to a group of false teachers who came to Corinth and troubled the church. The chaos this group caused devastated the apostle. Paul experienced much agony as he watched a church be shredded by false teaching—a church into which he had invested so much of his life. He even prayed three times for the Lord to remove this thorn, but he recognized that the Lord had sent it to pierce his otherwise proud flesh. Paul said the reason God sent this message of Satan was to keep him from exalting himself.

---

**It is when you come to the end of yourself that you experience the power of God.**

---

Paul had seen many revelations, had been to heaven and back, witnessed things unspeakable, was caught up to the third heaven, and had personal private appearances of the resurrected Lord Jesus Christ (2 Corinthians 12:1-7). This man had plenty to be proud of, and when the Lord needed to humble His otherwise proud servant, He sent a demon in the purposes of His providence. In the midst of this pain, Paul knew that God's grace was sufficient and that God's power would be perfected in his weakness. Beloved, it is when you come to the end of yourself that you experience the power of God.

## A Lesson on Humility

In Luke chapter 9, Jesus taught a lesson on humility. At this point, the disciples had been with Jesus for more than two-and-a-half years, twenty-four hours a day, seven days a week. They were constantly in the presence of Jesus, and every location was a classroom and everything was a lesson. These followers experienced relentless teaching, and everything Jesus taught them was absolutely right. Every word Jesus spoke came from a divine mind and because of this, the disciples were taught perfectly.

In addition, the disciples were given authority to represent Jesus Christ by proclaiming the gospel of the kingdom from town to town and village to village. These men were given so much authority that if they went into a town that did not receive their message, they were to pronounce a judgment on those people, shake the dust off their feet, and leave. The disciples were also given the power to cast out demons and to heal diseases. Common, ordinary men received an immense amount of truth, authority, and divine power to wield in the name of Jesus Christ. As a result, their flesh was having a difficult time fighting pride, and it was necessary for our Lord to teach them what it meant to be humble. Jesus did exactly that in Luke chapter 9, and Jesus' class on humility applies to us as well.

In the beginning of Luke 9 we read that the disciples were given power and authority to cast out demons, heal diseases, proclaim the kingdom, pronounce judgment on cities, and shake the dust off their feet. With this power and authority they went "preaching the gospel and healing everywhere" (Luke 9:6). To add to that, Peter, John, and James were taken up to a mountain with Jesus, where He pulled aside His flesh and was transfigured (verses 28-29). On that mountain, those three disciples saw the shining glory of God and met Moses and Elijah. These men experienced an astonishing, unique, and unequaled event.

With all that they had experienced, it was difficult for the disciples to stay humble. So as they came down the mountain, they had an argument "as to which of them might be the greatest" (9:46). You can imagine what was said during that argument. One of them may have said, "Well, you never know, it could be me." And James could have responded, "Well if it was going to be you, you would have been on the mountain with us." Instantly, the group would have been narrowed to three. One might have said, "We were taken up on the mountain, you weren't." Then another may have chimed in, "In the last village we visited, how many people did you heal?" The answer would've come, "Well, I had some minor healings." The retort, "Ha! I had five major healings." One can just imagine the argument taking place between the disciples.

It is important to remember that the disciples are listed in Matthew, Mark,

Luke, and Acts. In each of the lists, three groups of four disciples are mentioned. The groups appear in the order of their descending intimacy with Christ. Every time those lists are given, each disciple stays in his group, and the first name in each group never changes. This means that there were leaders over each of the groups. Peter was the first name listed in the most intimate group. He was the leader amongst the other leaders. So to put it simply, there was a pecking order. The first group was very bold. Peter was in this group along with James and John, also known as the Sons of Thunder. And because the disciples lived in a world of hierarchical understanding, they were arguing over who the greatest was by comparing all of their spiritual experiences, opportunities to display power, personal moments with Jesus, and even the incredible event on the mountain.

Evidently the argument was so intense that James and John asked their mother to go to Jesus and plead their case to sit at His right and left hands. The Sons of Thunder did this because their mother was related to Jesus' mother, and they assumed they had the inside family track. These men had the right message and were God's chosen representatives, yet they still faced the issue of pride. In this text, Jesus taught the disciples—and us—a needed lesson on humility.

### Pride Ruins Unity

The first principle Jesus taught is that pride ruins unity. Luke wrote, "An argument started among them" (9:46). The Greek word translated "argument" entails a battle in which unity is fractured. The disciples were a team, and they were not supposed to be competing with one another. This first generation of gospel preachers needed to give their lives for Christ and yield their hearts to one another. Instead, they were destroying their unity in the midst of a crucial mission. Pride is capable of destroying the most intimate kind of unity. Even Jesus, while on the verge of suffering on the cross, spoke to the disciples about His own personal suffering yet could not hold their attention because they were too busy alienating one another with their desire for personal glory. Pride has the capability of destroying relationships.

For example, pride destroyed relationships between the believers in Corinth. In 2 Corinthians 12:20, Paul wrote that he feared a visit to their church because he was concerned that he would find among them strife, jealousy, anger, disputes, slander, gossip, arrogance, and disturbances. He did not know if he could handle the factions that had stemmed from pride.

Pride is capable of causing much harm, and that is why Paul wrote in Philippians 1:27 that believers were to be "striving together for the faith of the gospel." He urged the Philippians to not compete with one another but to maintain unity:

If there is any encouragement in

Christ, if there is any consolation of love, if there is any fellowship of the Spirit, if any affection and compassion, make my joy complete by being of the same mind, maintaining the same love, united in spirit, intent on one purpose. Do nothing from selfishness or empty conceit, but with humility of mind regard one another as more important than yourselves; do not merely look out for your own personal interests, but also for the interests of others. Have this attitude in yourselves which was also in Christ Jesus, who, although He existed in the form of God, did not regard equality with God a thing to be grasped, but emptied Himself, taking the form of a bond-servant, and being made in the likeness of men. Being found in appearance as a man, He humbled Himself by becoming obedient to the point of death, even death on a cross (2:1–8).

As a pastor you can preach on the topic of unity until you are blue in the face, but as long as pride exists in the church, it will continue to destroy relationships.

## Pride Raises Relativity

The second principle Jesus taught is that pride raises relativity. The essence of the argument is to determine who is comparatively greater. Pride desires superiority over others, seeks to elevate itself, and compares itself with everyone else. That is exactly what Jesus accused the Pharisees of doing. These leaders loved to be noticed by men, loved the place of honor at banquets, loved the chief seats in the synagogues, loved respectful greetings in the marketplace, and loved to be called rabbi. A proud heart is incessantly fighting for the top and raising relativity by comparing itself with others. However, Jesus had and continues to have a different definition of greatness: "Everyone who exalts himself will be humbled, and he who humbles himself will be exalted" (Luke 14:11).

## Pride Reveals Depravity

A third principle Jesus taught is that pride reveals sin and depravity. Luke wrote that Jesus knew "what they were thinking in their heart" (9:47). Jesus always knows what is in the heart of a person. How would you like to spend three years with God constantly reading your thoughts? That may be the greatest evidence of God's grace in using imperfect vessels. Though He knows all our thoughts, He still utilizes fallible and weak people.

No matter how much you may try to avoid creating disunity or some sort of spiritual pecking order, given enough time, the sins of the heart will still come out. Time and truth go hand in hand. A proud pastor may keep his pride under wraps for a while, but eventually the congregation will find out that he is driven by a proud heart. That is one of the main reasons some pastors have a short ministry.

The Lord, in His response, was not reacting only because of the damage pride causes, nor because of the relativity that occurs, but because of its sinfulness. Jesus knew what the disciples were thinking in their hearts as He "took a child and stood him by His side" (9:47). It was a child small enough to hold (see Mark 9:36), and yet grown enough to stand up before Jesus. This image depicts a person who comes to the Lord with no achievements, no accomplishments, and void of any self-worth. God does not care how many degrees you have, how widely you've read, how clever you are in communication, or how strong a leader you are. The only way you can approach Him is as a meek and humble child.

In that culture, children were considered the weakest, most ignored, and most vulnerable of all people. They were viewed as having little value, and many of them didn't survive to become adults. Jesus used this little child to teach the disciples that they were viewing themselves as kings when they were acting like children. The sin of pride fails to recognize the complete and utter dependence on God that a person needs to have. Pride reveals sin and depravity.

### Pride Rejects Deity

Fourth, pride rejects deity. Jesus said in Luke 9:48, "Whoever receives this child in My name receives Me, and whoever receives Me receives Him who sent Me." The child is representative of those who are Jesus' disciples. Jesus made it clear that unless one becomes like a child, he will not enter the kingdom. Therefore, those who reject Christ reject the presence of God in other believers. These children of God are precious to the Lord, and they must be precious to us as well.

As pastors, may we never say that we do not have time for other Christians, because the Holy Spirit dwells in every believer. The disciples felt that Jesus was wasting His time by interacting with children, but note His response to them: "Permit the children to come to Me; do not hinder them, for the kingdom of God belongs to such as these" (Mark 10:14). We must be very careful when it comes to rejecting, offending, or belittling other believers, because when we do, we're offending Christ, who dwells in them. Pride thinks it's better than another believer in whom Christ dwells, and thus pride rejects deity.

### Pride Reverses Reality

The fifth principle Jesus taught is that pride reverses reality. "The one who is least among all of you, this is the one who is great" (Luke 9:48). This truth upsets the world and overturns conventional wisdom. Worldly wisdom claims that whoever is the most popular, the most widely known, the most influential, and the most powerful is the greatest. Pride attempts to reverse the reality that it's the servant who is the greatest. Paul stressed this truth in 1 Corinthians 1:26-28 when he wrote about the Lord establishing His church with not many noble, not many mighty, but instead the lowly, the base, and the weak. He did this so that the glory might be His and that there would be no other explanation for the existence of the church other than the purposes of God.

Beloved, we are the lowly and the least. Our battle should focus on seeing who can serve the most, because "whoever wishes to become great among you shall be your servant" (Matthew 20:26). Pride attempts to reverse reality, and this is seen even in the Christian world. People who are honored, popular, and have accomplished all kinds of things tend to become relentlessly self-promoting. As ministers of God, this is a battle we have to fight, and we are to strive to be lowly like Jesus.

### Pride Reacts with Exclusivity

Sixth, pride reacts with exclusivity. For this lesson we look at Luke 9:49: "John answered and said, 'Master, we saw someone casting out demons in Your name; and we tried to prevent him because he does not follow along with us.'" Here we see John reacting with exclusivity. John was a dynamic, driven man; he was not meek. What did not help was that he had just come down from the mountain of transfiguration. It is in the midst of all this that John came across someone casting out demons in the name of Jesus Christ, and

John attempted to hinder him because that person was not one of the disciples who followed Jesus. John basically said, "Hey, you're not in our group. You don't wear our label."

We read that this individual not only tried to cast out demons, he was casting them out in the name of Jesus. Maybe he was one of the seventy who were sent out, but he was not a part of the Twelve. To be doing something in Jesus' name indicates consistency with Jesus' identity and mission. Apparently this individual was a believer, though not an apostle, and he was serving for the glory of Christ. The original Greek text indicates that the man kept doing what he was doing, and John and some others were trailing along, trying to stop him. They did this because he wasn't in the group.

Pride is always sectarian and narrow. This man was not an unbeliever like Simon Magus, who was trying to buy the Holy Spirit's power (Acts 8:18-19). However, he was not directly affiliated with Jesus' group of disciples, and John had a problem with that.

I sometimes get questioned why I associate with a specific organization or person, and why they associate with me. If I were to limit my associations only to people in my group, then the world would be a lonely place. Pride wants to do exactly that. Pride says, "I know more than you. I don't know if I can work with you. You need correction. You need help. You're not quite there. Once you get there, then I'll work with you." Humility says,

"If you're doing this in the name of Christ and doing your best to serve Christ, I'll come alongside you," because there is latitude and generosity among the humble.

Jesus made it clear that there is no middle ground. If someone is for Christ and is doing his best to serve Christ, then stop trying to hinder him. Jesus replied to John, "Do not hinder him; for he who is not against you is for you" (Luke 9:50). The true church is a very diverse place. I have been all over the world, and it is evident that cultures, styles, and expressions of worship vary from region to region. Though I might do certain things differently, if they are for Christ, then I am called to not hinder that effort. But it's difficult to be humble when you think you're right. We must humble ourselves and realize that we are all still in-process.

---

**Humility belongs to those who understand that the way down is the way up.**

---

Humility pursues unity by seeking to exalt others. Humility refuses relative comparisons. Humility purifies the inner person of all selfishness. Humility belongs to those who exalt God alone as the object of worship, and recognizes that they should not reject fellow believers, but honor and love them. Humility belongs to those who understand that

the way down is the way up. Humility is characteristic of those who embrace the diversity of true believers.

*Pride Restrains Mercy*

The seventh and final principle Jesus taught is that pride restrains mercy. As we approach the end of Luke 9, we read that the Galilean ministry has ended and the days were approaching for Jesus' ascension to Jerusalem and ultimately the cross (verse 51). The scene changes, but the lesson on humility continues, and here we find an illustration of how pride restrains mercy. To show mercy is to be generous, kind, and selfless. The opposite is a lack of mercy, which is reserved for the rankest kind of people—those filled with vengeance, vitriol, and viciousness. On this occasion, we read that some of the disciples were merciless: "He sent messengers on ahead of Him, and they went and entered a village of the Samaritans to make arrangements for Him. But they did not receive Him, because He was traveling toward Jerusalem. When His disciples James and John saw this, they said, 'Lord, do You want us to command fire to come down from heaven and consume them?'" (Luke 9:52-54).

The Samaritans were a mixed race of Semite pagans left over from the Northern Kingdom. After the Northern Kingdom was invaded by the Assyrians, the people who were left intermarried with pagans and became loyal to the Assyrian king. They were hated by the Jews because they were considered to be half-breeds who had rejected their race and their faith.

While the Jews rejected the Samaritans, Jesus did not. In John 4, we read about ministering to these people because the gospel was intended for the Gentiles too. So in Luke 9, Jesus visited a Samaritan village to preach the kingdom. As He approached, Jesus sent out messengers to make preparations. However, the townspeople rejected Jesus and prevented Him from coming. They refused Him because He was journeying with His face toward Jerusalem, and they despised the Jews. Because the Samaritans were not allowed to worship in Jerusalem, they had to build their own place of worship at Gerazim. To make matters worse, in 128 BC, their temple at Gerazim was destroyed. This made them hate the Jews even more.

When James and John saw this rejection, they asked the Lord, "Do You want us to command fire to come down from heaven and consume them?" Well, that's a strange reaction to unbelief. They didn't show a missionary heart. And when did these disciples ever have the ability to express such a power? Where did they get that idea? Remember that they had just been with Elijah at the transfiguration, and most likely they were recalling an incident that is recorded in 2 Kings 1.

There, we read that Ahaziah, the king of the Northern Kingdom, sent 50 men along with a captain to take Elijah prisoner. When the captain saw Elijah, he said, "O man of God, the king says, 'Come down'" (verse 9), which was another way of saying, "You're under arrest." Elijah answered, "If I am a man of God, let fire come down from heaven and consume you and your fifty" (verse 10). And fire came down from heaven, and consumed the men. The foolish king sent another group of men, and the captain of this group said, "O man of God, thus says the king, 'Come down quickly'" (verse 11). Elijah answered, "If I am a man of God, let fire come down from heaven and consume you and your fifty" (verse 12). Once again the fire of God came down from heaven, and this group was consumed.

The king sent a third group. At least this captain was rational—he came before Elijah, bowed on his knees, and pleaded, "O man of God, please let my life and the lives of these fifty servants of yours be precious in your sight" (verse 13). He continued, "Behold fire came down from heaven and consumed the first two captains of fifty with their fifties: but now let my life be precious in your sight" (verse 14). As a result, the angel of the Lord said to Elijah:

"Go down with him; do not be afraid of him." So he arose and went down with him to the king. Then he said to him, "Thus says the LORD, 'Because you have sent messengers to inquire of Baalzebub, the god of Ekron—is it because there is no God in Israel to inquire of His word?—therefore you shall not come down from the bed where you have gone up, but shall surely die'" (verses 15-16).

We learn in verse 17 that the king died "according to the word of the LORD."

Going back to Luke 9, the disciples remembered what Elijah had done and wanted to call fire down from heaven as well. Instead of receiving confirmation, however, the disciples received a rebuke from the Lord: "He turned and rebuked them, and said, 'You do not know what kind of spirit you are of; for the Son of Man did not come to destroy men's lives, but to save them.' And they went on to another village" (verses 55-56).

Jesus was on a mission of mercy, but the disciples' pride restrained their mercy. We can never turn the opponents of the gospel into the enemy. If we attack everyone who disagrees with us by labeling them, assaulting them, and calling them names, then we are distancing the mission field from ourselves. The lost are not the enemy; they are the mission field. The fire will come one day, but until that day, we are commissioned to participate in a mission of mercy.

That little Samaritan village was saved from physical fire. And later we read in Acts 8 that Philip, a deacon in the early church, preached in Samaria. Perhaps many of the Samaritans were also saved from the eternal flame by Philip's preaching.

As pastors, we are on a mission of mercy, and we cannot alienate the very people we are called to reach. Yet pride will do just that because pride restrains mercy. We know the truth, and we have the truth. But we should not let this knowledge make us proud; rather, we are to preach the truth with love and humility. Jesus said, "Be merciful as your Father in heaven is merciful. And be humble, as Christ who humbled himself."

# PRAYER

Father, Your Word is precious. Your Word is rich. Your Word is powerful. May we learn well these principles on humility. Jesus could have brought down fire from heaven, but instead, He just went to another place. Help us manifest all the characteristics of humility and none of the ugly characteristics of pride. We commend ourselves again to Your grace and to Your Word, which is able to build us up and give an inheritance to us, which we wait for with joy. In Christ's name, Amen.

# 2

# Purity in the Camp

*Ligon Duncan*
*Shepherds' Conference 2007*

*Numbers 5:11-31*

For the last eight years, I have consecutively preached my way through a book of the Pentateuch on Sunday mornings, followed by a book of the Psalms on Sunday evenings.

While preaching through the Pentateuch, I dreaded coming to the book of Numbers. My friend John Currid, who is in the midst of writing a commentary on the whole of the Pentateuch, wrote on the books in this order: Genesis, Exodus, Leviticus, Deuteronomy, and then he went back to Numbers. So even a scholar of the Old Testament like John Currid approached the book of Numbers with some fear and trepidation.

Numbers may well not be your favorite book in the Bible, and perhaps you are not particularly excited about learning from it. You might not have read the book in a long time, much less preached a sermon from it. The book consists of 36 chapters, 1288 verses, laws, sand, desert, grumbling, and wandering. Doesn't sound too hopeful, does it?

But I want you to see how important, exciting, practical, and applicable the book of Numbers is. Yet at the same time, there are some challenges facing us when we come to it.

## Challenges to the Book of Numbers
### A Book of History

For one thing, Numbers is a book of history, and in the modern world, we dislike history because we don't know much about it. At the beginning of the twentieth century, Henry Ford taught us that history is bunk. We rarely think that the events that happened 20 years ago have anything to do with today, and if they do, we still choose to not remember them. One British scholar, Ambrose Bierce, said, with tongue firmly planted in cheek, that "war is God's way of teaching Americans geography."[1]

I would add history to that statement as well.

Like it or not, the Book that we preach is a book of history. Even if you don't love history, biblical history is like none you've ever read. Californians will remember their former governor, Ronald Reagan, who was capable of telling history through stories that would draw you into the experience. Moses was able to do that as well. He told history in such a way that he planted you into the middle of the story. He made you realize that these are your people; this is your story. I grew up in the Deep South. My father used to take me to graveyards and say, "Son, these are your people." (Trust me when I say Southerners are strange.) Moses, from 3400 years ago, was saying to us, "These are your people. Learn from them."

### A Book of Disobedience

Another challenge to teaching, preaching, and learning from the book of Numbers is that it's filled with stories about people behaving terribly. Who wants to hear about that? Instead, let's be positive, optimistic, upbeat, and hopeful about human nature. But we're pastors. Like our Master, we have not been called to the righteous, but to sinners. Even in our

churches there are individuals still battling with indwelling sin. Individuals who, by the powerful operation of the Holy Spirit, have been called to faith in Christ and united with Him. Individuals who have been gloriously converted from the inside out by that sovereign regenerating work of the Holy Spirit, yet still struggle with sin.

The pastor's life consists of dealing with people behaving badly. What better book to go to than Numbers? We are just like the Israelites, and though we'd rather not think about our sin, it is so important that we do. We need to think about it, we need to own it, we need to see its danger and its consequences, and we need to repent and deal with it. Numbers will help us do that.

### A Book Uniquely Organized

Third, this book is filled with stories, and the flow of these stories is sometimes interrupted by what seem like arbitrary sections of laws and bizarre procedures. Moses was not only a great storyteller, he was also an excellent organizer. You will find that the story sections of this book are related to the law sections of this book. And the law sections are related to the procedure sections. There is an underlying logic to it all. Of course, Moses had a great ghostwriter: God, the Holy Spirit, authored these words. And once you understand the logic of the organization, you appreciate the book all the more because of the different ways that Moses drove home the truth.

## Nine Things Paul Said About Numbers

Just in case you're not yet convinced of the importance of studying Numbers, I want to take you to the New Testament—to the apostle Paul and 1 Corinthians 10. After that, I want to look at a hymn that we all know and love. All this is to try to convince you of how applicable, helpful, important, and edifying Numbers is.

Look with me at 1 Corinthians 10:1-13. Everything that Paul talked about in this passage happened in the wilderness and was recorded by Moses in either Exodus or Numbers. The key point that the apostle wanted to make to the Christians in Corinth comes right out of the book of Numbers. Paul was saying how Numbers is important, helpful, applicable, and edifying. But he said more than that—he was telling us that the book of Numbers was written for us. He said that the events recorded in Numbers happened for our benefit, and that God wants us to learn from them how we are to live today.

Let's look at what Paul wrote:

I do not want you to be unaware, brethren, that our fathers were all under the cloud and all passed through the sea; and all were baptized into Moses in the cloud and in the sea; and all ate the same spiritual food; and all drank the same spiritual drink, for they were drinking from a spiritual rock which followed them; and

the rock was Christ. Nevertheless, with most of them God was not well-pleased; for they were laid low in the wilderness.

Now these things happened as examples for us, so that we would not crave evil things as they also craved. Do not be idolaters, as some of them were; as it is written, "The people sat down to eat and drink, and stood up to play." Nor let us act immorally, as some of them did, and twenty-three thousand fell in one day. Nor let us try the Lord, as some of them did, and were destroyed by the serpents. Nor grumble, as some of them did, and were destroyed by the destroyer. Now these things happened to them as an example, and they were written for our instruction, upon whom the ends of the ages have come. Therefore let him who thinks he stands take heed that he does not fall. No temptation has overtaken you but such as is common to man; and God is faithful, who will not allow you to be tempted beyond what you are able, but with the temptation will provide the way of escape also, so that you will be able to endure it.

I want you to notice nine things in this passage that the apostle Paul said about the book of Numbers.

> Our focus should be on the redeeming
> work of Christ and how that particular
> story contributes to the development
> of that grand biblical theme.

*First,* notice Paul wrote that the events that occurred in the wilderness serve as examples "for our instruction." It's very popular today, in some circles, to say, "All our preaching must be redemptive historical," in the sense that it only draws attention to the big picture of God's redeeming purposes in any particular passage. This view endorses that there should be no application and we should never preach examples from the Old Testament because that's moralism. Instead, our focus should be on the redeeming work of Christ and how that particular story contributes to the development of that grand biblical theme.

There are many helpful things emphasized by those who are interested in promoting redemptive historical preaching, and it is a helpful corrective to non-cross-centered, non-gospel-centered exposition. But it has a slight problem, and that problem is with the New Testament. The New Testament uses examples from the Old Testament and applies them to Christians, both negatively and positively. That's exactly what the apostle Paul was doing in 1 Corinthians 10:1-13. He was referencing what the children of Israel did in the wilderness, as recorded in Numbers, and he wrote to the Corinthians and to

us and said, "See what they did? Don't do that."

Jesus did the same thing when He turned to His disciples and said, "Remember Lot's wife" (Luke 17:32). James did the same and gave a positive example when he said, "I have to get these guys to pray like Christians. Let's see what illustration could I use...Elijah! Pray like Elijah. There was a drought in the land until that man started praying, and God sent down rain. That's how you pray, Christians—like Elijah" (see James 5:16-18).

The New Testament is filled with examples of the inspired writers of Scripture using the Old Testament to encourage and to exhort believers to live the Christian life. That's what Paul was doing in 1 Corinthians 10—he said the events that occurred in the wilderness occurred as examples for us (verses 5-6).

*Second,* notice Paul said that the events that occurred in the wilderness were designed to provide a moral warning to us. Look at verse 6: "Now these things happened as examples for us, so that we would not crave evil things as they also craved." Those events served as moral exhortations designed to warn us about the danger of sin.

*Third,* notice again in verse 6 that the apostle did not simply say these things were recorded as examples for us. He wrote, "These things *happened* as examples for us." Our breath ought to be taken away by this; men lost their wives, women lost their husbands, parents lost their children, children lost their parents and their grandparents in the desert. Paul was in no way belittling the experiences of the people of God in the wilderness. But he made it clear that, in God's design, this happened in order that He could give an example to you. That is how much God loves you, and that is how much He cares for you. He does not waste life, for He created it. He does not treat the lives of His people flippantly and glibly, and yet the lives of thousands and thousands of people were affected in the course of His providence. The apostle Paul said, "This happened for you." All the more that we should say, "Those are my people."

*Fourth*, the events of Numbers provide exhortation to Christians. Look at verse 7: "Do not be idolaters, as some of them were." Then look at verse 11: "Now these things happened to them as an example, and were written for our instruction, upon whom the ends of the ages have come." God, in His providence, has in view New Covenant believers in the events recorded in the book of Numbers.

*Fifth*, notice that Paul specifically applied these exhortations to New Testament believers in four areas. One, "do not be idolaters" (verse 7). The whole Bible was written as a full-scale assault on idolatry. The first thing that Paul wanted us to learn from Numbers is not to be idolaters. You can't imagine how crucial this is for life in the Christian congregation. If we're going to be disciples, and not just a bunch of people who merely sit on the pew, we must be committed to

the worship of the one true God in all of life. That means not being idolaters.

Two, Paul declared from the story of the Israelites in the wilderness that we are not to be immoral. Many people under the assault of our toxic culture are beginning to think, *We've been too narrow on moral issues, and the Christian church ought to be big enough to handle the various types of sexual diversities that exist in our culture.* Contrary to that, the apostle Paul wrote in verse 8, "Nor let us act immorally, as some of them did, and twenty-three thousand fell in one day."

Three, notice Paul wrote that we're not to presumptuously test the Lord like Israel did.

And four, we're not to grumble against providence like they did (verses 7-10). Those are the specific ways Paul applied moral exhortation to New Testament believers.

*Sixth*, not only did these events happen for Christians, but we're told in verse 11 that they were *written down* for Christians. God intentionally had these events recorded for us: "Now these things happened to them as an example, and they were written down for our instruction, upon whom the ends of the ages have come." The inscripturation of this story had in view a benefit to God's New Covenant people.

*Seventh*, the apostle Paul warned us in this text against thinking that we will not fall like the Israelites did. "Don't think, New Covenant Christian," he was saying, "that just because you have seen the glories of the cross that you are impervious to the temptation to fall like the children of Israel in the wilderness" (paraphrase).

*Eighth*, we are to learn from the Israelites' temptations and failures in order to escape our own (verse 13). You've heard the platitude that he who does not learn from history is doomed to repeat it. Well, this is the spiritual corollary to that platitude: "Look at their failures. Look at their temptations and escape yours, Christian."

Then *ninth*, the apostle Paul said that Christ is right at the center of this whole wilderness account (verse 4). He's the rock that followed the people. This is all about exalting Christ.

### Hymnal Support

Now, if Paul hasn't convinced you, let me ask you to consider a song found in hymnals. William Williams, the greatest of the Welsh Christian poets, wrote a hymn called "Guide Me, O Thou Great Jehovah." That hymn is the book of Numbers applied to Christians. If you've sung that song before, you've been singing about Numbers being applied to modern-day believers. "Guide Me, O Thou Great Jehovah" is William Williams' Christian meditation on the story that is recorded in Numbers.

### Introducing Numbers 5

I hope by now you are seeing that Numbers is a glorious, profitable, applicable, and exciting book to study. Now we turn to Numbers 5. This chapter can

be outlined into three parts: Verses 1 to 4 recount physical impurities that can defile you and require you to be removed from the camp. Verses 5 to 10 recount certain moral offenses that can defile you and require you to be removed from the camp. And verses 11 to 31 deal with domestic tensions eventuated either by marital infidelity or the fear of it. These sections are grouped in this chapter and have to do with issues that defile the camp.

The first five chapters of Numbers discuss how to live with God in your midst. He is holy, and there are certain requirements for His people to meet so they can be holy as He is. Therefore, chapter 5 is essential because it clarifies what defiles the camp and dishonors God. Consequently, the Israelites were to deal with defiled people with the utmost seriousness.

Numbers 5:1-10 immediately reveals the practical significance of separation from the defiled. The listed physical impurities were a potential danger to the camp, literally to their lives.

There were no antibiotics back then, which meant disease could spread like wildfire through the camp. Coming into contact with the dead and the bacteria that they carried, or a person with a blood disease and the bacteria that he or she carried, or a leper and the dangerous infections that lepers carried could be detrimental to the community. There are obvious reasons why you would want to isolate people with such physical impurities from the camp.

Of course, there is also an obvious theological reason that such separation was to be done. This whole passage is teaching us what God is like. In this context, the emphasis is that God is holy and He is present. Because He is holy and He is present, we must meet certain requirements if we are going to dwell near Him. The laws themselves are God-centered. They point us to Him. They teach us about whom He is and what He has done.

That portion of the chapter is basically self-explanatory. Next, I want to draw your attention to what appears to be a bizarre and seemingly inapplicable section that looks at strained marital relations. Look with me at verses 11 to 31:

Then the LORD spoke to Moses, saying, "Speak to the sons of Israel and say to them, 'If any man's wife goes astray and is unfaithful to him, and a man has intercourse with her and it is hidden from the eyes of her husband and she is undetected, although she has defiled herself, and there is no witness against her and she has not been caught in the act, if a spirit of jealousy comes over him and he is jealous of his wife when she has defiled herself, or if a spirit of jealousy comes over him and he is jealous of his wife when she has not defiled herself, the man shall then bring his wife to the priest, and shall bring as an offering for her one-tenth of an ephah of barley meal; he shall not pour oil on it nor put frankincense on it, for it is a grain offering of jealousy, a grain offering of memorial, a reminder of iniquity.

'Then the priest shall bring her near and have her stand before the LORD, and the priest shall take holy water in an earthenware vessel; and he shall take some of the dust that is on the floor of the tabernacle and put it into the water. The priest shall then have the woman stand before the LORD and let the hair of the woman's head go loose, and place the grain offering of memorial in her hands, which is the grain offering of jealousy, and in the hand of the priest is to be the water of bitterness that brings a curse. The priest shall have her take an oath and shall say to the woman, "If no man has lain with you and if you have not gone astray into uncleanness, being under the authority of your husband, be immune to this water of bitterness that brings a curse; if you, however, have gone astray, being under the authority of your husband, and if you have defiled yourself and a man other than your husband has had intercourse with you" (then the priest shall have the woman swear with the oath of the curse, and the priest shall say to the woman), "the LORD make you a curse and an oath among your people by the LORD is making your thigh waste away and your abdomen swell; and this water that brings a curse shall go into your stomach, and make your abdomen swell and your thigh waste away." And the woman shall say, "Amen. Amen."

'The priest shall then write these curses on a scroll, and he shall wash them off into the water of bitterness. Then he shall make the woman drink the water of bitterness that brings a curse, so that the water which brings a curse will go into her and cause bitterness. The priest shall take the grain offering of jealousy from the woman's hand, and he shall wave the grain offering before the LORD and bring it to the altar; and the priest shall take a handful of the grain offering as its memorial offering and offer it up in smoke on the altar, and afterward he shall make the woman drink the water. When he has made her drink the water, then it shall come about, if she has defiled herself and has been unfaithful to her husband, that the water which brings a curse will go into her and cause bitterness, and her abdomen will swell and her thigh will waste away, and the woman will become a curse among her people. But if the woman has not defiled herself and is clean, she will then be free and conceive children.

'This is the law of jealousy: when a wife, being under the authority of her husband, goes astray and defiles herself, or when a spirit of jealousy comes over a man and he is jealous of his wife, he shall then make the woman stand before the LORD, and the priest shall apply all this law to her. Moreover, the man will be free from guilt, but that woman shall bear her guilt.'"

## Learning from Numbers 5

There are five things we should note in this passage. *First*, we should see the larger theological significance of this ritual because it seems bizarre at first glance. It may even appear to be chauvinistic. *Second*, we should observe what this ritual teaches us about the importance of sexual purity for all of the people of God. Sexual purity is not just an issue about you individually. It's not just an issue about you and your relationship with God. It is an issue that impacts the whole of the people of God. *Third*, we need to see what this ritual teaches us about the appointed ordinances of God in Scripture, and even about baptism and the Lord's Supper. *Fourth*, we should see what this ritual teaches us about the importance of the marriage bond and how that relates to us as the people of God. And *fifth*, we should note what this ritual teaches about the work of Christ on the cross.

Let me say all that in another way for sake of clarity: *One*, see the big picture. *Two*, see why it is that sexual purity matters to all the people of God. *Three*, see this passage as a pictured oath. *Four*, see what this passage has to say about the sacredness of marriage. And *five*, see what it has to say about the atoning work of Christ.

### The Big Picture

First, it is important to understand the primary purpose of this text. You don't have to know much about the ancient Near East to know that the trial described here is not wholly different from the trials of ordeal that are often found in other cultures. In the ancient world, when crimes committed could not be proven, trials of ordeal were used to reveal either the guilt or the innocence of the person who was suspected of the crime.

Now, that is where the similarity ends, and the differences found in this passage point us to the fact that God's ways are just and wise even when they're seemingly unfathomable to the finite mind. For instance, we learn from the Mauryan laws and from other cultural artifacts that in the ancient world you were assumed guilty until you were proven innocent. Furthermore, cruel tests were often used in these trials of ordeal. For example, suspected adulteresses would be told to submerge one hand into a pot of boiling water. If they removed it

unscathed, they were considered innocent. Sometimes suspects were forced to grasp a red-hot rod. If they released that rod from their hand and there was still flesh on their hand, rather than clinging to the rod, then they were innocent.

However, in Numbers 5 we see something entirely different. We notice how this whole test is dependent upon the effectual working of the Word of God. There is no magic here. There are no cruel trials. Instead, this trial assumes that the Word of God is effective, and that it can search out even the deep things of the heart.

The Word of God, in this case, is literally drunk by this woman, and the Word's judgment will find her out. By contrast, this test, unlike other trials of ordeal in the ancient Middle East, was physically safe. It was probably unpleasant to drink water with dust in it, but there was nothing physically harmful about ingesting it. It's important to remember that this process was controlled and was public.

---

**You cannot love God and live like a pagan. Instead, you must love God and live like a disciple.**

---

So the big picture is that God's version of a trial of ordeal is just and wise, though it may seem unusual to our culture. But the question that should still be lingering in your mind is, "Why is this text here?" The answer is very simple and straightforward and drawn from the passage: because adultery defiles, and thus pollutes the camp. If leprosy defiles the camp, if hemorrhages defile the camp, if dead bodies defile the camp, then adultery also defiles His camp. It is God's way of saying belief and behavior go together, truth and practice go together, and faith and life go together. You cannot love God and live like a pagan. Instead, you must love God and live like a disciple.

This whole passage presses on God's great concern for a consistent discipleship amongst His people—a consistent discipleship where heart, profession, and life are connected.

### Sexual Purity Matters

Second, this passage makes it clear that sexual purity matters to the whole people of God, including your individual sexual purity and mine. Isn't it interesting that this aggrieved or suspicious man is not allowed to take matters into his own hands, no matter what the temperature of his jealousy is? Instead, he is forced to go to the priest. Do you hear an echo of that in Jesus' teaching, "Tell it to the church" (see Matthew 18:15-20)? And the Westminster Confession, the Baptist Confession of 1689, and the Savoy Confession, when it comes to issues of adultery and divorce, stress that individuals must not be left up to their own consciences, but must bring their concerns to the church. Moses, in Numbers,

was teaching the people of God that sexual immorality is a spiritual issue, and it affects all the people of God. Your individual sexual immorality or even unwarranted jealousy is a matter that impacts the whole people of God.

You may be asking here, "Why is there a law only for a jealous husband? Isn't that a little chauvinistic?" I have three answers for you. *First*, I don't know. In fact, we don't even know whether this law—from what we learned in the rest of the Old Testament—was ever used. There is no record of it anywhere else in the Old Testament. So, I don't know why the law was given only for jealous husbands and not jealous wives.

But *second*, this does not mean that God's law was chauvinistically tilted toward husbands, because the laws regarding adultery extended to both the husband and the wife. Moses had already covered that both a husband and a wife who committed infidelity were under the death penalty. So, it's not as if God has left husbands off the hook and put poor, defenseless women on the hook.

In fact, *third*, there may well be a logic here that is designed to protect a wife who is unjustly suspected of infidelity. In other cultures around the world, even today, if the husband is jealous of his wife, she just disappears. The chief in the village isn't consulted and the husband takes matters into his own hands. In this passage, the husband is not allowed to do that; he must bring the suspected wife to the priest. Furthermore, if this publicly embarrassing exercise can't convince a husband that his wife is innocent, nothing will. Men tend to be tempted to ungodly jealousy in a way that wives are not, and therefore God, in His wisdom and providence, provided a safe way for the people of Israel to deal with ungodly temptation.

This text teaches that sexual immorality is a spiritual issue, and unwarranted jealousy over suspected sexual immorality is a spiritual issue. And both are matters that affect the whole of the people of God.

### A Pictured Oath

Third, we have a self-maledictory oath—an oath in which you call down curses, destruction, and judgment on yourself, as pictured through the actions of this ritual. Notice in verse 17 that the suspected wife must drink the holy water that contains dust from the tabernacle floor. It's important to remember that the dust from the tabernacle floor had been close to the Mercy Seat, which was the visible and tangible expression of God's presence with His people. The dust came off of holy ground. But remember too that the recipients of the five books of Moses were the children of Israel, who had in the back of their minds a story about a serpent who once had to lick the dust. They remembered their own forebearers, some of their own parents, even some of themselves who were there that day the children of Israel had to drink the dust of a golden calf. The woman suspected of adultery had to take into her body holy things that had been close to the Ark of the Covenant—things that would serve as a reminder of the judgment of God.

According to verse 18, the suspected woman had to hold an offering to the Lord in her hands as the oath was administered. It may be helpful to remember Jesus saying, "Therefore if you are presenting your offering at the altar, and there remember that your brother has something against you, leave your offering there before the altar and go; first be reconciled to your brother, and then come and present your offering" (Matthew 5:23-26). The point of Jesus' teaching is to not be a hypocrite while making the offering. Therefore, for the suspected woman to give an offering would press home to her, "If you do this and you're guilty, you are a hypocrite worshipping in the house of God. May God's curses come down upon you."

Now, pastorally speaking, understand that every component of this ritual presses home upon the woman the importance of being truthful and repentant if guilty. This is God's kindness on display! He knows that our sin is deceitful and it will hide in the smallest corners of our hearts; it never wants to be publicly revealed. As a result, God constructed a ritual that would aggressively pursue that sin and give every opportunity for that person to admit that sin and the need for grace and repentance.

Essentially what we have here is a picture of an oath. This woman is acting out a picture, the word curses of God. This is what is at work, in a positive direction, in the ordinances of baptism and the Lord's Table. The waters of baptism remind us of our union with Christ through the work of the Holy Spirit. The Lord's Table reminds us that we are invited to slide our knees up under the table of God and fellowship with Him, in Christ alone. Just as in Numbers 5 we have a picture of a curse, so in baptism and the Lord's Table we have pictures of promise.

### The Sacredness of Marriage

Fourth, Numbers 5 affirms for us the sacredness of marriage. These public measures highlight the importance of marriage. They also reveal that marital fidelity is a spiritual issue that impacts the whole community and our relationship with God. Moses' point was that marital infidelity is incompatible with membership in the people of God. The New Testament presses this idea home when it tells us that marriage is a picture of the gospel. It is a picture of union with Christ. It is a picture of the relationship, which is obtained by grace, between God and His people, and therefore, for the gospel's sake, we must live out the gospel in marriage. That's why Peter told husbands who are not dealing with their wives rightly, "Your prayers will be hindered"—because marriage is a picture of the gospel (see 1 Peter 3:7).

I say this especially to these who are leaders of God's church: What's at stake in your marriage? The gospel! If your

relationship with your wife—though you love Christ, she loves Christ, and you love to serve His people—is not right, then it must be your priority to make it right because it is your greatest gospel opportunity. If you neglect your marriage, then it doesn't matter what else you do because marriage matters to the gospel, to the people of God, and especially to the marriages of those whom we shepherd. One of Paul's qualifications for an elder is that he should be a man of one wife and a good leader of his household (1 Timothy 3:2-5). That logic goes all the way back to Numbers.

It's not surprising, then, that the apostle Paul wrote in 1 Corinthians that those who are unfaithful to their spouses have no place amongst the people of God (6:12-20). Or that John, in the book of Revelation, told us that there will be no immoral people in the kingdom (Revelation 22:15). This, however, does not mean that sexual infidelity is the unpardonable sin. What it does mean is that it is absolutely serious and strikes at the very heart of the gospel. It means that the only way out is a tangible repentance that expresses itself in a changed life.

### The Work of Christ

Fifth, Numbers 5 points us to the atoning work of Christ. No Christian can read about the drinking of these curses without being reminded of another who drank the curse. Look at verses 23-24: "The priest shall then write these curses on a scroll, and he shall wash them off into the water of bitterness. Then he shall make the woman drink the water of bitterness that brings a curse, so that the water which brings a curse will go into her and cause bitterness." Luke even picked up on Numbers 5:1-4 when he wrote about the leper, the hemorrhaging woman, and the dead little girl. Whereas every Old Testament member of the people of God would have told Jesus, "Don't touch this person, Jesus. It will make you unclean," instead, we are told by Luke that when Jesus touched the leper, He didn't become unclean; instead, the leper became clean (Luke 5:12-16).

A few chapters later, in Luke 8:40-56, Jesus was on His way to the house of a leader who would soon lose a child, and a woman who was hemorrhaging touched Him. Every Hebrew person there was thinking, *Oh no, she's unclean.* Yet something extraordinary happened, Luke recorded that Jesus didn't become unclean; rather, the woman became clean. A few moments later, Jesus came into the presence of a dead child and said, "Child, arise!" (verse 54). Even though Jesus had been in the proximity of a dead body, He was not made unclean. Rather, He restored life to this girl. We are told by Luke that this Lord Jesus is absolutely extraordinary; He makes the unclean clean.

Just after the apostle Paul referenced Numbers 5 in 1 Corinthians 11, he wrote, "In the same way He took the cup also after supper, saying, 'This cup is the new covenant in My blood; do this, as often as you drink it, in remembrance of Me'"

(1 Corinthians 11:25). Then Paul said, "A man must examine himself, and in so doing he is to eat of the bread and drink of the cup. For he who eats and drinks, eats and drinks judgment to himself if he does not judge the body rightly" (1 Corinthians 11:28-29). Jesus knew what was in that cup, and the only One who could drink it was Him, or those who are in Him by the Spirit, by grace, through faith. For anyone else to drink that cup meant that they would come under its just condemnation. But He drank the cup, and He drank it to the dregs.

Jesus wrestled in the Garden of Gethsemane over this: "My Father, if it is possible, let this cup pass from Me" (Matthew 26:39). He spoke this way because He knew what was in the cup. Just as the priests wrote the words of this curse, scraped them into the water, and handed the water to the woman, do you see what your Savior was doing for you on the cross? He was drinking your cup. Like those good Hebrews who watched Him come near to touch the leper, the hemorrhaging woman, and the dead child, we're all saying, "Lord God, don't drink that cup of mine. Don't infect Yourself with my judgment, my condemnation. My sins are written on that sheet. Don't take that into Your body."

But He still drinks the cup, and He drinks to the dregs for those from every tribe, tongue, people, and nation, men and women, and boys and girls, all who trust in Him. By the taking of that cup, and by the shedding of His blood, He made you clean. Hallelujah, what a Savior! Lead your people to find their purity in Christ alone by being clothed in His righteousness. And lead them to live out practically what they are positionally, because impurity affects the entire camp.

---

## PRAYER

Our Lord and our God, we believe that Your Word is inspired, but we doubt it at times. We come to passages like this, and we think that the light of the gospel cannot burst forth from them. Oh, how we love it when You prove us wrong. We thank You for the glory of this passage, for the way that it points to the requirement of living out the Christian life, and most of all, how it points to our Savior. He took the cup of judgment and cursing in our place that we might become the righteousness of God in Him. No one can pluck us out of His hands. Guide us, indeed, O Thou, our great Jehovah. In Jesus' name, Amen.

# Hallowed Be Your Name: The Leader on His Knees

*Tom Pennington*
*Shepherds' Conference 2013*

*Luke 11:1-13*

Nothing comes more naturally to us than breathing. From the doctor's first slap, it's involuntary. As you read this you are breathing somewhere between 12 and 15 times a minute, and today you will breathe 20,000 times. We can vary the rate of our breathing. We can even hold our breath for a short time, but it is impossible to voluntarily stop breathing entirely. If we don't inhale, carbon dioxide builds up in our blood and we experience what scientists refer to as "overwhelming air hunger."

This reflex is essential to human life. Without breathing, the body's oxygen level drops dangerously low in a short period of time. Within three to six minutes the brain is irreversibly damaged, and minutes later, death follows. You can live for weeks without food. You can survive for days without water. But you can live for only a few minutes without oxygen.

Breathing is so crucial to living that breath is a metaphor for life itself. That's why the English Puritan Thomas Watson's statement is so arresting and compelling: "Prayer is the soul's breathing."[1] What breathing is to the body, praying is to the soul. We absolutely cannot survive without it. John Calvin referred to prayer as the soul of faith. Just as the body dies when the soul leaves; even so, faith itself dies when prayer is gone.

Remarkably, in spite of the importance of prayer and our understanding of it, we pray very little. It's like exercise—we all know it's important, but for many of us, the greatest exertion each day is forcing the ice cream scoop into a frozen half-gallon container of ice cream.

## A Shocking Census

Nearly 30 years ago, 17,000 Christians attended a conference sponsored by a major denomination. While they were there, they completed a survey about their spiritual habits and activities. It remains, as far as I know, the largest survey of its kind. Some 17,000 evangelical Christians were asked questions, including a question about how much time they spent in prayer on a daily basis. They reported that they prayed, on average, less than 5 minutes a day. At the same conference there were 2000 pastors and their wives, and they were asked the same question. On average, 2000 evangelical pastors and their wives reported that they prayed less than 7 minutes a day.[2]

It appears that prayer has in fact become the pastor's most neglected duty. Sadly, it's unlikely that those numbers have changed much in the ensuing years. In fact, I think in today's man-centered, shallow Christian culture, the situation is probably far worse. What makes those statistics so tragic is that Scripture tells us that the one true and living God actually listens to the prayers of His people. Psalm 34:17 says, "The righteous cry, and the LORD hears." Because of that spiritual reality, the hearts of the righteous have always beat with a passion for speaking to God.

## The Blessing of Prayer

Before the fall, Adam and Eve walked and talked with the second member of the Trinity in the Garden. The first reference to prayer, as we know it, comes in Genesis chapter 4. We read that in the godly line of Seth, "men began to call upon the name of the LORD" (verse 25). From that point onward, prayer permeates the pages of the Old Testament. In the New Testament, prayer remains foundational to man's relationship to God. A devotion to prayer was the consistent pattern of the early church. According to Acts 2:42, believers "were continually devoting themselves to the apostles' teaching and to fellowship, to the breaking of bread and to prayer."

Prayer was also the great priority of the apostle Paul. You're familiar with the many times he referred to his prayers. First Thessalonians 3:10: "We night and day keep praying most earnestly." Second Timothy 1:3: "I constantly remember you in my prayers night and day."

---

**Nothing is more foundational to the health of our own Christian faith than prayer.**

---

Throughout church history, godly men have joined the chorus, emphasizing the importance of prayer. Augustine wrote, "Prayer is the protection of holy souls…the preserver of spiritual health[3]…the column of all virtues, a ladder to God…[and] the foundation of faith."[4] Martin Luther said, "As it is the business of tailors to make clothes, and of cobblers to mend shoes, so it is the business of Christians to pray."[5] In his *Institutes*, John Calvin called prayer "the chief exercise of faith by which we daily receive God's benefits."[6]

**Reasons We Don't Pray**

Nothing is more foundational to the health of our own Christian faith than prayer. We all say we believe that and we affirm it. So the question is, Why don't we pray? What are the reasons we give for not praying? There really is only one reason that we typically offer, and it's that we don't have time. "I would like to pray more, but I'm just too busy" is the common excuse. But we must strip away that excuse for a moment and honestly remind ourselves that this is not the reason we don't pray. Busyness is just an excuse, a feeble attempt to justify our lack of obedience to the clear will of God. So what are the real reasons that we don't pray? Let me give you a few to consider.

*One reason we don't pray is a lack of humility.* We are by nature, as fallen sinners, fiercely independent. But independence is not a reflection of, nor is it the path to, spiritual maturity. Instead, spiritual maturity is marked by believing what our Lord taught us in John 15—that apart from Him we can do nothing. In

1 Peter 5, Peter called on us to humble ourselves under the mighty hand of God, to accept His providence in our lives (verses 6-7). That humility is expressed by casting all of our care upon Him, because He cares for us. When we are truly humbled before God, we will recognize our need of Him and we will pray. In fact, the clearest measure of our pride is our neglect to pray.

*A second reason we don't pray is a lack of faith.* Often we don't pray because, frankly, we haven't seen results when we have prayed. Past results, however, don't justify our lack of future efforts. This is a greater problem than we are willing to admit. Though we would never say prayer doesn't work, if we really believed that there would be clear, visible, verifiable results within five minutes of praying, then we would become prayer warriors. It often comes down to our doubting whether anything will happen when we pray. This frame of mind means nothing will happen, because, as James wrote, "Ask in faith without any doubting, for the one who doubts is like the surf of the sea, driven and tossed by the wind. For that man ought not to expect that he will receive anything from the Lord" (James 1:6-7).

*A third reason we don't pray is a lack of obedience.* We are commanded to pray. Romans 12:12: Be "devoted to prayer." Colossians 4:2: "Devote yourselves to prayer." First Thessalonians 5:17: "Pray without ceasing." Prayer is to be the constant daily pattern of our lives. So let's be honest with ourselves and with the Scriptures, and acknowledge that if we are not personally devoted to prayer, it is sin. We must obey our Lord and we must devote ourselves to prayer.

## Growing in Prayer

The key question that arises is, How can we grow in our understanding and practice of this discipline? Nowhere do we learn more about how to pray than in what is traditionally called the Lord's Prayer. Two versions of the Lord's Prayer have been preserved for us through divine inspiration. One is in Matthew 6:9-13, and the other in Luke 11:1-4. Now, these are not parallel passages. In harmonizing the Gospels, we discover that Jesus probably preached the Sermon on the Mount—recorded in Matthew 6— in the summer of AD 29, or the summer before His crucifixion if you hold to a different date of His death. A few months later, probably in the fall of that same year, Jesus taught Luke 11. This prayer, then, is one that Jesus repeated on at least two occasions, and He probably used it a number of other times throughout His ministry as a pattern for His disciples' prayers.

Luke's version of the Lord's Prayer is extremely insightful for us because of the circumstances in Luke 11:1-13. In verse 1, a disciple requests instruction on prayer, and that is followed in verses 2 through 4 by the Lord's Prayer. Our Lord gives us a pattern, then, for prayer. Verses 5 through 8 record the parable of the reluctant friend, a parable about God's eagerness to hear our prayers. In verses 9 through 10, our Lord gives us direct affirmation that God hears and answers prayer: "Ask, and it will be given to you; seek, and you will find; knock, and it will be opened to you. For everyone who asks, receives; and he who seeks, finds; and to him who knocks, it will be opened." In verses 11-13, Jesus ends this lesson on prayer by giving us an illustration from family life, which shows that God is even more responsive to the requests of His children than human fathers.

Notice the first four verses of Luke 11:

> It happened that while Jesus was praying in a certain place, after He had finished, one of His disciples said to Him, "Lord, teach us to pray just as John also taught his disciples." And He said to them, "When you pray, say: 'Father, hallowed be Your name. Your kingdom come. Give us each day our daily bread. And forgive us our sins, for we ourselves also forgive everyone who is indebted to us. And lead us not into temptation.'"

I want to focus primarily on verse 1 because it turns the spotlight onto Jesus' personal example of prayer. And it shows the impact that Jesus' example of prayer had on the disciples, and the impact it should have on us. By observing Jesus' example, we learn three crucial lessons about our own prayer life.

### Prayer Requires Commitment

The first lesson is that prayer is a spiritual priority that requires great commitment. In verse 1 we read, "It happened that while Jesus was praying in a certain place…" The word Luke uses here for "praying" is the Greek word we expect. It's part of the family of words that the New Testament uses most frequently for prayer. In secular Greek, this word simply meant to speak to a deity. In Scripture, it is used of man's approach to God. It is, as Calvin defined prayer, "conversation with God."[7]

Here, our Lord speaks to God. Nowhere do we witness firsthand the importance and priority of prayer more than in the life of our Lord. The writer of Hebrews wrote, "In the days of His flesh, He offered up both prayers and supplications with loud crying and tears to the One able to save Him from death, and He was heard because of His piety" (5:7). Now, it's tempting to think that Jesus spent time in prayer because He missed the communion that He had always enjoyed with the Father, but this doesn't pass the theological test. Jesus' divine nature didn't change when He took on humanity. Although His human nature was bound to a body and could be in only one place at any time, His divine nature continued to fill the universe. The communion that the Son had enjoyed with the Father from all eternity continued throughout His earthly life, except for during those dark hours on the cross.

This is foundational to our grasping the priority of prayer—Jesus' prayer life was a reflection of His human nature, not of His divine nature. It was as the perfect man living the life you and I should live that He prayed.

And He prayed often. In fact, nine times in this Gospel, Luke tells us about Jesus praying. We are told Jesus began his public ministry with prayer: "Now when all the people were baptized, Jesus was also baptized, and while He was praying, heaven was opened, and the Holy Spirit descended upon Him in bodily form like a dove, and a voice came out of heaven, 'You are My beloved Son, in You I am well-pleased'" (Luke 3:21-22). Jesus' public ministry, initiated at His baptism, began with prayer.

Luke wrote that this was Jesus' regular practice. For example Luke 5:16 says, "Jesus Himself would often slip away to the wilderness and pray." Literally, the text says, "He was withdrawing and was praying." Luke intended to stress for us the fact that this was a consistent pattern of Jesus' life. We also learn that Jesus prayed all night before making a strategic decision. For example, He prayed before He chose the Twelve: "It was at this time that He went off to the mountain to pray, and He spent the whole night in prayer to God. And when day came, He called His disciples to Him and chose twelve of them" (Luke 6:12-13). The choice of the Twelve came out of a night of prayer.

According to Luke, it was while Jesus

was praying that He was transfigured before the disciples. Luke 9:28-29 says, "Some eight days after these sayings, He took along Peter and John and James, and went up on the mountain to pray. And while He was praying, the appearance of His face became different, and His clothing became white and gleaming." The Father chose to reveal His glory while Jesus was praying. In Luke 22:39 we find Jesus in Gethsemane praying, "And He came out"—that is, out of the upper room—"and proceeded as was His custom to the Mount of Olives; and the disciples also followed Him…" "And He withdrew from them about a stone's throw, and He knelt down and began to pray" (22:41). He even died praying: "Jesus, crying out with a loud voice, said, 'Father, into Your hands I commit My Spirit.' Having said this, He breathed His last" (23:46). Jesus' last words were a prayer of trust.

Now Mark's Gospel gives us additional insight. Mark makes it clear that Jesus' typical day was filled with prayer. In Mark 1:35 we discover that Jesus prayed early in the morning. This was His practice: "In the early morning, while it was still dark, Jesus got up, left the house, and went away to a secluded place, and was praying there." What makes this truly remarkable is that it happened on Sunday, after a very busy Sabbath. Notice in verses 21-22 that Jesus had begun His day by teaching in the synagogue in Capernaum. While He was there, He cast a demon out of a man (verses 23-28). He

returned to Peter's home and there healed Peter's mother-in-law (verses 29-31). All of this occurred before lunch, but the day was not over for Jesus. In fact, after dark, when the Sabbath was over, the entire city showed up outside of Peter's home (verse 33). This passage emphasizes Jesus' personal interest in individuals; one by one He healed them and cast out demons. Undoubtedly, that went on late into the night.

Early the next morning, Sunday, after that long day and night of ministry, Jesus got up to pray while it was still dark. So much for the excuse that we don't have time. Jesus "went away to a secluded place"—literally to a wilderness (verse 35). He strategically slipped out of Peter's house, quietly left the city of Capernaum, and found a quiet, secluded place in order to have an extended time of prayer.

Not only did Jesus pray in the morning, He also prayed in the evening after a long day's work. We read in Mark 6:45-48,

Immediately Jesus made His disciples get into the boat and go ahead of Him to the other side to Bethsaida, while He Himself was sending the crowd away. After bidding them farewell, He left for the mountain to pray. When it was evening, the boat was in the middle of the sea, and He was alone on the land. Seeing them straining at the oars, for the wind was against them, at about the fourth watch of the night He came to them, walking on the sea.

Now again what makes this remarkable is what had transpired earlier that day. Jesus' time of prayer came at the end of a long day, during which a crowd of more than 15,000 people had tracked Him down. Jesus' compassion led Him to heal the sick and, according to Mark 6:34, He taught them many things. Late that afternoon, on the same day, He had miraculously fed this crowd of 5000 men, which probably means more than 15,000 people altogether. It was after a day of intense ministry that Jesus spent time in prayer.

Jesus' example demonstrates that next to the Word of God, prayer was His greatest duty.

He also made it clear that He expects us, as His disciples, to pray as well. In Luke 11:2 our Lord said, "When you pray." In Matthew 6:5-7, He used that same phrase three separate times— "When you pray...when you pray... when you are praying." The first time He used a plural pronoun. It's as if He were saying, "When you—that is, *all* of My disciples—pray, and I'm assuming and expecting that you will."

But He went beyond expecting that we would pray—throughout the New Testament, He commanded us to pray. Read Ephesians 6:18: "With all prayer and petition pray at all times in the Spirit, and with this in view, be on the alert with all perseverance and petition for all the saints." In Colossians 4:2 we are told, "Devote yourselves to prayer." The Christian life is not merely about the indicatives of the gospel, but as a result of our justification, there are also imperatives we are to obey. Praying is one of those spiritual imperatives, a command from our Lord Himself.

---

**The priorities of Jesus and the priorities of His apostles must be our priorities as well.**

---

No matter how busy we are, there is absolutely no excuse not to pray. The two compelling priorities in Jesus' ministry were the Word of God and prayer. The apostles, like us, could be pretty dense, but they eventually got this. In Acts 6:4, you read that the apostles in the Jerusalem church were devoting themselves to prayer and the ministry of the Word. The priorities of Jesus and the priorities of His apostles must be our priorities as well.

### Prayer Is Necessary for Effective Ministry

Prayer is essential for all Christians, but it is even more vital for us who are the leaders of His church, because it is the foundation of all ministry. You see this in the apostle Paul, specifically his prayers, because they were the foundation of the effective ministry that he

222 THE JOHN MACARTHUR HANDBOOK OF EFFECTIVE BIBLICAL LEADERSHIP

enjoyed. Paul's ministry existed because God responded to his prayers.

We also see this in the examples of other Christian leaders in the church, specifically the example of Epaphras, who was a leader in the church in Colossae. When Paul addressed the Colossian church, he wrote, "Epaphras, who is one of your number, a bondslave of Jesus Christ, sends you his greetings, always laboring earnestly for you in his prayers, that you may stand perfect and fully assured in all the will of God" (4:12). John Owen, the great English Puritan, said, "He that is more frequent in his pulpit to his people than he is in his closet for his people is but a sorry watchman."[8] Jonathan Edwards wrote of David Brainerd, "His history shows us the right way to success in the work of the ministry...How did he labor always fervently...in prayers day and night, wrestling with God in secret...until Christ [was] formed in the hearts of the people to whom he was sent!"[9] Prayer is a spiritual imperative.

### Prayer Is Necessary for Effective Preaching

Prayer is also essential to effective preaching. The apostle Paul understood this and asked the Ephesians, "Pray on my behalf, that utterance may be given to me in the opening of my mouth, to make known with boldness the mystery of the gospel" (Ephesians 6:19). Augustine wrote, "A preacher must labor to be heard with understanding, with willingness, and with obedience. Let him not

doubt that he will affect this with fervent prayers more than with all the power of his oratory."[10] Richard Baxter wrote, "Prayer must carry on our work as well as our preaching. For he that does not pray for his people will not preach powerfully to his people."[11]

### Prayer Is Necessary for the Battle with Temptation

It is also through prayer that we win the personal battle with temptation and sin. In Luke 22:39-46, our Lord connected prayer with the power to overcome temptation. "Watch and pray that you do not enter into temptation." Commenting on the final petition in the Lord's Prayer, John Calvin wrote, "We conclude from this petition that we have no strength for living a godly life except so far as we obtain it from God. Whoever implores the assistance of God to overcome temptations acknowledges that unless God deliver him he will be constantly falling."[12] J.C. Ryle wrote, "What is the reason that some believers are so much brighter and holier than others? I believe the difference, in nineteen cases out of twenty, arises from different habits about private prayer. I believe that those who are not eminently holy pray *little*, and those who are eminently holy pray *much*."[13] It sounds simplistic to say that our spiritual struggles stem from the neglect of either Scripture or prayer. But when people come into the pastor's office seeking counsel, nine times out of ten they have been inconsistent either in private prayer, in the Word, or both. If you are losing in your struggle with a sin habit, it is probably because you are neglecting one or both of the basic means through which God extends His grace to us, and that is through His Word and prayer. John Owen, in his classic work on sin and temptation, makes this point:

A man finds any lust…[that] is powerful, strong, tumultuating, leads captive, vexes, disquiets, takes away peace; he is not able to bear it; wherefore, he sets himself against it, prays against it, groans under it, sighs to be delivered: but in the meantime, perhaps, in other duties—constant communion with God—in reading, prayer, and meditation—he is loose and negligent. Let not that man think that ever he shall arrive to the mortification of the lust he is perplexed with…Do you think he will ease you of that which perplexes you, so that you may be at liberty to that which no less grieves Him? No. God says, "Here is one, if he could be rid of this lust I should never hear of him more; let him wrestle with this, or he is lost." Let not any man think to do his own work that will not do God's. God's work consists in universal obedience; to be freed of the present perplexity is their own only… The rage and predominance of a

particular lust is commonly the fruit and issue of a careless, negligent course in general.[14]

As the disciples watched Jesus' life, they saw Him praying. It's clear from Luke 11:1 that they came to the conclusion that prayer was a spiritual priority in His life, and therefore must be in their own lives as well. Without prayer, spiritual growth is impossible, and ministry will be totally ineffective.

**Lessons About Prayer**
*Prayer Requires Deliberate Time*

The first lesson we learn from Jesus' example is that prayer is a spiritual priority that requires great commitment. If that is true, why do we so frequently neglect this duty? I think we can see why in the second lesson that we learn from Luke 11:1—prayer is an intentional practice that requires deliberate time.

Notice again verse 1: "It happened that while Jesus was praying in a certain place, after He had finished…" The clear implication of this statement is that the disciples saw Jesus praying, they saw the priority in His life, and they had to wait until He finished praying. In other words, Jesus devoted time to prayer. In other places, the Gospel writers tell us that our Lord spent considerable time in prayer. He often withdrew to a lonely place to pray, and that would have been pointless if He intended to spend only a short time in prayer. We are told that on at least two occasions, Jesus prayed all night.

We can gain further insight into our Lord's prayer life by looking at what happened during the Passion Week. The Thursday night before His crucifixion, Jesus and His disciples assembled in the upper room to celebrate the Passover. In Luke 22, we learn that Jesus had prayed for Peter, that his faith not fail. Of course, as they gathered to celebrate the traditional Passover celebration, Jesus, as the host, would have offered a number of prayers. In addition to that, He inaugurated the Lord's Table and gave thanks for both the bread and the cup. When the supper was over, Jesus prayed what is the longest recorded prayer from Him in Scripture—it appears in John 17 and is often called His high-priestly prayer.

Afterward, Jesus and the disciples left the upper room and went to Gethsemane, where again Jesus prayed—three times. Jesus prayed long enough that Peter, James, and John fell asleep. It's likely that Jesus prayed at least an hour and maybe as long as two hours. Our Lord offered all of those prayers in just one evening between sunset and midnight. Clearly, He devoted deliberate and intentional time to praying. Yet we are tempted to use Paul's words, "Pray without ceasing" (1 Thessalonians 5:17) to justify our lack of time spent in prayer. This is how we salve our consciences. It's true that our lives are to be lived in a spirit of prayer, but the same apostle who wrote "Pray without ceasing" also wrote "Devote yourselves to prayer" (Colossians

4:2). Prayer requires deliberate and intentional time.

But why is prayer not the habitual practice of our lives? At a practical level, one reason is that we simply don't have undistracted time. The average person is interrupted by his smartphone, phone calls, text messages, and Facebook updates every three minutes. According to Nielsen Media Research, the average person in the US spends five hours a day watching videos, and another hour using the Internet. If you're between the ages of 18 and 34, you spend almost three hours a day playing video games.[15] Although we should pray, we are constantly distracted by our electronic tools and toys. Turn off the television, turn off the game console, silence the smartphone, close the computer, and deliberately, intentionally get alone with God in prayer just as our Lord did.

A more subtle enemy to prayer is evident in Acts 6:2-4, where we read about the problem of feeding the widows in the church. The Twelve summoned the congregation of the disciples and said, "It is not desirable for us to neglect the word of God in order to serve tables. Therefore, brethren, select from among you seven men of good reputation, full of the Spirit and of wisdom, whom we may put in charge of this task. But we will devote ourselves to prayer and to the ministry of the word." Ministry itself and the legitimate needs of people threatened to destroy the apostles' devotion to the Word of God and to prayer. The same is true for us. The good is often the enemy of the best, and the busyness of ministry can destroy our devotion to the Word of God and to prayer. Like the apostles, we must not allow the busyness of ministry to eclipse prayer. Instead, find capable people who can come alongside you and free you for devotion to the Word of God and prayer.

Throughout Scripture we find others who intentionally set aside time each day for prayer. David, in Psalm 55:17, wrote, "Evening and morning and at noon, I will complain and murmur, and He will hear my voice." According to Daniel 6:10, even though Daniel knew about the decree prohibiting worship, he continued to kneel on his knees three times a day and pray and give thanks before his God as he had always done. In Acts 3:1, we read that Peter and John went up to the temple at the ninth hour, the hour of prayer. In Acts 10:9, we see that Peter went up on the housetop about the sixth hour, or noon, to pray. There was a daily, intentional pattern to these people's prayers.

Martin Luther's barber, Peter Beskendorf, once asked Luther about prayer. Luther wrote him a 40-page response. A portion of that response reads:

A good clever barber must have his thoughts, mind and eyes concentrated upon the razor and the beard and not forget where he is in his stroke and shave. If he keeps talking or looking around or thinking of something else,

he is likely to cut a man's mouth or nose—or even his throat. So anything that is to be done well ought to occupy the whole man with all his faculties and members. As the saying goes: he who thinks of many things thinks of nothing and accomplishes no good. How much more must prayer possess the heart exclusively and completely if it is to be a good prayer?…It is a good thing to let prayer be the first business in the morning and the last in the evening. Guard yourself against such false and deceitful thoughts that keep whispering: Wait a little while. In an hour or so I will pray, I must first finish this or that. Thinking such thoughts we get away from prayer into other things that will hold us and involve us till the prayer of that day comes to naught.[16]

The main difference between those who pray and those who don't is that those who pray *plan* to pray. Calvin included an entire section in the *Institutes* entitled "Prayer At Regular Times," in which he suggested a daily pattern of prayer: When you first get up, when you start your work, before meals, and at the end of the day.[17] We've learned from the life of our Lord that prayer was an intentional practice for which He deliberately set aside time. If it was so important for Him to make time to pray during a ministry of only three-and-a-half years, how much more important is it for us! His ministry was far more demanding than ours, and yet He made time to pray. May we never insult our Lord again by saying the reason we don't pray is because we don't have enough time. Jesus' example teaches us that prayer is a spiritual priority that requires great commitment, and that prayer is an intentional practice that requires we deliberately set aside time for it.

### Prayer Requires Careful Instruction

The third lesson we learn from Luke 11:1 is that prayer is a practical skill that requires careful instruction. "It happened that while Jesus was praying in a certain place, after He had finished, one of His disciples said to Him, 'Lord, teach us to pray just as John also taught his disciples.'" One of the Twelve—we aren't told here which one—makes this specific request: "Lord teach us to pray." "Teach" here is translated from a common Greek verb that refers to oral instruction. The disciples already had a basic understanding of prayer because they had read the Old Testament and the examples of prayer that appear there. They had grown up in Jewish homes in which they had heard praying, and they themselves had prayed. By the time this incident occurs in Luke 11, they had lived with Jesus Christ day and night for more than a year. They had undoubtedly heard Him pray many times before. And just a few months earlier—in the summer of

that year—Jesus had taught them how to pray when He taught the Sermon on the Mount. But they still had not mastered the skill.

In one sense, praying is just the natural cry of a child to his Father, but mature praying doesn't come naturally. It is a skill that must be taught and learned. The disciples knew that their prayers still needed help, and they weren't the only ones to acknowledge their inadequacy in this area. They said, "Teach us to pray just as John [the Baptist] also taught his disciples." We have no record of John's prayers or of his teaching on prayer, but clearly this was an essential part of his ministry. In fact, in Luke 5:33, the Pharisees said to Jesus, "The disciples of John often fast and offer prayers." John's disciples needed to be taught how to pray, just as the apostles requested Jesus to teach them how to pray.

This point should be very comforting. We aren't the only ones who need help with prayer. We get in line behind the disciples of John and behind the apostles when it comes to learning how to pray. We also see here that prayer is a skill we can acquire with the right instruction. Of course, the best One to teach us how to pray is Jesus Himself. The amazing truth is that, by the grace of God, we have an inspired record of how our Lord taught His disciples to pray. The answer to the request in verse 1 is found in verse 2: "He said to them, 'When you pray, say...'" and of course what follows is the Lord's Prayer. Jesus gave the most comprehensive version of this prayer a few months earlier, when He preached the Sermon on the Mount.

In Matthew 6:9, Jesus began, "Pray, then, in this way." Jesus here provided us with a model and a pattern to fashion all our prayers after. Just as the Ten Commandments condensed God's law into ten Hebrew words that even a child could memorize, this prayer condenses everything that should be a part of our prayers into a small package that even a child can learn. Hugh Latimer, the English Reformer and martyr, described it this way: "This prayer is the sum and abridgment of all other prayers. All other prayers are contained in this prayer."[18]

In this remarkable prayer, our Lord gave us a model that our prayer should follow. It is important for us to make a couple observations about this prayer that ought to encourage us to study our Lord's instruction more carefully.

## The Elements of Prayer

There are three elements of this prayer: a preface, six petitions, and a conclusion. The preface, "Our Father who is in heaven," teaches us the attitude that we should have as we come before God in prayer. "Our" is a plural pronoun. Prayer is not an individualistic, self-absorbed practice. Rather, we are to pray as a member of a family. The word "Father" reminds us that we are to pray as a child to his father. We've been adopted, and therefore we're talking to our Father. The balance comes in the expression

"who is in heaven." This means that we are not only to come to Him as to our Father, but also as a subject to a King.

The six petitions that follow identify six categories of prayer. They outline the kinds of requests that should come from our lips and our hearts. We are to pray for *the glory of God*—"hallowed be Your name." That is, may His name and everything connected with Him be set apart and treated as holy. We are to pray for the *kingdom of God*—"Your kingdom come." We should pray for the advancement of God's spiritual kingdom in people's hearts and for the coming of the literal kingdom when our Lord returns and establishes it. Third, we are to pray for *the will of God*—"Your will be done on earth as it is in heaven." Fourth, we are to pray for *the needs of this life*—"Give us this day our daily bread." Fifth, we are to pray for *the confession of sin*—"Forgive us our debts as we have forgiven our debtors." And sixth, we are to pray for *the pursuit of holiness*—"Do not lead us into temptation, but deliver us from evil."

Notice the proportion of these requests: half are about God, and half are about us and our needs. Notice the balance in this model prayer—Jesus divided the requests that we should be making of God into six categories, and yet most of our prayers fall into only two of them: the needs of this life, and the confession of sin. That means our prayers are significantly out of balance. Also, observe the order of the requests, which is obviously by design and tells us volumes about the focus of our prayers. The first three are all about God. Our needs come only in the second half of this prayer. That means our prayers must begin with and be preoccupied with God, His glory, His kingdom, and His will. Only then are we ready to ask for the things that we need.

What is remarkable about this prayer is that Jesus taught us to pray the same way He prayed. Jesus often began His prayers by addressing God as His Father and acknowledging that He is in heaven. Luke 10:21: "I praise you, Oh, Father, Lord of heaven and earth." He was always concerned in prayer that His Father's name be hallowed: "Father, glorify Your name" (John 12:28). We read in John 17:1, "Lifting up His eyes to heaven, He said, 'Father, the hour has come; glorify Your Son, that the Son may glorify You.'"

Jesus constantly prayed that God's kingdom would advance. In John 11:41-42 He said, "Father, I thank You that You have heard Me. I knew that You always hear Me; but because of the people standing around I said it, so that they may believe that You sent me." Jesus' concern was that God's will be done on earth. In the Garden of Gethsemane He prayed, "Father, if You are willing, remove this cup from Me; yet not My will, but Yours be done" (Luke 22:42). He prayed regarding the needs of this life, including the need for daily bread. We always find Jesus praying before meals and praying before He miraculously produced food for the crowds.

Although Jesus never asked forgiveness for His own sins—because He had none—He did pray for the forgiveness of others. In Luke 23:34 He asked, "Father, forgive them." He also prayed for the spiritual protection and growth of others—in Luke 22:32 He told Peter that though Satan wanted to sift him like wheat, "I have prayed for you, that your faith may not fail." In John 17:17, Jesus prayed for His apostles and for us when He said, "Sanctify them in the truth; Your word is truth." When you pray in the same categories that appear in the Lord's Prayer, you join your prayer with the Lord Himself. Right now, our great High Priest continues to offer these same petitions with us and for us. He ever lives to make intercession for us.

Our Lord has shown us the priority of prayer in our lives and ministries by His own personal example. He has shown us the practice of prayer by the time He deliberately and intentionally invested in it. And He has taught us the skill of prayer by His careful instruction. He has given us everything that we need. Now we need to simply ask for the grace to determine, as His apostles did, that we will devote ourselves to the ministry of the Word and to prayer.

# PRAYER

Father, forgive us for excusing our lack of obedience. Forgive us for our lack of faith. Forgive us for sinning against You and our people by not praying as we should, by not being devoted as our Lord was to prayer. We pray that today, You would give us a renewed commitment to devote ourselves daily to intentional, deliberate prayer. We pray in Jesus' name, Amen.

# 4

# A Leader Who Suffers Well

*John Piper*

*Shepherds' Conference 2001*

*Colossians 1:24*

**Opening Prayer**

Father, I ask that the effect of our efforts would be radical obedience. I also pray for a readiness to suffer for the cause of Christ, and a readiness to take risks that would look foolish and be foolish where there is no resurrection from the dead. I pray that we would be freed from the American vise grip of ease, comfort, security, and safety. I pray that You will keep me faithful to Your Word now, balanced in its proportions, protected from the devil, and filled with Your Spirit, leaving out anything unhelpful and including all that should be mentioned for the strengthening of God's people. In Jesus' name, Amen.

**Tribulation and Joy**

We read in 1 Thessalonians 1:6, "You also became imitators of us and of the Lord." In this text there are two people

who are models of something, namely Jesus and Paul. Here is what they are models of: "having received the word in much tribulation with joy of the Holy Spirit." Jesus was a man who received the Word of God in tribulation, but was sustained by joy. We read in Hebrews, "For the joy [that was] set before Him [He] endured the cross" (Hebrews 12:2). Paul was a man who received the Word of God and was told in receiving of it, "I will show Him how much He must suffer for My name's sake" (Acts 9:16). Yet the apostle said over and over again that he rejoiced in tribulation. We are called to be imitators of Jesus and Paul. We are called to receive the Word in much tribulation, but with joy.

Paul lived a life of suffering. The question is: What was the function of suffering in the apostle's life? Or what is the function of the suffering in the pastor's life, the missionary's life, and the saint's life? Is it something that just happens to a pastor, and then that person can honor God because of the way he deals with it? Or is there a purpose for it in the church? Can a pastor suffer for his church? Can he suffer for his mission field?

Is suffering just something that comes because the devil is a bad person and we then convert it into sanctifying influences through the power of the Holy Spirit? Or could it be that when God said to Paul, "I will show you how much you must suffer," that then there is a design and strategy in this suffering? I bring these questions and this topic up because leaders need to hear about suffering. Most pastors come from well-to-do churches, where very few people realize that they suffer by design.

## Suffering as Strategy

Richard Wurmbrand was a Romanian pastor who suffered for 14 years in prison for the sake of the gospel. I learned from him by literally sitting at his feet, since he takes his shoes off and sits down when he speaks. It was about 15 years ago when I was with about 12 other pastors sitting low at Richard's feet, and it was then that he sowed into my heart the seed of embracing suffering as a strategy.

He asked questions like, "If you and the man next to you knew that both of you were about to have a child, one disabled, the other whole, which would you choose to have?" Even that question had a profound impact on me, and I've

recently seen some ways it has influenced my flock. At Bethlehem Baptist, dozens of babies are adopted—from all over the United States and all over the world. Families are willing to endure suffering by adopting these little children from orphanages in Ukraine. The result is pain, and if God is merciful, glory. Some of these families have endured such pain that they've had to consider letting these kids go, and the pain of that is incredible. These families have put themselves in life-threatening situations because of their choice to love and ultimately because of their choice to suffer.

Richard Wurmbrand has also impacted me through a story that he told. It was a story about a Cistercian monk, which is an order in the Catholic Church that is always quiet. A radio interviewer in Italy asked this abbot of the Cistercian monastery, "What if you were to realize at the end of your life that atheism is true, and that there is no God?" And the abbot replied, "Holiness, silence, and sacrifice are beautiful in themselves. Even without the promise of a reward, I still will have used my life well." Paul, however, would have given the exact opposite answer, because he did give the exact opposite answer in 1 Corinthians 15:19. Paul wrote, "If we have hoped in Christ in this life only, we are of all men most to be pitied." There's not a text in the last ten years of my life that has caused me more difficulty than this passage, brought me to my face, called my ministry into question, and threatened to change my future more than this text.

This passage says that if there is no resurrection from the dead, then the choices I am making and the life I am living are absolutely absurd. This kind of thinking is shocking in America because almost nobody sells Christianity this way. People sell Christianity as love, joy, peace, patience, kindness, better marriage, and more obedient kids. Even a God who perhaps prospers your business. Consequently, if Christianity is a delusion, then it does not make a difference as long as you've lived a good life.

However, Paul had the opposite view. We are of all men most to be laughed at, pitied, regarded as foolish and absurd if we are not raised from the dead after this hellish life. Paul did explain in the same chapter the alternative option if there is no resurrection from the dead. He wrote, "Let us eat and drink" (15:32). Now, he didn't mean by that we should all become drunkards and gluttons if there's no resurrection. To be a glutton and be overweight means having a heart attack when you're 36. Or to be a drunkard entails a difficult life. Nobody looks at those modes of life and says, "There's the life." What Paul meant is, "Just be normal." Eat, drink, be normal, avoid any excessive risks, keep the security high, and enjoy reasonable comforts. That is how one is to live if there's no resurrection from the dead. Normal, simple, ordinary, cultural Christianity if there is no resurrection.

Paul further explained how the truth of the resurrection impacted his life in 1 Corinthians 15:29-31: "If the dead are not raised...why are we also in danger every hour?" I read that on the plane today and thought to myself, "Good night." If I'm in peril even one hour, I will try to fix it. I naturally do not want to be in peril, but Paul chose it. For Paul, it wasn't just one hour, it was every day, all day. Danger on the seas, danger on the roads, danger in the city, danger from faulty brethren, and danger from the enemy. Paul did not have security, and it seems like he was always in danger.

I've been in danger just a few times in my neighborhood when threats have come. As a result, it's tough to concentrate and do ministry. How are you going to prepare to talk to the Muslims tomorrow if the mob is outside tonight? Though in peril every hour, Paul went on to write, "I affirm, brethren, by the boasting in you which I have in Christ Jesus our Lord, I die daily" (15:31). Now that's foolish if there's no resurrection from the dead. If there's no assurance of resurrection from the dead, then you should get maximum life every day. This man thought this way, this man made these kinds of choices because he knew true joy. Paul's answer for suffering well is found in Colossians 1:24.

## An Intimidating Text

In John MacArthur's office there is this brass statue of a man on his knees with his hands out. On the statue is written, "I will trust in the Lord." This statue of a man cringing face down before Almighty God is how I feel before these types of passages. As pastors, we are sometimes tempted to use the Bible in order to escape the Bible. We use expository preaching as the means for ministry to protect ourselves from passages that stretch us to minister in other ways. Don't get me wrong, I believe in expository preaching with all my heart, but God calls us to be more than just expositors.

### Rejoice in Suffering

We read in Colossians 1:24, "Now I rejoice in my sufferings for your sake." We don't know what to do with a verse like this. Almost everyone in my church does the complete opposite—they grumble when they suffer; they ask God, "Why?" and they don't rejoice. What's wrong with the apostle Paul? Does he come from another planet? Yet the biblical pattern of life is so supernatural, so radical, and so different that very few pastors and laymen are living it.

We continue reading, "Now I rejoice in my sufferings for your sake, and in my flesh I do my share on behalf of His body, which is the church, in filling up what is lacking in Christ's afflictions." Paul labels his suffering as the "filling up what is lacking in Christ's afflictions." Suffering is designed to accomplish something called "filling up" what is lacking in Christ's afflictions. What does this mean? We all know what it does not mean. We know from Paul and Jesus that

this verse does not mean that the apostle Paul improves upon the atoning work of the cross. When Jesus declared, "It is finished," He meant an infinitely valuable and perfect sacrifice has been made, and nobody can ever improve upon that sacrifice. What has been paid on the cross is paid in full, and no one can make any contribution to the payment that was made for the forgiveness of sins and the justification of lives before a holy God. Jesus alone has done this, and we find our security by resting in it.

So if that is what this verse does not mean, then what does it mean? What is lacking in the afflictions of Christ is not the perfection of the value of its atoning worth, but the personal presentation to those for whom He paid the price. Christ, by the Father's design, means for His atoning sufferings to be offered and presented to all those for whom He died, in every people group in the world; and this is to be done through suffering.

---

**Joy is the only way you'll survive your mission in this world if you decide to suffer for Christ.**

---

However, this suffering must be accompanied with joy, because without it one will never survive. For the joy that was set before Christ, He endured the cross. And for the joy that is set before you, you will endure the choices that you make, which make no sense if there's no resurrection from the dead. Joy is the only way you'll survive your mission in this world if you decide to suffer for Christ. The joy of the Lord will be your strength through choices that nobody understands.

**A Parallel Example**

Now, why do I think this passage means what I just said it means? Because of the parallel use of language in Philippians 2. I took the two key terms in this passage, "fill up" and "lacking," and searched where else these terms were paired. The clearest parallel example is found in Philippians 2, when Paul wrote about Epaphroditus. Epaphroditus was the individual who took the gifts from the Philippians to Rome, where Paul was. Paul responded to the Philippians with this letter and commended Epaphroditus because he risked his life almost to the point of death, according to Philippians 2:27. Epaphroditus made a choice that would have been pretty foolish to the world, but nonetheless, he made it. We read that he survived because "God had mercy on him" (verse 27). Therefore, Paul told the church to receive him with joy and to hold him and others like him in high regard.

In verse 30 we read that Epaphroditus "came close to death for the work of Christ, risking his life to complete what was deficient in your service to me." We see in this verse the two words found in Colossians 1:24, *lacking* and *fill up*. Here we have a very close parallel. The

Philippians had a love gift for Paul; they were willing to sacrifice in order to serve a fellow brother in Christ. Yet this gift is incomplete until the Philippians get it to be where it was designed to be—in Rome. And Epaphroditus fills up what is lacking with the cost of almost his own life.

Marvin Vincent, who wrote a commentary on Philippians a little over 100 years ago, wrote on this passage, "The gift to Paul was a gift to the church as a body. It was a sacrificial offering of love. What was lacking was the church's presentation of this offering in person."[1]

Paul represented Epaphroditus as supplying what was lacking by his affectionate and zealous ministry. And that's my interpretation of Colossians 1:24—I think that's exactly what's going on in that verse. Jesus Christ has an affectionate sacrifice and offering for the world. He has designed that it not be telecast or radioed only, but embodied. Now, here's the question: If the design is to get the atoning, effective, powerful, gospel-feeling sufferings of Jesus into the lives of those for whom it was designed, by what means shall it happen? Paul made it very clear by what means in Colossians 1:24: "I rejoice in my sufferings for your sake... in filling up what is lacking."

The method for the "filling up" the "lack" of personal presentation is what happened to Paul's body when he preached:

Five times I received from the Jews thirty-nine lashes. Three times I was beaten with rods, once I was stoned, three times I was shipwrecked, a night and a day I have spent in the deep. I have been on frequent journeys, in dangers from rivers, dangers from robbers, dangers from my countrymen, dangers from the Gentiles, dangers in the city, dangers in the wilderness, dangers on the sea, dangers among false brethren; I have been in labor and hardship, through many sleepless nights, in hunger and thirst, often without food, in cold and exposure (2 Corinthians 11:24-27).

Suffering is essential! Don't be a pastor if you don't believe that. God means for you to reach His people among all of the people groups of the world and in our neighborhoods with faithfulness in the midst of suffering. He means for those people to see Jesus, the real crucified Jesus, in your crucifixion. That's what Paul was writing in Colossians 1:24.

## A Common Occurrence

I recently received a letter, and I'm going to use some false names here because I don't know if this person wants this out. The letter reads, "Two weeks ago, my brother, Joe, was shot as he sat in his hut in a northern Uganda village. Joe and his wife, Frances, are missionaries to the Muslim tribe Aringa in northern Uganda, which is three miles from Sudanese border. Frances and Joy,

their five-month-old daughter, had just arrived in the States for a short visit since they'd been gone over a year. Joe remained in Africa. Two days after Frances's arrival, Joe and Martin were sitting together in the living area in the hut in the evening when they heard a strange sound outside. Joe suspected trouble. He jumped up, kicked the door shut just before the spray of bullets was released. The bullets exploded through the door, hit Joe in his shoulder and Martin in the lower arm."

The letter continues to explain that the assailants broke in, demanded money as they dragged the two men around, and these men cried out for Jesus to save them. What happened? The soldiers lowered their weapons and walked away. The men spent five hours without any medical aid and they still survived. That story had a happy ending, but we all know the stories that have the less "earthly" happy ending.

This is normal! Woe to the church that doesn't teach their young people that this is normal. Paul wrote, "I rejoice in my sufferings for your sake…in filling up what is lacking." Now, is this just apostolic? No, because Jesus declared, "For whoever wishes to save his life will lose it, but whoever loses his life for My sake and the gospel's will save it" (Mark 8:35).

**The truth of suffering for the glory of God applies to everyone.**

Beloved, the path of salvation is the path of losing one's life for the sake of the gospel. We also read in 2 Timothy 3:12, "Indeed, all who desire to live godly in Christ Jesus will be persecuted."

That truth of suffering for the glory of God applies to everyone. And the reason this truth finds so little echo in the American church is because we have so domesticated the word *godliness*—so much so that we scarcely can begin to comprehend what Paul meant by it. Godliness is limited to reading your Bible, going to church, and keeping the commandments. But that's not all there is to godliness because the Pharisees did all of those things. Godliness is being so ravished by God, so satisfied by God, so filled with God, so driven by Jesus that you live in a way that the only explanation for your life is the promise of God raising you from the dead. That's why I'm always praying, "Lord, get me and my wife ready for our next decision."

We will never be Christ's church until we choose to take risks that can only be explained by the resurrection from the dead. That's the only way that we'll be the church that we ought to be and finish the Great Commission.

## Joy Is the Key to Suffering

The last word to investigate here is *joy*. "I rejoice in my sufferings." The Calvary road is a hard road filled with joy and Paul's joy seems to me to be absolutely boundless. He wrote to the Corinthians, "Sorrowful yet always rejoicing"

(2 Corinthians 6:10). What is the key to this joy? We find it in Romans 5:2: "We exult in hope of the glory of God." Paul continued, "Not only this, but we also exult in our tribulations." I just read this morning an article by Marvin Olasky on the topic of proselytizing in the current issue of *World* magazine. He mentioned that Christianity has excellent examples of how to proselytize. But he also uses an illustration of bad ways to do it. He wrote that 100 years ago, in Turkey, Muslims lined up Armenian Christians and certain Muslim leaders would walk down the line and ask the question, "Do you worship Christ or Allah?" If the answer was "Christ," a sword was thrust to the abdomen. Now, how many people do you watch that happen to before you make up your mind as to what you will answer? Joy in Christ at that moment is not optional; it is the only hope of obedience. That's why Paul says here, "I rejoice in my sufferings."

## Filling Up What Is Lacking

I want to conclude with an illustration from J. Oswald Sanders, a great statesman missionary. Sanders died a few years ago, and he was 89 when I heard him last. He gave an illustration which so perfectly embodies Colossians 1:24. Sanders talked about an Indian evangelist, a brand new believer who wanted to tell everybody about Jesus. He traveled the whole day and after a very difficult journey came to a village. He wondered whether he should wait until the morning to evangelize to this village. But then he decided to go into the village and preach the gospel before resting. The evangelist got the crowd around him, preached the gospel, and they scoffed at him. He quit because he was tired and discouraged, walked out of the village, and laid down underneath a tree to sleep.

A few hours later as the sun was going down, he woke up startled with the whole village around him. He saw one of the leaders of the village over him and thought, *Oh, they're going to hurt me or kill me.* The leader said, "We came out to see you and noticed the bloody feet that you have. We've decided that you must be a holy man and that you care about us because you came so far as to have feet like this. We would like to hear your message again."

Pastor, we rejoice in our sufferings, and in our flesh we fill up what is lacking in the afflictions of Jesus. One thing that is lacking in the afflictions of Jesus is a personal, embodied, bloody presentation of His cross to those for whom He died. We must be that presentation. I've preached this message multiple times because I feel burdened to call the church to get ready not for what may happen, but for what *should* happen if we're living Paul's life. You are being called through my mouth by God Almighty to make choices in your ministry, in your marriage, and in your parenting. If you are hovering right on the brink of a radical decision, I'm excited for you. I want to push you over the edge and reinforce what God is calling you to do, and that is to make choices in the service of love, not masochism—a service of suffering and sacrifice that can only be explained if Christ will raise you from the dead.

# PRAYER

Father, I pray for pastors who teach these truths to their people. I pray that these leaders may build radical, out-of-sync, risk-taking, sacrificial, love-displaying, and Christ-exalting congregations. Congregations that can only be explained by the truth that Jesus has so satisfied their souls, that they can say, "Let goods and kindred go, this mortal life also; the body they may kill; God's truth abideth still; His kingdom is forever."[2] But Lord, You will never build these kinds of congregations if we don't embrace those risks of love. Show every person now the steps they are to take for the world to be stunned and give glory to our Father in heaven. In Christ's name I pray, Amen.

# 5

# A MINISTRY OF INTEGRITY

*John MacArthur*
*Shepherds' Conference 2010*

*2 Corinthians 5:11-15*

I never think about the cross in vague or general terms. I always think about the death of Christ in a very personal way, mindful of the fact that Jesus bore in His own body my sins and credited His righteousness to my account. This truth lifts my worship to Him, and it reminds me that I am called to be a leader with integrity.

I recently spoke to a pastor who called me because he had put himself in a position of compromise. His actions were public and the people who were nearest and dearest to him were concerned about his behavior. I reminded him, along with any leader who reads this, that pastors are called to have integrity.

## Levels of Integrity

*First*, integrity must be manifested in the pastor's family. You must make sure that the life you live so well matches the message that you preach to your children, wife, and the people close to you.

*Second*, the pastor is called to have integrity in the church. One of the downsides of spending nearly half a century in the same church is that there are no secrets. I don't have any secrets personally, nor does my family. There is a great level of exposure in long-term ministry. The upside is if by the grace, goodness, and kindness of God a pastor can survive with his integrity intact, there is a joy and a level of trust that exists in the church family that is difficult to describe.

*Third*, a pastor must have integrity with the people beyond his own church who are influenced by his preaching and teaching. They need to know that the individual they are listening to can be trusted. David wrote in Psalm 25:21, "Let integrity and uprightness preserve me." And he prayed to the Lord in Psalm 41:12, "You uphold me in my integrity." That is constantly my prayer as well—for the Lord to never let me live before my family, before my church, before a watching world in any way that is divergent from what I preach and what I say I believe.

> **Integrity should mark all believers,
> but most of all, the one who has
> the most at stake—the mouthpiece,
> the spokesman, the model,
> the example, the leader.**

In addition, not only do I want to maintain integrity in my own life, I want to be surrounded by people who have integrity. In Psalm 101:6 David looked at his kingdom, along with whom he wanted around him, and said, "He who walks in a blameless way is the one who will minister to me." In fact, the alternate reading of that psalm is, "He who walks in a way of integrity…" Integrity should mark all believers, but most of all, the one who has the most at stake—the mouthpiece, the spokesman, the model, the example, the leader.

### Defining Integrity

The Hebrew word translated "integrity" means whole or complete. Every part of a believer's life must be in perfect order with every other part. The word is used for what is flawless, what is perfect, what is blameless, and what is consistent. Even the English word *integrity* comes from *integer*, which is a mathematical term meaning one. The dictionary would define *integer* as the quality of being undivided. A few synonyms for integrity would be *honesty* or *without hypocrisy* or *without duplicity*. In other words, you live with integrity when you haven't covered anything up. First Timothy 3 reminds us that if a man wants to be an elder, he must be blameless and above reproach. All too often today's church leaders are focused on ministry efforts and goals that are defined by courage, energy, enthusiasm, optimism, entrepreneurship, and imagination. But Scripture is far more concerned about integrity.

### An Attack on Integrity

Now, having mentioned that, the most precious commodity that I have as a pastor is my personal relationship to Christ. Therein lies the integrity of my ministry. As soon as it becomes obvious to my own children, family, church, or the watching world that I'm something different than what I preach, all is lost. Yet it is difficult to try to defend your integrity against your critics. I have had many critics and I have had them for a long time, but with the Internet, they've gone interplanetary. My daughter went to work for *Grace to You* a few years ago. She thought everyone loved her father because she lived in a microcosm of this church. Her responsibility at *Grace to You* was to process the letters sent by mail. She was shocked by all the hate mail that came in against me and was so crushed by it that she began clandestinely answering all these people. She would write back, "You don't know my father. Stop saying these things about him."

The most challenging part of ministry is receiving false accusations of being unfaithful, unbiblical, or guilty of any other sin. I remember, when I began in ministry, saying to my father, "Dad, will you pray for me?" He responded, "I will pray for you and I will pray for two things specifically—that God will protect you from sin, and that God will protect you from people who accuse you of sins you don't commit." My father knew that pastors need to be protected from false accusations. As a pastor, you will be maligned, and sometimes these enemies are very close. Sometimes they're on the church board, and this will make the attacks painful.

## An Integrity Worth Defending

The first step to defending your integrity is to have an integrity that is worth defending. But even then, defending oneself is tricky business, because it is difficult to do it without seeming self-serving or self-centered. I don't like defending myself, but I also know that when unfounded, unwarranted, untrue accusations and criticisms come against me, they destroy people's trust in my ministry. False

accusations cut me off from an opportunity to bring the truth to the people who are under my influence. A pastor protecting his integrity is a pastor protecting the flock he shepherds.

In 1 Corinthians 4:3, Paul wrote that it is a small thing what men say of him, because God brings the final verdict. And in one sense it is not about personal feelings, self-esteem, self-protection, or making sure you go through life blissfully, but about how the words of certain men affect your ministry opportunity. It hurts to have your ministry maligned because it cuts you off from the people who buy into those lies and you no longer have the opportunity to be a servant of the Lord to them. That is especially painful when it occurs in the church. This has happened at Grace Community Church, where in one fell swoop, more than 200 people left in a protest against me under the assault of a false accusation some years ago. But I learned that if you have a life worth defending, then you're caught in this very awkward position of having to defend yourself.

## Persuading Men

If you find yourself in this position, then you're in good company with the apostle Paul. You could take just about any passage in 2 Corinthians and the text would eventually get you to the place of looking at how Paul viewed his ministry and how he dealt with others who questioned his integrity. More specifically, there are three words that stand out in

2 Corinthians 5:11: "we persuade men." What exactly was Paul persuading men to? Was he talking about eagerly being engaged in persuading people to believe the gospel? Because Paul does that in other places in Scripture—for example, we read in Acts 18:4 that Paul was reasoning in the synagogue in Corinth every Sabbath, trying to persuade Jews and Greeks. And in Acts 28:22 a group came to Paul, and he was trying to persuade them concerning Jesus, from both the Law of Moses and from the Prophets, from morning until evening (verse 23). Paul was persuasive when it came to the gospel.

Yet the reference in 2 Corinthians 5:11 is not about persuading people to believe the gospel. Rather, Paul wrote about persuading men about his own integrity, which was a key issue in 2 Corinthians. At this time, Paul was under a full-scale assault by false teachers in Corinth who were teaching a mangled mixture of Christianity, Judaism, and pagan religions. In their attempt to successfully teach these lies and fulfill their satanic agenda, these false teachers had to destroy that congregation's trust in the reigning teacher, Paul.

Consequently, Paul wrote to persuade the Corinthians of his own integrity, for it had been illegitimately assaulted. In chapter 1, he wrote about all the suffering he had endured. The false teachers claimed that Paul's suffering was due to divine judgment. But Paul reminded the church that though he was suffering, he was suffering for the sake of the gospel. In chapter 4, Paul stressed that this suffering was occurring so that he could comfort the church. He was even attacked about his honesty. His critics were saying, "You don't do what you say you're going to do. You said you were coming, and you didn't come." Paul responded by reminding the people in the church that he could only do what the Lord allowed him to do. The apostle had to defend his own integrity. Then the false teachers attacked his virtue, and he replied that he did not have a secret life of shame and that there was no other Paul.

The false teachers accused Paul of being proud and wanting to elevate himself, and he reminded the church that he was nothing more than a clay pot, an earthen vessel. The teachers questioned his openness, and he wrote back, "Our heart is opened wide" (6:11). He was accused of being in the ministry for sexual favors and money. He responded, "We wronged no one, we corrupted no one, we took advantage of no one" (7:2). They attacked his apostleship, as if it was illegitimate, and he reminded the people that he was not inferior to any apostle. They attacked his giftedness, saying that his persona and his speech were unimpressive and contemptible, and they even attacked his message. They hit him every way they could. Their accusations were flying all over the Corinthian church and they were landing on Paul to such a degree that Paul admitted that he was depressed (7:6). I've been there, and you've been there. We are looking at our life like Job and doing our best to walk the walk and to live what we preach. We hate to become defensive because we don't want to seem overly self-protective, but we still understand what is at stake.

As a result, "we persuade men" (5:11). This phrase unlocks the door to this little portion of Scripture and to how we defend our integrity. Paul used a plural pronoun because he was talking about himself, yet at the same time he was also strategically avoiding saying "I." The Greek word translated "persuade" is *peithomen*, the same term used in Galatians 1:10, in the negative sense, where it means to seek the favor of men. In Galatians, Paul did not care about seeking the favor of those who rejected the true gospel. But in 2 Corinthians he was on the opposite end—he was seeking a favorable response from the church because he was defending his own integrity.

### Appealing to God

I speak to pastors who contact me to talk about the terrible assaults that are going on against them in their churches. My response is, "Defend yourself if you have a life worth defending." Likewise, Paul wanted the favor and the trust of his church. Note the phrase that follows "we persuade men"—"but we are made manifest to God" (5:11). As a leader, if you are going to say, "I want to persuade you of my integrity," then you are also going to have to say, "And God knows the truth about me." God is the one who knows our true spiritual condition and our heart. In these types of situations, we must be willing to gladly stand before God's court and take whatever discipline is deserved.

Another court that Paul appealed to was his own conscience. In 2 Corinthians 1:12 he wrote, "Our proud confidence is this: the testimony of our conscience, that in holiness and godly sincerity, not in fleshly wisdom but in the grace of God, we have conducted ourselves in the world, and especially toward you." No matter what was said against Paul, what accusations came his way, what slander was spoken, what book was written against him, his conscience was clear. Though some people were accusing Paul, his conscience was not. In chapter 1 Paul appealed to the court of his conscience, but in chapter 5 he went to even a higher court—God Himself, who knew the sincerity and integrity of the apostle's heart. Pastor, what peace will come to your soul when you can say, "God knows my heart."

In Acts 23:1, Paul mentioned that he had lived his life with a perfectly good conscience, and in Acts 24:16, he said he had done his best to maintain a blameless conscience. Now that is an integrity and life worth defending. It is only when one has a clear conscience and knows that by the grace of God he has lived in holiness and godly sincerity that he can rise to a legitimate defense of his integrity for the sake of the One he represents.

> If there is any one thing that undergirds the teaching of the Word of God, it is the sincere integrity of the minister.

## Reasons for Defending Your Integrity

The integrity of the messenger is a critical aspect of making the message acceptable. At the end of 2 Corinthians 5:11, Paul wrote, "I hope that we are made manifest also in your conscience." Paul wanted these people to trust him, to not have doubts about him, to not believe all the lies about him, to not listen to all the evil criticisms of the false teachers, and instead to listen to their own conscience. Paul was saying, "I trust your conscience more than I would trust those false teachers, because you belong to Christ and you know me personally. Your conscience has been formed by the truth of God, informed by the truth of God, and is operating under the influence of the Spirit of God." The evidence of Paul's sincerity was critical to the effect of his ministry. If there is any one thing that undergirds the teaching of the Word of God, it is the sincere integrity of the minister. Paul knew that and was willing to fight to defend himself.

### Reverence for the Lord

Why is it important to defend your ministry and integrity? The *first* reason is a reverence for the Lord. Paul wrote, "For we must all appear before the judgment seat of Christ, so that each one may be recompensed for his deeds in the body, according to what he has done, whether good or bad" (verse 10). Paul then transitioned to this in verse 11: "Therefore, knowing the fear of the Lord, we persuade men." We are to have reverence and fear toward being examined by the Lord and the possibility that He would determine our deeds are "bad" (Greek, *phaulos*), which means worthless.

I suppose the strongest driving force in my life is reverence for the Lord. My view of God drives and compels me. It is my view of God that drives my view of Scripture. Paul wrote, "Knowing the fear of the Lord..." The Greek word translated fear is *phobos*, from which we get the word *phobia*. It is a strong word that can even be translated as "terror." However, Paul was not intending to speak of God as the One who judges and condemns. Rather, he was writing about the admiration, respect, and worship that the Lord excites in his soul—the compelling desire to worship Him, honor Him, and glorify Him.

One difficult aspect of being criticized is that it's disheartening to know there are people who think that I would do something that would bring shame on the name of Christ. The last thing I would ever want to do is dishonor the Lord. To know the fear of the Lord is the ultimate form of accountability. What controls the heart is a healthy fear of the Lord, or awe and reverence. Paul wrote that he knew this fear—the word "knowing" refers to a settled knowledge. Paul had the settled knowledge of God as a Lord to be adored, and his obedience stemmed from this proper knowledge of God.

We find the opposite response in Jonah, whom God commanded, "Go to Nineveh." Jonah's reply was, "I'm not going to Nineveh. I know the kind of God You are. You'll save those people." Sadly, a proper knowledge of God led Jonah to be disobedient. For Paul, however, this knowledge led to obedience. It is as if Paul was saying, "I know what kind of God I have. I love Him, I adore Him, and I want to glorify Him." Paul cared about his integrity because he cared about the name of Jesus being worshipped.

The apostle wanted nothing to undermine the truth of his faithfulness to the Christ he proclaimed. He certainly wanted to face the judgment seat of Christ and hear, "Well done, good and faithful servant." If his reputation was ruined, the Lord's name would be shamed, and his usefulness would be gone. His fruitfulness would be curtailed. Consequently, Paul lived in holiness and godly sincerity because he did not want God to be dishonored.

### Concern for the Church

The *second* reason Paul defended his integrity was because of his concern for the church. We understand what happens to the church when integrity is shattered. Paul wrote, "We are not again

commending ourselves to you but are giving you an occasion to be proud of us, so that you will have an answer for those who take pride in appearance and not in heart" (5:12). When Paul spoke about "those who take pride in appearance and not in heart," he was referring to the false teachers who were into works-based righteousness. False teachers always come along and take pride in appearance and not in heart. For them, it's all about looking good externally, because false religion can never change the heart.

As pastors, we want to live with integrity so that the church would be proud of us and defend us against false accusers. Paul realized it was necessary to defend himself because the false teachers were harming the church's confidence in him. He knew their attacks on his integrity would create discord, retard growth, and cripple the church's testimony. Paul's concern for his reputation was for the church's sake. He was not attempting to be newly vindicated; this was just an opportunity for the congregation to step up and demonstrate that they were proud of Paul by answering the critics. Yet apparently they did not do this.

In fact, the last time Paul made a visit to Corinth, someone in the church stood up and falsely accused him. And when no one defended him, he left with a broken heart. That's why Paul was hesitant about coming back. He did not know if he could stand the pain. The apostle was hoping these people would rally around their minister, rally around the truth that he taught, and take the initiative against the intruders.

I met a very prominent TV preacher on a flight one night from Chicago. He happened to be inebriated about half an hour into the flight, and when he saw me, he treated me with significant disdain. I responded, "This is interesting because I'm now in the process of writing a little article about you." A few days after I got back to Los Angeles, I received an envelope in the mail from him. It read, "Dear John: Thanks for the wonderful fellowship on the flight from Chicago…" He of course had written this letter so that if I brought up anything about his drinking, he could deny it. Along with the letter from him, he had attached about 12 other letters, all from different people praising him. We understand that it matters to be defended by people other than ourselves. But this defense did not work for me, because I was on the plane and saw the reality of his condition. In 2 Corinthians, Paul also did not want to write only a testimonial to himself, even though it was believable he did have integrity. He knew it is better when a congregation rises up to a pastor's defense.

The apostle wanted his Corinthian friends to boldly confront the enemies of the church and rise to protect their faithful minister and shepherd. Paul would prefer to "let another praise you, and not your own mouth" (Proverbs 27:2). He wrote that he and his fellow workers were

giving the Corinthian believers "an occasion to be proud of us" (2 Corinthians 5:12). He wanted the church to boast of him, in the right sense of the word. They needed to take up his case. They needed to answer his detractors. They had all the information, because they had sat under his ministry for nearly two years. What else could Paul write that had not been already written and said?

That was the situation Jonathan Edwards found himself in as well. He had ministered for more than 20 years in one church and was a catalyst for the Great Awakening, but the church threw him out and spread the word against him so far and wide that he was reduced to ministering to a settlement of Indians. Spurgeon experienced this when the Baptist Union threw him out with an overwhelming vote that was seconded by his own brother, who was his assistant pastor. Paul understood that a minister has to defend himself for the sake of the strength and unity of the church.

### Devotion to the Truth

The *third* reason we defend our integrity is for devotion to the truth. "If we are beside ourselves, it is for God; if we are of sound mind, it is for you" (2 Corinthians 5:13). Paul was not defending himself in a self-serving manner, but out of devotion to the people in the church and to God. "Beside ourselves" means to be out of one's mind. This entails that the people were calling Paul crazy, claiming he had lost his mind. But this same term is used to describe excitement and enthusiasm. Paul was saying, "If I appear over-the-top excited and enthusiastic, it's for God. If I am passionate and seem insane, there is a reason for it. I'm a fanatic about God and His truth."

How could Paul not be enthused, passionate, and zealous when what he did was all for God? For the divine truth that had been given to him and needed to be passed on to others so they could believe.

Next, Paul wrote, "And if we are of sound mind"—that is, if there are times when we are moderate, sober-minded, calm, cool, collected, meek, humble, and restrained—"it is for you." There's a part of a pastor that is passionate, zealous, and over the top. But there is also a part that is sober-minded, analytical, and careful in all the things he does and says. Paul was reasonable when he needed to be reasonable, and he was passionate when he couldn't contain his love for the truth and the God of that truth.

### A Gratitude for Salvation

A *fourth* reason for defending integrity is a gratitude for salvation, or a gratitude for saving love. "For the love of Christ controls us" (5:14). Everything that Paul did was because of the fact that Christ's love controlled him. What had come into Paul's life took over him completely. He wrote, "For the love of Christ controls us, having concluded this, that one died for all, therefore all died; and He died for all, so that they who live might no longer live for themselves, but for Him who died and rose again on their behalf" (5:14-15).

Paul was defending his integrity because he was constrained to maintaining a place of effective ministry, usefulness, and believability. The apostle was willing to fight on account of Christ's great love for him. He knew that one way to show gratitude for that love was by giving himself in sacrificial ministry on behalf of the gospel. Pastor, do you love Christ enough to make all the sacrifices necessary to live a life of gratitude? To clarify, a life of gratitude is a life of holiness and godly sincerity that gives back in gratitude the integrity of ministry that pleases the Lord and says, "Thank You for Your unspeakable gift" (see 2 Corinthians 9:15).

Paul wanted to minister because "One died for all." This is one of the greatest theological statements you'll find anywhere in the epistles. Now let's get a little technical here by asking who fits into the category of "all." Fortunately, the word "all" is qualified in verse 14: "therefore all died." If you assume that "all" refers to all of humanity that has ever lived, then you are holding to a Universalist perspective. Do you believe everybody who has ever lived is going to heaven? If your answer is no, then you understand that Christ's atonement has limits.

The "all" whom Christ died for are those who believe in Him. He rose on their behalf only. The text itself tells us that this is a specific death, an act of substitution. Do not allow yourself to think that Jesus did the same thing on the cross for all the people in hell as He did for the people in heaven. That would mean He died for nobody in particular. Some people see Christ's death as a potential that is actualized when a person comes to believe in Jesus. But how can spiritually dead sinners activate a potential atonement? Jesus did not die a vague death; He died for all those who are His elect children. He said, "I am the good shepherd, and I know My own and My own know Me, even as the Father knows Me and I know the Father; and I lay down My life for the sheep" (John 10:14-15).

Paul had a heart of gratitude because he understood the actual atoning substitutionary death that Christ had died for him. It was this overwhelming reality—the fact that before he ever came into existence, God in His eternal and sovereign love had purposed that Jesus Christ would bear his sins in His own body on the cross—that led to Paul's gratitude.

Paul then wrote in verse 16, "Therefore from now on we recognize no one according to the flesh; even though we have known Christ according to the flesh, yet now we know Him in this way no longer." Paul, at one point, thought Jesus was a charlatan and a fraud. He would have been screaming, "Crucify Him" with everybody else in that crowd before Pilate. But because that was already history, he expressed his opposition to Jesus by persecuting Christians. Paul originally had a human view of Christ: "We have known Christ according to the flesh." Yet after his conversion, "We know Him in this way no longer." Paul's view was transformed. He was, as he said in verse 17, "A new creature; the old things passed away; behold, new things have come."

## Defending Your Own Integrity

Paul was transformed through his faith in Christ and Christ's substitutionary atoning death on his behalf. This truth of the cross leads to an all-consuming gratitude for salvation that results in a defense of integrity. How could Paul not defend the nature of his new identity, which was purchased by the precious blood of Christ? Likewise, as a pastor, seek to possess an integrity that is worth defending, and defend it because the cross has made you a new creation.

# 6

# OPPOSITION AND HOPE

*Mark Dever*
*Shepherds' Conference 2007*

*Daniel 1–6*

Recently I was surprised by a publication that instructed Muslims about the correctness of killing Christians in Saudi Arabia. The book encouraged Muslims to fight their own personal jihad and work to expose what they see as an evil cabal controlling the American government.

As Christians, at least in the West, we feel more troubled and uncertain than we may have felt 30 years ago. At the very same time, there seems to be growing among us indigenous threats to our public ministries and liberties, as well as challenges to the free practice of the Christian faith in this land. There is the entrenched secularism of our elites, which dismisses the validity of Christianity and eats away at the residual cultural empathy that there is for the gospel. And there is also the innervating and

exhausting reality of our unchallenged addiction to comfort amidst perilously growing material affluence.

With our ideas marginalized by the elites and with our eyelids growing heavy through the warm embrace of worldly ease, we find ourselves particularly unprepared to combat a fairly new phenomenon in this country—the phenomenon of legal intolerance toward an exclusive faith like Christianity. Hate crimes, which are detestable things, are increasingly described as the inevitable result of hate speech. Speech that others deem as incitement to violence, even nonphysical violence, is increasingly regarded as socially disruptive and wrong. Condemnations of homosexuality are taken to be incitements to personal violence against people. The ground is being prepared at local, state, and federal levels alike to make statements decrying homosexuality or even statements denying the truth of other religions be categorized as hate speech.

In short, any statements that might prove inflammatory are to be classified as illegal. Christians who have for so long dominated the scene in America, and at least have been widely tolerated in the West, are now beginning to face the prospect of living in a world that does not so easily accept our freedoms to make certain claims and denials. As pastors, we are on the front line of this change, and if you don't realize that now, you will within the next few years.

What do we do when we're told that it's illegal to say another religion is false or homosexuality is wrong? You may say, "Well, Mark, that's on your mind because you're a pastor on Capitol Hill in Washington, DC. A third of your congregation is made up of lawyers." Friend, I wish that was the only reason we should think about this, but there are already many places around the world where these threats are realized. We have to remember that many of our brothers and sisters this very day are facing oppression, whether from Latin American Roman Catholics, Indian Hindu nationalists, Muslims, communists, or secularists. It's fair to say that even while we enjoy the freedom of meeting in this country, there is no such freedom for Christians in many other places around the world.

But what if our laws here in America become like the laws of most nations around the world today? What if there were more public intolerance toward our faith that makes it difficult to have a public meeting? What should we do?

## The Example of Daniel

We find our answer in the Old Testament, and there are few portions of the Bible that are as instructive for us in this matter as the book of Daniel. Most Christians are familiar with at least the first half of this book, since it is full of famous stories regularly mined by parents who want to prevent their kids from going with the crowd. In chapter 1, Daniel stood up for his diet. In chapters 2 through 6 he stood up for his faith. These chapters are full of human drama and valor in the face of danger, truth in response to threats, uncompromising faithfulness in places full of the temptations of power and wealth. In these biographical chapters of Daniel, you have two sieges, four kings, and lots of dreams and visions. The rest of the book, chapters 7 through 12, is no longer a story of Daniel, but focuses on Daniel reporting about his visions. Here we will focus on the first six chapters.

As vivid as Daniel's story is, it is often misunderstood. It's often interpreted and applied as a religious "how to succeed" manual. Certainly there is much we can learn from Daniel's example. In chapter 1, Jerusalem was besieged by the most powerful king in the ancient Near East, the Babylonian emperor Nebuchadnezzar. As a young man, perhaps even a teenager, Daniel was taken into captivity.

Once in Babylon, he was selected for a special program so he could be trained as an advisor to the king. He was successful and was treated with favor by those in charge. He was allowed to eat his own food so that he wouldn't become ceremonially unclean according to his own religion, and he gained great knowledge and understanding.

In chapter 2, King Nebuchadnezzar made an impossible demand of his wise men regarding a vision that he'd had. It was Daniel alone who was able to describe the vision and interpret it for the king. The rest of the story in these first six chapters continues in the same vein, with Daniel being both outstandingly faithful and a model of prosperity at the same time. Outstandingly faithful as he faced real opposition, and yet he always prospered.

## The Purpose of Daniel

Of course this isn't just a story about Daniel. If you look back to Daniel 1:2, you see that Nebuchadnezzar's conquest of Jerusalem was possible because God allowed it. Though it may seem like Judah's God had been defeated, this verse makes it clear that it was the Lord who delivered Jerusalem into the hands of the Babylonians. And the official who showed favor to Daniel's dietary restriction was provoked by God (verse 9). As for Daniel gaining understanding, we see that it was God who gave him knowledge and wisdom (verse 17). Daniel served in the court as a wise man and advisor for

almost 70 years after he was deported to Babylon. That's longer than Winston Churchill's public career, and that too was a result of God's favor. As for Daniel interpreting Nebuchadnezzar's dream, we read that the mystery was revealed to Daniel in a vision that came from God. Even the purpose of the dream and its interpretation was to show to Nebuchadnezzar that his power came from God: "The God of heaven has given [you] the kingdom, the power, the strength and the glory" (2:37-38).

We don't know exactly when this vision came to Nebuchadnezzar. And we see that the king would not tell the astrologers what his dream was, because if he had told them, then he wouldn't know if he should trust their interpretation. However, the astrologers were against Nebuchadnezzar's demand. We read in Daniel 2:10, "There is not a man on earth who could declare the matter for the king, inasmuch as no great king or ruler has ever asked anything like this of any magician, conjurer or Chaldean." They were right—only the true God could reveal this vision and its meaning.

Daniel accepted this impossible task because he knew God was able.

The king said to Daniel, whose name was Belteshazzar, "Are you able to make known to me the dream which I have seen and its interpretation?" Daniel answered before the king and said, "As for the mystery about which the king has inquired, neither wise men, conjurers, magicians nor diviners are able to declare it to the king. However, there is a God in heaven who reveals mysteries, and He has made known to King Nebuchadnezzar what will take place in the latter days" (Daniel 2:26-28).

---

**The message of this book is that God causes His faithful to survive, and that's a message pastors need to hear.**

---

Surely we, along with all the readers of this story for the last millennia, must admire Daniel's courage and his willingness to stand alone for the truth. But is this the point of these stories in Daniel? I want us to look at Daniel as an example, but in a way that's different than what is often taught in Sunday school. I want to look at Daniel more as an example of what God does with faith. The message of this book is that God causes His faithful to survive, and that's a message pastors need to hear. We'll look at three lessons we can learn from the first six chapters of Daniel.

### Lessons to Learn from Daniel

#### God Is Our Hope

The first lesson we must learn is that God is our only hope. The book of Daniel exposes the myth of the godless world that we are left in this world without

hope. Whether you are a refugee from a defeated nation, a religious minority under an unjust sentence of death, have your friends persecuted and executed, are called to speak difficult things to people above you and stationed in power, or you are a pastor with your back against the wall, you still have hope, and it is in God, who is the true sovereign of the world. You do not stand at the mercy of an election or legislation, for God is the one who is sovereign.

God's faithfulness is the explanation for Daniel's survival and prosperity. All throughout the book of Daniel, God is shown to be powerful and in control. We certainly see God's power in the wonderful story about Shadrach, Meshach, and Abednego. We read their response to Nebuchadnezzar in Daniel 3:17: "If it be so, our God whom we serve is able to deliver us from the furnace of blazing fire; and He will deliver us out of your hand, O king." Even Nebuchadnezzar referred to God as the "Most High" (verse 26). In verse 28 we read the king's proclamation, "Blessed be to the God of Shadrach, Meshach and Abednego who has sent His angel and delivered His servants who put their trust in Him, violating the king's command, and yielded up their bodies so as not to serve or worship any god except their own God." The central feature of this book, then, is not Daniel's faithfulness, but God's faithfulness. If you understand this truth, then it will be wonderful news to your soul.

Before Nebuchadnezzar condemned

Shadrach, Meshach, and Abednego, he seems to have entirely forgotten the lessons he had learned earlier when he had his troublesome dream. He blustered in verse 15, "What god is there who can deliver you out of my hands?" Then we have that amazing response we just read in Daniel 3:16-18—Shadrach, Meshach, and Abednego were faithful to God and trusted Him completely. Theirs was a confident, trusting, humble, and joyful statement that persecuted Christians ought to say to their persecutors. We know our God is sovereign, and He may exercise His sovereignty in ways that we don't understand right now, but even if He chooses not to save us, He is a wise and good God, and we can trust Him.

Daniel's friends made evident the confidence that we as Christians are to have. They were sentenced to a fiery death: "Then Nebuchadnezzar was filled with wrath, and his facial expression was altered toward Shadrach, Meshach and Abednego. He answered by giving orders to heat the furnace seven times more than it was usually heated" (3:19). The furnace was so hot that the flames killed the men who tied up and put Shadrach, Meshach, and Abednego into the furnace. There, in that blazing furnace, the very place where earthly power like Nebuchadnezzar's would seem to be at its absolute height, Nebuchadnezzar saw the limits of his power. His earthly power was unmasked by the sovereign God, in whose hand is all power. Nebuchadnezzar was amazed, for in this place

that he meant to show his power, instead, he found out who was the real ruler of the world. And after he saw the power of God, he praised the true God.

Yet even this conviction eventually faded away. In chapter 4, we see that the king's pride had grown again. The historical setting seems to be near the end of Nebuchadnezzar's reign. Commentators speculate that it was around 570 BC, when most of his building projects would have been finished, and it was then that Nebuchadnezzar provided an account of the Lord humbling him. The king said, "It has seemed good to me to declare the signs and wonders which the Most High God has done for me. How great are His signs and how mighty are His wonders! His kingdom is an everlasting kingdom and His dominion is from generation to generation" (verses 2-3). Then in verse 17: "The Most High is ruler over the realm of mankind, and bestows it on whom He wishes and sets over it the lowliest of men." Daniel echoed this statement in verse 25: "The Most High is ruler over the realm of mankind and bestows it on whomever He wishes." Nebuchadnezzar closed the chapter by saying, "I blessed the Most High and praised and honored Him who lives forever; for His dominion is an everlasting dominion, and His kingdom endures from generation to generation" (verse 34). Nebuchadnezzar offered praise to the most high.

You might think that because you're not the emperor of a great empire, but rather, the pastor of a small church, that pride cannot reside in your own heart. Not true. Nebuchadnezzar is proud here. He may have been able to capture Jerusalem, but Jerusalem's God was still unassailably sovereign over him, even in the capture. Nebuchadnezzar may have had a long reign, but God has a reign that will never end. Nebuchadnezzar may have built one of the great wonders of the ancient world, but it was God who made the world.

It is simply false and distorting when we begin thinking of ourselves in mighty ways because we are not our own best hope—God is! There is no Utopia in this fallen world. There is hope for eternity through the life, death, and resurrection of our Lord Jesus Christ. Through Christ, God becomes our hope just as He has been the hope and help of others. I'm reminded of the letter that Adoniram Judson wrote to Luther Rice when he was trying to raise money for Christian missions. Judson was overseas, and Rice was getting complaints about Judson's missionary work being hopeless and pointless. Judson wrote, "If they ask again, 'What prospect of ultimate success is there?' Tell them, 'As much as there is in almighty and faithful God, who will perform His promises, and no more.'"

Friend, the only hope we have today isn't our integrity, hard work, fortune, cleverness, or even courage. Our only hope is the same as Daniel's—God Himself. This book is here to remind us that only God can give us the faith and faithfulness we need. It's when we have exhausted our own strength that we are then in the perfect place to trust the Lord. Like that fiery furnace that Shadrach, Meshach, and Abednego went through or that deacons meeting you just went through, remember, you are a child of God. Do not despair, but realize that God is building a stage upon to which make clear His power and His faithfulness. Please remember that in your ministries. And remember to teach this to your people and deconstruct their false and deceptive hopes. Liberate them from lies and serve them by emancipating them from error with the message of these chapters, which tell us that God is our only hope.

### You Can Survive Opposition

A second lesson we learn in Daniel 1–6 is that you can survive opposition. Daniel's survival is meant to be an inspiration to us, more than just a "how-to" instruction guide. Daniel is to be a motivation for the hope that we need. Also, it's amazing to see Daniel survive as long as he did! The kings he served had such great power—they were absolute monarchs, unchecked by any parliament or popularity, by press or poll. Yet Daniel survived the king that had destroyed his native city, carried him to exile, and even sentenced him to death.

In chapter 5 we see Daniel, probably the only survivor in the king's court, still within the orbit of the king in 539 BC, only it's clear that the king has changed. The king is now Belshazzar, who was shaken when he saw the hand that wrote a message on the wall. Belshazzar promised Daniel that if he could properly interpret the writing, then he would make him the third ruler in the kingdom. The reason for the third position was because the Babylonian emperor was Nabonidus, and Belshazzar was his son. Because Nabonidus was still alive, Belshazzar was considered number two in the kingdom. So by offering Daniel the third place in the kingdom, Belshazzar was offering Daniel the highest place available.

By this time Daniel was nearing his eighties. And he responded with the courage that approaching death gives: "Keep your gifts for yourself or give your rewards to someone else" (5:17). He then confronted the king:

> Yet you, his son, Belshazzar, have not humbled your heart, even though you knew all this, but you have exalted yourself against the Lord of heaven; and they have brought the vessels of His house before you, and you and your nobles, your wives and your concubines have been drinking wine from them; and you have praised the gods of silver and gold, of bronze, iron, wood and stone, which do not see, hear or understand. But the God in whose hand are your life-breath and all your ways, you have not glorified (verses 22-23).

Daniel then explained the writing on the wall, which was an indictment from the Lord: "This is the interpretation of the message: 'MENĒ'—God has numbered your kingdom and put an end to it. 'TEKĒL'—you have been weighed on the scales and found deficient. 'PERĒS'—your kingdom has been divided and given over to the Medes and Persians" (5:26-28). What is most amazing of all is that after this took place, Daniel prospered again. He had taken unusual risk to speak honestly to the king. And later that night, it wasn't Daniel who was slain; it was Belshazzar. We read in Daniel 5:30, "That same night Belshazzar the Chaldean king was slain." Darius the Mede took his place. Even though the Babylonian Empire had come to an end, Daniel once again survived—not only an emperor, but a whole empire.

---

**Let's treasure the gospel and let's resolve afresh to hold out the good news of Jesus Christ around us, because this is how we will survive in this world and the next.**

---

As a pastor, do you not see from this that there are no worldly circumstances that you will face that should ever drain your hope dry? All opposition to God's people, whether in this life or the next, will end. Therefore, let us labor to keep our hope in the gospel. Let's try to evacuate our hopes from every place else they may be, and put them in the gospel. When we keep our hopes on earthly matters, we keep them at our peril. They're either dashed, or worse than that, they appear to succeed, and so distract us. Jesus said, "Where your treasure is, there your heart will be also" (Luke 12:34). Let's treasure the gospel and let's resolve afresh to hold out the good news of Jesus Christ around us, because this is how we will survive in this world and the next.

### Opposition Will Come

The third lesson is that you will face opposition. The book of Daniel exposes the myth that we live in an amoral world. In fact, the world is so fallen that it is normal for the godly to face opposition, and God's dealings with Daniel remind us of this reality. Pastor, wake up! You will face opposition. You don't hear this from evangelical pulpits, or in churches in the United States. Sometimes I fear that Christians are more like used car salesmen when it comes to the faith. They point out the good, cover up the difficult points, and do not sound like Jesus in the gospels or the apostles in Acts.

Daniel continued to face persecution even in the final years of his life. The man had survived three kings, and still faced opposition. It isn't clear when exactly Daniel died, but the events of chapter 6 must have taken place near the end of his life. It was at this time that the Babylonian Empire had fallen, but Daniel continued to prosper. We read in Daniel 6:1-2,

"It seemed good to Darius to appoint 120 satraps over the kingdom, that they would be in charge of the whole kingdom, and over them three commissioners (of whom Daniel was one)." It's a whole different empire, and yet Daniel was still on top. Verse 3 continues, "Then this Daniel began distinguishing himself among the commissioners and satraps because he possessed an extraordinary spirit, and the king planned to appoint him over the entire kingdom." Daniel is in his seventies or older, and the king planned to set him over the whole kingdom.

But as is so often the case, there were unprincipled men who were willing to challenge Daniel and harm him. Daniel 6:5 reveals their thinking: "We will not find any ground of accusation against this Daniel unless we find it against him with regard to the law of his God." And the same still happens today. We must understand that we live in a fallen world and cannot expect a Utopia or perfect government. Though virtue may prevent us from being persecuted for doing wrong and it is commendable to work up our courage and integrity as Daniel did, the fact we are righteous is no guarantee that we will avoid trials.

This generation of evangelical ministers is called to tar the Ark before the flood of God's judgment comes upon our land. You are to teach believers that they will face opposition in a fallen world. Don't sell people lying nostrums in order to create apparent prosperity in your church. You are called to teach your people about the fall and the implications of the fall. Pastors who are from other places in the world will be lovingly bemused that this is news or that anyone could be surprised by this because they've lived under far more difficult circumstances.

The liberty and material prosperity in America, though it has been an obvious blessing from God, has crippled the church in some ways. We must prepare ourselves by reading the book of Daniel, understanding that even the most virtuous will face opposition. The fallen world is so bent that when God Himself appeared in the flesh, He was opposed, persecuted, and crucified. But there is good news: If you go on to read the rest of Daniel and the visions in chapters 7–12, you'll see that ultimately, God wins.

A consistent element of these visions is that the saints are under attack in this world. For example, we read in Daniel 7:21, "I kept looking, and that horn was waging war with the saints and overpowering them." Moreover, "He will speak out against the Most High and wear down the saints of the Highest One" (7:25). Chapter 8 reveals this about suffering for God's people:

> It grew up to the host of heaven and caused some of the host and some of the stars to fall to the earth, and it trampled them down. It even magnified itself to be equal with the Commander of the host; and it removed the regular sacrifice from Him, and the place of

His sanctuary was thrown down. And on account of transgression the host will be given over to the horn along with the regular sacrifice; and it will fling truth to the ground and perform its will and prosper. Then I heard a holy one speaking, and another holy one said to that particular one who was speaking, "How long will the vision about the regular sacrifice apply, while the transgression causes horror, so as to allow both the holy place and the host to be trampled?" He said to me, "For 2,300 evenings and mornings; then the holy place will be properly restored" (10-14).

The interpretation is found in verses 24-25:

> His power will be mighty, but not by his own power, and he will destroy to an extraordinary degree and prosper and perform his will; he will destroy mighty men and the holy people. And through his shrewdness he will cause deceit to succeed by his influence; and he will magnify himself in his heart, and he will destroy many while they are at ease. He will even oppose the Prince of princes, but he will be broken without human agency.

From this exile that God's people were enduring to the various trials that are mentioned in Daniel 9, it is clear that being the people of God won't be a walk in the park. Mighty rulers will show favor to those who forsake God. Temptations and troubles will multiply. Pressure will be brought to bear on those who have been faithful to God, and many will lose their lives. In Daniel 12:7 we read, "They finish shattering the power of the holy people." My intent is not to get into the particular eschatology of these verses because we can understand them to refer to a final tribulation. What is evident here is that from the cross of Christ until His return, the world will be at enmity with God.

By our very nature, we don't like and want to avoid trials. Yet real Christianity doesn't presume to deliver from suffering in the present moment. You will have trials as a Christian, and we see from the book of Acts that the early Christians did so regularly. Jesus said, "Remember the word that I said to you, 'A slave is not greater than his master.' If they persecuted Me, they will also persecute you" (John 15:20). Our present situation of almost no visible persecution is actually unusual in the history of Christianity, even among the Christians who live in other parts of the world today. So I warn you to not get comfortable. Worldly comfort only serves to make cavities in our souls, to weaken us, to misguide us, and to misdirect our efforts.

Some think that maneuvering correctly in politics can help Christianity avoid suffering. While politics is a noble calling, and many ills have been alleviated by this noble public work, in our fallen world, Christian politicians will no more be able to eliminate persecution than Christian doctors will be able to eliminate death. We are in a fallen world at enmity with God, and our brothers and sisters in politics cannot promise less persecution. The day we don't suffer for following Christ is an odd day. Therefore, we are not to run away from pain and suffering, but to walk with God through those trying times and let Him teach us how to turn each bit of suffering into positive learning about the depths of God's love.

I guarantee that Shadrach, Meshach, and Abednego had more confidence in God the night after they were thrown into the fiery furnace. Likewise, cancer, surgery, unemployment, death, bereavement, and broken relationships will help an individual see something of the riches that God has committed toward strengthening the believer's faith. Persecution and trials are platforms that God has built to show His power, sufficiency, and loving-kindness toward His people.

Your congregation is a treasury of sufferings, from arthritis to loneliness, from bereavement to confusion. And God allows you to be a living testimony about having Him, trusting Him, and knowing that being His child is better than having happy marriages, or never-ending earthly friendships, or even legal toleration of Christians. Knowing Christ is better than all else.

A commitment to God's glory above

our own will normally bring suffering in this world. Peter wrote,

> If when you do what is right and suffer for it you patiently endure it, this finds favor with God. For you have been called for this purpose, since Christ also suffered for you, leaving you an example for you to follow in His steps, who committed no sin, nor was any deceit found in His mouth; and while being reviled, He did not revile in return; while suffering, He uttered no threats, but kept entrusting Himself to Him who judges righteously (1 Peter 2:20-23).

Is this what is expected when someone becomes a Christian? Is this what is expected when someone goes into the ministry? It is vital to consider carefully your expectations, because wrong expectations are a danger to souls. Let your expectations be shaped by what God promises in His Word. Consider all the trials Daniel faced even though he was a blessed man. The way you prepare for trials is by growing in your love for Christ.

Although we want to live in such way that people around us like us, we cannot expect that this will happen. Especially if the courts uphold certain kinds of hate speech legislation, we can't be too surprised if pastors will be charged with public crimes the way they have been in Canada, Australia, Norway, England, and elsewhere for doing nothing other than preaching the Bible. If there

are individuals in the pastorate who are expecting worldly prosperity, then they should get out now before they're publicly and eternally embarrassed. However, we will endure all circumstances when we have found something that we love more than this world's praises and prosperity.

## An Example of Suffering

I had the joy of listening to J. Smith recently in Manhattan. J. Smith is an American evangelist who lives in London and ministers to Muslims. He goes to Hyde Park Corner to debate Muslims and stands up on a soapbox to declare the truth. He shared with us about how some of the individuals who were found guilty in the London subway bombings were familiar faces who were among the crowds that he regularly spoke to at Hyde Park Corner. After the bombing, he asked the Muslims who had gathered near him, "How many of you think what these guys did was a good thing?" About 30 hands went up. He then said, "How many of you want to do this yourself?" About 15 hands went up. J. Smith then told our gathering, "We Christians should all be willing to be killed. My wife knows that someday I'll be killed because of the work I do." Friend, can you imagine having that kind of mind-set? I believe Daniel had that kind of mind-set. And I hope you have that kind of mind-set as well—that you are willing to endure opposition faithfully because you possess the ultimate hope of spending eternity with your Savior.

# PRAYER

Lord, we thank You for Your example of enduring persecution. Even more, Lord, we thank You for Your being persecuted for us and enduring the wrath we deserve. We know we'll never experience the full extent of persecution we deserve because of Your kindness and amazing love to us in Christ. We pray that You would give us strength, educate our hearts, and inflame our lives with love for You above all things. We pray in Jesus' name, Amen.

# 7

# The Leader and His Flock

*Rick Holland*

*Shepherds' Conference 2011*

*1 Peter 5:1-4*

First Peter 5:1-4 is familiar territory to anyone who is in ministry. In four simple verses, we get Pastoral Theology 101 all the way to the PhD, and we learn what it means to be a pastor, a leader, an overseer, and a shepherd:

> Therefore, I exhort the elders among you, as your fellow elder and witness of the sufferings of Christ, and a partaker also of the glory that is to be revealed, shepherd the flock of God among you, exercising oversight not under compulsion, but voluntarily, according to the will of God; and not for sordid gain, but with eagerness; nor yet as lording it over those allotted to your charge, but proving to be examples to the flock. And when the Chief Shepherd appears, you will receive the unfading crown of glory.

## The Imagery of Sheep and Shepherds

The Bible is a zoo. It is full of animals and it should be, because the variety of animals speaks to the creativity of our Lord and Savior, Jesus, the agent of creation. The Bible mentions over 70 types of animals. The Old Testament contains 180 words to reference animals, while the New Testament has about 50 words. There are clean and unclean animals, domesticated animals and wild beasts. There are cattle, goats, horses, camels, donkeys, pigs, dogs, snakes, frogs, bears, leopards, lions, foxes, jackals, wolves, fish, sparrows, eagles, vultures, worms, caterpillars, locusts, and even leviathans and behemoths.

Of all the animals, the sheep is the most frequently mentioned in the Bible, with more than 400 references. This is for good reason—sheep were a central part of the economy of Israel. They were raised for milk, meat, and wool. Sheep were also a central part of the sacrificial system. Because they were so essential, there also had to be shepherds. And if you want to comprehend the Bible's figurative references for shepherding people, then understanding the job of a shepherd in the ancient Near East is vital.

The conditions and the practices of shepherds back then were far different from what they are today. There were no fences, and the sheep could not be left by themselves inside an enclosure. Thus the sheep were completely dependent on their shepherds, who were responsible for protecting their flock against predators, sheltering them from threatening heat and cold, and leading them to pastures where they could feed and graze. In short, the shepherd was a provider, a protector, a guide, and an authority. Above all, the shepherd was a constant companion to his sheep.

Though shepherds were vital, they were not an esteemed part of the populace in Bible times. They were viewed as an odd sort because they lived nomadic lives in the wilderness. Their sole purpose was the care of their flock. They were hard-working blue-collar men. Yet these men were also special and respected at a certain level. Everyone knew that the welfare of the sheep, as well as the welfare

of the sacrificial system itself, was due to the faithfulness of these shepherds.

This lesson on sheep husbandry is necessary because understanding the task of a shepherd is essential to grasping the pastoral imperative before us in 1 Peter 5:1-4. In verse 2, Peter instructed spiritual leaders to "shepherd the flock of God." The simple command is to be a shepherd and to shepherd the flock of God. Most dictionaries and encyclopedias that I consulted about shepherding made mention of the stupidity of sheep. Sheep don't survive very well unless they are protected. If they are left to themselves or subjected to even the smallest predator, they will not survive. Sheep can't find their way back to a fold even when it's within sight. Some have witnessed sheep running off a cliff simply because they were mimicking other sheep.

Therefore, as we look at this familiar text, it's too easy to focus on the people we shepherd as lacking intelligence, being dependent, or being prone to wander. It's too easy to forget something very important: *We are sheep too.* When a man becomes a pastor, he does not become an under-shepherd for God; rather, he becomes a sheepdog. For the term *under-shepherd* is too much of a compliment. As pastors, we are the sheepdogs God sends out into the pasture to round up and care for His flock. We are those "unintelligent" and "dependent" sheep as well.

> God is the ultimate shepherd of His people, but He has graciously called us to help with this work.

God's purpose for pastoral ministry is illustrated in the image of a shepherd. It's a metaphor he uses more than any other illustration in the Bible concerning spiritual oversight. In Jeremiah 3:15, the prophet lays this foundation by saying, "I will give you shepherds after My own heart." God is talking about that great day when the Messiah establishes His kingdom. How will we know these shepherds are after God's own heart? The next phrase tells us: "who will feed you on knowledge and understanding." God's standard of shepherding is a shepherd who is after His own heart. This passage provides the lens through which to view other passages about shepherding— the faithful shepherd looks to God his Shepherd and shepherds like God does. God is the ultimate shepherd of His people, but He has graciously called us to help with this work.

## The Realities of Pastoral Ministry

In 1 Peter 5:1-4, Peter shows us what it means to be a shepherd-leader. Let me warn you: This is not for the fainthearted. Pastoral ministry is not for wimps. Pastoral ministry is not a social alternative to another job in the world. It's one of the most difficult, rigorous, painstaking, and crushing endeavors any human can undertake. This passage is about promoting the Great Shepherd while diminishing our role as shepherds.

In this passage, we observe three sobering realities of pastoral ministry, with the first one being…

### Pastoral Ministry Is a Serious Responsibility

In verse 1 we read, "Therefore, I exhort the elders among you, as your fellow elder and witness of the sufferings of Christ, and a partaker also of the glory that is to be revealed…" Peter's exhortation is very specific, as it targets the elders. The term "elder" literally means someone who's older. However, when you study the semantic domain of this word and its usage in Jewish society, an "elder" was either senior in age or senior in experience. Sometimes there were younger men who were more senior in experience than older men. Someone once said, "It doesn't matter how long you've been in the canoe that determines how far you've gone across the lake, but how hard you've been pulling on the oars." There are younger men in ministry who pull very hard on the oars.

Three terms in this passage triangulate the vision and the responsibilities of a church leader—overseer, pastor, and elder. Verse 1 employs "elder" from the Greek term *presbuteros,* whereas verse 2 uses the verbal form of the Greek term *poimanate,* which means "shepherd" or "pastor," and the Greek word *episkopos,* which means "to exercise oversight."

These three titles describe the office of an elder, who must be mature, wise, and has a heart and an ability to guide.

These three titles do not describe different kinds of men, nor different offices or roles, but characteristics that must converge in a spiritual leader. It is important to mention that though this passage references an office clearly outlined in the pastoral letters (1–2 Timothy and Titus), there are people who perform "overseeing" pastoral work as an extension of God's love for His flock without ever occupying a formal office. Paul had a similar understanding of these three terms. In Acts 20:17-28, he deployed the same three words—pastor, overseer, and elder—synonymously when he spoke to the elders at Ephesus. This signifies he was talking about a single office.

Peter wrote his first epistle to a group of believers whose lives were threatened because of their faith. And there are places in the world today where this experience is the reality for Christians. I have never suffered persecution that threatened my life. I've never been in a prayer meeting interrupted by a knock on the door and feared that Nero's guards had come to arrest me and take me to the lions. But that is the cultural context in which Peter's readers lived.

A noteworthy feature of Peter's letter is that instead of encouraging his readers with temporal comfort amidst persecution, he stressed that comfort would come at death. And until then, they were to be faithful. But if his emphasis was on faithfulness amidst persecution, then why did he shift to a discussion about elders at the close of his letter? Peter wanted to ensure that as the recipients encountered persecution and prosecution, someone was overseeing their lives, helping them have the proper perspective, and calling them to obedience. Persecution was no excuse for disobedience. Peter also wanted to make sure that the elders and pastors did not shrink away from shepherding people because of the oppression they might incur. After all, to be a pastor during this period was to make oneself a larger target for persecution.

That is why Peter began with the admonition to recognize the serious nature of ministry. Verse 1 begins with "therefore," which reverts the reader back to 1 Peter 4:17-18, where "judgment" is said to "begin with the household of God." Therefore, the strictest judgment and weight is on the leaders who are developing the maturity of the house of God. In addition, this verse contains the most extensive self-description of Peter in the epistle—"I'm your fellow elder and witness of the sufferings of Christ." Peter chose to identify himself not with an apostolic business card, but as a fellow elder: "I'm just like you. I'm a fellow elder. I'm a fellow overseer. I'm a fellow pastor." The bottom line? Peter was not asking the elders and pastors to do anything that he was not willing to do. Suffering exists for spiritual leaders too, and Peter understood their fears, temptations, and responsibilities. There's an important principle here: It's always the spiritual leaders who bear the brunt of persecution first. Peter embraced God's call on his own life as a leader in a church, a calling that would eventually lead to his martyrdom in Rome. And he was not asking other leaders to do anything that he was not doing himself.

Interestingly enough, Peter wrote that he was a "witness" of Christ's sufferings. Some scholars conclude from this that the author of this epistle cannot be Peter because Peter wasn't present at the cross. But how do we know Peter wasn't observing the cross from a distance? Though we have no evidence that he was present, neither do we have evidence that he was not. Tom Schreiner writes, "Peter did observe Christ in His ministry. He saw the opposition mount against Him, was present when He was arrested, and may have found his way to the cross even after denying Him."[1] Maybe, maybe not, but there's no reason to use this phrase to doubt that Peter wrote this epistle. Peter did witness the outcome of Christ's suffering.

The main point here is to beware. To take on the position and responsibility of spiritual leadership is to make yourself vulnerable to the same forces that killed Jesus. Think that through for a moment. If we take Peter seriously, to be a spiritual leader is to submit ourselves as vulnerable participants in and against those same principalities that were at war

to put Christ on the cross. Not only the demonic forces, but also those who hate the morality of our God and the glory of our Savior Himself. And so Peter charges us to recognize that we have a serious responsibility.

### Pastoral Ministry Is a Delegated Responsibility

In verses 2 and 3, Peter presented the second sobering reality of pastoral ministry: It is a delegated responsibility. After the resurrection, Peter had an unforgettable interview with the risen Lord on the shore of the Sea of Galilee. The same Peter who cut off a person's ear, ran for his life after the crucifixion, and went back to Galilee to fish once again now had an opportunity to converse with Jesus. We read in John 21:15, "When they had finished breakfast, Jesus said to Simon Peter, 'Simon, son of John, do you love me more than these?'" Peter must have choked on his fish as he heard Jesus' words. Jesus asked again, "'Simon, son of John, do you love me?' He said to Him, 'Yes, Lord; You know that I love You.' He said to him, 'Shepherd My sheep'" (verse 16). Once again the same verb appears that is translated "to shepherd the sheep." He said to him the third time, "'Simon, son of John, do you love me?' Peter was grieved because He said to him the third time, 'Do you love me?' And he said to Him, 'Lord, You know all things; You know that I love You.' Jesus said to him, 'Tend My sheep'" (verse 17).

In most of the books that examine

this passage and in most of the sermons I have heard on this text, the emphasis has been placed on why there are different Greek words used for love. I have done that as well. But may I suggest to you that's not the point? There's a repeated imperative that should be noted: "If you love Me, then pastor people." The point is to tend to the Lord's flock, to feed His sheep, and to pastor His people. Don't get lost in the debate over love: get busy about the work of tending the flock.

Jesus' command to shepherd is an interesting exhortation because it's something that we are to both do and be. Ephesians 4:11 says, "He gave some as apostles, and some as prophets, and some as evangelists, and some as pastors." The final word in the Greek text of that verse is the same word translated as "shepherd." C.H. Spurgeon said, "With all His maturity and firmness, the spiritual Father is full of tenderness and manifests an intense love for the souls of men."[2] Spurgeon continued that this pastor "was born on purpose to care for other people and his heart cannot rest until it is full of such care."[3]

According to Ephesians 4:11, pastoring people is more than something you do. It defines you. We were "born on purpose" to care for others. And to care for others is always a self-denying fight against our own flesh. As we investigate 1 Peter chapter 5, the first phrase in verse 2 is the most important in the entire passage. We find in it an impossible responsibility: to shepherd the church which is

"the flock of God." Peter didn't say, "Shepherd your flock." He said, "Shepherd the flock of God among you." This is God's flock, not ours. These sheep are God's lambs. He commands us to tend them for Him, to pastor them for Him, and to care for them because they belong to Him.

Also, notice that the ministry is localized—this flock is "among you." Peter is not talking about the Internet or blogosphere. I'm thankful for websites and blogs; I read some daily and they are very helpful. However, we have to be careful not to neglect the local flock by engaging with others in the blogosphere, which is not the church.

Peter continued by challenging shepherds to be "exercising oversight." In the original Greek text, this terminology referred to political overseers or leaders who had all the knowledge or wisdom of a city, village, or a town as they exercised oversight. He was referring to service that requires careful and wise oversight. However, Peter was not naïve. He recognized that there are special temptations associated with spiritual leadership, and so he mentions three sins and three antidotes through three contrasting phrases.

*Not Under Compulsion*

The first warning is to oversee the sheep not forcefully, but according to the will of God. Peter put it this way: "exercising oversight not under compulsion"—not because you're forced, not because someone's making you do it, but "voluntarily, according to the will of God."

We shepherd people not because we have to but because we want to. Have you ever heard a pastor talk about their call to ministry by saying, "I was called into the ministry kicking and screaming. I didn't want to do it, but the Lord grabbed me by the collar and threw me into the pulpit?" When someone says that, I often want to reply, "I don't think it was God who did that."

Pastoral ministry is something you do willingly, something you were born to do, something you desire to do. Spurgeon declared that if you're a pastor who doesn't want to be in ministry, you're better off being a plumber. God doesn't call men into the ministry kicking and screaming. In 1 Timothy 3:1, Paul wrote, "If any man aspires to the office of overseer, it is a fine work he desires to do." Who wants to be under a pastor who says, "Well, I was going to make a million dollars, but God gave you to me to shepherd"? We must shepherd the flock willingly.

### Not for Sordid Gain

Peter followed the charge of not serving under compulsion with a challenge concerning motivation. We are to pastor "not for sordid gain, but with eagerness" (1 Peter 5:2). The Authorized Version of the English Bible translates the phrase "sordid gain" as "filthy lucre"—in other words, for financial benefit or gain. First Timothy 3:3 informs us that an elder is to be "free from the love of money." Paul told Titus very clearly that elders and deacons are not to be fond of sordid gain (1:7).

It is important to observe that 1 Timothy provides instructions about remunerating elders who are worthy of double honor for their teaching and preaching. Paid pastors are part of God's economy. You don't muzzle the ox; you let him eat some of the fruit that he's helping to bear. Yet I get very disturbed when I hear of pastors and preachers who charge fees and require contracts when they are asked to speak at a conference or elsewhere. If you do pulpit supply or preach at conferences, does your decision to accept or decline the invitation depend on the size of the speaking fee? Do you consider the financial gain that you can appropriate because of ministerial relationships? You know what that's like— you're the pastor, you go to lunch, and you employ the fake reach for the check. You wait until the other person reaches, and then you reach. Pay for lunch, and don't be a freeloader! Peter's primary focus in his warning is for pastors to not profit from the ministry, because that adulterates the ministry.

### Not Lording It Over People

Third, Peter wrote, "Nor yet as lording it over those allotted to your charge, but proving to be examples to the flock" (1 Peter 5:3). Note that Peter never says that the flock is yours. Rather, the charge is to be an *example* of what you teach, not an *exception* to what you teach. Peter implied that elders should not govern through threats, emotional intimidation, power, or the use of political force. Rather, you are to govern by example.

This, however, does not negate the authority of the elder. In verse 5, the congregation is commanded to "be subject to your elders." This implies that elders have genuine governing authority in the church, and that there are times when they have to give directions to the church. Wield this authority by example.

Jesus taught His disciples the same lesson in Mark 10:42: "Calling them to Himself, Jesus said to them, 'You know that those who are recognized as rulers of the Gentiles lord it over them; and their great men exercise authority over them.'" In contrast to this secular model, Jesus challenged His disciples as follows: "But it is not this way among you, but whoever wishes to become great among you shall be your servant; and whoever wishes to be first among you shall be slave of all. For even the Son of Man did not come to be served, but to serve, and to give His life a ransom for many" (verses 43-45). Spurgeon wrote,

> Whosoever will be chief among you, let him be your servant. Let us be willing to be doormats at our master's entrance hall. Let us not seek honor for ourselves, but put honor upon the weaker vessels with our care for them. In our Lord's church, let the poor, the feeble, the distressed have the place of honor and let us, who are strong bear their infirmities.

> He is highest who makes himself lowest. He is greatest, who makes himself less than the least.[4]

When Peter's audience read the words in 1 Peter 5:3-4, Ezekiel 34 must have been echoing in their minds. The prophet spoke on behalf of God in verse 1, saying, "The Word of the LORD came to me..." Upon hearing Ezekiel proclaim these words, his listeners may have been thinking, *Great, it's coming. We're going to hear of the judgment of the nations. We're going to hear more of the social injustices put in their place.* But here is what the spiritual leaders of Israel heard: "Son of man, prophesy against [drum roll] *the shepherds of Israel.*" The spiritual leaders must've thought, *Time out—we're on the same team!*

But Ezekiel continued, "Thus says the Lord GOD, 'Woe, shepherds of Israel who have been feeding themselves! Should not the shepherds feed the flock? You eat the fat and clothe yourselves with the wool, you slaughter the fat sheep without feeding the flock'" (Ezekiel 34:2–3). Ezekiel's words must have rocked the world of the kings, prophets, priests, synagogue leaders, and all those who were exercising any kind of spiritual oversight.

The shepherds were eating the fat and clothing themselves with the wool. They were only taking and not feeding. Ezekiel continued, "Those who are sickly you have not strengthened, the diseased you have not healed, the broken you have not bound up, the scattered you have not brought back, nor have you sought for the lost; but with force and with severity you have dominated them" (verse 4). Does that sound familiar? Domineering with severity and force. This passage had to be in Peter's mind. The fold of Israel was scattered because the people lacked a shepherd. In our modern context, I have heard that more people leave churches because they were uncared for than because they didn't like the preaching.

We continue reading in Ezekiel 34:5-6: "They were scattered for lack of a shepherd, and they became food for every beast of the field and were scattered. My flock wandered through all the mountains and on every high hill." They went to the hilltops because that was the only place sheep could find shelter from predators. Ezekiel continued,

My flock was scattered over all the surface of the earth, and there was no one to search or seek for them. Therefore, you shepherds, hear the word of the LORD: "As I live," declares the Lord GOD, "surely because My flock has become a prey, My flock has even become food for all the beasts of the field for lack of a shepherd, and My shepherds did not search for My flock, but rather the shepherds fed themselves and did not feed My flock; therefore, you shepherds, hear the Word of the LORD: 'Thus says the Lord GOD,

"Behold, I am against the shepherds"'" (verses 6-10).

Imagine for a moment God saying, "I am against the pastors." Then He says, "I will demand My sheep from them and make them cease from feeding sheep. So the shepherds will not feed themselves anymore, but I will deliver My flock from their mouth, so that they will not be food for them." God has to deliver His people from pastors because they are after the flock to exploit them for their own personal gain.

As pastors, we are not celebrities; we are servants. It's easier to stand high in the pulpit than to stoop low to wash feet. It's easier to preach at conferences than to visit widows and orphans. It's easier to lead seminars in public than to pray in solitude for our people. Ezekiel and Peter's emphasis is simply this: You pastor because you love God and you care for His flock.

---

**How much time do you spend in the pulpit versus time with people?**

---

Do you care? After you preach and you walk down from the pulpit, most of the people who want to talk to you are not coming to say, "You're great." They're coming to say, "Please notice me. Please care for me. You have said something that had spiritual attraction and divine authority, and I want to be shepherded." Your hearers typically don't come up to talk about your great exegesis; they want you to shepherd them. Preaching is an important part of the shepherd's crook. However, there are just a few verses about preaching, and there are a lot about pastoral care. How much time do you spend in the pulpit versus time with people?

All this comes back to what is written in Jeremiah 10:21: "The shepherds have become stupid and have not sought the LORD; therefore they have not prospered, and all their flock is scattered." The problem with some shepherds is that they have not sought the Lord. Care for your people and have them enjoy a better walk with Jesus because you're their *spiritual* leader.

### Pastoral Ministry Is an Honorable Responsibility

The third sobering reality of pastoral ministry is that it is an honorable responsibility. First Peter 5:4 says, "When the Chief Shepherd appears, you will receive the unfading crown of glory." Peter stated the incentive for spiritual oversight—namely, the eternal reward to come. Ultimately a pastor's reward is not measured by financial remuneration or worldly glory, but by hearing Jesus say, "Well done, good and faithful servant, enter the joy of the Master" (see Matthew 25:23). One of the most beloved and familiar passages in the Bible is Psalm 23. When Peter uses the term, "Chief Shepherd," he echoed the psalm.

Psalm 23 has been a comfort to many. It's so familiar that even nonbelievers know it. Read the psalm and pay attention to how it portrays the Chief Shepherd, who is our example.

In Psalm 23:1-2 we read, "The LORD is my shepherd, I shall not want. He makes me lie down in green pastures." Green pastures were rare in the ancient Near East. The land was mostly brown rubble and the shepherds would pick out patches of grass between rocks. The psalmist continued, "He leads me beside quiet waters. He restores my soul; He guides me in the paths of righteousness for His name's sake. Even though I walk through the valley of the shadow of death, I fear no evil, for You are with me" (verses 2-4). How many times do you get called to the hospital with a person who is about to die and what they want is for their pastor to pray and hold their hand as they take their final breath? "Your rod and Your staff, they comfort me. You prepare a table before me in the presence of my enemies; You have anointed my head with oil; my cup overflows. Surely goodness and lovingkindness will follow me all the days of my life, and I will dwell in the house of the LORD forever" (verses 4-6).

If you want to take a class on shepherdology, just read Psalm 23 and say, "I want to do that for my people." That's the nature of God's care. The analogy of God as a shepherd is obviously connected to the understanding that His people are the sheep, but it doesn't stop there. We read in Hebrews 13:20 that God "brought up from the dead the great Shepherd of the sheep through the blood of the eternal covenant, even Jesus our Lord." Jesus is our Chief Shepherd, and Peter wrote about this in 1 Peter 2:25: "You were continually straying like sheep, but now you have returned to the Shepherd and Guardian of your souls." God's shepherding is done primarily through proxy, through an approved stand-in for His name. In other words, God uses men to be shepherds for His sheep, and He still calls men to shepherd His flock today.

Remember as well what Jesus said in John 10:11: "I am the good shepherd; the good shepherd lays down His life for the sheep." And we see the contrast in John 10:12: "He who is a hired hand, and not a shepherd, who is not the owner of the sheep, sees the wolf coming, and leaves the sheep and flees, and the wolf snatches them and scatters them." The hired hand is in it for sordid gain and not for the care of the flock. This hired hand flees because he is a hired hand and is not concerned about the sheep.

Then Jesus said, "I am the good shepherd, and I know My own and My own know me, even as the Father knows Me and I know the Father; and I lay down My life for the sheep. I have other sheep, which are not of this fold; I must bring them also, and they will hear My voice; and they will become one flock with one shepherd" (John 10:13-16).

I read an article about shepherding that said shepherds in the Middle East usually have upwards of a 100 sheep that graze the same ground with three or four other shepherds. That means a pasture or hillside could have 300 to 400 sheep and several shepherds. And if one of the sheep happens to wander, the shepherd will call the sheep and it will respond to him because it knows his voice. This is what Jesus has in mind in John 10. Richard Baxter wrote to pastors, "We must feel toward our people as a Father toward his children. Yay, the most tender love of a mother must not surpass ours. We must even travail in birth until Christ is formed in them. They should see that we care for no outward thing."[5] The prophet Samuel said to the people of Israel, "Far be it from me that I should sin against the LORD by ceasing to pray for you" (1 Samuel 12:23). Interestingly, Samuel said that after he was out of a job.

## The Goal of a Shepherd-Leader

All of what has been covered in this chapter is an introduction to Hebrews 13:17: "Obey your leaders and submit to them, for they keep watch over your souls as those who will give an account." Before you ask God to double the size of your church, make sure you're ready for double the amount of accountability. Before you ask God to fill the pews, make sure you're ready to pray for those who sit in them. Before you ask for a larger ministry, make sure you're asking for more time to be able to care for those people. Because the accountability and responsibility a shepherd has for the souls of God's flock is serious. When you think of the people as eternal souls with bodies, it changes the spectrum, dimensions, and depth of what you want to do.

The goal of a shepherd-leader must be to shepherd his people so that they draw near to love and cherish the Chief Shepherd of their souls, Jesus Christ.

# PRAYER

Father, I pray for spiritual leaders. Oh Lord, give us faithfulness. Give us an idea of our responsibilities before You make us responsible. Remind all of us that the flock we have is Your flock and they are Your sheep. Guard our hearts from filthy lucre, from prideful ambition, from domineering leadership, and from pastoring out of duty instead of delight. Help us take our cue from Jeremiah, who said that if we seek You, then and only then will we be shepherds after Your own heart. Oh Father, help us to extend Your pastoral care to Your flock through our humble efforts. In Jesus' name we pray, Amen.

# 8

# GUARDING THE GOSPEL

*Steven J. Lawson*
*Shepherds' Conference 2009*
*Galatians 1:6-10*

I am amazed that you are so quickly deserting Him who called you by the grace of Christ, for a different gospel; which is really not another; only there are some who are disturbing you and want to distort the gospel of Christ. But even if we, or an angel from heaven, should preach to you a gospel contrary to what we have preached to you, he is to be accursed! As we have said before, so I say again now, if any man is preaching to you a gospel contrary to what you received, he is to be accursed! For am I now seeking the favor of men, or of God? Or am I striving to please men? If I were still trying to please men, I would not be a bond-servant of Christ.

Every generation of believers in the church has had to fight for the purity and the exclusivity of the gospel of Jesus Christ. There is no exception. Beginning with Clement of Rome, Ignatius, and Justin Martyr, these men gave their own lives to preserve and to protect the purity of the gospel of Jesus Christ.

In the second century, Irenaeus fought Gnosticism, and Polycarp opposed the Roman proconsul at the cost of their lives. Cyprian fought apostasy in the third century and was sentenced to death. He removed his garments, knelt down, and only said, "Thanks be to God."[1]

In the fourth century Athanasius fought Arianism, which denied the deity of Christ and, thus, was a frontal attack against the gospel. Athanasius was unmoved, and he stood *contra mundum* against the world. He was willing to be one man standing for the gospel in the face of the entire world.

Augustine warred against Pelagius and his denial of the fall of the human race. John Wycliffe, John Huss, and Martin Luther attacked the perverted gospel of the Roman Catholic Church and its corrupt system of human works and merit. John Calvin fired volley after volley against Rome and its foul gospel, as well as against the Libertines, the Unitarians, and all other false sects.

In subsequent generations, Christian leaders continued to pay the ultimate price in order to preserve and protect the exclusivity of the gospel of Jesus Christ. John Rogers and the 284 Marian martyrs fought against the Roman Catholic Church over the nature of the Lord's Supper, which was in reality a fight over the nature of the purity of the gospel itself. Thomas Cranmer, Nicholas Ridley, and Hugh Latimer were burned at the stake at Oxford for the honor of the gospel. Latimer asserted to Ridley, "Be of good comfort, Master Ridley, and play the man: we shall this day light such a candle, by God's grace, in England, as I trust shall never be put out."[2] Six months earlier, Cranmer was physically removed from his pulpit and taken directly to the martyrs' stake and there he gave his life to uphold the standard of sound words.

Jonathan Edwards fought for the purity of the gospel against Arminianism and antinomianism. When the gospel was all but silenced in the Church of England, George Whitfield took to the open air and went out into the highways and the open fields. With a loud voice he proclaimed, "I have come here today to talk to you about your soul."[3] Asahel Nettleton fought for the gospel against Charles Finney, and Charles Spurgeon fought the Down-Grade Controversy over the message and the method of the gospel. So it goes in every generation. Every Christian leader worth his salt has fought for the gospel, and so must we.

This is exactly what Paul did in Galatians 1:6-10. He was waging war for the purity and the exclusivity of the gospel of Jesus Christ, and it is a hill worth dying on.

## Fighting the Good Fight for the Gospel

The apostle Paul spent virtually his entire life fighting for the gospel. He opposed incipient Gnosticism among the Colossians. He waged war against secular philosophy, Jewish legalism, Eastern mysticism, and strict asceticism among the Galatians. He battled against those in Corinth who denied the resurrection of Christ. He even wrestled with fanaticism among the Thessalonians.

In Galatians, Paul contended against the Jewish legalism that had been brought into the church. This struggle would prove to be one of the most demanding conflicts of his life. In his defense of the gospel, Paul waged war against a group of false teachers known as the Judaizers. This group sought to mix law with grace, works with faith, and to put believers and unbelievers alike under the law of Moses. They claimed salvation must be earned by the law and that sanctification must be achieved by the works of the flesh. In response, the apostle Paul wrote this letter to the churches of Galatia, in which he heroically and valiantly fought the good fight for the gospel of Jesus Christ.

This epistle was Paul's most passionate letter. He dictated his other letters, but to write Galatians, he took his pen and wrote it himself. He wrote it in boxcar-size letters so large that anyone could clearly read what he was saying. He minced no words and breathed holy fire as he told all perverters of the gospel that they may go to hell before they deceive others. Along with rebuking the Judaizers, Paul was shocked that the Galatians had so quickly and so easily fallen for this false gospel. The time had come for Paul to address the issue directly and to have an adult conversation with the church.

## Guarding the Gospel Today

We, as well, live in exactly such an hour. Not unlike the first century, the gospel of Jesus Christ is coming under attack again and again. There are many assaults upon the purity and the exclusivity of the gospel from cults, false religions, the Roman Catholic Church, the new perspective on Paul, the non-lordship advocates, the social gospel proponents, the Universalists, and many others. There are many attacks upon the gospel, and it will fall upon each and every leader of Christ's church to act like men and to stand strong in the grace of God in defending the gospel. There is an ad in an athletic arena that reads, "We must protect this house." Shepherds, we must protect this gospel.

We need to heed Paul's words in these verses. We need to heed this warning that was sounded by him, and it must grip our hearts again. Let these words be as a trumpet in our ears. Let them be a drumbeat by which we march. Let them arrest our hearts and summon our souls.

We will categorize these verses into four main headings. *First*, Paul's amazement in verses 6 and 7. *Second*, Paul's adversaries at the end of verse 7. *Third*, Paul's anathemas in verses 8 and 9. *Fourth*, Paul's aim in verse 10.

## Paul's Amazement

Paul expressed his astonishment over the Galatians in verse 6 as he wrote, "I am amazed." This word "amazed" is a strong word that means to be astounded, bewildered, and shocked. Paul was dumbfounded and perplexed at the news that he had received from the Galatians. He went on to say what he was amazed at: "That you are so quickly deserting Him" (1:6). He was shocked that the Galatians had abandoned the very gospel of Jesus Christ, which he had brought to them. The term "deserting" was used in the military to refer to a soldier who abandoned his position or post. It means to go AWOL. The Galatians had deserted their loyalty to God and their allegiance to the Lord Jesus Christ. The Greek verb is in the present tense, which reveals they were committing this action while Paul was writing the letter. At that very hour and at that very moment, they were in the process of deserting God Himself. Moreover, the Greek verb is in the middle voice, which implies that the Galatians were personally responsible for that act.

In deserting the gospel, the Galatians were deserting God. They were not merely deserting a system of theology, as important as that is, but the very God of that system. It is as if Paul was saying, "You are turning your backs on Almighty God. You are like military deserters. You are spiritual turncoats. You are defectors of the worse kind. I was just with you and delivered you the message, and now you are so quickly abandoning God." We can come to this conclusion because "God himself is the gospel." Therefore, to move away from the gospel is to move away from God. The gospel is God's gospel, and Romans 1:1 reminds us that the gospel is God's truth, God's power, God's message. And to abandon God's message is to abandon God Himself.

Every attribute of God is most beautifully put on display in the spectacle of the theater of the gospel of Jesus Christ. In Psalm 19:1 we read, "The heavens are telling of the glory of God." How much greater is the glory of God put on display in the message that tells us how to go to heaven? If God's glory is put on display in His creation, it is put on even greater display in His new creation through

the gospel. Remember, it is in the gospel that we most clearly see the holiness of God. We see that God is transcended and majestic, high and lifted up, and is infinitely separated from defiled sinners.

The holiness of God comes shining forth brightly in the gospel of Jesus Christ, and begs for the solution to come from God. It is in the gospel that we see the wrath of God most vividly displayed. We see sin under judgment at the cross, and we see our sin judged by God in Christ. We behold Christ who became a curse for us, suffering in our place, receiving divine vengeance on our behalf. But it is also in the gospel that we see the righteousness of God. We see the righteousness of God that has been provided for us in the perfect obedience of Jesus Christ, in His sinless life, and in His substitutionary death. It is in the gospel that we see the grace of God providing righteousness for sinners.

---

**All of the lines of theology proper intersect in the gospel of Jesus Christ, and all of the attributes of God intersect in the person and work of Christ, who is the gospel for us.**

---

It is in the gospel that we see the immutability of God, that there is but one unchanging way of salvation from beginning to end. It is in the gospel that we behold the power of God that is able to save the chief of sinners and that is able to transform and sanctify the vilest of rebels. It is in the gospel that we see the truth of God and the reality of His saving enterprise made known to us. It is in the gospel that we see the sovereignty of God, saving all of His elect, all those chosen by the Father and entrusted to Christ. All of the lines of theology proper intersect in the gospel of Jesus Christ, and all of the attributes of God intersect in the person and work of Christ, who is the gospel for us. To defect from the gospel is to defect from God Himself.

In verse 6, Paul continued, "I am amazed that you are so quickly deserting Him who called you by the grace of Christ." The Galatians deserted God after He had provided for them salvation through sovereign, irresistible, and effectual grace. This grace had called them, overpowered their resistance to God, and drawn them to Himself to be trophies of His grace.

This God who had called them by His pure, sheer, and unadulterated grace was rejected when they turned to a "different gospel."

There are only two kinds of gospels. There is the true gospel, and there is the false gospel. There is the gospel that saves, and a false gospel that condemns. Paul was claiming that the Galatians had deserted the gospel of divine accomplishment for a gospel of human achievement. This different gospel, or *heteron* gospel, denotes another of a totally different kind. A modern-day comparison is the idiom that we are comparing apples to

oranges. This message that had crept into Galatia was a totally different message that was a nonsaving and nonsanctifying gospel of legalism. It was a counterfeit gospel, a sham salvation, and a rip-off religion. As a result, Paul pleaded with them to turn back to the true gospel.

At the beginning of verse 7, Paul wrote concerning this different gospel that it "is really not another"—which is to say there is only one true gospel. There is only one true way of salvation, and any other message is soul-damning. There is only one way of salvation because Jesus said, "I am the way, and the truth, and the life; no one comes to the Father but through Me" (John 14:6). Peter preached, "There is salvation in no one else; for there is no other name under heaven that has been given among men by which we must be saved" (Acts 4:12). Paul wrote, "There is one God, and one mediator also between God and men, the man Christ Jesus" (1 Timothy 2:5). To desert this gospel is to be removed from the only way of salvation.

Jesus is the only way of salvation because no one else has been born of a virgin, lived a sinless and perfect life, given His perfect righteousness, died in the sinner's place, bore the sins of man, suffered the wrath of God, reconciled sinners to an infinitely holy God, redeemed us out of our slavery to sin and Satan, raised for our justification, and is seated at the right hand of God the Father. No one else has ever done all this—not Buddha, Allah, Mary, the pope, some Unitarian being, Joseph Smith, Mary Baker Eddy, and certainly not me on my own behalf. No one else but Jesus Christ sent from God.

Paul was amazed that the Galatians had deserted this one true saving gospel and so should we be astonished whenever we see such desertion in our own day. We should be bewildered when we see evangelicals want to sign something like an ECT (Evangelicals and Catholics Together) document and pretend that there is no difference between Rome and the gospel of Jesus Christ.

We should be astonished when we see certain so-called Christian leaders go on television and punt away the gospel. Larry King interviewed a known pastor and started the conversation with the following words: "We've had ministers on our program who said you either believe in Christ or you don't. If you believe in Christ you're going to heaven. If you don't, no matter what you've done in your life, you aren't." The response from his guest, a prominent so-called Christian leader, was, "Yeah, I don't know. I believe you have to know Christ, but I think that if you know Christ, if you're a believer in God, that you're going to have some good works. I think it's a cop out to say, 'I'm a Christian, but I don't ever do anything.'"4

King responded, "What if you're Jewish? What if you're a Muslim and you don't accept Christ at all?"5 The answer, "You know, I'm very careful about saying who would and who wouldn't go to heaven. I don't know." King responded, "If you believe you have to believe in Christ, they're [Jews and Muslims]

wrong, aren't they?" His guest responded: "I don't know if I'd believe they're wrong. I spent a lot of time in India with my father. I don't know about all their religion, but I know they love God. I don't know. I've seen their sincerity."

No, they do not love God; they hate God. Give us leaders who know the truth, who will declare the truth, who will stand with Athanasius, Polycarp, Calvin, Luther, Whitfield, and Edwards, and who will declare from the housetops that the gospel is the only power of God unto salvation. Paul was amazed that some were willing to desert the gospel, and so should we be astonished and bewildered at this hour of history.

### Paul's Adversaries

Second, in Galatians 1:7, we see Paul's adversaries. The problem of the false gospel was with the opponents, who were corrupting and disturbing the believers. We observe in the middle of verse 7 Paul mentioning the false teachers for the first time, though not by name: "Only there are *some…*" (emphasis mine). Draw a circle around the word "some." These *some* are the Judaizers who were trying to bring their legalism into the church and put the people under the law; as a result, they are "disturbing you." *To disturb* is the Greek word *tarassontes,* and it means to trouble, to agitate, or to shake up. These false teachers had come into the vacuum during Paul's absence and they had filled it up with their corrupt gospel.

The false teachers were shaking up

the allegiance of the believers to God Himself. In so doing, they were disturbing and troubling the church. For if you take away the gospel, you have taken away everything. "Only there are some who are disturbing you and want to distort the gospel of Christ" (verse 7). The word "distort" means to transform something into the very opposite of what it is. The Judaizers were changing the true gospel and morphing it into a false gospel. They were tampering with the message, deluding its purity, and distorting its essence. These Judaizers were teaching Christ, grace, and faith, but these alone were inadequate to save and to sanctify. They were saying human works are also necessary for salvation and religious effort is required for acceptance with God. However, Paul wrote in 2:21, "If righteousness comes through the Law, then Christ died needlessly." If we can achieve our own salvation apart from the sufficiency of the cross, then Calvary is the blunder of the ages.

There are many adversaries of the gospel today. They acknowledge a place for the cross, they speak of grace, they pontificate about faith, but simultaneously they claim that faith is not enough to be right with God. They claim that salvation is by faith and good works, faith and water baptism, faith and church membership, faith and speaking in tongues, faith and Hail Marys, faith and the mass, faith and the last rites, faith and the treasury of merit, faith and buying indulgences. They claim that all of these are necessary for salvation, and as a result they damn the souls of men.

Of course, there are adversaries to the gospel of a theological kind. They deny the Trinity, the absolute deity of Jesus Christ, the lordship of Christ, the virgin birth, the sinless life of Jesus, substitutionary death, the bodily resurrection of Jesus, and Jesus' second coming. Others reject the exclusivity of salvation in Christ alone and say, "Jesus is only one of many roads that lead to the mountaintop where God is." But if Jesus is not the only way to heaven, then He is none of the ways to heaven, for Jesus claimed to be the only way of salvation, and a liar cannot be our Savior. J.C. Ryle wrote that if we truly believe that Christ is the only way of salvation, then it will mark our preaching and empower our proclamation. As ministers, we will speak of Christ and our sermons will be filled with Christ because He is the only way of salvation.[6]

The true gospel is centered on God's salvation through His Son, the Lord Jesus Christ. Jesus, who is fully God and fully man, sacrificed Himself on the cross for our sins. On the cross, He became sin for us, bore our sins, died in our place, and suffered under the wrath of God so that sinners may be rescued from this present evil age. This whole world is a planet under judgment. We read in Romans 1:18, "The wrath of God is revealed from heaven against all ungodliness and unrighteousness of men who suppress the truth in unrighteousness."

Right now, this very hour, we are a planet under judgment from a holy God. There is only one way of rescue, and it is to come to the cross of the Lord Jesus Christ and by faith believe upon Him. This is the gospel.

Paul affirmed this truth in Galatians 2:16: "A man is not justified by the works of the Law but through faith in Christ Jesus." Justification is the forensic declaration of the holy judge. Justification is God's declaration of the righteousness of Christ being imputed to sinners who believe upon Jesus. This declaration and imputation is by grace alone, through faith alone, in Christ alone. Luther said, "This is the chief article from which all other doctrines have flowed. It alone begets, nourishes, builds, preserves, and defends the church of God. Without the church of God, it cannot exist for one hour."[7] Luther went on to say that the doctrine of justification is the chief matter upon which the church stands or falls.[8] This was the master truth that those who had come into Galatia had corrupted, perverted, and tainted. It was the truth of justification that Paul defended as he spoke out against the false teachers.

### Paul's Anathemas

We have beheld Paul's amazement and adversaries, and third we see Paul's anathemas. These Judaizers sought to undermine Paul's teaching of the gospel, and in Galatians 1:8 Paul put forward an extreme hypothetical situation in order to make his point. He began with

a radical statement when he said, "Even if we…" Even if Paul, Barnabas, Timothy, Luke, or "an angel from heaven"—Michael the archangel; Gabriel, one of the chief angels or one of the ruling angels or guardian angels; one of the seraphim, cherubim, or any of the elect angels—"should preach to you a gospel contrary to what we have preached to you, he is to be accursed!"

If any of these persons should preach a gospel that was contrary to salvation by grace through faith in Christ, that individual was to be "accursed" (Greek, *anathema*). That is a potent word, for it means to be devoted to destruction or to be consigned to the flames of eternal hell below. In other words, it means to be damned to hell. To put it bluntly, Paul was saying, "They should go to hell before they take anyone else with them into the pit below." This is the man who can be worked up over that which works up the heart of God.

Martin Luther provided a colorful commentary on this passage when he wrote, "Paul is breathing fire. His zeal is so fervent that he almost begins to curse the angels themselves."[9] There was no room for neutrality, no room for indifference, no room for passivity, for this was a time for Paul to defend the gospel. James Montgomery Boice wrote, "How can it be otherwise? If the gospel Paul preaches is true, then the glory of Jesus Christ and the salvation of men are at stake. If men can be saved by works, then Christ has died in vain. The cross is emptied of power. If men are taught a false gospel, they are being led from the one thing that can save them…to destruction."[10] How true are these words spoken by Boice, because those who corrupt the one true saving gospel contribute to the damnation of lost souls.

Paul reloaded in verse 9 and dogmatically asserted that his message was consistent to what the Galatians had heard before. He wrote, "As we have said before…" Paul referred to the time he was in Galatia amidst the churches. He was emphatic in underscoring that he had not altered his message, which he received not from men but from Christ. He said, "If any man"—whether an apostle, an angel, or a self-appointed religious leader—"is preaching" (notice the present tense) "to you a gospel contrary to what you received, he is to be accursed!" Paul repeated this shocking statement to emphasize the severity of the judgment that awaits the false prophet. The hottest place in hell is reserved for those false teachers who distort the gospel of Christ and drag others down into the pit below.

I would remind us that Paul put these words on the front porch of this book. This is where Paul, in his other epistles, usually expressed his thanksgiving to God for the churches. Paul would normally write early in his letter, "Oh, how I thank God for you. You are in my every thought. You give me so much joy." Yet there is none of that in the epistle to the Galatians. Instead of being thankful, the apostle was rightly filled with holy zeal because the glory of God and of Christ had been contaminated with this false message. Paul was worked up about this because the only saving gospel and sanctifying message was at stake.

In doing this, Paul was following in the steps of his Master. Jesus Himself warned against false religious leaders who would pervert the true way of salvation. Jesus said, "Enter through the narrow gate; for the gate is wide and the way is broad that leads to destruction, and there are many who enter through it. For the gate is small and the way is narrow that leads to life, and there are few who find it" (Matthew 7:13-14). Jesus concluded by saying, "Beware of the false prophets, who come to you in sheep's clothing, but inwardly are ravenous wolves" (7:15). Paul's anathemas were rightly spoken. This was no time for dialogue. This was the time for declaration.

### Paul's Aim

Fourth, we see Paul's aim, which should be the aim of every single leader who shepherds God's flock. This is what every preacher and every Christian must wrestle with: "Am I now seeking the favor of men, or of God?" (Galatians 1:10). There are no other categories and no other options. Either we live our life to receive the approbation of God in heaven, or we play to the applause of the crowd. If Paul was seeking the favor of men, he would have toned down his rhetoric. But Paul was not courting the popularity of the world. He was not even courting the popularity of the church and the churches to whom this book was written. Paul was writing that he might receive his "Amens" out of heaven. Paul was seeking the approbation of God by writing what God had said. This harsh language was hardly calculated to win the approval of men, for men-pleasers simply do not hurl anathemas against those who proclaim false gospels. Paul was not concerned about that because he sought to please God.

> Ministry is simple—we ultimately must seek the favor and the approval of the Almighty God.

## Who Will You Please?

Here is that with which you and I must come to grips. If we seek to please God, it does not matter whom we displease. If we displease God, it does not matter whom we please. Ministry is simple—we ultimately must seek the favor and the approval of the Almighty God. Paul wrote, "If I were still trying to please men, I would not be a bond-servant of Christ" (Galatians 1:10). In the ultimate sense, pleasing men and pleasing God are mutually exclusive, not inclusive. Either you seek to please men, and if so you will displease God; or if you seek to please God, then you are willing to displease men. Even our Lord said in Matthew 6:24, "No one can serve two masters; for either he will hate the one and love the other, or

he will be devoted to one and despise the other." Jesus understood we can have only one master and as slaves of Christ, we report to Him and seek His approval.

Paul wrote in 1 Thessalonians 2:4, "Just as we have been approved by God to be entrusted with the gospel, so we speak, not as pleasing men, but God who examines our hearts." Paul realized that he was chosen by God, called by God, set apart by God, saved by God, redeemed by God, commissioned by God, enlightened by God, instructed by God, appointed by God, empowered by God, and directed by God. Why on earth would he suddenly seek to please men?

Paul knew that in the last day, it will be God before whom we stand. We will be judged, not by men or angels, but by God, and we will either be rewarded or passed over. Therefore, it is God whom we must please, and there is only one message that pleases God: the true gospel of Jesus Christ, which is salvation by grace alone, through faith alone, in Christ alone.

## An Example to Follow

One of the most courageous men to walk this earth with the gospel was John Knox. I had the privilege, a couple of years ago, to stand with Dr. MacArthur where Knox is buried, and to step in Knox's pulpit. John Knox, a Roman Catholic priest in Scotland, was converted by the power of the gospel and became a bodyguard of George Wishart. Wishart was martyred and his ministry was passed on to Knox. He began to preach in St. Andrew's castle and was soon captured and taken aboard a French ship. He served in the hull of that ship for the next 19 months as a captive of war. When he was released, he came back to Scotland to preach the gospel.

When Bloody Mary took the throne, Knox fled Scotland and went to Geneva to pastor an English-speaking congregation. He even played a role in the production of the Geneva Bible. However, once Bloody Mary was removed from the throne, Knox returned to Scotland. Mary, Queen of Scots, took on the throne, and on her very first Sunday as queen of Scotland, she went into the solitude of her own chapel, where she received a private mass. This news reached the ears of John Knox, and on the very next Sunday, at St. Giles Church in Edinburgh, Scotland, he ascended into to the pulpit and called out the queen. He declared from the pulpit, "One mass is more fearful to me than if 10,000 armed enemies were landed in any part of this realm." Knox said, "I have learned plainly and boldly to call wickedness by its own terms. I call a fig, a fig and a spade, a spade."[11]

When word reached Mary, Queen of Scots, she was infuriated. She summoned Knox to appear before her in order to give an account of his declaration. Knox came in, and the queen took the offensive. She launched with three indictments and charges to be brought against John Knox, and yet the charges deflected off of him like water on a duck's back. Knox did not mince words when he declared to her the idolatry of the mass, asserting that the mass could have no place in Scotland, for it would invite the judgment of God upon the nation. Knox was unrelenting in preaching to her the one true pure saving gospel of grace in the Lord Jesus Christ. Consequently, she was reduced to a puddle of tears. Knox recorded that she began to howl like a wounded animal. The cause of the Reformation in Scotland turned as a result of a series of six encounters between the thundering Scot, John Knox, and Mary, Queen of Scots.

When Knox died on December 24, 1572 in Edinburgh, the region of Scotland spoke these long-remembered words over Knox's grave: "Here lies a man who in his life never feared the face of man."[12] Perhaps Knox is best summarized by the closing words of the Scots Confession that he penned in 1560 upon his return to Scotland: "Arise, O Lord and let thine enemies be confounded. Let them flee from thy presence, that hate thy godly name. Give thy servants strength to speak thy word with boldness, and let all nations cleave to the true knowledge of thee."[13]

Where are such leaders today? As someone once observed, the problem with preachers today is no one wants to kill them anymore. Where are those who will say with Paul, "If any man is preaching to you a gospel contrary to what you received, he is to be accursed!" (Galatians 1:9)? I hope there are such men reading these words even now.

# PRAYER

Rise up, O men of God, have done with lesser things. Give heart and mind and soul and strength to serve the King of kings. Let us preach the gospel, teach the gospel, live the gospel, explain the gospel, and expand the gospel, and let the chips fall where they may. Let us please God. Let us not become men-pleasers. Amen.

# 9

# NO LITTLE PEOPLE, NO LITTLE SERMONS

*Albert Mohler Jr.*
*Shepherds' Conference 2010*
*John 9:1-42*

W e proclaim Him, admonishing every man and teaching every man with all wisdom, so that we may present every man complete in Christ" (Colossians 1:28). That is what the preacher of the Word gets to do. That is what the preacher of the Word is assigned to do. That is what the preacher of the Word had better do. God is calling men to preach His Word by supernaturally equipping them to accomplish this task. Yet not everyone heeds this mandate.

I recently had the opportunity to preach at a convention. As I was walking into the hotel ballroom to preach, I noticed strobe lights and all kinds of special effects, but I did not see a pulpit. They said, "Don't worry, it's electronic." I said, "My worry is it's invisible." They responded, "Don't worry, it will appear when you get ready to preach," and I was forced to practice faith. Then when it was time to preach, behold the floor opened and pipes appeared. On top of thin purple pipes there sat a wooden plate. On top of the wooden plate there stood a microphone, and I assumed that I was to stand behind the pipes and the plate.

As I got up behind the pipes and the plate—improvised as a pulpit—I thought, *I'm not sure exactly what this symbolizes. It could symbolize the cross-cultural power of the pulpit, or it could symbolize the disappearance of the pulpit because it is so conveniently put away.* In far too many churches there is an absence of the pulpit because there is an absence of preaching. The disappearance of the pulpit is the hallmark of the age. Have you noticed the unbearable lightness of so much of what is called preaching? Have you noticed the unbearable lightness of so many sermons being "small"? "Big" sermons are important, but big does not always equate to long. In the New Testament, some brief sermons have huge implications. Today, however, many long sermons actually contain small amounts of truth.

### Bringing Weight to Our Sermons

As pastors, our efforts will be weighed in the balances, and we will find out how "big" the ministry was. We will stand before our Maker, the judge of all, and find out how large our sermons were. We worship an infinite God and proclaim an infinite gospel. The New Testament describes the eternal weight of glory that is at stake. Francis Schaeffer wrote a book entitled *No Little People, No Little Places*. I hope if nothing else, that title encourages you. There are no little people, no little places, and the weight of a ministry is not determined by its size. Since there are no little people, there had better be no little sermons. Little sermons will not do.

---

*As leaders, we need the reminder that people are important. Therefore, we must recognize the need to bring weight to our sermons.*

---

As a leader of God's flock, you cannot overestimate the power of His Word. This is affirmed in the ninth chapter of the Gospel of John with the account of a man born blind who is healed. We see here a fascinating set of discussions, interrogations, and the revelation of the glory of God. This passage contains much irony—blindness, light, sight, eyes that will not see, eyes that are opened to see, and eyes thrown out from the temple because they now see. We are told that as Jesus passed by he saw a man blind from birth. The disciples, however, did not see a man. They saw a question. In seeing the man, Jesus reaffirmed that there are no little people. As leaders, we need the reminder that people are important. Therefore, we must recognize the need to bring weight to our sermons.

### Seeing the Question vs. Seeing the Man

Jesus' disciples looked at the man and asked, "Rabbi, who sinned, this man or his parents, that he would be born blind?" (John 9:2). This question is not foolish. As a matter of fact, in the teaching context of Jesus, that question would come to mind to anyone who is theologically inquisitive. There must be a reason or rationale for the blindness. Surely, we can identify a causative agent. A sin or an entire complex of sin must explain this.

Now, the problem is more complicated than it may appear. The direct linkage between sin and consequence may be apparent in some cases. For example, someone might have become blind due to traceable sin like fetal alcohol syndrome or another clear causative explanation. However, there is no direct explanation here that makes any sense to the disciples other than sin. Like the friends of Job, they immediately followed the conventional theological thinking of the time and imagined this misfortune was caused by someone's sin. Because the man was born blind, they suggested it could be the parents' fault. Perhaps some other explanation existed. So the disciples asked, "Rabbi, who sinned, this man or his parents, that he would be born blind?"

Theologically, the answer is sin because we live in a Genesis 3 world. Every disaster found in Scripture points to the fall and explains, in non-negotiable terms, that every single thing that goes wrong—all sin, evil, and even what we might define as natural or moral evil—is traceable directly to the fall. Earthquakes, tsunamis, mosquitoes, and tapeworms are all because of Genesis 3. In one sense, sin is the right answer. It is not the sufficient answer, however, to the disciples' question. And Jesus responded in a way that did not fit the conventional wisdom of their theology.

## The Errors of Assigning Suffering

The disciples asked this question presumptuously. John Calvin suggested three reasons why we err in assigning a reason for suffering and tying it to specific sin.[1] *First*, we err because we see sin and its consequences far more easily in others than we do in ourselves. The *second* reason is what he called immoderate severity. By that he meant we are poor judges of quantifiable suffering. How would we presume to have some adequate insight to measure why the consequence of this sin might be this suffering? Calvin said we have no meter that can guide us with any kind of accuracy there. It's sheer presumptuousness and arrogance on the part of the creature to try to determine this.[2] *Third*, Calvin wrote that there is now no condemnation for those who are in Christ Jesus. Yet, those who are Christ's still suffer.[3] That ought to warn us against presumptuousness. The disciples saw an understandable question, but Jesus saw a man and healed him. However, before He healed him, He made a comment to His disciples that was both a response and a retort. He said, "It was neither that this man sinned, nor his parents; but it was so that the works of God might be displayed in him" (verse 3).

Jesus affirmed that the focus was not on whether this man or his parents sinned. The causative agent here has a very different agenda, plan, and purpose in mind. This man was born blind so that the works of God might be displayed in him. Jesus went on to say, "We must work the works of Him who sent Me as long as it is day; night is coming when no one can work. While I am in the world, I am the Light of the world" (verses 4-5). Every human, every believer in the Lord Jesus Christ, and especially every preacher needs to hear that word. We must be aware of this command to work the works of Him who called us while it is day, since night is coming, when no man can work. There is a set time for our ministry. We and our ministries are finite. With every tick of the clock, turn of the calendar, and breath we take, we move closer to our death than to our birth. We progress closer to that time when no man can work. Thus, we must do what Jesus commands. We must work the works of Him who sent us while it is day. Night is coming, when no man can work.

Then Jesus began to teach about His identity, similar to what He had told us already in John 8. There He said, "I am the Light of the world; he who follows Me will not walk in the darkness, but will have the Light of life" (John 8:12). In response, the Pharisees confronted Him and said, "You are testifying about Yourself; Your testimony is not true" (verse 13). Jesus answered, "Even if I testify about Myself, My testimony is true, for I know where I came from and where I am going; but you do not know where I come from or where I am going" (verse 14). Jesus revealed Himself as the light of the world, but the Pharisees rebuked and rejected Him.

When Jesus spoke to His own disciples, He repeated the same phrase: "I am the Light of the world" (John 9:5). As the light of the world, Jesus healed the blind man so that the works of God would be displayed in him. Notice how Jesus healed this man. He spat on the ground, made clay out of the spittle, applied the

clay to the man's eyes, and said to him: "Go, wash in the pool of Siloam" (verse 7). The man did exactly what he was told to do, but the healing was passive. He merely received what the Lord had done for him. Jesus' actions are powerfully symbolic as we are all made out of clay— the dust of the ground.

We continue in the narrative and read the stunning words of John 9:7: "So he went away and washed, and came back seeing." He went away a blind man, feeling his way to the pool of Siloam, and he came back seeing. How could anyone preach a little sermon about that? Blindness became sight. Darkness became light. The disciples saw a question, but Jesus saw a man. Jesus made clear to His disciples that this man's blindness was not an occasion for them to ask a theological question. Instead, it was an occasion for the incarnate Son of God, the light of the world, to spit on the very ground that He had made, take the spittle, put it on the man's eyes, and send him to wash. The blind man went, washed, and came back seeing. You cannot preach a little sermon about that, and that's not even the end of the text. After darkness and blindness had become light and sight, the questioners came to figure out what this meant.

## The Neighbors See a Question

Now that the man was no longer blind, his neighbors saw him as a question. The narrator wrote, "Therefore the neighbors, and those who previously saw him as a beggar, were saying, 'Is not this the one who used to sit and beg?'" (John 9:8). The neighbors had not failed to notice him since by definition, in the New Testament era, a blind man was a beggar. They knew him and had identified him. Yet they ignored him, felt superior to him, and may have even felt pity upon him.

Note what doesn't happen in this passage: No one celebrated that this blind man could now see. His neighbors did not. His parents did not. The Pharisees surely did not. Notice the question the neighbors posed: "Is this not the one who used to sit and beg?" They knew him as the blind man who sat and begged, but now he sees. We continue reading: "Others were saying, 'This is he,' still others were saying, 'No, but he is like him.' He kept saying, 'I am the one'" (verse 9). Notice the confusion here. Others were saying, "No, but he is like him." In other words, if you get used to ignoring people, they all look alike. But he kept saying, "I am the one. I was blind, but now I see. You were the people who saw me when I was blind, when I could not see. Now I see, and you do not see me."

The people asked him other questions. Evidently they came to an adequate confidence that this was the blind beggar: "So they were saying to him, 'How then were your eyes opened?'" (verse 10). He explained, "The man who is called Jesus made clay, and anointed my eyes, and said to me, 'Go to Siloam and wash'; so I went away and washed, and I received sight" (verse 11). The answer was accurate and pristine. Then,

"they said to him, 'Where is He?' He said, 'I do not know'" (verse 12). His response was legitimate. The man had done what Jesus had told him to do. When he came back, he knew who had healed him, but he did not know where Jesus was.

The next question that arose was a theological one: Was the man clean or unclean? We are not able to exhaustively trace the biblical system of determining what was clean or unclean. What would have determined if this man was to be recognized as clean was the adjudication of the nature of this miracle. The miracle was unprecedented in terms of their experience and demanded some kind of explanation. As a result, the people brought the healed man to the experts— Theologians "R" Us—the Pharisees. The narrator wrote, "They brought to the Pharisees the man who was formerly blind" (verse 13). Now matters get complicated because it was the Sabbath when Jesus made the clay and opened the man's eyes. Jesus had a pattern of healing people on the Sabbath: the man at the Pool of Bethesda, the man with the withered hand, and now this man. If there was anything the Pharisees could not stand, it was a miracle on the Sabbath.

The Pharisees were confronted with a man who was formerly blind and was healed on the Sabbath: "Now it was a Sabbath on the day when Jesus made the clay and opened his eyes. Then the Pharisees also were asking him again how he received his sight. And he said to them, 'He applied clay to my eyes, and I washed, and I see'" (verses 14-15). It was a three-stage operation: clay, wash, see. "Therefore some of the Pharisees were saying, 'This man is not from God, because He does not keep the Sabbath.' But others were saying, 'How can a man who is a sinner perform such signs?' And there was a division among them" (John 9:16). One of the interesting ironies embedded in this account is that the formerly blind man had not identified Jesus as the one who had healed him. Nonetheless, the Pharisees already know who it was.

A division formed among the Pharisees over whether or not a man who was a sinner could perform such signs. They returned to the blind man and said to him, "What do you say about Him, since He opened your eyes?" (verse 17). Now that's a fascinating question. John, inspired by the Holy Spirit, gave us the most incredible weight of irony here. The Pharisees, the ones who couldn't see, asked the question, "What do you say about it?" Now remember, the man was brought to them because they were the experts, and yet they were saying to him, "Provide input." He did, and said, "He is a prophet" (verse 17).

Here was a formerly blind man who had been ignored by virtually everyone. Now they were asking him for answers. He had become the theologian. He had a category for Jesus: prophet. This once-blind man didn't know everything, but he knew that no sinner could have healed him.

In verse 18 we read, "The Jews then did not believe it of him, that he had been

blind and had received sight, until they called the parents of the very one who had received his sight." When the Pharisees didn't receive the answer that they wanted, they assumed that he was not who he said he was. So the people called in the man's parents and brought them to the Pharisees. This would have been a terrifying experience for them because for them to give the wrong answer might cause them to be cast out from the synagogue. The parents were confronted with their own son, and they must have had many of the same questions as the Pharisees: Why was he blind? How did this happen? Now their son, who was blind and a beggar, sees. Having been ignored, he's now the center of attention, and so are the parents. The Pharisees asked, "Is this your son, who you say was born blind?" (verse 19). We must remember that blindness was considered a blight and a curse. The Pharisees continued, "Then how does he now see?"

The parents responded, "We know that this is our son, and that he was born blind; but how he now sees, we do not know; or who opened his eyes, we do not know" (verses 20-21). They knew this was their son, and they knew he was born blind. But as to how he now sees, "We do not know." Or who opened his eyes? "We do not know." Then, in effect, they throw their own son under the bus: "Ask him; he is of age, he will speak for himself" (verse 21). We are told that his parents said this because "they were afraid of the Jews; for the Jews had already agreed that if anyone confessed Him to be Christ, he was to be put out of the synagogue" (verse 22).

The scene shifted again, and the man was brought back for a second interrogation: "So a second time they called the man who had been blind, and said to him, 'Give glory to God; we know that this man is a sinner'" (verse 24). This statement was a warning to be careful. Then we find out just how much of a theologian this fellow is in verse 25: "He then answered, 'Whether He is a sinner, I do not know; one thing I do know, that though I was blind, now I see.'" His primary concern was not a matter of theological nicety and attempting to resolve the Pharisees' dilemma. He would not be entrapped by their corrupted way of thinking. Instead, his response was, "You put that question aside, here's what I know: I was blind—ask my parents—and now I see."

That is the paradigmatic Christian testimony. John 9 is not just an account about a man who was born blind who now sees. This entire chapter is about the display of the glory of God through the blind receiving sight. John weaved the narrative together to show that those who are spiritually blind are unable to see spiritual realities.

The Pharisees then asked the man, "What did He do to you? How did He open your eyes?" (verse 26). They had already asked that question, and it had already been answered. But he answered yet again, "I told you already and you did not listen; why do you want to hear it again? You do not want to become His

disciples too, do you?" (verse 27). Here's what we discover about this man: Not only was he a theologian, but he was also incredibly perceptive and brave. He had the courage to ask the Pharisees, "You do not want to become His disciples too, do you?"

## The Man Sees Jesus as He Is

The disciples saw a question, Jesus saw a man, and the man saw Jesus as He was. The man mockingly asked the Pharisees, "Is that what's going on here? Do you want to become His disciples?" How did they respond? "They reviled him and said, 'You are His disciple, but we are disciples of Moses'" (John 9:28). These were the same folks who said, "We are the children of Abraham" (see John 8:33). Jesus responded, "No, you're not, because before Abraham was, I was. Abraham knew Me. You're no sons of Abraham."

Now they say to this man, "We are disciples of Moses." The Pharisees think they know something when they say, "We know that God has spoken to Moses, but as for this man, we do not know where He is from" (John 9:29). Just imagine this man's experience. He was blind and now he could see. And he has discovered that the world wasn't as he thought it was. The world was not made up of sighted people. It was made up of blind people! Up till now he had assumed that he was blind and everyone else had sight. Now he has come to understand that blind people have surrounded him all his life.

The man then said, "Here is an

amazing thing, that you do not know where He is from, and yet He opened my eyes. We know that God does not hear sinners; but if anyone is God-fearing and does His will, He hears him" (verses 30-31). How many times must the man have prayed to receive sight during all those years of sitting there begging? He never received sight, and then one day came Jesus. Now he could see. He continued, "Since the beginning of time it has never been heard that anyone opened the eyes of a person born blind. If this man were not from God, He could do nothing" (verses 32-33). This layman told the panel of theologians— the experts in the law—that if this man was not from God, He could do nothing.

Their response was an affirmation of only one thing: "They answered him, 'You were born entirely in sins, and are you teaching us?'" (verse 34). They only affirmed their faulty theological position. They hadn't learned a thing and still thought God's judgment was upon the man. What do you do when you have a theological problem you can't resolve? The only answer is that a sovereign God has acted. If you're the Pharisees, however, you "put him out" (verse 34). And that's what they did.

"Jesus heard that [the Pharisees] had put the man out, and finding him, He said, 'Do you believe in the Son of Man?'" (John 9:35). This man had been asked many questions. He had answered honestly and directly with amazing courage and remarkable candor. He had also answered with the knowledge that could come only to a man who had been touched by the Savior. Now the very One who gave him sight asked him a question. The man answered, "Who is He, Lord, that I may believe in Him?" (verse 36). He was ready to believe anything that this Man told him.

Notice how Jesus answered: "You have both seen Him, and He is the one who is talking with you" (verse 37). The man responded with a simple profession of faith: "Lord, I believe" (verse 38). Salvation had come not only to his eyes, but also to his soul. He did not only see, but he came to believe. He not only professed with his lips, but he also worshiped Jesus. Then Jesus clarified all that had happened as only He can: "For judgment I came into this world, so that those who do not see may see, and that those who see may become blind" (John 9:39). Jesus came to confirm the world's blindness. Earlier, John taught us that Jesus came to His own, and His own received Him not (1:11).

## When Some Remain Blind

In stark contrast to the narrative, the Pharisees then asked a pathetic question: "We are not blind too, are we?" (John 9:40). If you have to ask whether you are blind, you just might be blind. Jesus answered them with a word of severe judgment: "If you were blind, you would have no sin; but since you say, 'We see,' your sin remains" (verse 41). Their problem was not with physical blindness, but with a blindness of a completely different category. They were willfully, spiritually, and theologically blind.

They could not see because they would not see. The deadly reality of blindness is evident in this exchange between Jesus and the Pharisees. Though Jesus came into the world as light to illuminate it, the world did not know Him. Isaiah wrote, "On that day the deaf will hear words of a book, and out of their gloom and darkness the eyes of the blind will see" (Isaiah 29:18). In Isaiah 35:5-6 we read, "Then the eyes of the blind will be opened and the ears of the deaf will be unstopped. Then the lame will leap like a dear, and the tongue of the mute will shout for joy." Moreover, in Isaiah 42:6-7 we read, "I am the LORD, I have called You in righteousness, I will also hold You by the hand and watch over You, and I will appoint You as a covenant to the people, as a light to the nations, to open blind eyes, to bring out prisoners from the dungeon and those who dwell in darkness from the prison." The light of the world brings light because He is light. What are you going to do with this information? Are you going to preach just a little sermon? The light of the world displays the radiant glory of God.

**God's Glory Displayed**

Though John 9 is a complicated narrative, the hinge of it all is in verse 3: "It was neither that this man sinned, nor his parents; but it was so that the works of God might be displayed in him." Now do we believe that or not? If we believe

that, it makes all the difference in the world. A limitless universe of theology exists here. It is an earth-shaking reality. This man was born blind so that the works of God might be displayed in him.

The Pharisees were only the first to reject that theology. Preachers today look at this truth and explain away its threatening power. They domesticate it into a fascinating miracle account about Jesus the wonder worker. They moralize it by exhorting the blind to strain their eyes to see. They eviscerate it by denying the brute force of Jesus' words. They try to make it just mere literature filled with irony the literate love to enjoy. They apologize for it by explaining it as a crude theology that we have now overcome. They develop principles from it by offering a set of practical insights and observations for the wise and prudent. Or they transform it into therapy, encouraging all to abandon the unauthentic and find the sight of authenticity.

But Jesus said, "It was neither that this man sinned, nor his parents; but it was so that the works of God might be displayed in him." This is true about every one of us. It's true about every single human being who ever lived or will live. In fact, it's true about every atom and molecule of the cosmos. Why does anything exist? Why is anything as it is? Why is there anything at all? That the works of God might be displayed! This is way too much voltage for many. This means that in the ages past God determined that there would be a man who

298   THE JOHN MACARTHUR HANDBOOK OF EFFECTIVE BIBLICAL LEADERSHIP

was blind. He was born blind so that Jesus would come along and spit into the ground, anoint the man's eyes, send him to wash, and he would come back seeing.

If you can handle that truth, then you can't preach a little sermon. There is no little moralism here. There aren't just a couple of principles here that we can apply. There is an entire universe of meaning that throws the world, as we know it, upside down. That's the reality of the gospel—it comes and mixes up our categories. It destroys all conventional wisdom. It tells us that we are blind and that God is working all things out for the display of His own glory. The great question is: Do we trust Him or not?

When this man had the opportunity to see Jesus, he did not ask, "Why was I blind?" Instead, he wanted to know who the Lord was. Christ is the light of the world who opened not only this man's eyes, but also the eyes of all who see Him as Savior and Lord. As a pastor, what will you do with this truth? Will you preach a little sermon? Shepherd, there are no little people. How many people do we pass every day who desperately need the gospel? Yet we do not see them.

Jesus saw a man and healed him. May we see that there are no little people—only the fellow blind who desperately need sight. There must be no little sermons if we believe that every particle

and every single human being exists so that the works of God may be displayed. There are no little people. There are no little texts, because all display the glory of God. If there are no little texts, then there must be no little sermons.

Billions of stars and all the infinitude of expanding space exist for one purpose alone: that God determined to save the people on this planet through the blood of His Son. The entire cosmos is nothing but a theater for the story of the drama of God's redemption. We know the secret to the universe. We know the secret to creation. We know the secret to the meaning of life. There is no excuse for any of us to keep saying, "I don't know." If you don't know, don't preach. If you don't know, find out. We know, so we preach. Since we know, there is no little text. And there are no little sermons.

If we understand this and establish our ministries on this, then we will never see a little person. We will never declare a little God. We will never proclaim a little gospel. We will never know a little truth. We will never work up a little message. We will never be driven by just a little conviction. We will never be fueled by just a little passion. We will never preach a little sermon. But if we don't believe this and stake our ministry on this, then just any little old sermon will do.

# PRAYER

Our Father, we come before You to pray that there be no little sermons. We pray that You will use Your leaders to preach Your powerful Word. We pray to see Your glory in all endeavors and to see the miracle of the spiritually blind obtaining sight. To the glory of God, in the name of Jesus Christ our Lord, Amen.

# 10

# CONFRONTING HYPOCRISY

*John MacArthur*
*Shepherds' Conference 2005*
*Luke 11:37-44*

I t has been my heart's passion to call pastors to go to battle for the truth in a day in which we are losing it. From the very opening of Jude's letter we are called to earnestly contend for the faith which was once for all handed down to the saints, which is the basis of our common salvation. This command is a serious one, since certain persons have crept into the church unnoticed and are wreaking havoc on the truth; and this long war on the truth began with the fall of Satan and will go on until we reach the eternal state.

It is our time and our place in this world to be the warriors who defend the truth. While we can learn much from Jude about this, I want to take you to a completely different passage. I want to give you a glimpse of the greatest of all warriors for the truth, the Lord Jesus Christ, and how He dealt with one of

the paramount enemies of the truth, hypocrisy.

## The Encounter with a Hypocrite

In Luke chapter 11, we find an illustration in which Jesus confronted one of the many embedded spiritual terrorists of His day. This enemy was one of the many who had inserted themselves within the religious structure of Israel and had been accorded the highest place of respect and regard. They were so effective and efficient that they were accepted and honored by everyone and were able to turn the whole nation against the long-awaited Messiah. In verses 37-44, we witness a meal that took place between Jesus and one of these spiritual enemies, a Pharisee.

Now when He had spoken, a Pharisee asked Him to have lunch with him; and He went in, and reclined at the table. When the Pharisee saw it, he was surprised that He had not first ceremonially washed before the meal. But the Lord said to him, "Now you Pharisees clean the outside of the cup and of the platter; but inside of you, you are full of robbery and wickedness. You foolish ones, did not He who made the outside make the inside also? But give that which is within as charity, and then all things are clean for you.

"But woe to you Pharisees! For you pay tithe of mint and rue and every kind of garden herb, and yet disregard justice and the love of God; but these are the things you should have done without neglecting the others. Woe to you Pharisees! For you love the chief seats in the synagogues and the respectful greetings in the market places. Woe to you! For you are like concealed tombs, and the people who walk over them are unaware of it."

This is our great leader warring against a purveyor of error. For most readers it must seem strange that the most severe warnings and denunciations that Jesus Christ ever uttered were against the religious people of His day. In today's culture, we're supposed to embrace anybody and everybody who's religious, as if we were all engaged in worshiping and serving the same God. Since Jesus was, after

all, a religious figure, it would seem that He would respect and affirm religious people more than anybody else, especially Jews who were devoted so fastidiously to the Old Testament law. But just the opposite was true.

## The Disparagement of False Religion

Jesus, who is truth personified, perfectly understood true religion. He taught only what was true and what came from God, and understood damning deception when He saw it. Jesus knew what force in the world had the greatest power to destroy souls forever. He knew that of all the evils in the world, false religion—especially apostate Judaism and apostate Christianity—was the worst. The severest eternal judgment will be for the religious, especially those who pervert the Old and New Testaments.

Hebrews chapter 2 reveals that the judgment of God falls on those who have disregard for His law; and Hebrews 10 discloses that there is a horrific escalated judgment on those who disregard the New Testament and trample underfoot the blood of the covenant, counting it unholy and in some way perverting it. The leaders of the Jewish religion were apostates because they had perverted the Old Testament and rejected the Messiah and His salvation. These apostate leaders also manipulated the Romans into carrying out the execution of Christ that they themselves sought. Consequently, the Pharisees' judgment was to be severe, not only in a temporal sense with the destruction of Jerusalem, but in an eternal sense with the damnation of their souls.

Going back to Luke 11:29, we read that Jesus had been speaking to this crowd and said, "This generation is a wicked generation." Jesus was talking about the people of His own nation. Back in verse 14 of the same chapter, Jesus had cast a demon out of someone who had been made dumb by the demon. When the evil spirit came out, the dumb man spoke and the multitude marveled, while others said, "He casts out demons by Beelzebul, the ruler of the demons" (11:15). Since the populace was concluding that Jesus had supernatural power, there were only two options: either the power came from God, or it was from Satan. The crowds believed the Pharisees' lie that Jesus was from Satan, not God. They claimed that Jesus could not be from God because He contradicted the Pharisaical religious system, which was prescribed to be "from God." Their approach to religion was disastrous, and Jesus called them a wicked generation.

In verses 24-26, speaking to the same crowd, Jesus said,

When the unclean spirit goes out of a man, it passes through waterless places seeking rest, and not finding any, it says, "I will return to my house from which I came." And when it comes, it finds it swept and put in order. Then it goes and takes along seven other spirits more evil than itself, and they go in and live there; and the last state of that man becomes worse than the first.

Jesus taught that the worst possible condition a person can be in is to be moral and religious, but without God.

## The Indictment of Hypocrisy

In another diatribe that Jesus pronounced on the Pharisees, He made it very clear how He viewed them: "Woe to you scribes and Pharisees, hypocrites because you travel around on sea and land to make one proselyte; and when he becomes one, you make him twice as much a son of hell as yourselves" (Matthew 23:15). In verse 33 He added, "You serpents, you brood of vipers, how will you escape the sentence of hell?" Pastor, if you are going to go to battle for the truth, then you have to confront the enemy.

The account in our text is a story of a religious Pharisee who was headed for hell. While on his way, he was making others "twice as much a son of hell" than he himself was. Like an extremist, he was taking the souls of others while condemning himself. Now, the Pharisees possessed moral sensitivities—apparently an active conscience, and strong religious convictions. Technically, they should have found some common ground and gotten along with Jesus, but just the opposite was true. Jesus said He was far more accepting of prostitutes, tax collectors, criminals, and the social riffraff than with the religious establishment. That was the case because

Jesus did not come to call the righteous, but sinners to repentance.

Religion blinds people to the truth of their sin, makes them self-righteous, feeds pride, fuels vanity, and produces skilled hypocrites. The Pharisees were the most devout among the Jews and were the main spiritual models for the people, yet their warped and distorted interpretation of the Old Testament not only cut themselves off from God, but others as well. I do not think all the Pharisees sought to be hypocrites, but that is how it turns out when you are religious on the outside and evil on the inside. False religion forces an individual to become skilled at covering corruption and adept at external morality and ritual so as to carry on a deception. The Pharisees had no love for God, knew no power from the Holy Spirit, had no knowledge of the truth, and possessed absolutely no righteousness. They were actors and, like all hypocrites, the more they did it, the more convincing they became.

The Pharisees were very good at faking religion. We read in Matthew 23:13, "Woe to you...hypocrites...for you do not enter in yourselves, nor do you allow those who are entering to go in." Verse 15 adds, "You travel around on sea and land to make one proselyte; and when he becomes one, you make him twice as much a son of hell as yourselves." They cared about the little ritualistic details and neglected big moral issues (23:23). Jesus said, "You clean the outside, not the inside" (see verse 25). And in verse 27 He said, "You are like whitewashed tombs." The Pharisees provided superficial homage to the prophets, but they did not care about righteousness (verse 29). Jesus completely exposed these false leaders using the most incisive and graphic language.

---

> As pastors, we need to remember that we have an obligation not to accept false teachers, but to evangelize them.

---

### A Lesson on Confronting Hypocrisy

Though Jesus confronted hypocrites, He did so with a merciful purpose in mind. As pastors, we need to remember that we have an obligation not to accept false teachers, but to evangelize them. In Luke 11:37-44, Jesus taught us how to confront a religious deceiver. But this lesson does not entail that the response will always be positive, for Jesus' situation with the Pharisees did not end well: "When [Jesus] left there, the scribes and the Pharisees began to be very hostile and to question Him closely on many subjects, plotting against Him to catch Him in something He might say" (verses 53-54).

We see how our Lord mercifully confronted the Pharisees to expose their true condition. Contrary to Jesus' approach, in our modern day, evangelicals are quick to embrace false religionists and hypocrites. It is as if there were some ground to be gained in doing this, but all that evangelicals are doing is aiding and abetting the damnation of hypocrites. As students of God's Word, we have the responsibility to confront false teachers about their own condition. Religious hypocrites have unchanged hearts, are cut off from God, and are left to define their religion and their spirituality by what they do externally. These individuals do not need cover; they need confrontation.

The Pharisees' religion was external, and when all you have is the external, then you expand on it. They expanded the ceremonies, the rituals, and the prescriptions. They had nothing on the inside, so they took the basic law of God in the Old Testament and they inflated it by adding to it until it was beyond comprehension. This is essentially what the Roman Catholic system has done—adding endless regulations, supposed revelations, and requirements to further define their godliness by giving attention to ceremonial minutia. Therefore, to expose their true condition is perceived as an attack on their system. Jesus did exactly that when in Luke chapter 11 He launched His confrontation with the Pharisee. Jesus' strategy was to step right into the situation and immediately violate the man's conventions.

"When he had spoken" indicates that Jesus had completed His teaching to the multitude, in which He told them what a wicked generation they were and how they had plenty of light but no sight (Luke 11:37). After this talk, a Pharisee asked Jesus to have a meal with him. Pharisees were not priests, but laymen who were extremely devoted to the law and tradition. They had effectively obscured the law by adding to it. They had become known as the spiritual authorities in Israel to whom the people looked. And by Jesus' time, they were self-righteous, evil, degenerate, hypocritical, filled with pride, and abusive to the people.

One of them, for reasons that are not disclosed, invited Jesus to eat with him. This is shocking because the animosity between the Pharisees and Jesus had already been made evident. In fact, the Pharisees had even begun plotting Jesus' death. Yet there is no indication that this Pharisee in Luke 11:37 had an evil motive, and there is no indication what his motive was.

Now in ancient Israel, there were two main meals—a late morning lunch, and a late afternoon dinner. This man invited Jesus to come and have lunch with him. This event started off innocently because Jesus agreed to the invitation, came in, and reclined (verse 37). The usual posture for somebody who was going to eat at a social meal was the reclined position. There would be a couch or elongated place to sit, and guests would come to stay, recline, converse, and eat. For someone to invite a guest in this way was so that the people involved could get to know one another. It is at this point in the narrative that we learn the characteristics of false religion and hypocrisy.

## The Characteristics of Hypocrisy
### A Love of the Symbolic

The first characteristic of false religion is that it loves the symbolic. This is not true in just this case; it's generally true in every false religion. Whether you're discussing the Roman Catholic Church, the Greek Orthodox, or whatever other false religion, you learn that reality is absent and symbols are substituted. "When the Pharisee saw it, he was surprised that [Jesus] had not first ceremonially washed before the meal" (11:38). Jesus purposely walked right in, went to the table, and reclined. He knew what was expected of Him, and He did not do it. He knew the expected ritual, for He had been raised in that culture. As a result, the Pharisee was surprised—literally amazed—that Jesus had not first ceremonially washed.

The key word here is "ceremonially." The issue was not with dirt or hygiene, but with a ceremonial symbol developed in Judaistic practice. In case a Jew had touched a Gentile that day, or touched something a Gentile had touched, or had touched something unclean, he was required to symbolize the desire to be clean of all defiling contacts in the world by ceremonially washing himself.

According to Jewish tradition, there were certain ways the washing was to be done. But can these details be found in the Old Testament? No, because they have nothing to do with the Old Testament. This was an empty act of ceremonial purity that did nothing for the corruption of the heart. That is exactly what Jesus was talking about in Matthew 15 when He said that the religious leaders had substituted the traditions of men for the commandments of God. They could

not keep the commandments of God, so they invented foolish traditions.

Jesus walked in, sat down, and in effect said, "I'm not interested in your symbols, and I don't want to belong to your club." Jesus was willing to insult the man in order to confront his spiritual condition. The man was obsessed with symbols because false religion is stuck on symbols. Hypocrites have a love for the symbolic.

### A Love of the Sinful

The second characteristic of false religion is a love of the sinful. Though Jesus and the Pharisee had not said anything yet, Jesus knew exactly what the Pharisee was thinking. The Pharisee just stood there in shock because Jesus had not taken water and dribbled it across his fingers (Luke 11:38). Did the Lord say to the man, "Thanks for inviting me to lunch"? No. Did He say, "It's nice to meet you. So glad you're religious. You know we worship the same God, Jehovah"? He did not say any of that. Rather, He said, "Now you Pharisees clean the outside of the cup and of the platter; but inside of you, you are full of robbery and wickedness" (verse 39). Jesus instantly got to the heart of the matter and exposed that the Pharisee actually loved what was sinful. Jesus read the man's mind; the man was troubled by Jesus rejecting the symbolic, so Jesus immediately and unapologetically confronted the man's superficiality.

Jesus' choice of analogy was a very good one, since they were sitting at a table ready to have lunch. Whoever heard of washing just the outside of a dish when it is the inside that holds the food? It is pointless to wash only the outside and put the food on the inside. Jesus implied that this man was clean where it didn't matter. The ritualistic washing may have cleaned the outside of the body, but inside, he was "full of robbery and wickedness" (verse 39). The word "robbery," means to plunder, pillage, rape, to take something violently by force. The Pharisees were pillaging people's lives and abusing them as spiritual terrorists. Jesus also mentioned that the Pharisee was full of "wickedness," which entails an evil disposition, since its synonym is villain.

The more I study the Gospels, the more impressed I am with the direct approach that Jesus used. Jesus saw that this man was like the false prophets before him, who devoured the poor, plied their hypocrisy for personal gain, and abused people's souls. This hypocrite had a love for the sinful.

### A Love of the Simplistic

The third characteristic of false religion and hypocrisy is that it loves the simplistic. Jesus insightfully continued, "You foolish ones, did not He who made the outside make the inside also?" (verse 40). The Pharisees were ceremonialists who were shallow in their theology. It is necessary to clarify here that something that is simple has a clear meaning and is not complex. However, *simplistic* means to be

overly and irrationally simple. One has to be a fool to be in a false religion and to be a purveyor of it, because he lives with the simplistic reality that God only cares about the outside. The Greek word translated "foolish ones" could be stretched to mean "you brainless ones," or "you simpletons." The Pharisees were destitute of the knowledge of the truth and lived their lives before the God they claimed to worship, thinking He would be satisfied with the outside and not concerned about the inside. Hypocrites know what they are on the inside. In 1 Corinthians 2:11, Paul wrote, "Who among men knows the thoughts of a man except the spirit of a man which is in him?" Everyone knows their own heart. To be a human being means that you are self-conscious and know what's going on inside of you.

It's axiomatic to say that the spirit of a man knows what's in a man. Therefore, why would anyone think that a holy God is content with an individual being ceremonially clean with no regard for the inside? It certainly wouldn't seem to be a leap of intelligence to understand that if the Creator was concerned about the outside, He was also concerned about the inside. How ridiculous and sophomoric were these Pharisees? They were supposed to be teachers of deep divine truth, to know God, to be righteous, and to be the standard of virtue and holiness. And yet they thought that God was not interested in what was going on in their wretched hearts. Paul wrote in Romans 2:29, "He is a Jew who is one inwardly;

and circumcision is that which is of the heart." Even the Jews knew that God cared about the internal.

In Luke 11:41, Jesus continued, "Give that which is within as charity, and then all things are clean for you." Jesus basically told the man to take care of his heart—to let his heart go out to the poor and those in need. It is as if Jesus were saying, "You've got all your superficial almsgiving, all your phony prayers, all your phony fasts, all your hypocritical ceremonies, and yet you plunder people for the sake of self-gain. You use, and abuse, and rob them blind. You can't believe God doesn't care about your heart."

The Pharisees weren't alone in loving the simplistic. That still happens today. For example, ask yourself how a Roman Catholic priest can be so simplistic as to go around wearing the garb, partaking in all the ceremonies and rituals, representing himself as a holy man of God, and going out and being sexually immoral as a way of life?

In the Pharisees' case it might not have been sexual immorality, but it definitely involved devouring the poor and abusing people. How does one not go mad with guilt to stand and portray himself as a holy person and be in habitual sin? Sadly, this is an epidemic in every false religion because the heart has never changed. And there are even men who preach the true gospel who become very adept hypocrites. The longer they do it, the more skilled they become, and the

more they quiet their conscience, the bigger the disaster is when it finally becomes known. So we must remember that God is the God of the inside and the outside. We cannot be simplistic like the Pharisees.

## A Love of the Secondary

The fourth characteristic of religious hypocrites is that they love the secondary. Note Jesus' rebuke in verse 42: "Woe to you Pharisees! For you pay tithe of mint and rue and every kind of garden herb, and yet disregard justice and the love of God; but these are the things you should have done without neglecting the others." Now, it is important to remember that Jesus had been invited to lunch so the man could find out more about Jesus. But Jesus unmasked this man's love of the symbolic, sinful, and simplistic. In the next three verses Jesus pronounced three curses on the man—and not just on this Pharisee, but on all Pharisees. Jesus made the diagnosis instantly, and He pronounced the judgment almost as instantly.

"Woe" has already been used in the Gospel of Luke on several occasions against cities upon which our Lord pronounced judgment. "Woe" is not a sentiment of sorrow; it is a declaration of judgment. In Mathew 23, Jesus said "woe" multiple times as He spoke to the sons of hell who were headed for destruction, and who would have a greater condemnation. Therefore, when Jesus said "woe" in Luke 11, He spoke a word of judgment on this man. Why? "You pay tithe of mint and rue and every kind of garden herb, and yet disregard justice and the love of God" (verse 42).

The Pharisees did not understand what was primary, and loved the secondary. Like all religious people who don't know God, the Pharisees did only the external things they could do, and not those things that stem from the heart. The Old Testament required that a tenth of a person's grain, wine, oil, and flock be given to the Levites (Deuteronomy 14). Another tenth was to be provided for the national feast (Leviticus 27). Also, every third year, another tenth was to be given for the poor (Deuteronomy 26). All this giving was intended to help fund the theocracy, but there was no command in the Old Testament to tithe at this Pharisaical minute level. Can you imagine going to the temple with a bag of seeds and dropping one out of every ten seeds into a receptacle? In fact, the Mishnah states that the condiments like salt were exempt from the tithe. The Pharisees' observations were ridiculous!

The Pharisees had no heart for justice and no heart for God. They could not love the Lord their God with any part of their heart, any part of their mind, any part of their soul, or any part of their strength. Nor could they love their neighbor as themselves. Instead, they fussed with what did not matter, and fiddled with the minutia.

### A Love of Status

The fifth characteristic of hypocritical religion is a love of status. We read in verse 43, "Woe to you Pharisees! For you love the chief seats in the synagogues and the respectful greetings in the market places." False religious leaders love being accorded reverences, elevated positions, veneration, and admiration. They seek long, drawn-out designations that somehow give them higher esteem with the people. The chief seats in the synagogues faced the congregation, and these leaders sat there for everyone to witness their splendor. They desired to promote themselves.

In Mathew 23:5-12 we learn that these men loved to be called father, Rabbi, and teacher. They loved to be greeted in the marketplace. Yet their desire for status in the people's eyes was a form of idolatry. In John 5:44 our Lord asked the Jewish leaders, "How can you believe, when you receive glory from one another and you do not seek the glory that is from the one and only God?" Now that is the picture of false religious leaders—they claim to love God, love people, have insight into spirituality and religion, be holy and righteous and virtuous, but in reality all they care about is receiving glory and praise from people. They are spiritual terrorists who literally take people to hell with them.

Jesus concluded this indictment in Luke 11:44: "Woe to you! For you are like concealed tombs, and the people who walk over them are unaware of it." The Lord was saying, "I pronounce damnation on you because of what you do to the people who get near you." This time the judgment was not of their own evil, but of the evil transmitted to others. The whole nation of Israel had bought into their lies and hypocrisy. They followed in the same wickedness, and their end was the same judgment.

Jesus used the analogy of tombs because the Old Testament prohibited Israelites from touching a dead body (Leviticus 21). If a person touched a corpse, he was considered ceremonially defiled and could not observe the Passover according to Numbers 29. To become clean once again, he had to participate in ceremonial purification. In fact, Numbers 19 describes a seven-day purification process that was a nuisance to carry out. Because of the law's prohibitions, all graves were marked to ensure that no one accidently touched them. Tombs were whitewashed so that people wouldn't go near them and be defiled.

---

Those of us who serve in the ministry must learn Jesus' model for confronting evil for the merciful sake of the person who is the purveyor of evil.

---

Jesus said that the Pharisees were like an unmarked grave. People came in contact with them and had no idea that they were being defiled. And the defilement they experienced was not only ceremonial, but spiritual as well because their soul was in harm's way. Jesus knew how critical it was to address this issue.

Mercifully, He gave this Pharisee every opportunity to see himself for who he really was, but in the end, the response was hostility (Luke 11:53).

**The Responsibility to Expose Hypocrisy**

Those of us who serve in the ministry must learn Jesus' model for confronting evil for the merciful sake of the person who is the purveyor of evil. We have a responsibility to expose that person to himself as well as to others. Jesus' meeting began as a private one, but He took it from there and expanded it to the larger group, and later the larger group got the message and was duly confronted.

We also need to make sure we do not become anything like these men. We do not want to get caught up in symbols; we want to be the real thing. We do not want to live in some simplistic kind of schizophrenia where we carry on self-deception by being clean on the outside, while on the inside our minds and hearts are full of sin. We do not want to spend our lives fiddling around with secondary issues and rearranging deck chairs on the Titanic. We do not want to fool with what does not matter. We do not want to be guilty of seeking status, exaltation, or glory. Rather, we must be those who love righteousness, love God, love Christ, love biblical truth, love others, and love lowliness and humility. So that those who are under our charge, when they bump into us, are not defiled and exposed to death, but to life.

# PRAYER

Father, we thank You for Your Word and the opportunity to witness this Pharisee's lunch with our Lord. We see Jesus as a solitary figure with the whole nation against Him. He was the only One able to fight the battle to expose deceivers and to unmask the spiritual terrorists. Our Savior was always merciful to tell the truth about someone's spiritual condition. May we go forth in the spirit of our Lord Jesus to bring compassion to the broken sinner, and confrontation to the religious hypocrites. Help us speak the truth in love with mercy, but also to hold nothing back. Protect us from being hypocrites, living one way before our people and another way before You. We want to stand with our Savior in whose name we pray, Amen.

# 11

# WHAT IS MISSING FROM YOUR CHURCH SERVICE?

*Austin T. Duncan*
*Shepherds' Conference 2014*
*Selected Scriptures*

What is missing from your church service? Is it a fresh approach to welcoming visitors, new songs on the set list, or a need to revisit the ban on coffee in the auditorium? Your church may miss these things, but new songs, coffee, and a new announcement guy are not integral to a biblical church service. Although most congregants in America observe baptism, partake of the elements, sing together, and sit under preaching, they often forget two key elements to a biblical church service: the public reading of Scripture and pastoral prayer. Scripture commends these forms of worship, which are not only biblical but tremendously beneficial to your congregation. As pastors, we must strive to benefit our people by publicly reading God's Word and corporately praying to God in compelling and effective ways.

## The Problem

When public reading of Scripture happens, pastors often carry it out without proper care, regard, or attention. Few take into consideration oral interpretation, producing sloppy readers of Scripture whose helter-skelter reading conveys an equally sloppy view of Scripture. Church leaders deliver announcements with more flourish than they do when reading God's matchless Word. When it comes to congregational prayer, churchgoers experience "free for all" intercession for Aunt Edna's narcoleptic cataplexy, or things of that nature. Sometimes corporate prayer becomes a gossip session, a more spiritual version of church announcements, or a WebMD catalog of illnesses. As pastors, we need to be more effective in these areas, for the ingredients of our worship services are not up to us but are ultimately established by God. Corporate reading thunders God's voice, and pastoral prayer moves mountains. In short, they matter.

### Public Reading of Scripture: Biblical Support

Geoffrey Kirkland writes, "The public reading of Scripture is the reverential, repetitive, corporate and audible reading from the word of God in the regular gathering of believers for the purpose of reinforcing what God has said, recommitting one's self to obedience, and recognizing both the holiness of God and the holiness that God demands from His worshipers."[1]

The key words are *reverential, repetitive, corporate,* and *audible*. This public reading is distinct from the reading of the text for the sermon.

In Deuteronomy 31:9-13, Moses inaugurated a pattern of public reading of Scripture:

> So Moses wrote this law and gave it to the priests, the sons of Levi who carried the ark of the covenant of the LORD, and to all the elders of Israel. Then Moses commanded them, saying, "At the end of every seven years, at the time of the year of remission of debts, at the Feast of Booths, when all Israel comes to appear before the LORD your God at the place which He will choose, you shall read this law in front of all Israel in their hearing. Assemble the people, the men and the women and children and the alien who is in your town, so that they may hear and learn and fear the LORD your God, and be careful to observe all the words of this law. Their children, who have not known, will hear and learn to fear the LORD your God, as long as you live on the land which you are about to cross the Jordan to possess."

Before Israel entered Canaan, Moses prescribed regular reading of the Torah to ensure their covenant faithfulness. The people needed to be exposed to the Book of the Law by regularly hearing the reading of the Word. To hear the Word was a reminder that the source of this Word was not the people or even their leadership, but God. And though future generations would not hear God's voice audibly like the former generation did in Sinai, they would still hear His voice in His revelatory Word. The goal of public Scripture reading was to preserve the Israelites as a holy people, always dependent on the Word of God.

Throughout the momentous events in the life of Israel, the tradition of audibly reading the Word of God continued in Exodus, Joshua, and Nehemiah. The Psalms too commend audible reading, since certain psalms are intended to be antiphonal or for responsive reading. Antiphonal reading is done with two groups of people speaking or singing to each other different parts of the Psalms. Like a musical duet, priests and the people of Israel together sing praises to the Lord. In Deuteronomy 27 and Joshua 8, the people recount God's words to each other. The reading of the Word was a confession of the truth, a reinforcing of the covenant and a reminder of the importance of God's revelation to his people.

Between the Testaments, synagogues formed in which God's people assembled and followed a scheduled reading. Everett Ferguson writes, "The synagogue service included Scripture readings, interspersed with psalms, chants, sermons, prayers, alms-giving. We find the same elements in the early accounts of Christian worship, reading, singing, preaching, praying and giving."[2] That sounds very much like a church service.

In Luke 4, Jesus the Rabbi opened the scroll of Isaiah, reading powerfully from God's Word and saying, "Today this Scripture has been fulfilled in your hearing" (verse 21). That was not an unusual practice; it was the norm for the worship conducted in Jesus' day.

The New Testament practice of Scripture reading continued after the resurrection of Christ. First Timothy 4:13 reads, "Until I come, give attention to the public reading of Scripture, to exhortation and teaching." Without getting overly technical, a case can be made that this passage is not about merely reading a passage for the sake of exposition, but instituting a separate practice that was to be done by the Christians. The most obvious evidence for this is that there are three elements listed here: the public reading of Scripture, exhortation, and teaching. Three clearly separate elements are identified, and Paul exhorted Timothy to apply himself to doing all three in the context of pastoral ministry. This is how Phillip Towner describes it: "A community practice designed to steer the congregation out of the unorthodox backwaters of the heretical reading of certain texts, and back into the mainstream of the biblical story."[3] The people were prone to falling for myths and apocryphal tales, and Timothy was commanded to read the Scriptures so that the people would stay true to the Word of God.

The epistles provide further examples of the early church reading Scripture publicly. Christians shared these letters among churches, read them aloud in their gatherings, and treated them as Scripture. Peter confirmed that the apostolic writings were on par with the Old Testament (2 Peter 3:16), and Christians were to continue reading the Old Testament as well as the apostolic epistles in order to know the full revelation of God (Ephesians 5:19; Colossians 3:16). This is reason enough for us to engage in the public reading of Scripture.

### Public Reading of Scripture: The Benefits

Not only is the public reading of Scripture biblical, it is also beneficial. Let's look at four benefits the public reading of Scripture provides.

### Combats the Anemic Use of Scripture

First, reading Scripture publicly energizes your use of Scripture. When you open God's Word and you read it without a comment, introduction, or necessary explanation, it reinforces what you believe about Scripture when you hear Scripture that is from God. There is a difference between a church service that focuses on solely horizontal aspects of worship and a church service that fixes its gaze vertically by intentionally hearing from God.

There is a reverence that comes from the plain reading of God's Word that just doesn't fit in most worship services, because most worship services are concerned with not overwhelming the congregation with the Bible. Pastors don't want to distract from the message they have prepared or their zingy introduction. Such actions show that a church's leadership does not understand the nature and power of Scripture. Your doctrine of Scripture is weak if you don't have room for the public reading of Scripture. The practice of reading Scripture publicly connects the church body to Scripture and to a robust doctrine of Scripture by giving them an awareness of the power of the Word.

The churches I grew up in and served in before I came to Grace Community Church never did this. So the first time my wife and I attended Grace Community Church, we listened to Pastor MacArthur open the Bible and read through an entire chapter. This reading was immediately followed by a lengthy pastoral prayer that was focused and sobering. At first I wasn't used to so much standing, but it was clear that comments like, "Ladies and gentlemen, let's hear you make some noise for Jesus," or "Put your hands together for the Lord" would not fit in such a setting. When one hears the sustained reading of the Word of God, it forces him to realize that this church holds the Word of God in high regard.

> **The public reading of God's Word directs the entire service toward the God who speaks in Scripture.**

Pastor, when you implement this practice into your worship service, and do it well, it teaches your people to love the Word of God and to depend on Scripture alone. It has the double-edged effect of Hebrews 4:12. It reminds us that we are not central. The Word of God can and will work apart from our expository insights. A story from C.H. Spurgeon's life illustrates this double-edged effect. When Spurgeon was testing the acoustics of the Crystal Palace in London, he climbed up into the pulpit and said, "Behold the Lamb of God, which taketh away the sin of the world" (John 1:29 KJV). A workman who was in one of the galleries heard this declaration and was soundly converted. This serves as a reminder of the inherent power of the Word of God. Does the effectiveness of Scripture make you less important? Yes! And isn't it great that the power is not in you?

The public reading of God's Word directs the entire service toward the God who speaks in Scripture. It reminds us that revelation itself is a mercy. It shows the power of God to save and always accomplish His purpose (Isaiah 55:10-11). It confronts the sin in a congregation (James 1:23-25). Though you may not be preaching on sexual immorality during a given week, perhaps there's someone in the congregation who needs to hear a warning about that specific sin and your reading of 1 Thessalonians 4 addresses it. Praise God in His providence that He has a word for your people that you did not prepare!

Yet many evangelical churches send the reading of Scripture to boarding school, keeping it out of sight and mind. "It's ironic," writes one author, "that among even evangelicals, the people who above all see themselves as Bible people, there is so little enthusiasm for the public reading of the Bible."[4] But reading the Bible is powerful because we believe in the perspicuity of Scripture; we believe the Scripture is inherently clear. David F. Wells, in his book *God in the Wasteland*, speaks on the issue of inerrancy:

> The issue of inherency basically focuses on the *nature* of the Bible. It is entirely possible for those who have sworn to defend the concept of biblical inherency to function as if they had no such word in their hands. Indeed it happens all the time. And the sad fact is that when the nature of the Bible was being debated, the Bible itself was quietly falling into disuse in the church…Without this transcendent Word in its life, the church has no rudder, no compass, no provisions. Without the Word it has no capacity to stand outside its culture, to detect and wrench itself free from the seductions of modernity. Without the Word the church has no meaning.[5]

### Cures Historical Amnesia

Second, reading Scripture aloud cures historical amnesia. Ferguson writes, "It must be remembered that the principal opportunity for most Christians to become acquainted with the Scriptures was through hearing them read in the church."[6] Therefore the regular consecutive reading of the Bible occupied a key place in the early church's history. Obviously, the early church did not have a personal leather-bound or quilt-covered copy of Scripture. The congregants did not have a stack of Bibles at home. Instead, they listened to the reading of Scripture when they gathered. The public reading of Scripture is not just a personal practice but a community practice that has been done throughout the history of the church.

Public reading was first done in the synagogue, and as soon as the apostolic age was over, we witness the testimony of a man like Justin Martyr, who wrote, "On the day which is called Sunday, an assembly of believers, through town and country, takes place upon some common spot, where the writings of the apostles, or the books of the prophets, are publicly read so long as the time allows." That was written in approximately AD 158. As you continue through church history, in the fourth century there emerges a dominant liturgical pattern that includes multiple readings: one from the Old Testament and two from the Gospels. During the final reading, the people would stand. Now, I'm not calling the church to emulate these particulars of the historical tradition. Rather, I want to point out why our churches look so different from churches a thousand years ago and even hundreds of years ago. For 2000 years, the church observed the public reading of Scripture. Where did the practice go?

The church today is preoccupied with making an awesome contemporary video for Father's Day or putting a bed on the rooftop to promote a series on marital intimacy. It's what Thomas Bergler writes about in his book *The Juvenilization of American Christianity*. He calls the modern-day church a youth group on steroids. I'm not condemning youth groups, but there is something to be said about letting our corporate worship time be prescribed by God instead of culture. We need to seek to please God in our worship, not pander to the lowest common denominator. Church history can expose our folly and show us a more mature way. Christians have been reading the Bible in their worship services for 2000 years; there are many more examples of the public reading of Scripture in church history (see Bryan Chapell, *Christ-Centered Worship* 2nd ed. [Grand Rapids, MI: Baker, 2009], pp. 220-33). Let's not trade that heritage for a Fourth of July slideshow.

### Cornerstone to Expository Preaching

Third, the public reading of Scripture constitutes the cornerstone to expository preaching. Preaching begins with learning to read your Bible aloud. The first time I listened to Pastor MacArthur preach, I was shocked by how he read the Bible. I could tell that he understood what it meant. Before he got into any explanation or before he gave any outline, he provided interpretation even with how he paused and emphasized certain portions of the passage. I'm also reminded of a Shepherds' Conference that took place approximately ten years ago when Mark Dever was here. He read from Ezekiel chapter 1 and I was undone like Ezekiel by just hearing the passage read. In their readings of Scripture, it was clear that both of these men held the Word in high regard. The cornerstone of good preaching is good reading.

Jeffery D. Arthurs, in his book *Devote Yourself to the Public Reading of Scripture,* writes, "In many churches, public reading of the Bible is little more than homiletical throat-clearing before the sermon."[7] When you read the Scripture without explanation, you are saying something about the foundational and revelatory nature of Scripture. As expositors, we of all people ought to have confidence that God's Word can speak for itself. And that is precisely what it does during the public reading of Scripture.

### Counters the Man-Centered Service

Fourth, reading Scripture publicly counters a man-centered service. It cultivates the reverence and sobriety that I've already mentioned. A church that reads the Word is a church that is pointed toward heaven. What a joy it is to be under the spoken Word in the presence of other people who are saying, "We submit to this holy Word. This is our guide. This is our God. He has spoken." This isn't something you can livestream.

### Public Reading of Scripture: How to Do It Well

So that we might do well at the public reading of Scripture, I want to provide a few tips.

### Read for Interpretation

The *first* tip is to read for interpretation. A member of the orchestra does not determine the speed or the meter of a piece of music before him. The speed and the meter are written in the music and guided by the conductor. The musician is called upon to faithfully interpret the genius who wrote the piece. Likewise, the one who reads Scripture publicly must give expression to the author's intent and convey the message that's set before him.

For example, Luke 2:16 says, "And they went with haste [long pause], and found Mary and Joseph, and the baby lying in a manger" (ESV). If the second half of that sentence is read too fast without a pause, it sounds like Mary, Joseph, and Jesus were all lying in the manger. That's a big trough. If the text is read wrong, the interpretation is wrong. Let's try it again: "And they went with haste, and found Mary and Joseph [long pause], and the baby lying in a manger." Now it is evident that only Jesus was lying in the manger. By reading well, the pastor provides interpretation and teaches his people good hermeneutics—to mind the paragraph, to mind the punctuation, and to mind the grammar.

A pastor can fail to group words or phrases properly, or even miss the tone of the text. He needs to make climactic what the writer intended to make climactic and to show feeling appropriate for the sense of the passage. This is what oral interpretation is about, and it used to be a fundamental component of any seminary curriculum that intentionally taught preachers to read before teaching them to preach. Reading well is a tool for discovering the treasures that are in the passage. You note things like genre as you read a narrative with movement and emotion. You read poetry mindful of its beauty and symmetry. In Psalm 18, you want to convey the terror and awe of the theophany. Psalm 3 begins with despair, leads to confidence, and ends with assurance. As you read God's Word, you can convey those varying emotions and you don't have to have your Screen Actors Guild card to figure out how to relay assurance when you read, because if you have a heart of faith, you already understand the comfort assurance brings. This is not putting on a show, but reading with interpretation.

In reading the epistles, you emphasize the verbs, follow the arguments, and articulate the writer's ironclad logic. You have to understand the text if you're going to read it well, and you can't fake it. A pastor cannot just get up and rely on his giftedness, because when he gets to Romans chapter 16, he's in trouble if he doesn't know how to greet Tryphaena, Tryphosa, Asyncritus, and Phlegon. When you don't take time to pronounce properly, ultimately, you teach your people that there is irreverence and lack of concern with regard to certain aspects of Scripture. As a preacher, you have to remember that even the genealogies are included in Scripture by God, and are useful for teaching, rebuking, correcting, and training in righteousness.

### Read Prepared

This leads me to the *second* tip: Be prepared. Do not fake, wing, or ad-lib a reading. One has to study to read publicly, just like he has to study to present a sermon. The pastor has to let the message soak in, to understand it, and to own it. This may not entail memorizing the passage, but rather, gaining a deep familiarity of the text. Keep in mind the tricky bits, obey the punctuation, and use tools that will help you to know the meaning and the pronunciation of certain words.

### Read as a Believer

The *third* tip is to read as a believer. Stephen Olford wrote, "Read it as though you believe it."[8] Faith, assurance, and confidence must be in your voice to stress that you believe in the sufficiency of Scripture. After all, you are reading the Word of God, and the Word is true, sure, and reliable. Read the Bible in such a way that you exemplify trust in the author (see Psalm 19:7-9).

### Read with Appropriate Awareness

The *fourth* tip is to read with an appropriate awareness of yourself. This means being mindful of your body, your head, your face, your arms, your hands, and even your feet. Gestures ought to be natural and may need regulation when they're unhelpful. Some preachers look like they're being attacked by a swarm of bees. If you struggle with this, then enlist a helper, someone who will speak the truth to you. Don't say, "Come to Me, all who are weary and heavy-laden, and I will give you rest" (Matthew 11:28) while you put your arms forward, palms facing outward in a stopping motion. That distancing gesture does not convey the welcoming tone of that passage. Again, the goal is to be natural, mindful, appropriate, and prevent from being distracting. As you preach, make sure you carry out the task in a way that it's not about you, but about the Scripture.

Chapell says it this way: "The reader of Scriptures...is the most conspicuous component in the transmission of the Word, and at the same time the least important character in the spiritual drama between God and the assembled audience."[9] This is a good reminder to remove yourself from the experience. It's not about you, and it's not about your skill as a reader. It's about getting out of the way and enabling your people to hear God's Word unmixed with anything else.

### Practice Reading

The *fifth* and final tip is to practice reading. I would encourage you to listen to a recording of yourself, which may be excruciatingly painful. But if you never do it, then you won't find out your verbal tics. As you practice reading, read in a normal and natural tone of voice—responsibly, respectfully, and reliably. Read with meaning, sympathy, real expression, and emphasis. Read

with expectation, humble submission, and confident faith. Good preachers are plentiful compared to good readers. To become a good reader will require practice.

Allen Ross summarizes the matter well in *Recalling the Hope of Glory*:

> The reading of Scripture and the exposition of it are primary acts of worship in the church; they are offerings given to God in reverence and devotion. Reading God's holy Word in the assembly without understanding, interpretation, or enthusiasm undermines the foundation of all worship, which is to hear from God. When the reading of Scripture is with clarity, conviction, and power, it sets the Word of God before the people in a way that demonstrates its authority and demands a response. The reading of Scripture should be one of the most powerful parts of worship—every word spoken from the Word is from God.[10]

The public reading of Scripture is neglected in many churches today, but I don't know if it's as neglected as leading in pastoral prayer.

### Pastoral Prayer: Biblical Support

Corporate pastoral prayer is directly connected with the public reading of Scripture because it is another aspect of worship that is prescribed by God. The biblical support for this is extensive. In

1 Kings chapter 8, Solomon prayed at the completion of the temple. The corporate nature of the prayer is evident by the use of plural pronouns us, our, and we:

> When Solomon had finished praying this entire prayer and supplication to the LORD, he arose from before the altar of the LORD, from kneeling on his knees with his hands spread toward heaven. And he stood and blessed all the assembly of Israel with a loud voice, saying: "Blessed be the LORD, who has given rest to His people Israel, according to all that He promised; not one word has failed of all His good promise, which He promised through Moses His servant. May the LORD our God be with us, as He was with our fathers; may He not leave us or forsake us, that He may incline our hearts to Himself, to walk in all His ways and to keep His commandments and His statutes and His ordinances, which He commanded our fathers. And may these words of mine, with which I have made supplication before the LORD, be near to the LORD our God day and night, that He may maintain the cause of His servant and the cause of His people Israel, as each day requires, so that all the peoples of the earth may know that the LORD is God; there is no one else. Let your heart therefore be wholly devoted to the LORD our God, to walk in His statutes and to keep His commandments, as at this day."

This powerful benediction was not focused on Solomon, but on Solomon and Israel together as the recipients of God's blessing. This type of prayer is also evident as the prophet Ezra prays for the people of Israel in 1 Chronicles 29 and Ezra chapters 9 through 10. Then in the New Testament, we read in Acts 2:42 that the people of God were dedicated to praying together. In today's individualistic society, we are often thoughtful toward our individual responsibility to read the Bible, pray, and have times of devotion and solitude. Yet the far greater emphasis in the Scriptures is toward corporate spiritual disciplines and corporate prayer. And in Acts 4:23-31, it is clear what kind of prayer meetings the early church experienced. Believers were not praying about Aunt Bertha's chronic liver issues. Instead, we read,

> When they had been released, they went to their own companions and reported all that the chief priests and the elders had said to them. And when they heard this, they lifted their voices to God with one accord and said, "O Lord, it is You who made the heaven and the earth and the sea, and all that is in them, who by the Holy Spirit, through the mouth of our father David Your servant, said, 'Why

did the Gentiles rage, and the peoples devise futile things? The kings of the earth took their stand, and the rulers were gathered together against the Lord and against His Christ.' For truly in this city there were gathered together against Your holy servant Jesus, whom You anointed, both Herod and Pontius Pilate, along with the Gentiles and the peoples of Israel, to do whatever Your hand and Your purpose predestined to occur. And now, Lord, take note of their threats, and grant that Your bondservants may speak Your word with all confidence, while You extend Your hand to heal, and signs and wonders take place through the name of Your holy servant Jesus." And when they had prayed, the place where they had gathered together was shaken, and they were all filled with the Holy Spirit and began to speak the word of God with boldness.

*Teach by Example*

The only way people will pray like this is if they are taught to pray like this. This means such prayer needs to be modeled by the pastor. He must show the people that prayer isn't just closing one's eyes and letting everything come out. Instead, prayer is careful, thoughtful, composed, articulated, and strategic—especially for public worship. First Timothy 2:1-4 is a great affirmation of this.

Here, Paul instructed Timothy on how the church should function:

> I urge that entreaties and prayers, petitions and thanksgivings, be made on behalf of all men, for kings and all who are in authority, so that we may lead a tranquil and quiet life in all godliness and dignity. This is good and acceptable in the sight of God our Savior, who desires all men to be saved and to come to the knowledge of the truth.

In this prescription, you have a clear diagnosis and even a recipe for what a pastor's congregational prayer should include. As well, this type of prayer keeps us from being self-focused and self-motivated.

Christians used to be known for their prayers, which were a major part of the service. Nowadays the prayer is just tacked on to the end of the sermon. Pastors no longer like to write conclusions and tend to end their sermons with, "Let's pray. God, grant us to live out the outline that I just preached." In contrast, church history is full of long and powerful prayers that have much variety. This is a helpful counterbalance to where most modern American evangelical churches are—the free prayer, because we think it's more spiritual to shoot from the hip than to plan in advance what you're going to say to God on behalf of your people. In *Lectures to My Sudents,* Spurgeon provides this counsel: "Let me, therefore, very earnestly caution you, beloved brethren, against spoiling your services by your prayers: make it your solemn resolve that all the engagements of the sanctuary shall be of the best kind."[11]

---

**Corporate prayer…is a great reminder that we have congregational commitments and responsibilities to pray together and for one another.**

---

Pastor MacArthur is a master of this, and I had the opportunity to ask him why he prays the way he does on a Sunday morning. He had a very simple answer: "I intend to lift up the people before God. I want to pray for them, with them, and on their behalf."[12] This is how we as pastors have to think about the role of pastoral prayer. Corporate prayer is the perfect antidote to the individualistic approach that is all too common today. It is a great reminder that we have congregational commitments and responsibilities to pray together and for one another.

Like it or not, every church has a liturgy. Perhaps you don't use the Book of Common Prayer, but even something as simple as welcoming the visitors, singing, and a sermon is a liturgy. And the question is, Are you doing all that God has intended for you to do in this gathered time of worship as Christians have been

doing for thousands of years? The modern-day liturgy all too often looks like this: welcome, sing four songs, worship leader prays, sermon, concluding prayer, closing song, and everybody goes home. And that outline is absolutely historically impoverished, especially as it relates to prayer.

*Types of Prayers*

There are many kinds of prayers and a plethora of resources to help you develop variety in your corporate prayers. There are invocational prayers, which are intended to help the people cry out to God and call upon Him (Psalms 8; 100; 113). It is a profoundly biblical kind of prayer for starting a church service. A second kind of prayer is adoration and praise. This prayer recognizes God's greatness and grace. Third, there are prayers of confession, and you'll find these all through the Bible. These prayers simply acknowledge our sin and our need for grace. Usually they are done individually, but they ought to also be done corporately, as in Psalm 40:11-13 or 1 John 1:9: "If *we* confess our sins…" It makes sense for a pastor to pray, "Lord, we your people have sinned." You are not absolving them in some Roman Catholic ritual, but reminding them what God says about His grace—that there is full and free forgiveness in Christ.

The fourth type of prayer is a prayer of illumination. The apostle Paul prays this way in Ephesians 1:17-19. Fifth, you also need to have prayers of thanksgiving for all of God's good graces. Then sixth, along with prayers of thanksgiving, pastors need to pray prayers of intercession. The Reformers understood such prayers to include petitions for governing authorities, the welfare of the church (especially hurting individuals within it), and the progress of the gospel. Whenever Paul prayed for the progress of the gospel, he was offering up a prayer of intercession.

### Pastoral Prayer: How to Do It Well

The *first* tip to better pastoral prayer is to prepare. Asking God for illumination is a wonderful place to start: "Open my eyes, that I may behold wonderful things from Your law" (Psalm 119:18). It is important to be thoughtful about what you're going to pray, to consider what the needs of the congregation are, and to be mindful of what your goal is in this prayer. This prayer does not necessarily need to be written out, but it's also not an extemporaneous prayer, for it's a prayer that you've thought about. It has been helpful for me to write down a brief list of points before I lead the church in prayer because I want to have a thoughtful structure to my prayer.

It's essential that we learn to differentiate between these kinds of prayers and our personal prayers. It's good to pray about circumstances, jobs, sickness, and events. Those things are naturally on everyone's mind. But we need to teach our people to pray bigger—to teach them to pray for wisdom, holiness, purity, and the advancement of the gospel. If you do not

teach your people to pray like this, you'll have many earnest young men, worship leaders, and pastors default into their regular mode of prayer, which tends to be rote sentences that repeat the same catch phrases we are all familiar with. A practical way you can get prepared for a pastoral prayer is to pray Scripture.

A *second* tip is to not explain things to an omniscient God. This is a very common problem in corporate prayer. An example: "Lord, just as John Calvin once said a dog barks when his master is attacked, I would be a coward if I saw that God's truth is attacked and yet would remain silent." Are you telling God what John Calvin said? Should you put footnotes in your prayers?

Another example of this is what a good friend of mine, a pastor, prayed one Sunday morning: "Lord, your *ruach*, which means 'spirit…'" Afterward I asked him, "So you translate Hebrew for the Lord?" Your corporate prayer is intended to edify your people and even teach them how to pray. But remember that you are still talking to God, so stop telling Him what He already knows.

A *third* tip is to not preach or include announcements in your prayer. For example, inserting exhortations in your prayer can be awkward: "And Lord, help these hard-hearted people." You're talking to God, not preaching to your people. Spurgeon said, "Preach in the sermon and pray the prayer."[13] Nor is this the time to make announcements: "Lord, we pray that the junior high parents will get the deposits in by November 11 for the ski trip…At the men's ministry meeting, men whose last names start with A through J should bring donuts." Instead, use the time of prayer to consider God, His kingdom, and His people.

Make it your practice to pray well in public worship. It might be the best part. Spurgeon said, "Let your petitions be plain and heartfelt; and while you may sometimes feel that the sermon was below the mark, may they also feel that the prayer compensated for it all."[14]

## Two Vital Components

The public reading of Scripture and corporate pastoral prayer can help transform a worship service. These two God-entranced and God-focused practices are not just a matter of getting rid of verbal tics or unnecessary lip smacks. Ultimately, we want to build our worship services to bring God honor and glory with excellence. We gather to worship God, and He has taught us how to worshop.

## PRAYER

God, it is our desire to be equipped, to be thoughtful, to be engaged, and, ultimately, to hear from You. Father, may we grow in reverence for Your Word. Teach us to lead our people purposefully and to truly help them encounter You in worship. Thank You that we have access to You in prayer, and that this access reminds us of what Jesus accomplished at Calvary. Give us the courage to be men who lead your people in conviction, with humility, as You have directed us. May we please You in our lives, our ministries, and in the church. Amen.

# 12

# FOSTERING FELLOWSHIP

*John MacArthur*
*Shepherds' Conference 2014*
*1 Corinthians 12:12-27*

Most pastors are familiar with the topic of church fellowship. Yet I want to take the opportunity here to raise your understanding of fellowship and your sense of responsibility for it, and to stress the urgency of implementing all of the elements of fellowship in the life of the church. With that in mind, we will examine 1 Corinthians 12:12-27.

Even as the body is one and yet has many members, and all the members of the body, though they are many, are one body, so also is Christ. For by one Spirit we were all baptized into one body, whether Jews or Greeks, whether slaves or free, and we were all made to drink of one Spirit.

For the body is not one member, but many. If the foot says,

"Because I am not a hand, I am not a part of the body," it is not for this reason any the less a part of the body. And if the ear says, "Because I am not an eye, I am not a part of the body," it is not for this reason any the less a part of the body. If the whole body were an eye, where would the hearing be? If the whole were hearing, where would the sense of smell be? But now God has placed the members, each one of them, in the body, just as He desired. If they were all one member, where would the body be? But now there are many members, but one body. And the eye cannot say to the hand, "I have no need of you"; or again the head to the feet, "I have no need of you." On the contrary, it is much truer that the members of the body which seem to be weaker are necessary; and those members of the body which we deem less honorable, on these we bestow more abundant honor, and our less presentable members become much more presentable, whereas our more presentable members have no need of it. But God has so composed the body, giving more abundant honor to that member which lacked, so that there may be no division in the body, but that the members may have the same care for one another. And if one member suffers, all the members suffer with it; if one member is honored, all the members rejoice with it.

Now you are Christ's body, and individually members of it.

The essence of church life is expressed graphically in the aforementioned metaphor. The life of the church is communal and is an intensely shared personal relationship with a spiritual thrust. This is what apostle Paul expressed in his extended metaphor of the body, and we find that truth repeated throughout the New Testament, particularly in Paul's epistles. For example, in Galatians 3, Paul emphasized that we are all one in Christ Jesus. In Ephesians 4:15-16, he wrote that we are all growing together to the fullness of the stature of Christ and that the Lord is fitting every part of the

body together as one. In Philippians 2, Paul reminded us about caring for others more than ourselves, humbling ourselves, and having the attitude of Christ, which is selfless. This is what life in the church is to be like, and these passages re-establish in our minds the urgency of this matter of fellowship in the church.

## The Blessing of Fellowship

Dietrich Bonhoeffer was very influential in my life, especially when I began pastoral ministry. His book *Life Together* had a profound impact on me. At that time I was studying the pastor's responsibility in developing fellowship in the church, and I was not able to find much on the topic. While Bonhoeffer's book is not particularly theological—it's more devotional—I found it to be insightful and extremely helpful, particularly in light of how his life ended. On a gray dawn in April 1945, in a Nazi concentration camp at Flossenburg, Dietrich Bonhoeffer was executed by the order of Heinrich Himmler, who was Hitler's executioner. Bonhoeffer had been arrested about two years prior, and he was transferred from camp to camp: Tegel, Berlin, Buchenwald, Schoenberg, and Flossenburg.

During his transfers, Bonhoeffer lost all contact with the outside world. He became isolated from the people that he knew and loved. In fact, he was separated from all fellowship. And he had written *Life Together* a few years before that concentration camp experience. In that book, he wrote, "The physical presence of other Christians is a source of incomparable joy and strength to the believer. A physical sign of the gracious presence of the triune God, how inexhaustible are the riches that open up for those who, by God's will, are privileged to live in the daily fellowship of life with other Christians?"[1] He continued, "Let him who has such a privilege thank God on his knees and declare it is grace, nothing but grace that we are allowed to live in fellowship, in community with Christian brothers."[2] This man understood the blessing of enjoying fellowship with believers.

**Jesus' Prayer for Fellowship**

Multiple New Testament metaphors emphasize Christian fellowship. As Christ's church, we are bound to one husband. We are one set of branches connected to one vine. We are one flock with one shepherd, one kingdom with one king, one family with one father, and one building with one foundation. An even more intimate metaphor appears in 1 Corinthians 12—we are one body with one head. The metaphor of the body appears only in the New Testament, and thus is a unique way to understand the church.

---

Trinitarian fellowship is the model for fellowship in the church: a shared life, shared love, shared purpose, shared truth, and shared power. This is fellowship.

---

The church's fellowship is profound, spiritual, and real. It is a shared common life that is absolutely essential. It is what our Lord prayed for in His famous prayer in John 17, where He repeatedly said, "I pray that they may be one." Jesus was not praying for some kind of a social oneness, but for a spiritual reality. That prayer was answered when the church was born.

Jesus prayed that the Father would make His children one, just as He and the Father are one. What an amazing parallel! We are one in the way that the Son, the Father, and the Spirit are one. Trinitarian fellowship is the model for fellowship in the church: a shared life, shared love, shared purpose, shared truth, and shared power. This is fellowship.

In the New Testament, the Greek verb *koinoneo* is used eight times, and seven of those instances are translated "share," while in one instance it is translated "participates." The noun *koinonia* or *koinonos* appears about thirty times and has many different translations—"sharing," "contribution," "partnership," "participation," and sometimes "fellowship." The concept of fellowship then, refers to linking as partners and sharing a common life and cause. This is at the heart of life in the church, and this is what the church is.

**Headed the Wrong Direction**

It has been disturbing to witness in recent years that this has not been the direction the church has pursued. The church does not seem to be seeking a deeper, more profound expression of spiritual fellowship. Back in the 1980s, a Jewish humanist by the name of Neil Postman wrote a little book titled *Amusing Ourselves to Death*. Here is a Jewish humanist who is critiquing evangelical Christians and saying that they've lost their ability to think seriously because they are succumbing so much to entertainment. In the book he discusses the mind-crippling power of television, which does not engage people on an intellectual and meaningful level, but rather, causes them to sit like zombies and stare transfixed at a screen.

I do not think Neil Postman ever imagined that screens would consume so many American lives. The result has been devastating hyper-privacy. Screens are so private now that you can bring in the world of your own choosing through smartphones. Every person has become like a god, a creator of his own private universe, a secret world of preferences, downloading what he or she wants, eliminating what he or she does not want, and it has become a sphere of preferences and temptations. The smartphone is the most selfish necessity ever devised, and technology has put in our hands the most constant, the most accessible, the most visual private world of self-centered indulgence and temptation that humanity has ever known. You choose your music, your teachers, your entertainment, your friends, and like God, you become the creator of your world. The forest of temptations with

which you can indulge yourself is devastating to fellowship.

Carl Trueman wrote on this topic, "The language of friendship is hijacked and cheapened by the Internet social networks, Facebook friends."[3] This is part of what some call the juvenilization of the church. Trueman continued, "The language of Facebook both reflects and encourages childishness. Childishness is a textually transmitted disease."[4] Research shows that the average high school student is on the Internet nine hours a day. Think about being a pastor and trying to create a fellowship with the next generation. Trueman wrote about the social media epidemic and said, "Such are human amoebas subsisting in a bizarre non-world that involves no risk to themselves, no giving of themselves to others, no true vulnerability, no commitment, no sacrifice, no real meaning or value. They are self-created avatars."[5]

Real fellowship does not exist in that digital world. Christianity is not a private experience; instead, privacy devastates the church. We are rapidly heading toward the norm of people creating their own virtual world and virtual self. I tweet, therefore I am. This is who I am—the perfect, indomitable me, self-actualized like some technologically created science-of-mind projection.

Tragically, the culture is becoming more isolated, consumeristic, and self-absorbed. Consequently, developing fellowship is very difficult. Sadly, the evangelical church for decades has been trying to give the culture what it wants—privacy, convenience, and no accountability. The culture wants fellowship to die, and church life is falling victim to this seductive design.

Even attendance in many megachurches is on the decline because the trend is for people to belong to the first church of iTunes. One of the largest churches in America is an online church. I read an advertisement by a church that proclaimed, "Join an e-group." This is the trend, because at a real church you might have to face someone you don't agree with. At a real church you might have to sit next to somebody you're not too fond of. At a real church you might hear a message from a preacher who doesn't say what you want to hear. Worst of all, you might have to sing an old hymn in 4/4 time led by a senior citizen. Can you imagine the horror? That would be way too much for those who prefer an individualistic self-created world. For many, all information, all experience, and all relationships are based upon their own defined entitlement. That rules out truth, accuracy, credibility, rationality, sacrifice, deferred gratification, and meaningful relationships.

This is illustrated in a *Christianity Today* article by Kevin Miller. He wrote about Donald Miller, Rob Bell, and Brian McLaren all leaving the church. Ironically, ten years ago they were considered the most influential evangelicals in the world. These leaders were part of the Emergent Church movement that imploded because of personalized

entitlement religion. They had a bias against the accuracy, authority, and clarity of the Word of God. They formed a personalized religion that collapsed when people began to realize that there was no reason to get together. Donald Miller says on his blog, "I don't connect with God by singing to Him." He poses the question, "So do I attend church? Not often, to be honest."[6] In another instance he discusses having communion along the side of the road with chocolate chip cookies and cocoa. The idea is to create your own sacraments and your own hyper-individualized faith.

The sad reality is that in the last 20 years, the church has succumbed to a weak ecclesiology. Even in the midst of a revival of reformed theology, we are losing a whole generation to individualistic antifellowship habits. Even as a pastor, you feel pressure when someone asks, "What are you doing in your church with technology? What are you doing with social media?" Like most other things, technology has its value and can be a tool for good, but it is also an outlet for disastrous evil. As leaders, we cannot let the cyberspace replace real fellowship. Everything about the church fights against privacy, isolation, and narcissism.

## What We Need to Know About Fellowship
### The Basis of Fellowship

To help correct the church's errant trajectory, we have to understand the basis of fellowship. First John 1:1 is probably the most definitive verse on the basis of fellowship: "What was from the beginning, what we have heard, what we have seen with our eyes, what we have looked at and touched with our hands concerning the Word of Life…" John was writing about his firsthand experience with the incarnate God in Christ. He went on to say, "The life was manifested, and we've seen and testify and proclaim to you the eternal life, which was with the Father and was manifested to us—what we have seen and heard we proclaim to you also, so that you too may have fellowship with us; and indeed our fellowship is with the Father, and with His Son Jesus Christ" (verses 2-3).

---

**The goal of the gospel is not just individual salvation for people who then are privileged to do what they want, but rather, to create a fellowship.**

---

The basis of fellowship is the word of salvation. The proclamation of the gospel was so that "you too may have fellowship with us, and indeed our fellowship is with the Father, and with His Son." John was stressing that the proclamation of the gospel has a goal in mind: to create a partnership, a shared life, a shared purpose, a shared power, and a shared ministry. The goal of the gospel is not just individual salvation for people who then are privileged to do what they want, but rather,

to create a fellowship. This is what Jesus prayed for, and here John wrote about the answer to Jesus' prayer.

When Jesus was praying that His followers become one, He wasn't talking about some kind of social unity; He was praying about a real unity that is fulfilled in the work of the Spirit of God, who comes and creates the body of Christ by His own indwelling. In 1 Corinthians 6:17 Paul wrote, "The one who joins himself to the Lord is one spirit with Him." Therefore he who is one with the Lord is one with all those who are the Lord's. It is common to hear people say, "This member or that member is out of fellowship." Yet that's not accurate because if you are out of fellowship, you are an unbeliever. For if you are a believer, then you are in fellowship, because the basis of that fellowship is salvation. As a result, that puts all believers in union with each other. Every saved person is then mandated and entitled to full involvement in that fellowship. Our responsibility extends to others, for God has put our lives together for spiritual purposes.

After John makes it clear that the basis of fellowship is salvation, he draws a contrast in 1 John 1:5-7:

> This is the message we have heard from Him and announce to you, that God is Light, and in Him there is no darkness at all. If we say that we have fellowship with Him and yet walk in the darkness, we lie and do not practice the

truth; but if we walk in the Light as He Himself is in the Light, we have fellowship with one another, and the blood of Jesus His Son cleanses us from all sin.

An individual is either in the light or in the darkness, either saved or lost, either in fellowship or out of it. Believers are always in the fellowship, for they are in the light.

One wants to be careful about saying that another person is out of fellowship. Some may experience a time of wandering like David did, during which he said, "Restore to me the joy of Your salvation" (Psalm 51:12). Or as Donald Grey Barnhouse used to say, "There is a great difference between falling down on the deck of a ship, and falling overboard."[7] If you are on the deck of fellowship, though you may stumble and fall into sin—in fact, you will sin (1:8-10)—that is not fatal because, as 1 John 2:1 says, "If anyone sins, we have an Advocate with the Father, Jesus Christ the righteous; and He Himself is the propitiation for our sins; and not for ours only, but also for those of the whole world." We may fall on the deck, but that's not terminal, for the fellowship of the believers is forever.

Bonhoeffer wrote,

I am a brother to another person through what Jesus Christ did for me and to me. The other person has become a brother to me through what Jesus Christ did for Him. This fact that we are brothers only through Jesus Christ is of an immeasurable significance. It is not what a man is, he writes in himself, as a Christian, his spirituality and piety, that's not the basis of our fellowship. What determines our fellowship is what that man is, by reason, of Christ. Our fellowship with one another consists solely in what Christ has done in both of us. It remains so for time and eternity.[8]

Moreover, he wrote, "Christian fellowship is not an ideal which we must achieve. It is a reality created by God in Christ." Again, salvation is the basis of fellowship.

### The Nature of Fellowship

After we've established that salvation is the basis of fellowship, it is necessary to examine the nature of fellowship. In Acts 2, Peter preached a powerful sermon, and 3000 souls were added to the church by receiving the Word and being baptized (verse 41). These believers then continually devoted themselves to the apostles' teaching, fellowship, the breaking of bread, and prayer (2:42). Even beyond that,

all those who had believed were together and had all things in common; and they began selling their property and possessions and were sharing them with all, as anyone might have need. Day by day continuing with one mind in the temple, and breaking bread from house to house, they were taking their meals together with gladness and sincerity of heart, praising God and having favor with all the people. And the Lord was adding to their number day by day those who were being saved (verses 44-47).

The reality of fellowship is togetherness and sharing—sharing in a spiritual way as well as in a temporal way. We are told that the early church continually devoted themselves to all these things collectively. They expressed their partnership and spiritual union even in temporal ways. History reveals that many people were converted in that great event, and subsequent to that, lingered in Jerusalem because it was the only church in the world. They had come from the Diaspora back for the events of Passover and Pentecost. And since this was the only church at the time, they stayed, were cared for, and had their needs met.

That is why people began selling their property and possessions, "and we're sharing them with all, as anyone might have need" (verse 45). The verb tense of the Greek word translated "selling" is imperfect, which means they began continually sharing their resources. They gave to such an extent that they sold and liquidated their property to provide for each other. The impact of this is evident in verse 47: They were "having favor with all the people. And the Lord was adding to their number day by day those who were being saved." A church with genuine, sacrificial, and loving fellowship is a powerful testimony to the world. In John 13:35, Jesus said, "All men will know that you are My disciples, if you have love for one another." This is not a reference to the emotion of love, but the expression of it. That is fellowship.

Aristides, a pagan looking at Christians, wrote the famous statement, "They abstain from all impurity in the hope of the reckonings that is to come in another world. When there is among them a man that is poor and needy, and if they have not abandons of necessities, they fast two or three days that they may supply the needy with the necessary food, such is the law of the Christians and such is their conduct."[9] The church is to be a powerful testimony to the world. Yet in today's context that is being lost, particularly with the prosperity gospel, which feeds the selfishness and childishness of the so-called "church." The testimony of the church must stay intact, but privacy and solitude are hindrances to that.

### The Symbol of Fellowship

Next, I want to look at the symbol of fellowship, which we read about in 1 Corinthians 10:16-17: "Is not the cup of blessing which we bless a sharing in the blood of Christ? Is not the bread which we break a sharing in the body of Christ? Since there is one bread, we who are many are one body; for we all partake of the one bread." The symbol of fellowship is the Lord's Table. This is where we all end up on our knees at the foot of the cross. This is the leveler where there is neither Jew nor Greek, male nor female, bond nor free. It is a magnificent symbol of our common shared life grounded in Christ's atoning work.

As the pastor of Grace Community Church, one of the things I have tried to do through the years is emphasize that communion is looking back at the cross, but it also presently looks at the body of Christ as one group of sinners who together are humbled on their knees before the sacrifice of the Son of God. The church body has a common partnership in salvation. However, this truth is being diminished. Once when I was out of town I visited a large and well-known church, and it was a painful experience. At the end of his gross mishandling of Scripture, the pastor said, "This is communion Sunday. There is some bread and juice by the exits. Just grab some on your way out." I endured up to that point, but could no longer bear it, for treating the Lord's Table in that manner is abominable.

Though there is no prescription in the Scripture as to how often we are to partake in the Lord's Table, whenever we do, we are to be looking at the cross in deep and honest self-examination, and we should also stress the fellowship aspect of the ordinance. The church is all one body of people who are equally unworthy, equally graced with eternal life. We are all equally redeemed by Christ, and we are all equally bearing eternal life from Him and sustained in Him. The Lord's Table humbles us, levels us, and calls us to serious self-examination. But it also vividly celebrates our union with each other. Make much of the Lord's Table and treat it seriously, not casually.

*The Danger to Fellowship*

Fourth, we must be warned of the danger to fellowship, which is sin. Sin not only brings discipline on the believer, but it devastates the fellowship, shatters the unity, restricts the ministry, holds back the power, and confuses the purpose. That is why in 1 Corinthians 11:27 we read, "Whoever eats the bread or drinks the cup of the Lord in an unworthy manner, shall be guilty of the body and the blood of the Lord." Sinful habits and lack of proper self-examination are so serious that the Lord may make people sick and some of them may end up dying. In verse 31 Paul reinforced this: "If we judged ourselves rightly, we would not be judged." The rationale behind this is found in 1 Corinthians 5:6: "A little leaven leavens the whole lump of dough." As pastors, we are called to shut people out of partaking in the symbol if they are unwilling to confess all their sin. Individuals who do not take this seriously do not understand the significance of the unity of the church.

Matthew 18 contains the first instruction in the New Testament that mentions the church, and here is the charge:

> If your brother sins, go and show him his fault in private; if he listens to you, you have won your brother. But if he does not listen to you, take one or two more with you, so that by the mouth of two or three witnesses every fact may be confirmed. If he refuses to listen to them, tell it to the church; and if he refuses to listen even to the church, let him be to you as a Gentile and a tax collector (verses 15-17).

I'm convinced that the future of the church does not depend on cultural relevance, or marketing, or technology. Rather, the future of the church depends on the church's holiness. For the sake of fellowship, you must deal with sin in the church.

Note what Paul wrote in 2 Corinthians 12:15 when he was brokenhearted by the way the church in Corinth had treated him: "I would most gladly spend and be expended for your souls." Paul would have given his life for the spiritual well-being of the Corinthians. He then said,

> All this time you have been thinking that we are defending ourselves to you. Actually, it is in the sight of God that we have been speaking in Christ; and all for your upbuilding, beloved. For

I am afraid that perhaps when I come I may find you to be not what I wish and may be found by you to be not what you wish; that perhaps there will be strife, jealousy, angry tempers, disputes, slanders, gossip, arrogance, disturbances; I am afraid that when I come again my God may humiliate me before you, and I may mourn over many of those who have sinned in the past and not repented of the impurity, immorality and sensuality which they have practiced (verses 19-21).

Paul was burdened about the purity of the church. The same should be true of you as a pastor. This is the hard work of the ministry. The future of your ministry corresponds directly to your passion for the truth and the holiness of your church. Media cleverness may get crowds, but it does not produce holiness. But holiness does bring Jesus Christ to church, because where two or three are gathered together in a discipline situation, Christ is there in your midst. Sin endangers pure fellowship, so prevent the privacy of sin.

### The Duty of Fellowship

Up to now we have seen that the basis of fellowship is salvation. The nature of fellowship is a shared life, both spiritual and temporal. The symbol of fellowship is the Lord's Table. And the danger to fellowship is sin. Fifth, we must understand the duty of fellowship.

In Matthew 18, we see the negative aspect of the duty of fellowship: "Whoever causes one of these little ones who believe in Me to stumble"—that is, sin— "it would be better for him to have a heavy millstone hung around his neck and be drowned in the depth of the sea" (verse 6). It would be better off for you to drown with a millstone around your neck than to cause a fellow Christian to stumble. In verse 7 Jesus continued, "Woe to the world because of its stumbling blocks!" In verse 10 He said, "See that you do not despise one of these little ones." The principle is prescribed from a negative standpoint: Do not lead another believer into sin.

Someone can cause other believers to stumble by flaunting a liberty, despising them, belittling them, withholding what they need from them, ridiculing them, treating them with indifference, defrauding them, taking advantage of them, or even by failing to confront their sinfulness. Then note the contrasting positive statement in verse 5: "Whoever receives one such child in My name receives Me." When you welcome another believer into your life, no matter who that believer is, you're receiving Christ. Positively, you want to receive other believers; negatively, you don't want to offend other believers. That's the pattern that is required of you, for that is the duty of fellowship.

There are a few reasons given in Matthew 18 for why we should not offend fellow Christians. First, because of the relationship that believers have to angels: "See that you do not despise one of these little ones, for I say to you that their angels in heaven continually see the face of My Father who is in heaven" (verse 10). That's an amazing statement reminiscent of the custom in Eastern courts, in which highly respected men chose servants who would stand on their behalf before the king and look into the king's face. We know, according to Hebrews 1:14, that angels minister to the saints—they watch, guide, provide, protect, deliver, dispatch answers to prayer, and do more for all who belong to God. Therefore, we ought to be careful how we treat other believers because the angels are watching.

Second, we want to treat other Christians with care because of Christ. Jesus said, "Whoever receives one such child in My name receives Me" (Matthew 18:5).

Third, fellowship reflects your relationship to God. Matthew wrote,

What do you think? If any man has a hundred sheep, and one of them has gone astray, does he not leave the ninety-nine on the mountains and go and search for the one that is straying? If it turns out that he finds it, truly I say to you, he rejoices over it more than over the ninety-nine which have not gone astray. So it is not the will of your Father who is in heaven that one of these little ones perish (18:12-14).

We care for one another in the body of Christ by making sure we receive other believers as we would receive Christ, and by never having a negative influence and leading another believer into temptation or sin. Our duty in fellowship is to be an instrument of holiness in the lives of other believers, which embraces the "one anothers" of the New Testament. Christian fellowship consists of confessing your sins one to another, forgiving one another, loving one another, exhorting one another, edifying one another, teaching one another, admonishing one another, and praying for one another. That is fellowship, and it is personal because it militates against privacy, isolation, narcissism, and self-centeredness.

## The Result of Fellowship

The result of this kind of fellowship is simply stated in 1 John 1:3-4: "What we have seen and heard we proclaim to you also, so that you too may have fellowship with us; and indeed our fellowship is with the Father, and with His Son Jesus Christ. These things we write, so that our joy may be made complete." When biblical fellowship is understood and cultivated, the result is joy. Where you have a congregation of people pursuing the realities of fellowship, you have a manifestation of joy that transcends all the pains of life and comes out of shared sacrifice and meaningful spiritual relationships. I can testify that the joy in my own life and the joy in our church is the product of living in the fullness of fellowship.

## PRAYER

Lord, it is appropriate for us to consider what the apostle Paul wrote: "Finally, brethren, rejoice, be made complete, be comforted, be like-minded, live in peace; and the God of love and peace will be with you. Greet one another with a holy kiss. All the saints greet you. The grace of the Lord Jesus Christ, and the love of God, and the fellowship of the Holy Spirit, be with you all" (2 Corinthians 13:11-14). That's our benediction. May it be so, in Jesus' name, Amen.

# NOTES

## Chapter 2—Purity in the Camp (Ligon Duncan)

1. Geoffrey J. Martin, *American Geography and Geographies: Toward Geographical Science* (New York: Oxford University Press, 2015), 864.

## Chapter 3—Hallowed Be Your Name (Tom Pennington)

1. Thomas Watson, *The Lord's Prayer* (http://www.ccel.org/ccel/watson/prayer.txt), 516.

2. Don Whitney, *Spiritual Disciplines of the Christian Life* (Colorado Springs: NavPress, 1991), 62.

3. Augustine, Letters, "Letter to Proba," Letter 130.

4. Augustine, "Sermons to Brothers in the Desert."

5. Whitney, *Spiritual Disciplines*, 64.

6. John Calvin, *Institutes of the Christian Religion* (Philadelphia, PA: Westminster, 1960), 850.

7. Calvin, *Institutes*, 853.

8. John Owen, "Sermon II: A Memorial of the Deliverance of Essex County, and Committee," on Habakkuk 3:1-9.

9. Jonathan Edwards, *The Works of Jonathan Edwards* (Peabody, MA: Hendrickson, 2003) v. 2, 455.

10. Quoted in Richard Baxter, *The Reformed Pastor* (Portland, OR: Multnomah, 1982), 17.

11. Baxter, *The Reformed Pastor*, 18.

12. John Calvin, *Calvin's Commentaries*, vol. XVI (Grand Rapids, MI: Baker, 2005), 328.

13. J.C. Ryle, *A Call to Prayer* (Grand Rapids, MI: Baker, 1979), 35.

14. John Owen, Kelly Kapic, and Justin Taylor, *Overcoming Sin and Temptation* (Wheaton, IL: Crossway, 2006), 86-88.

15. See http://www.nielsen.com/us/en/insights/news/2012/the-cross-platform-report-how-and-where-content-is-watched.html.

16. As cited in John Piper, *Brothers, We Are Not Professionals* (Nashville, TN: Broadman & Holman, 2002), 63.

17. Calvin, *Institutes*, 917.

18. John Watkins, *The Sermons of…Hugh Latimer* (London: J. Duncan, 1824), 2.

## Chapter 4—A Leader Who Suffers Well

1. Marvin Vincent, *Epistle to the Philippians and to Philemon* (Edinburgh: T. & T. Clark, 1897), 78.

2. Martin Luther, *"A Mighty Fortress Is Our God."*

## Chapter 7—The Leader and His Flock (Rick Holland)

1. Thomas Schreiner, *The New American Commentary, 1, 2 Peter, Jude* (Nashville, TN: Broadman & Holman, 2003), 232.

2. As cited in Larry J. Michael, *Spurgeon on Spiritual Leadership* (Grand Rapids, MI: Kregel, 2003), 153.

3. Michael, *Spurgeon*.

4. Michael, *Spurgeon*, 154.

5. Richard Baxter, *The Reformed Pastor*, 4th ed. (Glasgow: Oliver & Boyd, Wm. Whyte & Co., and Wm. Oliphant, 1835), 181.

## Chapter 8—Guarding the Gospel (Steven J. Lawson)

1. David A. Lopez, *Separatist Christianity: Spirit and Matter in the Early Church Fathers* (Baltimore, MD: The Johns Hopkins University Press, 2004), 83.

2. John Phillips, *Exploring Proverbs: An Expository Commentary*, vol. 1 (Neptune, NJ: Loizeaux Brothers, 1995), 286.

3. J.C. Ryle, *A Sketch of the Life and Labors of George Whitefield* (New York: Anson D.F. Randolph, 1854), 29.

4. See http://www.cnn.com/TRANSCRIPTS/0506/20/lkl.01.html.

5. See http://www.cnn.com/TRANSCRIPTS/0506/20/lkl.01.html.

6. J.C. Ryle, *Simplicity in Preaching* (http://gracegems.org/18/Ryle-%20Preaching.htm).

7. Martin Luther, *What Luther Says*, vol. 2, 702-4, 715.

8. Luther, *What Luther Says*.

9. Martin Luther, *Luther's Works*, 26. 55.

10. James Montgomery Boice, "Galatians," *Expositor's Bible Commentary*, vol. 10 (Grand Rapids, MI: Zondervan, 1976) 429.

11. John Knox, *The History of the Reformation of Religion in Scotland* (Edinburgh: Banner of Truth, 1982), 250; Joseph Adolphe Petit, *History of Mary Stuart: Queen of Scots* (London: Longman, Green), 244.

12. John Knox, *The Works of John Knox*, vol. 6, liii.

13. Scots Confession of 1560.

## Chapter 9—No Little People, No Little Sermons (Albert Mohler Jr.)

1. John Calvin, *The Gospel According to John 1–10* (Grand Rapids, MI: Eerdmans, 1995), 237.

2. Calvin, *The Gospel According to John 1–10*.

3. Calvin, *The Gospel According to John 1–10*, 237-38.

## Chapter 11—What Is Missing from Your Church Service? (Austin Duncan)

1. Jeff Kirkland, *An Historical, Biblical, and Practical Analysis of Public Scripture Reading in Corporate Worship Gatherings* (Sun Valley, CA: The Master's Seminary), 2.

2. Everett Ferguson, *Early Christians Speak* (Abilene, TX: Biblical Research Press, 1981), 86.

3. Philip H. Towner, *The Function of the Public Reading of Scripture in 1 Timothy 4:13 and in the Biblical Tradition* (http://www.sbts.edu/wpcontent/uploads/sites/5/2010/07/sbjt_073_fall03_towner1.pdf), 53.

4. Mark Earey, "This Is the Word of the Lord: The Bible and Worship," *Anvil 19*, no. 2 (2002): 92.

5. David F. Wells, *God in the Wasteland* (Grand Rapids, MI: Eerdmans, 1994), 150.

6. Ferguson, *Early Christians Speak*, 87.

7. Jeffery D. Arthurs, *Devote Yourself to the Public Reading of Scripture* (Grand Rapids, MI: Kregel, 2012), 14.

8. Stephen Olford, "Why I Believe in Expository Preaching," audiotape of pastors' luncheon message at Dauphin Way Baptist Church, Mobile, Alabama, March 22, 1999.

9. Bryan Chapell, "The Incarnate Voice: An Exhortation for Excellence in the Oral Reading of Scripture,"', *Presbyterion* vol. 15, no 1 (Spring 1989(, 42-57, 42-43.

10. Allen Ross, *Recalling the Hope of Glory* (Grand Rapids, MI: Kregel Academic, 2006), 506.

11. C.H. Spurgeon, *Lectures to My Students,* First Series (New York: Sheldon and Company, 1875), 85.

12. A collection of John MacArthur's pulpit prayers have been compiled in the book *A Year of Prayer* (Eugene, OR: Harvest House, 2011).

13. Spurgeon, Lectures to My Students, 92.

14. HelmutThielicke, *Encounter with Spurgeon* (Cambridge: James Clark, 1964), 135.

## Chapter 12—Fostering Fellowship (John MacArthur)

1. Dietrich Bonhoeffer, *Life Together: Prayerbook of the Bible* (Minneapolis, MN: Fortress, 2004), 29.

2. Ibid., 30.

3. See http://www.reformation21.org/counterpoints/wages-of-spin/no-text-please-im-british.php.

4. See http://www.reformation21.org/counterpoints/wages-of-spin/no-text-please-im-british.php.

5. See http://www.reformation21.org/counterpoints/wages-of-spin/no-text-please-im-british.php.

6. Donald Miller, http://storylineblog.com/2014/02/03/i-dont-worship-god-by-singing-i-connect-with-him-else where/.

7. Donald Grey Barnhouse, *Your Questions Answered from the Bible* (Philadelphia, PA: The Evangelical Foundation, 1957), 29.

8. Bonhoeffer, *Life Together*, 25.

9. The Apology of Aristides, *Syriac text and translation*. Cited in *Encyclopedia Britannica*, vol. 1 (Chicago: Encyclopedia Britannica), 346.

# PART 3:

# THE SHEPHERD AS THEOLOGIAN

# 1

# The Lord's Greatest Prayer, Part 1

*John MacArthur*
*Shepherds' Conference 2016*

*John 17*

No profession in the world suffers from a more serious lack of clarity, when it comes to the basic requirements of the job, as the pastorate. Everyone but pastors seems to know what their job is. In fact, if we are honest, clergy malpractice goes on everywhere, all the time. It is ubiquitous. It is pandemic. There is widespread confusion about what it means to be a pastor, and widespread indifference to prescribed biblical duties. As a result, the church has no concept of what the pastor is to be or do.

## Where Is the Pastor-Theologian?

One thing is clear: Most pastors have no interest in being theologians, nor do their congregations expect them to be. The devolution of theology and biblical scholarship as a serious matter for Christians can be traced back to the absence of doctrine and careful biblical scholarship in the pulpit. This is a dereliction of duty. This is clergy malpractice. The pastorate is no longer an intellectual calling, and no longer do pastors provide serious intellectual leadership. Today's pastors do not move in the realm of theology; instead, they manage programs. They give uplifting talks, apply culturally invented principles, and pour their energy into everything but scholarship—everything but an intense study of the text, which yields sound doctrine.

They are practitioners rather than theologians. At best, today's pastors broker other people's ideas, which are selected carefully by their own whims and desires and the popularity of certain people. Pastors have become middle managers who broker other people's theology and other people's ideas. Whatever happened to speaking the things fitting for sound doctrine? For the goal of biblical exposition is doctrine first—to draw out of the text the doctrine, the truth—and then to show its implications, application, and exhortation. Above all other things, the pastor is to teach doctrine.

Not only that, but the pastor is also the guardian of sound doctrine. He is to protect the theological integrity of divine truth before his people, in his place, and in his generation. For a couple of centuries now, pastors have outsourced doctrine to the academy.

If you were to go back to the nineteenth century, the majority of university presidents in the United States were ordained pastors. Things have changed since then. In 1977 (after I had been at Grace Community Church for about 8 years), I received a phone call from James Montgomery Boice, and he asked me if I would come and serve on the International Council on Biblical Inerrancy that produced the Chicago Statement on Biblical Inerrancy. I was shocked. I was just a local pastor here at Grace Community Church, I was in my thirties, and I was out of my league. When I got to the first meeting in Chicago, I was stunned by the fact that there were only 2 pastors—myself and Jim Boice. The other 98 men came from academic institutions. And the fact that they picked me says something about how difficult it was to find somebody

else to go with Boice! While there I sat in conversations with Jim Boice and Roger Nicole, I kept my lips sealed. I did not want them to know how ignorant I was, so I just nodded like I understood what was going on.

Pastors have abandoned their high calling and substituted it with lesser functions. Their success, reputation, and sense of accomplishment is achieved by musical content, fashion, novelty, personality, and marketing savvy. Rarely do you find a pastor known as a theologian—as a biblical scholar. Rarely are their minds given to the mastery of Scripture and its doctrinal truth. Sadly, it is a difficult time for those who do understand their calling and who are experts in the interpretation, exposition, and doctrine of the Bible, because they are considered to be an anomaly. This has to change. Pastors must become theologians, biblical scholars, and guardians of sound doctrine.

In reality, de facto pastors are the theologians of the church, not the professors in institutions. The church understands theology from their pastor, and not from professional academics. Sinclair Ferguson said, "We have made little or no impression on the world for the very reason that gospel doctrine has made a correspondingly slight impression on us."[1] That is a tragic reality. Every significant pastor in church history, the names of whom you know, has been a heavyweight in theology. They all developed pastoral training institutions because the highest form of matured ecclesiology is the multiplication of pastor-theologians.

It was around 1650 that the Westminster Confession was developed. There were 121 scholars that spent years refining that great confession. They were the brightest minds, the theological heavyweights, and the biblical scholars of their day. Of the 121, all of them were pastors. We need to take theology back in the church. The academy has proven to be a very unsafe place for the Bible, and we need to take it back.

The academy started taking over after the Enlightenment took theology away from the church, and since the nineteenth century, pastors have been steadily forfeiting scholarly biblical theological influence. In our lifetime, the pastors who recognize the need to correct this travesty have all been working to salvage the Bible from academia.

## Theology's Significance

How important is theology? The word itself means a divine propositional truth revealed in Scripture, which is the pastor's stock-in-trade. Doctrine is the foundation of absolutely everything. Doctrine is the structure of one's beliefs and convictions—the things that control our lives.

In 2 Corinthians 5, Paul made an interesting comment as he described what motivated him. We all understand how much the apostle endured for the sake of Christ, how much he suffered, and how challenging his ministry was. As he neared the end of his life, he wrote that even everyone in Asia had forsaken him. The agonies that he went through are laid out in 2 Corinthians. We look at a man like that and ask, "What drove him? What moved him and kept him on course?" The answer is given in this statement: "The love of Christ controls us" (verse 14). It was the love of Christ that drove Paul.

If you were to ask most people about this today, they would say God loves everyone in the world equally and unconditionally. So what is Paul talking about? He explained, "Having concluded this, that one died for all, therefore all died; and He died for all, so that they who live might no longer live for themselves, but for Him who died and rose again on their behalf" (verses 14-15). Those two verses teach particular redemption— limited atonement. Jesus died for the all who died in Him. Paul was saying that his motivation was not that the death of Jesus Christ was some kind of potential expression of love, but that Christ died and rose for Paul personally. It was the apostle's understanding of particular redemption and a limited atonement that motivated him. He was Christ's!

Does theology matter? Does it change how you view life? Yes! But sadly, the church has doctrinal anemia, and that is why so many pastors who are considered to be successful have no interest in it.

## Theological Revival from John 17

My concern is to help you to think about theology. To do that, let's look to

John 17. Deep into the darkness of the Friday morning of Passion Week, Judas was already gathering the group that would come into the Garden of Gethsemane. Jesus had left the upper room, gone through Jerusalem to the east, and was heading toward the garden, where He would be arrested, and later that day, crucified. He had given promises and warnings to His disciples through chapters 13, 14, 15, and 16. Then, in their presence so they could hear, Jesus prayed the words of John 17. It is a breathtaking experience to read that prayer.

Back in Exodus 28, God had established the tabernacle, the priesthood, and even went so far as to define the clothing that the high priest was to wear. The priest was to put on a garment that represented the 12 tribes of Israel so that when he went in to the Holy of Holies to offer atonement on the Day of Atonement, and to offer incense as a symbol of prayers, he carried on his shoulders and over his heart the people of God, Israel.

That is exactly what happened in John 17. The great high priest, the Lord Jesus Christ, had gone into the heavenly holy of holies and was carrying His beloved people on His shoulders and on His heart. He did this in the presence of the Father. In the Old Testament, the high priest went into the Holy of Holies on the Day of Atonement and came out rapidly. But Christ went in, sat down, and He is still there. We are reminded in Hebrews 7 that He is ever living to make intercession for us—He is praying

us into heaven. And John 17 depicts for us the present work of the Lord Jesus. Hebrews tells us that He is doing it; John 17 shows us His very words.

---

**This high priestly prayer is the greatest ministry of the Lord Jesus Christ.**

---

It is sad to me, given the incomparable uniqueness of this event, how it has been diminished in the church. I don't know that I've ever heard a sermon on John 17. We love to talk about the cross. We love to talk about the death of Christ and His resurrection—and we should. We love to talk about the cross and the resurrection as the fulfillment of prophecy, as actual history recorded in the Gospels, and as it is reflected on by the New Testament writers. I submit that both of those glorious events—the death and the resurrection of Christ—fall below the reality of John 17. This high priestly prayer is the greatest ministry of the Lord Jesus Christ. Does that surprise you? If you want to contemplate something that will contribute to your sanctification, you need to learn this work of Jesus.

### "Much More Then"

Paul wrote in his letter to the Romans, "Therefore, having been justified by faith, we have peace with God through our Lord Jesus Christ, through whom also we have obtained our introduction by faith into this grace in which we stand; and we exult in hope of the glory of God" (Romans 5:1-2). The focus of this text is that we have been justified.

Paul went on to write, "For while we were still helpless, at the right time Christ died for the ungodly. For one will hardly die for a righteous man; though perhaps for the good man someone would dare even to die. But God demonstrates His own love toward us, in that while we were yet sinners, Christ died for us" (verses 6-8). We love that truth of the cross, and we must!

Now look at the first words of verse 9: "Much more then…" Much more than the cross? "Much more then, having now been justified by His blood, we shall be saved from the wrath of God through Him." Paul declared that having now been justified by Jesus' blood, "we shall [continue to] be saved from the wrath of God through Him." The apostle went on, "For if while we were enemies we were reconciled to God through the death of His Son, much more, having been reconciled, we shall be saved by His life" (verse 10).

Paul's comparison is that though the cross and resurrection of Jesus is an amazing truth, there is more to our salvation, which is the truth that we are being saved by His life. In verse 15, the apostle wrote, "The free gift is not like the transgression. For if by the transgression of the one the many died, much more did the grace of God and the gift by the grace of the one Man, Jesus Christ, abound to the many."

Paul was comparing Adam to Christ, and he used the same exact words that we just read earlier in verse 9: "much more."

Verse 17 says, "If by the transgression of the one, death reigned through the one, much more those who receive the abundance of grace and of the gift of righteousness will reign in life through the One, Jesus Christ." Understand that the work of Christ is much more, comparatively speaking, than the work of Adam. We acknowledge how significant that "much more" is. And as the work of Christ is much more than what Adam did, so what Christ does for us alive is much more than His death.

Hebrews 9:12-14 reads,

> Not through the blood of goats and calves, but through His own blood, He entered the holy place once for all, having obtained eternal redemption. For if the blood of goats and bulls and the ashes of a heifer sprinkling those who have been defiled sanctify for the cleansing of the flesh, how much more will the blood of Christ, who through the eternal Spirit offered Himself without blemish to God, cleanse your conscience from dead works to serve the living God?

Christ's sacrifice is much more than the animal sacrifices. Christ is much more than Adam, and so the work of Christ, who ever lives to bring us to glory, is much more than the work of the cross.

He died in hours. He rose in days. He ever lives to make intercession!

Hebrews 7:23-25 should help solidify this truth: "The former priests, on the one hand, existed in greater numbers because they were prevented by death from continuing, but Jesus, on the other hand, because He continues forever, holds His priesthood permanently. Therefore He is able also to save forever those who draw near to God through Him, since He always lives to make intercession for them."

How does this escape us? And in light of this truth, all of a sudden John 17 becomes a precious treasure of incalculable value. This is Jesus' intermediary mediating ministry. In John 17 we meet the mediator, the Lord Jesus Christ Himself, and here He prays for His people.

## Comfort in Theology

The entire prayer in John 17 is theology and doctrine. Apparently, if you do not have theology, not only can you not preach, you can't even pray. Here we find Jesus basing His entire ministry of intercession on sound doctrine; He pleads doctrine before His Father. This portion of Scripture is essentially a prayed systematic theological document on soteriology. And why would we expect anything less of Jesus, since He is the truth? Jesus prayed in the hearing of the 11 and all of us, for He wants all of us to understand this prayer.

We read in John 17:13, "Now I come to You; and these things I speak in the world so that they may have My joy made full in themselves." There is only one reason this prayer is here: for the Christian's joy. We know that the disciples that night needed a lot of joy. This is the Christ who comforts all of us with sound doctrine. He prays the theology of the Father back to the Father, knowing the Father will answer.

For whom does He pray this? Verse 9 says, "I ask on their behalf; I do not ask on behalf of the world, but of those whom You have given Me; for they are Yours." Jesus asked on behalf of the disciples and all those who believed. Also in verse 20: "I do not ask on behalf of these alone, but for those also who believe in Me through their word." Jesus prayed for all believers—those present at that time, and those who would follow through the rest of redemptive history. I am convinced that this is the most comforting chapter in the Bible because the security of the Christian's salvation is the most comforting truth we can know.

## Into the Holy of Holies

Let us go into the holy of holies here and listen to the divine theologian praying us into heaven. This prayer is a preview of what Jesus would be doing after His ascension until the end of redemptive history. It reveals a transition from His earthly ministry to believers to His heavenly ministry for believers. The requests we find in John 17 have been offered constantly by Jesus for the last 2000 years, and He will continue to offer them until all of God's children are safely in heaven. This is the real Lord's Prayer, because only He could pray it. The prayer in Matthew 6 is not the Lord's Prayer, it is the Disciples' Prayer because the Lord could not pray it. He could not say, "Forgive us our transgressions," for He never sinned. John 17 is the Lord's Prayer, and the Lord prayed in the opening verses for the Father to bring Him to heaven—to bring Him safely through the dramatic events that were going to take place immediately after this time of prayer.

John 17:1-5 is a prayer for Jesus' own glory. He asked to be glorified so that He could be put in place to intercede for the redeemed. From verse 6 to the end of the chapter, He lifts an intercessory prayer for believers—for us. And this mediating ministry of Jesus Christ is going on even at this very moment. We see here the theology from the perfect theologian with absolutely perfect theology.

**Salvation and the Trinity**

Salvation begins with the doctrine of God, and Jesus teaches us about the Father in His prayer. We read in John 17:11, "Holy Father," and verse 25, "righteous Father." In verse 3 we learn that there is only one true God, the only eternal noncontingent being, and no one is like Him; everything else is contingent and dependent on Him for existence. However, to say that God is righteous, holy, and the only God does not inherently compel any act of kindness toward anyone. This is where there has been

confusion recently regarding God and Allah. They are not the same. For Allah has been designed as a single solitary eternal being, not a trinity, who by virtue of his eternal singleness cannot love because there has never been anyone to love. Forever he has been one and only one. Allah possesses no relational attributes. How could he be loving when he is a single solitary person everlastingly? Allah is a form of the devil, and that is why there is no love, grace, mercy, and compassion in Islam.

In verses 23 and 24 of this chapter, Jesus made an amazing statement as He spoke to the Father: "I in them and You in Me, that they may be perfected in unity, so that the world may know that You sent Me, and loved them, even as You have loved Me. Father, I desire that they also, whom You have given Me, be with Me where I am, so that they may see My glory which You have given Me, for You loved Me before the foundation of the world." He continued in verse 26, "And I have made Your name known to them, and will make it known, so that the love with which You loved Me may be in them, and I in them." Jesus was saying that the definition of relationship in the Trinity is everlasting love. The true God is love because the true God has always loved.

There is more about the doctrine of God in verse 1: "Father, the hour has come; glorify Your Son, that the Son may glorify You." Here we meet the eternal Son. Again in verse 5: "Father, glorify

Me together with Yourself, with the glory which I had with You before the world was." Now we know that the Father and the Son are defined by a loving relationship that has been from all eternity. The Father and the Son share an eternal nature, eternal love, and eternal glory.

That is why John began his Gospel account, "In the beginning was the Word, and the Word was with God, and the Word was God. He was in the beginning with God. All things came into being through Him, and apart from Him nothing came into being that has come into being" (John 1:1-3). In verse 14 of that same chapter he wrote, "And the Word became flesh, and dwelt among us, and we saw His glory, glory as of the only begotten from the Father, full of grace and truth." Then in verse 18 we read, "No one has seen God at any time; the only begotten God who is in the bosom of the Father, He has explained Him." The apostle Paul also understood this when he explained that in Christ "are hidden all the treasures of wisdom and knowledge" (Colossians 2:3); "in Him all the fullness of Deity dwells in bodily form" (2:9).

The foundation of salvation is a triune, holy, eternal, and loving God. A single god with no capacity to love has no interest in saving anyone. But the God of the Bible is defined by love. Jesus is preexistent with God, co-existent with God, and self-existent with God.

In John 17, the Son was asking to be taken back to heaven and back to the eternal unity, love, and glory that He everlastingly had shared with the Father. It is as if Jesus was saying, "Father, take Me back because of who I am. You gave Me authority over all flesh; You have allowed Me to give eternal life. This is who I am. I am the eternal life because of what I've done. I've glorified You on the earth. I've accomplished the work You gave Me to do. Now take Me back." Here is the real personhood of the Trinity being demonstrated. Salvation exists because God is triune and God is love.

Another stunning statement about the nature of God is found in John 17:10: "All things that are Mine are Yours, and Yours are Mine." As mere mortals, we could join in the first part of this verse and say, "All things that are mine are Yours," but we could not say the second half: "All things that are Yours are mine." The only being who could make that statement is God.

The doctrines of salvation begin in the relationship of the Father and the Son in the Trinity. Paul wrote to Timothy about this God "who has saved us and called us with a holy calling, not according to our works, but according to His own purpose and grace which was granted us in Christ Jesus from all eternity" (2 Timothy 1:9). Redemptive history began as a plan within the Trinity, and because God is love, He desired to bring to Himself many more sons to love.

### Salvation and Election

The second important doctrine within soteriology is the doctrine of election. The people to whom the eternal Son gives eternal life are clearly identified. Jesus said in John 17:2, "He may give eternal life." To whom does He give that eternal life? He gave us the answer in verse 9: "I do not ask on behalf of the world." Jesus was uniquely praying for all whom the Father had given to Him (John 17:2). Then in verse 11, Jesus used the same language: "Holy Father, keep them in Your name, the name which You have given Me." As clearly as the Father has given a name to the Son, He has given people to the Son.

This is not the first occurrence of this truth in John's Gospel. In John 6:37, Jesus said, "All that the Father gives Me will come to Me, and the one who comes to Me I will certainly not cast out." It is important to note that all the Father gives to Jesus will come to Him, and those who come to Him, He will not reject. This falls into the category of what theologians have called irresistible grace. Why? "For I have come down from heaven, not to do My own will, but the will of Him who sent Me. This is the will of Him who sent Me, that of all that He has given Me I lose nothing, but raise it up on the last day" (verses 38-39). Again He said in verse 44, "No one can come to Me unless the Father who sent Me draws him; and I will raise him up on the last day." Then again in verse 65: "For this reason I have said to you, that no one can come to Me unless it has been granted him from the Father." This is the doctrine of divine sovereign election.

How did God choose whom He would give to Jesus? The only answer to that is found in two places. First, John 17:6 says, "I have manifested Your name to the men whom You gave Me out of the world; they were Yours and You gave them to Me." Then in John 17:9 we read, "I ask on their behalf; I do not ask on behalf of the world, but of those whom You have given Me; for they are Yours." Believers belong to God based on His sovereign decree and uninfluenced choice. This is clearly what is meant when Scripture says, "He chose us in Him before the foundation of the world" (Ephesians 1:4).

The book of Revelation contains a reference about certain names written, from before the foundation of the world, in the Lamb's book of life. The Father draws them at the appropriate time in history and gives them as a love gift to the Son. The Son receives them, and then His responsibility is to make sure they get to glory, and that is why He incessantly prays us into heaven. For every purpose of God there is a means. The purpose of God is to bring us to glory, and the means is the intercession of Jesus Christ. Jesus said in John 17:9, "I ask on their behalf." Jesus prays for those who are the Father's by choice—He does not ask for the world. Then in verse 20 we read, "I do not ask on behalf of these alone, but for those also who believe in Me through their word." Jesus' prayer stretches through all of redemptive history.

Now, there are many people who

say, "Christ died for the whole world." If Christ died for the entire world, then His will was at odds with the Father's. For the Father willed to save those whom He chose; therefore, Christ could not have died for the whole world or He would have been out of the will of the Father. It would be like saying the Father was a Calvinist and the Son was an Arminian, which is audacious, for there is only one will in the Trinity. Jesus does not pray for those who are not the Father's, nor did He die for those who are not the Father's.

What about Judas? John 17:12 explains, "While I was with them, I was keeping them in Your name which You have given Me; and I guarded them and not one of them perished but the son of perdition, so that the Scripture would be fulfilled." Judas was not an exception, for he did exactly what Scripture said he would do. He never was a son of God; he was always a son of destruction and damnation.

God is defined as love, and His love is so vast that it stretches beyond even the fulfillment of loving the Son and the Spirit. He wants many sons to love, and so He chooses them, gives them to the Son, and the Son grants them eternal life and intercedes for them.

**Salvation and the Incarnation**

For all of this to have taken place, sinners needed a Savior, for the Father could not bring unrighteous people to heaven. That leads to the third doctrine—the doctrine of the incarnation.

We have already seen the deity of Christ indicated as we looked at the Trinity, but we also see His humanity in John 17. In verse 8 Jesus said, "I came forth from You." That is the incarnation, the virgin birth. Similarly, in verse 3 we read, "Jesus Christ whom You have sent." Then again in verse 18, "As You sent Me into the world"; verse 21, "You sent Me"; verse 23, "You sent Me," and verse 25, "You sent Me."

Nearly 30 times in the Gospel of John, Jesus said He was sent by the Father. He indicated His humanity again in John 17:4: "I glorified You on the earth, having accomplished the work which You have given Me to do." And in verse 13, He anticipated returning back through the ascension. There are indications all through this chapter of Jesus' deity and humanity.

More importantly, consider also His work. In verse 4 Jesus prayed, "I glorified You on the earth, having accomplished the work which You have given Me to do." Understanding the incarnation entails you to understand not only the nature of Christ, but also the work of Christ. He was given the task of providing eternal life to the chosen, and by what work would He do that? There were two necessary realities.

*Atonement*

First, Jesus had to make atonement for sins. Theologians call this passive righteousness. He came to give His life a ransom for many. He bore in His own body our sins: "He was pierced through for our transgressions, He was crushed for our iniquities" (Isaiah 53:5). He had to die as a substitutionary sacrifice for His bride. He had to pay the price of death in order to satisfy the Father's justice, propitiating the Father. And then He was raised from the dead as the Father validated His sacrifice. He had to die, but He also had to live.

### Righteousness

Second, notice Jesus said in John 17:4, "I glorified You on the earth." The Father affirmed that the Son had done just that when He spoke, "This is My beloved Son, in whom I am well-pleased" (Matthew 3:17). Jesus did nothing but glorify God on earth; He was holy, harmless, and undefiled. In John 17:19 we read, "For their sakes I sanctify Myself." That is a powerful statement regarding active righteousness. Jesus lived a perfect life in order for that full life to be credited to our account. He died a substitutionary death so that death could be credited to our account. This is the substitutionary work of Jesus Christ passively and actively.

Then in verse 12 He added, "While I was with them, I was keeping them in Your name which You have given Me; and I guarded them and not one of them perished." While Jesus was on earth, He was living a perfectly righteous life that would be credited to His followers. He was going to die a substitutionary death for sinners. And throughout that entire process, He was also protecting and securing His own.

Often we get the idea that because the Lord says we are secure and our salvation is forever, it just automatically happens. Yet there are divine means the Lord had for guarding His own while He was on earth. Because He sanctified Himself and lived a righteous life to be credited to the people whom God had chosen, because He died a substitutionary death and satisfied the justice of God in the place of sinners, He was given authority over all flesh to give eternal life. As Jesus said to the Father in John 17:3, "This is eternal life, that they may know You, the only true God, and Jesus Christ whom You have sent."

In summary, salvation is to know God, to know Christ. This knowledge comes from the theology revealed to us in His Word. May we once again be reminded that theology is not merely optional.

# PRAYER

Lord, we are so blessed to have been able to reach down into this incredible portion of Scripture and pull up some of the richness in it. To look back at the cross and what Christ did and to contemplate the resurrection is a wonderful thing, but how much more exhilarating and comforting is it to know that this very moment He is alive at Your right hand, Father, praying us into heaven. What a sanctifying realization! Accomplish Your perfect purpose in every life, we pray, for the sake of our Savior. Amen.

# 2

# The Lord's Greatest Prayer, Part 2

*John MacArthur*
*Shepherds' Conference 2016*

*John 17*

As pastors, we need to take up the duty of being biblical scholars and theologians. By that I mean we are to know the Word of God well enough so that we can communicate it effectively to God's people. The example of a theological mind, of course, is our own Lord Jesus Christ. In John 17 we see how theology essentially governed everything that He said, not only in His preaching, but also in His praying. The book of Hebrews has much to say about the Lord Jesus Christ as our great high priest, but only in John 17 do we have a sample of that mediating intercessory ministry. This is the only example in Scripture of what He has been doing in heaven incessantly since His ascension.

This intercessory work is of utmost importance—not to say that we diminish in any way the significance of the cross or the resurrection. However, the cross was accomplished in hours, the resurrection in days, but several thousand years have already passed in the course of His intercessory work. We read in Hebrews 7:25, "He always lives to make intercession for them." For 2000 years, Jesus has been praying us into heaven against the force of sin that assails us. We get a sample of this in the darkness of the Friday morning of Passion Week as Jesus was about to enter the Garden of Gethsemane to be arrested and then crucified. He prayed this prayer in the hearing of the 11, and on behalf of them. But according to John 17:20, He was praying not only for them, "but for those also who believe in Me through their word." He was praying for believers in all the rest of redemptive history, and His prayer is soteriological doctrine.

As we have already seen, the gospel begins with God, and our Lord's prayer started with God; He spoke to the holy and righteous Father. We observed in the prayer that God is triune. Therefore, God is love, because eternally there has been relationship between the Father, Son, and Spirit, and that relationship is defined by an incomprehensible, infinite, and intimate love. Second, we noticed that embedded in this prayer are multiple statements about the doctrine of election. And third, we witnessed in this prayer the doctrine of the incarnation—the Father had sent Jesus into the world. Jesus said in verse 4, "I glorified You on the earth, having accomplished the work which You have given Me to do."

**Divine Revelation**

There is yet another doctrine that this prayer teaches us—the doctrine of revelation. The elect for whom Christ died and lived have to believe the gospel to be saved. If there is no gospel, there is no salvation. And that gospel must be presented in an unalterable and fixed way. Truth has to be delivered to the world so that it can be preached throughout the rest of redemptive history. We see in Jesus' high priestly prayer that the Son has delivered this truth. Read verse 6: "I have manifested Your name to the men whom You gave Me." Jesus revealed God to the disciples. He revealed God's will to them, for He did only what His Father told Him to do. The Son's food was to do the will of Him who sent Him (John

4:34). And He manifested the fullness of who the Father is.

In John 17:26, right at the very end of the chapter, Jesus said essentially the same thing: "I have made Your name known to them, and will make it known." He will keep on revealing God through all of redemptive history. How did He—and how does He continue to—reveal God and make His name known?

First, Jesus revealed God in His person. In John 1:14 we read, "The Word became flesh, and dwelt among us, and we saw His glory, glory as of the only begotten from the Father, full of grace and truth." In verse 18 we are told, "No one has seen God at any time; the only begotten God who is in the bosom of the Father, He has explained Him." A synonym for "explained" is *exegete*. Jesus has exegeted the Father. Jesus went so far as to say, in John 12:45, "He who sees Me sees the One who sent Me." Again in John 14:9, "He who has seen Me has seen the Father."

We read in Colossians, "In Him all the fullness of Deity dwells in bodily form" (2:9). In Hebrews 1:3 we read, "He is the radiance of His glory and the exact representation of His nature."

Jesus revealed God in His person, and He also revealed God in His words. For example, in John 12:44-50 we read,

> Jesus cried out and said, "He who believes in Me, does not believe in Me but in Him who sent Me. He who sees Me sees the

One who sent Me. I have come as Light into the world, so that everyone who believes in Me will not remain in darkness. If anyone hears My sayings and does not keep them, I do not judge him; for I did not come to judge the world, but to save the world. He who rejects Me and does not receive My sayings, has one who judges him; the word I spoke is what will judge him at the last day. For I did not speak on My own initiative, but the Father Himself who sent Me has given Me a commandment as to what to say and what to speak. I know that His commandment is eternal life; therefore the things I speak, I speak just as the Father has told Me."

Jesus is the inherent, infallible, and divine revelation of God. In John 17:8, He said, "The words which You gave Me I have given to them; and they received them and truly understood that I came forth from You, and they believed that You sent Me." In verse 14 He said, "I have given them Your word."

Though Jesus clearly had a commitment to the Old Testament—in the Gospels, there are about 80 instances in which He made reference to different Old Testament books…27 of them—He also knew that what He was saying was new revelation. Jesus knew the power of the New Testament when He said in John 17:17, "Sanctify them in the truth; Your word is truth." He was not only reaching back to the Scriptures that had already been written, but He was looking forward to what would be written—that which would be absolutely essential for the sanctification of His people—so that they may be, as verse 19 states, "sanctified in truth."

Our Lord had already, on that very night, acknowledged the role of the Holy Spirit in the coming days. He said in John 14:16-17, "I will ask the Father, and He will give you another Helper, that He may be with you forever; that is the Spirit of truth, whom the world cannot receive, because it does not see Him or know Him, but you know Him because He abides with you and will be in you." We learn more from verse 26: "The Helper, the Holy Spirit, whom the Father will send in My name, He will teach you all things, and bring to your remembrance all that I said to you." That is why the apostles and their associates were able to record their Gospel accounts and be absolutely inerrant and accurate.

John 15:26-27 reads, "When the Helper comes, whom I will send to you from the Father, that is the Spirit of truth who proceeds from the Father, He will testify about Me." In 16:12-13 we see, "I have many more things to say to you, but you cannot bear them now. But when He, the Spirit of truth, comes, He will guide you into all the truth; for He will not speak on His own initiative, but whatever He hears, He will speak; and He will disclose to you what is to come." Again, in verse 15, "All things that the Father has are Mine; therefore I said that He takes of Mine and will disclose it to you."

The truth was passed down from the Father, to the Son, to the Spirit, to the apostles. The Father, the Son, and the Spirit are truth. Our Lord had a clear view of revelation and the integrity of Scripture. This revelation is directly associated with salvation, because our transformation depends on what is completely external to all of us: The incarnate Son declared His gospel.

In Romans 10:13-15 we have the familiar necessity of preaching articulated perhaps more clearly than anywhere else: "'Whoever will call on the name of the Lord will be saved.' How then will they call on Him in whom they have not believed? How will they believe in Him whom they have not heard? And how will they hear without a preacher? How will they preach unless they are sent? Just as it is written, 'How beautiful are the feet of those who bring good news of good things!'" We continue in verse 17, "Faith comes from hearing, and hearing by the word of Christ." That is why Peter wrote in 1 Peter 1:23, "You have been born again not of seed which is perishable but imperishable, that is, through the living and enduring word of God."

In John 17:8 Jesus explained that the disciples had received the Word, understood the Word, and believed the Word. Consequently, that is what marks the faith that saves. This revelation from God not only has the power for salvation, but also for sanctification. "Sanctify them in the truth; Your word is truth" (verse 17). The Spirit of Christ has inspired the Scripture, and the Scripture stands forever. When a person receives, understands, and believes, that person receives eternal life from the Son.

## Regeneration

That leads to the next doctrine in this string of pearls: the doctrine of regeneration, or the work of God that makes repentance and belief possible. We were born in darkness, blindness, ignorance, and inescapable sin. Thus, we have to be made spiritually alive.

John 3 records an interesting conversation Jesus had with Nicodemus. The religious leader came to the Lord because he had a question on his heart different from the one on his lips. Nicodemus wanted to know how to be born again, how to enter the kingdom of God. Jesus responded in verse 3, "Truly, truly, I say to you, unless one is born again he cannot see the kingdom of God."

Nicodemus's reply is found in verse 4: "How can a man be born when he is old?"

Jesus' answer is amazing: "Truly, truly, I say to you, unless one is born of water and the Spirit he cannot enter into the kingdom of God. That which is born of the flesh is flesh, and that which is born of the Spirit is spirit. Do not be amazed that I said to you, 'You must be born again'" (verses 5-7).

Notice we still haven't seen an answer

to the question "How?" In verse 8, Jesus said, "The wind blows where it wishes and you hear the sound of it, but do not know where it comes from and where it is going; so is everyone who is born of the Spirit." What a strange answer. Jesus explained to Nicodemus that salvation is the Spirit's work—and He does it to whom He wills, when He wills.

In John 17:2-3 we read, "He may give eternal life. This is eternal life, that they may know You, the only true God, and Jesus Christ whom You have sent." Eternal life is a present reality, and to have it is to know God, know Christ, and to come out of death, darkness, ignorance, alienation, and blindness into life and light. It is to move, as Paul would put it, from being a natural man who understands not the things of God to someone who has the mind of Christ.

In John 10:27, Jesus stated, "My sheep hear My voice, and I know them, and they follow Me." And we find out something else in John 8:19: "So they were saying to Him, 'Where is Your Father?' Jesus answered, 'You know neither Me nor My Father; if you knew Me, you would know My Father also.'" It is a package deal. If you do not know both the Father and the Son, you do not know either.

What is eternal life? It is the true transforming knowledge of God. First John 5:20 reads, "We know that the Son of God has come, and has given us understanding so that we may know Him who is true; and we are in Him who

is true, in His Son Jesus Christ. This is the true God and eternal life." Eternal life is not something God gives you; it is you being in God, and God being in you. In being regenerate, you have been drawn up into the realm in which Christ exists. You have been removed from the world. That is why Jesus said,

If you were of the world, the world would love its own; but because you are not of the world, but I chose you out of the world, because of this the world hates you. Remember the word that I said to you, "A slave is not greater than his master." If they persecuted Me, they will also persecute you; if they kept My word, they will keep yours also. But all these things they will do to you for My name's sake, because they do not know the One who sent Me (John 15:19-21).

The world and the kingdom of Christ are two colliding kingdoms. And when you have been regenerated, you have been drawn up and out of the world. That is why verses 24-25 read, "If I had not done among them the works which no one else did, they would not have sin; but now they have both seen and hated Me and My Father as well. But they have done this to fulfill the word that is written in their Law, 'They hated Me without a cause.'"

But as regenerated children who are

no longer a part of the world, we still have a job in the world:

> I tell you the truth, it is to your advantage that I go away; for if I do not go away, the Helper will not come to you; but if I go, I will send Him to you. And He, when He comes, will convict the world concerning sin and righteousness and judgment; concerning sin, because they do not believe in Me; and concerning righteousness, because I go to the Father and you no longer see Me; and concerning judgment, because the ruler of this world has been judged (John 16:7-11).

You may be thinking, *How does that have any relationship to me at all?* John 17:18 gives us the answer: "As you sent Me into the world, I also have sent them into the world." Christ came to save sinners, not the righteous. He came to preach the gospel, and then gave us the task to keep preaching the gospel to this world. The Holy Spirit's internal work of conviction that sends sinners fleeing to the Savior is a mandate for the character of our evangelism. We are God's prosecutors. As a Christian, you indict sinners. Ephesians 5:11 explains how this takes place: "Do not participate in the unfruitful deeds of darkness, but instead even expose them." We expose and indict sinners. First Corinthians 14:24 affirms this: "If all prophesy, and an unbeliever or an

ungifted man enters, he is convicted by all, he is called to account by all." If you are not prosecuting sinners, you are not doing your job.

In the Old Testament, indictment, conviction, and prosecution were the dominant features of the forensic ministry of the prophets. Jude 14-15 affirms this: "It was also about these men that Enoch, in the seventh generation from Adam, prophesied, saying, 'Behold, the Lord came with many thousands of His holy ones, to execute judgment upon all, and to convict all the ungodly of all their ungodly deeds which they have done in an ungodly way, and of all the harsh things which ungodly sinners have spoken against Him.'"

That is not how people preach today. Old Testament prophets were God's prosecutors. John the Baptist was God's last Old Testament prosecutor, and it cost him his head. Jesus indicted Israel by telling them a parable about a man who kept killing the messengers who came back to his vineyard, and finally the man sent his son, and they killed him. The Jewish leaders killed Jesus because He stressed their unrighteous state. After we experience regeneration, we instantaneously become the prosecutors of the world. This has to be a vital part of our ministry, for the gospel must be seen as a rescue from damnation.

There is, of course, a positive side to regeneration. In John 17:10, Jesus said, "I have been glorified in them." Before we were regenerated, we fell short of God's glory. Now that we have been regenerated, He is glorified in us. The glory of God shining in the face of Jesus Christ becomes embodied in us, and we become the temple of the Lord Himself. At the same time, we are ripped out of the world, and we are so alien to it that it is violently hostile toward us.

## Union with Christ

That leads us to a sixth doctrine in Jesus' high priestly prayer, and that is the doctrine of union with Christ. The reality of eternal life involves a real union with the Trinity. In John 17:11, Jesus asked the Father "that they may be one." This is not some kind of superficial unity, for Jesus specified that His followers be one "even as We are." The Trinity does not have trouble getting along. The verse is not trying to communicate to us that if we work hard enough, we can kind of get along with each other. What Jesus is talking about here is ontological, not experiential. He is talking about being one in the common life of God.

In verse 21 Jesus prays "that they may all be one; even as You, Father, are in Me and I in You, that they also may be in Us." He prays further about this unity in verse 23: "I in them and You in Me, that they may be perfected in unity." It feels as though we are getting lost in the Trinity. It is the Father and the Son, and the Son and the Father, and the Spirit in both, the Spirit in us, and us in the Spirit. This union is so powerful that the result is

this: "that the world may know that You sent Me" (verse 23).

---

**Being one with God is infinitely more joyous, infinitely more blessed than all the riches and comforts of this world.**

---

This is such a staggering concept to understand, the profound reality of what salvation brings. In John 14:16-20, Jesus said,

> I will ask the Father, and He will give you another Helper, that He may be with you forever; that is the Spirit of truth, whom the world cannot receive, because it does not see Him or know Him, but you know Him because He abides with you and will be in you. I will not leave you as orphans; I will come to you. After a little while the world will no longer see Me, but you will see Me; because I live, you will live also. In that day you will know that I am in My Father, and you in Me, and I in you.

This is absolutely overwhelming. We have the privilege of being wrapped up in the Trinity. We share the same life. "Jesus answered and said to him, 'If anyone loves Me, he will keep My word; and My Father will love him, and We will come to him and make Our abode with him'" (verse 23). Salvation is not just a ticket to heaven, not just the forgiveness of sins, and not just escape from judgment; salvation is being caught up in the eternal life of the Trinity. We know God, Christ, and the Holy Spirit not as distant or secondhand, but near and firsthand. We know the triune God not vaguely, as if unclear, but distinctly and without confusion. We know God not doubtfully as if insecure, but confidently and boldly.

Because of this oneness with God, sin must appear to us to be far more alien than we ever imagined. Maybe that will help you understand Paul's exhortation in 1 Corinthians 6:19: "Do you not know that your body is a temple of the Holy Spirit who is in you, whom you have from God, and that you are not your own?" You are inseparable from the triune God. Being one with God is infinitely more joyous, infinitely more blessed than all the riches and comforts of this world. If it is not, then heaven will be less for you. If God is not all your joy here, then heaven will be less for you.

### Sanctification

Union with the triune God must impact our lives. Though we are perfect in Christ positionally, Jesus still taught about the importance of sanctification. John 17:15 reads, "I do not ask You to take them out of the world." We are left on this earth, but Jesus is praying that the Father would "keep them from the evil one" (verse 15). We are safe in the eternal sense, but unsafe in the temporal sense, for we live in imminent danger. One of the most amazing statements in this entire chapter is in verse 16: "They are not of the world, even as I am not of the world." Jesus was saying that His disciples were as He was with reference to the world, but they had to stay on earth, for He was going to the Father and they were not. It is as if Jesus declared, "My work is done, but theirs is beginning."

For us believers who are left in the world, there are imminent dangers. First John 5:19 reads, "The whole world lies in the power of the evil one." The evil one, Satan, seeks to devour, deceive, and destroy. We are to resist him so that he flees. We are to arm ourselves so that we are not vulnerable. We are to be knowledgeable of his devices. This is summed up in John 17:17: "Sanctify them in the truth; Your word is truth." That can only happen through the Word, in the power of the Spirit. We have an example from Christ, in verse 19: "For their sakes I sanctify Myself, that they themselves also may be sanctified in truth." When Jesus stated that He had been sanctified in truth, He was saying He had been set apart from sin perfectly.

What does being set apart look like? Jesus said in John 4:34, "My food is to do the will of Him who sent Me and to accomplish His work." In John 5:19, He said, "Truly, truly, I say to you, the Son can do nothing of Himself, unless it is something He sees the Father doing; for whatever the Father does, these things the Son also does in like manner." And in John 5:30 He said, "I can do nothing on My own initiative."

We also read in John 6:38, "I have come down from heaven, not to do My own will, but the will of Him who sent Me." Again, in 7:18: "He who speaks from himself seeks his own glory; but He who is seeking the glory of the One who sent Him, He is true, and there is no unrighteousness in Him." Jesus sought God's glory and will while on earth.

Sanctification comes through obedience, and perfect obedience is perfect sanctification. Jesus sanctified Himself demonstrably—manifestly—by His perfect obedience. Sanctification is perfect obedience to the Word and will of God. By what power did He do this? Of course He was God, but everything He did in His incarnation was by the power of the Holy Spirit working through Him. What a perfect model for us—Jesus walked in the Spirit, and that is why His life was characterized by love, joy, peace, gentleness, goodness, faith, meekness, self-control, and never anything else.

## Glorification

The final doctrine we find in Jesus' prayer is the doctrine of glorification. We see this truth multiple times in this one chapter. John 17:1 says, "Jesus spoke these things; and lifting up His eyes to heaven, He said, 'Father, the hour has come; glorify Your Son, that the Son may glorify You.'" Again in verse 5: "Now, Father, glorify Me together with Yourself, with

the glory which I had with You before the world was." And in verse 24: "Father, I desire that they also, whom You have given Me, be with Me where I am, so that they may see My glory which You have given Me, for You loved Me before the foundation of the world."

Jesus wanted His followers to see what it looks like to be loved by the Father forever from before the foundation of the world. The whole intent of the redemptive work of Christ, and the intercession of the eternal Son, is to bring all those who were chosen by God's sovereign election, and were given to the Son as His bride, and have been used to preach and write and proclaim the Word of God, and who have believed the Word of God, and have been sanctified by the Word of God—to take all of these people who possess eternal life, whose sins have all been paid for by the Son's death, and whose lives are covered by His perfect righteousness—and bring them all to heaven.

Jesus said in verse 12, "While I was with them, I was keeping them in Your name which You have given Me; and I guarded them and not one of them perished." Back in verse 11 He said, "I am no longer in the world; and yet they themselves are in the world, and I come to You. Holy Father, keep them in Your name." He will keep us till the end, and that wonderful truth is reaffirmed in Jude verse 24: "Now to Him who is able to keep you from stumbling, and to make you stand in the presence of His glory blameless with great joy." Guess what? We are all going to make it! We have an eternal salvation from the almighty God.

Why does God do all of this? Why save us, keep us, protect us, and bring us to eternal glory? Hours away from the cross, Jesus revealed His motivation for the suffering that stood in His path. In John 13:1 we find some of the most beautiful words you will ever hear: "Before the Feast of the Passover, Jesus knowing that His hour had come that He would depart out of this world to the Father, having loved His own who were in the world, He loved them to the end." He loved us to the end!

We have to admit that, as unredeemed sinners, we were not the most lovable people. But when God loves His own, He has only one way to love them, and that is infinitely. That infinite love was stated at the end of Jesus' prayer:

> I in them and You in Me, that they may be perfected in unity, so that the world may know that You sent Me, and loved them, even as You have loved

Me. Father, I desire that they also, whom You have given Me, be with Me where I am, so that they may see My glory which You have given Me, for You loved Me before the foundation of the world (17:23-24).

I don't even know what to do with that amazing truth. Jesus wants to take us to glory so that we can see and know what it is to be eternally, intimately, and infinitely loved by the Father. How can the Father love us as He loved the Son? Because we are in His beloved Son. When the Bible says that God loves us, it is not speaking of a superficial love. The eternal and infinite God loves us intimately.

The Son prayed and continues to pray for us based on all these incomparably glorious doctrines in order to bring us into heaven—so that we will be loved forever in the same way the Father loves the eternal Son. In our role we must be like Christ and not only know and teach theology, but have it permeate us so thoroughly that we pray it as well.

# PRAYER

Father, we thank You for these truths in Scripture that are beyond comprehension. We smile as our souls are just swept away. To be loved as Christ is loved? To be taken to glory so that we can be loved as He has always been loved? What a great plan, what a great salvation, what a great Savior!

Lord Jesus, even now, as You are interceding for us, we praise Your name. We thank You for Your unceasing vigilance to keep us from stumbling. You bring all of the Father's sons into the fullness of His eternal love. We are utterly unworthy of this, but Lord, may it speak to our hearts in such a way that not only does it bring joy and comfort, but it reminds us how alien sin is to those who live in the Triune God, and in whom the triune God lives. Use us to proclaim the glories of the gospel. We pray in our Savior's name. Amen.

# Adam, Where Art Thou? Rediscovering the Historical Adam in the Pages of Scripture

*William Barrick*

*Shepherds' Conference 2013*

*Selected Scriptures*

The historicity of Adam is a debated topic as of late. Just within the last several months, there have been multiple articles and books published on the subject. Indeed, as I write, I am preparing to speak at a symposium on the issue. In fact, it seems that everywhere I go I find that people are interested in what has been labeled "Rediscovering the Historical Adam." It is confounding that this is the chosen title, because Adam has been there all along.

Back in the day when vehicles had bench seats, my wife used to sit next to me. As car design and safety regulations developed, the car manufacturers switched to bucket seats and seat belts. Now my wife sits on what feels like the other side of the car, and she'll occasionally mention that she misses sitting together. I say to her, "Well, I haven't moved." That is the way it is with the historical Adam. He has been there in the text all along, and it is something of a misnomer to suggest that we are "rediscovering him." If God is allowing Adam to see, from heaven, the discussion that's taking place now, he is probably wondering what is going on.

However, this discussion is necessary because some key questions have arisen: Was Adam the first of the human race? Or was he just the head of a clan, a tribe, or a nation? Maybe he was merely symbolic and not a real individual? Is he a product of evolution? If he is a product of evolution, what does that look like, and what are the implications for Eve? She has the same DNA as Adam, which makes sense if you take a part out of his side and use it to make a woman. But how does that work with evolution? I want to take some time and provide a biblical analysis of the historicity of Adam.

## How Important Is Adam?

Duane Gish, a leader in the creationist movement, recently went home to be with his Lord and Savior at the age of 93. Years ago, he was speaking at a conference and said, "God and Adam were talking in the Garden of Eden. Adam said, 'Lord, I want a woman. She must be beautiful, charming, a good cook, a housekeeper, and willing to wait on me hand and foot.' God said, 'I can make you a woman like that, but it will cost an arm and leg.' Adam's response, 'What can I get for a rib?'"

Many of those who remember Duane Gish recall him telling that joke far better than I can. It relates to the crux of the problem: Namely, did Adam really exist? Many today suggest that the story of Adam is merely myth, legend, or allegory—spiritualized truth. People seem to be willing to accept miracles in the New Testament, as if God could do something special there through Jesus, but not so in the Old Testament. People do not struggle to accept the virgin birth as much as they do God creating the heavens, the earth, and a man.

Here at The Master's Seminary and Grace Community Church, we affirm that Adam was a historical person and the originating head of the entire human race. There was no man before him; there is no such thing as a pre-Adamite race. Indeed, when we look at the historical Adam, we see that his existence is essential to many areas of biblical understanding. The historical Adam is foundational to all creative activity, for if we cannot believe that God created Adam out of the dust of the ground and breathed into his nostrils the breath of life, then how can we believe that God created the universe?

The historical Adam is foundational to the history and nature of the human race. His existence determines our understanding of mankind—whether or not man is made in the image of God as a special creation, with a specific design distinct from all other parts of creation. The historical Adam is also directly connected to the origin and nature of sin. How is sin conceived in the human race if Adam is not its original head? If he is one of a thousand others—and there are supposedly fossil humanoids in the rocks dating prior to Adam—then how does his sin get attributed to those who lived before him?

The historical Adam is foundational to the existence and nature of human death. Paul said in Romans 5:12 that "through one man sin entered into the world, and death through sin." Therefore, the historical Adam is also foundational to the reality of salvation from sin. If the first Adam is merely allegorical, then what about the second Adam, Jesus Christ? If the second Adam is allegorical, then how is He capable of producing a literal sacrifice acceptable to God for the sins of mankind?

The historical Adam is foundational to the account of historical events in the book of Genesis. As Dr. MacArthur often says, if you don't accept the literal nature of the first chapters of Genesis, when do you start accepting the literal record of the Word of God? Thus the historical Adam is fundamental to the authority, inspiration, and inerrancy of the Bible.

### Evaluating Presuppositions

There are certain presuppositions that we need to reject and others that we need to affirm when approaching this topic. First, we reject the concept of an old earth. The earth may be many thousands of years old, but it is not millions of years old.

Second, we also reject the documentary hypothesis—that the Torah can be divided up into various source documents like the JEDP (Jahwist, Elohist, Deuteronomist, Priestly) documents—and that it was composed and compiled over many centuries.

Third, we affirm that the author of Genesis is God Himself. This is evident from the creation account because there was no one else present other than God. We read that God said to Job, "Where were you when I laid the foundation of the earth?" (Job 38:4). His point was that

if Job was there, then he would be God. If Job was God, then he would be able to create, to call the stars by name, to set the course of celestial bodies. Job was not able to do these things, nor was he able to see into the hearts of men, or judge mankind—he was not omniscient, omnipotent, or omnipresent. He was not God.

For that reason, Job was not able to deliver himself from his difficult circumstances or from the power, presence, and penalty of sin. Job had to put his hand over his mouth because he had been so busy trying to protect his own integrity that he was willing to impugn the integrity of God. God corrected Job's thinking—He is the ultimate author of the Scriptures, He was the eyewitness of creation, and it's His account that we have in Genesis 1.

Fourth, we affirm and uphold the independent historical accuracy of the Scriptures, from Genesis chapter 1 through Revelation chapter 22.

Fifth, we employ one consistent hermeneutic for interpreting all of Scripture. We don't change hermeneutics after Genesis 11. Instead, we use the same means of interpretation throughout.

Finally, we affirm the universal scope of Genesis 1 through 11—that is to say, it is pre-Israelite. Genesis 1 to 11 is not an exclusively Israelite book written for that nation alone. Moses penned it, but the record of the history of those chapters precedes Moses; it pertains to the time of the patriarchs. From where did Moses get the information? He may have had documents that were preserved that he could utilize (much like Luke used documents to write his Gospel), or God the Holy Spirit could have given Moses divine revelation, directly telling him what had occurred.

Regardless of how Moses obtained the information, the first 11 chapters of Genesis are not about Israel. This is where Old Testament scholar Peter Enns makes his mistake. He says that Adam is an Israelite, and that his story is about Israel, and it is for Israel.[1] This is not the case. Rather, Genesis 1–11 provides the foundation of the worldwide scope of salvation, redemption, and kingdom that God establishes and plans in His program. These chapters lay out God's design and purpose for all of mankind. They are universal in scope, for all people begin here, and all people are addressed here. In support of this, we observe that both the Old and the New Testaments assume a common human origin in Adam. Considering first the Hebrew Scriptures, Malachi 2:10 says, "Do we not all have one father?" I believe the translators of the New American Standard update have rightly left father uncapitalized, for the prophet is not talking about God, but man. Mankind has one father—namely, Adam.

The New Testament teaches the same truth. In Acts 17:26, the apostle Paul said, "He made from one *man* every nation of mankind." The New American Standard update adds the word "man" in italics to indicate the referent. It becomes clear from the preceding verse what Paul is talking about: He explains that all mankind owes its existence to a God who created them and breathed the breath of life into them—into that one man. The context makes it very clear that the apostle is referring to the original man, Adam, and explaining that all of mankind is made from him.

## Adam and Evolution

Oftentimes those who reject the historical Adam do so on the basis of evolutionary science. They affirm biological evolution such that they must jump through hoops to interpret the Scriptures differently from what the Scriptures appear to say. Evolution factors into many people's presuppositions when they approach the historicity of Adam—they begin with evolutionary science and the concept of an old earth, accepting the dictates of modern science. But just as with reading and interpreting Scripture, we must examine the evidence for scientific assertions and interpret them. We must not take the opinions of scientists as evidence itself. Rather, we must realize that they are presenting their interpretation of the evidence.

## Was Israel a Prescientific Culture?

There are some who accuse Christians of ignoring the fact that Israel was a prescientific culture. They believe that the biblical writers had a rudimentary worldview; specifically, that the Israelites believed in a flat earth—a disk on top of the sea with a solid dome for the sky—a three-storied earth, as it were. They suggest that the sky was viewed as a vault resting on foundations, perhaps mountains, with doors and windows that let in the rain, and that God dwelt above the sky hidden in the clouds, and the world was secured or moored on the water by pillars. The earth was the only known domain; the realm beyond was considered unknowable. If the biblical writers had such a prescientific worldview, then the question is asked: How can we accept Scripture's account to be accurate when it has nothing to do with science or history?

By way of a response, we must question the presupposition. Is this an accurate portrayal of how the pre-Flood patriarchs viewed the world? Genesis 4 talks of metallurgy, of working with iron and of making musical instruments. That implies an ability to make music, the composition of which is sophisticated. The people referred to in Genesis 4 lived many hundreds of years before Israel came on the scene, but they were certainly not prescientific.

**Literary Devices in the Ancient World**

Also, critics say we must assume that the ancient Israelites had no understanding of literary devices—that they could not use similes, metaphors, and figures of speech. But in Job 9:6, Job speaks about God in this way: "Who shakes the earth out of its place, and its pillars tremble." Does Job refer to pillars literally or figuratively here? Later, in Job 26:7, Job said

this of God: "He stretches out the north over empty space and hangs the earth on nothing." Either Job is contradicting himself—the earth hanging on nothing and yet on pillars—or he is employing a metaphor. Similarly, Job said, "My days are swifter than a weaver's shuttle, and come to an end without hope" (Job 7:6). Rather than take this as a literal statement, we should understand that Job was intelligent enough to use figures of speech.

If a man living contemporary or prior to the time of Abraham, before 2000 BC, had that capability, then why not the Israelites? Why could they not understand the use of metaphors? Indeed, it is somewhat anti-Semitic to suggest that the worldview of the Israelites must be interpreted apart from the use of metaphors, because we allow for such things in symbols written by the ancient Chinese, the ancient Sumerians, and the ancient Egyptians. We acknowledge such forms of communication with other cultures, but with respect to Israel 2000 years later, there seems to be a rejection of it.

Consider the fact that written language dating back to 1600 BC has been found on the walls of Egyptian mines from Serabit el-Khadim down in the Sinai Peninsula. That means the people were not only able to write, but to read and understand. Those inscriptions date to 200 years before Moses wrote the Pentateuch. Even the slaves were literate, and on those walls we find written the same name used for God in Genesis 21:33— El Olam, or the eternal God. We have allowed liberal theologians to treat the Jews with disrespect—to treat them and their evidence differently from any other evidence found in other cultures elsewhere in history and time. That ought not to be.

The biblical writers held a different worldview than other people; that is why we have a Bible, it's why they are the people of God, and it's why God revealed Himself to them. They are the representatives of the Creator God—the one God who is all-powerful and all-wise. There is only one Yahweh, and the Israelites were chosen to bear His testimony. They did not accept the myths and legends of other peoples, but stood contrary to them and combated their wrong views.

Throughout the ancient Near East, different peoples and cultures produced a variety of creation and Flood stories, but those stories are not uniform in the way that they approach creation or the Flood. Today, we are told the Bible must have borrowed from those cultures because of the fact that the Bible refers to the same events. The assumption is that the biblical writers must have borrowed information from other cultures. Yet we reject that assumption, along with the idea that the Old Testament writers were prescientific.

## Debunking the Prescientific Concept

It is a modern fantasy to think that the Israelites believed in a flat earth and

a solid-domed sky. The biblical evidence is clear; here are some helpful resources regarding the prescientific discussion. In 1991 Jeffrey Burton Russell published a book titled *Inventing the Flat Earth*, in which he debunks the prescientific concept of the ancient Near East. He suggests that we have imposed this worldview upon them because we think we who live in the modern age are more sophisticated.[2]

In 2006, Noel Weeks, who is from Australia, also wrote a response to a prescientific view of Israel in the *Westminster Theological Journal*, called "Cosmology in Historical Context."[3]

And Jonathan F. Henry addressed the same matter in a 2009 issue of *Journal of Dispensational Theology* with his article "Uniformitarianism in Old Testament Studies."[4]

## Dissecting the Creation Account

In Genesis 1:1-25, there is an orderly progression of six days—that is, six literal days of creation. The days are described as having both morning and evening. If these words don't hold their normal, literal meaning, then questions must be raised concerning the significance of each day. However, if "morning" means morning and "evening" means evening, then Genesis 1 speaks of literal days.

In Exodus 20:8-11, a commandment is given to observe the Sabbath, and it is predicated upon the creation account. Because God worked for six days, man must also work six days. If, however, the days in Genesis 1 are actually millions of years, then we must work millions of years for our first day, millions of years for our second day, and so on. Consequently, we would never get to a Sabbath.

As mentioned earlier, the creation has a universal focus. Adam is the head of all mankind, not just the father of Israel. The creation account is theocentric—it is about God, who He is, and how different He is from the views that other cultures have of Him. He is the all-powerful and omniscient Creator who spoke the world into existence. Unlike what certain ancient Near Eastern myths have proclaimed, He did not urinate on some preexisting eternal matter to produce this world. He did not hover and create a cosmic egg out of which we have hatched. Rather, He spoke everything into existence, perfectly preparing the earth for the life that He placed upon it.

## Adam and the Image of God

It is important to note that in the creation account, the word "seed" appears 6 times in the first 25 verses—each time in reference to plants. And we are told that plants would produce after their own kind. Then in Genesis 1:26–2:3 we see the first-person plural pronoun used in connection with God: "Then God said, 'Let Us make man in Our image, according to Our likeness'" (1:26). The pronoun must be interpreted as a reference to a plurality within the Godhead—that is, the Trinity.

It is not referring to a divine council of the angels, nor is it referring to the popular view of God speaking of Himself in a royal way. Indeed, Paul Joüon, in his Hebrew grammar, emphasizes that there is no such grammatical concept in biblical Hebrew.[5] Rather, this type of statement comes at key points in Scripture and it helps signify the importance of the event that follows. In this case, the emphasis is on man being created in the image of God. No animal is created in the image of God. Nor is mankind created and the image of God inserted at some later point. People were created in the image of God from the very start— "male and female He created them" (Genesis 1:27). In this account we are given the bare outline of what happened. The details come when Moses further elaborates on the event in chapter 2.

Incidentally, Moses used this technique throughout Genesis. He often gave a general description of events—as with the Tower of Babel—then he filled in the details after the broad overview was complete. Genesis chapters 1 and 2 are not two different creation accounts, nor are they two different creations. Notice they are internally consistent if properly read in the light of strict Hebrew grammar. The chronology is not changed, or mistaken—it is the same account, but with a detailed focus on man and how God gives mankind a divine mandate to be fruitful, multiply, and fill the Earth. The ancient reader is thinking at the end of chapter 1, *Well, how are they going to do that?* Genesis 2:4-24 gives the answer, with more information about man and how he is to fulfill the mandate given by God.

The Hebrew word for man is *Adam*. The first time any noun of major importance occurs in the Genesis record, it is usually without the definite article. Thereafter, the article is used as a means of referring back to the first occurrence of the noun. Interestingly, the word *adam*, as a name, does not occur until Genesis 2:20. Adam was naming all of the animals, but no counterpart was found for him. The first time his name is given, it happens in the midst of his naming the animals. Why is this significant? Because God named things when He created them. As part of the divine image that we are given, we have the authority to name things. Adam demonstrates this authority as he names the animals. He also demonstrates the use of language, speech, and reasoning—he is a sophisticated, fully operational human being with highly technical linguistic, mental, and psychological skills. And he exercises the image of God in him when he names the animals.

Notice in Genesis 2:7 that it is clearly a single individual whom God formed out of the dust of the ground. God breathed into this individual's nostrils the breath of life, and Adam became a living being—*one* living being. God placed him into a garden specially prepared for him. In verse 8 we read that "the LORD God planted a garden toward the east, in Eden; and there He placed the man whom He had formed."

We then see in verse 17 that God commanded man not to eat the fruit from the tree of the knowledge of good and evil, and in verse 18 He said that "it is not good for the man to be alone." It is important to remember that this occurs before the end of the sixth day—before Genesis 1:31, when God declares all things to be very good. Part of the reason they are said to be "very good" is because this issue of "not good" was resolved on day six. Why did God say, "It is not good…"? Because man was alone. But Adam cannot be alone if he is a tribe. He is not alone if he is a nation. He is not alone if there are pre-Adamite races. The text tells us that there is only one man. He is alone, and that is not good. God's ultimate design is for him to not be alone. So God searched the animals for an adequate counterpart, and none was found. If Adam were a product of evolution— of animals—you would think that God would have found something suitable for him, but that wasn't so, because none of the animals were made in the image of God.

An adequate counterpart would have to be a bearer of the image of God, just like Adam. Thus God uses Adam's side to produce that counterpart—a woman (2:21-22). This woman then inspires poetry from Adam. The first words that Scripture records from Adam are a poem—a three-lined poem with a triple repetition of "this one." In a climactic fashion, this is the one who is his bone and flesh. This account tells us much about the historicity of Adam. Also, it pushes back on the theory of evolution, for a person who is intelligent and capable enough to produce the sophisticated qualities and cadences of poetry must come from a perfect and omniscient God.

**Adam and the Fall**

The narrative of Genesis continues as that one man and one woman's story carries on into chapter 3, into the account of the Fall. It is not the fall of a tribe. It is not the fall of a nation. It is the fall of one man. The account is clearly historical, for history is found in the next chapter, with the record of the first murder—the history of Cain and Abel. History is also found in chapter 5 with the generations of Adam to Noah. This account cannot be taken as being mythological; it should be understood as historical and literal. So why would we treat Adam any differently?

Concerning the Fall and the subsequent curse, notice that there is a heritage of real pain, toil, and death. It is not allegorical pain, nor is it figurative toil and death. It is real death, real toil, real pain. There is a literal expulsion of that first man and woman from the garden. Genesis 1:31 affirmed that everything was very good, and then things were not good— they went terribly wrong. But it is not as if God was caught by surprise and had to move to Plan B. God had already set the program of redemption in motion even before He created the earth. He was still following His original plan. That is why

we find the mention of a seed in Genesis 3:15. The explanation of the seed here helps to explain how mankind also produces after its kind. The One who is produced as the seed of the woman will have victory over the seed of the serpent.

Also, notice that throughout Genesis 3, the second person singular pronoun is used. That is, God always addresses Adam. This is because, as Paul said, "It was not Adam who was deceived, but the woman" (1 Timothy 2:14). Adam went in with his eyes wide open. He purposely rebelled against God and was accountable for what had occurred. And in the same way that we accept the historicity of Jesus, the promised seed of redemption, we are to accept the historicity of the man who caused the Fall.

**Adam and the Canon**

Ezekiel 28:13 refers to the Garden of Eden as a historical and literal place. Similarly, Malachi 2:15 looks back and states, "Let no one deal treacherously against the wife of your youth," based upon God's design given in Genesis 2. These are indications that the Genesis record is to be accepted as absolutely true, literal, and historical—not an allegory.

Also, in 1 Chronicles 1:1, we have a genealogy that begins with Adam. The reason that is significant is because in Jesus' day, Chronicles was the last book of the Old Testament. In Luke 11:51-52, when Jesus talked about the murder of God's prophets, He spoke of this as having taken place "from the blood of

Abel" (pointing back to Genesis 4) "to the blood of Zechariah" (who was the last prophet recorded in the book of Chronicles—2 Chronicles 24:22). These are the first and the last books of the Old Testament, and Jesus cites them as bookends. So the Old Testament begins and ends with Adam.

> The New Testament…can only be built upon a literal historical Adam. It cannot be built on a figurative Adam that is a figment of someone's imagination.

The first book of the New Testament begins with the same terminology: "The record of the genealogy of Jesus the Messiah…" (Matthew 1:1). The writer was carried along by the Holy Spirit to write, in effect, that there is a new Adam, Jesus Christ. And you need to understand the first Adam before you can understand the second Adam. Furthermore, if you read the genealogy in Matthew 1 carefully, it is evident that the word *genesis* occurs several times in the Greek text. It is the same as the title of the book of Genesis—the concept of beginning and birth. Thus the author intentionally ties the Word of God together—the Old Testament begins and ends with Adam, and the New Testament begins and ends with the second Adam in a new heavens and a new earth. It is purposeful, it is

designed, and it can only be built upon a literal historical Adam. It cannot be built on a figurative Adam that is a figment of someone's imagination.

## Adam and Jesus Christ

In Luke 3:38, the genealogy states that Adam is "the son of God." In other words, he is produced by God. In Romans 5:12, Paul wrote, "Just as through one man sin entered into the world, and death through sin, and so death spread to all men, because all sinned." Paul continued in verse 14, "Nevertheless death reigned from Adam until Moses." Paul then explained the response: "For if by the transgression of the one the many died, much more did the grace of God and the gift by the grace of the one Man, Jesus Christ, abound to the many" (verse 15). Paul was moving through history, from the first Adam to the second Adam. The first Adam brought death; the second Adam brought the response—life.

In like manner, 1 Corinthians 15 refers to the first man and the last man in the context of the historicity of Christ's resurrection. If we deny the legitimacy, historicity, and reality of a literal Adam in 1 Corinthians 15, then we must question the second Adam and His resurrection. And if we do not have a literal and historical resurrection, we of all men are to be most pitied. It is important to note that Paul's message was not in agreement with the rabbis of his day. They had already departed from the truth of God's Word. They were unbelievers who had rejected the Messiah, the prophecies in the Old Testament, and even the literal nature of many of these things—including the existence of Adam as the single historical head of the human race.

The historicity of Adam has a bearing on the historicity of Christ. Thus, the historicity of Adam is a gospel issue. If we deny Adam as a historical man, we must deny Christ's resurrection. If we do that, we destroy the foundations of the Christian faith.

**Who Will You Trust?**

There is an overemphasis in scholarship today on the similarities between the Bible and ancient Near Eastern materials. However, if we do a comparative analysis, we find out that there are more dissimilarities than there are similarities. Therefore we should not attempt to interpret the Bible in light of ancient Near Eastern material, which affirms polytheism, whereas the Bible affirms monotheism. The ancient Near Eastern texts suggest that physical images were gods, whereas the Bible teaches that idols must be destroyed. The ancient Near Eastern texts have a low view of man, whereas the Scriptures have a high view of man. In the ancient Near Eastern texts you have conflict and chaos in the creation account; in the Bible, there is no chaos. In the ancient Near Eastern texts there are no uniform standards of ethics; in the Scriptures, there is an expectation of obedience to laws founded upon the character of God.

Despite all of these dissimilarities, it is true that there are certain similarities that exist due to a shared memory of actual events, such as creation and the Flood. God probably explained to Adam how He created everything and why Adam existed. Technically, Adam would be considered the first messenger of God's creation account. And like everything else in a fallen world, that shared memory was skewed by various ancient cultures as they came up with all kinds of myths that relate back to the original creation account.

We must not lift ancient Near Eastern texts above Scripture. Anytime we accept extrabiblical evidence over the biblical record, we denigrate the authority of Scripture.

In sum, there are three possibilities with regard to spiritual authority. One is the authority of the Lord in His written revelation. Another is the authority of the church and its infallible "pope"— not necessarily referring to Catholics, but a teacher, or the chairman of an elder board, or a pastor. A third option is the authority of human reason with its self-styled sovereignty because it does not make sense to understand things the way the Scripture presents them. Which will you choose? Which will you follow as your authority on this issue?

**The Word Stands Forever**

The Bible requires that we rethink evolution. Methods do not make certain claims true. Scientists are merely interpreters, and the science of origins differs from operational science because it is not possible to reproduce creation in the laboratory. Furthermore, science does not remain the same. Forty years ago, scientists were proclaiming that mountains were formed by isostasy, the accumulation of deposits on the surface on the earth through sedimentation that caused parts of the surface to sink, thereby pushing up other parts and forming mountains. No one believes that today. Rather, it is by the subduction of the tectonic plates that mountains are formed. This change in understanding has occurred in the span of 40 years. That is evidence that science does not remain the same; it changes.

But the word of God is dependable. "The grass withers, the flower fades, but the word of our God stands forever" (Isaiah 40:8). My plea for you is to make God and His Word the authority in determining the historicity of Adam and everything else connected to the creation account.

# Why Every Self-Respecting Calvinist Must Be a Six-Day Creationist

*John MacArthur*

*Shepherds' Conference 2009*

*Genesis 1–2*

Theology was once called the queen of the sciences, which is to say what the Bible taught trumped all other categories, including science. That's a proper title, for the Word of God prompts all other ideas and is absolutely true and accurate. The Bible is not theory, but is instead fact, reality, and truth. The Bible does not take a backseat when it comes to getting things right scientifically, especially when it comes to the creation account.

## A God Who Knows

Whoever created the universe and all that is in it understands how it works. Since our God created it, He is not waiting for scientific advances in order to comprehend it. He is not waiting for somebody to discover a system and inform Him about how it works. Since the Creator designed and sustains the universe, He knows the earth is spherical and turns on an axis. He knows it is suspended on nothing, sweeping through space in a fixed rotation in a massive solar system. He knows the staggering riches of the galaxies—the countless stars—and understands black holes better than Stephen Hawking. This Creator knows the cycles of air and water, about chemistry and biology. Whoever is intelligent enough and powerful enough to design, create, and sustain the incalculable complexity of the universe is certainly intelligent enough to do the relatively simple task of authoring an accurate book that describes it. Therefore, what

He tells us will be logically consistent and understandable.

If the Creator had not written a book, no one would know about creation, since only the Creator was there. People could make certain observations and conclusions, but they could never know for sure how it came about.

If the Creator wrote a book about His creation, He would never say the moon is 50,000 leagues higher than the sun and has its own light. He would never say the earth is flat, triangular, and composed of 7 stages, including honey, sugar, butter, and wine; or the earth sits on the heads of countless elephants who produce earthquakes when they shake. That is what the Hindu holy book says—lies that we know were not written by God. The Creator would never say there are only 13 members of the body through which death can come, but that is what the Taoist holy book says. Or that earthquakes are caused by wind moving water, and water moving the land, as the sacred Buddhist source suggests. Or if the Creator of the universe wrote a book, He would not say that Adam fell that men might come into existence and only then they may have joy, as it says in the Book of Mormon.

The true Creator gets it and understands what He has created perfectly. Therefore, when we come to the revelation given to us by the Creator, we are going to get an accurate record.

## In the Beginning

With regard to origins, the Bible can be relied on just as it can be trusted with every other subject. Scripture opens with a very simple, clear, and unmistakable statement: "In the beginning God created the heavens and the earth" (Genesis 1:1). God has made it so clear that no one can possibly misunderstand what that means.

In 1903, the English philosopher Herbert Spencer died. He had rejected the Bible, God, and Christ, but was held as a genius because he said there were five categories into which everything that exists can fit: time, force, action, space, and matter. Yet Scripture already gave the world those categories: "In the beginning"—that's time, "God"—that's force, "created"—that's action, "the heavens"—that's space, "the earth"—that's matter. "In the beginning God created the heavens and the earth" is a profound statement, while at the same time a very simple one. God created, out of nothing, everything that exists—and He did it in six days. Now I want to help you to feel the strength of conviction with regard to the biblical account of creation by hanging some thoughts on three specific words.

### Fidelity

The first word we consider is *fidelity*. Simply put, either you believe what Scripture says, or you do not. You can either accept it or reject it, but you cannot alter it. The common response to a statement like that is, "But what about science? Do we not have to apply science to the Genesis account to be intellectually honest?" Christian, get past the idea that you have to have scientific information to understand creation. All science is based on observation, verification, and repetition. Creation had no observers, it cannot be verified as to its means, and it cannot be repeated.

All that creation scientists can do is show that evolution has not happened, and though they can make a good case for that, that doesn't tell us anything about creation itself. One thing we must acknowledge about creation is that it did not happen by any scientific laws; it was a massive miracle. If you deliver yourself from trying to come up with a science of creation, you will be freed from that useless effort. That is why in the Genesis account, and everywhere else in the Bible, we are told repeatedly that God *created*. There are no explicit references, nor are there any implicit references, to any evolutionary process anywhere in the Bible.

There is one historical record of creation in Genesis 1, and then an expansion of the creation of man in Genesis 2. You might say, "Well, do not plants chang , develop, and mutate within species?" Of course they do—both plants and animals do. But none of that has anything to do with creation; it does not tell us

anything about what happened in six literal days.

For example, let's say you met Lazarus the day after he was raised from the dead. If you were to interview him, you might ask him, "What were you doing when you were away? Where were you? Can I touch your hand? Can I feel your arm? Can I rub your face? How are you feeling? Do you think the same as you did before you died and were raised? Do you have memories from your past before you were dead?" You could interview him until you are blue in the face, and you could analyze all the processes of his life. You could look at how he eats, how he functions, how he thinks, how he speaks, and how he acts. But that will tell you absolutely nothing about how he came back to life, because that was a supernatural miracle.

When Jesus fed the 5000, you could have taken someone's lunch out of their hand and said, "I'm sorry, but I'm taking this for a scientific experiment. I'm going to analyze the fish and bread, because no one has ever seen fish and bread come out of nowhere." Then after finishing your analysis, let's say you talk to the people and ask them how the food tasted, and whether or not they responded to it the way they do to other food. You could do all that, and it would not tell you anything about how the fish and bread came into existence.

Creation cannot be understood any other way than as a massive miracle revealed by the Creator on the pages of Scripture. Now if you do not believe that, then just say you do not believe it. But do not try to impose upon that massive miracle, which cannot have a scientific explanation, some scientific idea. Doing that is no more helpful than trying to explain how Lazarus came back from the grave by looking at his body. Creation was not a scientific event, and natural law did not play a role, for it was in creation that natural law was created.

Creation is matched only by the future new creation, when God re-creates all things. Neither event is the product of any fixed, repeatable, measurable, or observable scientific laws. All that the reader has is the opportunity to believe or not believe. That is it—fidelity.

You may be thinking, *Well, couldn't God have used evolution?* The question is irrelevant and intrusive, but if you need an answer, no, He could not, because evolution requires death, and there was no death prior to creation and the Fall. Speculation is foolish, and Scripture tells us that God made everything in 6 days. That is either true or not. If it is not true, your problems have just begun, for now you have 66 books with potential errors.

Many people reject the creation account because they do not want God to be acknowledged—for God is not just the Creator, He is the Law-Giver and the Judge. Evolution was invented in order to eliminate the God of Genesis and obliterate the viability of His moral law. Evolution is the latest means fallen sinners have devised to suppress the innate knowledge of God, to distance themselves from any responsibility to the biblical testimony to which they are accountable, and by which they are either redeemed or condemned.

By embracing evolution, sinners have enthusiastically endeavored to avoid moral responsibility, guilt, and judgment. Evolution is so pointedly hostile to Christianity that it is unthinkable for Christians to embrace it in any way. It is a rejection of biblical revelation. So-called theistic evolution has demonstrated a lack of fidelity to the authority of Scripture, dethroning divine revelation and replacing it with evolutionary theory. Scripture, not science, is the test of everything. Trust in the Scriptures.

Just to give you an illustration, one of the three largest ministries in America claims to be a Bible-based, Christ-proclaiming, and gospel-centered ministry. A letter was sent to the president of this ministry asking their position on origins and Genesis. He responded and said that the ministry takes no stand on origins because it is a "secondary" doctrine. He said that their efforts are designed to bring people together based on the historically essential doctrines of orthodox Christianity, and that creation falls in the category of nonessentials, like eternal security and the rapture. I would suggest that if you want to ask any so-called Christian ministry or church one primary question to determine that ministry's fidelity to the

Word of God, ask them this: What is your understanding of Genesis 1?

The answer will reveal their attitude toward Scripture. If they reject Genesis 1 or 2, ask, "At which chapter do you start believing what is said?" Do they kick in at Genesis 3, 6, 9, or maybe Exodus? By the way, you'll want to ask if there are other chapters that they do not believe. How about Isaiah 53? The issue here is not creation; it is fidelity to the Word of God.

### Simplicity

The second word to consider is *simplicity*. The Genesis account is, by all honest considerations, very simple, plain, clear, perspicuous, uncomplicated, and unmistakable. There are other accounts of creation outside of Genesis 1: "In the beginning was the Word, and the Word was with God, and the Word was God. He was in the beginning with God. All things came into being through Him, and apart from Him nothing came into being that has come into being" (John 1:1-3). "For by Him all things were created, both in the heavens and on earth, visible and invisible, whether thrones or dominions or rulers or authorities—all things have been created through Him and for Him" (Colossians 1:16).

All biblical references sustain the simple clarity of divine revelation. Take Psalm 104, for example:

Bless the Lord, O my soul!

O Lord my God, You are
    very great;

You are clothed with splendor
    and majesty,

Covering Yourself with light
    as with a cloak,

Stretching out heaven like
    a tent curtain.

He lays the beams of His upper
    chambers in the waters;

He makes the clouds His
    chariot;

He walks upon the wings
    of the wind;

He makes the winds His
    messengers,

Flaming fire His ministers.


He established the earth upon
    its foundations,

So that it will not totter forever
    and ever.

You covered it with the deep as
    with a garment;

The waters were standing above
    the mountains.

At Your rebuke they fled,

At the sound of Your thunder
    they hurried away.

The mountains rose; the valleys
    sank down

To the place which You
    established for them.

You set a boundary that they
may not pass over,

So that they will not return to
cover the earth.

He sends forth springs in
the valleys;

They flow between the
mountains;

They give drink to every beast
of the field ;

The wild donkeys quench
their thirst.

Beside them the birds of the
heavens dwell;

They lift up their voices among
the branches.

He waters the mountains from
His upper chambers;

The earth is satisfied with the fruit
of His works (verses 1-13).

Or Psalm 148:

Praise the LORD!

Praise the LORD from the
heavens;

Praise Him in the heights!

Praise Him, all His angels;

Praise Him, all His hosts!

Praise Him, sun and moon;

Praise Him, all stars of light!

Praise Him, highest heavens,

And the waters that are above
the heavens!

Let them praise the name of the
LORD,

For He commanded and they
were created (verses 1-5).

If you deny the creation account, you diminish praise to God. We read in Isaiah 42:5-8:

Thus says God the LORD, who created the heavens and stretched them out, who spread out the earth and its offspring, who gives breath to the people on it and spirit to those who walk in it, "I am the LORD, I have called You in righteousness, I will also hold You by the hand and watch over You, and I will appoint You as a covenant to the people, as a light to the nations, to open blind eyes, to bring out prisoners from the dungeon and those who dwell in darkness from the prison. I am the LORD, that is My name; I will not give My glory to another."

God's creative power in salvation is tied to His power in creation. The worship of God is tied to Him as the Creator. According to the book of Revelation, the God to be worshiped is the one who made the heavens and the earth, and all that is in them. The pattern for worship is God as Creator, and God as the new

Creator of those who put their trust in Him.

Also, it is important to note the simple hermeneutic of interpreting Genesis 1–2. If we take everything in Genesis as literal narrative, then why would we consider the first two chapters to be poetic? Genesis is not poetry. There are poetical accounts of creation in the Bible—for example, in Psalm 104 and certain chapters in Job. And they differ completely from the first chapter of Genesis. Ancient Hebrew poetry had certain characteristics, and they are not found in the first chapter of Genesis. So the claim that Genesis 1 is poetry is no solution.

We have fidelity and we have simplicity, and as the church of the Lord Jesus Christ we need to take our stand on the Scriptures at the beginning of the Scriptures. First Timothy 3 teaches that the church of the living God is "the pillar and support of the truth" (verse 15). We are the guardians and the proclaimers of the true God and His true revelation, and that includes the uncomplicated testimony of creation given to us in Genesis.

### Priority

The third word for us is *priority*. The creation account is not secondary; it is essential and critical to the main theme of divine revelation and the internal purpose of God. What is God's priority? Why is the universe in existence? Why did God create man? What is the goal, the end, the purpose, the divine priority?

God does not do anything for which He does not have a purpose. The existence of the universe and the theater of the universe must have an ultimate goal. God is achieving something through the countless vast arrays of circumstances, contingencies, changes, and revolutions from person to person and from city to city. God's work does not occur through wild, random minutiae. There is a certain fixed objective to which everyone and everything moves, from creation through providence to consummation.

Jonathan Edwards said it this way: "Providence subordinates all successive changes that come to pass in the state of affairs of mankind."[1] Everything from creation to consummation is part of one great plan being worked out by God's powerful providence. Not one molecule operates outside that plan. History will end, but only when the divine purpose is accomplished—when God's great final goal is achieved. This universe is not eternal; it will end as it began, in a massive display of divine power. It will end, according to 2 Peter 3:10, in an implosion, in which the atoms that make up this universe will melt.

That will happen only when God's scheme is done and He has no further purpose for this universe. Meanwhile, divine providence subordinates, orders, overpowers, and controls all things to achieve that end. We read in Isaiah 46:9, "Remember the former things long past, for I am God, and there is no other; I am God, and there is no one like Me." That is to say there is only one God, so all that exists does so within the purposes of that one God.

We continue reading in Isaiah 46:10 that it is God who declares "the end from the beginning." That is another way of saying, "When I began it, I had already ordained how it would end. From ancient times, I have ordained all that has been happening, saying My purpose will be established, and I will accomplish all My good pleasure." In the end of verse 11 of that same chapter, it is written, "Truly I have spoken; truly I will bring it to pass. I have planned it, surely I will do it." That is a worldview you need to have. For if you reject God as the Creator of all things, you reject the divine purpose that is attached to that creation.

That is why Colossians 1 reminds us that all things were created by Him and for Him. And the grand design is redemption—to gather a bride for His Son, to collect the redeemed. And it will be over when the last person whose name was written in the Lamb's book of life, from before the foundation of the world, is redeemed. All God's work of creation and providence is only a means to achieving the goal of redemption. Every person, every act, every event is subservient to the great purpose of the redemption of sinners. All material realities are subordinated to spiritual objectives. The work of redemption and the work of salvation is God's purpose. The creation of a visible universe and world provides the setting for the creation of an eternal people not yet fully seen.

Paul taught this in Ephesians 3:8-11:

To me, the very least of all saints, this grace was given, to preach to the Gentiles the unfathomable riches of Christ, and to bring to light what is the administration of the mystery which for ages has been hidden in God who created all things; so that the manifold wisdom of God might now be made known through the church to the rulers and the authorities in the heavenly places. This was in accordance with the eternal purpose which He carried out in Christ Jesus our Lord.

The eternal purpose of God is to redeem a bride for His Son, to take that bride to heaven, and in all of these actions, to display the glory of His grace to the watching holy angels. That great theme is manifested in many ways in the very work of creation.

---

**If you start tampering with Genesis, you start tampering with the understanding of the doctrine of salvation.**

---

We read in 1 Corinthians 15:22, "As in Adam all die, so also in Christ all will be made alive." That is the impact of one man. As there is only one Christ in whom men live, there is only one Adam in whom men die. Romans 5:18 says, "So then as through one transgression there resulted condemnation to all men, even so through one act of righteousness there resulted justification of life to all men." If you start tampering with Genesis, you start tampering with the understanding of the doctrine of salvation. For salvation rests in the one man Christ, just as the doctrine of condemnation rests in the one man Adam.

Not many understand that there are a plethora of salvation analogies that draw from Genesis. One is in 2 Corinthians 4:6: "God, who said, 'Light shall shine out of darkness,' is the One who has shone in our hearts to give the Light of the knowledge of the glory of God in the face of Christ." The analogy is this: Just as God created instantaneous light, so He creates instantaneous spiritual light. This is not some long, drawn-out process. In creation, everything began in a dark and formless void, until God instantly brought light.

Likewise, in salvation, the sinner is in a dark void without form, until the shining glory of God in the face of Jesus Christ enlightens him by a divine miracle. The miracle of spiritual light is analogous to the miracle of physical light. The instantaneous recovery of the elect from the darkness by the power of God—who puts the darkness to flight by opening the heart to gospel light—is a parallel to the darkness that fled at the very words out of God's mouth, "Let there be light." This is not a process; this is a divine miracle.

After that original light was created, more followed in the subsequent days of creation. Jonathan Edwards suggested that this too is a picture of the believer who, though he has been given light and though he has been brought out of the darkness, still experiences the reality of the present darkness. As the creation progresses, there is more beauty and more perfection. It begins with God saying, "This is good." It ends with Him saying, "This is very good." The creation of man on the sixth day is a picture analogous to the creation of the sinner, who is given the light of the glory of God shining in the face of Jesus Christ. In the days after, the sinner moves toward the experience that is more beautiful and more fulfilled, an experience that can be called "very good." If we can keep the analogy going, there is coming a day when this sinner saved by grace will enter into a heavenly rest, where all is light, the eternal Sabbath.

### The New Creation

The creation account is also interconnected to the new creation that we as believers are waiting for. It is written in 2 Peter 3:10, "The day of the Lord will come like a thief, in which the heavens will pass away with a roar and the elements will be destroyed with intense heat, and the earth and its works will be burned up." That is Peter's description of the un-creation, of how it all ends. After that there will be a "new heavens and a new earth" (verse 13)—that is, the eternal state—in which righteousness dwells. We have hope that the God who said His creation was "very good" will restore it to that same and even greater status.

Sadly, evangelicals have become more consumed with environmental issues than the future kingdom. *Christianity Today* came out in favor of a recent global warming bill. One evangelical leader said, "The earth is God's body, and He wants us to look after it."[2] In another evangelical's declaration on the care of creation, it was written, "We have sinned in our stewardship of creation; therefore we repent of the way we have polluted, distorted and destroyed the Creator's work."[3] The declaration also said, "We commit ourselves to extend Christ's healing to the creation."[4]

How is it that God is healing the physical earth when He is the one who cursed it? The above-mentioned declaration said, "Human poverty is a consequence of an environmental degradation."[5] Actually, human poverty is a consequence of the failure to subdue the creation by all means necessary. God created everything good, but man sinned and corrupted all of creation. Consequently, the earth has deteriorated from its original goodness and will probably continue to get worse. But it is not because of what man has done to the earth; it is because God cursed it.

If it was not for human care, for using all of our brainpower through the history

of mankind to make life good here, this earth would be uninhabitable. You have to use the sweat of your brow to prevent the earth from killing you, but if you subdue it, look at the riches that come out of it. If it weren't for man and his efforts to rule the earth, its riches would never be extracted. The most advanced societies subdue the earth and all its resources for man's benefit. The least-advanced societies, however, live in wastelands of hunger and suffer at the mercy of their environment.

We do not need less energy; we need more. We do not need less technology; we need more. If we want to help the poor, we have got to stop crying about environmentalism, because it only destroys the most deprived people. Many people estimate that global warming efforts will actually kill many people in the next few years, because it halts progress that protects them from the deadly character of the curse. The fact that the scientific community does not rise up and protest the false science means they have been politicized and postmodernized.

The ploy used by postmodern, politicized pseudoscience is what one scientist calls consensus science. That is to say it isn't actually a science, but is a way to shut down real science. The work of science is not done by consensus; science requires only one investigator who is looking for the facts. Consensus is involved only in situations where there is a political, social, and financial agenda, and not scientific support.

A scientist named Bjørn Lomborg wrote a book titled *The Skeptical Environmentalist*. *Scientific American* magazine vilified him as a heretic for even suggesting that anyone had to truly investigate the global warming claims of environmentalists. He does acknowledge that the temperature of the earth has risen, according to some scientists, by one degree in the past 30 years. But 30 years of data is not enough. It is a short-term trend, and trends come and go.

The best information tells us that since 1880, the globe's average temperature has gone up and down. From 1940 to 1970 it was cooler, and from 1970 to the present it has gotten one degree warmer. Legitimate science recognizes a close correlation between sunspots and climate change. The more sunspots, the warmer the climate; so it is solar variations that produce climate change. The sun is the source of temperature changes because of its infrared variations.

There is absolutely no evidence that $CO_2$ contributes to warming; actually, the opposite is likely true—warming produces more $CO_2$. The sun warms up the oceans, and when the oceans are warm, they release more $CO_2$. There is not enough data to determine that a rising temperature globally is produced by people or industry.

Why bring all this up? Because if you let politics, the world, and pseudoscience determine your worldview, then you will be regularly tossed to and fro. Instead, may your fidelity be to the simple and clear Word of God, written for us by the Creator of all things.

We read in the Word that man is not the enemy of nature; he is the steward of it. God gave him this planet to use it. The earth is not a fragile ecosystem that has evolved over billions of years by random chance. It is a strong, robust system held together by God, who upholds all things by His power. This world was never intended to be left pristine; it was intended to be used.

God made the earth. He sustains it, and He tells us that its end will come. May we be ready for that, and may we get our people ready as well by having our focus on nothing but the clear and infallible Word of God.

# PRAYER

Father, we thank You for the way You have revealed Yourself. We praise You as the Creator, Sustainer, and Consummator of the universe. The wonder of the staggering reality that You could speak the universe into existence reminds us that You can speak it out of existence just as fast. In the meantime, You sustain it.

Father, only You can tell us the story of creation, and we thank You for doing just that. May we have a renewed commitment to Your Word, to proclaim Your Scripture, to be unequivocal in our devotion and fidelity to that truth. We ask all this in Christ's name. Amen.

# 5

# FAITH OF OUR FATHERS: DO WE HAVE THE SAME GOSPEL AS THE EARLY CHURCH?

*Nathan Busenitz*

*Shepherds' Conference 2012*

*Selected Scriptures*

It was just over 500 years ago in the fall of 1510 that a desperate Roman Catholic monk made what he thought would be the spiritual pilgrimage of a lifetime. Five years prior to that journey, this man had joined a German monastery, much to the surprise and dismay of his father, who wanted him to become a lawyer.

In fact, it was on his way home from law school that this young man, then 21 years old, found himself in the midst of a severe thunderstorm. The lightning was so intense, he thought for sure he was about to die. Fearing for his life and relying on his Roman Catholic upbringing, he called out for help. "Saint Anne, save me, and I will become a monk!" Fifteen days later, he left law school behind and embraced monastic life; the fear of death had prompted him to become a monk, and the fear of God's wrath would continue to consume him in the years that followed.

He became the most fastidious of all the monks in the monastery, doing everything within his power to placate his guilty conscience and earn God's favor. He dedicated himself to the sacraments, to fasting and penance, he even performed acts of asceticism—like going without sleep, enduring cold winter nights without a blanket, and whipping himself in an attempt to atone for his sins. He would later say about this time in his life that if anyone could have earned heaven by the life of a monk, it would have been him. Even his supervisor, the head of the monastery, became concerned that this young man had grown too introspective and too consumed with questions about his own salvation.

## The Righteousness of God

This young monk became particularly fixated on Paul's teachings about the righteousness of God in the book of Romans, especially Romans 1:17, where Paul wrote of the gospel: "In it the righteousness of God is revealed from faith to faith; as it is written, 'But the righteous man shall live by faith.'"

This man's understanding of that verse was clouded. Reading it through the lens of medieval Roman Catholic tradition, he twisted its meaning by thinking that he had to somehow become righteous, through his own efforts, in order to gain salvation. Therein was the problem—he knew he was not righteous. Despite everything he did to try to earn divine favor, he knew he fell short of God's perfect standard.

As he would later recount, he began to hate the phrase "the righteousness of God" because he saw in it his own condemnation. He realized that because God's perfect righteousness was the standard, and because he as a sinner could not meet that standard, then he stood utterly condemned. Out of frustration and despair, he plunged himself even more fervently into the strict practices of monastic life. Trying his best to work

his way to salvation, he grew increasingly discouraged.

Hence, it was five years after he became a monk—in the year 1510—that this desperate man made what he thought would be the spiritual pilgrimage of a lifetime. He and a fellow monk traveled in October of that year to the city of Rome. If anyone could help him calm the storm that raged in his soul, he thought, surely it would be the priests, cardinals, and the pope in Rome. Moreover, he was convinced that if he paid homage to the shrines of the apostles and made confession in that holy city, he would secure the greatest absolution possible. He was so excited that when he came within sight of the city, he fell down and exclaimed, "Hail to you, holy Rome, three times holy for the blood of martyrs shed here."[1]

## Disappointment in Rome

His excitement soon turned to severe disappointment. He tried to immerse himself in the religious fervor of Rome, visiting the graves of saints, and performing ritualistic acts of penance, but he quickly noticed the glaring inconsistency. As he looked around him—at the pope, the cardinals, and the priests—he did not see righteousness. Instead, he was startled by the corruption, greed, and immorality. The famous historian Philip Schaff explains that the young man was

...shocked by the unbelief, levity and immorality of the clergy.

Money and luxurious living seemed to have replaced apostolic poverty and self-denial. He saw nothing but worldly splendor at the court of Pope Julius II...[and] he heard of the fearful crimes of Pope Alexander VI, which were hardly known and believed in Germany, but freely spoken of as undoubted facts in the fresh remembrance of all Romans...He was told that "if there was a hell, Rome was built on it," and that this state of things must soon end in a collapse.[2]

Here was a desperate man on a desperate journey, having devoted his life to the pursuit of self-righteous legalism. He went to Rome looking for answers, and all he found was spiritual bankruptcy. He returned to Germany disillusioned and disappointed, convinced that "Rome, once the holiest city was now the worst."[3]

A few years after he returned to Germany, Martin Luther would openly defy the pope by calling him the very anti-Christ. He would condemn the cardinals as charlatans, and denounce the apostate tradition of Roman Catholicism for what it had become—a destructive system of works-righteousness. But before that would take place, Luther needed to find the answer to his spiritual dilemma. If he was unrighteous in spite of his best efforts, how could he be made right before a holy and perfect God?

## The Heart of the Reformation

In 1513 and 1514, while lecturing through the Psalms and studying the book of Romans, Luther came to realize the glorious truth that had escaped him for so long: The "righteousness of God" not only encompasses the righteous *requirements* of God (of which all men fall short), but also the righteous *provision* of God, whereby He imputes Christ's righteousness to those who repent and believe. Luther's own remarks sum up the glorious transformation that took place in his heart as a result of that discovery. He wrote, "At last, meditating day and night and by the mercy of God...I began to understand that the righteousness of God is that through which the righteous live by a gift of God, namely by faith...Here I felt as if I were entirely born again and had entered paradise itself through the gates that had been flung open."[4]

After a lifetime of guilt—including years of struggling to make himself righteous by trying to please God on his own—Martin Luther finally came to understand the heart of the gospel message. He discovered justification by grace through faith in Christ alone.

For Luther and his fellow Reformers, the doctrine of God's grace became a central part of their preaching and teaching, in direct contradiction to the Roman Catholic doctrine of their day. The five *solas* of the Reformation—*sola Scriptura* ("Scripture alone"), *sola fide* ("faith alone"), *sola gratia* ("grace alone"), *solus Christus* ("Christ alone"), *soli Deo gloria* ("glory to God alone")—summarized the heart and the basis of that Reformation gospel.

"Scripture alone" refers to the fact that God's Word is the church's highest and final authority. "Faith alone" means that justification is not merited on the basis of good works, but is received by "grace alone" through faith in the person and work of Jesus Christ. "Christ alone" emphasizes that the Savior's once-for-all sacrifice at Calvary was perfectly sufficient to pay sin's penalty for those who believe in Him. Consequently, because they can take no credit for their salvation, the redeemed must give all the "glory to God alone."

## Did the Reformation Present Something New?

All of this raises a key question: Was Luther's understanding of the gospel something new? In other words, did Martin Luther and the other Reformers invent the doctrine of justification by grace alone through faith alone based on the finished work of Christ alone?

Some Roman Catholics would certainly argue for that. It was in May of 2007 that Francis Beckwith, then president of the Evangelical Theological Society, announced that he was resigning the position because he was leaving Protestantism to join Roman Catholicism. His reasons were largely related to church history and included statements like, "The early church is more Catholic than Protestant," and Catholics have "more explanatory power to account for both all the biblical texts on justification as well as the church's historical understanding of salvation prior to the Reformation all the way back to the ancient church of the first few centuries."[5]

Another Roman Catholic apologist, with whom I interacted in an online forum, said it this way: "As far as Protestant Christianity goes, it did not exist until the 1500s. I challenge anyone to find the current Protestant beliefs and practices before the 1500s." Later he clarified his point by saying he was looking for someone to show him where Protestant doctrines, such as *sola fide* and *sola Scriptura*, existed before the sixteenth century. He claimed that the evangelical gospel did not exist before the Reformation, and that core Protestant teachings were essentially invented by Martin Luther and the other Reformers. Obviously, that charge would be devastating if it were true.

## Reforming Before the Reformation

The fallacious nature of such allegations can be immediately demonstrated by pointing to the pre-Reformers, showing that Luther was actually building on the work of men like John Wycliffe and Jan Hus. Many think of the Reformation as a year in history (1517) or a phenomenon that started with Luther. The reality is that it began to gain momentum as early as the twelfth century. In the

FAITH OF OUR FATHERS:
DO WE HAVE THE SAME GOSPEL AS THE EARLY CHURCH?

399

1100s, the Waldensians began to teach that the Bible alone is the authority for the church. They defied papal authority, committed themselves to preaching the Scriptures, and even translated the Word of God into regional dialects so that people could read it in their native language. In the sixteenth century, the Waldensians became part of the Reformation movement because they recognized their doctrinal alignment with the Reformers.

If we move ahead to the 1300s, still two centuries before Martin Luther, we find an English scholar named John Wycliffe, who criticized the corruption of the Catholic system and called for reform. Known as the "Morning Star of the Reformation," Wycliffe (along with fellow scholars at Oxford) translated the Bible into English. A generation later, in the early 1400s, a Bohemian preacher named Jan Hus, having been influenced by both the Waldensians and Wycliffe, opposed the papacy and taught that Christ alone is the head of the church. If Christ is the head of the church, then His Word is the authority in the church—*sola Scriptura*. And if His Word is the authority in the church, then the gospel it presents must be the true message of salvation.

In 1415, after being promised safe passage to the Council of Constance, Hus was arrested, tried, and burned at the stake. A century later, Martin Luther would discover the writings of Jan Hus. He found them so convincing that he became known as the Saxon Hus.

From the Waldensians in the twelfth

century, to Wycliffe in the fourteenth, to Hus in the fifteenth, it becomes clear that momentum for the Reformation began to build long before 1517. Luther did not see himself as an innovator, but as someone building on the work of those who had come before him. Nonetheless, this still leaves open the question of the early church: Did believers in the early centuries of church history hold to a gospel of grace alone through faith alone?

### *The Solas in Scripture*

Before answering that question from church history, we must first answer it from the Word of God. As evangelical Christians, Scripture alone is our authority. While we might look to history for affirmation and encouragement, it is not our final authority. Our understanding of the gospel must be established from the clear teaching of the Word of God. The doctrine of justification by grace alone through faith alone must be defended from Scripture, or it cannot be defended at all.

Many passages of Scripture could be cited to make such a defense. For the sake of space, we will reference only a few. In Luke 18:13-14, Jesus contrasted the prayer of a Pharisee with that of a tax collector. He made it clear that we are not justified through our own self-righteous works; rather, God justifies those who, like the unworthy tax collector, cry out in faith and depend on Him for mercy. Romans 3:28 states that "a man is justified by faith apart from the works of the

Law." Romans 4 presents Abraham as an example of that reality, and Romans 5:1 reiterates that because we have "been justified by faith, we have peace with God through our Lord Jesus Christ." In Galatians 3:8, Paul again emphasized "that God would justify the Gentiles by faith." Ephesians 2:8-9 reveals that sinners have been saved by the grace of God, through faith, which is the gift of God and not a result of works.

---

**We are justified then by His grace alone, through faith alone, in Christ alone.**

---

In Philippians 3:8-9, Paul reiterated the bankruptcy of trying to earn salvation on the basis of good works. He explained that he did not have "a righteousness of [his] own derived from the Law, but that which is through faith in Christ, the righteousness which comes from God on the basis of faith." Titus 3:5-7 says God saved us "not on the basis of deeds which we have done in righteousness, but according to His mercy." Later in the text, it states that we are justified by His grace.

Even a brief survey of these passages is sufficient to show that our righteous standing before God is not based on good works that we have done, but only on the finished work of Christ on the

cross. We are justified then by His grace alone, through faith alone, in Christ alone.

### The First Church Council

What about church history? How did the earliest Christians understand the biblical teaching on justification by faith? There is a place where both biblical truth and church history meet, and it is in the book of Acts. Written by Luke in the early 60s of the first century, the book of Acts includes the first 30 years of the history of the church, starting at Pentecost and ending with Paul's house arrest in Rome.

Acts begins where Luke's Gospel ends, immediately after the resurrection of Jesus Christ. The first chapter centers on the Great Commission, which serves as the outline of the book; Christ's followers were to go and make disciples in Jerusalem and Judea, Samaria, and the outermost parts of the earth. We see that mission unfold in Acts. In chapters 2–7, the church is founded and the gospel spreads throughout Jerusalem and Judea. In chapter 8, the good news is taken to Samaria. In chapter 9, Saul is converted; he is the one who will take the gospel to the Gentiles throughout the Roman world. In chapter 10, Luke introduces his readers to the first Gentile convert, Cornelius. In chapter 11, we have the establishment of the first Jew-Gentile church in Syrian Antioch. From there to the end of the book, after a brief note regarding James and Peter in chapter 12, we read about how Saul (whose Roman name was Paul) takes the gospel to the Gentile world on several missionary journeys.

The book of Acts celebrates the advancement of the gospel. Yet in the middle of Luke's historical record (in chapter 15), a serious controversy arises over the very nature of the gospel itself. The issue was so important that the apostles met together in Jerusalem to settle the controversy. That meeting of the apostles is known as the Jerusalem Council—the first council of church history. It met around AD 49 or 50, nearly 20 years after the church was established on the Day of Pentecost; and 275 years before the next major church council, the Council of Nicaea.

The Jerusalem Council convened to address one essential question: *"What is the essence of the gospel?"* Is it a message of grace alone? Or is it a message of grace plus works? The advancement of the gospel could not continue unless the right message was being proclaimed.

### The Proclamation of the True Gospel (Acts 13–14)

At the outset of church history, starting with the day of Pentecost (Acts 2), the church was composed entirely of Jewish Christians. It wasn't until the conversion of the Samaritans (in Acts 8) and Cornelius (in Acts 10) that non-Jews began to be incorporated into the body of Christ. After highlighting Cornelius's conversion, Luke detailed the spread of the gospel into Gentile lands (in Acts 11:19–24),

culminating in the formation of a predominantly Gentile church in Syrian Antioch.

The inclusion of Gentiles into the church represented a major paradigm shift for Jewish Christians. For the previous 1500 years, since the time of Moses, God had been working through the nation of Israel. But now, in the church, Gentiles were being saved without having to first become Jewish proselytes. Of course, God had prepared the apostles for this by saving Cornelius while Peter was present (Acts 11:1-18). So when the apostles heard about Gentile converts in Antioch, they rejoiced and sent Barnabas to pastor the believers there. A short time later, Barnabas went to Tarsus, found Paul, and brought him back to serve alongside of him in Antioch (Acts 11:25-26).

After a season of fruitful ministry, around the year AD 47, Paul and Barnabas embarked on an evangelistic mission to several Gentile cities in Southern Galatia, in modern-day Turkey. They travelled first to Cyprus, then to Perga, and then to Psidian Antioch. It was there, in Antioch, that they entered the synagogue and Paul preached a powerful gospel message to the Jewish people in attendance.

The content of that sermon is recorded in Acts 13:16-41, and it centered on the fact that Jesus is the Messiah whom God raised from the dead so that sinners might be saved through Him. In his emphasis on the gospel of grace, Paul declared in verses 38-39: "Therefore let it be known to you, brethren, that through this Man [Jesus Christ] is preached to you the forgiveness of sins; and by Him everyone who believes is justified from all things from which you could not be justified by the law of Moses" (NKJV).

In contrast to the popular self-righteous legalism of first-century Judaism, Paul asserted that faith in Christ can do what keeping the law of Moses could never do. Forgiveness and justification come only through believing in Christ, and not through keeping the works of the Law. That would have been a revolutionary concept for those who heard Paul preach in the synagogue that day. Not surprisingly, many of them rejected it (verses 45-46), forcing Paul and Barnabas to leave the city (verse 50).

In Acts 14:27-28, Paul and Barnabas finally returned home, after preaching the gospel in several other cities, establishing churches, and appointing leaders in those congregations. Their first missionary journey was over, and it had been a great success. Though it had lasted many months, and though Paul and Barnabas were severely persecuted and nearly killed, churches had been planted throughout southern Galatia. The gospel of faith alone had been proclaimed to the Gentiles. But controversy was about to erupt.

### The Perversion of the True Gospel (Acts 15:1-5)

Acts 14 ends with the church in Syrian Antioch rejoicing over the success of the first missionary journey. By contrast, Acts 15 opens with these words:

> Some men came down from Judea and began teaching the brethren, "Unless you are circumcised according to the custom of Moses, you cannot be saved." And when Paul and Barnabas had great dissension and debate with them, the brethren determined that Paul and Barnabas and some others of them should go up to Jerusalem to the apostles and elders concerning this issue. Therefore, being sent on their way by the church, they were passing through both Phoenicia and Samaria, describing in detail the conversion of the Gentiles, and were bringing great joy to all the brethren. When they arrived at Jerusalem, they were received by the church and the apostles and the elders, and they reported all that God had done with them. But some of the sect of the Pharisees who had believed stood up, saying, "It is necessary to circumcise them and to direct them to observe the Law of Moses" (verses 1-5).

On the heels of a successful missionary venture, the church suddenly found itself embroiled in controversy over the essential nature of the gospel. The fundamental issue could be summed up with

FAITH OF OUR FATHERS:
DO WE HAVE THE SAME GOSPEL AS THE EARLY CHURCH?

403

this question: What must sinners do to be saved? (cf. Acts 16:30).

In Acts 13:38-39, Paul declared that faith in Christ does what the Law of Moses could not do: It brings both forgiveness and justification. But these former Pharisees, who later became known as the Judaizers, claimed that the gospel Paul had been preaching was illegitimate unless it also incorporated works. In addition to faith, they argued that both circumcision (Acts 15:1-2) and keeping the Mosaic Law (Acts 15:5) were necessary for salvation. It is no wonder that great dissension and debate arose among them, for this was no small matter. To settle the matter, Paul and Barnabas traveled to Jerusalem to consult with the apostles and elders there. Is salvation by grace alone, or is it by faith plus circumcision and the works of the Mosaic Law?

You might be wondering what Paul was thinking when he came to the Jerusalem Council. He tells us in the second chapter of Galatians, a letter which he wrote shortly after these events. Paul wrote, "I went up again to Jerusalem with Barnabas, taking Titus along also. It was because of a revelation that I went up; and I submitted to them the gospel which I preach among the Gentiles, but I did so in private to those who were of reputation, for fear that I might be running, or had run, in vain" (Galatians 2:1-2).

Paul came to Jerusalem and, before the council convened publicly, met with some of the apostolic leaders privately,

explaining to them the gospel he had been preaching to the Gentiles—the gospel of grace alone through faith alone. The passage identifies these leaders as James, the brother of the Lord, Peter, and John. Notice what Paul said about the Judaizers in Galatians 2:4-5: "It was because of the false brethren secretly brought in, who had sneaked in to spy out our liberty which we have in Christ Jesus, in order to bring us into bondage. But we did not yield in subjection to them for even an hour, so that the truth of the gospel would remain with you." As those words make clear, Paul was determined not to compromise on the truth of the gospel.

### The Preservation of the True Gospel (Acts 15:6-11)

After Paul met with these apostolic leaders privately, the public council took place. Luke describes the scene, starting in verse 6:

> The apostles and the elders came together to look into this matter. After there had been much debate, Peter stood up and said to them, "Brethren, you know that in the early days God made a choice among you, that by my mouth the Gentiles would hear the word of the gospel and believe. And God, who knows the heart, testified to them giving them the Holy Spirit, just as He also did to us; and He made no

distinction between us and them, cleansing their hearts by faith. Now therefore why do you put God to the test by placing upon the neck of the disciples a yoke which neither our fathers nor we have been able to bear? But we believe that we are saved through the grace of the Lord Jesus, in the same way as they also are."

Notice that Peter affirmed that it was right for the Gentiles to hear the gospel and believe. In verse 8, he confirmed that the Gentiles had received the Holy Spirit just as the Jewish believers had on the day of Pentecost. In verse 9, he emphasized that God had cleansed their hearts by faith. In verse 10, he stated that the Mosaic Law was a burden that was not necessary for salvation. And in verse 11, he reiterated that all believers, both Jew and Gentile, are saved by the grace of the Lord. This was a clear affirmation by Peter of the gospel of grace, apart from the works of the law, through faith in Christ alone.

Verses 12 and following indicate that James and the rest of the Jerusalem Council agreed with Peter, noting that Gentile Christians did not need to keep the Mosaic Law.[6] The gospel preached by Paul and Barnabas was wholeheartedly affirmed by the apostles at the Jerusalem Council as being the true gospel. Consequently, Paul and Barnabas returned to Antioch greatly encouraged and filled with joy (Acts 15:30-31).

In spite of the council's clear decision, the Judaizers would continue to cause problems. In the very churches Paul and Barnabas planted on their first missionary journey, false teachers began to insist that faith alone was insufficient for salvation. Instead, they claimed that circumcision and law-keeping were required for Gentile believers to be saved. One can imagine how concerned Paul would have been.

He responded in two ways: by planning a follow-up visit to those churches (Acts 15:36), and by sending them a letter, in which he offered them a stern warning:

> I am amazed that you are so quickly deserting Him who called you by the grace of Christ, for a different gospel; which is really not another; only there are some who are disturbing you and want to distort the gospel of Christ. But even if we, or an angel from heaven, should preach to you a gospel contrary to what we have preached to you, he is to be accursed! As we have said before, so I say again now, if any man is preaching to you a gospel contrary to what you received, he is to be accursed! (Galatians 1:6-9).

The apostle went on to clearly explain that justification is not based on doing the works of the law, but is only granted by grace through faith in Christ (cf.

Galatians 3:1-14). That theme continued to be a primary emphasis throughout Paul's writings over the course of his entire ministry (cf. Romans 4–5; Ephesians 2:8-9; Philippians 3:7-11; Titus 3:4-7).

The biblical truth that salvation is only by grace, and not by our own efforts, is what liberated Luther and his fellow Reformers from the system of works righteousness in which they had been trapped. But what about the early leaders of Christianity who lived in the centuries after the apostles? Did they also understand justification to be by grace alone through faith alone in Christ alone?

### The Church Fathers

Evangelicals rightly conclude that the Reformation doctrine of *sola fide* is grounded in Scripture. But many wrongly assume that such an understanding of the gospel is absent from pre-Reformation church history. In reality, glimpses of "grace alone" and "faith alone" can be found throughout the writings of both the church fathers and a number of medieval theologians. A full survey would demand a book-length treatment.[7] However, a brief list is sufficient to illustrate the point.

### Clement of Rome (d. ca. 100)

Clement of Rome was the pastor of the church in Rome from about AD 90 to 100. As a church leader, he was a contemporary of the apostle John. He was likely a disciple of Paul, and may even be the Clement mentioned in Philippians 4:3.

The Roman Catholic Church considers Clement to be a pope, which makes his affirmation of *sola fide* all the more significant. His epistle to the Corinthians is likely the earliest Christian document that we have outside of the New Testament. In chapter 32 of his letter, he says of believers:

> And so we, having been called through his will in Christ Jesus, are not justified through ourselves or through our own wisdom or understanding or piety, or works that we have done in holiness of heart, but through faith, by which the Almighty God has justified all who have existed from the beginning; to whom be the glory for ever and ever. Amen.[8]

Clement clearly understood justification to be received by faith apart from any meritorious acts on the part of the believer. Though he does not use the word "alone," he excludes any category that might be added to saving faith ("ourselves," "our own wisdom or understanding or piety," "works that we have done in holiness of heart"). These categories cannot justify, because sinners are justified by grace through faith, apart from any works.

To Clement's testimony, a chorus of other voices might be added:

### Polycarp (ca. 69–155)

Polycarp pastored the church in Smyrna in the first half of the second century. His faithfulness, even in the face of death, is famously recorded in *The Martyrdom of Polycarp*. In his *Epistle to the Philippians*, his only surviving letter, Polycarp echoes the truth of Ephesians 2:8-9 when he writes:

> I also rejoice because your firmly rooted faith, renowned from the earliest times, still perseveres and bears fruit to our Lord Jesus Christ, who endured for our sins, facing even death, whom God raised up, having loosed the birth pangs of Hades. Though you have not seen him, you believe in him with an inexpressible and glorious joy (which many desire to experience), knowing that by grace you have been saved, not because of works, but by the will of God through Jesus Christ.[9]

As Polycarp articulates, salvation is a gift of God's grace and cannot be earned on the basis of good works.

### The Epistle to Diognetus (second century)

This anonymous epistle is an early evangelistic tract written to an unbeliever. Its beautiful presentation of the gospel makes it one of the most eloquent works of patristic literature. Notice the author's clear understanding of Christ's imputed righteousness given to those who embrace Him in saving faith:

> He gave His own Son as a ransom for us, the holy One for transgressors, the blameless One for the wicked, the righteous One for the unrighteous, the incorruptible One for the corruptible, the immortal One for them that are mortal. For what other thing was capable of covering our sins than His righteousness? By what other one was it possible that we, the wicked and ungodly, could be justified, than by the only Son of God? O sweet exchange! O unsearchable operation! O benefits surpassing all expectation! That the wickedness of many should be hid in a single righteous One, and that the righteousness of One should justify many transgressors![10]

Fourteen centuries later, Martin Luther would similarly celebrate the great exchange that takes place at the moment of salvation.[11] Christ bore the sins of believers on the cross so that they might be clothed in His perfect righteousness (2 Corinthians 5:21).

### Hilary of Poitiers (ca. 300–368)

In the fourth century, Hilary of Poitiers wrote a commentary on the Gospel of Matthew. Significantly, he included the phrase "faith justifies" or "we are justified by faith" more than 20 times in that work. For example, he writes, "Wages cannot be considered as a gift, because they are due to work, but God has given free grace to all men by the justification of faith."[12] Commenting on the hostility of the Pharisees, he remarks, "It disturbed the scribes that sin was forgiven by a man (for they considered that Jesus Christ was only a man) and that sin was forgiven by Him whereas the Law was not able to absolve it, since faith alone justifies."[13] These, and similar statements, indicate that Hilary understood that justification is received through faith, apart from works.

## Basil of Caesarea (329–379)

In his *Sermon on Humility*, Basil of Caesarea explains why believers can take no credit for their salvation:

> This is perfect and pure boasting in God, when one is not proud on account of his own righteousness but knows that he is indeed unworthy of the true righteousness and is justified solely by faith in Christ. And Paul boasts that he despises his own righteousness, seeking that righteousness that is on account of Christ, which is the righteousness of God by faith.[14]

Following Paul's lead in Philippians 3:1-11, Basil reiterates that believers are "justified solely by faith in Christ." Such an affirmation of faith alone (*sola fide*) motivates Basil to boast only in God for his salvation (*soli Deo gloria*).

## Ambrosiaster (fourth century)

The fourth-century Pauline commentator known as Ambrosiaster makes numerous statements affirming justification by grace through faith in his commentary on Romans. Here are three brief examples:

> They are justified freely because, while doing nothing or providing any repayment, they are justified by faith alone as a gift of God.[15]

> Paul tells those who live under the law that they have no reason to boast basing themselves on the law and claiming to be of the race of Abraham, seeing that no one is justified before God except by faith.[16]

> Those are blessed of whom God has decreed that, without work or any keeping of the law, they are justified before God by faith alone.[17]

## John Chrysostom (347–407)

Renowned fourth-century preacher John Chrysostom expresses the truth of justification by grace through faith alone on many occasions in his *Homilies*. Here is a small handful of examples:

> What is the "law of faith"? It is, being saved by grace. Here he shows God's power, in that He has not only saved, but has even justified, and led them to boasting,

and this too without needing works, but looking for faith only.[18]

Would you know how good our Master is? The Publican went up full of ten thousand wickednesses, and saying only, "Be merciful unto me," went down justified.[19]

Attend to this point. He Himself who gave the Law, had decreed, before He gave it, that the heathen should be justified by faith… They said that he who kept not the Law was cursed, but he proves that he who kept it was cursed, and he who kept it not, blessed. Again, they said that he who adhered to faith alone was cursed, but he shows that he who adhered to faith alone, is blessed.[20]

For the Law requires not only faith but works also, but grace saves and justifies by faith.[21]

For as people, on receiving some great good, ask themselves if it is not a dream, as not believing it; so it is with respect to the gifts of God. What then was it that was thought incredible? That those who were enemies and sinners, justified by neither the law nor works, should immediately through faith alone be advanced to the highest favor. On this head [topic] accordingly Paul has discoursed at length in his Epistle to the Romans, and here again at length. "This is a faithful saying," he says, "and worthy of all acceptation, that Christ Jesus came into the world to save sinners." As the Jews were chiefly attracted by this, he persuades them not to listen to the law, since they could not attain salvation by it without faith. Against this he contends, for it seemed to them incredible that a person who had misspent all his former life in vain and wicked actions should afterwards be saved by his faith alone. On this account he says, "It is a saying to be believed."[22]

[God] has justified our race not by right actions, not by toils, not by barter and exchange, but by grace alone. Paul, too, made this clear when he said: "But now the justice of God has been made manifest apart from the Law." But the justice [or, righteousness] of God comes through faith in Jesus Christ and not through any labor and suffering.[23]

### Marius Victorinus (fourth century)

In his commentary on Ephesians, Marius Victorinus writes, "[God] did not give back to us what was merited, since we did not receive this by merits but by the grace and goodness of God."[24] Later he adds, "The fact that you Ephesians are saved is not something that comes from yourselves. It is the gift of God. It is not from your works, but it is God's grace and God's gift, not from anything you have deserved."[25] And again, "Only faith in Christ is salvation for us."[26] Elsewhere, commenting on Galatians, he looks to the example of Abraham as the archetype of justification by faith:

> For the patriarchs prefigured and foretold that man would be justified from faith. Therefore, just as it was reckoned as righteousness to Abraham that he had faith, so we too, if we have faith in Christ and every mystery of his, will be sons of Abraham. Our whole life will be accounted as righteous.[27]

### Augustine (354–430)

Augustine was the most influential church father, at least in the West. Accordingly, his emphasis on God's grace in salvation significantly influenced the thinking of the Reformers. That emphasis is clearly seen in excerpts from Augustine's writings. Consider the following:

> When someone believes in him who justifies the impious, that faith is reckoned as justice to the believer, as David too declares that person blessed whom God has accepted and endowed with righteousness, independently of any righteous actions. What righteousness is this? The righteousness of faith, preceded by no

good works, but with good works as its consequence.[28]

What is grace? That which is freely given. What is "freely given"? Given, not paid. If it was due, wages would be given, but grace would not be bestowed. But if it was really due, then you were good. But if, as is true, you were evil but believed on him who justifies the ungodly. (What is, "who justifies the ungodly"? the ungodly is made righteous), consider what by right hung over you by the law and you have obtained by grace. But having obtained that grace by faith, you will be just by faith—"for the just lives by faith."[29]

Now, having duly considered and weighed all these circumstances and testimonies, we conclude that a man is not justified by the precepts of a holy life, but by faith in Jesus Christ; in a word, not by the law of works, but by the law of faith; not by the letter, but by the spirit; not by the merits of deeds, but by free grace.[30]

### Prosper of Aquitaine (390–455)

An early defender and systematizer of Augustinian doctrine was Prosper of Aquitaine. Following Augustine's emphasis on grace, Prosper declared:

Just as there are no crimes so detestable that they can prevent the gift of grace, so too there can be no works so eminent that they are owed in condign [deserved] judgment that which is given freely. Would it not be a debasement of redemption in Christ's blood [literally, would not the redemption of Christ's blood become valueless], and would not God's mercy be made secondary to human works, if justification, which is through grace, were owed in view of preceding merits, so that it were not the gift of a Donor, but the wages of a laborer?[31]

As Prosper explains, no crimes are so egregious that they are beyond the reach of God's grace. Conversely, no good works are so noble that they can merit salvation. The gift of salvation is given freely, which means it cannot be earned on the basis of works. To think that it can is a debasement of Christ's sacrifice on the cross.

### Theodoret of Cyrrhus (ca. 393–457)

Theodoret of Cyrrhus expresses a similar understanding of salvation by grace through faith apart from works. In his commentary on Romans, he states, "The doer of righteousness expects a reward, but justification by faith is the gift of the God of all."[32] Earlier in that same work, he writes:

The righteousness of God is not revealed to everyone but only to those with the eyes of faith. For the holy apostle teaches us that God foresaw [literally, planned] this for us from the beginning and predicted it through the prophets, and even before the prophets, had it hidden in his secret will…Paul quoted Habakkuk for the benefit of the Jews, because he wanted to teach them not to cling to the provisions of the law but to follow [their own] prophets. For many centuries before they had predicted that one day there would be salvation by faith alone.[33]

Theodoret's commentary on Ephesians evidences a similar perspective. Speaking of Christ, he explains,

Since He rose we hope that we too shall rise. He Himself [by His rising] has paid our debt. Then Paul explains more plainly how great the gift is: "You are saved by grace." For it is not because of the excellence of our lives that we have been called, but because of the love of our Savior.[34]

Again he writes,

All we bring to grace is our faith. But even in this faith, divine grace itself has become our enabler. For [Paul] adds, "And this is not of yourselves but it is a gift of God; not of works, lest anyone should boast" (Eph. 2:8-9). It is not of our own accord that we have believed, but we have come to belief after having been called; and even when we had come to believe, He did not require of us purity of life, but approving mere faith, God bestowed on us forgiveness of sins.[35]

Accordingly, Theodoret can use the language of *faith alone* to describe the hope of salvation: "I consider myself wretched—in fact, wretched three times over. I am guilty of all kinds of errors. Through faith alone I look for finding some mercy in the day of the Lord's appearing."[36]

## Anselm of Canterbury (1033–1109)

If we jump ahead to the medieval period, we still find glimpses of the gospel of grace through faith apart from works. For example, in his *Exhortation to a Dying Man*, Anselm of Canterbury instructed those on the verge of death to trust only in Christ for their salvation, and not in their own merits. He articulated this truth in the form of a question: "Do you hope and believe, that not by your own merits, but by the merits of the passion [death] of Jesus Christ, you may attain to everlasting salvation?" He then instructed his readers to respond by saying, "I do." In that same context, he wrote:

Come then, while life remains in you, in His death alone place your whole trust; in nothing else place any trust; to His death commit yourself wholly; with this alone cover yourself wholly; in this enwrap yourself wholly. And if the Lord your God wishes to judge you, say, "Lord, between Your judgment and me I present the death of our Lord Jesus Christ; in no other way can I contend with You." And if He says that you are a sinner; say, "Lord, I interpose the death of our Lord Jesus Christ between my sins and You." If He says that you have deserved condemnation; say, "Lord, I set the death of our Lord Jesus Christ between my evil deserts and You; and His merits I offer for those which I ought to have, but have not." If He says that He is angry with you; say, "Lord I set the death of our Lord Jesus Christ between Your wrath and me." And when you have completed this, say again, "Lord, I set the death of our Lord Jesus Christ between You and me."[37]

## Bernard of Clairvaux (1090–1153)

A final example comes from Bernard of Clairvaux. Four centuries later, Martin Luther and his fellow Reformers would be deeply impacted by Bernard's teaching on justification by grace through faith alone. Here are a few citations that demonstrate why the Reformers were drawn to Bernard. He writes:

> For what could man, the slave of sin, fast bound by the devil, do of himself to recover that righteousness which he had formerly lost? Therefore he who lacked righteousness had another's imputed to him…It was man who owed the debt, it was man who paid it. For if one, says [the apostle Paul], died for all, then all were dead, so that, as One bore the sins of all, the satisfaction of One is imputed to all. It is not that one forfeited, another satisfied; the Head and body is one, viz., Christ. The Head, therefore, satisfied for the members, Christ for His children.[38]

> I confess myself most unworthy of the glory of heaven, and that I can never obtain it by my own merits. But my Lord possesses it upon a double title: that of natural inheritance, by being the only begotten Son of his eternal Father; and that of purchase, he having bought it with his precious blood. This second title he has conferred on me; and, upon this right, I hope with an assured confidence, to obtain it through his praiseworthy passion and mercy.[39]

> As for your justice, so great is the fragrance it diffuses that you are called not only just but even justice itself, the justice that makes men just. Your power to make men just is measured by your generosity in forgiving. Therefore the man who through sorrow for sin hungers and thirsts for justice, let him trust in the One who changes the sinner into a just man, and judged righteous in terms of faith alone, he will have peace with God.[40]

It is hard to imagine a better summary of the Reformation doctrine of *sola fide* than that final line—namely, that sinners are "judged righteous in terms of faith alone" and therefore they "have peace with God."

## How We Got Here

As the above survey demonstrates, the claim that the doctrine of *sola fide* is without historical warrant is, itself, without warrant. That sinners are justified by grace through faith alone was not a Reformation invention. It was the clear teaching of the apostles in the New Testament, and echoes of that truth can be traced throughout church history.

But how did this message get lost in history, such that the Reformation was necessary? The answer to that question is complex—because the shift took place gradually over centuries of time, as man-made traditions began to obscure the purity of the gospel.

The medieval Catholic Church eventually came to define justification in synergistic terms (meaning that the church presented salvation as a cooperative effort between God and man). In the thirteenth century, at the Fourth Lateran Council (1215), the Roman Catholic Church officially made salvation contingent on good works by establishing the seven sacraments as the means by which sinners are justified.

As Norm Geisler and Josh Betancourt explain in their book *Is Rome the True Church?*:

> Roman Catholicism as it is known today is not the same as the Catholic Church before 1215. Even though the split between East and West occurred in 1054, most non-Catholics today would have been able to belong to the Catholic Church before the thirteenth century. Regardless of certain things the church permitted, none of its official doctrinal proclamations regarding essential salvation doctrines were contrary to orthodoxy.

> While the development of Roman Catholicism from the original church was gradual, beginning in early centuries, one of the most significant turning points came in 1215, when one can see the beginning of Roman Catholicism as it is subsequently known. It is here that the seeds of what distinguishes Roman Catholicism were first pronounced as dogma. It is here that they pronounced the doctrine of transubstantiation, the primacy of the bishop of Rome, and seven sacraments. Many consider this a key turning point in the development of Roman Catholicism in distinction from non-Catholic forms of Christianity.[41]

Thomas Aquinas (1225–1274), who was born ten years after the Fourth Lateran Council, also contributed greatly to confusion on the true nature of the gospel. As Gregg R. Allison explains:

> More than anyone else, Thomas Aquinas set down the medieval Catholic notion of justification and its corollaries of grace, human effort, and merit. Although a substantial departure from Augustine and the Augustinians of the Middle Ages, his theology became determinative for the Roman Catholic Church...[Thomas] emphasized the grace of God yet prescribed an important role for human cooperation in obtaining salvation. Certainly, God exercises the primary role in achieving and applying salvation, but people have their part to play as well. God moves by initiating grace in

a person's life; then that person moves toward God and moves away from sin, resulting in the forgiveness of sins. Thus, Aquinas believed in a synergy, or cooperative effort, between God and people in justification.[42]

To base salvation on a cooperative effort between God's grace *and* our good works presents a major problem, for it distorts the biblical teaching about grace. As Paul explained about salvation, "If it is by grace, it is no longer on the basis of works, otherwise grace is no longer grace" (Romans 11:6). To add works into the equation is to frustrate grace. Certainly, good works are the *fruit* of salvation, but they are not the *foundation* of it. And it was at that point that medieval Catholicism muddled up the gospel.

By the thirteenth century, then, the official doctrines of the Roman Catholic Church had become fully corrupt, which brings us back full circle to the pre-Reformers. By the middle of the twelfth century, the Waldensians were questioning certain errors they saw in the Roman Catholic system. In the fourteenth century, John Wycliffe; in the fifteenth century, Jan Hus; and then in the sixteenth century, Martin Luther saw these errors as well.

Importantly, the Reformers saw their teachings as the *recovery* of truth that was very old, not the *invention* of something new. They looked to Scripture as the authoritative basis for doctrine, but they also studied the church fathers—contending that their teachings were in line with historic orthodoxy. John Calvin explained the Reformers' perspective on the church fathers with these words, "[The Roman church] unjustly set the ancient fathers against us (I mean the ancient writers of a better age of the church) as if in them, they had supporters of their own impiety...But we do not despise them [the church fathers]; in fact, if it were to our present purpose, I could with no trouble at all prove that the greater part of what we are saying today meets their approval."[43]

Rather than rejecting the early church's understanding of the gospel, the Reformers worked tirelessly to recover the very gospel championed and cherished by the apostles and those who lived in the centuries after them. That reality should be encouraging for those of us who preach, believe, and love that same gospel today.

# 6

# Mastering the Doctrine of Justification

*R.C. Sproul*
*Shepherds' Conference 2005*

*Galatians 1:6-10*

There is no place in the entire corpus of the apostle Paul where he speaks as strongly as he does in Galatians 1 to those who are moving away from the purity of the gospel. The apostle Paul expressed his astonishment to the Galatians, saying,

> I am amazed that you are so quickly deserting Him who called you by the grace of Christ, for a different gospel; which is really not another; only there are some who are disturbing you and want to distort the gospel of Christ. But even if we, or an angel from heaven, should preach to you a gospel contrary to what we have preached to you, he is to be accursed (Galatians 1:6-8).

Paul went on to write, "For am I now seeking the favor of men, or of God? Or am I striving to please men? If I were still trying to please men, I would not be a bond-servant of Christ" (verse 10). The last thought Paul attached to the warning of departing from the gospel is that of pleasing human beings. The apostle learned early in his ministry that to please men can be to displease Christ—a reminder that we need every day as we seek to serve Him with faithfulness and preach the true gospel.

## A Few Introductory Questions

I would like to ask three questions: First, how many of you are Protestants? Second, how many of you are evangelicals? Third, how many of you have been ordained or are otherwise serving in some capacity in what we call the gospel ministry?

If you have answered yes to any of those, then here are a few follow-up questions: If you are Protestant, what are you protesting? If you are an evangelical, how has that term been defined historically? And if you have been separated unto ministry, what is the gospel to which you are testifying?

I ask those questions because I am assuming that the vast majority of people who define themselves as Protestants have no idea what they are protesting. Also, there is a real crisis in our day about the very meaning of the term *evangelical*. Historically it described those who, in the Protestant Reformation, rediscovered the *evangel*, which is Latin for the gospel. Since the sixteenth century, there has been no period of time within Protestantism that the doctrine of justification by faith alone, which is at the heart of the *evangel*, has been more deeply obscured among professing evangelicals than it is today.

Presently, there are people who call themselves evangelical while at the same time denying the historic and biblical doctrine of justification by faith alone. This occurs so often that we can no longer just use the term *evangelical* to describe where we stand theologically. Most concerning to me is the loss of the understanding as to what comprises the substance of the gospel.

For example, I was at a meeting in Washington a few years ago where some of the leading so-called evangelical representatives of the world had gathered. One leader in particular was asked by the press, "What is the gospel?" This man, whose name I will not reveal to protect the guilty, was quiet for a while, and then he said, "It means the good news that Jesus can change your life, and you can have a personal relationship with Him." He stumbled around for a few more minutes, but it was absolutely clear the man did not have a clue as to the meaning of the gospel in biblical terms. I am greatly concerned about that, which is why I am going to look with you at the doctrine of justification by faith alone.

## Painting a Caricature

I intend to proceed with an overview of the Roman Catholic doctrine of justification because I have found that teaching from this pedagogical perspective helps the student grasp the biblical doctrine of justification. It is extremely beneficial to teach this truth against the backdrop of what the controversy was about during the Reformation in the sixteenth century.

The second reason I always begin with the Roman Catholic view of justification when I teach this doctrine is because it has been my experience that the vast majority of pastors with whom I speak about the classic controversy with Rome have very little understanding of the Roman Catholic view of justification. They have bought into the myth that Rome has recently changed from its sixteenth-century version of itself. There is the idea abounding that Rome has altered its doctrine of justification and now embraces what Luther was trying to get her to embrace. Nothing, of course, can be further from the truth. Although Rome has changed with respect to certain things since the sixteenth century, there are far more problems to resolve today.

One reason that misperception permeates contemporary evangelicalism is because professing evangelicals do not know the Roman Catholic view. Part of that is because we have, in many cases, slandered the Roman Catholic community by vastly oversimplifying the difference between us and them, and by telling everybody that Rome believes we are justified by works, not by faith; by merit, not by grace; by ourselves, and not by Christ. Yet this is a terrible slander because the Roman Catholic Church in the sixteenth century, the twentieth century, and the twenty-first century has insisted and continues to insist that there is no justification apart from grace, no justification apart from faith, and no justification apart from Christ.

What we usually do is set up a caricature of the Roman doctrine of justification by describing what is actually classic Pelagianism, which the Roman Church repudiated early on and once again at the Council of Trent in the sixteenth century. In every official occasion that Rome has addressed this issue, she has categorically repudiated pure Pelagianism, which says that a person can get to heaven without grace, without Christ, without faith, and

simply by living a good life. If we are to be clear in our understanding of justification, we have to understand what Rome does teach as well as what she does not teach.

## Consistent Through the Years

During the Year of Jubilee, Catholic popes will open what's known as the Holy Door, through which people can come to visit the pope and get a plenary indulgence. This event occurs every 50 years in the Roman Catholic Church. It was soon after the most recent event that I had a conversation with a friend of mine who was the number one ranking pilot, in terms of seniority, in a major American airline. We were having lunch, and he said, "You're never going to believe what happened to me."

I asked, "What happened?"

He responded, "On my latest trip to Rome, it was the Year of Jubilee. I walked through the door and I met the pope." He started to weep and said, "I received a plenary indulgence so that all the sins I have ever committed were forgiven by the church, by the sacraments, by the power of the keys of St. Peter."

It was clear, as I spoke to this man, that the doctrine of indulgences is still very much a part of the Roman system. It is reaffirmed along with the treasury of merit, purgatory, and like matters in the Catholic catechism.

A few years ago I was in Rome taking a group of people on a tour. The tour guide asked me what I wanted to see most. I told him, "The thing I want to see more than anything else is the Lateran Church."

The tour guide said, "The Lateran Church? What's so special about the Lateran Church?"

I responded, "That is where the Scala Sancta are."

He did not know what that was, so I further explained that these were the sacred steps that the Crusaders brought back from Jerusalem. Supposedly these were the steps that Jesus actually walked on as He went to the judgment hall. They have become an important relic for the Roman Catholic Church. It is believed that if one goes up the stairs on their knees, saying specific prayers on each step, they can receive a significant indulgence.

It was in that exact location, when Luther visited in Rome in 1510, that he had his awakening experience of disillusionment. After he ascended the sacred stairs on his knees, reached the top, and stood up, he said out loud, "Who knows if it is true?" It was at this moment that the seed of Luther's awakening to the gospel of justification by faith alone was planted. I wanted to go and stand where Luther stood and had that crisis moment.

We went to the Lateran Church, but I was unable to get anywhere near the stairs because every square inch of every step was completely covered with pilgrims, most of them elderly, who were on their knees, praying, kissing the steps, and going through the ritual that would give them indulgences and reduce their time

in purgatory. There was a plaque beside the stairs that announced the indulgence value of making this pilgrimage. In that moment I thought, *I'd like every American evangelical to see this, because we keep being told that Rome has changed and does not believe in this system anymore.*

## A Marred View of Justification

We learn about Catholicism's view of justification by analyzing the sixth session of the Council of Trent, which was dedicated to establishing the canons and decrees concerning justification in the church. The church first defined their view of justification, and then proceeded to list the anathemas, which are the statements of denial following the formula, "If anyone says…," "let him be anathema," meaning, "let him be damned."

When those canons are read carefully, it becomes evident that any orthodox evangelical would be anathematized by the sixth session of the Council of Trent. In their positive exposition of justification we learn of how Rome understands the doctrine. We see that justification begins with the sacrament of baptism. Justification, according to Rome, is imparted sacerdotally, through the ministry of the church via the sacraments—most notably the sacrament of baptism, and secondarily the sacrament of penance.

As Rome spells it out, justification begins with baptism. This may seem a bit technical, but Rome defines baptism as "the instrumental cause of justification." That phrase, "instrumental cause," has its roots in Aristotelian philosophy, which was synthesized in the Middle Ages with Roman Catholic theology. When Aristotle defined motion and causality, he designated several different types of causes: efficient cause, formal cause, instrumental cause, final cause, and so on. He used the illustration of a sculpture. If a statue is to be beautiful it has to have a material cause; it must be built out of a block of stone, block of wood, or some other material. The efficient cause would be the sculptor who shapes it. The important piece of this puzzle is the instrumental cause; according to Aristotle, it was the instrument or instruments by which the change from a square block of marble into a magnificent statue was brought to pass. The sculptor did not just look at the block of wood and say, "Let there be a statue." Instead, Michelangelo and others had to use tools.

Rome used this language in articulating her theology and wrote, "The instrumental cause of justification is baptism." In the sacrament of baptism, this is what is said to happen: The receiver of the baptism has the grace of justification, or what is sometimes called the righteousness of Christ, infused into the soul, which means it is poured into the soul of the believer. There it resides and inhabits the soul. However, that grace supposedly can be augmented or diminished. Rome has a tendency to speak of that grace in quantitative terms rather than qualitative terms.

In any case, here at the beginning of justification, there is an affirmation that

grace and the righteousness of Christ are required, but how the sinner gets that righteousness is through an infusion of grace into the soul. Once that grace is infused, virtually automatically by the sacrament of baptism, then the recipients of baptism must give their cooperation to such an extent that they become actually righteous. Only when righteousness is "inherent" in those individuals (as a result of their cooperation with this infused grace) do they enter a state of justification. God will declare them just or righteous only when righteousness inheres within them.

Please note that they could not be righteous without the infusion of the righteousness of Christ, but they also could not be righteous without their own cooperation. Once both of these occur, they are righteous and in a state of justification, in which they remain unless or until they commit mortal sin.

## Center of Controversy

The Roman Catholic Church distinguishes between mortal and venial sin. Venial sin is real sin, but it is not serious enough to kill the justifying grace that is in the soul. Mortal sin is called mortal because it kills or destroys the grace of justification. Some of the mortal sins in Roman Catholic theology are adultery, murder, stealing, drunkenness, and missing mass on Sunday. If an individual commits one of these sins, then he loses his justification.

One would then think that if a person

lost his justification through mortal sin that the remedy would be to go back to the church and say, "Baptize me again." But Rome believes that even though someone may lose his justification, he still maintains an indelible mark from his original baptism. The sinner is not baptized again, but instead, the remedy comes from what the church defines as the second plank of justification, the sacrament of penance, "for those who have made shipwreck of their souls." It was the sacrament of penance that was at the center of the controversy in the sixteenth century that brought about the biggest schism in the history of Christendom.

To be clear, the sacrament of penance has several components to it, including confession, absolution, and works of satisfaction.

When I talk with evangelicals and ask, "What is the difference between you and a Catholic?" the most common response is this: "I don't have to go to confession." Yet that is not the most prominent difference, for Christians should not be opposed to confessing sins. The New Testament advises us to confess our sins one to another. Even Luther kept the confessional in the sixteenth century. We are uncomfortable with a priest saying, "I absolve you" because we acknowledge that we have but one priest, and it is Jesus Christ alone who gives anyone absolution.

But as evangelicals, once again we have to be careful to not paint a caricature, for historically, the Roman Catholic Church does not believe that the priest has some kind of inherent magical power to forgive sins. Priestly absolution, in terms of their doctrine, is what is understood as the priest speaking on behalf of Christ by announcing Christ's forgiveness of sins to those who repent.

At the time of the Reformation, it was not absolution and it was not confession that created the firestorm. It was the next part of penance, the works of satisfaction, which are necessary for the sacrament to work. As an integral and necessary part of the sacrament, the repentant sinner, to be restored to the state of justification, is required to perform certain works to satisfy the demands of God. When these works are completed, the sinner receives a specific type of merit that is needed to restore his standing before God.

It is helpful to note that there are different categories or types of merit. *Condign merit* is merit of such a high level of virtue that it imposes an obligation upon God, who is just and righteous to reward it. *Congruous merit* is merit good enough that it would be congruous or "fitting" for God to restore justification to an individual. *Supererogatory merit* is above and beyond what God requires of His people. There have been just a handful of people in history who, according to Rome, when they died, were in such a state of righteousness that they went directly to heaven.

**The Antithesis of Biblical Justification**

The overwhelming majority of people who die, even though they do not die in a state of mortal sin, still have abiding impurities on their soul. And as long as an individual has impurities in his life at the time of death, instead of going to heaven, he goes to purgatory, which is called purgatory because it is the place of purging—where impurities are cleansed. It is in purgatory that the impure man is molded, shaped, and made righteous enough to get into heaven. Some individuals may spend only a few hours in purgatory, while others may be there for years, and some even up to millions of years.

If I had to go to purgatory to be cleansed of the impurities that remain in my life, I would have a hard time knowing when my parole date was due. This reminds me of a time when I was introduced by John MacArthur at a conference. John said,

> Before I give my address, I have to confess this dreadful dream that I had last night. I dreamed that I died and I stood before the gates of heaven. There was Peter, and he said, "John, we have been waiting for you. We expected you, but we have a little exercise for you to go through before you can get in."
>
> Peter pointed over to the side, and there was a large ladder that stretched up through the clouds as far as the eye could see. He said, "You have to go over there and climb that ladder, and you have to put a mark on every rung for every sin that you have committed in your life." Angels came over to me carrying a big white log of chalk. And they put this log on my shoulder, and I could barely lift it, but I balanced it there.
>
> I got on the ladder and I leaned forward and checked the first rung. Then I went up and checked the second rung. I was on that ladder for two weeks and I could see no diminution in the size of that log. All of a sudden, I saw movement above me. I had to move my hand, because there was a foot coming down the ladder. I looked up...and it was R.C. Sproul coming down for more chalk.

We all had a good laugh. But beloved, there is not enough chalk in the world to get me to the top of that ladder. That is why the Roman Catholic gospel is no gospel. It is horrible news, and I would despair altogether in that schema. Luther said the true gospel has no place for the sinner claiming merit of any kind before almighty God; the only merit that can save is the merit of Christ and Christ alone.

Yet many poor souls have sought to gain merit in purgatory through indulgences. People in the Middle Ages made arduous journeys to Rome and to other places in order to receive indulgences that would supposedly reduce their sentence or their loved one's sentence in purgatory.

It is no wonder these people were driven to visit every place that had relics.

Frederick III, the Elector of Saxony, wanted his university in Wittenberg to rival all the other universities in Germany and in Europe. He had the same goal for his relic collection in Wittenberg. He had amassed more than 15,000 relics, and spent a fortune to bring them to Wittenberg. His collection included what was said to be a vial of milk from the breast of the Virgin Mary, pieces of the cross, and a hair from the beard of John the Baptist. The indulgence value of the collection of relics in Wittenberg at the time of the Reformation was said to be 1,907,000 years. Which meant that if a pilgrim came to Wittenberg and looked at each relic there, he could buy 1,907,000 years of time off from purgatory. The alarming thing about this is that the largest professing body of Christendom still practices it.

These indulgences could take time off of a purgatory sentence only by getting merit from the treasury of merit, which is like a celestial bank account in which the excess merits of a few are deposited. I mentioned earlier that the average person is going to spend a long time in purgatory before he gets to heaven, but Rome claims there are a few people who live lives that are righteous enough that they go directly to heaven. In fact, there are some in church history who are said to have been so righteous that they have accrued for themselves a surplus of merit—people like St. Francis, St.

Augustine, Francis Xavier, and Thomas Aquinas. Their surplus is deposited into the treasury of merit, and it is the church in general, and the pope in particular, who has the keys of the kingdom and access to that treasury of merit. Therefore, the pope has the authority to make withdrawals and apply those merits to people who are deficient in their righteousness.

Much of this system stems from when the church was building St. Peter's Basilica in Rome and it needed the finances to do so. One of the works of satisfaction tied to the sacrament of penance was the giving of alms. If a person was truly sorry for his sins and wanted to be restored to justification, one of the things he could do was show the sincerity of his repentance by giving alms to the church.

## A Monk and a Mallet

In the sixteenth century, Rome had made it clear that these indulgences were not to be understood as salvation for sale. The peasants were supposed to have it explained to them that the only way they would get these indulgences was if their alms-giving was from a true spirit of penitence, and not out of a crass sense of trying to buy their way into heaven.

Justification is by faith alone, not by faith and something else. Justification is by grace alone. Justification is by Christ alone.

However, the representative in Germany, Johann Tetzel, did not have time for such subtleties. Instead, he made up his little jingle: "Every time a coin in the kettle rings, a soul from purgatory springs." Luther was outraged and penned the 95 Theses, which mentioned the corruption of the sacrament of penance, the corruption of indulgences, the corruption of the treasury of merit, and raised questions about the whole system of purgatory and even beyond that, the whole system of justification. Luther understood that it was not faith plus works, not grace plus merit, not inherent righteousness plus the righteousness of Christ that becomes the means and the grounds upon which an individual is justified. Luther made use of a single word that became the buzzword of the Reformation—*sola*. Justification is by faith alone, not by faith and something else. Justification is by grace alone. Justification is by Christ alone. And the Reformation was off and running.

## Catholic Faith and Justification

The Roman Catholic Church does not delete faith's role in justification; it just creates an unbiblical perspective of it. The Council of Trent stressed the necessity of faith in order to be justified. According to Trent, faith helps justification in three ways: Faith is the *initium*, the *fundamentum*, and the *radix* of justification.

Faith being the *initium* of justification means that it initiates but does not accomplish justification. That is to say, it is a necessary condition for justification, but it is not a sufficient condition for justification. You cannot be justified without it, but its mere presence is not enough to justify you. Sadly, in Rome's view, a person can have true faith and not possess justification.

Second, faith is the *fundamentum*—that is, the foundation upon which justification is established. We would disagree and state that when true faith is present, it has the certificate of occupancy already because all that is necessary for justification has taken place because our faith is in Christ, who justifies the sinner.

Third, faith is the *radix* or the root of justification. Apparently you can have the initiation of justification, the foundation of justification, and the root of justification, yet no true justification. The only time and only way God will ever declare anyone just is if and when that person actually is just, according to Rome.

How lacking is this system of belief. A person gets a quick dose of justification at baptism. It lasts as long as the individual refrains from committing mortal sin. If mortal sin is committed, that person loses his justification, but can retrieve it through the sacrament of penance. If the individual has enough righteousness that inheres in his soul, he can go to heaven. If there is mortal sin left when he dies, he goes to hell. But if he is merely impure, he goes to purgatory. Not until after the purging flames of that place cleanse him of his impurities is he finally worthy to enter into the kingdom of God.

## Clinging to the True Gospel

The Roman Catholic gospel is no gospel. For there is no other gospel except the gospel that is set forth clearly for us in the New Testament. The day the Roman Church anathematized justification by faith alone, it anathematized itself. When the church in the Middle Ages committed apostasy, it stopped being the church.

Many ecumenical movements are arising. Even professing evangelicals are saying, as they join hands with members of the Roman Catholic Church, that they have a unity of faith in the gospel. I have said to them, "If you have a unity of faith in the gospel with these people, you do not have a unity of faith in the gospel with me." Why? Because the Roman Catholic Church is embracing the Tridentine Doctrine of Trent, their view of the gospel, which ultimately denies the gospel of Jesus Christ.

Beloved, if you are unwilling to contend for this, then get out of the way because you are pleasing men rather than Christ. Luther warned that this would happen, just as Jude, Peter, and Paul warned us too. Luther said at the end of his life that his great fear was that the light that had burst forth with the rediscovery of the gospel would go out again in the next generation, that the gospel would be eclipsed into obscurity. Why is there a temptation to let this happen? Because anytime the gospel is preached

boldly and accurately, it creates conflict, and as human beings, we naturally want to avoid conflict with others.

But the reality is that doctrine divides. It divided the prophets of Israel from the false prophets. It divided Jesus from the Pharisees. It divided the apostles from those who despised them. Anyone who has ever stayed the course of the gospel has known and will know conflict. At some point, we have to say with Luther, who in "A Mighty Fortress Is Our God" penned the words, "Let goods and kindred go, this mortal life also." Forsaking all, we cling to the gospel of Jesus Christ, for there is no hope elsewhere.

I did not grow up in an evangelical Christian home. I grew up in the heart of paganism. Christ saved me while I was still a sinner. He looked and found no inherent righteousness in me.

I understood right away that my only hope in life was in Christ. If I had to wait to become righteous or to be counted righteous, my condition was utterly hopeless. You take away justification by faith alone from me, you are taking away Christ and His gospel.

My dear friends, you must not shrink from this battle. God will hold you accountable on the last day. Proclaim the whole counsel of God to every one of those people whom God has entrusted to your care. You cannot love the world so much that you allow the gospel to go into eclipse. For that is no love at all. Remember Paul's warning: "Even if we, or an angel from heaven, should preach to you a gospel contrary to what we have preached to you, he is to be accursed" (Galatians 1:8).

## Our Monument

If you go to Geneva today you can visit the Reformation Wall, a huge wall that commemorates the Reformation. Chiseled into the wall are the words *Post Tenebras Lux*, Latin for "After darkness, light." My great fear is that the monument of our age will read, "After the light, darkness." May it never be. Master the gospel of justification by faith alone in Christ alone. And make sure that your people understand it in its fullness.

# PRAYER

Father, we understand that we stand before You by grace alone, through faith alone, and in Christ alone. We pray that You would increase our love for the sweetness of that gospel, that we might have a clearer understanding of it and a passion to communicate and defend it wherever that battle rages. We ask You in Jesus' name and for His sake. Amen.

# 7

# THE EXTENT OF THE ATONEMENT

*Phil Johnson*
*Shepherds' Conference 2003*

*Selected Scriptures*

For whom did Christ die? Did the Good Shepherd give His life for the sheep, or did He die for all people without exception? Did He merely make forgiveness possible for anyone and everyone, or did He actually secure redemption for the elect? What, precisely, did God intend to accomplish through the death of His Son—and will His design be fully realized? Above all, is there a limit to the worth or value of the atoning sacrifice Christ offered?

Those questions are all part of the perennial debate between Calvinists and Arminians regarding the extent of the atonement. They are important and valid questions—but only if we can first agree on the question of *how* the death of Christ made atonement for sin.

Scripture says "Christ died for our sins" (1 Corinthians 15:3)—"the just for the unjust" (1 Peter 3:18). God "made Him who knew no sin to be sin on our behalf, so that we might become the righteousness of God in Him" (2 Corinthians 5:21). "Christ redeemed us from the curse of the Law, having become a curse for us" (Galatians 3:13). He "was delivered over because of our transgressions" (Romans 4:25). "He was pierced through for our transgressions, He was crushed for our iniquities; the chastening for our well-being fell upon Him" (Isaiah 53:5).

Those statements are clear, and this is by far the most vital truth to understand about the crucifixion: *It was a substitutionary sacrifice.* Christ died in the place and in the stead of those whom He saves. His death on the cross paid the penalty of their sin in full. He suffered everything condemned sinners deserve under the wrath of almighty God. In return

He gives believers a right standing before God, with immense, eternal blessings that only He rightfully deserves. Those who trust Him alone as Savior are spiritually united with Him, and His righteousness counts as theirs. Having fully atoned for their sins, He now covers them with the glorious garment of His own absolute perfection.

One's view of the *extent* of the atonement is comparatively insignificant next to the all-important truth that Christ's suffering and death were a vicarious payment of sin's penalty—a *penal substitution*. On that issue all truly evangelical Protestants have historically been in full agreement. Individuals and denominations who have experimented with alternative theories about the atonement have invariably drifted into liberalism, pietism, sacerdotalism, or other forms of works-based religion. In other words, when someone abandons the principle of penal substitution, that person has already moved outside the circle of evangelical orthodoxy.

On the other hand, if you accept the fact that Christ's death on the cross was a penal substitution, you have already affirmed the central principle underlying the historic Calvinist position on the extent of the atonement. The Calvinist view is often referred to as "limited atonement," but that's an unfortunate and misleading name. It's an expression invented for the sake of the TULIP acronym (a mnemonic device for remembering the so-called "five points of Calvinism"). But

to describe the atonement as "limited" wrongly gives the impression that Calvinists believe the sacrifice Christ offered was of finite value. That is emphatically not the case.

## The Five Points

To speak of "the five points of Calvinism" is likewise misleading. John Calvin never outlined the doctrines of grace in five points, nor was he personally involved in the debate from which the five points arose. The Arminians—followers of James Arminius—were responsible for singling out and highlighting the five points. Nearly a half-century after Calvin's death they brought a complaint against the teaching of the Reformed churches of Holland. Their protest was delivered in the form of a document known as the Five Articles of Remonstrance. In response, the Reformed church convened the Synod of Dort in 1618, and they issued a list of written replies organized under the five heads of doctrine suggested by the Arminian remonstrants' five objections. The Canons of the Synod of Dort is therefore the original and definitive source of the principles popularly known as the five points of Calvinism.

It's not clear who first arranged the five points under the acronym TULIP. The arrangement seems to date back to the early twentieth century. It's an easy way to remember the five points but perhaps not the best way to understand them accurately.

The *T* stands for *total depravity.* That's the common theological shorthand label used to signify this principle, but it can be somewhat misleading. To say the human race is fallen and "totally depraved" is not to suggest that all people are as bad as they could possibly be. The idea instead is that sin has infected every aspect of our being: mind, emotions, will, body, soul, imagination, subconscious—and every other faculty capable of giving vent to what's in our hearts. Some prefer to use the expression "total inability," stressing the fact that sinners are so infected with sin that they cannot please God (Romans 8:8). That's what we mean when we say human depravity is total. It is an utter inability to do anything good to earn favor with God. Sin poisons the whole person. What we do, what we think, what we love, what we choose— all of it is contaminated with sin. We are thoroughly sinful. That doesn't mean we are as evil as we could possibly be. It just means that no part of our being is free from the taint of sin.

*U* is for *unconditional election.* This means God chooses who will be saved, and He does it not because of anything good He finds in the sinner. Lots of people try to tiptoe around the doctrine of election, but you can't do that and be faithful to the biblical text. Ephesians 1:4 distinctly says that God "chose us in Him before the foundation of the world." Furthermore, election is unconditional in the sense that it is not based on some foreseen act of faith (or any other good

thing in the person whom God chooses). It is determined solely by the good pleasure of God's own choice. According to Ephesians 1:11, we are "predestined according to His purpose who works all things after the counsel of His will." We don't elect ourselves by responding to the gospel. God chose us before time began. We were sovereignly drawn to Christ, as Jesus told the disciples in John 15:16: "You did not choose Me but I chose you." The expression *unconditional election* stresses the fact that God's choice was determinative. "We love, because He first loved us" (1 John 4:19).

*L* stands for *limited atonement.* This, of course, is the doctrine we are chiefly concerned with, and as noted, I'm not fond of the expression. *Particular redemption* is a more suitable term, stressing the fact that God had a definite plan in the atonement, and His design will be fully accomplished. (It's worth noting that *everyone,* even the rankest Arminian, believes the atonement is limited in some sense—unless you want to opt for a universal atonement, where everyone without exception will ultimately be saved. The notion of a completely *un*limited atonement is patently unbiblical.)

The *I* stands for *irresistible grace,* and this is another expression that sometimes misleads people. Dave Hunt claimed that those who call grace irresistible are in effect suggesting that God employs force or violence against the free will of whoever He draws to Christ. But that idea is expressly repudiated in virtually every classic Calvinist doctrinal statement. The Westminster Confession of Faith, for example, emphatically says that while God is absolutely sovereign, "neither is God the author of sin, nor is violence offered to the will of the creatures" (WCF 3.1). Rather, grace is "irresistible" in the same way we might say the laughter of a happy infant is irresistible. God's grace draws people by attraction; He does not compel us by force. He opens our eyes to the glory of Christ, and we find that glory *irresistible*. The actual point is that God's saving grace is always *effectual*. Jesus said in John 6:37, "All that the Father gives Me will come to Me." God will not fail to save those whom He elects.

And finally, the *P* in TULIP is for *perseverance of the saints*. The biblical doctrine of perseverance teaches that those who are in Christ will never fully or finally fall away (1 John 2:19). This doctrine seems particularly confusing for some. By no means should we ever imagine that we as believers might summon the power to persevere in the faith by our own power or through the independent exercise of human free will. Nor does it mean that a person can abandon the faith and yet remain certain of salvation and eternal security. Those who do fall away give irrefutable proof that they never really knew Christ (1 John 2:19). True believers always persevere, because God graciously *keeps* us in the faith. We "are protected by the power of God through faith for a salvation ready

to be revealed in the last time" (1 Peter 1:5). It's not that the saints have any ability to hold fast by their own power, but that God's grace sovereignly secures their perseverance. He is the one "who is able to keep you from stumbling, and to make you stand in the presence of His glory blameless with great joy" (Jude 24).

Those are the doctrines popularly known as the five points of Calvinism. I affirm them all, insofar as they are properly understood in light of Scripture.

But recognizing that many stumble when they encounter the principle commonly referred to as limited atonement, we need to take a closer look at that doctrine and consider carefully what the Bible says about it.

## Particular Redemption

First, let's acknowledge that this issue is the most difficult of all the five points to understand and accept. At least four out of five Calvinists will say that this is the last of the five points they came to grips with. It is not an easy issue, and we should not pretend that it is.

Second, because this is not a simple issue, it should not be considered simplistically. It's vital to understand that there is not just one view for the limited atonement position and another view for the unlimited atonement position, as if there are two polar opposites that compete against each other. This is not really an "either-or" question, even among Calvinists. In fact, historically, the most intense debates about limited atonement have been intramural, among people who hold to different flavors of Calvinism. There are at least three major divisions of Calvinists: high, moderate, and low Calvinists. They all have different views, and there are many shades and degrees in between. In fact, I doubt if you could find any two Calvinists who agree completely with one another on every text and every nuance related to this topic.

Questions related to the extent of the atonement caused a huge debate among Calvinists during the Marrow Controversy in Scotland in the 1700s. This was also one of the major issues on which Andrew Fuller contended with other Calvinistic Baptists during the late eighteenth century in England. It has been continual fodder for debate among Welsh Calvinists since the beginning of the 1700s. In 2002, The Banner of Truth Trust published the first English version of a classic Welsh book on this issue, *The Atonement Controversy in Welsh Theological Literature and Debate, 1707–1841.*

If you want to sample some moderate opinions on the extent of the atonement from leading mainstream Calvinist writers, read what Andrew Fuller, Thomas Boston, Robert L. Dabney, William G.T. Shedd, B.B. Warfield, and Charles Hodge wrote on the subject. They may surprise you. Read John Owen too, but do not imagine that Owen's book *The Death of Death in the Death of Christ* represents the only strain of Calvinist thought on the issue. It does not—in fact, far from it.

Anyone who studies this issue in depth will quickly discover that the classic Calvinist view on the extent of the atonement is a lot less narrow and a lot less cut-and-dried than some of today's young, aggressive Calvinists would like to admit. Historic Calvinism as a movement has generally acknowledged that there *are* universal aspects of the atonement. Calvin himself clearly did not hold the rigid views some of today's ultra-high Calvinists are trying to defend on the Internet. Despite what you might read in some of those militant Internet discussions, it's not necessarily unorthodox or anti-Calvinistic to "testify that the Father has sent the Son to be the Savior of the world" (1 John 4:14).

Let me also admit that this is one issue where historical theology is not overwhelmingly on the side of the Calvinists. Until some of the later Catholic scholastics raised this question and began to debate about it in the Middle Ages, most of the church fathers and leading theological writers in the church, both orthodox and heretical, assumed that Christ died for all humanity and that was the end of that. There are some exceptions, like Theodoret of Cyrus (AD 393–466), who wrote this about Hebrews 9:27-28: "It should be noted, of course, that [Christ] bore the sins of many, not of all: not all came to faith so He removed the sins of the believers only."[1]

Ambrose (AD 339–397), wrote this: "Although Christ suffered for all, yet He suffered for us particularly, because He suffered for the church."[2] Jerome (AD 347–420), a contemporary of Augustine, commented on Matthew 20:28: "He does not say that he gave his life for all, but for many, that is, for all those who would believe."[3] Those are classic Calvinist statements. You can find little remarks like that here and there among the church fathers, but for the most part, when they wrote about the atonement, they treated it as universal.

My friend Curt Daniel has written an excellent syllabus that I want to recommend, titled *The History and Theology of Calvinism* (Dallas: Scholarly Reprints, 1993). It is the best single overview of Calvinism I have encountered. It is filled with copious quotations and wonderful insight, and he covers the differing opinions Calvinists have expressed regarding how to explain the universal and particular aspects of the atonement. Another resource I recommend is Paul Helm's *Calvin & the Calvinists* (Edinburgh: Banner of Truth, 1982). This work makes a persuasive case to show that Calvin himself was indeed a five-point Calvinist. Several popular authors have tried to argue otherwise, but Helm convincingly refutes their thesis.

I'll cite just one quotation that settles the question of whether Calvin held to the doctrine of particular redemption. Commenting on 1 John 2:2, he wrote, "Under the word *all* or whole, he does not include the reprobate, but designates those who should believe as well as those who were then scattered through various parts of the world."[4]

I have said all this to stress that this is the most despised and controversial of all the teachings of Calvinism. And even among Calvinists, there is a lot of debate.

## Infinitely Sufficient

Now, you may be asking, "If you admit that this wasn't held by many of the church fathers and only loosely held by Calvin himself, why make an issue out of it at all?" Because there is an important point of truth in seeing how the atoning work of Christ applies to the elect in a particular sense by the design and purpose of God.

The average person thinks this debate is all about the sufficiency and the value of Christ's atoning work, but that is not the disagreement. In the Second Head, Article 3 of Canons of the Synod of Dort we read, "The death of the Son of God is the only and most perfect sacrifice and satisfaction for sin, and is of infinite worth and value, abundantly sufficient to expiate the sins of the whole world." That is the canonical Calvinist manifesto. Calvinists have *always* believed and emphatically affirmed that the sacrifice of Christ was of infinitely sufficient value.

In other words, if one more person had been elect, Christ would not have had to suffer more than He did. Not one more blow from the Roman scourge would have been necessary. Not one more thorn would have been added to

His crown. He would not have needed to spend one more moment under God's wrath in order to atone for those additional souls, even if God *had* sovereignly chosen to save every person who ever lived. Not only that, but if God had intended to redeem Adam alone and leave the rest of us to bear the curse and the punishment of our sin in eternal hell, Christ would have not had to suffer any less than He did. Infinite value, by definition, cannot be diminished or added to in any respect.

I occasionally meet Calvinists who bristle or balk whenever someone says the atonement Christ offered was "sufficient for the whole world but efficacious only for the elect." But to say that is simply to affirm an important truth that the Canons of the Synod of Dort specifically singled out and stressed—namely, that the death of Christ was of infinite value and dignity.

Now, I should mention that there are indeed a few Calvinists who hold to a limited-sufficiency view of the atonement. They do not like saying that the atonement is of infinite value. Tom Nettles, for example, does not seem to agree with the Synod of Dort on this. In the book *By His Grace and for His Glory*, Nettles traces the roots of Calvinist doctrine throughout Baptist history. I recommend the book even though I would disagree strongly with Nettles on this point about the atonement. Nettles argues that if Christ's death was substitutionary, then He died for particular sins of particular people. If He died for particular sins,

then He did not die for other sins than those. Nettles seems to see such a one-for-one equivalence between our sins and the price of their atonement that he denies the sufficiency of the atonement to save anyone but those for whom it was designed to save. He writes, "The just nature of God does not permit him to inflict more wrath on the substitute than actually becomes effectual for forgiveness of the criminal. Nor does the love of God for the Son permit such an overkill."[5] Nettles apparently holds a view that some would call *equivalentism*. It is the notion that Christ suffered just so much, a finite amount in relation to the sins of the elect.

It pains me to disagree with Tom Nettles, but it needs to be said that his position stands in opposition to the Synod of Dort and the mainstream of historic Calvinism. His basic argument is that if Christ's atonement was substitutionary, then it had to be for particular sins and therefore it had a specific, finite value. I would argue instead that if the atonement Christ offered is substitutionary, then it *had to be of infinite value* for two reasons. One, as the Synod of Dort points out, the Person who submitted to the punishment on our behalf was not only really a man and perfectly holy, but also the only begotten Son of God, of the same eternal and infinite essence with the Father and the Holy Spirit. Because the Person who died on the cross was infinite in His glory and His goodness, His death was an infinite sacrifice.

Second, the punishment due each person for sin is endless wrath. An eternity in hell is not sufficient to atone for sin. So the price of atonement is infinite, and therefore the atonement itself, in order to be accepted, had to be of infinite value. That is precisely what the principle of *penal substitution* means—that Christ bore an immeasurable outpouring of divine wrath on the cross, taking on Himself everything sinners deserve. If Christ's death was not sufficient to atone for all, then it was not sufficient to atone for even one—because atonement for sin, even for one person, demands an infinite price.

**The Crux of the Matter**

The real debate between Calvinists and Arminians is not about the *sufficiency* of the atonement. The real issue is the design and the application of the atonement. Was it God's purpose to save specific people, or was He trying indiscriminately to save as many people as possible? What was His intent? What was His design? *Did Christ's death perfectly fulfill the plan of redemption as God ordained it?*

If you answer that question yes, you are affirming the principle underlying the Calvinistic position. Here are some even more important questions: Will all of God's purposes for sending Christ to die ultimately be accomplished? Did God intend something by the atonement that will not come to pass? Is there any divinely ordained purpose in Christ's dying that will ultimately be frustrated?

Asking those questions puts the importance of the whole issue in a totally different and clearer light.

The earliest Christians firmly believed, as I do, that the death of Christ will accomplish everything God's hand and His purpose predestined (Acts 4:28)—no more, no less. If we believe God is truly sovereign, we must ultimately come to that position. God is not going to be frustrated throughout all eternity because He was desperately trying to save some people who just could not be persuaded. That is how many Christians think redemption works. It is a grossly unbiblical way of thinking about God. The one true God who reveals Himself in Scripture says He planned and ordained the end of all things before the beginning of time, and He distinctly adds this: "My purpose will be established, and I will accomplish all My good pleasure" (Isaiah 46:10).

Christ's atoning work also accomplishes no *more* than God intended it to accomplish. If benefits accrue to nonbelievers because of Christ's death, then it is because God designed it that way. If Christ's dying means that the judgment of the whole world is postponed, then unregenerate people reap the benefits and the blessings of common grace *through the atonement*. That is exactly the outcome God designed. It did not happen by accident.

So this is my position (and it has been the teaching of most Calvinists throughout history): Some benefits of the atonement are universal, and some benefits of the atonement are particular and limited to the elect alone.

## Substitutionary Atonement

It is important to mention that ultimately, we cannot escape the limited and particular aspects of the atonement if we believe Christ's death on the cross was substitutionary. Let me illustrate: Did Christ suffer for Pharaoh's sins in Pharaoh's place and in his stead? Certainly not, because when Christ died on the cross, Pharaoh was already in hell suffering for his own sin. Those who suffer in hell all suffer for their own sin. Christ does not suffer on their behalf in the same way He did for people who are ultimately redeemed and delivered from hell. That's a rather obvious point, if you think about it.

The substitutionary aspects of the atonement therefore ultimately belong to the elect alone. Jesus bore their punishments so that they will not have to. If He had suffered vicariously for the sins of Judas in the same way He suffered in Peter's place, then Judas would not be suffering right now for his own sins. That is the inevitable ramification of vicarious atonement.

## Universal Ramifications

At the same time, there are universal aspects of the atoning work of Christ, and historic Calvinism has always recognized this. That is exactly the meaning of 1 Timothy 4:10, which is perhaps the best,

clearest text in all of Scripture to settle this whole question: "We have fixed our hope on the living God, who is the Savior of all men, especially of believers." R.B. Kuiper famously said he preferred to speak of Christ's dying *especially* for the elect rather than *only* for them. He wrote, "God designed to save *the elect* through the death of His Son...[But] the statement, so often heard from Reformed pulpits, that Christ died *only* for the elect must be rated a careless one."[6] To those who believe, Christ is Savior in a special and particular sense. His death had a particular reference to them in the ultimate design of God.

Curt Daniel gives a helpful illustration of how this is true by pointing to the parable in Matthew 13:44: "The kingdom of heaven is like a treasure hidden in the field, which a man found and hid again; and from joy over it he goes and sells all that he has and buys that field." Buying the field ensures that the man buys the treasure. The treasure was the object and the aim of his purchase. The treasure was the reason for His great joy. The treasure was the reason He made this deal in the first place. But He did not purchase the treasure only; He purchased the whole field. That is a good way, I think, to look at the atoning work of Christ.

Read Romans 14:9: "To this end Christ died and lived again, that He might be Lord both of the dead and of the living." Notice that the verse is teaching us that because of Christ's death and resurrection, He is Lord of all men in a special way. His death on the cross purchased the right for Him, as perfect man and perfect God, to rule as Lord over all the earth—over both the dead and the living, over the redeemed as well as the reprobate. That is also the same message we find in Philippians 2:8-10: "Being found in appearance as a man, He humbled Himself by becoming obedient to the point of death, even death on a cross. For this reason also, God highly exalted Him, and bestowed on Him the name which is above every name, so that at the name of Jesus every knee will bow, of those who are in heaven and on earth and under the earth."

That is a very clear statement that there is a universal ramification of the atonement. Christ's death, in some sense, purchased Him an exalted position of lordship over all. There is a true sense in which Jesus purchased the whole world in order to get the treasure, the church. Meanwhile, there are certain benefits of the atonement that accrue directly to those whom God has not chosen for salvation, the reprobate.

## Blessings of Common Grace

Spurgeon said it well in a sermon entitled, "Good Cheer for Many That Fear." He preached, "We believe that by His atoning sacrifice, Christ bought some good things for all men and all good things for some men."[7] What specifically did Spurgeon have in mind when he said that "Christ bought some good things for all men"? Clearly, he was speaking of common grace—the goodness of God and the common blessings of life that are shown to all men. This is the grace that keeps the evil in the world from being as bad as it could possibly be. Common grace is the grace that permits all sinners to live and enjoy life under a temporary reprieve from judgment and justice. Even though sinners are worthy of instant damnation, common grace delays that. Common grace pleads tenderly and earnestly with sinners to repent and to be reconciled to God, even though their hearts are set against Him.

According to Matthew 5:45, "He causes His sun to rise on the evil and the good, and sends rain on the righteous and the unrighteous." God loves the world! For those of you who feel like breaking out the torches and pitchforks whenever someone declares that God loves the whole world, I plead with you to tread lightly, because Scripture does not stop short of stating that truth. This goodness that God shows even to the reprobate is sincere, bona fide, compassionate *love*. It is not the same eternal, redemptive love that God has set on the elect from all eternity. It is love of a different sort, but it is true and genuinely well-meant love nonetheless.

Think carefully about it, and you will realize that every good thing God gives us—including the blessings of common grace—are made possible by the atonement. Because if God had no intention to save anyone ever, He would have instantly damned the whole human race the minute Adam sinned. That is what He did with the angels who fell. They were cast out of heaven at once, and no atonement will ever be made for the sins of any angel.

By contrast, the human race fell, and for the most part, still lives and enjoys life in a world where only we are blessed to an amazing degree with the providential care of a benevolent "God, who richly supplies us with all things to enjoy" (1 Timothy 6:17)—even though we are under the curse of sin. We see beauty and we enjoy the taste of our food. John MacArthur points out that if God wanted to, He could have made all our food taste like sand. But instead, He is good to us. "He Himself gives to all people life and breath and all things" (Acts 17:25). We laugh, experience joy, appreciate love, and we relish the good things of life. All these things are ultimately made possible by the atoning work of Christ. None of them would have been possible at all if Christ had not intended to die to save sinners. God would have instantly damned us all instead. In a superb book on the extent of the atonement, Robert Candlish included a key chapter titled "The Universal Dispensation of Gracious Forbearance—Its Connection with the Atonement," in which he argued persuasively that all the blessings of common grace are made possible by the atoning work of Christ. He wrote,

It is, then, a great fact, that the death of Christ, or his work of

obedience and propitiation, has procured for the world at large, and for every individual—the impenitent and unbelieving as well as the "chosen, and called, and faithful"—certain definite, tangible, and ascertainable benefits; benefits, I mean, not nominal, but real; and not of a vague, but of a well-defined and specific character. Of these the first and chief—that which in truth comprehends all the rest—is the universal grant to all mankind of a season of forbearance, a respite or suspension of judgment, a day or dispensation of grace.[8]

The reprobate therefore benefit from Christ's death, for the crumbs that fall from the table God spreads for His elect are a veritable feast for everyone. They experience all the blessings of common grace. That is a side benefit of the cross and an expression of God's goodness toward sinners.

High Calvinists and hyper-Calvinists sometimes argue that common grace is not really an expression of love or goodness toward the reprobate, because it only increases their damnation. It is true, in the words of Romans 2:4, that unbelievers "think lightly of the riches of His kindness and tolerance and patience"—and they will be held guilty for treating His grace with such contempt. But it is a serious affront to the character of God to suggest that His only purpose in showing common grace to the reprobate is to increase their guilt. One of the most important ways God acts graciously toward the wicked is by restraining the expression of their sinfulness. Most people are not as bad as they could be. None are as bad as they *would* be if God left them to themselves without any grace whatsoever. It should be obvious to anyone who understands human depravity that, on the whole, common grace decreases the severity of human guilt. A.A. Hodge wrote, "The entire history of the human race, from the apostasy to the final judgment, is, as Candlish says, 'a dispensation of forbearance' in respect to the reprobate, in which many blessings, physical and moral, affecting their characters and destinies for ever, accrue even to the heathen."[9]

R.B. Kuiper wrote in a similar vein: "The blessings of common grace, although resulting only indirectly from the atonement, were most surely designed by God to result from the atonement. The design of God in the atoning work of Christ pertained primarily and directly to the redemption of the elect, but indirectly and secondarily it included all the blessings of common grace."[10]

## The Free Offer of Salvation

Kuiper identified several universal benefits of the atonement—more than just common grace. For example, he wrote, "No other blessing of the common grace of God is as great as *the universal and sincere offer of salvation*, nor is

any other more obviously a fruit of the atonement."[11] He continued, "At no time is the gospel confined to any nation or for that matter, to any particular class of men. It is intended for Jews, Greeks, barbarians, and Scythians."[12]

Scripture supports this truth that the gospel does not discriminate. Colossians 3:11 says, "There is no distinction between Greek and Jew, circumcised and uncircumcised, barbarian, Scythian, slave and freeman." In Matthew 11:28, Jesus said, "Come to Me, all who are weary and heavy-laden, and I will give you rest." About those verses Kuiper wrote, "To say that such invitations... are intended only for those who, having been born again through the grace of the Holy Spirit, have come to realize their lost condition, is to limit the meaning of Scripture without warrant. Let it be said emphatically that the Reformed theology does not teach, as some allege, that the gospel invitation is only for the elect and the regenerate."[13]

There is no necessary contradiction between God's eternal sovereign design to save the elect and His sincere pleas for the reprobate to repent. When we preach the gospel, according to 2 Corinthians 5, it is our duty to plead with all who hear the message that they be reconciled to God. Paul wrote in 2 Corinthians 5:20, "We are ambassadors for Christ, as though God were making an appeal through us; we beg you on behalf of Christ, be reconciled to God." If you are not proclaiming the gospel to everyone with the confidence that they can be saved, you are not a good ambassador for Christ. If you are a Calvinist and you hesitate to extend God's offer of mercy freely to all—if you recoil from inviting men or pleading with them to repent and be reconciled to God—then you are not a good Calvinist.

In Ezekiel 18:23, God says, "Do I have any pleasure in the death of the wicked…rather than that he should turn from his ways and live?" Commenting on that text, Calvin wrote,

God desires nothing more earnestly than that those who were perishing and rushing to destruction should return into the way of safety. And for this reason not only is the Gospel spread abroad in the world, but God wished to bear witness through all ages how inclined he is to pity…It follows, then, that what the Prophet now says is very true, that God wills not the death of a sinner, because he meets him of his own accord, and is not only prepared to receive all who fly to his pity, but he calls them towards Him with a loud voice, when He sees how they are alienated from all hope of safety…We hold, then, that God wills not the death of a sinner, since he calls all equally to repentance, and promises himself prepared to receive them if they only seriously repent.[14]

Any variety of Calvinism that denies the free offer of salvation is out of step with John Calvin and a departure from the historic mainstream of Calvinist conviction. The gospel's call to faith and repentance is meant to be proclaimed indiscriminately to all. "God is now declaring to men that all people everywhere should repent" (Acts 17:30).

The Canons of the Synod of Dort expressly affirm that the gospel invitation is to be freely and openly broadcast to all: "The promise of the gospel is that whosoever believes in Christ crucified shall not perish, but have eternal life. This promise, together with the command to repent and believe, ought to be declared and published to all nations, and to all persons promiscuously, and without distinction, to whom God out of His good pleasure sends the gospel" (Second Head, Article 5).

To sum up, unbelievers receive a number of benefits from the atonement: delayed judgment, all the blessings of common grace, and the free offer of salvation through the gospel. Those are universal effects of Christ's atoning work, and that is why Charles Hodge, the great Calvinist theologian, wrote, "There is a sense, therefore, in which [Christ] died for all, and there is a sense in which He died for the elect alone."[15] That simply echoes the words of 1 Timothy 4:10: "We have fixed our hope on the living God, who is the Savior of all men, especially of believers."

## Particular Redemption

There is of course a definite, specific reference to the elect in the atoning work of Christ. First Timothy 4:10 plainly states Jesus is "the Savior of all men," but Jesus is not the Savior of all men equally, for He did not die for each and every individual alike. "This One is indeed the Savior of the world" (John 4:42)—but "especially of believers" (1 Timothy 4:10).

Jesus said in John 10:11, "I am the good shepherd; the good shepherd lays down His life for the sheep." The context makes Jesus' meaning inescapable. The Good Shepherd does not die for the goats or the wolves in the same way He sacrifices Himself for the sheep. He says it again in verse 15, "I lay down My life *for the sheep.*"

The apostle Paul told the elders at Ephesus, "Be on guard for yourselves and for all the flock, among which the Holy Spirit has made you overseers, to shepherd the church of God which He purchased with His own blood. I know that after my departure savage wolves will come in among you, not sparing the flock" (Acts 20:28-29). Christ purchased *the church* with His blood. It was those in the church—not the grievous wolves who were threatening the church, but the people of God—who were the object of Christ's affection, and their salvation was the main reason for which He died. The benefits that accrue to the reprobate are secondary effects of that reality.

In what sense did Christ purchase the church? In Ephesians 5:25, Paul used language that evokes the imagery of a marriage price: "Husbands, love your wives, just as Christ also loved the church and gave Himself up for her." For what reason did He purchase her? "So that He might sanctify her, having cleansed her by the washing of water with the word, that He might present to Himself the church in all her glory, having no spot or wrinkle or any such thing; but that she would be holy and blameless" (verses 26-27).

Those for whom Christ died are loved with the highest and purest kind of love. It is a particular love, and its closest earthly parallel is the love of a husband for his wife—a type of love that is not dispensed indiscriminately to everyone alike. In fact, what do we call a man who shares conjugal love with his neighbor and does not reserve it exclusively for his wife? We call him an adulterer. What would you call someone who indiscriminately showed every woman the intense ardent affection men reserve only for their wives? You would call him a philanderer.

Christ's love for His church is pure. It's more tender, more personal, and an infinitely greater love than the love of a husband for his wife.

Here is an excerpt from Curt Daniel's notes on this:

> The key is the analogy of Christ the husband dying for His bride. To understand this, we need to understand the Hebrew concept

of marriage. First, the man and the woman were betrothed to each other. This may have occurred even before either of them were born. Their parents may have arranged the betrothal. From the moment of the betrothal, they were in a sense married…nothing except death or divorce could legally prevent the marriage itself. But before the actual marriage could occur, there had to be an exchange, as it were. The father of the bride provided a dowry, and the groom provided the marriage price. In that sense, the groom "bought" his bride, even though he was already legally obliged to marry her. Then at the appointed time, they came together as man and wife.

This is a perfect type of Christ and the church…The elect were given to Christ by God the Father, and Christ was given to us also by the Father…

But, Christ the groom had to pay the marriage price for His bride. How did he do this? Because of our sins, the price was death. [Christ had to redeem us before He could take us as a bride.] Therefore, Christ gave Himself for the elect in death. The atonement purchased us for Him…

…The order here is crucial. First,

Christ loved the church; this is election (vs. 25). Next, he pays the marriage price; this is the atonement (vs. 25). Then, He prepares her for the wedding; this is salvation applied (vs. 26); lastly, He presents her to Himself in marriage; this is the final consummation of our union and glorification (vs. 27).

The point is simply this: Christ died with a special intent for His betrothed that He did not have for the rest of mankind.[16]

Notice that as a part of Jesus' mediatorial work in His high-priestly prayer, Jesus said this: "I do not ask on behalf of the world, but of those whom You have given Me; for they are Yours" (John 17:9). Now remember, when Christ prayed that prayer, He had already entered into the mediatorial office of the high priest. *He expressly excluded the world at large from His high-priestly prayer.* It seems clear from Scripture that Christ's redemptive work had a special reference to His chosen people. When He prayed that prayer, the work of atonement had begun, and He made it a point to exclude the world.

We read in Titus 2:14 that Christ "gave Himself for us to redeem us from every lawless deed, and to purify for Himself a people for His own possession, zealous for good deeds." That statement cannot apply to the reprobate. Did you realize that even your faith is a fruit of the atonement? It is a gift of God (Acts 16:14;

Romans 12:3; Philippians 1:29). Even repentance is God's work in us (Acts 5:31; 11:18; 2 Timothy 2:25).

In John 10:26, Jesus said, "You do not believe because you are not of My sheep." Now if Jesus were an Arminian, He would have said, "You are not of My sheep because you believe not." Instead, He said the exact opposite. The Good Shepherd laid down His life for the sheep, and their faith is part of His gift to them.

Jesus said in Matthew 26:28, "This is My blood of the covenant, which is poured out for many for forgiveness of sins." Paul said in Romans 5:15, "The free gift is not like the transgression. For if by the transgression of the one the many died, much more did the grace of God and the gift by the grace of the one Man, Jesus Christ, abound to the many." The author of Hebrews wrote in Hebrews 9:28, "Christ also, having been offered once to bear the sins of many, will appear a second time for salvation without reference to sin, to those who eagerly await Him." Jesus said in John 15:13-14, "Greater love has no one than this, that one lay down his life for his friends. You are My friends if you do what I command you." The reprobate are never called friends of Jesus, but those who do what He commands are His friends; and it is for them that He laid down His life.

Now let me go back to the point I began with: If the atoning work of Christ is substitutionary, it must be limited to those whom Christ actually redeems. In other words, when we understand that the atonement is substitutionary, we must see that in a certain way it applies to particular people. That is the inevitable ramification of vicarious atonement. Again, Christ did not suffer for the sins of Judas in the same way He suffered for Peter's sins. Taking Matthew 26:24 at face value, it seems clear that Judas will suffer for his own sin. "He who does not obey the Son will not see life, but the wrath of God abides on him" (John 3:36). All who die in unbelief will suffer "in their own persons the due penalty of their error" (Romans 1:27). Christ is in no sense their substitute.

Here's another way to say it: The aspects of the atonement that are substitutionary are inherently efficacious. The very reason believers do not have to fear condemnation in the final judgment is that Christ has already paid the price of their sin in full as their substitute. The atonement of Christ did not just make salvation possible; it actually purchased redemption for those who will be saved. He literally bought them, paid their debt, wiped it off the ledger, sealed their pardon, and assured their eternal salvation.

## Problem Passages

The key passage referenced by those who reject particular redemption is 1 John 2:2: "He Himself is the propitiation for our sins; and not for ours only, but also for those of the whole world." We have to remember here that the apostle was writing to a primarily Jewish audience. We read in Galatians 2:9, "Recognizing the grace that had been given to me, James and Cephas and John, who were reputed to be pillars, gave to me and Barnabas the right hand of fellowship, so that we might go to the Gentiles and they to the circumcised." That passage reveals that John was an apostle to the Jews. The recipients of his epistles would therefore have been predominantly, if not exclusively, Jewish.

John reminded this Jewish audience that Christ is the propitiation for sins, and not for the sins of Hebrews only, but also for the sins of Gentiles from every tongue and nation throughout the whole world. That's the proper sense of 1 John 2:2. There is little doubt that is exactly how John's initial audience would have understood this expression. The phrase "the whole world" means people of all kinds, including Jews, Gentiles, Greeks, and Romans, as opposed to "ours only," meaning the Jewish nation. The grammatical construction of 1 John 2:2 is an exact parallel to John's analysis of the unwitting prophecy issued by Caiaphas in John 11:51-52: "He prophesied that Jesus was going to die for the nation, and not for the nation only, but in order that He might also gather together into one the children of God who are scattered abroad."

Another verse that those who reject particular redemption turn to is 2 Peter 2:1: "False prophets also arose among the people, just as there will also be false teachers among you, who will secretly introduce destructive heresies, even denying the Master who *bought them*, bringing swift destruction upon themselves." This verse poses no problem if we understand two things.

First, the word "Master" in the phrase "the Master who bought them" is a Greek word that speaks of a sovereign master; it has a strong emphasis on the strength of God's sovereignty and lordship. If you understand this as a reference to Christ, it could simply refer to what Philippians 2:8-10 teaches—that Christ's death obtained for Christ a position of absolute lordship over all. These false teachers who were part of the field Christ purchased in order to obtain the hidden treasure of the church were denying the Lord who bought them. That's one interpretation of the verse.

But nowhere else in the New Testament is this Greek word used to designate Christ. It is an expression normally used to speak of the Father. And if these false teachers were Jewish false teachers, as it appears they were, then Peter may have been paraphrasing an Old Testament passage, Deuteronomy 32:5-6: "They have acted corruptly toward Him, they are not His children, because of their defect; but are a perverse and crooked generation. Do you thus repay the LORD, O foolish and unwise people? *Is not He your Father who has bought you?*" That passage plainly refers to the nation's temporal deliverance from Egypt. Peter may have simply meant that these false teachers were guilty of denying the God who had redeemed their ancestors from the nation of Egypt.

There is a third possible interpretation. Peter may have been making the point simply that although these false teachers had identified with the people of God and claimed to trust Christ, their preaching was a denial of the God they claimed to have been redeemed by.

Those three interpretations are all in perfect harmony with a Calvinistic view of the atonement, and they do not even exhaust the viable interpretations of 2 Peter 2:1. Moreover, the point of the verse is about the enormity of these false teachers' wickedness; it is not about the extent of the atonement. So the verse proves nothing against the Calvinistic doctrine of particular redemption.

### An Amazing and Uplifting Truth

Years of wearying debate over limited atonement (much of it unnecessarily acrimonious) has left many Christians with the uneasy feeling that questions about the design and extent of the atonement raise matters best avoided for the sake of peace in the church. It is unfortunate that the doctrine of particular redemption is so controversial, because in reality it is a truth that can only strengthen one's faith

that all things do indeed work together for good for those who love God. It underscores the personal nature of God's love for His elect. It greatly clarifies the doctrine of election. It illuminates *all* the doctrines of grace, for that matter.

My appeal to pastors and church leaders with regard to this doctrine is twofold: On the one hand, don't run away *from* this doctrine. It's neither as confusing nor as divisive as you might think. On the other hand, don't run away *with* it. Too many treat this doctrine as if it nullified everything Scripture teaches about common grace and the general benevolence of our loving God. It does not.

Remember, "The LORD is good to all, and His mercies are over all His works" (Psalm 145:9). "He causes His sun to rise on the evil and the good, and sends rain on the righteous and the unrighteous" (Matthew 5:45). But to the elect in particular, Jesus said, "Do not be afraid, little flock, for your Father has chosen gladly to give you the kingdom" (Luke 12:32). "Many are called, but few are chosen" (Matthew 22:14). There is glorious comfort and encouragement in all those truths, for those who have eyes to see.

He "is the Savior of all men, *especially* of believers" (1 Timothy 4:10).

8

# A Biblical Case for Elder Rule

*Tom Pennington*
*Shepherds' Conference 2003*

*Selected Scriptures*

Several years ago I watched a brief film entitled *Unlocking the Mystery of Life*. It described the journey of several scientists away from evolution to intelligent design. The focus of the video, which will never likely be a bestseller, was the bacterial flagellum—a tiny hair that protrudes from a single-cell bacterium. It is what enables the bacteria to move. When it is viewed under powerful electron microscopes, amazingly it is clear that the entire flagellum assembly is a tiny motor! It has all the components of the motors that run our electrical appliances—and the hair serves as a simple rotor.

When I saw the complexity of one single-celled bacterium, I was not only awed that our God has produced such amazing variety in creation, but I was also struck with the reality that He is a God of order—order we witness in even the smallest cells. In fact, the video went on to show that every human cell contains a number of tiny motors, including even a sophisticated DNA assembly line. That is how God designed the human body.

## Meticulous Design

Given that our God is a God of meticulous order, even down to the smallest living thing He has made, it surprises me to hear church leaders say that how the church is structured is unimportant. For example, George Barna writes, "The Bible does not rigidly define the corporate practices, rituals, or structures that must be embraced in order to have a proper church."[1] Likewise, Donald Miller writes, "No particular structure of church life is divinely ordained."[2] So God cares about the structure of the bacterial flagellum but doesn't care about how the church—the only entity that He promised to build and bless—is structured?

Miller adds: "Any form which the Holy Spirit can inhabit and to which He may impart the life of Christ must be accepted as valid for the church. As all forms of life adapt themselves to their environment, so does the life of Christ by His Spirit in the church."[3] That is evolutionary theory applied to the structure of the church. Some churches may have a kind of government that is best described as survival of the fittest, but that is not a biblically ordained structure.

Although some dismiss the structure of church government as unimportant, this issue is absolutely crucial, because structure determines how people think and act. As Alexander Strauch writes in *Biblical Eldership*,

> Some of the worst havoc wrought to the Christian faith has been a direct result of unscriptural forms of church structure. Only a few centuries after the apostles' death, for example, Christian churches began to assimilate both Roman and Jewish concepts of status, power, and priesthood...Under Christ's name an elaborately structured institution emerged that corrupted the simple, family structure of the apostolic churches, robbed God's people of their lofty position and ministry in Christ, and exchanged

Christ's supremacy over His people for the supremacy of the institutional church.[4]

What should matter most to us is what Scripture says about the structure of the church and its leadership. The church will always have some structure, but what structure—if any—does Scripture prescribe? I want to consider the evidence that in Scripture the normal pattern is a plurality of godly men leading each church. And then I want to examine the biblical evidence that God intends for every church to follow that pattern. But first let's survey the primary models of church government in contemporary Christianity.

## Forms of Church Government

### Episcopalian

The Episcopalian model maintains that there are three legitimate church offices: bishops, presbyters (also called rectors or priests), and deacons. In this model, bishops alone have the authority to appoint other bishops, presbyters, and deacons. This is a hierarchy in which men outside a local church usually choose those who will lead each church.

Some Episcopalians trace the authority of the bishop back to the apostles, or apostolic succession. Other Episcopalians don't attempt to trace succession back to the apostles but argue it appeared very early in church history and that lends weight to this position. Still others embrace this model because they think it is functionally the best for the structure and organization of the church.

There are four primary denominations that practice this form of church government: the Orthodox, the Anglicans, the Roman Catholics, and some Methodist denominations. The defense for this model is primarily church history. For example, J.B. Lightfoot wrote about the office of bishop, "History seems to show decisively that before the middle of the second century each church or organized Christian community had its three orders of ministers, its bishop, its presbyters, and its deacons."[5] So the Episcopalian form of government likely began in the early 200s, and by the 300s the three offices were common.

Others argue that in Acts 15 James exercised the office of bishop during the Jerusalem Council. Some similarly point to Titus's oversight of a number of churches (Titus 1:7). Another argument sometimes put forward is that this model is not distinctly forbidden in the New Testament. However, the more important question is this: Is it *prescribed* in the Bible?

### Presbyterian

In the Presbyterian model, churches are not ruled by bishops, but by elders. Some elders also have authority within the denomination regionally or even nationally.

"The local church is governed by the session, which is composed of ruling elders elected by the membership, with the teaching elder or minister as presiding officer."[6] Typically the congregation elects the ruling elders, or laymen, from the congregation, to serve as representatives of the members. Together the teaching elder and those ruling elders constitute the session and govern the local church.

"The next highest-ranking body is the Presbytery, which includes all the ordained ministers or teaching elders and one ruling elder from each local congregation in a given district. Above the presbytery is the synod, and over the synod is the general assembly, the highest court. Both of these bodies are also equally divided between ministers and laymen or ruling elders."[7]

The denominations that practice this form of government are primarily Presbyterians and various Reformed churches.

To defend this structure, some point to 1 Timothy 5:17, where Paul makes a distinction between elders who rule and those who teach. Some point to Paul's instruction to Titus (1:5) to ordain elders in every church, drawing the implication of regional or national oversight.

However, the Bible nowhere explicitly calls for elders to have or exercise authority beyond their own local flock. Some argue that Acts 15 is one possible exception, when the Jerusalem church elders sent an authoritative letter to other churches. But that passage cannot be used to defend Presbyterian government. After all, the apostles were still present and the ultimate authority behind that letter, and there are no apostles with such authority today. Also, the church in Antioch voluntarily requested the assistance of the Jerusalem church, likely because of the presence of the apostles. In addition, Acts 15:22 says that the *entire Jerusalem church* sent the letter to the other churches. In light of that, Wayne Grudem writes, "If this narrative gives support to regional government by elders, it therefore also gives support to regional government by whole congregations."[8]

### Congregational

A third form of church government is congregational, where ultimate authority for each local church resides within each church—which is completely autonomous. The denominations that follow this form are Congregational, Baptist, Mennonite, Evangelical Free, independent, and others. The congregational form of church government has a number of variations and expressions.

A very common congregational model is that of a single elder or pastor supported by a deacon board. Those who follow this approach often teach that 1 Timothy 3 prescribes a single elder in each church with a plurality of deacons, since the word *elder* is singular in that passage. However, the singular can also be used collectively as opposed to a single individual.

Another congregational structure is the corporate board model, in which the congregation chooses its pastor and also selects members to exercise oversight over the pastor (as CEO) and the entire organization, just like the board of a corporation.

Another form of congregationalism is pure democracy. Churches that practice this kind of government often seriously struggle with unity. My father-in-law pastored in the South for many years and once witnessed a serious breach in unity in a nearby "democratic" church. The contention centered on the color of shingles to use on the church's roof. The debate was so heated they decided the only way to keep the church from splitting was to put one color of shingles on half the roof and another color on the other half. Sadly, for years the members sat only under the half of the roof that had been shingled with their preferred color.

### A Plurality of Elders

A final form of church government, and the model I will argue Scripture teaches, is that in every church there should be a plurality of godly men chosen by the elders and affirmed by the congregation. One of those elders usually serves as the primary pastor-teacher, the one delegated the chief responsibility to teach the Word to the flock.

### Plurality in the Old Testament

The background for this type of church government is first found in the pattern of leadership in Old Testament Israel, which created a mindset among the Jewish people who formed the earliest churches. There are two primary words translated "elder" in the Old Testament. The first is זָקֵן [*zaqen*], which means "old or mature in age." This word is usually found in the plural form and occurs 178 times in the Old Testament—about 100 of those occurrences refer to men in a position of authority. The other word is הַבְיָשׂ [*siyb*], an Aramaic word used five times in the post-exilic book of Ezra. This word means "gray-headed" and speaks of age and maturity.

When we examine how these two words are used in the Old Testament, we find the primary reference to elders occurs within the context of family: within the tribe, clan, and house or family. This usage is clear in Genesis 50:7: "Joseph went up to bury his father, and with him went up all the servants of Pharaoh, the elders of his household and all the elders of the land of Egypt." Second Samuel 12:17 tells us that "the elders of [David's] household stood beside him in order to raise him up from the ground, but he was unwilling and would not eat food with them [after his child died]." The elders of David's household sought to end his mourning and encourage him.

In the Old Testament, elders also ruled over cities administrating the local government. For example, in Ruth 4:1-2 we read, "Boaz went up to the gate and sat down there, and behold, the close relative of whom Boaz spoke was passing by, so he said, 'Turn aside, friend, sit down here.' And he turned aside and sat down. He took ten men of the elders of

the city…" Within the family there were elders. And elders oversaw the life and government of the city (cf. Numbers 22:4, 7; Deuteronomy 19:12; 21:1ff, 19; 22:15; Judges 8:14).

There were also elders over nations—a plurality of men who served as leaders and advisors. This was common throughout the ancient world, even in the nations around Israel. For example, Numbers 22:7 refers to the elders of Moab and Genesis 50:7 to the elders of Egypt.

And the structure of elders over the nation was common in Israel and existed as early as the time of Moses. Exodus 4:29-30 tells us that in Egypt "Moses and Aaron went and assembled all the elders of the sons of Israel; and Aaron spoke all the words which the LORD had spoken to Moses." Before Moses officially began his ministry, there was already a body of men, the elders of Israel, to whom Moses presented what the Lord had spoken (cf. Exodus 3:16; 4:29; 12:21; 17:5; 18:12; 24:1, 9, 11, 14). In Numbers 11, Moses appointed 70 men to assist in leading the people of Israel. Some Jewish scholars point to that event as the beginning of the Sanhedrin—the 70 elders of Israel, as they referred to them.

This group of elders continued to serve as an advisory body during the monarchy (1 Samuel 8:4; 2 Samuel 3:17; 5:3; 17:4, 15; 19:11; 1 Kings 20:7; 21:8; 23:1). Even though there was a king on the throne and there were prophets to keep the king in check, Israel still had this body of elders, which continued even into the New Testament era. Elders were also influential during the exile in Babylon. According to Ezekiel 8:1, the elders continued to wield considerable influence (cf. Jeremiah 29:1; 14:1; 20:1). After the return from exile, they were called on a number of occasions to help mediate specific problems and issues (Ezra 5:9ff; 6:7; 10:8, 14). And, of course, in the Gospels we find many references to the elders of Israel functioning as the Sanhedrin and highest ruling body of Judaism.

Clearly, in the first-century Jewish mind, the word *elders* referred to a plurality of godly leaders. With that history, it was natural for the concept of elder rule to be adopted by the first churches, which were primarily Jewish and under the responsibility and leadership of the apostles.

**Plurality in the New Testament**

In addition to the Old Testament pattern, the New Testament and the apostolic example provide overwhelming evidence for a plurality of godly men leading each church.

Elders played a dominant role in the life of the church in Jerusalem and at the Jerusalem Council. Throughout the book of Acts, Luke refers to the church in the singular but to elders in the plural form. Each church had a plurality of elders. That pattern permeates the New Testament.

For example, in Acts 15:4 we read, "When they arrived in Jerusalem, they were received by the church [singular] and the apostles and the elders [plural],

and they reported all that God had done with them." Notice that same pattern appears in verse 22: "It seemed good to the apostles and the elders [plural], with the whole church [singular], to choose men from among them to send to Antioch with Paul and Barnabas" (cf. Acts 11:30; 15:2, 6, 23; 16:4; 21:18).

James was written to Jewish believers dispersed because of persecution—probably the persecution of Herod mentioned in Acts 12. Written in the mid-40s AD, it may have been the first New Testament book written, so the formation of the church would have been at an early stage. James wrote to small groups of believers dispersed across Eastern Europe, and yet there is already a pattern of multiple elders within each church. In James 5:14, he writes, "Is anyone among you sick? Then he must call for the elders [plural] of the church [singular] and they are to pray over him, anointing him with oil in the name of the Lord."

Acts 14 is a crucial passage because it contains the first mention of elders in a *Gentile* congregation, near the end of Paul's first missionary journey. In verse 23, Luke writes: "When they had appointed elders [plural] for them in every church [singular], having prayed with fasting, they commended them to the Lord in whom they had believed." Luke uses the Greek preposition *kata* in a distributive sense: "having appointed for them church by church, elders." He is referring to the churches in Antioch of Pisidia, Iconium, Lystra, and Derbe. So one of the key steps in organizing a new church was appointing elders. This was Paul's pattern everywhere he went.

In Acts 20, Paul concluded his third missionary journey and headed to Jerusalem for the Feast of Pentecost, around May AD 57. Earlier on that same journey, Paul had established the church in Ephesus and ministered there for about three years. On his way to Jerusalem, Paul's ship docked in Miletus for several days to load and unload cargo. Miletus was only 40 miles south of Ephesus, so Paul seized the opportunity to summon the Ephesian elders with whom he had ministered for three years. His words in Acts 20 are the only record of Paul speaking directly to a group of elders in the entire New Testament. Verse 17 says that "from Miletus he sent to Ephesus and called to him the elders [plural] of the church [singular]." In verse 28, Paul warned these elders, "Be on guard for yourselves and for all the flock, among which the Holy Spirit has made you [plural] overseers." There was one flock, and these elders were responsible to oversee it. The church in Ephesus had a plurality of godly men who led and pastored it. Timothy also later ministered in Ephesus. In 1 Timothy 5:17, we discover that there were still multiple elders in that church.

Philippians 1:1 was written later in Paul's ministry. He wrote "to all the saints in Christ Jesus who are in Philippi, including the overseers and deacons." At that point, the church in Philippi was more than ten years old. Paul was under

house arrest in Rome, and this church with its heart for the apostle had sent him an offering and had also sent Epaphroditus to minister to him. In his response (the letter to the Philippians), the apostle identified two offices in this church: the office of overseer, and the office of deacon. Both are mentioned in the plural form, and we know there was only one body of believers, one church in Philippi. Fifty years later, Polycarp wrote to the Philippian church: "to the Church of God which sojourns at Philippi." He called the church (singular) to submit to its deacons and elders (plural).[9]

According to Acts 27:7, the ship taking Paul to Rome had taken shelter on the south side of Crete. And after release from his first Roman imprisonment, he visited Crete. By the time Paul wrote Titus, his son in the faith, the churches on Crete were probably already established. But they were weak, having been assaulted by false teachers (Titus 1:10-16; 3:9-11). Because of that relentless assault, Paul left Titus there for a specific purpose: "For this reason I left you in Crete, that you would set in order what remains and appoint elders [plural] in every city [singular]" (Titus 1:5). Since Crete is a small island with small cities, it is likely there was only one church in each city, and elders—plural—were to be appointed in each of those churches.

## A Leader Among Leaders

Whenever the word *elder* is connected to the word *church* in the New Testament, we find a singular flock overseen by a plural number of elders. That pattern is consistent even with our Lord and His ministry. He gave the early church a plurality of leaders: He appointed 12 apostles. Then He sent the 12 out two by two, with equal rank and authority. But obviously even among the apostles there were leaders among leaders. In Scripture, the apostles are always listed in three groups of four. The same men are always in the same group of four. And the first name in each group is always the same—apparently there was a leader of each group. And Peter's name is always mentioned first. So even the apostles illustrate the principle of a plurality of leaders and of leaders among leaders by virtue of experience, age, and skills. Christ ordained the basic concept of plurality even with the apostles.

**Elder, Overseer, and Shepherd**

Both the Old and New Testaments provide ample evidence for the concept of a plurality of elders in the church, but there is one more important line of argument based on the Greek words that describe the office of elder. These words not only help us understand the number of elders required but also their duties.

First, the Greek word translated "elder" is *presbyteros*. It has two primary uses in the New Testament. One use is to describe older men. For example, 1 Timothy 5:1 tells us not to rebuke an older man, but to appeal to him as a father. This word is also used as a title for a community official. There is no specific age demanded

by this word, but it does imply maturity, dignity, experience, and honor. When the Bible connects a particular age to the commencement of spiritual leadership, the examples point to about thirty years of age. For example, a man who belonged to the descendants of Aaron could enter full service in the priesthood at 30 (Numbers 4:46-47). Our Lord began His earthly ministry at about that age as well (Luke 3:23). Many commentators believe Timothy was in his early thirties (1 Timothy 4:12). Although those examples of age are not binding on the office of elder in the local church, they can help provide a general guideline.

The same word is used 28 times in the Gospels and Acts to refer to the Sanhedrin. It is used 12 times in Revelation to describe the 24 elders who are representatives of the redeemed in heaven. It is also used 19 times in Acts and the epistles to refer to a group of leaders in each church.

The second Greek word, *episkopos*, is translated "overseer" and in some versions, "bishop." The word was commonly used to refer to secular officials of various kinds, especially local officials such as superintendents, managers, controllers, and rulers.

The Septuagint uses this word of military officers (Numbers 31:14), tabernacle administrators (Numbers 4:16), supervisors of temple repair (2 Chronicles 24:12, 17), temple guardians (2 Kings 11:18), city supervisors, and mayors (Nehemiah 11:9). It appears only five times in the New Testament. Once it is used of Christ

(1 Peter 2:25) and the other four times of church leaders, especially in the context of Gentile congregations like that in Ephesus. It is a general word like *supervisor*, *manager*, or *guardian*.

It is necessary to examine multiple passages that address this concept of managing and supervising to develop a clear picture of the responsibility of elders. In 1 Timothy 5:17, Paul wrote, "The elders who rule well are to be considered worthy of double honor, especially those who work hard at preaching and teaching." The Greek word translated "rule" [*proistēmi*] means "to set over, to rule." It is also translated several other ways in the New Testament. For example, it is translated "leads" in Romans 12:8 in reference to the gift of administration. It is translated "manage" in 1 Timothy 3:4-5 in reference to an elder's oversight of his household. It is translated "managers" in 1 Timothy 3:12 in reference to deacons managing their children and their households.

While all elders are to be able to teach, some elders labor at preaching and teaching (1 Timothy 5:17). Paul implies that some elders have greater teaching responsibilities, probably because of superior giftedness. But all the elders are to manage everything that happens in their local church. That does not mean that they must do all the work, but they must ensure everything is done decently and in order.

A third Greek word, *poimēn*, translates as "shepherd" or "pastor." The *noun* form occurs 18 times in the New Testament—of shepherds that keep animals, of Christ (e.g., Hebrews 13:20-21; 1 Peter 2:25), and once of church leaders. The *verb* form, used three times in the context of church leaders, emphasizes the pastor's primary role—teaching or leading his sheep. In John 21:16, Christ commanded Peter, "Shepherd My sheep." In Acts 20:28, Paul reminded the Ephesian elders that they were to *shepherd* the church of God. And in 1 Peter 5:1-2, Peter charged the elders scattered across Asia Minor to shepherd the flock of God.

All three words—*elder*, *overseer*, and *shepherd*—clearly refer to the same office. The qualifications for an *overseer* in 1 Timothy 3 and an *elder* in Titus 1 are almost identical. Also, Paul told Titus to appoint elders (1:5) and then called the same men *overseers* (1:7). First Peter 5:1-2 brings all three words and concepts together into one office: "I exhort the elders among you, as your fellow *elder*…[to] *shepherd* the flock of God among you, exercising *oversight*" (emphasis added).

Paul also uses these three terms interchangeably in Acts 20:17, 28: "From Miletus he sent to Ephesus and called to him the *elders* of the church…Be on guard for yourselves and for all the flock, among which the Holy Spirit has made you *overseers*, to *shepherd* the church of God" (emphasis added).

Together these three terms describe the office: *elder* emphasizes the man's character—his spiritual maturity. *Shepherd* and *overseer* refer to his function. A *shepherd* feeds, protects, and cares for his

454 THE JOHN MACARTHUR HANDBOOK OF EFFECTIVE BIBLICAL LEADERSHIP

people. An *overseer* rules or has charge over both the people and the ministry of the church. So *elder, shepherd,* and *overseer* all identify the same person, serving in the same office. But the New Testament pattern is a group of qualified elders leading every local church.

### Required Today?

One final question must be answered: Is this clear biblical pattern a mandate for churches today? For all who take the New Testament and the pastoral epistles seriously, it must be! The pastoral epistles were written to church leaders to dictate how they are to conduct themselves in the household of God (1 Timothy 3:15). Within these books, Paul insists on a plurality of leadership (cf. 1 Timothy 5:17; Titus 1:5). In addition, there is the weight of apostolic example. The apostles probably established elder rule in the Jewish churches (Acts 15:6). That is why James, who ministered alongside the apostles in Jerusalem and was the most influential leader in the Jerusalem church, expected elder rule in the Diaspora (James 5:14). Paul established elder rule in all the Gentile churches (Acts 14:23) and commanded Titus to appoint elders in every church as well (Titus 1:5). So this form of church government carries apostolic authority and has been prescribed for all church leaders with all the weight of inspired Scripture.

If a plurality of godly elders already leads your church, this should serve as a great encouragement. If not, carefully study what Scripture teaches about this topic. If you conclude that your church government needs to change, pray for wisdom and move very slowly.

The first step toward change is to establish the sufficiency and authority of Scripture. Remind your congregation that whatever Scripture says about any issue must be obeyed and followed, even if it requires difficult changes. Then begin slowly over time to teach the biblical pattern of church leadership. In the meantime, identify a few men who meet the qualifications for elders and begin to rely on them for help and counsel, even though they do not yet carry that title. Have them begin to function as elders, even if they do not yet occupy the office per se. It may take years but work toward the goal of your congregation embracing the biblical pattern. It will take time. Do not try to change your church to elder rule quickly. But do make moving in that direction a priority, because the Old Testament pattern, the New Testament evidence, and the Greek words for the pastoral office combine to form an unbreakable chain of evidence. God intends that a local church be governed by a plurality of godly men. Therefore, it is to that pattern that every biblical church must aspire.

# PRAYER

Father, we are overwhelmed by the grace You have shown us in Christ. We thank You, from the bottom of our hearts, that we stand righteous before You, wearing not a righteousness of our own, but a righteousness that comes to us from Jesus Christ. Father, we are further overwhelmed that not only have You given us the great privilege of belonging to You, but You have given us the incredible responsibility and opportunity to serve in Your body. We ask that You will make us faithful stewards of that calling. We pray these things in Jesus' name. Amen.

# The Great Commission as a Theological Endeavor

*Paul Washer*

*Shepherds' Conference 2014*

*Matthew 28:16-20*

The eleven disciples proceeded to Galilee, to the mountain which Jesus had designated. When they saw Him, they worshiped Him; but some were doubtful. And Jesus came and spoke to them, saying, "All authority has been given to Me in heaven and on earth. Go therefore and make disciples of all the nations, baptizing them in the name of the Father and the Son and the Holy Spirit, teaching them to observe all that I commanded you; and lo, I am with you always, even to the end of the age" (Matthew 28:16-20).

There are four things in particular to note from this passage. First, we see a reflection of our weakness. Second, we see a declaration of Christ—His absolute authority and power. Third, we see the preeminent task of the church. Fourth, if all this is too much, if it overwhelms us, we have the promise of His presence and power. For every man who has taken the Great Commission seriously, this last promise is the thing that holds him. It is what strengthens him and makes him go on.

## Our Weakness

Let's look first at a reflection of our weakness. Verses 16 and 17 read, "The eleven disciples proceeded to Galilee, to the mountain which Jesus had designated. When they saw Him, they worshiped Him; but some were doubtful."

Here we do not see great men of faith. Instead, we see men like us—a mixture of faith and obedience, doubt and uncertainty. The Greek word that is used here for doubt is *distzo*, meaning "a double standing." That is to say, there was an uncertainty or a hesitancy about them. It is the same word that was used to describe Peter when he was commanded by Christ to come out of the boat and walk upon the raging sea.

Now, I want to be fair at this moment to these men. We should not just attribute this doubt to their weakness, but also to the magnitude of what they were being called to believe and do. Let's think for a moment about Peter being called to walk out onto the Sea of Galilee, and yet that was nothing compared to what they were being called to do at this very moment.

These men were being called to walk out into the sea of humanity—a radically depraved humanity. They were being sent out as lambs in the midst of wolves. They were being called to cast down every earthly power and authority, to do so by faith and by the proclamation of the most scandalous message that the world has ever known, which was first spoken by a carpenter. We can see that there is at least something of a reason for their doubt.

One of the greatest things I have ever learned from Scripture regarding the apostles is that they were like us. But we see here that they would be transformed to become something more than mere men. How would that happen? They grasped, by the power and ministry of the Holy Spirit, the reality of the absolute authority of Jesus Christ, as is evident in the book of Acts.

When we talk about missions and those who participate in missions, there are at least three qualifications that are absolute essentials. First, we need men who are constantly growing in their knowledge of the person and work of Christ—who He truly is and what He has truly done. Second, we need men who will renounce once and for all every fleshly means of planting churches and doing missions. And third, we need men who are constantly, unceasingly crying out for greater manifestations of the life and power of the Holy Spirit in their own life.

Just because there are so many wrong men teaching so many wrong things about the Holy Spirit doesn't mean we should overreact against them and turn our Trinity into something less than it is. Do not allow false prophets to rob you of your inheritance of the Spirit. We cannot fulfill the Great Commission apart from the power, the teaching, the righteousness, the holiness, and the life of the Holy Spirit.

## Declaration of His Power

Having looked at the reflection of our weakness, let's see now the declaration of His power. Verse 18 reads, "Jesus came up and spoke to them, saying, 'All authority has been given to Me in heaven and on earth.'" Jesus knows their weakness, and

He goes out to meet them. How many times in your ministry has this been true? He knew your weakness at that moment, but He did not leave you. Instead, He went out to meet you—He came for you. What a blessed Savior, what a broad-shouldered God we have. He knows our frame. He knows that we are dust. There has never been a great man of God, nor will there ever be; only tiny little faithless men of a great and a merciful God. He went out to meet them.

A young person came to me and said, "But the Great Commission is so great and I'm so weak." My response was, "Yes, but as someone once wrote, 'Christ does not call men who are worthy. Christ makes men worthy by virtue of the calling.'"

What exactly did Christ do here? He came out and He countered the disciples' doubt and uncertainty. He did so with a declaration of His absolute authority over everything, without limitation, jurisdiction, or exception. This is His power.

David Brown, a well-known Scottish theologian and exegete, said, "What must have been the feelings which such a Commission awakened? We who have scarce conquered our own misgivings—we, fishermen of Galilee, with no letters, no means, no influence over the humblest creature, conquer the world for Thee, Lord? Nay, Lord, do not mock us.'"[1]

The Lord did not mock. He responded, "All authority has been given to Me in heaven and on earth. Go therefore…and lo, I am with you always, even to the end of the age" (verses 18-20).

Our strength—our everything—is not found in us; it is all found in Him. A wonderful illustration of Christ's authority is found in Genesis 41:44: "Pharaoh said to Joseph, 'Though I am Pharaoh, yet without your permission no one shall raise his hand or foot in all the land of Egypt.'" The resurrected and exalted Christ stands before the Father, and all authority is given to Him in heaven and on earth. It is as though the Father said to the Son, "Without Your permission, Son, no one will raise his hand or his foot in all the cosmos."

Even the hand that was raised to throw the first stone at Stephen was under the sovereign jurisdiction of the Lord Jesus Christ. Knowing this is what will make a weak man strong. What does this kind of authority mean for our missionary endeavors? It means that he who goes to and fro weeping, carrying his bag of seeds, will come again with a shout of joy, bringing his seeds with him. Is this authority just some theological speculation, something to be talked about in a seminary? Absolutely not! It is essential for everything we do in world missions. His authority means that there will be a great multitude which no one can count standing before the throne and the Lamb. They will be clothed in white robes, and each one will have in his hand a palm branch, and they will cry out with a great and unified voice, "Salvation to our God who sits on the throne, and to the Lamb"

(Revelation 7:10). His authority means we will win, because He has won. What an open door lies before us, and what strength He has given us in His name.

Most people involved in missions would give a hearty amen to everything I have said thus far. Jesus is Lord, and He has authority and power. But we must understand the implications of the sovereignty of Christ. If we are to go out *in* His authority, then we must go out *under* His authority. That means everything we do in missions and church planting, everything that we believe, everything that we practice, and all of our so-called strategies and methodologies must all be warranted by the Scriptures, or we have no authority at all. Our authority comes from our conformity to what this mighty Lord has commanded.

I believe the Achilles' heel of modern evangelical missions is that everyone is doing what is right in their own eyes. Our missions methodology and our church-planting strategies are not to be the invention of the anthropologist, the sociologist, or the expert in leading cultural trends. Then from where should our strategy and our methodology come? It should come from the Scriptures, drawn out of the Scriptures by the exegete, the theologian, and the church historian. But these have been all but removed from modern evangelical missions. That is our Achilles' heel.

I'm reminded of Moses being told to make everything in the tabernacle according to the pattern that was shown to him on the mountain. Now if God can say that about the tabernacle, how much more the greatest of all causes. See to it that you do this Great Commission according to the pattern that has been shown in the Holy Scriptures.

God has given the church and her ministers the Scriptures so that we might be equipped not for some good works, not for certain good words, but for every necessary work of the kingdom. God has also given the Scriptures to the church so that we might know how to conduct ourselves in the household of God—the church of the living God, the pillar and the support of the truth.

The Reformation, the Puritans, Spurgeon, Calvin, Lloyd-Jones—none of them were wrapped up in Calvinism. They were wrapped up in the sufficiency of Scripture. Of course part of that is a right understanding of soteriology. But all over America, I see men who are supposedly going back to the truth, but only with regard to soteriology. If I look at their church planting and their way of doing missions, it looks just like every other evangelical. It is not just about reforming your soteriology, for the Puritan genius was this: They sought to take every aspect of life and ministry, and submit it to a book, the Scriptures. Yet there is this prevalent idea of taking the Puritans, and the Reformers, and dressing all of it up to fit the culture so that other people today will appreciate it. We must cling to what is written, and we must do our church planting, our church life, our missions, our families, and everything else according to what is written and not what is right in our own eyes.

Someone came to me and said, "Brother Paul, I believe in the inerrancy of Scripture." I replied, "Good for you, because the inerrancy of Scripture means nothing unless you also practice the sufficiency of Scripture." They are twin sisters. Inerrancy—you can hold onto that without being changed—but to take that doctrine and move on to sufficiency, now that is a whole other ball game.

If we are going to fulfill the Great Commission, we must lay aside every fleshly strategy and methodology. We must go into the Scriptures and follow the pattern that is given to us there. The more we, as a people, hold on to the works, strategies, and methodologies of the flesh, the less that we will see God. What must we do? We must rip from us—like a poison, like a plague, like a scab—Saul's armor, and we must go out and pick up the smooth stones of the gospel that for too long have been neglected. Beloved, that is the only way we are ever going to go out and slay this Goliath called world missions.

**The Church's Preeminent Task**

Let us now look at what specifically the church is called to do. Matthew 28:19-20 reads, "Go therefore and make disciples of all the nations, baptizing them in the name of the Father and the Son and the Holy Spirit, teaching them to observe all that I commanded you;

and lo, I am with you always, even to the end of the age." Please note that I call this point the church's preeminent task and not the church's preeminent command. The church's preeminent command is to love the Lord your God with all your heart, soul, mind, and strength. The second command is to love your neighbor as yourself. Only men who have been changed through the regenerating work of the Holy Spirit and the renewal of their mind in the Scriptures can have a love for God that propels them to do great things in God's name.

*A Labor of Love*

The Great Commission is a labor of love. We love God, and therefore we desire that the knowledge of the glory of God be upon this earth like the waters that cover the sea. We desire that the name of God be great among the nations, from the rising to the setting of the sun. We love Christ, and therefore we desire that the Lamb receive the full reward of His suffering. We love men—and if you don't love men then you need to get out of ministry—and we cannot tolerate their suffering; therefore, we want to see God glorified in their salvation. It is a labor of love.

We must remain under His authority, and He commands us to love Him and our neighbor. We must constantly, daily, not only in our public life, nor only in our pulpit ministry, but also in our private life, remain under His authority. He bought you, He owns you, and you are not your own, so take that truth and drive it like a stake straight through the heart of the flesh. You are His!

Young men, if you have not settled that matter before you graduate, all the degrees in the world will not help you. We go out in His name because we love Him. We love Him because He first loved us. When you go and preach on the street and the people listening turn on you after about five minutes—they grab your little pulpit, megaphone, all your tracts and Bibles, and even you and throw it all off the plaza into the street— it is going to take a lot more than simple love for people for you to pick up everything and march right back to that plaza again. For that kind of persistence and endurance to exist, it is going to take the love of Christ manifested in your life—the reality of what He has done for you. Although your suffering might not be that dramatic, it is oftentimes more intense. In order for you to keep going, serving, blessing, though unnoticed and unappreciated by men, it is going to take this standard and comprehension of the reality of Christ.

### Make Disciples

Jesus then said to His followers, "Make disciples" (verse 19). The phrase "make disciples" has the prominent idea of instruction and teaching. Making disciples is the means of communicating truth. What is a disciple? It is someone who is like his master. So the end of church planting and the end of the Great Commission is not recording decisions

or counting converts; it is taking the gospel of Jesus Christ and boldly proclaiming it to the lost. And when those lost are soundly converted, then we enter into a lifelong labor with the full counsel of God's Word for their sanctification. That is what we are called to do.

Now this is difficult work. You will leave this wonderful, necessary, and edifying conference and go back to this difficult task. But the hard work pays off, for I would take one sound disciple over 10,000 so-called converts that evangelicalism is producing today. The idea of making disciples is further clarified by Paul in his letter to Timothy: "The things which you have heard from me in the presence of many witnesses, entrust these to faithful men who will be able to teach others also" (2 Timothy 2:2). This text is so often used out of context by individuals who reference it to stress that the moment someone is converted they need to go and disciple someone else who has been converted more recently. That type of discipleship has its place, but that is not what Paul is talking about here. Paul is telling Timothy to raise up leaders, to raise up men of God, and to raise up men who are qualified to be elders and biblical deacons.

We are called to make disciples even when the circumstances are not ideal. It is amazing that Jesus never said, "The harvest is great, but the money is few." Money is not the problem. Men of integrity—biblical men who have lashed themselves down to Scripture—that is the rarity. Christians who are making disciples is the gem, and we are called to this task. Although these kinds of men are being produced at The Master's Seminary and at other good seminaries that the Lord has raised up, never forget that this work is the primary task of the church.

Jesus then said that this work is to be done in all nations. If you have had a measure of success in the ministry and you are content, then it shows that you have a very small, shriveled heart. There is a sense in which the man of God who has been obedient, regardless of so-called success, is able to lay his head down at night and sleep. However, we should not be content just because we have had some measure of success in our little fishbowl. We should not be content until the name of Jesus Christ is proclaimed to every person of our generation, until His flag flies on every hill, mountain, and valley. We can be content when His name is glorified on every inch of this planet.

There has never been a time in the history of the world when an effectual door has been as opened as it is now. I'm not a prophet nor the son of a prophet, but through studying church history, human history, and secular history, I would tell you that a shadow is growing in the West. I don't know how long we will have this privilege to go out to all the nations, for it could be very soon that we are running for our lives. So while it is day let us work, for night comes when no man labors.

I used to write all the time in the back of our magazine, "Just what part of 'go' do you not understand?"[2] Then I realized that with regard to the evangelical community, the answer is that most individuals don't understand "go." Now you all know that "go" is not the primary command in the passage—"make disciples" is. Craig Blomberg, in his commentary on Matthew, gives this helpful insight: "Too much and too little have often been made of this observation."[3] It is emphasized too much when a church or a minister thinks that they are called to bloom only where they are planted—that they are doing the work because they are doing ministry in their Jerusalem. They are not granted that luxury because though they must minister in Jerusalem, they cannot forget the nations.

Also, too much emphasis is placed on "go" and not enough on "make disciples." This is the great sin of evangelicalism today, when we frantically give in to blatant pragmatism. When we look at the need of the world, too often we act in a way that is not biblical—that is, by sending people into the mission field who should not be on the mission field. This means individuals who do not meet the requirements set forth in Titus 1 and 1 Timothy 3. We cannot keep sending young, untrained people who do not even understand the word *propitiation* to the mission field. We must send qualified men, for this is an absolute necessity.

Another way in which we emphasize "go" too much is when we succumb to the carnal strategies that are being put before men today with regard to how to do missions and how to plant churches.

These strategies are absurd. They are made by little boys who know nothing of the power of God, who know nothing about intercessory prayer, and who do not believe in the power of proclamation. We need to lay aside these strategies once and for all, and use what the Scriptures give us to use.

The missionary enterprise is actually quite simple. You can divide it up into two ministries. You are either called to go, or you are called to send those who are going. Either way, the same devotion is required. William Carey told men, "I will go down [in the mine that is India], if you will hold the rope."[4] Missions is either you go down the rope into the mine, or you hold the rope for those who go down. Either way, there will be scars on your hands and exhaustion on your faces. Where are your scars? Where are the scars of your church? Where is the exhaustion? Where is the labor?

Pastors can be the greatest catalyst or the greatest hindrance when it comes to involving people in sacrificing for missions. The church is looking at their pastor. Is he concerned for the Indonesians who do not know the gospel? Is he concerned for countless good men, genuinely converted, trying to labor in some jungle somewhere, but do not have a clue how to interpret the Scriptures because they have not had the privileges you have? You must involve your people in missions. You must go, or you must send.

We live in an age of media, cyberspace, computers, Internet, and technology, and I praise God for that because we are able to send books, literature, and other things into closed countries. But we cannot fulfill the Great Commission online. It must be through incarnational missions. When God decided to send the gospel, He became a man and dwelt among us, and He is calling the church to do the same—to send flesh and blood. There should be no reason why we do not have missionaries all over the world. There should never be a reason why a missionary is walking around beggarly, trying to find a few books or raise a little money. Where is our faith, and where is our boldness?

I embrace fully the Westminster Confession and the 1689 London Confession with regard to their statements concerning the sovereignty of God. But sometimes I pray, "God, what do You want me to do in this situation?" Now, I don't hear a voice in response, but often this thought comes into my head: *Well, what can you believe Me for? How far do you want to take this?*

Just how big is your God? I'm so tired of men hiding behind the sovereignty of God. It is not a catalyst to permit us to remain passive; it is a catalyst to compel us to fight. I do not need a lightbulb to explode in my study while I'm praying to know that the gospel needs to be preached more in Indonesia. He has said, "Go, and to every nation, but go properly."

### Baptize Them

Jesus also said that as we make disciples we are to baptize them. There are a few things to mention concerning this. First, our converts must accept the full and unique Christian teaching. The text mentions baptizing in the very specific name of the Father, the Son, and the Holy Spirit. The God of the Bible is not the God of the Koran. The God of the Bible is not just like all other gods with a different name. The God of the Bible is not merely optional among many other religious options. He is the Name, the Way, the Truth, and the Life. You and I can end the 2000-year war between the secular world and the church by just changing an article—from a definite article to an indefinite article. All we have to do to be the toast of the secular world is to say that we believe in Jesus and that He is *a* way, *a* truth, and *a* life. But if we say that, we destroy the power of the gospel and we damn our own souls. There is no other name.

Also, our converts must publicly profess Jesus Christ as Lord. So many missionaries respond to me, "But if they do that they'll suffer." I don't say this lightly—yes, they will. I'm not saying we should lay aside all wisdom, that we should go out and try to be persecuted, or that we should demand these things from brothers in persecuted countries. But missions and suffering go hand in hand. Much of the missionary strategy today is designed so that missionaries and their converts do not have to suffer, but suffering is a part of representing Jesus Christ. In many of the countries with the greatest persecution of Christians, if you go home

and tell everybody you believe in Jesus, they won't have a problem with it, even in some Muslim countries. It is when you identify with Jesus Christ and His church, through baptism, and renounce all other religions, gods, and doctrines—that is when all hell breaks loose. Converts must identify with Christ publicly. The apostles never sought to teach people how to avoid suffering. Rather, they predicted suffering, and were determined to prepare people for it.

The last thing to say about baptism is that we are not called to leave in our wake a bunch of disconnected individual disciples. We are called to bring those disciples together in a church. Not a Bible study, not a worship group, but a church. And we are to labor until that church has a mature leadership, mature doctrine, is autonomous, strong, and biblical. Lately, missionaries have been trying to build culturally sensitive churches instead of biblically faithful churches. We should not take Western culture and force it on another culture. We should challenge the West and its culture, and when we go into other cultures, we must do the same. The standard that challenges culture is the Word of God.

The Great Commission is didactic. It is a theological endeavor. It is not about sending missionaries per se; it is about sending the truth through missionaries—to teach all to observe the truth. The Great Commission is not just about *gnosis*, it is about *praxis*; it is not just about orthodoxy, it is about orthopraxy. This is very clear in the teaching of Christ when He says, "Take My yoke upon you and learn from Me" (Matthew 11:29). The two always go hand in hand. To learn from Him is to submit to His sovereignty.

*Teach Them*

Then Jesus said in the Great Commission that we are to be "teaching them to observe all that I commanded you." What is the source? From where are we to teach people? What is to be our source of information? To teach them "all that I commanded you" (verse 20). We teach the words of Christ, the Word of the living God. Missions is not about sending missionaries; it is about sending God's truth through missionaries. I mention this simple statement again because we have more missionary activity today than at probably any other time in history, and yet most of it is smoke and mirrors. Dust! And when it all settles, I do not know how much truth will remain.

Because we are sending truth, the missionary must be an exegete. He must be a theologian. He must be both a proclaimer and a scribe. One of the best illustrations of a missionary, even though to his own people, was Ezra, for he set his heart to study the law of God, to practice it, and to teach its statutes and ordinances in Israel (Ezra 7:10). That is a missionary.

A young man contacted me years ago while I was in Peru and said, "I want to come down there, brother Paul, and I want to work with you." I replied, "Talk to me about your time in the Word, talk to me about your knowledge, your study of the Scriptures." He said, "That's not my area. I just want to come down there and give my life away." I responded, "Well, then talk to me about intercessory prayer." He said, "That's really not my area. Brother Paul, I just want to come down there and give my life away." I did take the young man under my wing, but this is what I said to him, "Nobody in Peru needs your life. They need someone who can come here, open his mouth, and proclaim to them the Word of the living God. They need the life, death, and resurrection of Jesus taught to them."

The command to make disciples through teaching proves that the Great Commission is a theological and doctrinal endeavor. But if we look at the great majority of missionary work in the world today, we see that doctrine does not have a high priority—although at one time it was the queen of all sciences. Lacking theology, mission work today in many cases has become a glaring contradiction, even an absurdity.

There are a few ways in which that's going on. Number one, it has become the popular opinion that Christians should lay aside their doctrine and rally around a common confession of Jesus. There is only one problem: There are multiple Christs being preached in the world today, not only in so-called Christendom, but even in the realm of evangelicalism. Are we to preach a Christ that is so vague and so general that we tell the world to follow an undefined Jesus and contradictory opinions with regard to His Word? Absolutely not!

Number two—and this may be the most absurd thing that was ever birthed in the mind of a man—we need to lay aside our doctrine and rally around the Great Commission. However, since we have already come to the conclusion that the Great Commission is a doctrinal or theological endeavor, to lay aside doctrine and theology while fulfilling the Great Commission is suicide. This is the problem today, and it is the same problem for every generation of the church—a depreciation of truth. Yet Christianity is a truth religion, and the Great Commission is about the proclamation of the truth.

If you want to be an ivory-tower theologian who sits and pontificates and meditates, then you can have all kinds of undefined doctrine. If you want to be a seminary student who just argues theology in the student center, you can have all kinds of undefined doctrine. But when you go to plant a church and you are dealing with real people with real problems, defining the small stuff becomes very important. It is the common practice of missionary organizations to reduce their doctrinal statement down to the lowest common denominator so that they can bring in more

candidates for the mission field and more supporters for those candidates. In many cases that is done by men with a desire to do something right. But it is a blatant surrender to pragmatism, and in the end, we lose our soul.

## His Presence and Power

Jesus concludes the commission with these words: "Lo, I am with you always, even to the end of the age" (Matthew 28:20). The first word in that sentence communicates the idea of looking, seeing, beholding, taking notice. It is as though Christ was looking at these men and saying, "Look at Me! Look at Me! I am now going to give you the greatest of all encouragements. I will be with you always, even into the end of the age."

By these words, as I have previously suggested, Christ shows that in sending the apostles, He does not entirely resign His office as if He ceased to be the teacher of His church. For He sends away the apostles with this reservation: that they will not bring forward their own inventions, but will purely and faithfully deliver from hand to hand, as we say, what Jesus entrusted to them. That is the word of missions—to faithfully deliver to our hearers what has been entrusted to us. God will bless that kind of work in the mission field.

# 10

# WHY EVERY SELF–RESPECTING CALVINIST MUST BE A PREMILLENNIALIST

*John MacArthur*
*Shepherds' Conference 2007*

*Selected Scriptures*

I have a heartfelt concern for an area of theology that needs more careful attention than it has been given. The topic is sovereign election, Israel, and eschatology. One of the strange ironies in the church and in Reformed theology is that those who are most in love with the doctrine of sovereign election, who are most unwavering in their devotion to the glory of God, the honor of Christ, the work of the Spirit in regeneration and sanctification, who are adamant about the veracity and inerrancy of Scripture, who are fastidious in hermeneutics, who are the most careful when it comes to doctrine, who are guardians of biblical truth, and who are laboring with all their powers to determine the true interpretation of every text in divine

revelation, yet at the same time are disinterested in applying those passions and skills to determining the end of the story, and are rather content to be in playful disagreement to the vast biblical data on eschatology.

## Does Eschatology Matter?

Does the end matter to God, and should it matter to us? The culmination of all redemptive history is important. History is headed to a divinely designed conclusion, and it is significant enough that God has revealed it to us. God filled the Scriptures with end-time prophecies, and it has been estimated that nearly a quarter of the Bible, at the time it was written, relates to the eschaton.

Did God in this significant volume

of revelation somehow muddle His words so hopelessly that the high ground for theologians is simply to recognize the muddle and abandon any thoughts of the perspicuity of Scripture with regard to eschatology? Is in fact working hard to understand prophetic passages needless and impossible because they require a spiritualized or allegorized set of interpretations? Are you comfortable with the notion that the tried-and-true principles of interpretation have to be set aside every time you come to a prophetic text?

### Reclaiming a Literal Interpretation

There are a number of amillennialists and postmillennialists who state that many prophetic passages require a spiritualized or allegorized interpretation. The common view held by these two camps is that the kingdom promised to Israel, as identified in the Old Testament, was never meant to be fulfilled in a literal sense. O.T. Allis, a well-known amillennialist, acknowledges that a simple and literal interpretation of these Old Testament prophecies would require that the promises to Israel be realized by national Israel: "The Old Testament prophecies if literally interpreted, cannot be regarded as having been yet fulfilled or being capable of fulfillment in the present age."[1]

Floyd Hamilton, in *The Basis of Millennial Faith*, elaborates: "Now we must frankly admit that a literal interpretation of the Old Testament prophecies gives us just such a picture of an earthly reign of the Messiah as the pre-millennialist pictures."[2] Lorraine Boettner wrote, "In the meaning of the Millennium, it is generally agreed that if the prophecies are taken literally, they do foretell a restoration of the nation of Israel in the land of Palestine, with the Jews having a prominent place in that kingdom and ruling over the other nations."[3]

All three of these cases required a severe alteration in hermeneutics in order to avoid a premillennial conclusion, which apparently, in their view, is a fate worse than death. To protect some kind of preconceived theological position, it is necessary for them to change the rules of interpretation. However, if we're going to change those rules we better have clarity from the Lord that those rules need to be changed. But there's no evidence that God wants us to change the rules of interpretation.

For example, when we go to the first three chapters of Genesis, God is not pleased when we come up with progressive creationism, theistic evolution, or any kind of day-age theory. Instead, God is exalted as the Creator in the full glory of His creative power when we have a literal interpretation of the first three chapters of Genesis. Nothing in the text gives mandate to indicate that this descriptive account is something other than specific, literal, normal, and factual language. One cannot justify calling it poetry because a recent study conducted by one of our professors at The Master's College, using linguistic software to compare the difference between prose and poetry, led to the conclusion that the narrative account is distinctly prose and not poetry. We don't want anyone tampering with the beginning; why are we so tolerant of people tampering with the end?

We do not want to allow someone to arbitrarily introduce their own hermeneutic into Genesis, and yet we are content to allow people to introduce their own hermeneutics into prophetic passages throughout the Bible, and particularly in the book of Revelation. Where is the divine mandate on the pages of Scripture to do such a thing? What chapter and verse is that found in? Who then decides the new rules for engagement?

## A Clarion Call for Change

Going back to my introductory thought, it is ironic that those who celebrate God's sovereign grace of unilateral, divine, unconditional, and irrevocable election to Christians unashamedly deny the same for elect Israel. This is a strange division, for Scripture teaches the perpetuity of the elect church to salvation glory, and in similar language Scripture affirms the perpetuity of ethnic Israel to a future salvation of a generation of Jews that will fulfill all the divine promises given to them by God. In both cases, this is the work of and the result of divine sovereign election.

Of all the people who could be premillennialist, it should be those who love sovereign election—Calvinists. Arminians make great amillennialists because

the two views are consistent—God elects and preserves no one. We can leave amillennialism to the process theologians or the open theists, who think God is becoming progressively better because as every day goes by He gets more information to figure out whether or not in fact He can keep some of the promises He previously made. Let's leave amillennialism to the charismatics, the semipelagians, and other sorts who reject the security of salvation, since it makes sense with their theological position—Israel sinned, became apostate, killed the Son of God, and forfeited everything.

How is it possible to reconcile the idea that God is the only one who can determine who will be saved and yet proclaim that the church inherits all of Israel's promises because they do better than Israel? Amillennialism does not compute because it basically says Israel, based on their disobedience, forfeited all the promises. Do you think that they on their own could have done something to guarantee that they'd receive these pledges? If you think that Israel lost their place in God's economy because they did not do what they were supposed to, then you have rejected election and embraced Arminian theology. In Isaiah 45:4, God called Israel "my elect." He said, "For the sake of Jacob My servant, and Israel My chosen one, I have also called you by your name." Isaiah 65:9 speaks of Israel being God's elect and says that they will inherit the promise. In Isaiah 65:22, once again national Israel is called God's elect. God repeated this title a number of times in the Old Testament.

Now that leads us to the conclusion that if one's interpretation of God's election and Israel's promises is accurate, then their eschatology will be accurate as well. Never will you migrate from one view to another just depending on the last book you read, the last lecture you listened to, or the last influential person you interacted with.

How does one have a proper view of Israel? To get Israel right, you get the Old Testament covenants and promises right. To get the Old Testament covenants and promises right, you get the interpretation of Scripture right. To get the interpretation of Scripture right, you stay faithful to a legitimate hermeneutic. The end result of this is that God's integrity is upheld.

The Bible calls God "the God of Israel" more than 200 times. There are more than 2000 references to Israel in Scripture, with 73 New Testament uses of *Israel*. None of those references means anything but national Israel. This includes Romans 9:6 and Galatians 6:16, which are the only two passages that amillennialists reference in their attempt to convince us that the two cancel out the other 1998. However, those two passages can easily be interpreted as a reference to Jews who were believers.

It should also be noted that Jews still exist today. That becomes an interesting fact when you ponder whether or not you've ever met a Hittite, an Amorite, or a Jebusite. Anybody know any of those folks? Do you know that the Israeli immigrant bureau in the land of Israel requires DNA tests where Jewish ancestry is questioned, and they actually know what Jewish DNA looks like? Somebody asked John Stott in a European conference what was the significance of Israel's existence today, and he replied, "It has no biblical significance." That's a strange answer, because three-fourths of Scripture is the story of Israel, and the nation is still in existence.

The foundation for an accurate understanding of eschatology is having a working concept of election and Israel. The two go together and are inseparable. How is it that we have come to understand election and totally missed Israel? I'm confident that God did not reveal prophetic truth in such a way to hide or obscure the truth, but to reveal it for our blessing, our motivation, and ultimately His glory. My words to you here are a call to reconnect these two truths. Return the sovereignty of God in election to its rightful place, and therefore return the nation Israel to its rightful place in God's redemptive history. As a result, all eschatology will unfold with magnificent beauty through the normal hermeneutic you can take to every passage.

Now that the Spirit of God is moving the church to reestablish the glorious high ground of sovereign grace in salvation, it is time to reestablish the equally high ground of sovereign grace for a future generation of ethnic Israel during the messianic earthly kingdom with the complete fulfillment of all God's promises to Israel.

## A Tested Eschatology

I have thought through these great realities for almost 50 years. The clearer I understand sovereign electing grace, the clearer the place of Israel in God's redemptive plan gets. I have not moved away from the biblical eschatology I was convinced of when I began in the ministry. One of the benefits of being the pastor of Grace Community Church for nearly 40 years is that I'm forced to keep moving, since I can't preach old sermons. These dear people—can you imagine hearing the same preacher for almost 40 years? Not so good for them, but beneficial for me because I have had to continually teach all portions of the Bible. I'm getting close to preaching through the entirety of Luke, which leaves our church family with only the Gospel of Mark before I've preached through the entire New Testament. For 40 years I have taught and preached through every verse, every phrase, every word of the New Testament, then gone back and written commentaries. Through all of this my eschatology has had to stand the test of every New Testament verse. My conviction has not changed; it only has been strengthened and refined.

I've also preached through many Old Testament books. Early in my years here at Grace Community Church I started in Genesis. I've preached through prophetic books. In and out of Daniel, Ezekiel, Isaiah, Zechariah, and the minor prophets. A fair test of a cohesive eschatology is to drag it through every single text, and I've done my best to do exactly that. I am unwaveringly committed to the sovereign election of a future generation of Jews to salvation and the full inheritance of all the promises and covenants of God given to them in the Old Testament. This isn't a personal ambition; God's Word is at stake.

## Dispensationalism?

Now, at this point I imagine some of you are saying, "Oh no—we came to a pastor's conference, and it's turned into a dispensational conference. Next thing he's going to do is drag out Clarence Larkin's charts, give out really nice leatherbound copies of the Scofield Study Bible, and then we'll all be gifted the Left Behind® series. He's probably going to tell us there are seven dispensations, two kingdoms, two new covenants, two ways of salvation." My response: Relax and forget dispensationalism, because I'm not talking about that. Even though, as a side note, every one of you is a dispensationalist. Let me test this hypothesis. Do you believe that God dealt with man one way before the Fall, after the Fall, before the law, after the law, before the cross, after the cross, now and in eternity? Exactly.

However, I reject the cartoon eschatology and the crazy interpretations of the locusts of Revelation 9 being helicopters. I don't think that Henry Kissinger is the Antichrist and that Hillary Clinton is the harlot of Babylon. Though I don't agree with all of dispensationalism, it is no more peculiar than the interpretation of many amillennialists, who have fictionalized that Jesus reads everything into AD 70. Another common objection is, "Well, didn't the dispensationalists invent premillennialism?" In the modern era, two books reintroduced premillennial views, neither of them written by a dispensationalist. The first was called *The Pre-Millennial Advent of Messiah*. It was written in 1836 by an Anglican named William Cuninghame.[4] The second was an English publication in 1827 written by Manuel Lacunza y Diaz, a Jesuit.[5] It is wrong to conclude that there is a direct and necessary connection between all that is strange in dispensationalism and a clear understanding of the kingdom.

## The Whole Truth

When Frederick the Great asked his chaplain for proof of the truthfulness of the Bible, he said, "Give me a brief defense." His chaplain replied, "I can do that in one word. Israel." Israel, understood as a people preserved by God for an eschatological kingdom, has immense apologetic value. We have to get the whole counsel of God right. We have to give the world the truth about the end of history and the climactic glory of Christ and the fulfillment of God's promises to Israel and the church. We delve into the discussion with a series of questions.

## Is the Old Testament Amillennial?

It is not legitimate to interpret the Old Testament as secondary to the New Testament. If you say that, then the Old Testament cannot be rightly interpreted apart from the New Testament, and you have denied the perspicuity of a large portion of God's Word. Walter Kaiser summarizes this well when he writes that you end up having "a canon within a canon." Without using the New Testament to reinterpret the Old, does the Old Testament itself propound an amillennial view?

It's inappropriate to revoke the true meaning contained in the Old Testament and make all of its promises related to the church. Even Paul acknowledged that the church is a mystery not mentioned clearly in previous revelation (Ephesians 3:1-6). The idea that the New Testament is the starting point for understanding the Old is where amillennialism comes from. Once again, if this is done, it damages the perspicuity or the clarity of the Old Testament in and of itself. It leads to exegetical spiritualization that goes beyond just prophetic texts and warrants the interpreter to lead New Testament Christian principles back into Old Testament texts, where they do not belong.

An example of this is what some individuals do with the book of Nehemiah. They interpret Nehemiah as being the Holy Spirit, the fallen walls of Jerusalem as the fallen walls of the human heart, and they say the Lord wants to rebuild the fallen heart by the use of mortar, which is speaking in tongues. Spiritualization puts the reader on a slippery slope.

It's rare to find a pastor who preaches the Old Testament with the interpretive lens of a person living at the time it was written. Please don't misunderstand what I mean—we can use the Old Testament for illustrations, we can use it for examples, and it has to have practical application to people in our cultural context. However, interpretation must begin with the clarity and perspicuity the original readers would have had.

*Replacement theology* ignores that principle and demands that the Old Testament promises be viewed through the lens of the New Testament. It also strikes a strange dichotomy since all the curses promised to Israel came to Israel and are still being poured out on them. If you're wondering whether the curses in the Old Testament were literal, you can see the tangible evidence of the nation of Israel bearing those curses. Yes, Israel is currently experiencing the promise of God that they will be perpetuated as an ethnic people; however, this current group of Jews that live in the world today, and in the nation Israel, are bearing a curse. They are apostate, they have rejected their Messiah, and they are under divine chastening. All the curses promised to Israel for disobedience to God came true and are coming true.

But now all of a sudden we're supposed to split all the passages of blessings and curses and say that Israel is experiencing literal curses, but the promises of blessing have been spiritualized and

given to the church? Where is the textual justification for such a split interpretation? Wouldn't you think that whatever way the curses were fulfilled would set the standard for whatever way the blessings would be fulfilled? Also, wouldn't you expect that all of the prophecies that literally came to pass during Jesus' advent would set the pattern for how the prophecies connected to His second coming would come to pass?

Is the Old Testament amillennial? Of course not. If you affirm normal hermeneutics and the perspicuity of the Old Testament, then you cannot use the New Testament to reinterpret the Old. The totality of Scripture must be interpreted, preached, and taught as clear revelation from God that is to be understood, believed, and applied by the people to whom it was given.

### What Are the Covenants?

To further understand this topic, we must ask a second question: What covenants are made in the Old Testament? The primary goal of this research is to behold the connection between these covenants and God's electing sovereignty. We read in Genesis 12:1, "Now the LORD said to Abram, 'Go forth from your country, and from your relatives and from your father's house.'" In this passage we have a great illustration of election. What did Abram do to set this in motion? Nothing, for Abram played no part in instituting this covenant. Now follow the use of the expression "I will":

"And *I will* make you a great nation, and *I will* bless you, and make your name great; and so you shall be a blessing; and *I will* bless those who bless you, and the one who curses you *I will* curse. And in you all the families of the earth *will* be blessed" (verses 2-3). The expression is used five times. We see here sovereign, unilateral, and unconditional election.

In Genesis 15, Abram wanted confirmation of this covenant coming to fruition. "O Lord GOD, how may I know that I will possess it?" (Genesis 15:8). God's response: "'Bring me a three year old heifer, and a three year old female goat, and a three year old ram, and a turtledove, and a young pigeon.' Then he brought all these to Him and cut them in two, and laid each half opposite the other; but he did not cut the birds" (verses 9-10). Then the birds of prey came down upon the carcasses, but Abram drove them away.

Now what did God do here? He took these animals, cut them in half, set them opposite of each other, and there's a path going through these split animals and the two dead birds—one bird on each side. This relates to the term in Hebrew, "cut a covenant." When you cut a covenant or make a covenant, you put out blood sacrifices as a way of demonstrating the seriousness of the promise. God prepared what would be a very traditional and typical way to engage in making a covenant. Only this occasion is different because we read, "Now when the sun was going down, a deep

sleep fell upon Abram; and behold, terror and great darkness fell upon him. God said to Abram, 'Know for certain that your descendants will be strangers in a land that is not theirs, where they will be enslaved and oppressed four hundred years'" (verses 12-13).

Well, does "four hundred years" actually mean four hundred? Yes it does! Our hermeneutic forces us to take that literally. And it's perfectly accurate because it's a prophecy of what will take place. "But I will also judge the nation whom they will serve, and afterward they will come out with many possessions. As for you, you shall go to your fathers in peace; you will be buried at a good old age" (verses 14-15).

Then we read in verse 17, "It came about when the sun had set, that it was very dark, and behold, there appeared a smoking oven and a flaming torch which passed between these pieces." God anesthetized Abram and God alone went through the pieces, visually indicating that this was a unilateral, unconditional, irrevocable promise that He made with Himself. There were no conditions for Abraham to fulfill. For on that day, the Lord made a covenant with Abraham, and it is a covenant that does not end.

We jump to Genesis 17:7: "I will establish my covenant between Me and you and your descendants after you throughout their generations for an everlasting covenant, to be God to you and to your descendants after you." God elected Abraham, elected the nation that would come out of his loins, and made a covenant and a promise to be their God. This is the foundational covenant in the Bible, a unilateral and unconditional promise of the Lord.

### The Mosaic Covenant

Fast-forward to when God gave the Mosaic Covenant to Israel—it became very apparent how sinful they were. Yet even in the midst of Israel's blatant sin, apostasy, idolatry, and violation of God's law, the nation still continued to be the object of His covenant love. In Ezekiel 16 there is a staggering chronicle by God of His choice of Israel. He speaks of Israel in graphic terms, comparing their election to finding a baby thrown away in a field. "On the day you were born your navel cord was not cut, nor were you washed with water for cleansing; you were not rubbed with salt [which they did to disinfect children] or even wrapped in cloths. No eye looked with pity on you to do any of these things for you, to have compassion on you. Rather you were thrown out into the open field, for you were abhorred on the day you were born" (Ezekiel 16:4-5). God said, "When I passed by you and saw you squirming in your blood, I said to you while you were in your blood, 'Live!' Yes, I said to you while you were in your blood, 'Live!'" (verse 6). There again we see God's sovereign election.

The story goes on to show how God took Israel as an unfaithful wife, cleansed her, and made her His own. "Moreover, you played the harlot with the Assyrians

because you were not satisfied; you played the harlot with them and still were not satisfied" (verse 28). Then in verse 36 we read, "Your lewdness was poured out and your nakedness uncovered through your harlotries with your lovers and with all your detestable idols, and because of the blood of your sons which you gave to idols." Indictment after indictment, we see that God is furious with them. Nevertheless, we read,

"I will remember My covenant with you in the days of your youth, and I will establish an everlasting covenant with you. Then you will remember your ways and be ashamed when you receive your sisters, *both* your older and your younger; and I will give them to you as daughters, but not because of your covenant. Thus I will establish My covenant with you, and you shall know that I am the LORD, so that you may remember and be ashamed and never open your mouth anymore because of your humiliation, when I have forgiven you for all that you have done," the Lord GOD declares (verses 60-63).

This is a reiteration of the terms of the covenant in the face of Israel's history of defection, disobedience, and apostasy. God's decision to set His love on Israel was in no way determined by Israel's performance nor by Israel's national worthiness, but purely on the basis of His independent, uninfluenced, sovereign grace (Deuteronomy 7:7-8). The Lord alone is the sole party responsible to fulfill the obligations, and there are no conditions which Abram or any other Jew could fulfill on their own.

A parallel can be made with the Christian's experience. Believers do not come to Christ on their own, but are given life by the Spirit of God according to His will. And the Lord alone is the sole party responsible to fulfill the obligations. Obedience is not the condition that determines fulfillment. Rather, divine sovereign power is the condition that determines obedience, which leads to fulfillment. Therefore, when God gave the unilateral covenant, He knew He would have to produce the obedience in the future to fulfill this plan.

### The Davidic Covenant

After the Mosaic Covenant, God gave the Davidic Covenant, which was instituted in 2 Samuel 7. It is here that God promised to David that he would have a greater son who will have an everlasting kingdom. This covenant is an expansion of the Abrahamic Covenant: "I will raise up your descendant after you, who will come forth from you, and I will establish his kingdom. He shall build a house for My name, and I will establish the throne of his kingdom forever" (2 Samuel 7:12-13). God promised to Abraham a seed, a land, and a nation; of course that embodies the kingdom and the promise of a perfect king. In establishing the Davidic

Covenant, once again we see God use the phrase "I will." God is the one who accomplishes His work.

It is important to clarify that this is not to say that the Abrahamic Covenant is only for Israel. We all participate in its spiritual blessings. When it comes to the Abrahamic and Davidic Covenants, all believers will participate, even those not of Israel, because we experience salvation and are citizens of the kingdom.

### The New Covenant

The final covenant is the New Covenant. There can be no fulfillment of the promises God gave to Abraham or David apart from salvation. And throughout history there has always been a faithful remnant of Israel—those who did not bow the knee to Ba'al. God has always had a people, His chosen. And not all Israel is the true Israel of God. Isaiah 6:13 reminds us that God will have a holy remnant, but in the future there will be a salvation of ethnic Israel on a national level. That is precisely the message of Jeremiah 31—the New Covenant given to Israel.

We enjoy discussing this covenant because we participate in the salvific provision of the New Covenant ratified in the death and resurrection of Christ. However, it is essential to remember that the application of the New Covenant is in a special way given to a future generation of Jews. "'Behold, days are coming,' declares the LORD, 'when I will make a new covenant with the house of Israel and with the house of Judah, not like the covenant which I made with their fathers in the day I took them by the hand to bring them out of the land of Egypt, My covenant which they broke, although I was a husband to them'" (Jeremiah 31:31-32). The Mosaic Covenant was not a covenant that could save, but this New Covenant from the Lord will change everything. What warrant do amillennialists have to say that the direct reference to "Israel" does not mean national Israel?

"I will put my law within them and on their heart I will write it; and I will be their God, and they shall be My people" (verse 33). "I will forgive their iniquity, and their sin I will remember no more" (verse 34). Is it possible that God has changed His mind about doing this for His people? "Thus says the LORD, who gives the sun for light by day and the fixed order of the moon and the stars for light by night, who stirs up the sea so that its waves roar; the LORD of hosts is His name: 'If this fixed order departs from before Me,' declares the LORD, 'then the offspring of Israel also will cease from being a nation before Me forever'" (verses 35-36). I haven't noticed that happen yet. Have you? There isn't another way to understand this passage other than the clear and literal meaning. If this text does not mean what it just said, then it's incomprehensible.

The New Covenant promises the salvation that incorporates all the promises of the Abrahamic Covenant, the Davidic Covenant, and all the extended promises throughout the entire Old Testament.

What is the key feature? God will put His law within them; on their heart He will write it. He will be their God, and He will forgive their iniquity.

The parallel passage of this promise is found in Ezekiel 36:24-27:

> I will take you from the nations, gather you from all the lands and bring you into your own land. Then I will sprinkle clean water on you, and you will be clean; I will cleanse you from all your filthiness and from all your idols. Moreover, I will give you a new heart and put a new spirit within you; and I will remove the heart of stone from your flesh and give you a heart of flesh. I will put My Spirit within you and cause you to walk in My statutes, and you will be careful to observe My ordinances.

The only way an individual is capable of walking in God's statutes and obeying His ordinances is if God Himself causes them to do it. When God gave unilateral, unconditional, sovereign, and gracious promises to an elect people, He guaranteed He would fulfill those promises through His divine power. When God said such covenant promises are irrevocable, we cannot, without impunity and guilt, for any seemingly convenient idea or assumption, say they are void.

Well, what about Israel's apostasy? Doesn't that revoke the promises?

Understand that the New Covenant promises given in Jeremiah and Ezekiel were given to Israel at the time when the nation was under divine judgment for apostasy. These blessings were not given when all was well and the people were living in obedience to God. At the time of this prophecy Israel is apostate, living out of the land, and God still says that even this rebellion will not revoke His promises.

Another fair question that arises is, "Didn't Israel reject their Messiah?" One of the strange theories of dispensationalism is that Jesus came and offered the kingdom, and because unbelieving Jews did not accept it and killed Him, He came up with Plan B, which entailed giving the kingdom to the church. That is completely wrong because the cross was not Plan B. We can read the description of what would happen at the cross in Psalm 22. Isaiah 53 prophetically described the crucifixion and the Suffering Servant, Jesus. The cross has always been part of the plan.

But how does national Israel connect with the cross? In Zechariah 12:10, we read, "They will look on Me whom they have pierced; and they will mourn for Him, as one mourns for an only son, and they will weep bitterly over Him like the bitter weeping over a firstborn." Then in Zechariah 13:1: "In that day a fountain will be opened for the house of David and for the inhabitants of Jerusalem, for sin and for impurity." A day will come when Israel will be saved and the totality of the New Covenant will be fulfilled! And if you continue reading into Zechariah 14, you'll learn about the coming of the kingdom. Zechariah chapters 12 to 14 do not make sense apart from a premillennial view.

### Were the Israelites in Jesus' Day Amillennial?

In an effort to answer this third question, Emil Schurer wrote a helpful study of first-century Jewish eschatology. It was first published in 1880, and a more recent edition was released by Hendrickson Publishers.[6] Shurer stated that the ancient Israelites believed the Messiah's coming would be preceded by a time of trouble. They believed that before the Messiah arrived, Elijah would come as a forerunner. They also believed that the Messiah would be the personal son of David, that He would have special powers to set up His kingdom, and that all the Abrahamic and Davidic Covenant promises would be fulfilled in Him.

They also believed that Israel would repent and be saved at the coming of the Anointed One, the kingdom would be established in Israel with Jerusalem at the center, and the messianic influence would extend across the world. As a result, the world would be renovated, peace and righteousness would dominate, and all people would worship the Messiah. This worship would involve a reinstituted temple. The culmination of this kingdom would be final judgment, and after that, the eternal state. That's

Jewish pre-New Testament eschatology. And it lines up perfectly with the premillennialist view.

Schurer is not the only evidence for this. Zacharias, the priestly father of John the Baptist, believed this. In the latter part of Luke 1, Zacharias's proclamation stems from the Old Testament passages about the Abrahamic, Davidic, and New Covenants. Zacharias knew what was happening—that the coming Messiah meant the covenants were to be fulfilled.

### Was Jesus Amillennial?

This fourth question is one of the most important we must answer. We read what Luke wrote about the resurrected Christ:

> The first account I composed, Theophilus, about all that Jesus began to do and teach, until the day when He was taken up to heaven, after He had by the Holy Spirit given orders to the apostles whom He had chosen. To these He also presented Himself alive after His suffering, by many convincing proofs, appearing to them over a period of forty days and speaking of the things concerning the kingdom of God (Acts 1:1-3).

Jesus spent His final 40 days with the disciples talking about the things concerning the kingdom of God. If Jesus was amillennial, this was His moment to launch amillennialism. But we see that after 40 days of instruction about the kingdom, the disciples were still confident that the kingdom, for national Israel, was still a future event. They did not ask if the kingdom would come to Israel. Instead, they asked when: "Lord, is it at this time You are restoring the kingdom to Israel?" (verse 6).

How did Jesus respond? Did He say, "Where did you get such a foolish idea? Where did you come up with that concept? Haven't you been listening to Me during the last forty days? I'm an amillennialist. How bizarre to think that I'm going to restore the kingdom to Israel. You didn't hear me—the church is the new Israel."

But Jesus didn't say there isn't going to be a kingdom. Rather, He responded, "It is not for you to know times or epochs which the Father has fixed by His own authority" (verse 7).

In Acts 1:7, the Greek verb "fixed" is in the middle voice, so it's better translated "the Father has fixed for Himself." It's about the Father's glory, exaltation, and the world finally experiencing paradise regained. The ultimate goal here is singular and unilateral. There is no Replacement Theology in the theology of Jesus; there is no supersessionism. This movement to establish that there is no earthly kingdom for Israel is absolutely foreign to the Old Testament, foreign to the New Testament, and foreign to Jesus.

### Were the Apostles Amillennial?

If the Israelites in Jesus' day and Jesus Himself did not hold to the amillennial view, then what about Peter? Was he the first amillennialist? To answer this fifth question, we listen in on Peter's sermon:

> The God of Abraham, Isaac and Jacob, the God of our fathers, has glorified His servant Jesus, the one whom you delivered and disowned in the presence of Pilate, when he had decided to release Him. But you disowned the Holy and Righteous One and asked for a murderer to be granted to you, but put to death the Prince of life, the one whom God raised from the dead, a fact to which we are witnesses (Acts 3:13-15).

"But the things which God announced beforehand by the mouth of all the prophets, that His Christ would suffer, He has thus fulfilled" (verse 18). This is a statement that we take literally; therefore, the next phrase that comes out of Peter's mouth should be taken literally as well: "Therefore repent and return, so that your sins may be wiped away, in order that times of refreshing may come from the presence of the Lord" (verse 19). "Times of refreshing" refers to the future kingdom. "That He may send Jesus, the Christ appointed for you, whom heaven must receive until the period of restoration of all things about which God spoke by the mouth of His holy prophets from

ancient time" (verses 20-21). I especially love verse 25: "It is you who are the sons of the prophets and of the covenant which God made with your fathers."

Peter did not cancel the covenant; he reinforced the validity of it: "Saying to Abraham, 'And in your seed all the families of the earth shall be blessed.' For you first, God raised up His Servant and sent Him to bless you by turning every one of you from your wicked ways" (verses 25-26). Peter had the perfect opportunity to nullify these promises, and yet he reminded his Jewish listeners that they were the sons of the covenant.

Was James an amillennialist? Read what he said:

> Simeon has related how God first concerned Himself about taking from among the Gentiles a people for His name. With this the words of the Prophets agree, just as it is written, "After these things I will return, and I will rebuild the tabernacle of David which has fallen, and I will rebuild its ruins, and I will restore it, so that the rest of mankind may seek the Lord, and all the Gentiles who are called by My name," says the Lord, who makes these things known from long ago (Acts 15:14-18).

The acceptance of the Gentiles was not the cancellation of Israel's promises. Instead, after Gentile conversion, God will rebuild the tabernacle of David, which has fallen, entailing that the Davidic Covenant and messianic promises will be fulfilled.

Maybe the apostle Paul was the first amillennial? He wrote in Romans 3:1-4, "What advantage has the Jew? Or what is the benefit of circumcision? Great in every respect. First of all, that they were entrusted with the oracles of God. What then? If some did not believe, their unbelief will not nullify the faithfulness of God, will it? May it never be!" If Paul had held the amillennialist position, he would have written, "Absolutely, it nullifies the promise of God." But he didn't do that. Note what he said:

> It is not as though the word of God has failed. For they are not all Israel who are descended from Israel [that is to say they are not all true Israel]; nor are they all children because they are Abraham's descendants, but: "through Isaac your descendants will be named." That is, it is not the children of the flesh who are children of God, but the children of the promise are regarded as descendants (Romans 9:6-8).

Just because some Jews hadn't come to belief didn't mean that God's faithfulness had been nullified. And just because there are some whom God chooses doesn't mean that He is not going to choose a whole duly-constituted generation of Jews to fulfill His promises.

Then perhaps most notably we see what Romans 11:26 says: "So all Israel will be saved." How else can you interpret that? One way is to say that Paul was not referring to national Israel. But where in the text does it say it's not Israel? "Just as it is written, 'The deliverer will come from Zion, He will remove ungodliness from Jacob.' 'This is My covenant with them, when I take away their sins'" (verse 26). The Israelites are enemies at the present time, but that is for the sake of the Gentiles. Why can we be sure that eventually God will save them? "For the gifts and the calling of God are irrevocable" (verse 29). If it depended on the people of Israel to obey God on their own, then theirs was an impossible task from the start. Only the One who made the promise can enable the obedience that is connected to the fulfillment of the promise.

### The Danger of Replacement Theology

Ronald Diprose wrote an excellent work titled *Israel and the Church*.[7] It first appeared as a PhD dissertation in Italian and has no connection to traditional dispensationalism. It shows how the effect of Replacement Theology helped to form the church of the Dark Ages—he explains how the church went from the New Testament concept to the sacramental institutional system of the Dark Ages, which we know as Roman Catholicism.

Diprose lays much of the blame at the feet of Replacement Theology, which stems from Augustine, Origen, and Justin. Why did the church implement altars, sacrifices, a sign parallel to circumcision, a priesthood, ceremonial rituals, and reintroduce mystery by speaking in a language that most people could not understand? Diprose traced the Roman Catholic ecclesiology to the influence of causing the church to be the new Israel. Replacement Theology justifies bringing in all the trappings of Judaism.

Another negative effect of Replacement Theology is the damage it does to evangelistic outreach to Jewish people. Imagine that you're speaking to a Jewish person and you say, "Jesus is the Messiah."

The response: "Really? Where is His established kingdom?"

"It's already here," you say.

The Jewish person's retort: "If that's the case, then why are we still being killed and persecuted? Why don't we have the land that was promised to us? Why isn't the Messiah reigning in Jerusalem, and why aren't peace and joy and gladness dominating the world? Why isn't the desert blooming?"

Then you say, "Oh no, you don't understand. All that's not going to take place literally. You're actually not God's people anymore; we are."

Then the Jewish person will respond with this devastating comment: "If this is the kingdom of Jesus, then Jesus is not the Messiah the Tanakh promises."

However, if you tell that nonbelieving Jew that God will keep every single promise He made to Israel, and that God is preparing for a great day of restoration for the Jewish people, then you have a chance to communicate to that individual. But you have to look to Psalm 22, Isaiah 53, and Zechariah 12:10 to understand that first the Messiah had to come, die, and be raised on the third day to ratify the New Covenant so He could forgive people's sins and inaugurate the kingdom.

## A Final Plea

As pastors, we have to get divine, sovereign, gracious, unconditional, unilateral, irrevocable election right, and we have to get God, Israel, and eschatology right. When we do, then we can open our Bibles and preach our heart out of any text and say what it says without having to scramble around and find some bizarre interpretation that fits a specific theological system.

Get it right, and God is glorified. Get it right, and Christ is exalted. Get it right, and the Holy Spirit is honored. Get it right, and Scripture is clear. Get it right, and the greatest historical illustration of God's work in the world is visible. Get it right, and the meaning of mystery in the New Testament is maintained. Get it right, and the straightforward meaning of the text is intact and Scripture wasn't written for mystics. Get it right, and the chronology of prophetic literature is intact. Get it right, and your historical worldview is complete. Get it right, and the practical benefit of eschatology is released on your people. Get it right!

A literal millennial kingdom of the eschaton is the only view that honors sovereign electing grace, honors the truthfulness of God's promises, honors the teachings of Old Testament prophets, the teachings of Jesus, and the teachings of the New Testament writers. Make your church a second-coming church, and make your life a second-coming life.

# PRAYER

Father, what a glorious, transcendent theme. May we live in the light of the coming of Christ. May we know that Your Word can be trusted and that we can preach every verse and proclaim what it clearly states. Thank You for these precious men who are here at the conference. Lord, fill us all with joy in the truth and in the privilege of serving You. In Christ's name. Amen.

# 11

# HEAVEN ON EARTH: EXPLORING THE GLORIES OF THE ETERNAL STATE

*Michael Vlach*
*Shepherds' Conference 2013*

*Selected Scriptures*

Many discussions on eschatology focus on the rapture, Tribulation, and millennium. Consequently, the eternal state often gets left out of detailed consideration. Yet the eternal state ought to excite us. When we look at the fallen world and experience its effects, it is good to think about our ultimate destiny. The new heavens and new earth with its New Jerusalem is where we will spend eternity. Even the thousand-year millennial kingdom, as long as it is, is significantly less than eternity.

Second Peter 3:13 reads, "According to His promise we are looking for new heavens and a new earth, in which righteousness dwells." The new heavens and new earth are our ultimate destiny, and it is to them that we should be looking.

Even the intermediate heaven, where saints go when they die, is temporary. It will give way to the new earth and the New Jerusalem. Therefore, we cannot neglect this important doctrine.

## Mistakes to Avoid

There are two mistakes to avoid when studying the eternal state. The first is avoiding this topic. For most of church history this has been a problem. Compared to other doctrines, there are not many works treating the eternal state.[1] A second mistake involves looking at eternity through what can be called "spiritual vision model" glasses. This occurs when we overspiritualize the eternal state and treat it as so transcendent and "other-than" that we lose how real it is. The spiritual vision model is a paradigm or approach to God's purposes that elevates spiritual realities to the exclusion of physical realities.

Spiritual vision thinking can be traced to the philosopher Plato, who made a strong distinction in value between spiritual and physical matters. His ideas influenced both Jewish and Christian scholars at times. Unfortunately, when Christians think about their eternal home they often perceive it as a static, colorless, spiritual existence. Studies have shown that roughly two-thirds of Americans think heaven is a bodiless spiritual existence. But that is not what the Bible teaches. When God created the world, He declared it "very good." This included the physical realm. Because the creation has a physical dimension, so too will the new earth.

We should not overspiritualize our future home and think God's purposes are only spiritual and not material. You may be familiar with cartoons where people in heaven are seen on a cloud with wings and a halo. That is a common cultural conception—heaven is static, still, contemplative, and boring. Many people think of heaven in those terms. There are even Christians who wonder, "Is heaven boring?" Nothing could be further from the truth.

Christian leaders need to teach people about our eternal home on the new earth. Doing so helps give people hope! If we are making the eternal state into something that it's not, then our hope is perverted. We must seriously examine passages related to the eternal state and draw sound conclusions when possible.

Revelation 21–22 is the most specific passage about the eternal state. There are some things in these chapters that we can know with a high degree of confidence. Also, some matters are more difficult to understand. Sometimes people can err on one of two sides. One is to think they can be certain on the meaning of every detail. Another is avoiding these chapters altogether.

I have put together a list of ten study points on the eternal state to help us better understand the glories of our home to come. But first, let's look at three key presuppositions:

### Key Presuppositions

First, we can have real and sufficient knowledge about the eternal state. This does not mean perfect or exhaustive knowledge. But just because we do not have exhaustive knowledge does not mean we cannot have true knowledge. God has revealed truths about our eternal destiny, and He wants us to understand them.

Second, the eternal state is not just a colorful way of describing our present salvation experience. It is not simply a picturesque description of our salvation. Second Corinthians 5:17 and Galatians 6:15 indicate we are new creatures in Christ, but Revelation 21–22 is describing the ultimate destiny of God's people. The details in Revelation 21–22 explain a real, literal, and tangible place that the people of God will dwell in.

Third, the eternal state of Revelation 21–22 follows the millennial kingdom described in Revelation 20:1-6. The chronology in Revelation describes a coming period of tribulation (chapters 6–18). This period culminates in the return of Jesus Christ to earth (chapter 19). Following Jesus' return to earth is the thousand-year reign of Jesus and His saints on the earth (chapter 20). Then the glories of the eternal state will occur (chapters 21–22:5).

## Ten Considerations About the Eternal State

### The Beginning and the End

First, strong parallels exist between the creation account in Genesis 1–2 and the new creation described in Revelation 21–22. The new creation is a restoration of the original and very good creation of God. So it is helpful to go back to the very beginning and then look at the very end. To use theological terminology, we should study both protology (beginning things) and eschatology (last things). We should study Genesis 1–2 and Revelation 21–22. As we do, issues regarding the fall and the work of Christ at His first coming become clearer.

There are striking comparisons between the first two chapters of the Bible and the last two chapters. In both, we see God as creator and maker. Genesis 1 says God created the heavens and the earth. Then in Revelation 21:1, John sees "a new heaven and a new earth." In the Genesis account, God said, "'Let there be light'; and there was light" (verse 3). Then in Revelation, there is no need for a lamp or light because the glory of God will illumine His people (22:5).

In Genesis 1–2 we learn about the Garden of Eden. In Revelation 21–22 we see the new heavens and earth and the New Jerusalem. Concerning the presence of God with man, the Lord God walked in the garden in the cool of the day with Adam. Then we are told in Revelation 21:3, "Behold, the tabernacle of God is among men, and He will dwell among them."

In Genesis, death was promised for disobedience—"In the day that you eat from it you will surely die" (Genesis 2:17). But Revelation 21:4 tells us death is removed. When it comes to the curse, Genesis 3:17 states, "Cursed is the ground because of you." But Revelation 22:3 tells us, "There will no longer be any curse." In the Genesis account, there was a river that flowed out of Eden. And there is a river in Revelation 22:1—the river of the water of life. Also, the tree of life is prominent in Genesis 2–3. After that we no longer see the tree of life. But Revelation 22:2 states: "On either side of the river was the tree of life." The tree of life was in the Garden of Eden, and it will show up again in the New Jerusalem.

With Genesis 1:26-28 we discover God's mandate for mankind to rule and subdue the earth as God's mediator. Then the last verse about the New

Jerusalem in Revelation 22:5 says God's people will reign on the earth—"They will reign forever and ever."

Satan deceived God's image bearers in Genesis 3, but when you get to Revelation 20:1-3, Satan is incarcerated in a spiritual prison called the abyss. A thousand years later he is sentenced to the lake of fire forever. The tempter is removed.

The importance of nations is discussed in Genesis 10–11, where we find an extensive table of nations listing people groups from the sons of Noah. Then in Revelation 21:24 we read, "The nations will walk by [the New Jerusalem's] light, and the kings of the earth will bring their glory into it." From Genesis 10 onward, nations are in conflict, but in Revelation 21–22 nations are at peace. Revelation 22:2 states that "the leaves of the tree [of life] were for the healing of the nations."

Do you see a pattern? As we study Genesis 1–2 and then Revelation 21–22, we see a strong connection between the creation account and the new creation account.

When it comes to the issue of the eternal state in the Old Testament, the prophets did not always make clear distinctions between the coming intermediate kingdom (i.e., the millennium) and the eternal state. When prophets like Isaiah looked at the days of Messiah and things to come, they offered details that could be true of both the millennial and eternal kingdom. However, later on in the scheme of progressive revelation, it becomes clearer that there is a distinction between the millennial kingdom and the eternal kingdom.

In Isaiah 65:20, we read that in a coming period, "the youth will die at the age of one hundred and the one who does not reach the age of one hundred will be thought accursed." The prophet is telling us that if someone were to die at the age of 100, we would think, *What happened? What went wrong?*

Can we say that is true in this present age we live in? If somebody dies at the age of 100, do we say, "Wow, that person must have done something wrong. What happened?" No; in fact, we are impressed that the person lived for so long. On the other hand, we know death won't occur in the eternal state. Death will have been removed. That tells us Isaiah 65:20 must refer to a different period. In what era is dying at age 100 viewed as a premature death? Certainly not in this age, since most people die before age 85. And it certainly cannot be in the eternal state, since no one will die at that time. The only era in which death at age 100 could be considered premature, then, is the intermediate kingdom known as the millennium (Revelation 20:1-6).

First Corinthians 15:20-28 explains that Jesus will bring the original creation back into conformity to the Father's will. Once Jesus successfully completes His reign upon the earth and has subjected all things to Himself, He will hand the kingdom over to God the Father and subject Himself to the Father. After the Messiah has reigned over every square inch of this previously rebellious planet, a transition will occur to the eternal kingdom, when God will be all in all (1 Corinthians 15:24, 28).

Revelation 21:1–22:5 describes the new earth and the New Jerusalem. Alan Johnson wrote: "It is remarkable that John's picture of the final age to come focuses not on a platonic ideal heaven or distant paradise but on the reality of a new earth and heaven. God originally created the earth and heaven to be man's permanent home."[2]

People often think of eternity as a purely spiritual destiny. Many are under the impression that our ultimate destiny is escaping earth and anything physical. Supposedly we will live in a spiritual realm forever. But that is not the picture that Scripture paints.

### Replacement or Renewal?

The second detail is that Revelation 21:1 says the new heaven and new earth will replace the present heaven and earth. The present heaven and earth will pass away. But what does this mean? Here we run into an issue on which many godly and intelligent Bible teachers disagree. The disagreement is not whether there is going to be a real, tangible, physical new earth. But there is debate concerning the relationship of the present earth with the coming new earth. Two differing views are: (1) an annihilation of the present earth with a replacement new earth, or (2) a renewal of the present earth so the new earth is this present earth restored.

Some believe the present earth is annihilated and replaced by an entirely new earth. Others believe the new earth is this present planet purged and restored.

Both sides point to evidence for their views. In favor of the annihilation view is Revelation 20:11, which speaks about the earth and heaven fleeing away. Second Peter 3:10-12 talks about destruction by fire and the elements being burned up. Some say this indicates a removal of the present order of things so much that there needs to be an entirely new universe. Psalm 102:26 states, "Even they [earth and heavens] will perish... all of them will wear out like a garment." Jesus said, "Heaven and earth will pass away" (Matthew 24:35). These texts are viewed as evidence that there will be an entirely new, out-of-nothing creation that replaces the current earth.

On the other hand, the renewal view makes much of Romans 8, which indicates the creation will be glorified when man is glorified. To explain further, when man fell, the creation was subjected to futility. The ground was cursed. But we are told, in verse 20, that it was subjected "in hope." Creation is personified as longing to be set free from its current corruption and slavery. When man is glorified, the earth is glorified as well.

Key biblical terms point to a renewal of the earth. Jesus speaks of a coming "regeneration" of the cosmos in Matthew 19:28. Regeneration can mean "renewal" in the sense of remaking something that was marred. In Colossians 1:20, Paul says

Jesus will "reconcile all things to Himself, having made peace through the blood of His cross." The "all things" in this context of Colossians 1:15-20 involves everything that has been created, including the world.

In Acts 3:21, Peter predicts a coming "restoration of all things" that the Old Testament prophets wrote about. This language of regeneration, reconciliation, and restoration refers to fixing what previously was broken. They do not seem consistent with an annihilation view.

Those who hold to a renewal view sometimes argue that this view highlights God's victory in saving the creation He created and deemed "very good" (Genesis 1:31). Satan does not get the victory over God's "very good" creation—God does! So God does not send His original creation into oblivion; He restores it!

I believe the restoration view is correct. The evidence, particularly Romans 8, indicates a strong parallel between creation and man. When man fell, creation fell. When man is glorified, creation will be glorified. When it comes to our future, God does not annihilate and start over with an entirely new person. We will receive a resurrection body, but there is continuity with who we are now. The fiery destruction of the universe in 2 Peter 3 is best understood in the sense of purging and purifying, not annihilation. The destruction of the earth in 2 Peter 3 is likened to the destruction of the world by the flood in Noah's day. This was a global catastrophic destruction, but it was not an annihilation of earth.

### Continuity or Discontinuity?

Third, Second Corinthians 5:17 says, "If anyone is in Christ, he is a new creature; the old things passed away; behold, new things have come." When a person becomes a Christian, he becomes a new creature. Old things have passed away. But a Christian does not become an entirely different person. There is still a one-to-one correspondence between who we are now and who we will be in the future. That is true of Jesus, who was the "first fruits" of the resurrection (1 Corinthians 15:20). When Jesus came out of the grave, He was transformed and glorified, but He was still the same person.

Revelation 21:1 says, "Then I saw a new heaven and new earth; for the first heaven and the first earth passed away." So clearly there is a discontinuity between the present universe and the one to come. The question is, are we looking at a discontinuity in the sense of a total replacement? This passage could be emphasizing removal of the world tainted by sin to one purged from the effects of sin.

Revelation 21:1 also tells us that no sea was seen on the new earth. There have been different understandings of what it means that there will be no sea. Some believe that "sea" in Revelation represents chaos. Daniel talks about bad Gentile powers coming from the sea, and in the ancient world, the sea was viewed as being hostile. While John wrote the book of Revelation, he was surrounded by the sea as he was imprisoned. However, if we are talking about a literal new heaven, a literal new earth, and a literal New Jerusalem, then it seems a bit odd to conclude that "sea" is just figurative for chaos.

Others believe that the statement "there is no longer any sea" simply means there will be no bodies of water or aquatic life on the new earth. Still others say that the saltwater seas and oceans that separate men now in a fallen world will be removed, but this does not mean the total removal of all bodies of water, such as large lakes, rivers, etc. For example, a river is mentioned in Revelation chapter 22. Perhaps this river flows to other bodies of water.

### The New Jerusalem

A fourth detail of the eternal state is the holy city, the New Jerusalem. This New Jerusalem was the ultimate hope of Abraham, as stated in the book of Hebrews. When it comes to this city, there have been some different views on what it actually is. Some have argued that the New Jerusalem itself is the new earth. So nothing exists outside the New Jerusalem because the New Jerusalem is new earth.

The next view is that the New Jerusalem will reside upon the new earth. This view is more likely. John saw the new heaven and earth, and then he spoke of a New Jerusalem coming down from heaven. This seems to be the capital city of the new earth. Revelation 21:24-26 mentions "the nations...and the kings of the earth [who] will bring their glory into [the city]." That the nations will

bring their glory *into* the city shows activity *outside* of the New Jerusalem. These nations outside the city will bring their cultural contributions into the city.

### God's Presence

Fifth, God will establish His presence fully with men. Revelation 21:3 says, "I heard a loud voice from the throne saying, 'Behold, the tabernacle of God is among men, and He will dwell among them, and they shall be His people, and God Himself will be among them.'" In the Old Testament, God's presence resided in the tabernacle and then the temple. With Jesus' coming, God resided with men. In this age between the two comings of Jesus, the Holy Spirit resides in His people. In the coming millennial kingdom, Jesus will be physically present on earth while the Holy Spirit continues to reside among God's people. Yet in the eternal state, the full presence of God will be on the new earth. The Father, the Lamb, and of course the Holy Spirit will dwell on the new earth with humankind.

In Revelation 21:3, some translations read, "They shall be His people." The literal translation is "peoples" (Greek, *laoi*) and probably refers to "the nations" of 21:24-26.

### The Death of Death

Sixth, God will remove the negative aspects of the previous world. Revelation 21:4 declares: "He will wipe away every tear from their eyes; and there will no longer be any death; there will no longer be any mourning, or crying, or pain; the first things have passed away." The day is coming when all the negative effects of the fall will be removed. There will be no more death, no more mourning, no more crying, and no more pain.

Living in a fallen world makes it seem like the negative aspects of sin are going to continue forever, but they are not! Sin and its effects will be removed.

### The Wicked Will Not Enter

The seventh detail about the eternal state is that believers will inherit the new earth while unbelievers will be barred from it. Revelation 21:8 states, "The cowardly and unbelieving and abominable and murderers and immoral persons and sorcerers and idolaters and all liars, their part will be in the lake that burns with fire and brimstone, which is the second death." We are reminded that the story does not end well for everyone. God's people will inherit the new earth, but the wicked will be banished from it. As preachers and teachers, we must be careful that we do not present the new earth and heaven as everyone's destiny, because it is not. Salvation comes through faith in Christ alone. Without this, no one will participate in the new earth.

### Exploring the New Jerusalem

Eighth, from Revelation 21:10 onward we read a glorious description of the New Jerusalem. According to Revelation 21:12, the city will have "a great and high wall, with twelve gates." At the gates will be 12 angels, and the names of the 12 tribes of Israel will be written on the gates. In verse 13, we read, "There were three gates on the east and three gates on the north and three gates on the south and three gates on the west." This suggests continuity with the old earth because navigational directions still exist. Verse 14 reveals that the city wall will have 12 foundation stones with the names of the 12 apostles on them. Verse 15 says the city and the wall can be measured: "The one who spoke with me had a gold measuring rod to measure the city, and its gates and its wall."

We are then given the dimensions of this great city: "The city is laid out as a square," which means the length, width, and height will be equal. "Its length is as great as the width; and he measured the city with the rod, fifteen hundred miles; its length and width and height are equal" (verse 16).

There are four different understandings as to what 1500 miles in width, length, and height actually means. Some say this refers to a pyramid shape. A more popular view is that the city is in the shape of a cube, and that we can draw connections with the shape of past temples and the Holy of Holies. The most holy place in the temple was in the shape of a cube, so this would mean that the New Jerusalem would be like an encased temple or building.

Still others have argued that the shape is that of a square and not a cube, so John was referring to a large land mass surrounded by a wall. Another view is that architectural shape is not in view here, but rather, emphasis is being placed on the city's perfection.

Another question with regard to the city is its sheer magnitude. The predominant view is that the city is 1500 miles long, wide, and high. If that is the case, the area covered would be 2,250,000 square miles, which is extremely large. The length and width of the city is roughly half the size of the United States.

A lesser-held view is that the city is 1500 miles in totality, which entails that its length, width, and height add up to 1500 miles. So if it is in the shape of a square, then each of the sides measures 375 miles. If you accept those estimates, then the city would be more the size of a large Midwestern state in the United States.

We learn about the size of the wall in verse 17: "He measured its wall, seventy-two yards, according to human measurements, which are also angelic measurements." Does this passage mean that this wall is 72 yards thick, or 72 yards high, or both? If you read certain Old Testament descriptions of walls, sometimes the height is given, sometimes the thickness is given.

If we go with the view that the city is a large skyscraper cube, then the 72 yards most likely does not refer to the wall's height, for a city that is 1500 miles in height is not contained by a wall that is 72 yards in height. So as the golden cube exists, it would be 72 yards thick. In ancient times, the emphasis of a wall was

on its height. So the 72-yard height would fit better if you were to take the view that the New Jerusalem is more like a land mass, and not so much an encased cube.

The New Jerusalem is made of precious materials ranging from stones to precious metals, all of various colors. Revelation 21:22 says there is no temple in the city because God and the Lamb are its temple. God and the Lamb's presence are so manifested in this city there is no need for a temple.

Verse 23 continues, "The city has no need of the sun or of the moon to shine on it, for the glory of God has illumined it, and its lamp is the Lamb." The New Jerusalem is so illumined by God that it does not need any other light source. This is not necessarily a statement that the sun or moon do not exist, but they are not needed to light the New Jerusalem.

Verse 24 says, "The nations will walk by its light, and the kings of the earth will bring their glory into it." This refers to literal geopolitical nations. Kings exist, which most likely means that governmental functions are taking place. And because we are on the new earth, these nations and kings are followers of the King. While nations are a post-Fall development (Genesis 10–11), their mention here indicates that God desires the presence of multiple nations on the new earth.

These rulers "will bring the glory and the honor of the nations into it" (verse 26). It seems these nations will use all their talents and gifts and some would even say cultural contributions for the glory of God, and they will make their contributions in the New Jerusalem.

### The Tree of Life

A ninth detail is the prominence of the tree of life. In Revelation 22:1-2 we read, "Then he showed me a river of the water of life, clear as crystal, coming from the throne of God and of the Lamb… on either side of the river was the tree of life." The last time anyone witnessed the tree of life was back in the garden in Genesis 3. After the fall, Adam and Eve were barred from eating from the tree of life. God sent an angel to guard the tree so that Adam and Eve would not have access to it. But in the New Jerusalem on the new earth, we will see the tree of life, and it will bear 12 kinds of fruit. It will yield its fruit every month, which seems to indicate that time will exist in the eternal state.

The leaves of the tree have a unique function—they will be used for "the healing of the nations" (verse 2). This does not mean nations will be at war with one another; instead, the leaves of the tree will maintain perpetual harmony among the nations. The nations once at war will be in harmony. Access to this tree will no longer be barred. It will be accessible to all on the new earth.

### Eternal Fellowship

The tenth and final observation concerns our fellowship with and service of God. "There will no longer be any curse; and the throne of God and of the Lamb will be in it, and His bond-servants will serve Him" (Revelation 22:3). We learn in verse 4 that we will see God's face and His name will be on our foreheads—an indication of intimate fellowship. "There will no longer be any night; and they will not have need of the light of a lamp nor the light of the sun, because the Lord God will illumine them" (verse 5). The new earth will enjoy the presence and light of God for all of eternity: "They will reign forever and ever" (verse 5).

The coming eternal state should thrill our hearts. Everything we do now and everything we are fighting for is pointing toward this period in history. No matter what we go through now, no matter what sorrow, tears, or tragedies we face, when we are on that new earth, it will all have been worth it. We are going to be so focused on God and what He has prepared for us that everything negative that ever happened in this life is going to be forgotten. We will fellowship with our God and Savior and all those who love Him.

# Notes

## Chapter 1—The Lord's Greatest Prayer, Part 1 (John MacArthur)

1. Sinclair Ferguson, *The Christian Life* (Edinburgh: Banner of Truth, 2013), 6.

## Chapter 3—Adam, Where Art Thou? (William Barrick)

1. Peter Enns, *The Evolution of Adam: What the Bible Does and Doesn't Say about Human Origins* (Grand Rapids: Brazos Press, 2012), 66.

2. Jeffrey Burton Russell, *Inventing the Flat Earth* (Westport, CT: Praeger, 1997), 76.

3. Noel Weeks, "Cosmology in Historical Context," *Westminster Theological Journal* 68, no. 2 (2006): 283-93.

4. Jonathan F. Henry, "Uniformitarianism in Old Testament Studies: A Review of *Ancient Near Eastern Thought and the Old Testament* by John H. Walton," *Journal of Dispensational Theology* 13, no. 39 (2009): 19-36 (esp. 25-28).

5. Paul Joüon, *A Grammar of Biblical Hebrew*, trans. and rev. T. Muraoka, *Subsidia Biblica* 14/I–II (Rome: Pontifical Biblical Institute, 1993), 2:376 (§114*e* n. 1).

## Chapter 4—Why Every Self-Respecting Calvinist Must Be a Six-Day Creationist (John MacArthur)

1. Jonathan Edwards, *Miscellany* no. 547, 1731.

2. Blaine Harden, "The Greening of Evangelicals: Christian Right Turns, Sometimes Warily, to Environmentalism," *Washington Post* (February 6, 2005), A01.

3. Declaration of the Care of Creation, Evangelical Environmental Network and *Creation Care* magazine, 1994, http://www.creationcare.org/evangelical_declaration_of_the_care_of_creation.

4. Declaration of the Care of Creation.

5. Declaration of the Care of Creation.

## Chapter 5—Faith of Our Fathers (Nathan Busenitz)

1. Cf. Philip Schaff, *A History of the Christian Church* (New York: Charles Scribner's Sons, 1916), 6:128.

2. Schaff, 129-30.

3. Schaff, 130.

4. Martin Luther. Trans. from James M. Kittelson, *Luther the Reformer: The Story of the Man and His Career* (Minneapolis: Fortress Press, 2003), 134.

5. Francis Beckwith originally published these comments on his blog in May 2007. Cf. Todd Pruit, "Beckwith Back to Rome," *The Alliance of Confessing Evangelicals* (July 30, 2007), http://www.alliancenet.org/mos/1517/beckwith-back-to-rome.

6.  In verses 20-21, James asked Gentile Christians to stay away from idolatry and immorality, and to be sensitive to the weaker consciences of their Jewish brothers and sisters, which fits perfectly with Paul's instruction about weaker brothers in Romans 14–15 and 1 Corinthians 8–9.

7.  Cf. Thomas Oden, *The Justification Reader* (Grand Rapids: Eerdmans, 2002). Also see Nick Needham, "Justification in the Early Church Fathers," in *Justification in Perspective*, ed. Bruce L. McCormack, 25–53 (Grand Rapids: Baker Academic, 2006), 40.

8.  Clement of Rome, *1 Clem.* 32.4. Trans. from Michael W. Holmes, ed. *The Apostolic Fathers* (Grand Rapids: Baker Academic, 2007), 87.

9.  Polycarp, *Pol. Phil.* 1.2-3. Trans. from Holmes, *The Apostolic Fathers*, 281.

10. *Diogn.* 9.2-5. Trans. from Oden, *The Justification Reader*, 65.

11. Cf. Martin Luther, *A Commentary on St. Paul's Epistle to the Galatians*, trans. Erasmus Middleton, ed. John Prince Fallowes (Grand Rapids: Kregel, 1979), 172.

12. Hilary, *Comm. Matt.* 20.7. *PL* 9.1030. Trans. from Hilary of Poitiers, *Commentary on Matthew*, The Fathers of the Church, trans. D.H. Williams (Washington, DC: The Catholic University of America Press, 2012), 212.

13. Hilary, 8.6. *PL* 9.961. Trans. from D.H. Williams, "Justification by Faith: A Patristic Doctrine," 658.

14. Basil, *Hom. humil.* 20.3. *PG* 31.529. Trans. from Elowsky, *We Believe in the Holy Spirit*, 98.

15. Ambrosiaster, *Ad Rom.*, on Rom. 3:24. *PL* 17.79. Trans. from Elowsky, *We Believe in the Holy Spirit*, 98.

16. Ambrosiaster, on Rom. 3:27. *PL* 17.80. Trans. from Bray, *Romans*, ACCS, 103.

17. Ambrosiaster, on Rom. 4:6. *PL* 17.83. Trans. from Bray, *Romans*, ACCS, 113.

18. John Chrysostom, *Hom. Rom.* 7 (on Rom. 3:27). *PG* 60.446. Trans. from *NPNF*, First Series, 11.379.

19. John Chrysostom, *Hom. 1 Cor.* 8 (on 1 Cor. 3:1-3). *PG* 61.73. Trans. from *NPNF*, First Series, 12.47.

20. John Chrysostom, *Hom. Gal.*, on Gal. 3:8. *PG* 61.651. Trans. from *NPNF*, First Series, 13.26.

21. John Chrysostom, on Gal. 3:12. *PG* 61.652. Trans. from *NPNF*, First Series, 13:26.

22. John Chrysostom, *Hom. 1 Tim.*, on 1 Tim. 1:15-16. *PG* 62.520-21. Trans. from Elowsky, *We Believe in the Holy Spirit*, 98.

23. John Chrysostom, *Adv. Jud.* 7.3. *PG* 48.919.

24. Marius Victorinus, *Ep. Eph.* 1 (on Eph. 2:7). *PL* 8.1255. Cf. Oden, *The Justification Reader*, 48.

25. Victorinus, 1 (on Eph. 2.9). *PL* 8.1256. Trans. from Oden, *The Justification Reader*, 48. Cf. Marius Victorinus, *Epistle to the Galatians* 2.3.21.

26. Victorinus, 1 (on Eph. 2:15). *PL* 8.1258. Trans. from Joseph A. Fitzmyer, *Romans: A New Translation with Introduction and Commentary by Joseph A. Fitzmyer*, The Anchor Bible, vol. 33 (New York: Doubleday, 1993), 361.

27. Marius Victorinus, *Epistle to the Galatians*, 1.3.7. Trans. From Mark J. Edwards, ed., Galatians, Ephesians, Philippians, ACCS, 39.

28. Augustine, *Enarrat. Ps.*, 31.7. *PL* 36.263. Trans. from John E. Rotelle, *Expositions of the Psalms 1–32* (Hyde Park: New City Press, 2000), 11.370.

29. Augustine, *Tractates on the Gospel of John*, John 1:15-18, Tractate 3.9 in *NPNF*, 7:21; cited from Gregg R. Allison, *Historical Theology*, 501.

30. Augustine, *Spir. et litt.* 13 (22). *PL* 44.214-15. Trans. from *NPNF*, First Series, 5:93.

31. Prosper of Aquitaine, *Voc. Gent.*, 1.17. *PL* 51.669. Trans. from Oden, *The Justification Reader*, 46.

32. Theodoret, *Interp. Rom.*, on Rom. 4:4. *PG* 82.88. Trans. from Bray, *Romans*, ACCS, 108.

33. Theodoret, on Rom. 1:17. *PG* 82.57, 60. Trans. from Bray, *Romans*, ACCS, 31.

34. Theodoret, *Interp. Eph.*, on Eph. 2:4-5. *PG* 82.520. Trans. from Oden, *The Justification Reader*, 113.

35. Theodoret, on Eph. 2:8-9. *PG* 82.521. Trans. from Oden, *The Justification Reader*, 44.

36. Theodoret, *Epist.* 83. *PG* 83.1269. Trans. from Elowsky, *We Believe in the Holy Spirit*, 99.

37. Both citations from Anselm of Canterbury, *Admon. mor. PL* 158:686-687. Trans. from *Meditations and Prayers*, 275-77.

38. Bernard of Clairvaux, *Epist.* 190.6. *PL* 182.1065. Trans. from John Mabillon, ed., *Life and Works of Saint Bernard, Abbot of Clairvaux*, trans. Samuel J. Eales (London: John Hodges, 1889), 2.580-581.

39. St. Bernard as recorded by William of St. Thierry, *S. Bern. vit. prim.* 1.12. *PL* 185.258. Trans. from Alban Butler, *The Lives of the Fathers, Martyrs, and Other Principal Saints*, vol. 8 (Dublin: James Duffy, 1845), 231.

40. Bernard of Clairvaux, *Serm. Cant.* 22.8. *PL* 183.881. Trans. from Franz Posset, *Pater Bernhardus*, 186.

41. Norman Geisler and Josh Betancourt, *Is Rome the True Church?* (Wheaton, IL: Crossway, 2008), 53-54.

42. Gregg R. Allison, *Historical Theology* (Grand Rapids: Zondervan, 2011), 505.

43. John Calvin, "Dedicatory Letter to Francis I," *Institutes*, section 4.

## Chapter 7—The Extent of the Atonement (Phil Johnson)

1. Robert Charles Hill, trans., *Theodoret of Cyrus: Commentary on the Letters of St. Paul*, vol. 2 (Brookline: Holy Cross Orthodox Press, 2001), 175.

2. Teodosia Tomkinson, trans., *Ambrose: Exposition of the Holy Gospel According to St. Luke* (Etna, CA: Center for Traditionalist Orthodox Studies, 1998), 201-202.

3. Cited in George Musgrave Giger, trans., *Francis Turretin: Institutes of Elenctic Theology*, 3 vols. (Phillipsburg, NJ: P&R, 1994), 2:462.

4. John Owen, trans., *Commentaries on the Catholic Epistles by John Calvin* (Grand Rapids: Eerdmans, 1948), 173.

5. Thomas J. Nettles, *By His Grace and for His Glory* (Lake Charles, LA: Cor Meum Tibi, 2002), 320.

6. R.B. Kuiper, *For Whom Did Christ Die?* (Grand Rapids: Eerdmans, 1959), 78 (emphasis added).

7. Charles Haddon Spurgeon, *The Metropolitan Tabernacle Pulpit*, 63 vols. (London: Passmore & Alabaster, 1903), 49:39.

8. Robert Smith Candlish, *The Atonement: Its Efficacy and Extent* (Edinburgh: Adam and Charles Black, 1867), 173.

9. Archibald Alexander Hodge, *The Atonement* (Philadelphia: Presbyterian Board of Publication, 1867), 359.

10. Kuiper, *For Whom Did Christ Die?*, 83-84.

11. Kuiper, *For Whom Did Christ Die?*, 84 (emphasis added).

12. Kuiper, *For Whom Did Christ Die?*, 85.

13. Kuiper, *For Whom Did Christ Die?*

14. Thomas Myers, trans., *Calvin: Commentary on the First Twenty Chapters of the Book of the Prophet Ezekiel* (Grand Rapids: Eerdmans, 1948), 246-247.

15. Charles Hodge, *Systematic Theology*, 3 vols. (New York: Scribners, 1872), 2:546.

16. Curt Daniel, *The History and Theology of Calvinism* (Dallas: Scholarly Reprints, 1993), 368.

## Chapter 8—A Biblical Case for Elder Rule (Tom Pennington)

1. George Barna, *Revolution* (Wheaton, IL: Tyndale, 2005), 37.

2. Donald Miller, *The Nature and Mission of the Church*, quoted in Robert Saucy, *The Church in God's Program* (Chicago: Moody Press, 1972), 105.

3. Miller, quoted in Saucy, 105.

4. Alexander Strauch, *Biblical Eldership* (Littleton, CO: Lewis & Roth Publishers, 1995), 101.

5. J.B. Lightfoot, "The Christian Ministry" in *St. Paul's Epistle to the Philippians* (London: MacMillan & Co., 1898), 186.

6. Robert Saucy, *The Church in God's Program* (Chicago: Moody Press, 1972), 112.

7. Saucy, *The Church in God's Program*, 112.

8. Wayne Grudem, *Systematic Theology* (Grand Rapids, MI: Zondervan, 1994), 926.

9. Polycarp, *Philippians*, 5, 6.

## Chapter 9—The Great Commission as a Theological Endeavor (Paul Washer)

1. Robert Jamieson, A. R. Fausset, and David Brown, *Commentary Critical and Explanatory on the Whole Bible*, vol. 2 (Oak Harbor, WA: Logos Research Systems, Inc., 1997), 64.

2. The magazine I refer to is *Heart Cry*. For more on this publication, see http://www.heartcrymissionary.com/heartcry-magazine-archive.

3. Craig Blomberg, *Matthew*, vol. 22, The New American Commentary (Nashville: Broadman & Holman Publishers, 1992), 431.

4. William Carey, as cited in Peter Morden, *Offering Christ to the World: Andrew Fuller (1754–1815) and the Revival of Eighteenth Century Particular Baptist Life*, Studies in Baptist History and Thought 8 (Carlisle: Paternoster, 2003), 136.

## Chapter 10—Why Every Self-Respecting Calvinist Must Be a Premillennialist (John MacArthur)

1. Oswald T. Allis, *Prophecy and the Church* (Philadelphia: P&R Publishing, [1945] 1947), 238.

2. Floyd E. Hamilton, *The Basis of Millennial Faith* (Grand Rapids, MI: Eerdmans, 1955), 38-39.

3. Herman Bavinck, *Reformed Dogmatics: Abridged in One Volume* (Grand Rapids, MI: Baker, 2011), 658.

4. William Cuninghame, *The Pre-Millennial Advent of Messiah Demonstrated from the Scriptures* (London: Nisbet, 1836).

5. Manuel Lacunza y Diaz, *The Coming of Messiah in Glory and Majesty* (London: L.B. Seeley and Sons, 1827).

6. Emil Schurer, *A History of the Jewish People in the Time of Jesus*, 5 volumes (Peabody, MA: Hendrickson, 1993).

7. Ronald Diprose, *Israel and the Church* (Downers Grove, IL: InterVarsity Press, 2004).

## Chapter 11—Heaven on Earth (Michael Vlach)

1. Randy Alcorn's book *Heaven* is one notable exception.

2. A.F. Johnson, "Revelation," in F.E. Gaebelein, ed., *The Expositor's Bible Commentary, Volume 12: Hebrews Through Revelation* (Grand Rapids, MI: Zondervan, 1981), 592.

# CONTRIBUTORS

*John MacArthur* is pastor-teacher of Grace Community Church in Sun Valley, California, and president of The Master's University and Seminary.

*William Barrick* is faculty associate and director of ThD studies at The Master's Seminary. He is also the Old Testament editor for the Evangelical Exegetical Commentary.

*Mark Dever* is senior pastor of Capitol Hill Baptist Church in Washington, DC, and the president of 9Marks.

*Ligon Duncan* is the chancellor/CEO of Reformed Theological Seminary and the John E. Richards Professor of Systematic and Historical Theology.

*Steven J. Lawson* is president of OnePassion Ministries and a professor of preaching at The Master's Seminary and at The Ligonier Academy.

*R.C. Sproul* was the founder and chairman of Ligonier Ministries and senior minister of preaching and teaching at Saint Andrew's in Sanford, Florida.

*Albert Mohler Jr.* is president of the Southern Baptist Theological Seminary in Louisville, Kentucky.

*Nathan Busenitz* is an assistant professor of theology at The Master's Seminary and an elder at Grace Community Church in Sun Valley, California.

*John Piper* is the chancellor of Bethlehem College & Seminary, Minneapolis, Minnesota. He ministered at Bethlehem Baptist Church for 33 years and now travels to speak, and writes regularly, through Desiring God.

*Tom Pennington* is the pastor-teacher of Countryside Bible Church in Southlake, Texas.

*Rick Holland* is the senior pastor of Mission Road Bible Church in Prairie Village, Kansas.

*Phil Johnson* is the executive director of Grace to You and primary editor of John MacArthur's books. He is also an elder at Grace Community Church in Sun Valley, California.

*Austin T. Duncan* is the college pastor at Grace Community Church in Sun Valley, California. He also oversees the preaching curriculum and the DMin program at The Master's Seminary.

*Alex Montoya* is the senior pastor at First Fundamental Bible Church in Whittier, California.

*Michael J. Vlach* is a professor of theology at The Master's Seminary and specializes in areas of systematic theology, historical theology, apologetics, and world religions.

*Paul Washer* is the founder of HeartCry Missionary Society, which supports indigenous missionaries throughout Africa, Asia, Europe, the Middle East, and Latin America.

To learn more about Harvest House books and
to read sample chapters, visit our website:

**www.harvesthousepublishers.com**

**HARVEST HOUSE PUBLISHERS**
EUGENE, OREGON